D0212447

Latin American Writers
on Gay and Lesbian Themes

Latin American Writers on Gay and Lesbian Themes

A BIO-CRITICAL SOURCEBOOK

EDITED BY
David William Foster

Emmanuel S. Nelson
ADVISORY EDITOR

GREENWOOD PRESS
Westport, Connecticut • London

Library of Congress Cataloging-in-Publication Data

Foster, David William.
    Latin American writers on gay and lesbian themes : a bio-critical
sourcebook / Edited [and compiled] by David William Foster.
      p.   cm.
    Includes bibliographical references and index.
    ISBN 0-313-28479-2 (alk. paper)
    1. Authors, Latin American—20th century—Biography. 2. Latin
American literature—20th century—History and criticism.
3. Homosexuality in literature. 4. Homosexuality and literature—
Latin America.   I. Title.
PQ7081.3.F62   1994
860.9'353—dc20   94-2191

British Library Cataloguing in Publication Data is available.

Library of Congress Catalog Card Number: 94-2191
ISBN: 0-313-28479-2

First published in 1994

Greenwood Press, 88 Post Road West, Westport, CT 06881
An imprint of Greenwood Publishing Group, Inc.

Printed in the United States of America

The paper used in this book complies with the
Permanent Paper Standard issued by the National
Information Standards Organization (Z39.48–1984).

10 9 8 7 6 5 4 3 2 1

Copyright Acknowledgment

This volume is dedicated to two of its contributors who have died since its inception: Dario Galaviz Quesada, the victim of homophobic murder in Mexico in August 1993, and Francisco Caetano Lopes, who died of AIDS at Stanford University in March 1994.

Contents

Preface

[I]t would be incorrect to say that lesbians associate, make love, live with women, for "woman" has meaning only in heterosexual systems of thought and heterosexual economic systems. Lesbians are not women.

Monique Wittig, *The Straight Mind and Other Essays*
(New York: Harvester Wheatsheaf, 1992), 80

I'm more man than you'll ever be and more woman than you'll ever get.

Popular Gay Comeback

de ángeles amándose jamás se construyó
una tumba y un tálamo sin alas
de alas ¿para quién? ¿de machos necios que acusáis al maricón
sin razón, sin ver que sois la ocasión de lo mismo que culpáis?;[1]

Manuel Ramos Otero, *El libro de la muerte*
(Río Piedras, P.R.: Cultural/Waterfront, 1985), 66

The emergence of Third World feminism, then, seemed imminent. Third World lesbians' disillusionment with the racism and classism of the women's and gay movements and the sexism and homophobia of Third World movements did much to force us to begin to organize ourselves autonomously in the name of Third World feminism.

Cherríe Moraga, *Loving in the War Years: Lo que nunca pasó por sus labios* (Boston: South End Press, 1983), 131

There is a twofold importance—and personal satisfaction—in presenting this compilation to the general and specialized user. On the one hand, it represents the first attempt to provide a comprehensive image of writing in Latin America that impinges on lesbian and gay issues. Although it has not been possible, for reasons of both space and availability of resources (more on this below), to present a thoroughly global view, the material presented here will go a long way toward establishing an inventory of sexual issues in Latin American writing that can no longer be ignored. Despite the diligent attempts in many scholarly sectors to ignore homoerotic motifs in Latin American writing—indeed, the effort remains a universal one in cultural and literary studies—one very positive contribution of this inventory should be to make it impossible to ignore these issues in a general way and as they relate to specific authors and specific forms of literary production.

On the other hand, this compilation brings together a group of scholars with a shared commitment to contributing to expanding the scope of Latin American cultural studies through attention to sexual matters. Included are approximately 130 entries prepared by some 60 scholars. Each will necessarily have a uniquely complex stance toward the area of queer theory, and for some the examination of the homoerotic—rather than being a circumscribed area of research in itself— is fundamentally a part of a larger view of cultural production, a view that refuses to be confined to the practices of a conventional literary scholarship that proscribes certain questions because they are ''not literary,'' ''biographical rather than textual,'' ''not subject to objective verification'' or simply ''none of anybody's business.'' For many, how anything can lie outside the scope of interest for the student of cultural production is beyond comprehension, and the primary imperative, thus, for the scholar must be such work on the margins of what is recognizable or comprehensible. Some of the contributors have already established a research program in the field, while others have used their collaboration in this publication to begin defining their research and ideological priorities. In a few cases, this reference work is honored to have individuals represented in the dual capacity of contributors and of authors whose works are studied by other scholars.

However, there has been a major problem associated with the organization of this project. Although there has been some inevitable give-and-take with respect to the identification of authors to be included, in the end it became relatively easy to define a list of essential figures. Much more difficult was the recruitment of critics to prepare the entries. Even with the enormous increase in the number of American scholars willing to go beyond canonical authors and safe topics, there remained a group of writers for whom it was impossible to prepare entries. While I am confident no writer of crucial importance has been omitted, it will remain for subsequent scholarly efforts to provide an even greater coverage than has been possible here. As it is, scholars from the United States writing in both English and Spanish are complemented by colleagues from Latin America writing in English, Spanish or Portuguese and, in a few cases, from European countries writing in Spanish. Part of the enormity of this task has been the preparation of suitable English translations of the material submitted in Spanish and Portuguese.

The letter of invitation to contribute to this volume set forth the parameters. The figures to be included would have contact with one of three definitions of gay topics: individuals with a professed gay identity, such that it would be productive to consider their total oeuvre from such a perspective (e.g., Manuel Puig); individuals who have written on gay themes, either with negative images

(José Donoso, Adolfo Caminha) or with positive images (Luis Zapata, Gustavo Alvarez Gardeazábal)—I realize that "positive" and "negative" here are problematical formulations; and, finally, any individual who, although not dealing overtly with a gay topic or professing a gay identity, has written works in which something like a gay sensibility can be identified, no matter how problematically (I venture to suggest René Marqués in this regard, as well as Jorge Luis Borges and Sor Juana Inés de la Cruz). I realize full well the possibilities of an intensely polemical reaction to inclusions in the third category, but this is precisely what I hope will make this volume a provocative contribution to Hispanic studies.

Coming from an ideological bias that rejects the neat and exclusivizing categorizations of subject identities, this position offers the potential to open a debate on crucial matters of cultural and literary politics in Latin Americanist scholarship, beginning with, say, the lack of a principled way of dealing with same-sex erotic poetry in Sor Juana or with the fundamentally homosocial universe of Jorge Luis Borges. Therefore, what is at issue is not just texts in which homosexual genital sex is showcased but, rather, writing that raises questions about the (hetero)sexist hegemony of Latin American culture and scholarship concerning that culture. Note that although literature is the obvious initial point of reference, other forms of cultural production must necessarily be included. Either because many of the authors in this volume belong to the most recent generation of Latin American cultural production or because the writing of older authors has only recently been examined in terms of sexual issues, secondary bibliographic references are often scant. All pertinent criticism, however, has been listed, and the registry for each author should be considered complete as of the closing of the project in 1993.

Clearly, I could expand the foregoing parameters and establish on my own an inventory of authors/texts/productions to be included and then proceed to identify potential authors for each entry. However, in the spirit of intellectual democracy (and protecting myself from the ideological perils associated with the single-handed forging of a canon), solicitation for collaboration in this project brought with it the request that collaborators contribute to the definition of the scope of the entries. It was immediately evident that women writers were underrepresented in this list, and I was anxious to expand coverage in every reasonable way. Their underrepresentation is due, obviously, to our lacking enough criticism to make accurate identifications of appropriate identities; it is also due to the simple and abiding fact that our points of reference continue to be so masculinist, precisely one of the problems this volume hoped to address.

In addition, definition of the corpus included the question of U.S. Latino authors, both those born in the United States and those with permanent resident status, and both those writing in Spanish and those writing in English. It was ultimately decided to be as inclusive as possible, in the interest of promoting an image of a continuum of Latin American cultural production that, as in the case of sexual definitions, refuses to respect borders, whether geographic or linguistic. In the case of Peru's César Moro, one has an example of a Latin

American author who wrote in French, a not infrequent phenomenon in Latin America in the precontemporary period (William Henry Hudson, who was a native of Argentina, is perhaps Latin America's most famous example of translinguistic writing, while Uruguay's Comte de Lautréamont is part of a distinguished nineteenth-century tradition in Latin American letters of writing in French.

Definitions and parameters are always a major problem in Latin American studies, part of its externally, as well as internally, maintained subalternity. Thus, there is no useful term the title of this volume could use to cover production in the United States, in either English or Spanish, by individuals identified with Hispanic culture. "Latino" is fast becoming the preferred term (although it is virtually never used in Arizona, for example, "Chicano" being still dominant). In the interests of avoiding a title that tries to cover every base, "Latin American" should be understood to include U.S. Latinos—which leaves untouched the question of how legitimately to distinguish between Puerto Ricans in Puerto Rico and Puerto Ricans on the U.S. mainland (first generation and after), since both groups are U.S. citizens, although the former are usually included under the heading "Latin American" and the latter customarily identify with Latinos. The other problem concerns Haitian writers, who are usually understood to be included in the denomination "Latin American," although they appear in any source with "Latin American" in the title, being almost exclusively associated with Francophone culture. I can only plead space problems, the difficulty of identifying scholars in a field virtually unknown to me, and the historically closer links between Spanish and Portuguese as reasons to leave Haitian writers for some future Greenwood volume.

Surveying in retrospect the enormous effort that has gone into the preparation of this volume, one could perhaps be pardoned for having almost unseemly pretensions for it: that it will serve as a major point of departure for beginning an adequate mapping of the intersection between queer theory and Latin American culture. Nevertheless, as will become evident in the examination of these entries, it is urgent that we understand that a Latin American homoerotic tradition cannot be examined by simply translating into Spanish or Portuguese the parameters that have been developed for a European or an American production. One must keep ever present the need not so much "to understand Latin America on its own terms" as not to view Anglo-European models as macro narratives that can be used to account for Latin America's cultural production. It is a given, one of the positive legacies of an almost bygone dependency theory, that such extensions produce distorted interpretations. But beyond this is the need to recognize another problem, which is the way such models, in addition to the distortions they produce, are incapable of taking into account essential dimensions of a nonnative cultural production.

Clearly, by even using a term such as *queer theory*, I am implying that a specific body of knowledge, legitimated by that (in itself highly problematic) term, is meaningful for the Latin American corpus, and I would have to acknowledge immediately that to most of the writers and a good number of the critics, the term is meaningless, whether in English or in something like a Spanish or Portuguese translation. This may be taken as a synecdoche, on the basic level of the conception of this compilation, of the problems inherent in publishing in English and in the United States an inventory like this one of such a vast range of Latin American authors and works. The important point is, to be sure, not the degree to which the weight of American cultural theories of the homoerotic, already represented by a distinguished bibliography, has been eluded by the critical opinions gathered here, but the extent to which a preoccupation is present as a form of metacriticism that can contain an injudicious reliance on hegemonic models and modes of interpretation.

Individuals who have contributed significantly to this project include my research assistants Gustavo Geirola, Guillermo Núñez Noriega, Melissa Lockhart, Darrell Lockhart, José B. Alvarez IV and Fabio Correa Uribe. As always, I am deeply grateful to the research programs at Arizona State University that have made possible the successful completion of this project. For almost thirty years, these programs have faithfully underwritten virtually my entire scholarly career, making possible the sort of intellectual and critical development that has led to the execution of projects such as this one.

NOTE

1. Translation of Otero poem:

    of angels loving each other there was never built
    a tomb nor a wedding bower without wings
    of wings for whom? for you stupid machos who denounce the queer
    without reason, without seeing that you are the occasion for that which you
        denounce?

Introduction

Lillian Manzor-Coats

Literature is a form of knowledge, with its own characteristics. . . . If we
begin from the basic proposition that any work of art orders reality according to who produces it, since in this order it is the artist expressing himself
[*sic*], implicitly there is a message that does not have to be political. Nevertheless, if we can understand how an apple can be political . . . we will
have understood why a story by Borges is political, or why a poem by
Sappho is.

Cristina Peri Rossi; quoted in Zeitz, 83

The project of a reference book of gay and lesbian writing in Latin America
places us in a mine field of contested theoretical and methodological questions
in U.S. academia and in Latin American studies. To begin with, the word *gay*
and its connotations do not have a one-to-one correspondence in Latin America.
Moreover, until very recently, the main theoretical questions that would allow
us to speak of ''gay'' and lesbian writing, mainly the relationship between writing and sexuality, have been absent from the field of Latin American studies.
Finally, while research in this field of Latin American studies in general, and
in literary studies in particular, takes place both in the United States and in Latin
America, the specific position of Latinos within U. S. academia, inside the site
of neocolonial ideology production, especially in relation to sexuality, cannot
go unnoted.

The category Latin America presents itself, from the very beginning, as problematic. On the one hand, we know that Latin America is a totalizing name that
refers to a vast geographical space in which different hybrid cultures, many
languages, and countries in different stages of putative development coexist. On
the other hand, Latin America misleadingly suggests one geographical space
with well-marked and stable boundaries and a linear history. Recent histories

have demonstrated the explosion of Latin America's geographical boundaries, both intracontinental—within the Americas—and intercontinental—between the Americas and Europe. The large Latino communities in Los Angeles, Miami, New York, Chicago, and other U.S. cities, as well as in Madrid, Barcelona, Paris, and Berlin, and Latino presence in U.S. academia, are examples of the fact that borders separating Latin America from the United States and from Europe are ever more porous. In spite of efforts by the INS and the European Community to solidify and close off borders, the Latin American nomad continues to cross geopolitical and cultural borders.

The impossibility of mapping a Latin American culture that is "all over the map" presents itself as my first obstacle. In other words, developing in this introduction a conjunctural analysis that tries to be historically and contextually specific becomes a Borgesian task of writing an encyclopedia-within-an-encyclopedia to introduce an encyclopedia. Needless to say, I have no such Borgesian goals. Acknowledging that there has not been any systematic treatment of the interconnections between individual national cultures and general configurations of Latin American society I believe that a more fruitful approach would be to analyze the ways in which Latin America and its individual national cultures are part of uneven inter-American and intercontinental global currents and flows.

I am using *culture* here in the way that Stuart Hall has theorized culture to mean both "the actual, grounded terrain of practices, representations, languages and customs of any specific historical society" and "the contradictory forms of 'common sense' which have taken root and helped to shape popular life" (26). However, by invoking a Latin American culture that is "all over the map," I am also suggesting that at present these cultural forms have no boundaries nor regularities. In other words, they are fundamentally fractal, as Arjun Appadurai has suggested (20). Clearly, in these fractal and overlapping cultural forms the imagination takes on a new role. Bringing together the Frankfurt School's idea of mechanically reproduced images, Benedict Anderson's idea of the imagined community and Jean François Lyotard's notion of the imaginary, Appadurai studies ways in which the imagination becomes a social practice based on "negotiation between sites of agency ('individuals') and globally defined fields of possibility" (Appadurai, 5).[1] Especially in what concerns issues of sexuality and cultural production, I suggest that any cultural studies approach to gay and lesbian writing in Latin America must take into account the ways in which specific practices are intimately tied to Latin America's sociopolitical history while being part of a continental, if not global, cultural economy. It is also of utmost importance to analyze the ways in which the intellectual work of Latin American cultural critics is also enmeshed in uneven contemporary relations of power within this global cultural economy.

GENDER CONSTRUCTIONS AND REPRESENTATIONS IN
LATIN AMERICA

> Para el análisis feminista, sin embargo, empezó a ser evidente que la razón
> de ser del autoritarismo o conservatismo femenino no radicaba en 'esencias'
> femeninas, sino que por el contrario, obedecía a una "razón de género" y
> por lo tanto a una pura construcción social, cultural y política, cuyos par-
> ámetros eran otros.[2]
>
> Julieta Kirkwood, 1983, 146

Any analysis of sexuality and gender categories in Latin America points toward the fact that none of these are natural, transhistorical categories.[3] As Michel
Foucault theorized, sexuality

> is the name that can be given to a historical construct: not a furtive reality that is difficult
> to grasp, but a great surface network in which the stimulation of bodies, the intensification
> of pleasures, the incitement to discourse, the formulation of special knowledges, the
> strengthening of controls and resistances, are linked to one another, in accordance with
> a few major strategies of knowledge and power. (105–106)

While Foucault was quite clear in theorizing sexuality as a "technology of sex,"
he did not directly address the differential ways in which that technology produced a set of effects in male and female subjects. For this reason Alicia Puleo,
a Latin American antropologist, redefined Foucault's notion of sexuality as a
mode of relating one's body with the bodies of others, a relation accompanied
by a preestablished social role that conditions our perception of others and of
ourselves (18).

What Puleo called a preestablished social role is precisely what in Anglo-
American feminist theory is called gender. Teresa de Lauretis, starting at the
point Foucault stopped, has offered the most incisive analysis of what she calls
the technology of gender, the ways in which "the construction of gender is the
product and the process of both representation and self-representation" (9). Puleo's avoidance of the term *gender* is perhaps due to the fact that in Spanish,
as in most Romance languages, the word *género* does not have as its primary
meaning the connotation of a person's sex. While de Lauretis also addressed
this linguistic difference in her essay (3–5), it is important to emphasize that
the Latin American feminists' resistance to this term is not grounded solely in
theoretical and linguistic differences. For some, using *gender* indiscriminately
presents an ethical and political question. As Amy Kaminsky has elaborated
brilliantly,

> [b]ecause of the reality of cultural imperialism and the resistance of North American
> feminists to practice it and of Latin American theorists on the left to permit it, the
> forgoing of translation altogether in favor of the English term "gender" is an untenable

solution to the terminology problem. At a time when Latin America is struggling against North American neocolonialism, the introduction of a North American term into a radical discourse is both undesirable and virtually impossible to achieve. (4)

It is important to note that Latin American social scientists have been using the word *género* since at least the mid-1980s. This is not surprising, given the fact that most of the academic feminist scholarship in Latin America is in the social sciences and not in the humanities. Feminist literary analysis, specifically, has been published much more frequently outside of Latin America, in the United States and Europe. Moreover, most feminist praxis in Latin America tends to be extra-academic in ways usually unreadable by Anglo-European feminists.

The ethical and political questions presented by the use of *gender* or *género* in Latin American feminist writing is one of many problems that Latin American cultural critics working outside of Latin America must address. I believe the answer does not lie necessarily in totally refusing the use of the term because it is foreign to us, but rather in analyzing our paradoxical subject position in relation to our research. On the one hand, Latin Americans as well as Latin Americanists are in a subordinate position within U.S. academia; feminists, doubly so. On the other hand, we are in a privileged position vis-à-vis our colleagues in Latin America and the subjects involved in our study. While we do not want to replicate the construction of Latin America effected by Anglo-American discursive and institutional regimes, these regimes do position us in a paradoxical, unwilling complicity. Herein lies the double bind: the ways in which we participate in the construction of knowledge of Latin America are prescribed and/or recuperable by Anglo-American regimes of knowledge as well as by academic and institutional demands (for an excellent analysis of this double bind within a postcolonial context, see Spivak, "Who Claims Alterity?''; also see Belnap's excellent analysis of Spivak's thematizations). Rather than propose an escape from structures of ideological violence—an impossibility in our transnational era—a more fruitful solution is to negotiate with these structures and tentatively disrupt them by bringing them, as Gayatri Spivak has suggested, into a productive crisis (1989). Not only must Marxist and feminist narratives productively interrupt one another, but Anglo-American and Latin American feminist narratives should productively interrupt one another (these problems will also surface in the use of the term *gay* in Latin America, as we will see later).

Acknowledging, then, that a resistance to the use of *gender/género* is a cultural resistance to the idea that differences between men and women are culturally constructed as opposed to natural, the next step is to look at specific ways in which masculine and feminine are constructed and represented in Latin America. Clearly, these constructions have to do with issues of sexuality, grammar, and representation in relation to our long and varied colonial and neocolonial legacy. For the most part, these traditional gender constructs are based on the codes of the *marianismo*/machismo dichotomy (see Araújo; Castro-Klarén; del Campo; Stevens). Within these codes, the construction of woman in terms of *marianismo* (from the name Mary) is based on the Virgin Mary and the role she has been assigned in Roman Catholicism.

The two most important elements taken from the Virgin Mary as symbol of woman are maternity and chastity: Mary as Mother of Jesus and Wisdom of God, Mary as New Eve and Perpetual Virgin. On the one hand, Mary as mother is translated into the image of *mater dolorosa* or *pietá*, the self-denying mother who lives and suffers for her son Jesus. On the other hand, the image of Mary as virgin and chaste obliterates woman's sexuality as pleasure and casts her solely into a reproductive role. Woman, then, is respected because of qualities related to her role as mother: "This spiritual strength engenders ab-negation, that is, an infinite capacity for humility and sacrifice. No self-denial is too great for the Latin American woman, no limit can be divined to her vast store of patience with the men of her world" (Stevens, 95). Like the Virgin Mary, woman—the white woman—is idealized, considered semidivine, re-spected for her conduct and moral superiority (Stevens, 90). The Indian and black woman did not follow these patterns of socialization. They are both coded outside the *marianismo* model (first in the form of whore, then as the panicky, hysteric female).

Masculinity within the codes of machismo seems to be guided by a simulatory move: to be male equals being macho, *macho* meaning the excessive and ex-treme presence of masculinity or male dominance. Male dominance as ma-chismo is translated as exaggerated aggression and stubborness in male-to-male relations, and arrogance and sexual aggression in male-to-female relations. Male-ness is thus culturally coded as hypermaleness; the difference between macho, the hypersimulation of maleness, and male disappears (for an analysis of mas-culinity as a simulatory move, see Manzor-Coats; Piedra).

Intimately tied to this dichotomy is a construction of masculinity and femi-ninity within a matrix of clearly differentiated active and passive roles in the cultural and sexual realms. Again, the specific ways in which these constructs of male/female are connected to class and racial issues, the ways to signify so-called active and passive, as well as the ways in which women's material op-pression occurs, vary historically from country to country and from region to region. However, these constructions and representations have in common the ways in which physical, sexual, and "colonial violence is en-gendered" in and through them (de Lauretis, 33). In Mexico, for example, masculinity is synon-ymous with the *chingón*, "the one who fucks." Octavio Paz explains it in the following manner:

The verb [*chingar*] is masculine, active, cruel; it stings, wounds, gashes, stains. And it provokes a bitter satisfaction. The person who suffers this action is passive, inert and open, in contrast to the active, aggressive and closed person who inflicts it. The *chingón* is the *macho*, the male; he rips open the *chingada*, the female, who is pure passivity, defenseless against the exterior world. (77; see Zlotchew for an analysis of linguistic metaphors connecting male sexuality and aggression)

In Nicaragua, during Augusto César Sandino's time, the U.S. troops were given the nickname *machos* by women ("The machos were around here with their jackets: a blue coat, beautiful M beautiful P which said 'polisman' so we may respect them. But we respected their arms and not themselves" [Tijerino, 23]). And in Brazil, the male role is also associated with violence and aggression, force and power. Masculinity is thus embodied in the figure of the *machão*, the macho or he-man: "To be a man, a real man, you have to be a *machão*. A *machão* in bed and in the street: you have, or you think you have, huge sexual potential, a big cock, and you fuck with anything that's a woman. The *machão* is a roughneck, too. . . . He goes out into the street and he's always ready to fight in order to defend his honor" (Parker, 44). All of these examples underline that playing the active role is what constitutes maleness. Moreover, macho or hypermaleness is based on the active role not only as penetrator in the sexual act but also as perpetrator of force and power in the social imaginary.

Although gender categories present themselves as allegedly natural—as if they were the true, the norm—within this Latin American context it seems clear that from the onset masculinity and femininity are both part of a simulatory move that underlines, as Judith Butler has suggested, that

gender is a kind of imitation for which there is no original; in fact; it is a kind of imitation that produces the very notion of the original as an *effect* and consequence of the imitation itself. In other words, the naturalistic effects of heterosexualized genders are produced through imitative strategies; what they imitate is a phantasmatic ideal of heterosexual identity, one that is produced by the imitation as its effect. In this sense, the "reality" of heterosexual identities is performatively constituted through an imitation that sets itself up as the origin and the ground of all imitations. (313; Butler's emphasis)

In other words, gender is performative insofar as the subject it produces is an effect of a stylized repetition of acts that are historically constituted within specific social contexts. Thus, *performative* here alludes to both the dramatic sense of an act that is scripted and to the sense of nonreferentiality: the model always is already a simulation, as Severo Sarduy has taught us.

HOMOSEXUALITY IN LATIN AMERICA

We call them [men] *picha dulce*, sweet dick, those who go to mail a letter, for example, and during the walk from home to post office fuck even one of us [queers] without endangering or putting into question his virility, the excuse being that he just couldn't resist.

Senel Paz, *El lobo, el bosque y el hombre nuevo*, 7; translation by
McClemont

She remembers
The horror in her sister's voice,
"Eres una de las otras,"

The look in her mother's face as she says,
"I'm so ashamed, I will never
be able to raise my head in this pueblo."
The mother's words are barbs digging into her flesh.
De las otras. Cast out. Untouchable.

Gloria Evangelina Anzaldúa, "Del otro lado"

It is also within the above performative gender constructs that one must understand the construction of the male homosexual in Latin America. The category homosexual is not necessarily occupied by the one who is involved in same-sex erotic practices, but by the one who deviates from the gender constructs. In other words, in most societies in Latin America a man who engages in homosexual activity with other men is considered to be queer, *maricón*, only if and when he does not play his role as macho—that is, when he assumes the sexual and social role of the passive, the open, the weak; when he assumes the position and plays the role of woman. As long as he plays his active role as macho properly, the gender of his sexual partner is inconsequential, and he remains indistinguishable from the rest of the male population.

The terms assigned to homosexual men in most of Latin America follow from the gender constructs and are thus connected to issues of grammar and representation. (*Homosexual* here, following the construction above, refers to the man who plays the socially and sexually passive role.) In other words, as Tomás Almaguer has pointed out within the Mexican and Chicano cultures, the different names given to the *maricón*—*maricón* being the least stigmatized of all, respond to the linguistically gendered codes consonant with Latin America's patriarchal cultures, in which women always occupy an inferior position. Thus in Mexico, for example, the feminized homosexual man, analogous to the U.S. sissy or fairy, is called a *joto* or *puto*. The *joto*, a name phonetically linked to *roto* (broken) and synonymous with *rajado* (split or cracked), suggests being broken or ripped open—in other words, the male version of the *chingada* (La Malinche; for a Chicana feminist critique of this position, see Alarcón). *Puto*, on the other hand, while linked to the feminine word *puta*, a prostitute or whore, is not a male prostitute. Both terms are related to the most stigmatized females in Mexican society, the *chingada* and the whore. In Nicaragua, as Roger N. Lancaster and others have studied, "The social definition of the person and his sexual stigma derive from culturally-shared meanings of not just anal passivity and penile activity in particular, but passivity and activity in general. 'To give' (*dar*) is to be masculine, 'to receive' (*recibir, aceptar, tomar*) is to be feminine" (114). *Cochón* is the term used to refer to the feminized man, the one who takes it in and accepts like a woman.

In Brazil, activity and passivity in terms of cultural and sexual relations also revolve around words that relate to sex. *Comer* (to eat), *foder* (to fuck), and *abrir as pernas* (to open one's legs) are all linked to acts of control and domination. As José, a Brazilian native informant, explains, "When you are fucking

(*fodendo*) someone, when you're eating (*comendo*) . . . then you are above someone. . . . You have a superiority. . . . You're on top of someone. . . . You're in a position of dominator, of trainer. . . . You're being the king during that moment'' (Parker, 42). Within this axis of sexual identity, the one who is not in control, the one who is passive, is the *marica* (little Mary) or *bicha* (literally, worm); in other words, like the *joto* and the *cochón* they are penetrable and thus symbolically occupy the position of woman, the passive feminine role. This proliferation of pejorative names, at times quite a baroque or neobaroque enterprise, is reminiscent of the proliferation of names and divinities studied by Lyotard in *Libidinal Economy*.

Within this active/passive matrix that organizes Latin American gender constructs, the lesbian exists in a vacuum of unreadability and unnameability both socially and sexually. When she is named, she is euphemistically othered socially, but not sexually, by being put in the position of ''one of the others.'' As Parker has suggested, ''The very idea of a female sexual conduct outside of a context which is in some way or another defined vis-à-vis male sexuality, is almost unthinkable'' (53). Lesbian sexuality is read as asexual insofar as the signs of sexuality— male sexuality—supposedly are excised from the lesbian relation. In other words, since there is no activity, no penetration—read as no power—lesbianism is easily recuperated as asexual. On the other hand, the lesbian, as may be expected, is the most threatening to traditional gender constructs because she is the one who departs most completely from both masculine and feminine norms of expected social and sexual behavior. The threatening aspect of the lesbian, that ''horror'' in Anzaldúa's poem, is automatically converged into her masculine character and appearance; in other words, when the lesbian is read, she is read only as ''butch.''

The most common Spanish term assigned to the lesbian underlines the ways in which she is defined less in terms of her sexual behavior than in terms of her supposedly fundamental masculine style and her ambiguous nonposition within the sexual hierarchy: *marimacha*. This term, an odd linguistic mixture of María and macho, suggests an androgynous being who does not properly fit either the female role (Marí*a*) or the male (mach*o*). In an analogous fashion, the Brazilian Portuguese terms for the lesbian dyke, *machona* and *sapatão*, underline the lesbian's masculine style or quality. While *machona* (a big *macho*, linguistically feminized) is easily recognizable by an Anglo reader, *sapatão* (big shoes) needs some clarification. The shoe's connection to feet, metonymically functioning as a phallic symbol, is not all that is suggested by the term *sapatão*. What is at play here, as Judith Parker has demonstrated, is the connection between the big shoe and the army boot in the Brazilian and Latin American social imaginary:

You can see that of all the terms for the dyke, ''army boot'' is the strongest. . . . It's the symbol of the Brazilian army. So it's the symbol of machismo, it's the symbol of the courageous man, it's the symbol of the strong man. . . . He puts on those leather shoes, those boots that come up to here, a thing to step in the mud with, to go to battle, to go to war.... So, it's very much a man's thing! Understand? So, the army boot is a shoe that stands up to everything and is strong. (52)

Clearly, strength and power, the performative signs of virility in machismo codes, are the links between the big shoe and the army boot.

While these presentations of gender and homosexuality in Latin America are based heavily on a performative, thus constructionist, model (it assumes that an individual's sexual identity is constituted in relation to the social and historical context), this model does not account for "how society comes to dwell within individuals or how individuality comes to be socially constituted" (Epstein, 23). In other words, it lacks the psychic or intrapsychic processes through which identification takes place. Judith Butler's development of psychic identifications is a step in that direction (316–318).

GAY AND LESBIAN AS A POLITICAL CATEGORY

> I believe that [in Mexico] our highest representatives of "machismo" are gay.
>
> > Jesusa Rodríguez: cited in Franco

Most historians of the gay liberation movement in the United States mark the 1970s as the decade in which gay and lesbian identities began to be institutionalized (see Epstein; d'Emilio; Weeks). Post-Stonewall politics saw the rise of so-called gay and lesbian communities and political organizing around the sexual/political category of gay and lesbian, many times embracing a rather essentialist conception of identity. Invoking an equal rights language, gays and lesbians constituted themselves as a minority group, much like ethnic minority groups. In other words, gays' and lesbians' organization and mobilization around a politics of identity as a sexual minority has "a clearly political utility, for it has permitted a form of group organizing that is particularly suited to the American [sic] experience, with its history of civil-rights struggles and ethnic-based, interest group competition" (Epstein, 20).

This model of political organization and mobilization in the 1970s United States has no counterpart in Latin American societies. Dictatorial military states characterized by violence, repression, torture, and institutionalized acts of disappearance were the sociopolitical reality in most of Latin America in the 1970s. These military states constructed themselves through representational strategies based on the codes of *marianismo* and machismo. Woman's role was to help constitute the fatherland, thus casting her as an instrument of reproduction. Her space of action was the private space defined by the domestic, the quotidian, the maternal. The military state cast itself in the role of father, protector, provider, and benefactor of the country/family. In order to restore and reconstruct an alleged national unity, putatively subversive elements had to be identified and eradicated. The role of subversive was occupied by Communists, student leaders, and, as may be expected, homosexuals. David William Foster noted:

Military tyranny only provides homophobia with its greatest value as spectacle. Homophobia . . . becomes under authoritarian governments part of the way in which the dictatorial/dictated reconstruction of the public dimensions of personal identity and behavior is characterized very loudly and repeatedly in the press, from the pulpit, and by official decree. ("Latin American Literature," 6)

Most political organizing in Latin America took place around issues of human rights in which feminism and countercultural identities, when taken into account, were considered in relation to a sociopolitical reality that affected everyone, not just feminists or gays and lesbians (Foster, *Gay and Lesbian Themes*, 63; see also Silva). Instead of organizing around issues that could invoke an equal-rights discourse, appeals to human rights in Latin America invoked an oppositional discourse against authoritarian and patriarchal dynamics of social and political repression (see, e.g., Vidal; Kirkwood 1983 & 1985).

The economic linkage of military states to multinational capital that speeded the pace of urbanization and the change of the international marketplace, as well as the return of democracy in the 1980s and the advent of AIDS, have contributed to the increased pace of the "modernization of sexual life" in Latin America (Parker, 85). This modernization is characterized by a proliferation of discourses on sexuality, especially in the urban areas. It is also in the urban areas where one begins to see a proliferation of public spaces where homosexuals gather, spaces that are clearly differentiated by class.[4] Moreover, most anthropological and sociological work on male homosexuality is based on fieldwork conducted mainly in urban areas.

Modernization in the sexual realm, as in the economic realm, has resulted in the coexistence of two classificatory models for male homosexuality, one traditional and one "modern." The traditional or "archaic" model (Fry; Perlongher 1990a & b) is the popular and hierarchical one. As previously described, this model is based on the relationship between the macho, who is not identified as homosexual, and the *marica*, the effeminate homosexual. The violence at the core of this paradigm, the same violence that is constitutive of the conventional model of masculinity, connects this archaic model with patriarchal and authoritarian forms of "micro-fascism" (Perlongher, "Avatares," 132).

In contrast to and coexisting with the above model, is the more recent, egalitarian "modern" model of homosexuality. In this model, is typical of the more urban middle classes, a subject who identifies himself as homosexual relates as an equal to another subject who also assumes a homosexual identity. In Perlongher's words, this model is based on a "gay/gay relationship" ("Avatares," 126). These modern homosexuals who assume a gay identity are generally considered to base their sexual practices on foreign sexual scripts. Thus in Mexico, for example, they are called *internacionales* (international people):

Gay Mexican males who fall into the *internacionales* category are difficult to assess as a group. . . . Most of them are masculine rather than feminine and during the early years of their sex lives play only the "activo" sexual role—the "pasivo" sexual role is incorporated later as they become more involved in homosexual encounters. Many "internacionales" state that although they may play both sex roles, they nevertheless retain a strong preference for one over the other. (Carrier, 231)

In spite of the incorporation of these more bourgeois and egalitarian conceptions of sexuality, masculinity is still privileged among Latin American males, whether heterosexual or homosexual. Carrier states that "Although attempts have been made in the gay liberation movement to get its more masculine members to view feminine male behavior in a more positive way, they have had little success" (248). For these reasons, Jesusa Rodríguez's words in the epigraph to this section are quite right; in Latin America, gay discourse and practices, regardless of archaic or modern identificatory processes, are intimately connected to machismo ideology.

It is important to note that in order to describe the modern model of homosexuality, Joseph Carrier and Néstor Perlongher, among others, resort to the English term "gay." It should be clear by now that a politics of gay identity and the notion of a gay community, as they function in the United States and in some areas in Europe, are not common or typical in most of Latin America. In spite of these differences, the word *gay* is practically commonplace in most of Latin America. In Brazil, for example, gay ghettos, mostly lower class, are called boca gay (Perlongher; *boca* means "mouth").[5] In Mexico, the Universidad Nacional Autónoma de México has institutionalized Gay Cultural Week as *La semana cultural Gay*. Mexican gay journals have titles like *Opus Gay* and *Macho Tips*. Even in Cuba, where there are no overt signs of a gay politics or gay identity, the term *gay* is often heard (for studies of homosexuality in Cuba, see Argüelles and Rich; Montaner; Young).

The use of the term *gay* in Latin America is generally seen as an appropriation of a "foreign" term to describe "foreign" sexual scripts. Even Richard Parker sees it as part of "a whole range of developments—again, more often than not, emanating from abroad and imported . . . by the highly educated urban elite" (87). I believe one has to analyze the currency of the term from a global perspective. If, following Arjun Appadurai, one looks at the disjunctures between economy, culture, and politics that characterize global cultural flows, one can see that sexuality and its discourse are an integral part of these imagined worlds, "the multiple worlds which are constituted by the historically situated imaginations of persons and groups spread around the globe" (Appadurai, 7).

In order to suggest how sexuality is at the core of the relationship between ethnoscapes, mediascapes, finanscapes, ideoscapes, and technoscapes, let me briefly refer, first, to Richard Parker, a Berkeley-trained anthropologist. He went to Brazil to conduct fieldwork sponsored by the Tinker, Fulbright, and Wenner-Gren foundations. While he eventually ended up as a professor of anthropology at the State University of Rio de Janeiro, Boston's Beacon Press published in English the results of his initial research. Perlongher, an Argentinian poet and anthropologist, lived and taught in Brazil until his death in 1992. He conducted research on Brazilian male prostitution, and the results of his research are published in both Spanish and Portuguese. Both are involved in AIDS research and activism.

From these two examples one can discern that within these unstable ethnoscapes, deterritorialized academics move from one country to another, affecting the construction of sexuality, sexual politics and sexual policies in an unprecedented fashion. Obviously, academics are not the only ones involved in this process. Consider Queers for Cuba, a group of mostly Anglo leftist queers who organize around their queerness and their active solidarity with Cuba. In spite of the U.S. embargo and U.S. and Cuban homophobia, they undertook a massive fund-raising campaign primarily for medicine and money, which they then took to the AIDS hospital in Havana in August 1993 as part of the Friendshipment. And add to this global ethnoscape the thousands of straight and gay U.S. tourists who vacation in Mexico, Brazil and now Cuba, as well as the middle- and upper-class Latin Americans who come to the United States to fulfill their erotic fantasies.

Different sexual practices and sexual scripts, then, not only coexist but travel via people, the media, and technology. The fluidity of our ethnoscapes and mediascapes allow these practices and scripts to be rehearsed and replayed differently, according to class, ethnicity, and age. In the United States, for example, interethnic and interclass sexual practices rework the archaic and modern scripts. Tomás Almaguer explains:

In so doing, . . . working-class Latino men often become the object of middle-class Latino's or the white man's colonial desires. In one expression of this class-coded lust, the effeminate *pasivo* becomes the boyish, feminized object of the middle-class man's colonial desire. In another, the masculine . . . *activo* becomes the embodiment of a potent ethnic masculinity that titillates the middle-class man who thus enters into a passive sexual role. (89)

On this very small scale, the Latin American use of the word *gay*, the redefinition of the category *homosexual*, and the creation of a small number of political action groups and publications aimed at the homosexual population are examples of much more than the appropriation of foreign ideas by the elite. Within the disjunctures of human movement, financial transfers, technological flow, and dissemination of images and ideologies, issues of gay identity and gay "rights" sit at the intersection of a variety of ideoscapes and mediascapes. Although traditional Latin American political cultures have not been organized around the issue of gay rights, sexuality continues to be shaped and transformed. Sexual practices and scripts, rather than appropriated, are "indigenized" in different ways (Appadurai, 9). The category *internacionales* and the spelling *guei* are two of many examples of this process of indigenization in the realm of sexuality.

Lesbians, again, have been absent from most analyses of homosexuality. While there is a small but growing anthropological, historical and sociological literature on male homosexuality in Latin America, to my knowledge there are only a handful of studies on lesbians; only one of them is a book (see Castro; Hidalgo and Hidalgo Christensen; Jones; Mott). From the scarce material that is available, it seems that the political mobilization and organization of lesbians in Latin America goes hand in hand with changes in Latin American feminist movements from a transnational perspective (for an analysis of the transnational nature of Latin American feminist movements, see Miller). In the 1980s, as these feminist movements began to reach broader sectors of the population, there emerged new issues for discussion, and sexuality was one of them. A writer for the Mexican journal *fem* succinctly described these changes in the following manner: "At the beginning of 1980, feminism was most engaged in the debate of the specificity of woman and relations between men and women. Then, there was the question of child care and equal salaries. Only later did we begin to speak of the personal, of our body, and of sexuality" (quoted by Miller, 234).

An important factor in the development of a lesbian consciousness in Latin America seems to have been the presence of lesbians at international conferences as well as their participation in the coalitions, dialogues, and networks between Latina lesbians in the United States and in Latin America. In the late 1970s, Latina lesbian groups were being created in such U.S. cities as New York, San Francisco, Los Angeles, Denver, Boston and Philadelphia. In New York, the Comité Homosexual Latinoamericano (Latin American Homosexual Committee) was created in 1977. Although Latina lesbians participated, this was mostly a gay Latino organization. As may be expected, Latinas began to have problems due to "the sexism of the Latino brothers" (Ramos, xiv). In 1980, Digna Landrove de la O. and Juanita Ramos organized the Colectiva Lesbiana Latinoamericana (Latin American Lesbian Collective) in New York City. This group formed the Latina Lesbian History Project. In 1981, Cherríe Moraga and Gloria Anzaldúa published the ground-breaking collection *This Bridge Called My Back*, which included a number of writings by Latina lesbians; most of these addressed the connections between racism in the Anglo community and homophobia in the Latino community (see, e.g., the works by Alarcón, Anzaldúa, Levins Morales, Moraga, Morales and Quintanales).

Lesbian organizations also began to appear in Peru, Brazil, Colombia, Chile, Mexico, Argentina, the Dominican Republic, and Puerto Rico (Ramos, xiii). Representatives from these organizations were present at the first three Latin American and Caribbean Feminist Encounters (Miller, 234).[6] The intercontinental dialogue between lesbians that began in the 1980s was followed by three meetings of Latin American and Caribbean lesbian feminists. Latina lesbians from the United States also participated. The first was held in Cuernavaca, Mexico, in October 1987, immediately before the fourth Latin American and Caribbean Feminist Encounter. Over two hundred women participated in this gathering, which was carried out in "a normal climate" (Cárdenas, 67). However, at the second meeting, which took place in Costa Rica in 1990, the group of *entendidas* (Spanish euphemism for lesbians) was verbally attacked by the church and the government on public television. Their peace caravan was stoned in the streets of San José, and they were attacked as "leftists" (Cárdenas, 98). This public assault underscores the issues of unnameability I addressed earlier. Although they were attacked verbally and physically, the words *homosexuality* and *lesbianism* were unspoken. That is, they remained verbally unnamed through the euphemism of *entendidas* and were "othered" socially as "leftists."

The lesbian movement in Latin America, much like the feminist movement, has to be considered within an intercontinental or global scope. It seems that the evolution of a Latin American lesbian consciousness and identity has been enabled by the fluidity of our ethnoscapes, mediascapes and technoscapes that has permitted transnational networking and political activism. Although the presence and activism of lesbians has put sexuality and lesbianism on the Latin American feminist agenda, lesbianism, while no longer a taboo subject, has been, and continues to be, a bone of contention among Latinas and Latin American feminists.

WRITING AND HOMOSEXUALITY

> —El personaje de mi novela es maricón—le digo. . . .
> —¿Y por qué? pregunta, al fin. Me toma de sorpresa: ¿acaso lo sé? Pero improviso una explicación.
> —Para acentuar su marginalidad, su condición de hombre lleno de contradicciones. También para mostrar los prejuicios que existen sobre este asunto entre quienes, supuestamente, quieren liberar a la sociedad de sus taras.[7]
>
> Mario Vargas Llosa, 335

Although many critics agree that gender and sexuality are fundamental categories in the organization of a subject's experience, the relationship between writing specifically and gender and sexuality appears to be more problematic. The methodological base for this volume, as presented in David William Foster's preface, is the identification of writers who fall within three definitions of gay topics: "those individuals with a professed gay identity . . . ; those individuals who have written on gay themes . . . ; and, finally, any individual who, although not dealing overtly with a gay topic or professing a gay identity, has authored works in which something like a gay sensibility can be identified, no matter how problematically" ("Latin American Literature," n.d.). It seems to me, then, that theoretical connections must be identified not only between writing and sexuality but also between reading and sexuality.

We know that in the construction of fictional worlds, literature represents models and patterns of sexuality, and this representation is part of the construction of sexuality. In other words, literature is a discourse about sexuality. What do we do or what should we do when we talk about sexuality in general, and homosexuality specifically, in relation to literature? Any discourse about homosexuality should be related, first of all, to the heterosexual or heterosexist hegemony that characterizes Latin American culture and cultural criticism. An analysis of this dialectical relationship between the two should be seen in connection with other forms of social political and economic determinations. Homo-versus heterosexuality considered in this fashion would take into account individual as well as collective forms of subject formation. This is probably one of the reasons why in Latin American writing homosexuality is intimately connected to other power structures within society.

Fry's and Perlongher's differentiation of an archaic and a modern typology of the male homosexual could be instructive for reading the ways in which Latin American literature has represented and constructed the homosexual in Foster's first two categories. We could say that the archaic literary construction uses the homosexual as a scapegoat to deal with either social marginality or politically and economically oppressive regimes. In these works, the homosexual can be read as a silent witness, so to speak, of sociopolitical repression. Typical of this scapegoating is the literary construction of the homosexual in José Donoso (1925), Elena Garro (1920), Mario Vargas Llosa (1936), Adolfo Caminha (1867–1897), and even Manuel Puig (1932–1990).

A modern or postmodern construction of the homosexual—and we do not have many examples—would look at homosexual love and relationships as natural, legitimate, and realizable. It would also have to deal with the heterosexist and partriarchal linguistic and literary codes that have traditionally "erased" or "written out" homosexuality as one of many dimensions of human affairs (Foster, *Gay and Lesbian Themes*, 114). In these texts, homosexuality and textuality are created as a space of opposition in which the political economy of the body's desires and longings can be articulated (see Schaefer-Rodríguez for an excellent analysis of this kind of reading and writing). Sylvia Molloy (1938), Rosamaría Roffiel (1951), and Luis Zapata (1951) fall into this category.

In this dialectical reading of homosexuality and textuality, literature is not seen as an unmediated record of the society that produced it. In other words, I am not suggesting that homosexual literature is solely the representation of homosexuality by and for homosexuals. Neither am I endorsing naïve assumptions about the transparency of language. On the contrary, the most interesting gay and lesbian writing in Latin America is trying to invent, to create a language appropriate and authentic to the homosexual experience, both personal and literary. This language, more often than not, comes out of and responds to a notion of a self, both self-knowing and self-representation, that is both fragmented and collective. Thus, these writings are quite different from the individualistic subject formation in Anglo-American queer narratives, where the coming-out story, the homosexual relationship, and the breakup have become formulaic (Anzaldúa, 260).[8]

Most postmodern texts that we may tentatively call homosexual underscore, moreover, that while literature is a discourse about homosexuality, the two are not one and the same. In other words, they emphasize the need to look at the sociohistorical realities that inform sexual categories so that homosexual practices connected to political praxis do not disappear (for a warning against this conflation of sexuality into textuality, see Van Leer, 9–10). Homosexuality in these texts is part of a revolutionary agenda in the political, social, sexual and literary realms.

For these reasons Foster's third category, that of a work in which one can identify "something like a gay sensibility," is highly problematic. In readings of Anglo-European literature, the concepts of homoeroticism, homosocial desire, and homosexual thematics have been commonplace since the publication of Eve Kosofsky Sedgwick's influential works. However, as David Van Leer has pointed out, by privileging a textual construction of homoeroticism, Sedgwick does not connect sexual preference to a social reality. Thus, "She avoids a more direct demonstration of the social operation of these categories by treating them as purely linguistic phenomena, implying that there is no sexuality outside of language" (11).

This would be the first problem to avoid in a reading of homoeroticism in any Latin American text. While it is important to analyze homoeroticism in the Cubans in Severo Sarduy (1937–1993) and José Lezama Lima (1912–1976), for example—I should add fellow Cuban Guillermo Cabrera Infante (1929)—this reading should connect homoeroticism not only to the persecution of homosexuals in Cuba but also to the homophobia in Cuban society at large. These readings must correlate, as Foster has suggested elsewhere, "the personal with the political, since questions of sexual politics are inevitably related to larger issues of social construction" ("Latin American Literature," 11). In so doing, the pitfalls of leaving out homosexuality as a social reality and practice would be avoided.

It seems to me that problems related to reading and interpretive strategies are implicit in David Foster's three definitions of gay topics. In other words, what is important is not solely to identify "texts in which homosexual genital sex is showcased" (Preface, this volume). Rather, the most important task at hand is to analyze what a nonheterosexist or queer reading practice would be. We know that Latin American critics are noteworthy for reading with a so-called "straight" mind. The lesbian or gay subtexts have rarely been considered. Even in cases where it is difficult *not* to read the lesbian or gay text, the issue of homosexuality is easily avoided. Cristina Peri Rossi (1941) is a case in point. Practically none of the criticism on her work has considered issues of lesbian sexuality and/or lesbian textuality. Kaminsky's excellent analysis of her work in a chapter entitled "The Question of Lesbian Presence" is the only exception. When Peri Rossi's novel *Solitario de amor* (Love Solitaire; 1988) was published, it was widely reviewed in the newspapers in Uruguay. Reviews noted that the novel tried to present love-passion from a masculine point of view, but that the erotic tone was purely feminine. Many critics commented jokingly, though not in print, "Cristina, no less" (Gandolfo, 85). They were clearly referring, without naming the word, to the lesbianism that is explicit or implicit in her work.

Peri Rossi is also a good example here because her work forces us to ask precisely the kinds of questions I was addressing above. In other words, we need to consider not only what lesbian literature is but, most importantly, what a lesbian critical stance toward a text might be when "it is not about love or sex, when traditional characterization disappears, when plot is minimized, when everything we attach to identity is disattached" (Kaminsky, 116). These are also the questions we need to address in order to approach Sarduy's work, for example, with a queer mind.

I have been trying to suggest that instead of focusing solely on gay or lesbian aesthetics in a text we should recast our concerns and focus on a gay or lesbian reading sensibility—in other words, in reading with a "queer *facultad*" (faculty), as Gloria Anzaldúa has suggested (257). Based on a model of identification and not of identity, inherently not very different from Judith Butler's psychic identification, Anzaldúa notes that reading is a process through which what is not familiar to us remains hidden in the text, is not perceived. Following Anzaldúa ("To(o) Queer the Writer"), I venture to say that to read with a queer *facultad* would mean

to "see into" and "see through" unconscious falsifying disguises by penetrating the surface and reading underneath the words and between the lines. . . . For me then it is a question of whether the individual reader is in possession of a mode of reading that can read the subtext, and can introject her experiences into the gaps. Some conventionally trained readers do not have the flexibility (in identity) nor the patience in deciphering a "strange," that is, different, text. (238)

Although Anzaldúa's essay does not refer to reader response theorists, any critic familiar with this extensive body of critical and theoretical work will immediately ask how Anzaldúa's mode of reading with a queer *facultad* is different from, say, the modes of reading theorized by Wolfgang Iser, George Poulet, Norman Holland, or Stanley Fish, to name a few. Although these theorists have different approaches to models of reading, we have learned from them to acknowledge the creative role of the reader, to identify the diachronic and synchronic processes through which the reader fills in gaps, and to analyze the interaction of text and reader (for an excellent analysis and critique of different approaches to reader response criticism, see Mailloux). This approach is summarized by Iser in the following fashion: "The phenomenological theory of art lays full stress on the idea that, in considering a literary work, one must take into account not only the actual text but also, and in equal measure, the actions involved in responding to that text" (274).

Jonathan Culler was one of the first theorists to interrogate reader response theories on the issue of gender:

If the experience of literature depends upon the qualities of a reading self, one can ask what difference it would make to the experience of literature and thus to the meaning of literature if this self were, for example, female rather than male. If the meaning of a work is the experience of a reader, what difference does it make if the reader is a woman? (42)

A decade of research in feminist theory has answered this question of "what is the *difference* of women's writing" (Showalter, "Feminist Criticism," 182) and reading. Moreover, this research has underlined that the importance lies not on a woman as reader but on feminist readings. As Patrocinio Schweickart has noted, "Feminist criticism, we should remember, is a mode of *praxis*. . . . We cannot afford to ignore the activity of reading, for it is here that literature is realized as *praxis*. Literature acts on the world by acting on its readers" (24).

Although the now classical approaches to reader response criticism do offer different accounts of the reading experience, they have all overlooked issues of race, gender, class and sexuality. Moreover, in these approaches, the nature of the reading material is inconsequential. Gloria Anzaldúa's model of reading with a queer *facultad* is based on these oversights. She underscores, first, that it is impossible to separate how we read from what we read. Second, how we read is dependent upon "the place one's feet are planted, the ground one stands on, one's particular position, point of view" (258).

Peri Rossi's words in the preface of this volume suggest that the connection between a literary text and *how* a community of readers might decode an apple or a poem by Sappho is political. I suggest that this *how* is by reading between the lines with the queer *facultad* with which the collaborators of this volume and I have approached our topics and authors. I hope that this volume will incite and excite you into joining this growing community of readers and writers with a queer *facultad*.

NOTES

1. To study the imagination as a social practice in our global culture, Appadurai looks at the relationship between flows of people (ethnoscapes), finance (financscapes), information (mediascapes), technology (technoscapes) and ideology (ideoscapes).

2. "For feminist analysis, however, it began to be evident that the reason for the existence of authoritarianism or women's conservatism did not lie in feminine 'essences'; on the contrary, it obeyed a 'law of gender' and, therefore, a pure social, cultural and political construction with other parameters" (my translation).

3. As Jeffrey Weeks has suggested, "what we define as 'sexuality' is an historical construction, which brings together a host of different biological and mental possibilities" (15).

4. In Montevideo, for example, after the return of democracy, middle-class gays went to a disco called Controversia, where all activity took place inside. Lower-class gays

went to another street and gathered on the sidewalks, creating, according to Elvio Gandolfo, a carnivallike atmosphere of exhibition (85). This is the space in which transvestites and others can perform, in Gandolfo's unconscious homophobic language, "gestures that are theatrically emphasized . . . and that the social gaze considers typical" (85).

5. A Brazilian informant told Parker, "There are gay or *guei* beaches in Copacabana and Ipanema. There are gay bars and nightclubs in Rio and São Paulo just like in New York or Paris" (Parker, 94).

6. The Encuentro Feminista Latinoamericano y del Caribe (Latin American and Caribbean Feminist Encounter) was held in Bogotá in 1981, in Lima in 1983, and in Santos, Brazil, in 1985.

7.

—The character in my novel is queer, I tell him. . . .
—And why? he finally asks, taking me by surprise. How do I know? But I improvise an explanation.
—In order to highlight his marginality, his condition as a man full of contradictions. Also in order to show the prejudices that exist about this issue among those who, supposedly, want to liberate society from its vices. (my translation)

8. Clearly, Anzaldúa is referring to coming out more as a narrative than as a social enactment or performance. For an excellent analysis of the difference between these two, see Van Leer, 39–42. In reference to the individual nature of the U.S. lesbian experience, specifically, Amy Kaminsky notes that "The desire to codify lesbian experience for a lesbian audience in the United States comes out of a tradition that values individual identity, a tradition that has by now been redesigned so that the body of the individual is as highly valued as the mind that has been abstracted from it" (116).

REFERENCES

Abelove, Henry, Michèle Aina Barale, and David M. Halperin, eds. *The Lesbian and Gay Studies Reader*. New York: Routledge, 1993.

Adam, Berry D. "Homosexuality Without a Gay World: Pasivos y Activos en Nicaragua." *Out/Look* 1.4 (1989): 74–82.

Alarcón, Norma. "Chicana's Feminist Literature.: A Re-Vision Through Malintzín/or Malintzín: Putting Flesh Back on the Object." In Moraga and Anzaldúa, 182–190.

Almaguer, Tomás. "Chicano Men: A Cartography of Homosexual Identity and Behavior." *differences: A Journal of Feminist Cultural Studies* 3.2 (1991): 75–100.

Anderson, Benedict. *Imagined Communities: Reflections on the Origin and Spread of Nationalism*. London: Verso, 1983.

Anzaldúa, Gloria. "Del otro lado." In *Compañeras: Latina Lesbians (an Anthology)*. Ed. Juanita Ramos. New York: Latina Lesbian History Project, 1987.

———. "To(o) Queer the Writer—Loca, escritora y chicana." In Warland, 249–263.

Appadurai, Arjun. "Disjuncture and Difference in the Global Cultural Economy." *Public Culture* 2.2 (Spring 1990): 1–24.

Araújo, Helena. "El modelo mariano, tema y variaciones." *Eco* [Bogotá] 248 (June 1982): 118–122.

Argüelles, Lourdes, and B. Ruby Rich. "Homosexuality, Homophobia and Revolution: Notes Toward an Understanding of the Cuban Lesbian and Gay Male Experience" *Signs: Journal of Women and Culture in Society* 9.4 (1984): 683–699; 11.1 (1985): 120–136.

Behares, Luis E. "La subcultura homosexual en Montevideo." *Relaciones* 64 (Sept. 1989): 13–24.

Belnap, Jeffrey. "Intellectuals in the Post-Colonial World." Ph.D. diss., University of California–Irvine, 1993.

Butler, Judith. "Imitation and Gender Insubordination." In Abelove et al., 302–320.

Campo, Alicia del. "Resignificación del marianismo por los movimientos de mujeres de oposición en Chile." In Vidal, 429–465.

Cárdenas, Nancy. "País que ataca a sus minorías, es un país emponzoñado por el fascismo." (interview with Patricia Ruiz Manjares). *Siempre* 1937 (Aug. 1990): 66–67, 98.

Carrier, Joseph M. "Gay Liberation and Coming out in Mexico." In Herdt, 225–253.

Castro, María. "El lesbianismo como una cuestión política." Mexico City: Ponencia, 1987.

Castro-Klarén, Sara. "Women, Self, and Writing." In Castro-Klarén et al., 3–26.

Castro-Klarén, Sara, Sylvia Molloy, and Beatriz Sarlo, eds. *Women's Writing in Latin America*. Boulder, Colo.: Westview Press, 1991.

Culler, Jonathan. *On Deconstruction: Theory and Criticism After Structuralism*. Ithaca, N.Y.: Cornell University Press, 1982.

de Lauretis, Teresa. *Technologies of Gender*. Bloomington: Indiana University Press, 1987.

d'Emilio, John. *Sexual Politics, Sexual Communities: The Making of a Homosexual Minority in the United States, 1940–1970*. Chicago: University of Chicago Press, 1983.

Epstein, Steven. "Gay Politics, Ethnic Identity: The Limits of Social Constructionism." *Socialist Review* 17.3–4 (May–Aug. 1987): 9–54.

Escritura y sexualidad en la literatura hispanoamericana. Madrid: Editorial Fundamentos, 1990.

Foster, David William. *Gay and Lesbian Themes in Latin American Writing*. Austin: University of Texas Press, 1991.

———. "Latin American Literature." In the forthcoming *Encyclopedia of International Lesbian and Gay Culture*. Claude J. Summers, ed. New York: Holt, Rinehart and Winston, n.d.

Foucault, Michel. *The History of Sexuality*, vol. 1. Trans. Robert Hurley. New York: Random House, 1978.

Franco, Jean. "A Touch of Evil: Jesusa Rodríguez's Subversive Church." *The Drama Review* 36.2 (1992): 48–61.

Fry, Peter. *Para inglês ver: Identidade e política na cultura brasileira*. Rio de Janeiro: Zahar Editores, 1982.

Gandolfo, Elvio E. "Montevideo sexual, una reflexión a pie." *Nueva sociedad* 109 (Sept.–Oct. 1990): 80–89.

Goldwert, Marvin. "Mexican Machismo: The Flight from Femininity." *Psychoanalytic Review* 72.1 (1985): 161–169.

Hall, Stuart. "Gramsci's Relevance for the Study of Race and Ethnicity." *Journal of Communication Inquiry* 10.2 (1986): 5–27.

Herdt, Gilbert, ed. *Gay and Lesbian Youth*. New York: Haworth, 1989.

Hidalgo, Hilda, and Elia Hidalgo Christensen. "The Puerto Rican Lesbian and the Puerto Rican Community." *Journal of Homosexuality* 2 (Winter 1976–1977): 109–121.

"Homosexuality in Cuba: A Threat to Public Morality?" *Connexions: An International Women's Quarterly* 2 (1981): 18–19.

Iser, Wolfgang. *The Implied Reader: Patterns of Communication in Prose Fiction from Bunyan to Beckett*. Baltimore: Johns Hopkins University Press, 1974.

Jones, Brooke. "Cuban Lesbians." *off our backs* 10 (Oct. 1980): 6, 16.

Kaminsky, Amy. *Reading the Body Politic: Feminist Criticism and Latin American Women Writers*. Minneapolis: University of Minnesota Press, 1993.

Kirkwood, Julieta. "El feminismo como negación del autoritarismo." *Material de discusión programa FLACSO—Santiago de Chile* 52 (Dec. 1983): 143–155.

———. "Feministas y políticas." *Nueva sociedad* 78 (July–Aug. 1985): 62–70.

Lancaster, Roger N. "Subject Honor and Object Shame: The Construction of Male Homosexuality and Stigma in Nicaragua." *Ethnology* 27.2 (1987): 111–125.

Lyotard, Jean François. *Libidinal Economy*. Trans. Iain Hamilton Grant. Bloomington: Indiana University Press, 1993.

Mailloux, Steven. *Interpretive Conventions: The Reader in the Study of American Fiction*. Ithaca, N.Y.: Cornell University Press, 1982.

Manzor-Coats, Lillian. "Who Are You, Anyway?: Gender, Racial and Linguistic Politics in U.S. Cuban Theater." *Gestos* 11 (1991): 163–174.

Miller, Francesca. *Latin American Women and the Search for Social Justice*. Hanover, N.H.: University Press of New England, 1991.

Monsiváis, Carlos. "Control y condón: La revolución sexual mexicana." *Nueva sociedad* 109 (Sept.–Oct. 1990): 99–105.

Montaner, Carlos Alberto. "Sexo malo." In his *Informe secreto sobre la revolución cubana*, 173–177. Madrid: Ediciones Sedmay, 1976.

Moraga, Cherríe, and Gloria Anzaldúa. *This Bridge Called My Back: Writings by Radical Women of Color*. Watertown, Mass.: Persephone, 1981.

Mott, Luiz R. B. *O lesbianismo no Brasil*. Pôrto Alegre: Mercado Aberto, 1987.

Parker, Richard G. *Bodies, Pleasures and Passions: Sexual Culture in Contemporary Brazil*. Boston: Beacon Press, 1991.

Paz, Octavio. *Labyrinth of Solitude: Life and Thought in Mexico*. Trans. Lysander Kemp. New York: Grove Press, 1961.

Paz, Senel. "The Wolf, the Forest and the New Man." Trans. David McClemont. Unpublished ms.

Perlongher, Néstor. "Avatares de los muchachos de la noche." *Nueva sociedad* 109 (Sept.–Oct. 1990a): 124–134.

———. *O negócio do michê: Prostituição viril e São Paulo*. São Paulo: Editora Brasiliense, 1990b.

Pescatello, Ann, ed. *Female and Male in Latin America*. Pittsburgh: University of Pittsburgh Press, 1973.

Piedra, José. "His/Her Panics." *Dispositio* 16.41 (1991): 71–93.

Puleo, Alicia. "Perspectivas antropológicas de un problema de crítica literaria." In *Escritura y sexualidad en la literatura hispanoamericana*, 9–20.

Ramos, Juanita. "Preface." In *Compañeras: Latina Lesbians*, xiii–xix. New York: Latina Lesbian History Project, 1987.

Sarduy, Severo. *Simulación*. Caracas: Monte Avila Editores, 1982.

Schaefer-Rodríguez, Claudia. "The Power of Subversive Imagination: Homosexual Utopian Discourse in Contemporary Mexican Literature." *Latin American Literary Review* 33 (1989): 29–41.

Schweickart, Patrocinio A. "Reading Ourselves: Toward a Feminist Theory of Reading."
In Showalter, *Speaking of Gender*, 17–44.

Showalter, Elaine. "Feminist Criticism in the Wilderness." *Critical Inquiry* 8 (1981):
179–187.

———., ed. *Speaking of Gender*. New York: Routledge, 1989.

Silva, Aguinaldo. *Primeira carta aos andróginos*. Rio de Janeiro: Pallas, 1985.

Spivak, Gayatri Chakravorty. *The Post-colonial Critic: Interviews, Strategies, Dialogues*.
New York: Routledge, 1990.

———. *Thinking Academic Freedom in Gendered Post-coloniality*. Cape Town: University of Cape Town, 1992.

———. "Who Claims Alterity?" In *Remaking History*, 269–292. Ed. Barabara Kruger
and Phil Mariani. Seattle: Bay Press, 1989.

Stevens, Evelyn P. "Marianismo, the Other Face of Machismo in Latin America." In
Pescatello, 87–103.

Tijerino, Doris. *Doris Tijerino: Inside the Nicaraguan Revolution as Told to Margaret
Randall*. Trans. from the Spanish by Elinor Randall. Vancouver: New Star Books,
1978.

Van Leer, David. "The Beast in the Closet: Sedgwick and the Knowledge of Homosexuality." In his *The Queening of America*. New York: Routledge, forthcoming.

Vargas Llosa, Mario. *Historia de Mayta*. Barcelona: Seix Barral, 1984. (*The Real Life
of Alejandro Mayta*. Trans. Alfred MacAdam. New York: Farrar, Strauss and
Giroux, 1989, p. 301).

Vidal, Hernán, ed. *Poética de la población marginal: Fundamentos materialistas para
una historiografía estética*. Minneapolis: Prisma Institute, 1987.

Warland, Betsy, ed. *InVersions: Writings by Dykes, Queers and Lesbians*. Vancouver:
Press Gang Publishers, 1991.

Weeks, Jeffrey. *Sexuality and Its Discontents: Meanings, Myths and Modern Sexualities*.
London: Routledge and Kegan Paul, 1985.

Young, Allen. *Gays Under the Cuban Revolution*. San Francisco: Grey Fox Press, 1981.

Zlotchew, Clark M. "Metáforas agresivo-sexuales en inglés y en español." *Foro literario*
12 (1984): 3–10.

A

ACOSTA, OSCAR ZETA (United States; 1935–1974?)

Acosta was born in El Paso, Texas, in 1935. His father, Manuel, was a descendant of Indians from Durango, Mexico; his mother, Juana, was a naturalized U.S. citizen of working-class origins. During World War II, when the father served in the military, the family relocated to the San Joaquin valley in central California. Acosta had five siblings: Anita, Marta, Sally, Roberto and Al. According to his own testimony, he began to abuse alcohol; and although he had the reputation of a *vato loco* (crazy dude), he entered the U.S. Air Force. His military service in Panama was marked by a conversion to Baptist fundamentalism, a belief he later rejected. Acosta married Betty Dowd; a son, Marco Federico Manuel, was born in 1960. He worked his way through college and law school after leaving the military and was admitted to the California bar in 1966. In 1967, he began to work as an attorney for an antipoverty agency.

Much of Acosta's life in the Los Angeles civil rights movement, during the turbulent late 1960s and 1970s, is detailed in his graphic and exaggerated biography, *The Autobiography of a Brown Buffalo* (1972). In 1970, Acosta published his first short story, "Perla Is a Pig," later anthologized in *Voices of Aztlan*. While writing, he was a leading attorney in civil rights cases such as *Castro* v. *Superior Court of Los Angeles County*, a precedent-setting decision concerning First Amendment rights, and *Carlos Montez et al.* v. *Superior Court of Los Angeles County*, a case involving systematic exclusion of Hispanics as jurors.

Simultaneoulsy, Acosta began his friendship with Hunter S. Thompson, the "gonzo" journalist of the 1970s. Thompson appears as Stonewall in Acosta's second novel, *The Revolt of the Cockroach People* (1973). Thompson reciprocated with the character Raoul Duke, a three hundred-pound Samoan attorney, in his work *Fear and Loathing in Las Vegas* (1972).

Acosta disappeared from a friend's sailboat in June 1974 near Mazatlán, Mexico. Neither the FBI nor the Coast Guard could confirm his death.

The work of Acosta consists of *Autobiography of a Brown Buffalo* (1972), *The Revolt of the Cockroach People* (1973) and "Perla Is a Pig." Both full-length works are considered significant documentary literary creations that reflect the political and social chaos of the 1960s and 1970s. *Autobiography* is Acosta's quest analysis, searching for the world from which he evolved spiritually, psychologically and sexually. *Revolt* portrays the societal conflicts of the Chicano community in Los Angeles marked by the mysterious death of a prominent journalist, Rubén Salazar. Other important incidents documented include the 1968 interruption of Christmas Eve services at Saint Basil's Cathedral, the educational protests of the Tooner Flats Seven, and the Vietnam protests. Psychological self-examination and sexual assertiveness mark the works.

General critical assessments reflect the sociopolitical expression of the Chicano movement and the particular Los Angeles and California settings. Biographical consideration emphasizes the parallelism of other multiethnic testimonial works, among them those of Piri Thomas in the New York Puerto Rican community. Both of Acosta's books were reissued in 1989 by Vintage Books with a forward by Hunter Thompson and an afterword by the author's son.

In his ground-breaking article, "Homosexuality and the Chicano Novel," Juan Bruce-Novoa cites the gay "leitmotif with a distinct negative signification" in Acosta's work. His essay details the continuous disrespectful use of *fag*, *faggot* or *homosexual* as the term that represents any individual Acosta does not like. His negative signifiers are directed at the Los Angeles police chief, Moctezuma, Timothy Leary, Mark Harris, Herb Gold, and Liberace, as well as unnamed judges, court stenographers, and passersby. The use of the term becomes gratuitous in the two works; homosexuality symbolizes the other, the enemy—a representation of the dress of society. "I live with cockroaches, winos, pimps, whores, junkies, fags, yoyos with bloody noses and bad breath" (*Revolt*, 48). Los Angeles is "a broken city filled with battered losers. Winos in tennies, skinny fags in tight pants" (*Revolt*, 23). San Francisco is a "fag's Baghdad by the Bay" (*Autobiography*, 18). The Polk district is peopled by "fancy assed fags selling flowers" (*Autobiography*, 36).

In his writing, one homosexual stands out: José Ramón Lerma. His description is somewhat positive:

The tall pimple faced man was a mystic of classic proportions, a Mexican fag who'd never gotten over catching his mother with some man in a Salinas grape vineyard where he learned all his Catholicism. Although the Polk district was filled with queers, butches and fags, José Ramón Lerma was one of the few homosexuals we tolerated at JJ's (local bar). Not only because he had learned to keep the beast in his pocket but because he was the only artist of the whole bunch of scags. (*Autobiography*, 47)

Federico García Lorca's homosexual identity must not yet have been revealed to Acosta: "I am the son of Lorca, I remind myself, the only poet this century worth reading" (*Autobiography*, 66). Responding to an apparent gay come-on, Acosta notices the short distance between the eyes, a distinguishing characteristic of faggots (according to Acosta), and when the other man reaches for a handshake, the author, cupping his cigarette, burns the man's hand. Maleness or machismo is a paranoid concern of Acosta's. Speaking of education, he stresses this preoccupation: "It seemed that the sole purpose of childhood was to train boys how to be men. . . . We were supposed to talk like *un hombre*, walk like a man, act like a man and think like a man" (*Autobiography*, 75).

In his *The Autobiography of a Brown Buffalo* and *The Revolt of the Cockroach People*, Acosta represents the homosexual as the evil, threatening other—the individual who threatens his masculinity and his status. In his personal search for definition and awareness of self, he glorifies the supermacho stud, simultaneously exaggerating his disdain for all other males. His chosen insult is *fag* or *faggot*.

WORKS

The Autobiography of a Brown Buffalo. San Francisco: Straight Arrow, 1972. Reiss. New York: Vintage Books, 1989. All quotations taken from the latter edition.
"Perla Is a Pig." In *Voices of Aztlan: Chicano Literature Today*. Ed. Dorothy Harth and Lewis M. Baldwin, 28–48. New York: Mentor, 1974.
The Revolt of the Cockroach People. San Francisco: Straight Arrow, 1973. All quotations taken from this edition. Reiss. New York: Vintage Books, 1989.

CRITICISM

Alurista. "Myth, Identity and Struggle in Three Chicano Novels: Aztlán . . . Anaya, Mendez and Acosta." In *European Perspectives on Hispanic Literature of the United States*. Ed. Genviève Fabré, 98–106. Houston: Arte Público Press, 1988.
Bruce-Novoa, Juan. "Homosexuality and the Chicano Novel." In *European Perspectives on Hispanic Literature of the United States*, Ed. Genviève Fabré, 98–106. Houston: Arte Público Press, 1988.
Kowalczyk, Kimberly A. "Oscar Zeta Acosta: The Brown Buffalo and His Search for Identity." *The Americas Review* 16 (Fall–Winter 1988): 198–209.
Rodríguez, Joe D. "The Chicano Novel and the North American Narrative of Survival." *Denver Quarterly* 16 (Fall 1981): 229–235.
———. "God's Silence and the Shrill of Ethnicity in the Chicano Novel." *Explorations in Ethnic Studies* 4 (July 1981): 21.
———. "Oscar Zeta Acosta." *Dictionary of Literary Biography*, 82: 3–10.
———. "The Sense of Meztizaje in Two Latino Novels." *Revista chicano riqueña* 12 (Spring 1984): 57–63.
Stavans, Ilan. "Bandido Vendido: The Life & Times of Oscar Zeta Acosta." *The Bloomsbury Review* 12 (Jan.–Feb. 1992): 4.

John C. Miller

AGOSTO, MOISÉS (Puerto Rico; 1965) _____

Moisés Agosto was born in San Juan, Puerto Rico, in 1965. After graduating from the University of Puerto Rico, he moved to New York in 1988 to study at the State University of New York at Stony Brook. Since 1989, when he joined the activist organization ACT-UP, Agosto had dedicated himself to the fight against AIDS. In 1991, he became a member of the People with AIDS Coalition, for which he is the editor of *Sidahora* (roughly, Aids Hour), a bilingual periodical that keeps the Hispanic community of the New York metropolitan area informed about medical, social, political and artistic issues related to the AIDS crisis. In spite of an extremely busy work schedule, which includes writing for *Sidahora* and traveling frequently to national and international conferences on AIDS, Agosto has written four collections of poetry and, with Joey Pons-Myers, the first book of poetry in Spanish totally dedicated to AIDS. He is writing a fictionalized autobiography.

At the beginning of each author's section in *Poemas de lógica inmune* (Poems of Immune Logic), Agosto (7) and Pons-Myers (27) identify themselves as "homosexual activists living with Aids." The texts that follow can equally be described as poems by homosexual activists living with AIDS. They are about both the homosexual experience and the experience of living with AIDS, as well as the experience of being Puerto Rican, and a Puerto Rican in the United States: a HIV-positive homosexual Puerto Rican in exile (territorial, sexual, medical). The sense of exile that permeates their poems is also literary (poetic, aesthetic). These are poems with functions other than the aesthetic; they are urgent poems with a need to communicate, to inform, to educate in the midst of a medical and social emergency. They are also therapeutic poems. Creating art can be a healing process and also a process of empowerment.

The poetry of Agosto (and Pons-Myers) is political because it represents AIDS as a political issue. Added to poverty and racism, AIDS threatens *el barrio* (the Puerto Rican communities) with genocide. Added to colonialism, AIDS is another form of the oppression of Puerto Rican people. The last poem of Agosto's section in *Poemas de lógica inmune* seems like a new version of the wandering Puerto Rican of René Marqués's play *La carreta* (The Ox Cart), and of songs like Noel Estrada's "En mi viejo San Juan" (In My Old San Juan). It is the Puerto Rican who has to leave the (poor, impoverished) island (of the Rich Port) in order to get treatment on the mainland, constantly going back and forth across the bridge mentioned in an article in the *New York Times* ("AIDS Travels NY–PR 'Air Bridge,' " 15 June 1990, B-1) between the metropolis and the colony. The Puerto Ricans face two deaths: national death by colonialism and physical death by AIDS. The only cure is revolution: AIDS poetry is an angry poetry.

Agosto represents AIDS poetically by transforming the (medical) language of AIDS, mixed with nostalgia for Puerto Rico and the Caribbean in the form of home/*santería* (veneration of folk saints) remedies into a language of (AIDS) poetry. The *lagarto* (lizard) becomes a symbol of people with AIDS, and AIDS becomes a sour tropical fruit: "SIDA, tamarindo del Caribe" (20). *Seca* (drought) refers to the fatigue experienced by people with AIDS; *SIDA* (AIDS) becomes a verb: *sidamitar*; *sarcoma*, from the skin cancer Kaposis' sarcoma, becomes *sarcomer*, based on the verb *to eat*; New York City (and the subway) becomes *el síndrome de hierro* (the iron syndrome, linked to the carrier metaphor) and, reversibly, the Acquired Immunodeficiency Syndrome becomes a subway (mass transportation vehicle); prescribed and home-made remedies juxtapose the foreign, the invader, and the familiar, exile and nostalgia: *Zovirax o Manzanilla* (Zovirax or Chamomile Tea); the cure is invoked by the rhythms of Caribbean *santería*; the back, the body, of the deflowered Christ (the lyrical subject, the PWA [Persons with Aids] subject) becomes a lethal weapon. In his three completed manuscripts and in a fourth in progress, Agosto develops further his poetical discourse of AIDS.

WORKS

"Inmunología poética. 1991. Unpublished MS.
"Para siempre florecer entre las tumbas." 1993. Unpublished MS.
Poemas de lógica inmune. San Juan: Publivisiones Pons, 1991. With Joey Pons-Myers, first author.
"Reciclajes." 1992. Unpublished MS.
"Tantas lujurias y un ojo dislocado." 1991. Unpublished MS.
See also poems on pp. 24–25 of Carlos A. Rodríguez, "Retazos: Poesía del sida en lengua hispana." *SIDAHORA* 13 (Winter 1992): 21–27.

CRITICISM

Santos-Febres, Mayra. *"Poemas de lógica inmune*: Testimonio de vida en tiempos del SIDA." In *Poemas de lógica inmune*, 5–6. Repr. *SIDAHORA* 10 (Spring 1992): 38.

Carlos A. Rodríguez-Matos

ALABAU, MAGALI (Cuba; 1945) _____

Alabau was born in Cienfuegos. After the Cuban Revolution, she received a government grant to study dramatic arts at the National Art School of Cubanacán. Along with fellow students she founded Teatro Joven (Young Theater), and she presented a work called *Los mangos de Caín* (Cain's Mangoes) by Abelardo Estorino. She left Cuba in 1967 and moved to New York City, where she has lived ever since. In New York, Alabau continued her acting and directing career. She has been involved in the theater as an actress (Greenwich Mews

Theater, INTAR, La Mama Experimental Theater) and as a director (Duo The-
ater/Medusa's Revenge). In 1988 Alabau won first prize in the *Lyra's Magazine*
poetry contest. In 1990 she received the Cintas Fellowship Award. In 1992,
Hermana (Sister) was awarded the Latin American Institute Writers Poetry Prize
for the best poetry book written in Spanish.

In Alabau's *Electra, Clitemnestra* we witness a vein of lesbian eroticism and
desire, her second book, *Hermana*, and her latest, *Hemos llegado a Ilión* (We
Have Arrived in Ilion; 1991), present a lesbian sensibility and emotional bonding
among women. In *Electra, Clitemnestra*, the author takes the Greek myths of
Electra and Clytemnestra and elaborates on them, adapting and transforming the
story. Through rewriting the classical myths, Alabau transforms their homosexual meaning into lesbian meanings. Rather than adapting the classical anecdotes,
she questions their significance. In Alabau's poetry the women, heroines who
in the classical story act for the sake of the patriarchal family, carry out a
personal desire. The traditional interpretation of the myth of Electra and her
desire for her father is transformed into desire for the mother. Thus, Alabau
deconstructs the myth of heterosexual love and replaces the Freudian incestuous
fantasy with a lesbian union. The exploration of the desire for another woman
is beautifully expressed in poems IV and VII through the use of erotic images
of great synthesis and economy. Alabau's style is concise, and all the words
and images produce a dramatic effect.

The lesbian unions in Alabau's first book challenge the predominance of
binary combinations and the assumption of a heterosexual matrix of love and
desire as it has been traditionally accepted. Poem VII of this collection transforms the Freudian notion of primary scene, in which the daughter or the son
is witness to the sexual encounter of the mother and the father. Instead, the
daughter and the mother are united in the sexual act. *Electra, Clitemnestra* is a
collection of great erotic charge in which the body of the woman is portrayed
as the locus of desire. Breast, nipples and clitoris are strongly eroticized. The
body of the mother, traditionally desexualized by motherhood, has been transformed into the paramount object of desire. If traditional views have denied
women access to pleasure because of the absence of a penis, in this collection
the clitoris is privileged, such that it is not associated with a single pleasure but
with multiple pleasures.

In *Electra, Clitemnestra*, women are unified by sexual and erotic desire. In *Hermana* and *Hemos llegado a Ilión*, Alabau presents communication and emotional
bonding between women while exploring the marginalization imposed by a heterosexist society on women whose sexual orientation is not the one prescribed. *Hermana* explores the fusion and the communion between two sisters, one who is in
exile and returns to her native country in search of herself, and one who remained in
her native country, living most her life in reclusion. The sisterhood of these women
can be understood as a metaphor for the emotional rather than the biological ties that
unite them. It can be said that here sisterhood is a metaphor for kindred spirits or
women who are united by the same sexual orientation.

Emotional communication among women is presented through the extensive poems that constitute *Hermana* and *Hemos llegado a Ilión*. In both, Alabau explores the poetic possibilities of a dual journey, one spatial and the other internal. She also presents a fragmentation of the I and the rupture of the speaker's identity in order to embrace and incorporate the identity of the other woman. In *Hermana* we witness the interchangeability of the I and the you, while in *Hemos llegado a Ilión*, the speaker's journey to her native country seems to be a metaphor for the reclaiming of a side of herself that was left behind. Thus a part of her identity that had been hidden is revealed. If in *Hermana* the fusion of the women is textualized through the combinations of the I and the you (Iyou), in *Hemos llegado a Ilión* there is a journey that the speaker undertakes in the company of female friends. As the I becomes a we, the poetic speaker's voice is transformed and united with other female voices, thereby giving way to a more inclusive female discourse.

In *Hermana* and *Hemos llegado a Ilión* there is the desire to return and reclaim another space and time. There is a dialectic of inside/outside and now/then, as well as references to masks, mirrors, and carnival that are reflective of lesbian themes and sensibilities. These references have been used extensively in lesbian texts to allude to the metaphorical exile suffered by lesbians, whose survival has long depended on the concealment of their identity.

WORKS

Electra, Clitemnestra. Concepción, Chile: Libros del Maitén, 1986.
Hemos llegado a Ilión. Madrid: Editorial Betania, 1991.
Hermana. Madrid: Editorial Betania, 1989. Bilingual edition as *Sister/Hermana*. Trans. Anne Twitty. Madrid: Editorial Betania, 1992.

CRITICISM

Alvarez Bravo, Armando. "El tono confesional recorre la poesía de Magali Alabau." *El nuevo herald*, Sept. 10, 1989, p. 5D.
García Ramos, Reinaldo. "Sobre dos libros de Magali Alabau." *Linden Lane Magazine* 6.1 (1987): 19.
Hernández, Librada. "Magali Alabau: *Hermana*." *Revista iberoamericana* 152–53 (July–Dec. 1990): 1381–1386.
Martínez, Elena M. "El constante vacío de la memoria. Entrevista con Magali Alabau." *Revista Brújula/Compass* (Instituto de Escritores Latinoamericanos/City College of New York) 14 (Summer 1992): 6.

Elena M. Martínez

ALARCÓN, FRANCISCO X.
(United States; 1954) ⸺⸺⸺⸺⸺⸺⸺⸺⸺⸺⸺

Poet, barrio activist and gay advocate, Francisco X. Alarcón has become, in less than ten years, the leading Chicano poet of homoerotic verse and social commitment, forging a human and artistic image of the Chicano/U.S. Latino homosexual. From 1980 to the early 1990s his socially organic verse helped fill the vacuum left by engagé Chicano poets of the 1960s and 1970s, and intellectually surpassed the indigenist voice found in early barrio poetry. Alarcón's poems feature many struggles faced in the 1980s by Chicanos and immigrants from Central America: racism, war, exile, women's oppression, AIDS, homelessness, environmental pollution and reified Aztec thought.

A third-generation Chicano born in Wilmington, California, Alarcón received his primary and secondary studies in both California and Guadalajara, Mexico. His residency and study in Mexico stimulated him to become a writer. As a doctoral student in Latin American literature at Stanford University, from 1978 to 1980 Alarcón edited the journal *Vórtice* (1976–1980). He won a Fulbright fellowship to do research in Mexican literature during 1982–1983 at the Colegio de Mexico.

Beginning with *Tattoos* (1985), which earned Alarcón the 1981 Primer Premio Latinoamericano de Poesía–Rubén Darío (Rubén Darío First Prize for Latin American Poetry), he has published nine poetry books. The most important are *Body in Flames* (1990), *De amor oscuro* (Of Dark Love; 1991), and *Snake Poems* (1992). As a unit, the three texts feature a unified homoerotic and activist vision. However, Alarcón experienced several changes from 1981 to 1989 before reaching such a worldview. In retrospect, *Ya vas, carnal* (All Right, Brother; 1985) stands as a transitional work. Featuring fifteen poems by Alarcón and a set each by Rodrigo Reyes and Juan Pablo Gutiérrez, the collection is the first publicly declared gay literary work published and distributed inside the Chicano/U.S. Latino literary circuit; it contains direct and highly sensual homoerotic images. Keeping both aspects in mind, *Ya vas, carnal* surfaces as a manifesto of Chicano/U.S. Latino gay writers. The remaining five books by Alarcón— *Quake Poems* (1989), *Loma Prieta* (1990), *Poemas zurdos* (An Outsider's Verse; 1992) and *No Golden Gate for Us* (1993)—are primarily situational or composed of poems from the above five works. For example, *Poemas zurdos*, prepared in Spanish for the Mexican reader, is a minianthology of poems from *Tattoos*, *Ya vas, carnal*, *Loma Prieta*, *Cuerpo en llamas* and *No Golden Gate for Us*.

Tattoos represents Alarcón's search for a gay poetic voice, one that vacillates and will not gain confidence until *Ya vas, carnal*. As featured in the poem "Prayer," where the poetic I demands a compassionate god who can experience all the world's injustices, the gay voice appears as a player in all social struggles, except homosexual rights, in such poems as "Poet in Prison," "Un Beso Is Not a Kiss," "Erós" and "Nocturno Marino" (A Sea Nocturne).

In *Ya vas, carnal* Alarcón presents a confident gay poetic voice, particularly in the last seven poems, of which "Shadow's Fate" is the only one that reiterates the need for homosexuals to hide from society. Otherwise, the poems exude homoeroticism—for example, "Bienaventurados" (The Blessed Ones) and "Lenguaje" (Language). Apparently an *ars poetica*, the latter symbolically celebrates, as the arms and tongue exchange bodily motion, a boundless love that must intensely touch and feel the lover. "Bienaventurados" praises the lovers who decisively confront silence and repression, thus carrying in the act of love the seed of true liberation. The marginalized and pathetic gay figures in *Tattoos*'s "Un Beso Is Not a Kiss" and in *Ya vas, carnal*'s "Fugitive," who needed to hide from all city residents, now claim gay love as a universal. As in *Tattoos*, the gay Chicano poetic voice in *Ya vas, carnal* seeks to better society, as illustrated in the poems "Zenthroamérika" (Central America) and "Patria" (Our Land), the latter suggesting a future utopia for Chicanos and the former protesting political violence in Central America. However, the poetic I still appears disjointed, perhaps due to tension between the personal and the political.

Body in Flames presents, in an introductory and in a closing poem framing four thematic sections, a unified gay Chicano poetic voice, one that is both homoerotic and activist (Muñoz). To achieve such a balance, Alarcón uses, with some revision, several poems from *Tattoos* and *Ya vas, carnal*. In this way, *Body in Flames* forms part of an established social continuum whose struggles remain identity, marginality, and regeneration. On the other hand, the new poems, "The Other Day I Ran into García Lorca," "Love Doesn't Exist" and "Mi Pelo" (My Hair), reintroduce the homoerotic dimension. Building on the recent rediscovery and publishing of lost gay poetry by Federico García Lorca (1898–1936), "The Other Day I Ran Into García Lorca" features an Andalusian poet who plants an intimate kiss on the mouth of the poetic I. In such an image, openness rules the gay poetic voice. "Mi Pelo," whose image of gray hair on the head of the poetic I symbolizes longevity, reclaims tenderness and playfulness as deep-seated in a gay relationship. In "Love Doesn't Exist," the image of the lovers' shadows embracing on a café window empties the semantic content of the title. Section III expands the homoerotic vision, claiming that gay love originates in the unsaid or the senses. Using hyperbolic metaphors in which geographical sites equal human body parts (thighs, the chest, the mouth, tongue), the opening poem, "Everything Is an Immense Body," illustrates this new sensuality. "Lo del Corazón" (Concerning the Heart) goes so far as to dethrone the heart as the symbol of love—a timeless tradition in heterosexual poetry. "Prophetic Anatomy" asserts that love's mystery resides in the lover's anatomy, specifically the arms, the lips, the shoulders, the hair, and the eyes.

In *Body in Flames*, the activist dimension experiences, section by section, equal development. Taken from *Tattoos*, the poem "I Used to Be Much Darker" marks the social continuum in Alarcón's activist voice. Section I details Chicano childhood in California during the 1960s and the 1970s: working-class neighborhood, racism, oral tales, graffiti, miseducation, writer's marginality, barrio allegiance and gay subordination. Expanding the subject's historical vision, Section II examines struggles of the 1980s in the Chicano/Latino community: women's rights, opposition to torture in Central America, revindication of gay love and self-defense. The poetic I sees in matriarchy a source of freedom and struggle. For example, "A Small but Fateful Victory" features a rebellious and triumphant sister and mother. Matriarchy becomes a recurring ideologeme [minimal unit of ideological meaning] in Alarcón's poetry; concomitantly, such a position means the rejection of patriarchy. In the poem "My Father," the poetic I feels like a stranger before his father and soon realizes that both reject "the nightmare called man" (35).

Body in Flames's unified homoerotic and activist dimension provides the poetic I with the ability to focus on one or the other with equal mastery in Alarcón's next two collections: *De amor oscuro* and *Snake Poems*. The latter examines Chicanos both historically and globally, and *De amor oscuro* immortalizes gay Chicano love. This last text is the first collection in Mexican American poetry wholly dedicated to the emotion of love. To date, no heterosexual poet, male or female, has attempted such a task. Two poems from *Body in Flames*, "Prophetic Anatomy" and "The Other Day I Ran into García Lorca," serve as *De amor oscuro*'s inspiration and sensual parameters. García Lorca's homoerotic poetry, *Inéditos de Federico García Lorca: Sonetos del amor oscuro* (*Collected Poems/Federico García Lorca*; 1984), inspired Alarcón to write his own collection of love poetry, furthering his pledge to be openly gay in his work and life.

Alarcón sees himself as an heir to a gay love tradition from García Lorca. In writing *De amor oscuro*, he uses the Andalusian poet's phrase "amor oscuro" in his own title and recruits as translator the same person, Francisco Aragón, who translated the rediscovered sonnets by García Lorca. In "The Other Day I Ran into García Lorca," the kiss on the poetic I's lips symbolizes the passing of a gay love tradition from the Andalusian poet to Alarcón. The latter's guest editorship of issue 26 of the journal *Quarry West* (1989), two years before the publication of *De amor oscuro*, stands as undeniable proof that García Lorca is the source of inspiration. Alarcón places as the opening texts two newly rediscovered gay sonnets by García Lorca and, after calling attention to suppressed Chicano homoerotic poetry, declares in the introduction:

We decided to begin this anthology by publishing two poems that exemplify suppressed writing, the case in point are [*sic*] the homoerotic sonnets by Spanish poet Federico García Lorca that had to wait more than four decades to see the light and still are unavailable in this country. We reclaim García Lorca's poems *as part of our legacy and struggle* against the suppression of desire and aspiration. (5)

"Prophetic Anatomy" establishes *De amor oscuro*'s sensual parameters in two ways: it privileges the senses as the source of love, and it places emphasis on the lover's body, particularly the upper extremities and their motion. After the introductory poem defines gay Chicano love as multivalent, sonnets 2 to 7 celebrate its sensual expression in the lover: the arms, the voice, the hands, the shoulders, the sleeping body and the legs. From a metaliterary level, these seven sonnets and number 8, which celebrates a gift from the lover, constitute the problem in a typical sonnet, here the existence of gay Chicano love; and the remaining six, the solution, not its suppression but its acceptance by the general community. Unlike the free, competitive and intense sensuality in John Rechy's novel *Numbers* (1967), the expression of homoeroticism in *De amor oscuro* is mythic, innocent, religious and mystical. Allegorized by Greco-Roman and Christian imagery and highlighted by the absence of genitalia, this conception of love stands as unique in Chicano poetry and letters. Despite *De amor oscuro*'s immersion in gay Chicano love, the activist dimension remains latent in Alarcón's verse. Even at this low level, the social concerns spur an achievement. In *De amor oscuro*, a farm worker figures as the poetic I's lover, socially marking the texts with the struggle of César Chávez and the United Farm Workers against the growers.

Antipodally to *De amor oscuro*, *Snake Poems* immerses the poetic I in the activist dimension. Except for an Aztec invocation speaking for lovers, this collection distances itself from both erotic and homoerotic verse. The social dimension weighs heavily on *Snake Poems*: the poetic I traces the Chicano social condition to Mexico's colonial period under Spain and examines the condition's present standing in the United States. Far from being an apocryphal text, *Snake Poems* intertwines, particularly in the six middle sections, Aztec invocations with a series of poems on the current Chicano condition, calling attention to today's social agenda. As a rule, each original poem addresses a particular issue: "Ololiuhqui" (a medicinal herb), section I, seeks a cleaner environment; "Spirits of the Forest," section 2, advocates wildlife preservation; "Canto a las Tortillas" (Tortilla Chant), section 3, praises a proven nutrient; "Potent Seeds," section 4, champions corn; "Wiser," section 5, advocates male tenderness; "Tonantzin," section 6, privileges female freedom and rebellion; and "Working Hands," also in section 6, identifies Chicano workers as the democratic voice of the community. That the sections "Tahui" and "New Day," which consist of original poems by Alarcón, frame the six sections made up of Aztec invocations marks the inversion of suppressed Aztec thought as necessary to understand colonization, and foregrounds Chicano subordination in the United States, a situation that conscious struggle can change.

Several themes in Alarcón's previous work code the poetic I's return to its activist dimension. As a structuring ideologeme, matriarchy claims attention, especially considering its considerable expansion in *Snake Poems*. Placed in the section "Healers," the poems "Matriarch" and "Tonantzin" mark the links between the figure of the grandmother in *Body in Flames* and Tonantzin. The figure of the matriarch has evolved to the level of goddess, a symbolically omnipotent yet liberating leader. Moreover, as the Virgin of Guadalupe, Tonantzin not only leads other goddesses, such as Coatlicue, Chalchihucueye and Citlacueye, but also holds for the Chicano people, considering their continued subordination, the banners of hope and rebellion. This matriarchal dimension has its roots outside *Snake Poems*. In joining Chicano feminists, Alarcón sees matriarchy's revindication as a necessary step in the formation of a nonsexist society. As for patriarchy, he again symbolically rejects the father in *Snake*

Poems, leaving the message that women's liberation is a revolutionary force in the struggle of the Chicano people. His rejection takes the form of glossing original Aztec invocations still used during Mexico's colonial period that Hernando Ruiz de Alarcón, his ancestor, sought to record and suppress in the *Tratado de las supersticiones y costumbres gentílicas que oy viven entre los indios naturales desta Nueva España* (Treatise on the Superstitions and Heathen Customs That Today Exist Among the Indians Native to New Spain; 1629). The glossing results in an ideological inversion that rescues and adapts Aztec thought to today's changing society.

In highlighting his development as a poet, his community activism, his personal objectives and his literary achievements, this essay does not seek to rhapsodize Alarcón's success in opening a creative space available to Chicano gay writers. Defense and support of homosexuals by Mexican-American intellectuals are limited. Few in the general Chicano/U.S. Latino community openly tolerate the public expression of a gay life-style. Ignorance, fear, and ridicule on the part of many heterosexuals still prescribe silence as proper gay behavior, and such silence marks the preferred literary genres of Chicano/U.S. Latino gay writers: the poem, the novel, the short story and the play form a readily available metaphorical discourse where only the conscious reader comprehends the gay dialectic.

Through his community activism, his consistent dedication to the Chicano/U.S. Latino literary circuit and his winning of literary awards and honors, Alarcón has molded in sequence a significant contribution in literature that includes a dual homoerotic and social vision; an authentic image of the Chicano homosexual based on openness about sexual and cultural preference; a poetic discourse that features community struggles from the 1970s to the 1990s; a vanguard role in the establishment of a creative space available to Chicano/U.S. Latino gays and lesbians; and an appropriation of model artistic forms as well as past and new linguistic signs.

WORKS

Body in Flames/Cuerpo en llamas. San Francisco: Chronicle Books, 1990.
De amor oscuro/Of Dark Love. Santa Cruz, Calif.: Moving Parts Press, 1991.
"Introduction." *Quarry West* 26 (1989): 5–6.
Loma Prieta. Santa Cruz, Calif.: We Press, 1990.
No Golden Gate for Us. Santa Fe, N. Mex.: Pennywhistle Press, 1993.
Poemas zurdos. Mexico City: Editorial Factor, 1992.
Quake Poems. Santa Cruz, Calif: We Press, 1989.
"Reclaiming Ourselves, Reclaiming America." *Before Columbus Review* 3.2 (Fall/Winter 1992): 19–21.
Snake Poems: An Aztec Invocation. San Francisco: Chronicle Books, 1992.
Tattoos. Oakland, Calif.: Nomad Press, 1985.
Ya vas, carnal. San Francisco: Humanizarte Publications, 1985.

CRITICISM

Arteaga, Alfred. "Before These Poems, and After." In Alarcón, *Snake Poems: An Aztec Invocation*, ix–xi.

Bellm, Dan. "Chants Encounter: Francisco X. Alarcón's Aztec Way of Knowledge." *Village Voice* (New York), Oct. 27, 1992, pp. 73–74.

Eng, Karen. "*Snake Poems: An Aztec Invocation* by Francisco X. Alarcón." *Shaman's Drum* (Summer 1992): 67–68.

Griffin, Noel, and Baile Átha Cliath. "Introduction/Réamhrá." In Francisco Alarcón, *Colainn ar Bharr Lasrach*. Trans. Gabriel Rosenstock. Indreabhán, Ireland: Cló Iar-Chonanchta, 1992. Gaelic trans. of *Cuerpo en llamas*.

Kessler, Stephen. "Consoling the Flowers." *Poetry Flash: A Poetry Review & Literary Calendar for the West* 223 (Aug. 1992): 1, 4–5, 8.

Leone, Robert. "Palabras heridas: An Interview with Francisco X. Alarcón." *Lector* 5.1 (Summer 1985): 18–21.

Muñoz, Elías Miguel. "Corpus of Words and Flesh: *Body in Flames/Cuerpo en llamas.*" *The Bilingual Review* 16.2–3 (1991): 235–240.

Quitner, Jeremy. "Dreamer's World." *Bay Area Reporter: Arts and Entertainment* 22.22 (28 May 1992): 29, 38–40.

Rodríguez del Pino, Salvador. "Francisco Alarcón." In *Chicano Writers: Second Series*, 3–7. Ed. Francisco Lomelí and Carl R. Shirley. Detroit: Gale Research, 1992.

Manuel de Jesús Hernández-Gutiérrez

ANGEL, ALBALUCÍA (Colombia; 1939) _____

Albalucía Angel was born in 1939 to an upper-middle-class family in Pereira. Although she did not begin to write seriously until her adult years, as a child she was an avid reader. She was encouraged by her grandmother, whom she sees as a major influence on her life and work. At the age of seventeen Angel went to Bogotá to study art and literature at the Universidad de los Andes. She became a student and friend of the writer and art critic Marta Traba, who encouraged her to continue her studies in Paris and Rome. Once in Europe, and in defiance of her conservative family, Angel left school and spent several years living and traveling in Europe, determined to make a living as a folk singer. In the late 1960s she started to write seriously, and in the 1970s, while residing both in Europe and in Colombia, she published her first four books: *Los girasoles en invierno* (The Sunflowers in Winter; 1970), *Dos veces Alicia* (Alicia Twice Over; 1972), *Estaba la pájara pinta sentada en el verde limón* (The Spotted Bird Was Sitting on the Lemon Tree; 1975) and *¡Oh gloria inmarcesible!* (Oh, Undying Glory; 1979). The first two of these works are set in Europe and reflect the author's experiences there. The last two focus specifically on Colombia. In *La pájara pinta*, which was awarded the Vivencias National Novel Prize in 1975, the context is both the author's childhood and the bloody period that began in 1948 and is referred to in Colombia as La Violencia (the Violence). Angel returned to Europe, where she wrote and published her two latest novels: *Misiá señora* (Miz Madame; 1982) and *Las andariegas* (The Raggedy Women; 1984). She has lived in London since 1980.

Angel's narratives tend to be experimental in form, especially in her use of nontraditional narrative structure and a variety of narrative voices. Much of her work is clearly autobiographical, and it often focuses on childhood and adolescence. All of Angel's narrative works feature a marked privileging of female experience and expression. Both *La pájara pinta* and her later works are markedly feminist in tone, and at points the narratives become an exploration and celebration of female sexuality, including lesbian sexuality. In *La pájara pinta*, same-sex eroticism is depicted as one element in a series of childhood and adolescent sexual experiences that includes heterosexual experimentation and molestation by adults. In this novel, adult sexual and emotional relationships are exclusively heterosexual. In *Misiá señora*, a novel that depicts its female protagonist during three periods of her life, the lesbian theme focuses on the protagonist's feelings of love and desire for other women, both as a child and as an adult. Here, however, the oppressive heterosexism of Colombian society is highlighted. Practically every reference to lesbian love in the novel is accompanied by a remembrance of feelings of fear and guilt, as the protagonist, Mariana, recalls the priest's probing questions during one childhood confession: "Have you ever fallen in love with a woman?" Still, in this novel, lesbian love is presented as a pleasurable and liberating alternative to the oppressive and often violent patriarchal heterosexual relations.

Las andariegas more closely resembles a long prose poem and a collage than a traditional novel. It includes short episodes written in terse, poetic language, unconventional spelling and punctuation, experiments with spacing and typography, drawings and epigraphs. This work is self-consciously feminist and woman-centered. Although it depicts, at times, what may be read as a woman's utopia, it is not necessarily a lesbian novel. It is probably seen as a lesbian work more by association than for its content. This is because the text is clearly inspired by French writer Monique Wittig's 1969 lesbian classic *Les Guérrillères* (French title, which means "Women Warriors," retained in English translation). In fact, the majority of the epigraphs in Angel's work are from Wittig. Like *Les Guérrillères, Las andariegas* attempts to present a rewriting of history in which women are the central characters; and the mythology that surrounds them, from both Western and indigenous American sources, is woman-centered. In the process, Angel depicts visions of a society where women wanderers, even in moments of adversity, are strong, united and independent. Most important, in re-creating a collective memory for women, Angel's text seeks to speak in a language and a form that is appropriate to the task, in order to reject old models and to represent a "new woman."

WORKS

Las andariegas. Barcelona: Argos Vergara, 1984.
Dos veces Alicia. Barcelona: Seix-Barral, 1972.
Estaba la pájara pinta sentada en el verde limón. Bogotá: Instituto Colombiano de Cultura, 1975.
Los girasoles en invierno. Bogotá: Bolívar, 1970.
Misiá señora. Barcelona: Argos Vergara, 1982.
¡Oh gloria inmarcesible! Bogotá: Instituto Colombiano de Cultura, 1979.

CRITICISM

Araújo, Helena. "Ejemplos de la 'niña impúdica' en Silvina Ocampo y Albalucía Angel." *Hispamérica* 38 (1984): 27–35.
———. *La Scherezada criolla,* 99–106. Bogotá: Universidad Nacional de Colombia, 1989.
Filer, Malva. "Autorrescate e invención en *Las andariegas* de Albalucía Angel." *Revista iberoamericana* 132–133 (1985):649–655.
García Pinto, Magdalena. *Women Writers of Latin America: Intimate Histories,* 45–78. Trans. Trudy Balch and Magdalena García Pinto. Austin: University of Texas Press, 1991.
Gerdes, Dick. *"Estaba la pájara pinta sentada en el verde limón*: Novela testimonial/documental de 'la violencia' en Colombia." *Revista de estudios colombianos* 2 (1987): 21–26.
Keefe Ugalde, Sharon. "Between 'in Longer' and 'Not Yet': Woman's Space in *Misiá señora.*" *Revista de estudios colombianos* 1 (1986): 23–28.
———. "El discurso feminino en *Misiá señora*: ¿Un lenguaje nuevo o acceso al lenguaje?" *Discurso literario* 4.1 (Autumn 1986): 117–126.
Mora, Gabriela. "El *bildungsroman* y la experiencia latinoamericana: *La pájara pinta* de Albalucía Angel." In *La sarten por el mango,* 71–81. Ed. Patricia Elena González and Eliana Ortega. Río Piedras, P. R.: Ediciones Huracán, 1985.
Williams, Raymond Leslie. "Albalucía Angel." In *Spanish American Women Writers: A Bio-Bibliographical Source Book,* 31–40. Ed. Diane E. Marting. Westport, Conn.: Greenwood Press, 1990.
———. "An Interview with Women Writers in Colombia." In *Latin American Women Writers: Yesterday and Today,* 155–161. Ed. Yvette Miller and Charles M. Tatum. Pittsburgh: Latin American Literary Review Press, 1977.

Karen S. Goldman

ANZALDÚA, GLORIA E. (United States; 1942)

A self-described "Chicana tejana feminist-dyke-patlache poet, fiction writer and cultural theorist" from the Rio Grande valley of south Texas, Gloria E. Anzaldúa was born to sixth-generation Mexicanos. She received a B.A. in English at the Pan American University, an M.A. at the University of Texas at Austin, and is completing a Ph.D. at the University of California, Santa Cruz. A well-known speaker, Anzaldúa has presented workshops and lectures in the United States and abroad. She has taught creative writing, Chicano/a studies, and feminist theory at several U.S. colleges and universities. Anzaldúa and her works have won numerous awards, including the Before Columbus Foundation American Book Award for *This Bridge Called My Back* (1983), the Lambda Lesbian Small Book Press Award for *Haciendo caras*, an NEA Fiction Award, and the Sappho Award of Distinction.

By positioning herself as a working-class "Chicana tejana feminist-dyke-patlache," Anzaldúa assumes an oppositional stance in her theoretical writings and explores a diverse range of issues, including Nahuatl spiritual-mythic traditions, U.S. white supremacy, and the interlocking systems of oppression that marginalize people who, because of their sexuality, gender, ethnicity, and/or economic status, do not belong to the dominant cultural group. In the prefaces to *This Bridge Called My Back* and *Making Face, Making Soul/Haciendo caras* (1990), her two edited anthologies of creative and critical writings by U.S. women of color, she exposes the exclusionary practices of the mainstream (white/Anglo) U.S. women's movement, examines the ways U.S. Third World feminists acquire personal and collective agency by (re)defining themselves and explores the possibilities of developing a multicultural feminist/lesbian movement. In "Speaking in Tongues," a widely anthologized essay analyzing the specific difficulties she and other women of color experience in their efforts to become published writers, Anzaldúa calls attention to the ways lesbians of color are silenced both by the dominant U.S. culture and by their own racial-ethnic communities.

In "La Prieta" (The Dark-Skinned Woman) Anzaldúa draws on her own experiences as a working-class Chicana dyke to investigate the destructive effects of externally imposed labels, the homophobia and sexism within Mexican American communities, the conflicts within and among U.S. Third World women and the ways horizontal oppression prevents members of subjugated groups from forming effective political alliances. Similarly, in "En Rapport, In Opposition" she challenges U.S. women of color to overcome their internalized oppression and establish alliances with women whose life-styles, sexualities, ideologies or even skin color differs from their own.

In *Borderlands/La Frontera: The New Mestiza* (1987), Anzaldúa develops many of her earlier themes, including her desire to mediate between diverse cultures, the overlapping forms of oppression experienced by Chicana lesbians and other marginalized groups, shamanic writing traditions, U.S. imperialism and the ostracism encountered by the "queers" of all nations. Although this collection of essays and poems defies easy classification, it can perhaps be described as a cultural autobiography, for Anzaldúa blends personal experience with history and social protest with poetry and myth in order to (re)construct her personal and communal identities. Even her style—most notably her abrupt shifts between first- and third-person narration and her transitions from standard English to working-class English to Chicano Spanish to Tex-Mex or to Na-huatl—indicates Anzaldúa's simultaneous construction of individual and collective identities. By interweaving accounts of racism, sexism and classism she experienced growing up in south Texas with historical and mythic analyses of the Aztec and Spanish conquests of indigenous gynecentric Indian tribes, Anzaldúa reclaims, without romanticizing, her political/cultural/spiritual Mexican and Nahuatl Indian roots.

Originally delivered at the Lesbian Plenary Session of the 1988 National Women's Studies Conference, "Bridge, Drawbridge, Sandbar or Island: Lesbians-of-Color Haciendo Alianzas" (1990) focuses on issues related to coalition-building in lesbian and feminist communities. As in her earlier writings, Anzaldúa employs personal experience both to emphasize the importance of self-naming and to explore the exclusionary practices of white/Anglo feminists. She calls for multicultural, or "mestiza," feminist communities and maintains that alliance work requires the flexibility to shift between identities. She challenges white/Anglo lesbian-feminists to examine the ways their monolithic description of female identity, coupled with their emphasis on gender-based oppression, ignores the multiple forms of oppression experienced by lesbians of color. Similarly, in "To(o) Queer the Writer—Loca, escritora y chicana" (1987), Anzaldúa challenges the exclusionary politics of mainstream lesbian and feminist women's movements by exposing the white, middle-class values implicit in the term "lesbian." This essay contains her most comprehensive discussions of "lesbian sensibility," "lesbian" writers, the ethnocentrism of academic "queer theory" and the ways culture, class, sexuality, and gender influence writing and reading practices.

Like her theoretical works, Anzaldúa's poetry and fiction synthesize autobiographical material, history, and myth to explore diverse sets of issues simultaneously. The Spanish and English poems collected in *Borderlands/La Frontera* include social protest, personal/metaphysical reflections on Anzaldúa's experiences as a writer and autobiographical accounts of childhood episodes. Other poems, like "Nightvoice" (1991) and "Old Loyalties" (1991) explore erotic and platonic dimensions of lesbian relationships. In "Del otro lado" (On the Other Side; 1987) Anzaldúa draws on her personal experiences as *una de las otras* (one of the others) to explore the sense of homelessness, as well as the internal and external struggles experienced by lesbians and gays of color. By depicting her characters at pivotal moments in their lives, her short fiction examines multiple, overlapping issues.

In "El Paisano Is a Bird of Good Omen" (1983), for example, Anzaldúa exposes the Mexican American community's sexism and homophobia and explores the implications of "passing" as heterosexual in her depiction of Andrea, a Chicana dyke, on the eve of her wedding. As she reevaluates her decision to marry a *loquería*, a gay male cousin, Andrea must choose between her connections to *familia* and the *tejana* land and her desire to express her sexuality freely. Similarly, "She Ate Horses" (1990) centers on Prieta's decision to terminate her relationship with her childhood friend and lover. In this story Anzaldúa employs *recuerdos* (memories, recollections), mythic encounters with La Llorona (a legendary figure who haunts the land, weeping for her dead children) and realistic dialogue and description to examine the interconnections between instinct, self-control, passion, autonomy and possessiveness in lesbian relationships. "La historia de una marimacho" (Story of a Dyke) (1989), Anzaldúa's only published story written entirely in Spanish, explores butch/femme roles in the Mexican American community.

Like *Borderlands/La Frontera, Prieta* defies conventional Western genre boundaries; Anzaldúa describes it as "a novel/short story collection." Although each story can be read on its own, many depict a Chicana named Prieta at various points in her life. But the title character is somewhat different in each story/chapter, and often her names subtly reflect this difference: in "Entremados de PQ" (PQ's Inner Structures), for example, she is Pura Prieta, a rancher and part-time student; in "Seguin 15" she is Urraca Prieta, a university student; in "Las Movidas of a Baby Butch," she is Quelite Prieta, a young *marimacha* (*movidas* = moves); and in "The Were-Jaguar Mouth," she is La Gata Prieta, a writer. Anzaldúa employs both first- and third-person narration and incorporates autobiographical material, mythic narrative and realistic Tex-Mex dialogue, settings and characters. She explores a diverse set of issues, including lesbian sexuality, butch/femme roles, bisexuality, Mexican Americans' homophobia and sexism, the medical establishment's treatment of women, other forms of violence against women, altered states of reality and heterosexual/homosexual relationships.

Anzaldúa and her works are often used to illustrate the diversity in Chicano/a, feminist and lesbian studies. However, there are few in-depth analyses of the ways her *campesina tejana* (Texas peasant) cultural background, her feminism, and her sexual preference shape her theoretical and creative perspectives. José David Saldívar, for example, borrows Anzaldúa's metaphor of *la frontera* and mentions her critique of U.S. capitalism in his discussion of contemporary south Texas border writers, yet almost entirely ignores the text's lesbian/feminist dimensions. In her discussion of the innovative strategies employed by contemporary Chicana feminists, Sonia Saldívar-Hull refers to Anzaldúa's sexual preference but does not fully explore the ways her sexuality influences her "border feminism." In her analysis of the construction of multiple identities in three Latina autobiographical narratives, Lourdes Torres includes a discussion of *Borderlands/La Frontera* and briefly describes how Anzaldúa's sexuality distances her from traditional Mexican American culture and further politicizes her work.

Other recent scholars like Bonnie Zimmerman, Diane Freedman, AnnLouise Keating, and Cherríe Moraga focus on the literary dimensions of Anzaldúa's writings. Although *Borderlands/La Frontera* cannot be considered a fictional work, Zimmerman incorporates an analysis of the text into her study of recent

U.S. lesbian fiction. She maintains that Anzaldúa's cultural autobiography provides an important corrective to the monolithic concepts of identity and community found in most recent white lesbian fiction. Freedman examines *Borderlands/La Frontera* in her study on U.S. women writer's "cross-genre compositional practices." In an examination of three lesbian-feminist writers of color, Keating argues that Anzaldúa's use of culturally specific historical and mythical material distinguishes her revisionist mythmaking from Euro-American lesbian writers' revisionist myths. Moraga provides one of the most sustained analyses of Anzaldúa's sexual preference to date in her review of *Borderlands/La Frontera*. She implies that the text itself is not "lesbian," for it does not explore "sexual desire between women" (155). However, as Anzaldúa notes in "To(o) Queer a Writer," Moraga's conception of "lesbian" writers is too restrictive and marginalizes the other dimensions of her work.

For Anzaldúa, sexuality cannot be separated from race, class, culture, gender or other systems of difference. Throughout her theoretical and creative writings she associates her sexual preference with her Mexican Indian heritage and her *campesino* upbringing in south Texas. She rejects the words "lesbian" and "homosexual" as white, middle-class labels and adopts terms like *tejana tortillera* (Texas dyke), *mitá y mitá* (half-and-half), *patlache*, and *mestiza queer* to describe herself. These self-inscriptions have significant performative effects and political implications. By repeatedly emphasizing the cultural and class-specific dimensions of her sexuality, Anzaldúa destabilizes monolithic (Anglo, middle-class) definitions of homosexual identity and exposes the ethnocentricity of U.S. academic "queer theory." Her fiction serves a similar function, for its focus on *marimachas*, Chicana dykes, and *tejana tortilleras* provides a necessary corrective to the homogeneous portrayals of lesbians found in most recent U.S. literature.

By reclaiming, without romanticizing, culturally specific labels to describe her own sexual preference, Anzaldúa combines visionary utopian thinking with critical analyses of the interlocking forms of oppression that affect homosexuals and other marginalized people. In *Borderlands/La Frontera*, for example, her self-description as *mitá y mitá*, half man and half woman, "a strange doubling, a deviation of nature that horrified," enables her simultaneously to expose Mexican Americans' homophobia and sexism and to develop alternative definitions of nonheterosexual identities, behaviors and modes of perception (19). She acknowledges the term's derogatory implications, yet maintains that such "deviance" can have revolutionary effects. By destabilizing male/female binary oppositions, *mitá y mitá* challenges Western culture's dualistic thinking. Thus she describes herself as a forerunner of a new race that will meld both woman and man into a new gender that is neither" (194). This both/neither thinking, with its simultaneous acceptance and rejection of traditional gender categories, problematizes current discussions of "sameness" and "difference" in queer theory.

Similarly, in both "La Prieta" and *Borderlands/La Frontera* Anzaldúa unites

visionary thinking with her critique of existing social systems. She acknowledges the diverse ways homosexuals of all colors are marginalized by the dominant heterosexual cultures, yet suggests that this oppression enables them to
form cross-cultural alliances. As she explains in the latter work, she envisions
a new cosmic race embracing the four worlds. Anzaldúa locates herself and
other queer mestizas at the crossroads of these diverse *razas*, for she believes
homosexuals to be "the supreme crossers of cultures." Because they exist on
the margins of all societies, lesbians and gay men can establish bonds with
dissimilar peoples and create a transcultural, multiethnic tribe. By thus demonstrating that it is possible to form alliances that do not suppress difference, she
explains, lesbians and gays of all colors represent a vital stage in the
(r)evolutionary process, "a blending that proves all blood is intricately woven
together" (80–84). As the Other in every nation, "the mirror reflecting the
heterosexual tribe's fear," they provide a serious challenge to the dominant
Western culture's concepts of (hetero)sexuality and identity. Thus Anzaldúa sees
her lesbianism as the ultimate denial of Western patriarchal standards, for by
rejecting the heterosexual life-style enforced by both Mexican American and
Anglo mores, she separates herself from existing heterosexist belief structures
and acquires a radical freedom to rename herself according to her own (forbidden) desires. In describing herself as "every woman's sister or potential lover"
(80), she defies the cultural dictates that define "woman" exclusively in relation
to "man" and indicates her willingness to establish bonds with women from
diverse backgrounds.

It is important to note that Anzaldúa's desire to form cross-cultural sisterhoods
functions simultaneously with her desire to create political alliances with gay
men of all colors and with other oppressed peoples. Unlike those (primarily
Anglo) lesbian-feminists who posit a radical difference between women and
men, Anzaldúa destabilizes all apparently fixed categories, and she provocatively
crosses sexual, cultural, and gender boundaries. In *Prieta*, for example, her depiction of Prieta's heterosexual relationship with a Latino, as well as her "impossible love" for a gay Anglo male, challenges the (apparent) permanence and
stability of the hetero/homo dichotomy. And in "Interface," a poem included
in *Borderlands/La Frontera*, she describes a metaphysical/sexual relationship
between herself and Leyla, an "alien" who only partially assumes physical
form.

Anzaldúa's simultaneous emphasis on multiple systems of difference enables
her to go beyond definitions of homosexuality that focus primarily on gender,
sexual object choice and sexual desire. In her theoretical and creative writings,
sexuality represents a component in a constantly shifting process of identity
(re)formation and political activism. As she explains in "To(o) Queer the
Writer" the "new *mestiza* queers" she envisions have "the ability, the flexibility, the amorphous quality of being able to stretch this way and that way. We
can add new labels, names, and identities as we mix with others" (249).

WORKS

Borderlands/La Frontera: The New Mestiza. San Francisco: Spinsters/Aunt Lute, 1987.

"Bridge, Drawbridge, Sandbar or Island: Lesbians-of-Color Hacienda Alianzas." In *Bridges of Power: Women's Multicultural Alliances.* Ed. Lisa Albrecht and Rose M. Brewer. Philadelphia: New Society, 1990.

"Del otro lado." In *Compañeras: Latina Lesbians (an Anthology).* Ed. Juanita Ramos. New York: Latina Lesbian History Project, 1987.

"En rapport, In Opposition: Cobrando cuentas a las nuetras." In *Making Face, Making Soul/Haciendo caras.*

Making Face, Making Soul/Haciendo caras: Creative and Critical Perspectives by Women of Color. Ed. Gloria Anzaldúa. San Francisco: Aunt Lute Foundation, 1990.

"Nightvoice." In *Chicana Lesbians: The Girls Our Mothers Warned Us About.* Ed. Carla Trujillo. Berkeley: Third Woman Press, 1991.

"El Paisano Is a Bird of Good Omen." In *Cuentos: Stories by Latinas.* Ed. Alma Gómez, Cherríe Moraga and Mariana Romo-Carmona. New York: Kitchen Table/Women of Color Press, 1983.

"La Prieta." In *This Bridge Called My Back.* Ed. Cherríe Moraga and Gloria Anzaldúa. New York: Kitchen Table/Women of Color Press, 1983.

Prieta. San Francisco: Aunt Lute Foundation, 1994.

"She Ate Horses—Version 1." In *Lesbian Philosophies and Cultures.* Ed. Jeffner Allen. Albany: State University of New York Press, 1990.

"Speaking in Tongues: A Letter to Third World Women Writers." In *This Bridge Called My Back.*

This Bridge Called My Back: Writings by Radical Women of Color. Ed. Cherríe Moraga and Gloria Anzaldúa. New York: Kitchen Table/Women of Color Press, 1983.

"To(o) Queer the Writer—Loca, escritora y chicana." In *Inversions: Writing by Dykes, Queers, and Lesbians.* Ed. Betsy Warland. Vancouver: Press Gang, 1991.

CRITICISM

Freedman, Diane P. *An Alchemy of Genres: Cross-Genre Writing by American Feminist Poet-Critics.* Charlottesville: University Press of Virginia, 1992.

Keating, AnnLouise. "Myth Smashing, Myth Making: (Re)Visionary Techniques in the Works of Paula Gunn Allen, Gloria Anzaldúa, and Audre Lorde." In *Critical Essays: Lesbian and Gay Writers of Color.* Ed. Emmanuel Nelson. New York: Haworth, 1993.

Moraga, Cherríe. "Algo secretamente amado." *Third Woman: The Sexuality of Latinas* 4 (1989): 151–156.

Saldívar, José David. *The Dialectics of Our America: Genealogy, Cultural Critique, and Literary History.* Durham, N.C.: Duke University Press, 1991.

Saldívar-Hull, Sonia. "Feminism on the Border: From Gender Politics to Geopolitics." In *Criticism in the Borderlands: Studies in Chicano Literature, Culture, and Ideology.* Ed. Hector Calderón and José David Saldívar. Durham, N.C.: Duke University Press, 1991.

Torres, Lourdes. "The Construction of Self in U.S. Latina Autobiographies." In *Third World Women and the Politics of Feminism*. Ed. Chandra Talpade, Ann Russo, and Lourdes Torres. Bloomington: Indiana University Press, 1991.

Zimmerman, Bonnie. *The Safe Sea of Women: Lesbian Fiction 1969–1989*. Boston: Beacon Press, 1990.

AnnLouise Keating

ARCIDIÁCONO, CARLOS (Argentina; 1929)

Carlos Arcidiácono, born in Lanús, province of Buenos Aires, holds a degree in art from the Argentine National Academy of Fine Arts. He began by teaching drawing, then became a radio commentator on cultural themes and traveled to Paris on a scholarship to further his skills in the broadcasting of cultural programs. As a literary, theater and cinema critic, Arcidiácono formed part of the permanent staff of *Sur*, the prestigious journal owned and directed by Victoria Ocampo. In 1966 he began working for the newspaper *La Prensa*, also as a critic.

Arcidiácono's first book of short stories, *La gallina loca* (The Crazy Hen; 1966), received the first prize of the National Art Fund of Argentina in 1966. His first novel, *Ay de mí, Jonathan* (Woe Is Me, Jonathan), appeared in 1976. Specifically a gay novel that is the interior monologue of a gay man whose lover does not call, it is made up of eleven untitled chapters, each preceded by an epigraph that has an ironic relationship to the chapter that follows. One has to do with the marvel of Creation and God's mercy, when the substance of the book is hopelessness, lack of love, and the basically lonely human condition. Another epigraph, on snakes devouring one another, precedes an episode in a Turkish bath where the homosexuals are ready to "eat" one another.

The book is an exorcism and a therapeutic exercise. The narrator has suffered a series of disappointments, and the most recent one seems to be the last straw: he must write in order to get rid of his pain as well as to understand himself and his situation as a gay man in need of love. A constant preoccupation with the act and process of writing stresses the fact that we are reading a *written* work. This, as well as the dominant form of compulsive confession, serves to establish a bond of intimacy and complicity between the writer and the reader. Another reason for writing is to shed some light on the situation he is going through, which turns out to be one of permanence.

Ay de mí, Jonathan is a very literary work of intertextual density, full of quotes and references to other writers, some of them gay or of gay sensibility, like Oscar Wilde, Walt Whitman, Federico García Lorca and T. E. Lawrence. Vladimir Nabokov's *Lolita* serves as central intertext. There is a link or a similarity between Arcidiácono's narrator and Nabokov's Humbert Humbert, both desperate for an elusive lover, both writing in the first person, both experiencing a deep emotional involvement that the world frowns upon and considers deviant. But whereas Humbert wishes to explain and justify himself to the reader, Arcidíacono's narrator is clearly aware of the world's stigmatization and the uselessness of the effort to try and *explain*. He even consults an analyst in his endeavor to become "normal," because, as he says, he doesn't fit the mold.

Ironically, Arcidíacono uses the culturally accepted code of the jilted lover, giving free rein to his despair and loneliness, to destabilize the convention, to the extent that the situation here is one of intermale sexuality. The use of this subversive strategy results in a parodic discourse, rich in the colloquialisms and taboo language of the Argentine Río de la Plata. The absent lover, Miguel, is mentioned on the second page, but it is yet not clear to the unprepared or unknowing reader that he is the object of the narrator's love. He could be the interlocutor, the recipient of the narrator's confession, his confidante. By the third page the reader has begun to suspect the truth but does not become fully conscious of the situation until page 20, when the narrator asks if it is not normal to fall in love with someone made in God's image, someone just like himself.

An initial tone of despair, a nervous, high-strung style verging on the brink of hysteria, finally gives way to the full realization that Miguel's call will never come. Between these two extremes of despair and resignation, the book intersperses incidents from the narrator's present life, like a trip to Tigre, on the Paraná River delta near Buenos Aires, a picturesque area where the river joins the Río de la Plata, forming several watercourses and islets with sandy beaches and grassy expanses. There are evocations from the past as well—for example, moments from the narrator's sojourn in France, visits to the working-class neighborhoods surrounding Buenos Aires and his first sexual experience, when being kissed by a young friend leads him to discover his sexual inclination. After that, his whole life has been an effort to recapture that first unforgettable moment, which he sees as the only opportunity to live fully.

Ay de mí, Jonathan has witty, campy commentaries and funny stories about homosexuals in Argentina in the 1960s and 1970s, such as the one about the lesbian who ends up accepting her homosexuality but asks her analyst to tell her which sex she belongs to. There are also some biting remarks about heterosexuality. The strength of this powerful, superb book lies in the rich presentation of the narrator's consciousness, his thoughts and memories, his fears and hopes, his insomnia and his loneliness. A rich gallery of characters makes a brief but memorable appearance, for instance, Luis Manuel, the boy who gave the narrator his first kiss; Soledad, a woman friend; Miguel, the absent object of his love and despair; Marcelo Méndez, diving master and champion who died when the springboard broke in two; and Dr. Zuccarini, the overzealous director of a scientific research institute, who denies a nurse her annual vacation on the grounds that taking a holiday is a form of madness and escapism.

This book is the first openly gay novel to appear in Argentina. That it was published and not banned is a miracle, for it came out in 1976, during the time of the military dictatorship, which called itself the Proceso de Reorganización

Nacional (Process of National Reorganization): it was a time when any violation of decorum was considered a serious transgression, when young men with long hair were taken to the police station, where their hair was cropped. There is a real abyss between the dominant macho regime and the gay sensibility of the book. Arcidiácono was brave enough to keep a close relationship (if not an actual identification) between the narrator of his novel and himself as author. Both are art critics and work for a newspaper. Both are named Carlos. The epigraph of the eleventh chapter is the statute of the credit union of *La Prensa*, the newspaper where Arcidiácono worked for many years. The ancestry of narrator and writer also coincides. Both are descended from Calabrian and Basque immigrants (189). Moreover, most characters are friends or acquaintances of Arcidiácono's, many under their real names, like Xul Solar and his wife, Lita, Marcelo Méndez, and Dr. Zuccarini.

The most suitable epigraph, suggesting the nature and emotion underlining *Ay de mí, Jonathan*, comes from a poem by Walt Whitman, "Out of the Cradle Endlessly Rocking":

> O past! O happy life! O songs of joy!
> In the air, in the woods, over fields,
> Loved! loved! loved! loved! loved!
> But my mate no more, no more with me!
> We two together no more.

WORKS

Ay de mí, Jonathan. Buenos Aires: Corregidor, 1976. A fragment of this novel appeared in English translation by Edward A. Lacey in *My Deep Dark Pain Is Love*. Ed. Winston Leyland. San Francisco: Gay Sunshine Press, 1983.
La gallina loca. Buenos Aires: Falbo Librero Editor, 1966.
La niña bonita. Buenos Aires: Corregidor, 1977.
"La vidente no tenía nada que ver." Unpublished MS.
La vista gorda. Buenos Aires: Celtia, 1983.

CRITICISM

Costa Picazo, Rolando. "La novela gay en la Argentina y los Estados Unidos." Paper presented at the 21st Annual Conference of the Asociación Argentina de Estudios Americanos, Buenos Aires, 1988.
Foster, David William. *Gay and Lesbian Themes in Latin American Writing*, 107-110. Austin: University of Texas Press, 1991.

Rolando Costa Picazo

ARENAS, REINALDO (Cuba; 1943–1990) _____

Poet, essayist, playwright, short-story writer and author of ten novels and novellas, Arenas is one of Cuba's most prolific and innovative literary voices of the twentieth century. Born to a poor family in rural Oriente Province, Arenas began to write at an early age. As a teenager he joined the rebel forces of Fidel Castro and fought against the dictatorial government of Fulgencio Batista. Two years after the triumph of the Revolution, he moved to Havana, where his literary career officially began. In 1967, when he was only twenty-four years old, his first novel, *Celestino antes del alba* (*Singing from the Well*), was published. This first work, which had been awarded an honorable mention in the Concurso Nacional de Novela Cirilo Villaverde (Cirilo Villaverde National Novel Competition) in 1965, heralded the arrival of this gifted and unconventional young writer. However, due to its limited number of copies (two thousand) Arenas's literary reputation was restricted to a small number of Cubans.

In the mid-1960s, when the Castro regime became open in its persecution of homosexuals, Arenas turned away from the Revolution. His dissatisfaction with the government deepened when his writings—transgressive, unconventional and supportive of the individual's right to self-expression—were declared antirevolutionary and censored. Soon the cultural policymakers of the Cuban government did not allow Arenas's books to be published on the island, thus forcing him to send his manuscripts abroad for publication, an act that infuriated the regime, which confiscated and destroyed Arenas's work and branded him persona non grata. For many years he lived a somewhat picaresque life in Havana, moving constantly and working at odd jobs to survive. Finally in 1980, as a result of a bureaucratic blunder, Arenas managed to escape from Cuba through the Mariel boatlift.

After his arrival in the United States, Arenas settled in New York City. Having been censored in Cuba for so long, he began, as if intoxicated with his newly found freedom, to write prodigiously: novels, short stories, poetry, dramatic pieces, essays, newspaper articles. For Arenas, writing was a necessity, a liberating act of self-expression, an act of fury in which he challenged, undermined and subverted all types of ideological dogmatism, all forms of absolute "truths."

On December 7, 1990, suffering from AIDS and too sick to continue writing, Arenas committed suicide. In a moving farewell letter received a few days later by the Miami Spanish newspaper *Diario las Américas*, he made it quite clear that his decision to take his life should not be interpreted as one of defeat. In the final lines of the letter he wrote: "My message is not a message of failure, but rather one of struggle and hope. Cuba will be free, I already am." These final words reveal the self-determination and indomitable spirit of this gifted writer and political activist.

Like many Latin American writers who find it impossible to separate their literary careers from the sociopolitical realities of their countries, Arenas was an outspoken critic of Fidel Castro's regime. But his criticism of the Cuban Revolution was much more than an attack against communism; it was an angry cry against injustice, against a system under which he, like many others, had been persecuted for being homosexual.

While there are implicit and explicit homosexual characters, episodes and
scenes in practically every text that Arenas wrote, it is in *Otra vez el mar*
(*Farewell to the Sea*; 1982), *Arturo, la estrella más brillante* (the second part
of *Old Rose: A Novel in Two Stories*; 1984), *Viaje a La Habana* (Journey to
Havana; 1990), *El color del verano* (The Color of Summer; 1991) and *Antes
que anochezca* (Before Night Falls; 1992), the author's autobiography, that we
find greater explicitness in the depiction of gay characters and homosexual desire. Yet Arenas's representation of homosexuality cannot be considered "positive" in the way that a great majority of Anglo-American gay literature has
striven to celebrate homosexual identity and represent ideal gay relationships
based on mutual respect and equal status. Nonetheless, if one carefully examines
Arenas's entire oeuvre, one finds a persistently resurfacing argumentative center
that supports the rights of all individuals, regardless of their sexual orientation,
a staunch defense of the individual's imaginative capabilities and right to self-
expression in a world beset by ignorance, intolerance and persecution.

Otra vez el mar (1982) is the third and central novel of a five-book sequence
(*Celestino antes del alba* [1967], *El palacio de las blanquísimas mofetas* [*The
Palace of the White Skunks;* 1980], *Otra vez el mar, El color del verano*, and *El
asalto* [The Assault, 1990]), described by the author as both a writer's autobiography and a metaphor of Cuban history. Rewritten three times over a period of sixteen years, *Otra vez el mar* is the story of Héctor, a sensitive and passionate young
man living under an institutionalized revolution who finds himself questioning his
alienation and tortured existence. His story depicts the increasing divergence between desire, passion and imagination, and a brand of revolutionary social reality
that becomes progressively more brutal and oppressive.

Structurally, *Otra vez el mar* is an interplay of two monologues of personal
frustration that work as a duo. Part I (the wife's discourse) and Part II (Héctor's
cantos) present the histories, dreams, memories and hallucinations of a Cuban
couple as they return to Havana by car after a six-day vacation at the beach.
Part I is a straightforward narration divided into six chapters, each corresponding
to one of the six days at the beach. Part II, narrated by Héctor, is a dramatic
meshing of poetry and prose divided into six cantos, each likewise corresponding to one of the six days of vacation. Furthermore, there is an intertextual web
that links both parts. Situations in Part I are continued or resolved in Part II.

The story commences when the six-day vacation has ended and the couple
leaves the beach to begin their trip home. At this moment both characters—first
the wife, then Héctor—begin to speak, to remember, to imagine, to dream, to
sing of their personal frustrations and disenchantment. Although the wife relates
the first part of the novel, she remains nameless throughout the text. The position
of dominance of her discourse within the textual linearity of the novel (Part I)
sets up the reader to rely on the authenticity of her voice. However, her discourse
and her very existence are challenged in the last sentences of the novel when it
is revealed that she is only an invention, a ghost or obsession of Héctor's imag-

ination. Like the child narrator of Arenas's first novel, *Celestino antes del alba*, Héctor has created an alter ego in order to survive in a repressive environment that, in his case, excludes and condemns him on two counts: for being a political dissident and for being homosexual. Yet it is through the negation of the wife— a developed and complex character who narrates her memories, dreams, hallucinations and fears over 193 pages of the text—that attention is called to Héctor's need to invent, create and compose as a way to defend himself from a rigid and intolerant society that is extremely hostile toward transgressions from the norm and that believes order exists in the preservation of an exemplary revolutionary social consciousness.

Throughout Part II of *Otra vez el mar* Héctor denounces the charades he finds himself forced to perform to hide his homosexuality. He sees himself acting out a role over which he has no control. For this reason, when he finally has the opportunity to fulfill his sexual desire with the young boy he meets at the beach, his paranoid fears prevent him from doing so. Instead, he chooses to believe that he has been set up. Thus he insults the boy and tells him of the lies and cover-ups he will be forced to promulgate if he expects to live as a homosexual in a socialist society that deems homosexuality a nonproductive behavior and emblematic of bourgeois decadence: "You know that you will never be able to be yourself; you'll always wear a mask, be ashamed, be a source of derision and scandal and revenge for other men, and of unending humiliation for yourself? For survival alone, you will have to betray and deny what defines you, what you precisely *are*" (343–344). Throughout *Otra vez el mar* Héctor's personal moments of inquietude and unhappiness are the consequence of living under a regime unwilling to accept any textual or sexual expression not contributing to the established order of the revolutionary hegemony. Thus, at the end of the novel, as Héctor's car approaches Havana, the possibility of continuing to sing his imaginary poem begins to disappear. Héctor is well aware that if he arrives, he will return to the slavery of the city, to conventionalism and conformity. For this reason he says, "Don't arrive, don't ever get here, because arriving is turning yourself over to them" (410). In the end, Héctor's car increases its velocity as it nears the city; suicide or apocalyptic freedom in death is the final outcome. As a result, the text is what remains after death. The voices that reach the reader are those that remain posthumously and will be repeated "otra vez" (again), as the title of the novel suggests.

Arenas's *Arturo, la estrella más brillante* ("Arturo, the Brightest Star"), first published in Barcelona in 1984, is a continuation of his earlier novella *La vieja Rosa* (First written in 1966). In 1990 these novellas—two texts that well exemplify the writer's earliest and most experienced work—appeared in English under the title *Old Rose: A Novel in Two Stories*. Together, these two texts, which were published eighteen years apart, tell the stories of Old Rosa, a powerful landowner whose desire for absolute control is undermined by the social changes of the Cuban Revolution, and her youngest son, Arturo, an individual imprisoned and persecuted both emotionally, by the memories of his domineering mother, and physically, by a revolutionary system that locks him up in a forced labor camp because he is a homosexual.

During 1980, the year Arenas escaped from Cuba through the Mariel exodus, he granted the *Nouvel observateur* an interview (translated into English in *Encounter*, January 1982) in which he spoke out against the hostility of the Cuban revolutionary regime to all subversive individuals, noncommitted writers as well as homosexuals. In his interview, Arenas maintained that while he lived in Cuba, the exteriorization of any form of difference or opposition was considered counterrevolutionary, for it went against the archetype of the disciplined revolutionary or *hombre nuevo* (new man). As early as 1965 forced labor camps under the name UMAP (an acronym for Unidades Militares de Ayuda a la Producción; Military Units for Aid to Production) were constructed in the province of Camagüey to correct "antisocial" and "deviant" behaviors that threatened the creation of a true revolutionary consciousness.

This period of repression was documented by Néstor Almendros and Orlando Jiménez-Leal in the 1984 film *Conducta impropia* (Improper Conduct). This film consists of individual testimonies that document the atrocities committed by the Cuban revolutionary government against homosexuals. In the film Arenas recounts his experiences with discrimination against homosexuals while living in Cuba. During the height of the purges of homosexuals, Arenas states, any individual who was identified as homosexual or "extravagant" was carted off to a UMAP camp for not adapting to the revolutionary model. Allen Young's account of homophobia in Cuba (*Gays Under the Cuban Revolution*; 1981) supports Arenas's accusations of the regime's intolerance of any manifestation of "extravagant" behavior. Young writes: "The people carted off to UMAP camps included youths who showed "too much" concern with their personal appearance (long hair, colorful clothing, etc.); they were said to be victims of *la enfermedad* (the disease) or of "cultural imperialism" (22).

The story of *Arturo, la estrella más brillante* is a fictitious account of one man's experiences in one of the many UMAP work camps in Cuba in the late 1960s. The desire to document the conditions of the UMAP camps is focused from a literary perspective. It is interesting to note, however, that Arenas's text, presented as pure fiction, was born out of a desire to remember his friend Nelson Rodríguez Leyva, whose unpublished book of stories about his experiences in a UMAP camp was confiscated and destroyed by the Cuban authorities. Far from being political propaganda, *Arturo, la estrella más brillante* is a defense of individuals' right to dream, to rise above the oppression that threatens their existence. The text has no paragraphs, blank spaces nor periods. Much like thoughts, memories and dreams, the narrative shifts and flows, without interruption, from one level of reality to another.

The first part of *Arturo, la estrella más brillante* focuses on Arturo's memories of his life before the UMAP camp. However, as the story progresses and Arturo must face the endless cutting of sugarcane, the extreme solitude and the constant humiliations and abuses of the guards, memories are not enough to distract him from his state of oppression. Thus he begins, like many of Arenas's characters, to dedicate his time to imagining and dreaming as a means of escaping his asphyxiating situation. When the vulgar realities of camp life reach unbearable proportions, Arturo's fictive flights of imagination take on a very specific task, that of dreaming an ideal male lover. Arturo's oppression is not solely the result of a repressive political system. Such a simplistic explanation would only convert the novella into political propaganda. Oppression is also evident in the "improper" conduct of certain homosexual prisoners who create their own oppressive hierarchy of power, a "sistership" as they call it, that does not tolerate individuals who do not assimilate.

Already subjugated by the abuses of the guards, Arturo realizes that he must fit into this gay subculture if he wishes to escape further persecution. Thus, he begins to take on the dizzying slang, the poses, the cant of this imprisoned gay ghetto until he finally becomes the star, "the Queen of the Captive Queers," of the transvestite shows performed at night in the barracks. Arturo discovers that he must destroy any expression of self that does not conform to the imprisoned gay world of the barracks, must bury any authentic self-expression underneath a facade of burlesque and vulgar mockery in order to be accepted. Yet as time passes, the wild extravaganzas of the barracks night life begin to leave him empty and unfulfilled. These feelings of frustration escalate after the tragic death of Celeste, one of the other stars of the transvestite shows. Thereafter, Arturo feels more and more desperate to escape his sordid surroundings; consequently, he takes on a new creative task, dreaming/creating a fantastic and fabulous castle where he hopes to meet his ideal lover.

Arturo's labor of love, which requires all his passion and strength, is constantly interrupted by the vile realities of the camp. To continue with his work, his only "real" refuge, he begins to give up sleep and meals, to take advantage of every free moment. Yet, this is not enough. In a desperate attempt to complete his imaginary castle, Arturo decides to escape from the camp. As he throws his machete down, he runs through the sugarcane fields until he reaches the vast esplanade where he hopes to give shape to his wonderful castle. In the few minutes (story time) before the soldiers reach him, Arturo is able to spend time (discourse time) carefully building and lavishly furnishing his fantastic domain. Precisely at the moment when Arturo completes his work, the squad of soldiers advances toward him, pointing their rifles. Arturo, who sees a choir of angels announcing the arrival of his lover, eagerly runs toward them. But as the "angels" get closer, Arturo discovers "with irrefutable, inarguable clarity" that these are not angels but soldiers led by his mother, Old Rosa, "boiling mad," who screams with gun in hand: "Faggot faggot faggot, you won't get away from me this time" (103).

A reading of *La vieja Rosa* by itself might suggest that the abusive authority of the main character—a reflection of Cuba's prerevolutionary social injustices—could be challenged and easily eliminated by the Revolution. Yet, in

Arturo, la estrella más brillante we see how this symbol of authoritarian oppression reappears, and this time with far more vengeance. Let us remember
that *La vieja Rosa* was written when the author was only twenty-three years
old, when his views on the subject were limited by his personal experiences.
On the other hand, *Arturo, la estrella más brillante* is a much more mature text,
and thus reflects the sinister ambiguities, the devious and insidious nature of
oppression that can resurface and assert itself under different forms and guises—
for example, in a government deciding to round up "deviants" and lock them
up, while presenting itself to the world as the champion of the underdogs and
the downtrodden.

Arenas subtitled *Viaje a La Habana*, *Novela en tres viajes* (Novel in Three
Trips). This work, published a few months before his death, is a collection of
three stories, each with its own plot, characters, and action. Yet all three stories
are connected by a central theme: the search for a homosexual identity that
produces a personal liberation (even when in one of the stories, "Mona," this
search ends with the destruction of the protagonist).

The first piece, "Que trine Eva" (Let Eve Scream) is the story of a couple,
Evattt and Ricardo, who, like the characters in *Otra vez el mar*, could well be
one character split into two personalities. As a result of the severe shortages on
the island, they dress themselves with clothes that are skillfully and creatively
sewn and knitted by Evattt, the wife, a Cuban Penelope (throughout the story
there are numerous parodies of both mythological and religious figures). Evattt's
and Ricardo's clothing soon is the talk of Havana. To maintain their reputation
the couple, always wanting to look their best and outdo their peers, dress in the
most outrageous and flamboyant wardrobe (their clothes truly reach hyperbolic
proportions). Everything goes smoothly until one day Ricardo starts to feel that
there is "someone" who does not admire them, who feels indifferent to their
sensational exhibitionism. Soon Ricardo's doubt turns into dissatisfaction and
fear, an obsessive feeling that drives him to want to find that individual, to
dazzle him and win him over with his wardrobe.

Thus, Evattt and Ricardo's trips begin, an odyssey that will take them, along
with their many suitcases filled with the most extravagant suits and dresses,
throughout the island in search of that "indifferent" being. After numerous trips
and excursions (which are reminiscent of Fray Servando Teresa de Mier's endless peregrinations in Arenas's *El mundo alucinante* [*Hallucinations*; 1969]), the
couple finally finds the one who is responsible for their journeys, a young fisherman whom both Evattt and Ricardo try to win over. That night, at a special
revolutionary celebration, after trying every form of dance and pose to get his
attention, Evattt sees the young man get up from his table, ignore her, and walk
over to Ricardo, to whom he extends his hand and walks with toward the sea.
Defeated and abandoned, Evattt returns home, where she dedicates herself to
knitting a black mourning dress that she plans to wear in the streets of Havana.

Among the many possible readings, "Que trine Eva" can be read as a carnivalesque (sub)version of the story of Adam and Eve, the biblical couple with

whom our oppressive Western sexual tradition began. Ricardo, unhappy and unsatisfied with his triumphs in Havana (a carnivalesque inversion of Eden) is the masculine (in)version of the biblical Eve that "lets herself" be tempted by the serpent (a recurrent symbol in all the stories of *Viaje a La Habana*). Evattt, who allows herself to be talked into these wild journeys as a result of Ricardo's whims, is the female (in)version of Adam, who allowed himself to be persuaded by Eve. This vertiginous game of inversions of traditional gender roles demystifies and subverts the biblical belief that Eve ("the weaker sex") was responsible for Adam's fall from grace.

"Mona," the second story of the collection, utilizes the techniques of the detective story and the gothic tale, with Arenas's typical sense of humor and irreverence, to tell the extraordinary and fatal story of Ramón Fernández, a Cuban immigrant from the Mariel exodus living in New York City, who is imprisoned for trying to destroy Leonardo da Vinci's Mona Lisa, on special exhibit at the Metropolitan Museum of Art. This story utilizes a number of literary devices of realistic-referential literature (including the use of direct testimony, detailed dates and footnotes) in order to present, and at the same time subtly subvert, Ramón's extraordinary story.

From his prison cell Ramón writes a testimony of how he came to know the mysterious Elisa, a lusting and fascinating woman, who turned out to be Leonardo da Vinci, painted himself onto the canvas (à la Dorian Gray), and thus gave himself eternal life in order to abandon the painting and find the sexual satisfaction with men that he was denied during his lifetime. The story ends with the death of Ramón in his cell and leaves the intratextual reader with a number of questions: Was it in fact suicide, or was Ramón persecuted and finally killed by Leonardo/Elisa, who wanted to protect his/her secret? On the other hand, was it all a paranoid hallucination resulting from Ramón's repressed homosexual feelings, or did everything occur the way Ramón declares in his testimony? This doubt makes the story a contemporary example of fantastic literature as defined by Tzvetan Todorov. With this story Arenas has provided the first example of what can be called gay fantastic literature.

The last, title story of *Viaje a La Habana* presents the theme of incest joined with homosexual desire, thus combining two of society's most closeted taboos in a single story. Arenas's treatment of these themes results in a sensitive and emotional tale of affection between two human beings in search of love. The protagonist of the story, Ismael (biblical name of an outcast and wanderer, but also an allusion to José Martí's *Ismaelillo*, a collection of poetry inspired by and dedicated to Martí's son) decides, with much trepidation, to return to Cuba to visit his wife and son after having departed the island fifteen years earlier. Ismael left Cuba after serving three years in prison, having been set up and later accused of sexual perversion and corruption of minors. After leading a repressed and solitary life in exile, Ismael decides to return to Cuba, a journey as much in time-space as a symbolic journey in search of a liberating identity.

Upon reaching the island, Ismael decides to spend a few days in Havana before going to his hometown of Santa Fe. In Havana he meets a young military man with whom he falls in love, a love that is seen by Ismael as a resurrection: "Don't you realize that I was dead and you resurrected me?" (146). Yet Ismael must pass through his own Calvary in order to achieve his resurrection (in Christianity, Jesus' resurrection brings about his reunion with God the Father). The last four pages of the text articulate the adversities and sufferings that Ismael endures to reach his home town, Santa Fe (literally Holy Faith) on December 25 (yet another biblical allusion). In the story's denouement, which can be read either as a dream or as reality (neither of which undermines the protagonist's coming to terms with his own homosexuality), Ismael discovers that the youth he had met in Havana is his own son, who confesses to Ismael that he had suspected since they first met that he was his father. "Viaje a La Habana" assimilates and gives new possibilities to various religious symbols and biblical passages to articulate a homosexual story of love, thereby transgressing the restrictive morality of Christianity toward homosexual desire.

In his autobiography, *Antes que anochezca*, Arenas informs us that although *El color del verano* is the fourth novel of his five-book cycle (*Celestino antes del alba*, *El palacio de las blanquísimas mofetas*, *Otra vez el mar*, *El color del verano*, and *El asalto*), it was in fact the last novel he wrote. He also tells of his determination, despite his precarious health, to complete the novel. In this respect *El color del verano* is a significant text, for with it. Arenas was finally able to give closure to a cycle of novels he had begun writing three decades earlier. Although *El color del verano* takes place in the summer of 1999, the entire novel is a carnivalesque document of what it was like to be young and homosexual in Cuba during the 1960s and 1970s. This is made evident in the prologue, which appears halfway through the text (246–250). Here the lines between fiction and metafiction are intentionally erased. First the "documentary" nature of this fourth novel of the quintet is underscored:

To a certain extent this work pretends to reflect, without flattery or high-sounding principles, somewhere between the picaresque and dissolute life of a great portion of Cuban youths, their desires to be young and to exist as such. The underground vision of a homosexual world, which surely will never appear in any newspaper, and much less in Cuba, predominates here in these pages. This novel is intrinsically tied to one of the most vital eras of my life and that of a great majority of people who were young during the sixties and seventies. If I didn't write about it, *El color del verano* is a world that would be lost and fragmented in the memory of those that knew and lived it. (249)

Who writes this prologue? The ambiguous but provocative answer lies in the fact that both Reinaldo Arenas (the flesh-and-blood author) and Gabriel/Reinaldo/the Tétrica Mofeta (the fictitious author[s] are the writers of a novel titled *El color del verano*. This *mise-en-abîme* undermines the authority of authorship while underscoring the concern of recording this particular era in Cuban history that would be forgotten and lost forever if not preserved in writing. The island on which the story of *El color del verano* is played out is explicitly identified as Cuba (124). It is the summer of 1999, and the dictator Fifo is celebrating fifty years in power: "fifty years which in fact are really only forty, he increased them because he loved . . . round numbers and publicity" (64). Under Fifo's tyrannical rule the people of the island must shield their true feelings for fear of recrimination, and are forced to live double, even triple, lives in order to survive: "On that island everyone led at least a double life: in public they would unceasingly praise the tyrant while secretly hating him and desperately hoping he would kick the bucket" (123). In addition to creating an internal dialogism that enriches the resonances of characterization, the splitting of characters underscores the dishonesty and fear present within this totalitarian state in which individuals must fragment themselves into a multiplicity of "selves," each fulfilling different social functions.

In *El color del verano* the first-person narrative voice is shared by Gabriel/Reinaldo/the Tétrica Mofeta (Gloomy Skunk). This trinity, like the poet Héctor in Part II of *Otra vez el mar*, is responsible for writing the anecdotes, letters, tongue twisters, and stories that make up the novel and in turn give voice to Cuba's excluded and marginal homosexual subculture of the 1960s and 1970s. The splitting of the protagonist in three is explained early in the text. Gabriel, returning from the United States to visit his mother in the small town of Holguín, imagines himself confessing to her his true self/selves: "I'm not one person, but two or three at the same time. For you I am Gabriel, for those that read what I write, which I'm rarely able to publish, I'm Reinaldo, for the rest of my friends with whom from time to time I can escape and be totally myself, I'm the Tétrica Mofeta" (101). In addition to underscoring how society's nonacceptance of homosexuality forces the homosexual to protect his true identity by hiding behind a mask, Arenas's poetic trinity is a parodic, sullen and blasphemous (sub)version of the Catholic Trinity (Father, Son and Holy Spirit in one divine Godhead) that reflects and gives voice to the very complex and contradictory human facets of the protagonist's personality.

Reinaldo is the writer–creator (God the Father) who gives life to his characters. The nostalgic recollections of Gabriel (a biblical name of one of the archangels who appears as a divine messenger) must be sacrificed, like the son Jesus Christ, in order for the Tétrica Mofeta (the protagonist's homosexual spirit of truth) to exist. In one of his last interviews, Arenas declared:

The gloomy skunk undergoes a metamorphosis so he can extend his existence through that of various characters. He is a homosexual who lives in Cuba, the victim of all sorts of persecution. In spite of it all, he's trying to write a novel which the government is trying to find and destroy. He's got a double in the United States, Gabriel, . . . [who] has a series of complexes he can't overcome . . . because he didn't fulfill his mother's dream. (80)

In *El color del verano*, four letters written to and by the alter egos (Reinaldo/Gabriel/the Tétrica Mofeta) are reproduced within the text. These letters poignantly capture the emotional weight, the trials and the tribulations of living under a revolution and in exile. The first three letters (84, 166, 288) are marked by a tone of despair, sadness and disillusionment at having to live in exile (Paris, New York and Miami). Although individuals are free to express themselves without fear in these cities, Reinaldo/Gabriel/the Tétrica Mofeta feels alienated and out of place. For example, the grayness and coldness of Paris is contrasted to the tropical climate of Cuba; the dirty beaches of Long Island are quite different from the warm blue waters of the Caribbean; and despite its tropical climate, Miami is presented as a plastic imitation, a mere shadow, of Cuba. The three letters written from exile also document the horrors of AIDS.

In the fourth letter (344) the Tétrica Mofeta, who finds himself in Cuba, writes to Reinaldo, Gabriel and the Tétrica Mofeta, who are living in exile. In this final letter the Tétrica Mofeta sympathizes with the sorrows and afflictions of his alter egos, but feels that their pain cannot compare with the horrors of living under a tyrannical system in which citizens must cooperate with the laws and whims of a dictator. In addition, living with AIDS under a system that persecutes homosexuals, and that cannot provide needed medical attention, is far more horrifying. But instead of concentrating on the negative, the Tétrica Mofeta goes on to talk about his (their) writings, which make up ''a single complete work in its entirety [whose] mocking and desperate spirit [is perhaps] that of our own country'' (344–345). In *El color del verano* the precision of historical facts and figures is sacrificed for the vital and dynamic ''documentation'' that only fiction can provide. The four letters of *El color del verano* poetically and intuitively capture the complex feelings of fragmentation, dissatisfaction and confusion that the protagonist (Reinaldo/Gabriel/the Tétrica Mofeta) experiences living both in and outside Cuba.

The last text Arenas wrote before his death was *Antes que anochezca*, his autobiography. Central to this memoir is the sexual and political repression the author had to endure in Cuba and about which he does not hesitate to write in the text. Far from being a traditional autobiography, *Antes que anochezca* utilizes a combination of historical facts and delirious and exaggerated fiction. Yet this mixing of fact and fiction in no way diminishes the strength of the testimony. For example, Arenas does not limit himself to simply declaring his homosexuality but graphically presents and exaggerates his sexual escapades, going beyond what many (Hispanic) readers would consider good taste. There is no denying that Arenas was quite aware of the hypocrisy and homophobia of his Hispanic audience and, rather than making concessions, allowing himself to be closeted by bigotry disguised as good taste, he expressed his experiences honestly, to the point of alienating certain readers. In 1992 Mario Vargas Llosa stated in his review of the autobiography: ''This is one of the most moving testimonies that has ever been written in our language about oppression and rebellion, but few will dare to acknowledge this fact since the book, although one reads it with an uncontrollable appetite, has the perverse power of leaving its readers uncomfortable'' (15).

Arenas has left the international gay community an important literary legacy. His writing, passionate, rebellious and irreverent, while fascinating the reader with literary innovation and experimentation, also provokes further dialogue and discussion concerning the homosexual's problematic relationship with society.

WORKS

Antes que anochezca (autobiografía). Barcelona: Tusquets Editores, 1992.

Arturo, la estrella más brillante. Barcelona: Montesinos, 1984. English trans. included with that of *La vieja Rosa*.

El asalto. Miami: Ediciones Universal, 1990.

Cantando en el pozo. New authorized ed. of *Celestino antes del alba*. Barcelona: Editorial Argos Vergara, 1982.

Celestino antes del alba. Havana: Ediciones Unión, 1967. English version *Singing from the Well*. Trans. Andrew Hurley. New York: Viking Penguin, 1987.

El central. Barcelona: Seix Barral, 1981. English version *El Central: A Cuban Sugar Mill*. Trans. Anthony Kerrigan. New York: Avon Books, 1984.

El color del verano. Miami: Ediciones Universal, 1991.

Con los ojos cerrados. Montevideo: Editorial Arca, 1972.

Final de un cuento. Huelva, Spain: Diputación Provincial de Huelva, 1991.

Lazarillo de Tormes (lecturas fáciles). New York: Regents Publishing Co., 1984.

Leprosorio (trilogía poética). Madrid: Editorial Betania, 1990.

La loma del ángel. Málaga, Spain: DADOR/Ediciones, 1987. English version *Graveyard of the Angels*. Trans. Alfred MacAdam. New York: Avon Books, 1987.

El mundo alucinante. Caracas: Monte Avila Editores, 1982. First published 1969. English version *Hallucinations*. Trans. Gordon Brotherson. New York: Harper & Row, 1971. Also *The Ill-Fated Peregrinations of Fray Servando*. Trans. Andrew Hurley. New York: Avon Books, 1987.

Necesidad de libertad (Mariel: Testimonios de un intelectual disidente). Mexico City: Kosmos Editorial, 1986.

Otra vez el mar. Barcelona: Editorial Argos Vergara, 1982. English version *Farewell to the Sea*. Trans. Andrew Hurley. New York: Viking Penguin, 1986.

El palacio de las blanquísimas mofetas. Caracas: Monte Avila Editores, 1980. English version *The Palace of the White Skunks*. Trans. Andrew Hurley. New York: Viking Penguin, 1990.

Persecución (cinco piezas de teatro experimental). Miami: Ediciones Universal, 1986.

Un plebiscito a Fidel Castro. Madrid: Editorial Betania, 1990.

El portero. Málaga, Spain: DADOR/Ediciones, 1989. English version *The Doorman*. Trans. Dolores M. Koch. New York: Grove Press, 1991.

Termina el desfile. Barcelona: Seix Barral, 1981.

Viaje a La Habana. Miami: Ediciones Universal, 1990.

La vieja Rosa. Caracas: Editorial Arte, 1980. English version *Old Rose: A Novel in Two Stories*. Trans. Andrew Hurley and Ann Tashi Slater. New York: Grove Press, 1989. Includes translation of *Arturo, la estrella más brillante*.

Voluntad de vivir manifestándose. Madrid: Editorial Betania, 1989.

CRITICISM

Béjar, Eduardo C. *La textualidad de Reinaldo Arenas*. Madrid: Editorial Playor, 1987.

Ette, Ottmar, ed. *La escritura de la memoria*. Frankfurt am Main: Vervuert, 1992.

Foster, David William. *Gay and Lesbian Themes in Latin American Literature*, 66–72. Austin: University of Texas Press, 1991.

Hernández-Miyares, Julio, and Perla Rozencvaig, eds. *Reinaldo Arenas: Alucinaciones, fantasía y realidad*. Glenview, Ill.: Scott, Foresman, 1990.

Olivier-Giesbert, Franz. "Pourquoi j'ai fui Fidel Castro." *Le Nouvel Observateur* 880 (Sept. 19–25, 1981): 64–68. Interview with Arenas. Repr. as "Dangerous Manuscripts: A Conversation with Reinaldo Arenas." *Encounter* 58.1 (Jan. 1982): 60–67.

Rozencvaig, Perla. *Reinaldo Arenas: Narrativa de transgresión*. Mexico City: Editorial Oasis, 1986.

———. "Reinaldo Arenas's Last Interview." *Review: Latin American Literature and Arts* 44 (Jan.–June 1991): 78–83.

Schwartz, Kessel. "Homosexuality and the Fiction of Reinaldo Arenas." *Journal of Evolutionary Psychology* 1–2 (Mar. 1984): 12–20.

Soto, Francisco. "*Celestino antes del alba:* Escritura subversiva/sexualidad transgresiva." *Revista iberoamericana* 154 (Jan.–Mar. 1991): 345–354.

———. *Conversación con Reinaldo Arenas*. Madrid: Editorial Betania, 1990.

———. "Reinaldo Arenas's Literary Legacy." *Christopher Street Magazine* 156 (May 1991): 12–16.

Valero, Roberto. *El desamparado humor de Reinaldo Arenas*. North Miami: Hallmark Press, 1991.

Vargas Llosa, Mario. "Pájaro tropical." *El País* (Lima), June 15, 1992, 15–16.

Young, Allen. *Gays Under the Cuban Revolution*. San Francisco: Grey Fox Press, 1981.

Francisco Soto

ARÉVALO MARTÍNEZ, RAFAEL
(Guatemala; 1884–1975) _____

Arévalo Martínez is Guatemala's most important modernist writer. Self-taught, as are the majority of Guatemalan writers, he was unable to complete high school because of health problems. Nevertheless, he is considered a founder of modern Latin American narrative.

On the basis of the publication date of his first book, *Maya* (1911), Guatemalan criticism groups Arévalo Martínez with the writers known as the Generation of 1910. In Central America the group represents the rather late incorporation of modernism into the literature of the region, a literature that was still tied to forms deriving from European Romanticism and realism of the nineteenth century.

A prolific writer, Arévalo Martínez developed in his poetry, short stories, novels, dramas and essays, in the period between 1911 and 1971, a complex autobiographical oeuvre in which he chronicles the story of the Decadent Poet. This creature, a martyr to neurasthenia and religious doubt, nevertheless represents the experiences of all men during those years of dramatic economic, political and social changes (the writer establishes a clear demarcation between the experiences of men and those of women). The story "El hombre verde" (The Green Man) demonstrates how Arévalo Martínez's autobiographical subject has no name; and if his narrator is anonymous or if he is identified as Rafael Arévalo Martínez, Manuel Aldano, Professor Cendal, Mr. Friend, or any other name, he could just as well be Oscar Wilde, St. Teresa, St. Francis of Assisi, Plato, or Jesus. This is because of all these names refer to the same entity, the Poet, who is the reflex of a nameless Unique Being who, since no other name is available, is called God.

Of all of the texts published by Arévalo Martínez, his first story, "El hombre que parecía un caballo" (The Man Who Looked like a Horse), continues to be the one with which most readers are familiar. Yet this story is no more than a fragment of one of the author's numerous narrative cycles. This group of stories might be identified as the Manuel Aldano cycle, since all of them chronicle fragments from the life of Aldano, whom critics are unanimous in seeing as the alter ego of Arévalo Martínez, and of Sr. de Artel, a semiveiled fictionalization of the Colombian poet Porfirio Barba Jacob, who share an intense spiritual adventure. Their experiences are the result of the deep friendship that binds them. This friendship, shaped in accord with the theories of love proposed by Plato and as subsequently developed by the Neoplatonists of the Renaissance (especially Marsilo Ficino and Leone Ebreo), represents an anomaly in Latin American literature. It is important to clarify that, as a Neoplatonist, Arévalo Martínez sees love as a strictly spiritual matter. One's friend, like a lover, seeks only to love the soul of the beloved, which, according to this doctrine, is imprisoned in a material body. In this soul one can perceive the reflection of the Unique Being of which both body and soul are an emanation. Moreover, as he explains in his novel *El mundo de los maharachías* (The World of the Maharachías), men, as a combination of spirit and matter, strive to become true human beings. But such a state can be attained only by means of the spiritualization of the body and of its needs and desires. Paradoxically, this implies the acceptance of their animal nature—that is, of a return to their natural state.

Thus, the story in question, as Arévalo Martínez did on several occasions, makes it clear that the visions the two friends experience are the result of the high degree of spiritual evolution they possess as poets. The idea that the two human beings must pass through a series of stages in their spiritual development before achieving true humanity, in which the animal and the spiritual are one— which Arévalo Martínez expresses in several of the poems in *Las rosas de Engaddi* (The Roses of Engaddi), is the result of the beliefs that he held with respect to metempsychosis, a concept borrowed not only from Plato but also from Madame Blatavsky, the most important figure associated with the doctrines of theosophy, and that he justifies on the basis of Darwin's ideas on evolution.

Another consequence of the cycle of reincarnations that the soul must undergo before attaining a total spiritualization and the return to the Unique Being from which it has fallen, is the "sexual complexity" that characterizes all exceptional beings. This theory, which seems to have originated with Arévalo Martínez, is explained in a Platonic dialogue with the title "Complejidad sexual." Arévalo Martínez, upholding the concept of personal soul and sexual polarization, undermines the idea of the individual as a specific being, defined by sex and by name, with the latter emblematic of the unity and coherence that all subjects imply.

As a consequence of the drastic opposition that Arévalo Martínez establishes between the quotidian world, which for the modernists represents the realm of the material, and the spiritual world, the sort of experiences that the friends in question come to live occurs on a level completely independent of the events the poet must face on a day-to-day basis. This can be seen in a short novel published in 1925, *La oficina de paz de Orolandia* (The Orolandia Peace Office), which narrates the problems that the narrator and protagonist, a poet named Félix Buendía, must confront on a daily basis in order to support his family. This satiric novel with political overtones portrays the corruption that characterizes the lives of human beings who are concerned only with drawing a salary. These experiences, as Arévalo Martínez explains in his essays, pertain to a degraded reality that is renounced by man as he progresses in the discovery of the spiritual aspects of the world—as his soul progresses in its development.

The idea that the material world is characterized by its degradation and that, therefore, work undertaken in order to survive in it plunges man even further into the depths of the nonhuman is also elaborated in Arévalo Martínez's poetry. In "Canto a Flamel" (Song to Flamel), a poem included in *Maya*, the poet criticizes the French alchemist Nicolas Flamel for having turned to action rather than limiting himself to the word. This opposition between action and contemplation is explored when the poet counterpoises the biblical figure of busy Martha with that of her contemplative sister, Mary. That in this well-known story from St. Luke, Jesus may have favored the transports of Mary over the industriousness of Martha justifies what, according to Arévalo Martínez, must be the function of the poet. The latter, like the birds in the parable, must reject all material work in order to limit himself to the contemplation of the world and to singing the only truth: the multiplicity that we perceive in the universe is illusory, and the force that provides it with its reality—its unity—is love.

Arévalo Martínez's frequent use of biblical figures in his texts fills his prose and poetry with religious resonances that he tends to contrast with the most important scientific theories of the period: references to Darwin's theory of evolution, to Cesare Lómbroso's typology, and to Max Nordau's ideas concerning decadence are common in his texts. They are juxtaposed not only to specifically Christian ideas but also to the doctrines of Plato and the ideas of theosophy. The writer nevertheless allows the reader to determine which of these two discourses, the religious or the scientific, presented as contradictory, is to be employed in order to interpret the facts described his narratives; this serves to underscore the role the reader plays in the elaboration of any text's meaning. If we add to this the extreme fragmentation of Arévalo Martínez's work—intertextualization as a strategy to suggest that every work is a unique text, while at the same time extending the texts of other writers and on occasion turning hallucinatory—we see that it is impossible to assign a univocal meaning to Arévalo Martínez's writings. Like all material forms, any literary text is only a fragment of an unattainable but real unity (the poem in the case of literature) that only the reader–poet can come to perceive, that is, can come to elaborate. In this fashion, Arévalo Martínez's literature must be seen as a totally imaginary adventure, as the creation of a language that resists any sort of facile incorporation into discourses that seek to identify themselves as canonical. If within his texts religious discourse criticizes and invalidates scientific discourse, the latter is ironically the means by which the author seeks to explain and justify his spiritualist vision of the universe.

By the same token, although the friendship between Aldano and Sr. de Aretal is described by means of erotic images that evoke the world of heterosexual love—the amorous intensity experienced by the newly married is one of these images—those images are nevertheless employed in order to define a strictly spiritual experience that, because of its sexual complexity, occurs between two men. By contrast, when spiritual attraction, which is the basis of the love that binds friends in Arévalo Martínez's literature, is absent, we have relations between ''inverts'' and transvestites, the terms employed by the narrator in ''Por cuatrocientos dólares'' (For Four Hundred Dollars), the story of two friends who, seeking only the satisfaction of their material needs, sacrifice their lives to the basest sort of mercantilism, able to perceive only the most abject forms of reality. Such relations, which Arévalo Martínez does not condemn because they take place between persons of the same sex (as is clear in an essay on Oscar Wilde), are, nevertheless, objectionable in his eyes for being the material version, and therefore a degraded version, of the spiritual love that binds true friends.

Thus, on a certain level, one of the reasons for these texts lies in the desire of the author to affirm the role that love plays in the revelation of the universe as an entity possessing a unitary and spiritual meaning. Yet such an affirmation is found in a discourse in which the contradictions function as a structural principle of an entire work, embodied in the theory of complementary opposites proposed by the author, whereby everything that exists in the universe is endowed with a soul. But these particular souls are fragments of a unique soul that exists in everything that can be perceived. In this way, literature is to be perceived as the material aspect of poetry, which in turn is one of the forms of love. Thus, the relation that binds the two friends in ''Hombre'' is reflected in the relation that the reader establishes with the poet.

With his exquisitely wrought prose, especially in the texts from his first period, which are overwhelming for the richness of their references and the surprising quality of their images, Arévalo Martínez's textual corpus attracts and seduces us. Nevertheless, as the author explains, in order for us to approach his work, in order for us truly to love it, we must go beyond its appearance, beyond its body, to discover the message it reveals to us, a message in which the irrelevance, the degradation of all matter is affirmed. Consistent with the paradoxical nature of his work, in the vision of love that Arévalo Martínez offers, to love a body, which is the same as loving the forms of literature, is to fall in love with a specter, to become impassioned over a chimera; it is to ignore the profound truth that, as a prisoner in matter, strives to reveal itself to us and, thus, to reveal authentic reality that, because it is spiritual, is unique and eternal.

WORKS

El hombre que parecía un caballo. Madrid: Compañía General de Artes Gráficas, 1931.
El hombre que parecía un caballo y otros cuentos. Guatemala City: Editorial Universitaria, 1951. San Salvador: Ministerio de Cultura, 1958.
Manuel Aldano (la lucha por la vida). Guatemala City: Talleres Gutenberg, 1922.
Maya. Guatemala City: Sánchez & De Guise, 1911.
El mundo de los maharachías. Guatemala City: Unión Tipográfica, 1938.
Obras escogidas. Guatemala City: Editorial Universitaria, 1959.
La oficina de paz de Orolandia. Guatemala City: Sánchez & De Guise, 1925.
Poemas de Rafael Arévalo Martínez. Guatemala City: Tipografía Nacional, 1965.
Las rosas de Engaddi. Guatemala City: Sánchez & De Guise, 1921.
La signatura de la esfinge (narración de J. M. Cendal, profesor universitario). Guatemala City: Imprenta Electra, 1933.

CRITICISM

Acevedo, Ramón Luis. *La novela centroamericana*, 215–272. Río Piedras, P. R.: Editorial Universitaria, 1982.
Albizúrez Palma, Francisco, and Catalina Barrios y Barrios. *Historia de la literatura guatemalteca*, 2:71–83. Guatemala City: Editorial Universitaria, 1982.
Algunos juicios de escritores guatemaltecos y extranjeros sobre la personalidad de Rafael Martínez y lista bibliográfica de su producción intelectual ordenada alfabéticamente por títulos. Guatemala City: Editorial del Ministerio de Educación Pública, 1959.
Arévalo, Teresa. *Rafael Arévalo Martínez: Biografía de 1884 hasta 1926*. Guatemala City: Tipografía Nacional, 1971.
Ayora, Jorge. ''Psicología de lo grotesco en 'El hombre que parecía un caballo.' '' *Explicación de textos literarios* 2.2 (1974): 117–122.
Branas, César. *Rafael Arévalo Martínez en su tiempo y en su poesía*. Guatemala City: Unión Tipográfica, 1944.
Carrera, Mario Alberto. *Las ocho novelas de Rafael Arévalo Martínez*. Guatemala City: Ediciones de la Casa de Cultura Flavio Herrera de la Universidad de San Carlos, 1975.

Estrada, Hugo. *La poesía de Rafael Arévalo Martínez*. Guatemala City: Tipografía Nacional, n.d.

Liano, Dante. *La palabra y el sueño*, 81–96. Rome: Bulzoni Editori, 1984.

Lonteen, Joseph Anthony. *Interpretación de una amistad intelectual y su producto literario: "El hombre que parecía un caballo."* Guatemala City: Editorial Landivar, 1969.

Salgado, María A. *Rafael Arévalo Martínez*. Boston: Twayne, 1979.

Francisco Nájera

ARIAS TRUJILLO, BERNARDO
(Colombia; 1903–1938) _____

Arias Trujillo's suicide cut short a very promising literary career and was felt for quite some time in Colombian literary circles. Born in the province of Caldas, a bastion of conservatism in western Colombia, Arias Trujillo hanged himself with his tie on March 4, 1938, in Manizales, the provincial capital. His work includes two novels, two books of essays, a few poems and translations, as well as short stories published in magazines and not yet collected.

Born into a humble family, Arias Trujillo was awarded a scholarship that enabled him to complete legal studies in Bogotá. Back in his native Manizales, he became a successful lawyer and journalist. He was appointed secretary of the Colombian consulate in Buenos Aires, a position that he held between 1932 and 1934. In Buenos Aires he published his first novel, *Por los caminos de Sodoma: Confesiones de un homosexual* (Sodom's Way: Confessions of a Homosexual; 1932), which appeared under the pseudonym Sir Edgard Dixon. Back in Colombia in 1934, he published a book of political criticism, *En carne viva* (Open Flesh; 1934), in which he questioned the Colombian government's perceived failure in its handling of the territorial dispute with Peru. In 1935 he published the novel *Risaralda: Película de negrumbre y vaquería filmada en dos rollos y en lengua castellana* (Risaralda: A Two-Reel Film about Blacks and Cowboys Filmed in Spanish; 1935), which brought him widespread recognition. In 1938 he published a book of literary essays, *Diccionario de emociones* (A Dictionary of Emotions; 1938). Arias Trujillo was also an active journalist, and in 1930 he founded and directed the first liberal newspaper in his region, *El Universal* (The Universal), which closed a few months later. Arias Trujillo used his newspaper to launch a campaign of political proselytism and criticism of the cultural heritage of almost half a century of conservative hegemony, which was nearing its end that year. His sharp criticism of the Catholic church, among other things, caused the Liberal party to order him to cease publication of his newspaper.

Arias Trujillo's poetry consists of only a few pieces, the most relevant being "A una muchacha deportista" (To a Sportswoman), "Letanía de la serpiente" (Litany of the Snake), and "Ruby Nelson," possibly the first—and certainly the best-known—male homoerotic poem in Colombian literature. Arias also wrote a polemical translation of Oscar Wilde's "Ballad of Reading Gaol."

Although today Arias Trujillo's literary reputation rests mainly on *Risaralda*, for many years "Ruby Nelson" was passed around in gay circles in Colombia, mostly through handmade copies, often adulterated, that were handed out in gay bars and at parties. *Por los caminos de Sodoma*, on the other hand, enjoyed a somewhat legendary reputation as the authentic and desolate confession of a homosexual. However, until 1990, when the novel was reissued, few people had access to the text, which fueled speculation about its nature and status.

Por los caminos de Sodoma resorts to a nonreliable narrator, although the text is essentially a third-person narrative: an anonymous narrator introduces Sir Edgard Dixon, a bilingual English nobleman. Dixon in turn introduces the story of David, which is mostly written in the third person. The novel presents homosexuality both as a legitimate option and as a deviation. One way to see this evident contradiction is to understand the author's need to lessen the shock that the publication of this novel would cause, especially among the most traditionally minded readers. This balance of having the public accept the novel while using the novel to plead for acceptance of the gay condition results in a text that is rather uneven in quality, possibly doing more damage than good in the long run because of the way it stresses certain homosexual stereotypes. The pleas of the protagonist, David, for acceptance are often unconvincing. His story recounts his lack of adaptation to his cultural milieu, his first romantic disappointment when the boy he loves platonically is seduced by a priest, his decision to leave his provincial town and then to reside in Buenos Aires, where he believes a man can love another man freely. There David meets Evans, a young circus artist, with whom he falls in love; however, this romance lands him in jail and makes him bitter and disillusioned with life.

The novel's confessional tone is pervasive from beginning to end, and it perpetuates a series of clichés about women. This consistent misogyny, and the validation of traditional heterosexual clichés such as the importance given to virginity, are features of the novel. For instance, although David finds sexual gratification with Evans, he constantly laments the fact that Evans was not a virgin when they met. This idea tortures David, who wishes to find a young man he can deflower. Such a vision of sexuality as sin, dirt, and guilt is, of course, not far from the traditional Christian perception of sex. Arias Trujillo's discourse in *Por los caminos de Sodoma* repeats much of Christian moralism regarding sex: venereal diseases are offered as proof that straight sex is polluted, although certainly this problem was not unknown in gay circles in the 1930s. The narrator finds the anatomy of women to be repulsive, although the terms used to describe it are an exact reversal of those traditionally used to dismiss homosexuality, and the implication is that heterosexual love is against nature. Last, Arias Trujillo's novel, although in essence a cry for recognition of homoeroticism, ignores the plight of lesbians in a patriarchal society. However, both his gay novel and his poetry, as well as his polemical translation of Wilde's poem, established him as a major figure in the creation and development of a gay identity in Colombian literature.

WORKS

Diccionario de emociones: Estampas móviles de hombres, sitios y ciudades. Manizales, Colombia: Editorial Zapata, 1938.

En carne viva. Manizales, Colombia: Editorial Zapata, 1934.

Por los caminos de Sodoma: Confesiones de un homosexual. Buenos Aires: Editorial Pagana, 1932. 2nd ed., Cali, Colombia: Ediciones BAT, 1990.

Risaralda: Novela de negrumbre y vaquería filmada en dos rollos y en lengua castellana. Manizales, Colombia: Editorial Zapata, 1935.

CRITICISM

Camacho Carreño, José. "Arias Trujillo, o el criollismo." In his *Diccionario de emociones*, 5–15. Medellín, Colombia: Bedout, 1963.

Mejía Duque, Jaime. *Bernardo Arias Trujillo: El drama del talento cautivo.* Manizales, Colombia: Editorial Papiro, 1990.

Williams, Raymond L. *The Colombian Novel, 1944–1987*, 137–140. Austin: University of Texas Press, 1991. Also in Spanish as *Novela y poder en Colombia: 1844–1987*, 182–185. Bogotá: Tercer Mundo, 1991.

Gilberto Gómez Ocampo

ARROYO, RANE (Puerto Rico; 1954) ⸺⸺⸺⸺

Rane Arroyo is a self-professed gay writer, a Puerto Rican poet, playwright, critic and performance artist, in that order. His creative voice speaks from the internalized ambivalence of living in two worlds: a Puerto Rican in the Anglo-American world, and a gay man in the straight world. These are very real themes in his work that reflect his background:

The memory of my first day at college. I was the first in my family to aspire and to achieve a "higher" education; when I took those first steps on campus, I felt as if I was trespassing and that "some invisible wild dog" was about to break loose and wrestle me to the ground. (Sheldon, "Interview")

Raised in Chicago and educated in its prosperous suburbs, Arroyo was given speech therapy in grade school to help him lose his "accent." It was successful in exterior terms. As the first Hispanic student in these white schools and on through college, Arroyo has continued to tread rough terrain as a dweller outside of both the "Chicagorican" ghetto and the gay ghetto. Indeed, his name, Rane (Ramón) Arroyo—partly Scandinavian but mostly Hispanic—becomes a metaphor for the duality of cultural voices that is his experience. This is partly the source for his remarkably philosophical writing and his grieving for an identity stolen from him by the white powers that be. In the third and final stanza of an early poem, "Why I Didn't Write This Poem," the narrator is mistaken for a thief on the basis of his ethnicity.

Arroyo won the Hart Crane Memorial Poetry Award in 1991 for his poem "Le Mal de Siam." His dramatic work *Other Couples* (three one-act plays) won the 1983 Jane Chambers Memorial International Playwriting Award. A 1986 Follett fellow in interdisciplinary arts education at Columbia College (Chicago), Arroyo wrote and performed art actions in Chicago for a number of years. Like the plays that came later, his avant-garde art actions combine the deep roots of storytelling and existential philosophy. Life and death and their interstices become foregrounded in life's simple day-to-day struggles. His characters are rich: Buddha, a tragic señorita who breaks men's hearts, a paraplegic in love with his dead daughter-in-law, and hustlers of every persuasion. Of his performance character Juan Angel (a bisexual rock singer who writes love songs inspired by men but addressed to women), Arroyo says:

I understand his problem very well. As a Puerto Rican from Chicago, most of my cultural identity was composed from popular music or movies like "West Side Story." I didn't know that I could become a poet and critic; I did believe that I could be a rock and roll singer or a movie star. (Sheldon, "Interview")

Although these dramas are not exclusively urban slices of life, the violence, the intercultural perspectives and the elements for divine coincidence combine to give the works an urban flair, particularly a Chicago flair. Arroyo is concerned about that landscape. Typically, his dramas do not shy away from violence and death in all its forms.

Arroyo is primarily a poet; his poetic works have been widely published by small presses for over a decade. There is evidence that Arroyo's gay identity partly emerges from the gay club scene. Inherent in the gay club scene (identity) is a superficial view of beauty; indeed, one of his dominant images is the anonymous "angel": a desirable but ultimately untouchable object of love. But Arroyo is not content to stop at that overly simplified metaphor because his angels prefer to wear leather, making them more earthly, dangerous creatures.

The previously mentioned early poem smacks of the produced one-act play *Buddha and the Señorita*, in which the Señorita hears the bullet in her gun lovingly call her name; the bullet "tells" her it loves her ... before she pulls the trigger and kills herself. Surely this duality, or ambivalence, is indicative of a deeper issue, identity as conflict (imaged within violence).

Attracted to the "double voicing" of the Russian literary theorist Mikhail Bakhtin, Arroyo believes his "assimilation" to be both a hindrance to greater success and a challenge to open the dialogue across cultures and identities. Arroyo's work is now archived in the Centro de Estudios Puertorriqueños (Hunter College), a major Puerto Rican studies institution. Of the archives, Arroyo (thirty-eight years old when this entry was written) states in a letter addressed to friends and colleagues:

It is important for me that the vision of my art and the political activism of my life be preserved holistically—without interference.

Consequently, with el Centro's enthusiastic response to my early career in poetry, playwrighting [*sic*] and criticism, I have decided to donate all my life's materials to the archive. Such a decision—which may seem premature to some—stems from several factors . . . [including] my need to remain a part of both the gay *and* Puerto Rican cultures. ("Letter")

Thus, Arroyo displays a positive view toward bridging issues of cross-cultural identity.

Arroyo's dramatic works, like *Tiara Tango* and *A Family in Figleaves,* revise the structure of the family; inherent in that social construct is not only identity but also definition(s) of love. In his recently published poetry, *Columbus's Orphan* (1990), Arroyo continues to grapple with "identities." He has long been revising the history of Spain and the American "Hispanic" identity. He opens historicosocial dimensions in *Columbus's Orphan.* There is an abundance of landscape in these poems, from the subtly colored prairies to the vivid Southwest deserts, that melds Catholic symbols of our world. An alchemist of light and sound, Arroyo hypnotizes the reader with stanzas of immense and powerful thoughts; the people in his poems roam these pages in thoughtful atheism.

Arroyo's catalog of pop culture icons would make a weighty study in themselves. Symbolist, realist and anticapitalist, Arroyo is a spiritual conquistador of the contemporary Hispanic identity and the diaspora forced upon people of color in anglicized America. From the beginning, critics have considered Arroyo to be a fairly involved poet, and his poetry to be reminiscent of the pastiches that Frank O'Hara put together.

Although many individuals have criticized Arroyo's creative works for their "blunt" nature and his unblinking stare at sex and power, the exploration of painful or controversial subjects is essential. Arroyo's plays produced in Pittsburgh—while he completed his doctorate—were critically overlooked or dismissed, but this is more symptomatic of the provincial, white elitism entrenched in that city's cultural milieu than of flaws in Arroyo's work; Chicago and New York, as well as Springfield, Illinois, and Indiana, Pennsylvania, have been infinitely more receptive to the same dramatic works. In the face of racism and homophobia (so potent in Pittsburgh), Arroyo would agree that artists must explore *all* subjects frankly. He adds, "The loss of innocence is not shocking, it's natural" (Sheldon, "Notes"). It opens one up to the "known world unknown."

WORKS

Buddha and the Señorita. In *Tough Acts to Follow: One-Act Plays on the Gay/Lesbian Experience,* 34–47. Ed. Noreen C. Barnes and Nicholas Deutsch. San Francisco: Alamo Square Press, 1992.

Columbus's Orphan. Arcadia, Fla.: JVC Books, 1993.

A Family in Figleaves. Dir. B. Keith Ryder. New Works Theatre, Arlington, Va., Aug. 17, 1992.

"I'm Here for You." *Berkeley Poets Cooperative* 29 (1987): 28.

"Infidelities in the Tropics." *Owen Wister Review* 16.1 (Fall 1992): 75.

"Le Mal de Siam: Father Pere Labat in the Caribbean 1697–1705." *Icon* 30.2 (Spring 1991): 8–11.

"Letter to Friends and Colleagues." Dec. 2, 1992. Rane Arroyo Papers. Centro de Estudios Puertorriqueños, New York.

Red Bed. Tucson: Sonora Review Chapbooks Series, 1993.

Tiara Tango. Dir. Paul Kawecki. Starring James Fischer and George Johns. Nat Horne Theatre, New York, Sept. 16, 1992.

"Why I Didn't Write This Poem." *The Evergreen Chronicles* 20.1 (Winter/Spring 1992): 12.

CRITICISM

Sheldon, Glenn. "Interview with Rane Arroyo." Rane Arroyo Papers. Centro de Estudios Puertorriqueños, New York.

———. "Notes on Rane Arroyo." Winter 1983–1984. Rane Arroyo Papers. Centro de Estudios Puertorriqueños, New York.

Glenn Sheldon

AYALA, WALMIR (Brazil; 1933) ———————

Though known in Brazil primarily as a writer of children's fiction, Ayala has also been a novelist, poet, editor, anthologist and dramatist. Born in Pôrto Alegre, Ayala studied at the Catholic Pontifical University of Rio Grande do Sul and moved to Rio de Janeiro in 1956.

Ayala's first venture into what may be termed a homosexual aesthetic was a text that may be more an example of gender-bending than specifically gay in its content. *Nosso filho vai ser mãe* (Our Son is Going to Be a Mother; 1965), is a play that does not offer any homosexual content, yet provides a critique of the hegemonic binary code of gender. Otávio feels it is unfair that he cannot conceive a child. It is hinted in the text that his desire to be a woman may be due in part to the fact that his mother, having wanted a daughter, used to dress him as a girl and have him sing opera for her friends. In the opinion of Luis Canales, the pregnancy of Otávio is metaphoric; he wants to give birth to himself—or, rather, to his homosexual dimension, the homosexual who "remains in the closet and who longs to liberated."

Ayala's play focuses on societal homophobia and the injustice of sexually prescribed roles. Otávio is forced to address the concerns of his neighbors—society—to defend himself, to defend the logic he sees in his desire to give birth. The play presents Otávio as a sympathetic protagonist searching for justice, a sort of Ibsenian *Enemy of the People*, as he argues against the hypocrisy and stupidity of the putatively good men (understood to mean heterosexual): "I was speaking, speaking about the most important things to me, and he has the same expression that you see on monkeys in the zoo. The same vacant eyes, the same thought process, the egoism, the utilitarian sense. We are completely lost" (40). At the end of the play, Otávio is betrayed by his mother, who places him in an asylum, one of the time-honored treatments for homosexuals. Otávio is never able to realize his dream. Religion, always a dominant motif for Ayala, takes its place at the end of the play when Otávio's mother is placed in the role of Judas.

Um animal de Deus (An Animal of God; 1967) is a candid homosexual love story written in a poetic manner. The homosexual themes in Ayala's work are dealt with not in explicit sexual terms but in those that express profound poetic love, a love enhanced throughout the novel with references to particular pieces of classical music (for example, at some of the culminating points in the narrative). This love story is between Mário and a handsome married man, Rafael. Ayala accentuates Rafael's spiritual dimension by calling him the Archangel. The novel deals with Mário's frustration at Rafael's response to his declaration of love, which he acknowledges but never fully accepts. Mário receives love letters from a homosexual friar, who decides that his desire for Mário is enough to cause him to leave his religion. Interestingly, this happens at the same time that Mário decides he may find peace from his obsession with Rafael by becoming a cleric. At the end of the novel, there is an extended reference to the Bible. After Judas's betrayal, a young man, naked except for a linen cloth, follows Jesus to convince himself of perdition or salvation. Thus, the novel revolves around the compatibility of religious love and homosexuality, and it introduces the possible ambiguity of this particular passage from the Bible. On the inside jacket of the text there is a note from Fausto Cunha, stating that for many years Ayala was hesitant to submit his novel for publication, possibly for fear of repudiation because of its content.

Diário III: A fuga do arcanjo (Diary III: The Flight of the Archangel; 1976) is the third of Ayala's diaries to be published, following *Diário I: Difícil é o reino* (Diary I: Difficult Is the Reign; 1962) and *Diário II: O visível amor* (Diary II: The Visible Love; 1963). Again, the author combines his religiosity with love in describing his relationship with a man designated only as X. The diary begins with a meditation on the nature of love: "Até que ponto um amor poder ser anormal?" (7; At what point may love be considered abnormal?). The diary reflects the autobiographical nature of the earlier novel, *Um animal de Deus*.

The story is virtually the same. This time, however, it is Ayala speaking about his life and his unrequited love for a married man. He questions the right of religious institutions or social dictates to circumscribe love. This is the same story as *Um animal de Deus*, but in a diary form, in the first person. The friar is present, renouncing his cloth at the end, as in the novel. Mário is present, in the form of Ayala, thinking of turning to religion at the end after losing X (cf. Rafael).

Interesting in this diary is the trepidation with which the text is greeted at the end by Ayala's editor. Ayala is advised that there may be a danger in publishing certain of the text's confessions, even though he feels it has a character that needs to be defended. Ayala writes that he is proud of who he is and feels no need to hide his true identity. This is notable, given the particularly constraining sociopolitical climate of its antecedent. If indeed the diary entries presented here gave rise to the earlier *Um animal*, then the time of gestation may be placed in the mid-1960s, not a time of particularly liberal ideologies in Brazil, given the military's dictatorial ascent to power in 1964.

Clearly, romantic homoerotic love has remained one of the more important motifs in Ayala's writing, continually coupled with poetry, music and religion. He also offers a sustained critique of prescribed social codes of behavior that propose to circumscribe by gender something as elusive and ephemeral as love.

WORKS

Um animal de Deus. Rio de Janeiro: Lidador, 1967.
Diário I: Difícil é o reino. Rio de Janeiro: Civilização Brasileira, 1962.
Diário II: O visível amor. Rio de Janeiro: Civilização Brasileira, 1963.
Diário III: A fuga do arcanjo. Rio de Janeiro: Editora Brasília/Rio, 1976.
Nosso filho vai ser mãe/Quem matou Caim? Rio de Janeiro: Letras e Artes, 1965.
A nova terra. Rio de Janeiro: Editora Record, 1980.
Partilha de sombra. Rio de Janeiro/Pôrto Alegre: Globo, 1981.

CRITICISM

Bins, Patrícia. "Walmir Ayala: *Os reinos e as vestes*." *Minas Gerais. Suplemento literario* 22.1080 (July 18, 1987): 10–12.
Canales, Luis. "O homosexualismo como tema no moderno teatro brasileiro." *Luso-Brazilian Review* 18.1 (1981): 173–181.
Chamma, Foed Castro. "*A selva escura*—romance de renúncia." *Minas Gerais. Suplemento literario*. 25.1170 (Sept. 28, 1991): 14.
Knowlton, Edgar C. "Walmir Ayala." In *A Dictionary of Contemporary Brazilian Authors*, 11. Comp. David W. Foster and Roberto Reis. Tempe: Center for Latin American Studies, Arizona State University, 1981.

Melissa A. Lockhart

AZEVEDO, ALUÍSIO (Brazil; 1857–1913) _____

Azevedo is considered the most important Brazilian naturalist author. In his famous novel *O cortiço* (*A Brazilian Tenement*; 1890), there is a homosexual relationship between Pombinha and Léonie, two secondary characters. Pombinha (her name means little dove) is a teenager who lives in the tenement, and Léonie is a French prostitute now living in Rio de Janeiro. It is important to bear in mind that Brazilian naturalism is an imported school of literature, an attempt to imitate work produced in Europe and to attain sophistication in the tropics. Sexuality in Azevedo's fiction, as well as in that of other authors of the day, adheres much more to the aesthetic principles of naturalism than to any radical position of the author. The elites of nineteenth-century Brazilian society were basically conservative, and it would be accurate to say that literature written and read by the upper strata of the social spectrum was a form of symbolic domination, a way of strengthening the hegemony of the ruling classes. Therefore, one should resist seeing the aforementioned homosexual relationship as a challenge to the authoritarian pattern evinced by Brazilian literature at the end of the century, and as more of an example of how to *épater le bourgeois*, which, so to speak, "exaggerates" sexuality in order to restate how the "good behavior" of patriarchal families, seen as pure and chaste, should be pursued and emulated as a social goal, thereby guaranteeing their prominence within the social stratification.

WORKS

O cortiço. Rio de Janeiro: Garnier, 1890. English version *A Brazilian Tenement*. Trans. Harry W. Brown. New York: R. M. McBride, 1926. Also New York: H. Fertig, 1976.

CRITICISM

Cândido, Antônio. "De cortiço a cortiço." *Novos estudos* 30 (1991): 111–129.
———. "Literatura-sociologia." *Cadernos da PUC* 28 (1976): 120–134.
Sant'Anna, Affonso Romano de. "*O cortiço*." In his *Análise estrutural de romances brasileiros*, 97–115. 4th ed. Petrópolis, Brazil: Vozes, 1977.
———. "Curtição: O Cortiço de mestre Cândido e o meu." In his *Por um novo conceito de literatura brasileira*, 213–235. Rio de Janeiro: Eldorado, 1977.

Roberto Reis

B

BALZA, JOSÉ (Venezuela; 1939) ⎯⎯⎯⎯⎯⎯⎯⎯⎯

Balza was born in a small town in the Orinoco delta region. From a very early age, with the same ceaseless passion with which he rowed and swam in the river, he read and wrote. He moved to Caracas in 1956, seeking more books and university courses in psychology. One might say that his entire literary work, including the texts he has yet to write, express the profoundly sensual and collective dimensions of this itinerary. The attention to artistry in Balza's work makes it difficult to classify, and both his novels and his stories are as much filled with moments of poetry as they are with essayistic meditations. By the same token his essays could well be narratives.

Any one of Balza's works would serve to demonstrate his attempt to express the multiplicity of the human psyche. The narrator, generally the main character, explores his memories, his dreams, his feelings and the associations activated by experiences and events. There is a permanent existential search based on fragments, recollections, spaces, sensations, anecdotes, friendships, love and the like. This series of intense experiences allows diverse characters to escape the stereotypical. In many of his "narrative exercises," Balza expresses one of the liberating functions of the imagination: the construction of a free and vital sexual existence.

In *Largo* (1968) the characters ponder the value of friendship and the possibility to achieve love by destroying controlling stereotypes. The main character, who will commit suicide, feels himself frustrated in life and is unsatisfied by the intense memory of love. The story suggests that he envies his friend Adriano, who fully lives his homosexual choice, free from guilt in his Greek concepts of friendship and love.

In *D* (1977), which deals with the early days of radio in Venezuela, characters are unsuccessful in their search for historical roots and political options, so they rely on their sexual liberty to make up for the other failure. Fer, the painter who is also on the verge of suicide, frequents a masturbators' club, but that is not enough for him.

Female characters also find existential fulfillment in sexual liberties that the dominant coordinates suppress and censor. In *Percusión* (Percussion; 1991), the main character, an old man, recalls a life of continual travel as he is about to return to his native land. Among his various lovers, he remembers Jenneke, who every now and then chose to sleep with someone else, although the greater part of the time she preferred to be with him. But what he most remembers is the great love he had for Harry, a boy from the interior whom he took with him to the city. There are many reflections on eroticism in this novel that are based on experiences in locales where broad sexual conventions and open family obligations serve as the basis of a social quest for sexual liberty. The question is not limited to the presentation of the narrator's bisexuality or his homosexuality, but extends to the exploration of his memories of love, his poetic illusions, his desire for sincere carnality.

In *Medianoche en video: 1/5* (Midnight on Video: 1/5; 1988), Balza's most recent novel, there is a ritual of celebration on the Orinoco in a ''1/5'' yacht. One of the characters, a doctor from the Andean region, resolves his entrapment in the dominant sexual code by developing amorous relationships with the gardener and the gardener's wife. The doctor's friends help him attempt to free himself from the resulting guilt and uncertainty. Another character, using jokes, explores his unconscious and that of the group.

In many of Balza's short texts, characters escape from the consciousness imposed by dominant sexual coordinates in the realm of sensuality. Whether it be a male dancer, a restless youth, or friends drinking together, Balza's characters express an intense mental and sensual activity that cannot be covered by a single explanation or label.

Although critics have recognized Balza as one of the most lucid voices to emerge from Venezuela in recent years and the most prominent figure in contemporary Venezuelan fiction, the general public seems to have ignored him. This is due principally to his determination to restore imagination to the place it has lost in the context of contemporary daily life. Balza insists on reflecting on reality via the senses in order to escape the influence of consciousness. The apprehension of reality, despite the predominance of sight, smell, and taste, is achieved through the pleasure of assembling memories and sensations in a new, uncertain and unclassifiable order. For this reason, Balza insists on teaching art; on commenting on contemporary painting, the movies of Wim Wenders and popular music in Venezuela; and on rereading *Don Quixote*, Lawrence Durrell, Marcel Proust and the best of Latin American and other poetry. For Balza, art in general is part of a body that one must discover and navigate as a permanent commitment.

WORKS

"Almond Trees in Tanvary." Trans. Bruce Morgan. *Tamaqua* 1.162 (Spring 1989): 30–36.

El cuento venezolano: Antología. Caracas: Ediciones de la Dirección de Cultura, Universidad Central de Venezuela, 1985.

Cuentos: Antología. Havana: Ediciones de Casa de las Américas, 1983.

D. Caracas: Monte Avila, 1977.

Ejercicios narrativos: Selección. Caracas: Ediciones de la Gobernación de Caracas, 1976.

Ejercicios narrativos: Volumen de cuentos. Cumaná, Venezuela: Ediciones de la Universidad de Oriente, 1967.

Este mar narrativo: Ensayos sobre el cuerpo novelesco. Mexico City: Fondo de Cultura Económica, 1987.

El fiero (y dulce) instinto terrestre: Ejercicios y ensayos. Caracas: Ediciones de la Academia Nacional de la Historia, 1988.

Jesús Soto, el niño. Caracas: Ediciones de la Galería de Arte Nacional, 1981.

Largo. Caracas: Monte Avila, 1968.

Marzo anterior. Caracas: Ediciones del Club de Leones de Tucupita, 1965.

Medianoche en video: 1/5. Mexico City: Fondo de Cultura Económica, 1988.

La mujer de espaldas: Ejercicios holográficos, 1980–1985. Caracas: Monte Avila, 1986.

Órdenes. Caracas: Monte Avila, 1970.

Percusión. Barcelona: Seix Barral, 1982; Bogotá: Tercer Mundo Editores, 1991.

Un rostro absolutamente: Ejercicios narrativos (1970–1980). Caracas: Monte Avila, 1982.

"The Sentence." Trans. Bruce Morgan. *Revista línea plural* 3 (1989): 12–15.

Setecientas palmeras plantadas en el mismo lugar. 2nd ed. Caracas: Monte Avila, 1981. Orig. Caracas: Síntesis Dos Mil, 1974.

Transfigurable (ensayos). Caracas: Dirección de Cultura, Universidad Central de Venezuela, 1983.

El vencedor: Ejercicios narrativos. Caracas: Contexto Audiovisual 3, 1989.

CRITICISM

Arias, Raquel. "Diálogo con José Balza." *Zona franca* 3a época, 10 (1978): 12–17.

Berrizbeitia, Josefina, et al. *Balza narrador.* [Caracas]: Ediciones Octubre, 1990.

Fauquié Bescós, Rafael. "José Balza: La mirada permanente." In his *Espacio disperso*, 155–160. Caracas: Academia Nacional de la Historia, 1983.

Mata Gil, Milagros. *Balza: El cuerpo fluvial.* Caracas: Academia Nacional de la Historia, 1989.

Moody, Michael. "Entrevista con José Balza." *Confluencia* 6 (1991): 111–115.

Roberto J. Forns-Broggi

BARBA JACOB, PORFIRIO (pseud. of Miguel Angel Osorio; Colombia; 1883–1942)

Osorio was born in Antioquia, Colombia, and died in Mexico City. His ambiguous identity can be symbolized by his use of pseudonyms such as Main Ximénez, Ricardo Arenales, and, his best-known, Porfirio Barba Jacob. According to the critics his best poems are "La estrella de la tarde" (The Afternoon Star), "Canción de la vida profunda" (Song of the Deep Life), "Elegía de septiembre" (September Elegy), "Un hombre" (A Man), "Los desposados de la muerte" (The Bridegrooms of Death), "El son del viento" (The Sound of the Wind), "Canción de la soledad" (Solitude Song), "Balada de una loca alegría" (Tune of a Wild Joy), "La reina" (The Queen), and "Futuro" (Future).

The most common themes in Barba Jacob's poetry are homosexuality, a quest for space, an existentialist crisis, ignorance, the emptiness of the soul, a conflict with the other/oppressor, and the vulnerability of the human being. A modernist poet, he used metaphor to transgress the rules of the patriarchal heterosexual society; and he never denied his homosexuality in order to face the dominant burgeois world, which demanded he follow established canons. Metaphor in his poetry allows the reader to defamiliarize the doubling of Barba Jacob as poet and individual in the face of a cultural crisis and a conflict that made him go against the heterosexual tide of his time.

"El son del viento," "Momento" (Moment), and "Los desposados de la muerte" are in *Poemas selectos* (Selected Poems), published to honor Barba Jacob on the centennial of his birth. Through metaphor and poetic language, the most common leitmotifs in his poetry, Barba Jacob describes and transgresses the cage that restrains his freedom.

"El son del viento" contains the themes of sexual doubling, the feminine role of the poet, joy in pleasure, a search for knowledge, the fleeting quality of love, and homosexuality as a consequence of his position in the conflict between homosexuality and heterosexuality, which forces Barba Jacob to struggle openly against narrow-minded oppressors. In the line "fui Eva . . . y fui Adán" (I was Eve . . . and I was Adam), the poet depicts a sexual doubling by making a biblical allusion through the use of the binary opposition Eve/Adam, which expresses a process of seduction. Adam is seduced by Eve, and he plays her game. There is a parallel between this quotation and Barba Jacob because it refers to the loss of paradisiacal space. Hence, Eve/Adam/Barba Jacob should search in other worlds for what has been taken away: freedom and space.

The poetic voice of homosexuality also is found in the poem "El son del viento." The homosexual element praises the concept of eros. Barba Jacob is very fond of the exotic and distant cultures of the Orient, Greece and the Middle East because they help the narrator fulfill his sexual fantasies with males, who may be more passionate, masculine and beautiful to the poetic voice. The howl at the end of the poem is moving because it expresses solitude, anguish, pain, breath, spirit, protest and rebirth of life that come from the heart of the poet. In "El son del viento," Barba Jacob alludes to a homosexual love from a triple perspective: a protest against the patriarchal heterosexual world that oppresses him sexually; a total acceptance of his sexual preference; and the concept of eros as a path to knowledge, wisdom, perfection and truth.

"Momento" describes a poetic voice that isolates itself from the mundane world because it is going through a period of doubt. The poet feels both powerful and dominated: powerful because he knows that the strength of his liberal ideology will give him the courage to keep going; dominated because he realizes how asphyxiating the dominant could be. The binary opposition I/the other is vital in this poem, since the I/poet represents those oppressed by the other/ heterosexual. The use of the personal pronoun I is fundamental because it shows the challenge, the innermost tone and the desire for individualization of the poet. The narrating voice goes on to demonstrate self-confidence and vanity, which allow it to fight the oppressor. However, the perennial problem is not the oppressed/homosexual nor the oppressor/heterosexual, but eternity.

"Los desposados de la muerte" has been considered one of Barba Jacob's best poems. In it he portrays the archetypes of males in society and he uses parts of the male body (hands, eyes, curls, forehead) to praise the beauty of that sex. The archetypes are the naïve (Michael Farrel), the adolescent (Emiliano Atehortúa), the ordinary (Guillermo Valderrama), the timid (Leonel Robledo), the harmonious (Stello Ialadaki) and the strong (Juan Rafael Agudelo). The archetypes of the poetic discourse correspond exactly with the characteristics that Eros inherits from his parents, Poros (richness) and Penia (poverty). From his father, Eros inherits virility and cleverness, and he searches after the beautiful and the good. From his mother he inherits dullness and indigence; he is not pretty or fragile, but a wanderer. We can see that once more the poet insists on the quest for wisdom and the craving for the beautiful (the male) through two literary devices: a modernist language and metaphors. The names of the males are a combination of exoticsm and regionalism, a dream of trips to distant countries that allow him to fulfill his sexual mythical fantasies; the rediscovery of Latin studs. The mythical heroes in the poem symbolize the rebirth of a sexual ideological emancipation that will guide the poet in the pursuit of his rights as an individual and as an intellectual. "Los deposados" represents his hope and his double nature as a man who seeks his identity and space in foreign countries and in his motherland.

Barba Jacob used metaphoric language to protest against the Colombian patriarchal society because it controlled his sexual needs. Nevertheless, he did not allow the other/heterosexual to castrate him either emotionally or ideologically. Therefore, he searched for a space and challenged the world that marginalized him and considered him a subversive human being because of his breaking of traditional norms. In his homoerotic poetry we can perceive the Greek concepts of Eros and Thanatos. Eros concerns his love for the beautiful male as a way to attain wisdom and perfection. Thanatos deals with his obsession for the fleeting nature of time. Barba Jacob expresses his desires to attain immortality and, like Plato, has been motivated by the strength of love.

WORKS

Antorchas contra el viento. Bogotá: Biblioteca Popular de Cultura Colombiana, 1944.
La canción de la vida profunda y otros poemas. Ed. Juan B. Jaramillo Meza. Manizales, Colombia: 1937.
Canciones y elegías, edición de homenaje al poeta. Mexico City: Alcancía, 1932.
"Cartas inéditas." *Armas y letras* 7.12 (1950): n.p.
El corazón iluminado. Bogotá: Impreso en la Editorial ABC, 1937.
"Poemas desconocidos." *The Americas* 57 (1948): 161–172.
Poemas selectos. Ed. Alberto Bernal Ramírez. Bogotá: Editorial Printer Colombiana, 1983.
Rosas negras. Ed. Rafael Arévalo Martínez. Guatemala City: G. M. Staebler, 1933.

CRITICISM

Arango L., Manuel Antonio. *Tres figuras representativas de Hispanoamérica en la generación de vanguardia o literatura de postguerra*, 49–69. Bogotá: Procer, 1967.
Cardoza y Aragón, Luis. "Relectura de Barba Jacob." In his *El río de caballería*, 37–50. Mexico City: Fondo de Cultura Económico, 1986.
García Prada, Carlos. *Estudios hispanoamericanos*, 219–225. Mexico City: El Colegio de México, 1945.
Holguín, Andrés. *La poesía inconclusa y otros ensayos*, 147–162. Bogotá: Instituto Colombiano de Cultura, División de Publicaciones, 1947.
Jaramillo Meza, Juan B. *Vida de Porfirio Barba Jacob*. Bogotá: Kelly, Librería Voluntad, 1956.
Legretti, Alvaro. *Rasgando la niebla*. Medellín, Colombia: Sanderio, 1983.
Maya, Rafael. *Alabanzas del hombre y de la tierra*, 149–163. Bogotá: Santafé, 1934.
Mejía Gutiérrez, Carlos. *Porfirio Barba Jacob: Ensayo biográfico. Centenario de nacimiento 1883–1983*. Medellín, Colombia: Imprenta Municipal, 1982.
Mejía Vallejo, Manuel. *El hombre que parecía fantasma*. Bogotá: Secretaría de Educación y Cultura y Recreación Municipal, 1984.
Méndez Plancarte, Alfonso, "Porfirio Barba Jacob." *Abside* 1.1 (1942): 88–98.
Posada Mejía, Germán. *Porfirio Barba Jacob, el poeta de la muerte*. Bogotá: Publicaciones del Instituto Caro y Cuervo, 1970.
Puerta Palacios, M. C. *Miguel Angel Osorio o Porfirio Barba Jacob: Su vida y poesía*. Medellín, Colombia: Tipografía Litografía Especial, 1984.

Juan Antonio Serna

BARBACHANO PONCE, MIGUEL
(Mexico; 1930)

Barbachano Ponce was born in Mérida, in the state of Yucatán. He studied at the Colegio Montejo in his hometown, then spent a year in Havana (1938).

Since 1939 he has lived in Mexico City. He received a law degree from the Universidad Nacional Autónoma de México, where he also studied philosophy. Barbachano Ponce is a dramatist, novelist, film critic and director of short features. As a film critic, he produced the cultural news bulletin *Cine-verdad* (Movie Truth; 1955–1974) and *Tele-Revista* (TV-Review; 1956–1977). From 1974 to 1977 he was a programming consultant for Canal 13 (Channel 13), and the producer between 1977 and 1982. From 1976 to 1979 he was a film critic for the newspaper *Excélsior*. Since 1971 Barbachano Ponce has been a professor of social and political science at the Universidad Nacional Autónoma de México, specializing in the evolution of film language, with a particular interest in the convergence of film conventions and information and communication strategies.

Barbachano Ponce has published two novels, five plays, one screenplay, a wide range of film criticism and a collection of short stories. Sexuality, class, race and the problems of domestic life are privileged themes in his writing. He made his debut as a playwright with *El hacedor de dioses* (Godmaker), which premiered in Mexico in 1954, followed by *Once lunas y una calabaza* (Eleven Moons and a Pumpkin) in 1958. Although both plays were well received, *Las lanzas rotas* (The Broken Lances), staged in 1959, gave him a wider audience, in part because of its subject: the Cuban Revolution. One of his most interesting and avant-garde plays remains *Los pájaros: Cinco obras en un acto* (The Birds: Five One-Act Works). Barbachano Ponce wrote *Los pájaros* in the 1950s and published it in 1961. Censorship prevented its staging ultil 1977. "El albatros" (The Albatross), one of the five works, presents a woman trying to come to terms with her lesbian desire. "Los murciélagos" (The Bats), "El cóndor" (The Condor), and "Atájacaminos" (Shortcut) call into question heterosexist gender constructions. In "El águila" (The Eagle), Barbachano addresses racial tensions in Mexico between Indians and non-Indians. While he brings forth the notion of race as a trope of difference, he complicates this notion by adding another dimension to the problem, the issue of homosexuality. The play stages the story of two young men: Jacinto, the mestizo whose Indian mother was seduced by an Englishman, and Fernando, the son of a landowner. After his studies, Fernando returns to his village with progressive ideas that include denouncing the exploitation of Indians. Jacinto, Fernando's father's former servant, is now a violent, resentful policeman who seeks revenge and rapes Fernando. Fernando cannot accept the humiliation, and he murders Jacinto.

In addition to his plays, Barbachano Ponce has written two novels. *Los desterrados del limbo* (Exiles from Limbo; 1971) combines reality, fantasy, and absurdity to narrate the story of a maid who works for an old and eccentric couple. Grotesque humor permeates the text as Barbachano Ponce carnivalizes the world of thought and speech in order to undermine a literature bound by literary and social constraints. *El diario de José Toledo* (The Diary of José Toledo; 1964) is the first novel in Mexico to deal openly with homosexuality. José Toledo, a young civil servant, is deeply in love with Wenceslao. However, Wenceslao denies him the possibility of engaging in a romantic relationship, a situation that leads José to commit suicide. The author did not find a commercial publisher for his novel until 1988, having published it, despite strong resistence, at his own expense in 1964. His most recent literary publication is a collection of short stories, *La utopía doméstica* (Domestic Utopia; 1981).

Barbachano Ponce's work has not received significant critical attention in Mexico, and he remains nearly unknown in the United States. However, the performances of his plays were reviewed positively in cultural supplements of prestigious Mexican newspapers. In 1962 the noted Spanish novelist Juan Goytisolo was one of the first critics to review *Los pájaros* at a time when Barbachano Ponce was unable to stage the play. Goytisolo praised Barbachano Ponce's innovative analysis of Mexican sexuality and particularly his revisionist approach to the concept of virility, while deploring the censorship it provoked. Marco Antonio Acosta, in his review of *Los pájaros* (1977), argued that if Barbachano Ponce's play had not been censored, Mexican drama would have developed differently. Despite the paucity of critical studies on Barbachano Ponce's works, at the time of its publication *El diario de José Toledo* attracted the most interest. María Elvira Bermúdez understood this novel as a call for "modern deference." Henrique González Casanova read José's drama as a symbol of the solitude all human beings experience at some time in their life. González Casanova acknowledged discomfort when confronted with the reality of the story. Yet the critic's acquaintance with the city in which the novel is set, the simplicity of the language and the commonness of the lives of the characters who impinge on José allow him to transcend the original feeling of estrangement. Federico Alvarez's pointed criticism focuses on the issue of representing male homosexuality. His essay seems to underscore the need to portray strong, virile homosexual characters in order for literature to avoid reproducing the social emasculation of the gay male. He condemns Barbachano Ponce for his construction of what he considers to be a pathetic and ordinary homosexual character lacking imagination and spiritual strength, attributes he associates with a "feminoid psychology."

David William Foster devotes a few pages to *El diario de José Toledo*. He argues that in this novel José's character mimics heterosexual behaviors, thereby denying himself the possibility of a differently defined identity. This raises the crucial question of mimicry and its implications in the process of identity formation.

Barbachano Ponce's originality lies essentially in his efforts to address courageously the question of "multifaceted alterity" and "deviant masculinities" at a time when the taboo surrounding these issues considerably hampered his career as a writer. The continuous censorship to which his work has been subjected accounts for the paucity of his literary production. Barbachano Ponce is probably one of the few male writers who as early as the 1950s denounced patriarchy and engaged in a reconceptualization of the semantically overcharged notion of virility in Mexico. In *El diario de José Toledo*, José's voice as he confides in a diary alternates with the voice of a narrator recording the events that determine Wenceslao's life, as well as the lives of the characters marginally present in José's diary. Although José states his sexual desire for Wenceslao, the text is extremely chaste in order to neutralize moral indignation. Barbachano Ponce sought to transcend the idea of difference by creating a character whose love for another is universal, and his diary can be compared to a humble love letter in which he expresses his emotions and his faithfulness to Wenceslao, who rejects his love. The simplicity and comprehensiveness of José's experience, his sincerity and the vocabulary of profound desire are meant to produce a rapprochement between the heterosexual reader and the homosexual character. Barbachano Ponce points to their shared characteristics rather than their dissimilarities in an effort to desatanize homosexuality and to debunk the myth built around the idea that homosexuals live a licentious love life. In a sense his literary approach to the theme of homosexuality prefigures current gender theories denouncing essentialism.

However, Barbachano Ponce's textual inscription of homosexuality (a result of his desire to transcend the notion of difference) opens a complex line of observations. Alvarez's critique shows that certain male readers could view José's sensibility as a "trope of the female soul in a man's body"; this could in turn tarnish and even threaten the masculine image they believe they have to preserve at any cost. Heterosexual males could contain José in the cultural stereotype that tends to associate femininity with homosexuality and ultimately to epitomize a rugged machismo. Men whose objects of desire are of the same sex could also read this model of homosexuality as prohibiting any acting out of masculine roles. But it could appeal to homosexuals who acknowledge femininity within their homosexuality. This novel, overflowing with ambiguity, offers a fascinating terrain for the study of the entangled rapport between masculinity, femininity, homosexuality and heterosexuality.

The conflation of the theme of race and homosexuality in "El águila" complicates earlier critical remarks. Jacinto, considered racially inferior because of his Indian heritage, attempts to reduce Fernando to an equivalent stage of inferiority. In order to undermine the master/slave dialectic, Jacinto tries to "conquer" and to "reduce" Fernando by raping him, thus reversing the master/slave relationship through having the slave rape the master. Since Jacinto will never be able to deprive Fernando of his power as a master, he seeks another way of establishing a new form of codependency based on homosexuality. Barbachano Ponce is the first writer in Mexican letters to bring together two tropes of difference, race and homosexuality.

WORKS

Los desterrados del limbo. Mexico City: Joaquín Mortiz, 1971.
El diario de José Toledo. Mexico City: Premià, 1988. First published in 1964.
Examen de muertos. Premiered Mexico City, 1958.
El hacedor de dioses. Premiered Mexico City, 1954.

Las lanzas rotas. Premiered Mexico City, Colección Teatro de México, 1959.
Once lunas y una calabaza. Premiered Mexico City, 1958.
Los pájaros: Cinco obras en un acto. Mexico Era, 1961. Premiered in 1977.
La utopía doméstica. Mexico City: Oasis, 1981.

CRITICISM

Acosta, Marco Antonio. "Los pájaros." *El nacional*, Nov. 9, 1977, p. 16.
Alvarez, Federico. "José Toledo contra Miguel Barbachano Ponce." *La cultura en México* 136 (Sept. 23, 1964): xvi–xvii.
Bermúdez, María Elvira. "*Los desterrados del limbo*." *Revista mexicana cultural* 158 (Feb. 6, 1972): 2.
———. "Literatura evocativa." *Revista mexicana cultural* 130 (June 6, 1982): 6.
———. "Un tema atrevido." *El Nacional*, June 9, 1969, p. 4.
Foster, David William. "The Deconstruction of Personal Identity." In his *Gay and Lesbian Themes in Latin American Writing*, 43–61, esp. 56–58. Austin: University of Texas Press, 1991.
Galindo, Carmen. "En la orilla letal de la palabra." *La cultura en México* 481 (Apr. 28, 1971): ix–x.
González Casanova, Henrique. "*El diario de José Toledo*." *La cultura en México* 136 (Sept. 23, 1964): xvii.
———. "*Los desterrados del limbo*." *La cultura en México* 485 (May 26, 1971): xiv.
Goytisolo, Juan. "Los pájaros." *La cultura en México* 6 (Mar. 28, 1962): xv.
Schneider, Luis Mario. "El tema homosexual en la nueva narrativa mexicana." *Casa del tiempo* 47.50 (1985): 82–98.

Marina Pérez de Mendiola

BERMAN, SABINA (Mexico; 1955) _____

Playwright, director, actress, poet, novelist and scriptwriter for films, Sabina Berman is one of the most widely recognized and active playwrights of her generation, receiving national recognition at a very early age. Several of her plays have been performed abroad, and four have received Mexico's National Theater Award (all are contained in *El teatro de Sabina Berman*). *Bill/Yankee* (1979) proposes identity as a creative process, focusing on the interrelationship between individual and national identities and on the influences that impinge upon their formation—a recurrent theme in Berman's work; *Rompecabezas* (The Puzzle; 1981) utilizes the techniques of documentary theater to examine the 1940 assassination in Mexico of Leon Trotsky by Jacques Mornard—not challenging the official historic record, but exploring the questions of ethnic and national identity of the two principal characters; with a similar focus, but as a satire, *Águila o sol* (Eagle or Sun; 1984) incorporates into historical discourse the traditionally excluded indigenous peoples' interpretation of the events from the arrival of the Spaniards to the death of Moctezuma; *Herejía* (Heresy; 1983) stages the Mexican Inquisition's persecution of Jews. Berman's first novel, *La bobe* (The Grandmother, in Yiddish; 1990), focuses on Jewish identity, narrating the relationship of a young Mexican girl and her Polish Jewish grandmother.

Berman has written and produced much highly praised children's theater, including *La maravillosa historia del Chiquito Pingüica* (The Wonderful Story of Small Pingüica; 1982), which received the National Theater Award for Children's Theater (1983), and *El árbol de humo* (The Smoke Tree; 1984), which won the Gorostiza Award in 1984. Other critically acclaimed plays include *El suplicio del placer* (The Pain of Pleasure; 1986), her most frequently staged play, and *Muerte súbita* (Sudden Death; 1988).

Berman's poetry has been published in numerous Mexican periodicals and in two volumes: *Poemas de agua* (Water Poems; 1986) and *Lunas* (Moons; 1988). Further attesting to her creative versatility, her work as a movie and television scriptwriter won her the Ariel Award for *Tía Alejandra* (Aunt Alejandra; 1979). She composed the dance scripts for the 1987 productions *Una luna una* (One Moon One) and *Ni puertas ni ventanas* (Neither Doors Nor Windows). In 1975 Berman won the Latin American Short Story Contest sponsored by the Committee for the Organization of the International Year of the Woman and was coauthor of *Volar* (Flying), a collection of journalistic essays on levitation.

Berman sees literature, especially the public forum and communal experience of theater, as an ideal space in which to explore the complexity of the creative process of constructing a self and a national identity, and to foreground the mechanisms of power that impinge upon such acts. The author's aesthetics, including her dramatic technique, thematic content, play titles and even her transformations of the allegedly arbitrary markings of gender in Spanish grammar, are directly related to her interpretation of the unstable status of reality and its relationship to fiction, which results in a "deformity" (Burgess 81; Nigro 8). This deformity is a linguistic, sociopolitical and gender one in which lies posing as truth become critical elements of the power struggle within all human relationships, notably in Mexico's rigid categories of social stratification that include the interlocking systems of gender, sexuality, race and class.

Much of Berman's literary production attempts to provoke a reconceptualization and reformulation of the categories of gender and sexuality. Her work participates in a contemporary revisionary feminist dialogue that focuses on the notions of sexual difference and sexuality as they relate to subjectivity. Berman suggests a "freedom" generated by the capacity to *choose* the forms of experience through which we constitute ourselves. She also echoes contemporary feminist theories when she sees the construction of identity as the repetition and stylization of acts. Berman equates this process with that of an actor creating a character on stage, where the individual subject engages in a continual reinterpretation and representation of the gendered self: as in real life, "On stage no one is automatically a Man or a Woman. One creates or becomes a Man or a Woman gesture by gesture, action by action . . . by the repetition of certain ideas, certain bioenergy, the repetition each day, each moment of the same body" ("On Theater" 3).

This recuperation of the possibilities of interpretation of the body is foregrounded in the three short plays that comprise *El suplicio del placer*, especially in the first, "El bigote" (The Mustache). Berman neutralizes the traditional gender markers of the categories of masculine and feminine—victim/perpetrator, strong/weak, active/passive, intellect/intuition—by not assigning her characters physical characteristics or behavior that normally mark gender, and through the introduction of a prop, a mobile mustache, that situates the process of signification of gender on the body. Besides the element of transvestism that points to the theatricalization of gender in which the assigned roles appear fictitious, who wears the mustache has the power—a masculine attribute and acquisition. The contradictory and illusive sign of the mustache gains signification within the context in which it is worn: in a farcical pop-Freudian analysis, without it both He and She are seen as lacking something; with it, a Lacanian lack is filled and the subject is restored to the Phallic Order.

Berman does not, however, perform a simple gender role inversion. She not only comments on or ridicules popular notions of subject constitution, but her initial neutralization of traditional gender markers also suggests that the identity of each individual is to be located in the other, but not as Derridean *différance*. A fluidity of signs is established, indicating a fluidity of two parts of a whole, as opposed to two separate beings. Neither is characterized by the markers of essential sexuality that traditionally define gender. Both are ambiguous identities, carrying bits and pieces of those gendered traits, sexual desire and sexuality that Mexico's patriarchal society has attributed—arbitrarily, according to Berman—to a particular sex.

Berman's attempt to explode the existing categories of gender and sexuality is most obvious in her book of poems, *Lunas*, where her poetic strategy moves toward a "lesbianization" of language that allows the feminine to become the universal, if not the absolute, according to Lydia Gil. Berman underscores the relation between body and language by transforming the arbitrary markings of gender of the Spanish language. In her exploration and celebration of the physical and emotional engagement of woman loving woman, she changes from masculine to feminine such nouns as *body* (*cuerpo* to *cuerpa*) and *nipples* (*pezones* to *pezonas*), thus retrieving the female body from the masculine order embedded in Spanish grammar.

A careful examination of her work and her discussions, however, evidences a slippage in her discourse. Berman has not yet reconciled the contradictions in her conceptualization of gender, caught between essentialism and biological determinism, and the idea of gender as a social construct. Although engaging in a critical exposition of the discourses of power whose locus is the body and attempting to define a space in which freedom to interpret that body is permitted, Berman reverts to an essentialist characterization. For example, in the final lines

of "El bigote," after struggling to create a subjective space free from preestablished definitions, the characters engage in dialogue in which inner weaknesses
are displayed and suggest that this attempt at "freedom" is frustrated by innate
human nature—and, in fact, constitutes a theatrical strategy for control of the
other.

Similar ambiguities can be found in Berman's discussions and lectures. When
asked by an actress playing "She" in a production of "El bigote," "Don't you
believe that there are Women and Men? Do you think it is a question of choice
that I have breasts?" Berman replied, "Not only in theater is it valid to select
the Sexual Gender of the body. It is also valid that within one body there exist
three Persons, or that three bodies comprise one Person" ("On Theater" 8).
On other occasions, however, she insists on the identifiable difference between
men's and women's writing and on the existence of a "strictly feminine writing" that is a result of the particular and peculiar experiences of women (personal interview). This essentialist universalization of Woman contradicts her
affirmation of the ability and right to choose and re-create oneself, and it negates
the differences of class and ethnicity that deny the possibility of any seamless
identity of Woman as a category.

Nonetheless, Berman's work is essential to the ongoing process of liberation
in Mexico, where official and self-imposed censorship limits the possibilities of
artistic and self-creation; of the creative resolution of that country's economic
and environmental crisis; and of the institutionalized violence against marginal
groups including women, indigenous peoples and homosexuals. Berman's critiques of representation, in which gender is central to any account of social
processes, and her foregrounding of the concept of gender as a semiotic process
involving the complex system of cultural, social, ethnic, psychological and historical differences, are seen by feminists as essential in Mexico. The importance
of her uncommon courage to place lesbian love, sexuality and sensibility in the
public sphere—in a Mexican society intolerant of lesbianism—must not be un-
derstated. Finally, Berman's hesitation to subscribe to French or Anglo-
American feminist theories and strategies is indicative of Mexican feminists'
move toward the formulation in their own terms of strategies of change reflecting
the sociocultural realities of that society.

WORKS

La bobe. Mexico City: Editorial Planeta Mexicana, 1991.
Lunas. Mexico City: Editorial Katún, 1988.
"On Theater." Unpublished paper, read at SUNY-Buffalo, November 1992.
Personal interview with Roselyn Costantino, Mexico City, March 1991.
Poemas de agua. Mexico City: Editorial Shanik, 1986.
El suplicio del placer. In *El teatro de Sabina Berman*, 265–299. Mexico City: Editores
        Unidos, 1985.
Volar, 3rd ed. Mexico City: Posada, 1989.

CRITICISM

Burgess, Ronald D. *The New Dramatists of Mexico, 1967–1985*, 80–91. Lexington: University Press of Kentucky, 1991.

Gil, Lydia. "Sabina Berman and the Lesbianization of Language." Unpublished MS, 1992.

Nigro, Kirsten. "Sexualidad y género. La mujer como signo escénico en el teatro latinoamericano." Unpublished MS, 1989.

                                                   Roselyn Costantino

BIANCO, JOSÉ (Argentina; 1909–1986) _____

Although himself the focal point for many years of an informal *tertulia* (circle) of gay Buenos Aires intellectuals, Bianco never wrote explicitly about homosexuality. Homoerotic energy is, however, present in all of his fictional work, from the early story "El límite" (The Limit), about a classmate's epileptic fit, to his last novel, *La pérdida del reino* (The Loss of the Kingdom; 1972). In his critical essays he also expresses a constant interest in the erotics of male writing (particularly in the essays on Marcel Proust).

Sombras suele vestir (Shadow Play; 1941), the first of Bianco's three major fictional works, defines his fascination with the figure of the go-between, though by the end of the novella it is not clear where the erotic investments lie in the complex series of interlocking triangles. The novella is divided into three sections, each focused on a different character: first on Jacinta Vélez, then on Bernardo Stocker, then on Stocker's partner, Sweitzer. By the end of the novella it appears that Vélez committed suicide in the middle of the first segment and that, refusing to acknowledge that possibility, Stocker has transferred his affections to Vélez's autistic brother Raúl. But is Raúl a stand-in for Jacinta or vice versa? Is Stocker most fascinated by Jacinta when she is no more than a ghost— that is, when carnal contact with her is no longer possible? And is Sweitzer's fascination with the triangle a signal of the erotic attention he grants to Stocker? The novella delicately skirts questions of hetero/homosexual identity but is thoroughly infused with erotic energy.

Las ratas (The Rats; 1943) is also centered on a love triangle, this time fairly explicitly including a homosexual component. The novella is narrated by Delfín Heredia and tells of the affair between his mother and his half brother, Julio. The novella ends with the revelation that Delfín has poisoned Julio, allegedly out of anger over Julio's manipulative treatment of his stepmother (Delfín's own mother). Throughout the novella, however, Delfín catches himself spying on Julio, and the final description of Julio's half-naked body—watched by Delfín, who is hidden in a closet—emphasizes the male beauty that fills Delfín with repugnance. The murder, then, is motivated as much by the narrator's struggle with his homosexual feelings as by his unresolved Oedipal problems.

Bianco waited almost thirty years before publishing his last work of fiction (and his only full-length novel), *La pérdida del reino*. A long and intense novel about a failed writer, Rufino Velázquez, the work is cast as a reworking by an unnamed narrator of the materials for Velázquez's autobiography. The story revolves around two close friends of Rufino's, Luisa Doncel and Néstor Sagasta. The reader gradually comes to understand that the main motivating factor in Rufino's life is a desire to do everything that Sagasta does—to go to the same places, to sleep with the same women, to think the same thoughts—and that this desire has led to his inability to function as an individual. He is not even able to write his novel; instead, the loose papers are gathered up after his death by Luisa Doncel and entrusted to the narrator. Once again the narrative turns on homosexual desire that is never acted upon, which is the key to Rufino's failures as a writer and as a man.

In one of his several essays on Proust, Bianco notes that Proust, by including homosexual love in *Recherche* on the same terms as heterosexual love, made more of a contribution to changing attitudes toward the "persecuted homosexual minority" than did André Gide with the "fallacious arguments of *Corydon*." At the end of his life Bianco often talked to friends about his intentions of writing a gay novel along the same lines as some of Yukio Mishima's, though more graphic and more violent. Perhaps that unwritten novel was unnecessary, since Bianco's three published novels, without positing a rigid homosexual identity for any of their characters, show the polymorphous nature of desire.

WORKS

Ficción y realidad. Caracas: Monte Avila, 1977.
Ficción y reflexión. Mexico City: Fondo de Cultura Económica, 1988.
La pérdida del reino. Buenos Aires: Siglo XXI Editores, 1972.
Las ratas. Buenos Aires: Ediciones Sur, 1943. Trans. Daniel Balderston as *The Rats*. In *Shadow Play and The Rats: Two Novellas by José Bianco*, 35–88. Pittsburgh: Latin American Literary Review Press, 1983.
"Sombras suele vestir." *Sur* 85 (1941): 23–66. Also in book form. Buenos Aires: Ediciones Sur, 1942. Trans. Daniel Balderston as *Shadow Play*. In *Shadow Play and The Rats*, 1–33. Pittsburgh: Latin American Literary Review Press, 1983.

CRITICISM

Bastos, María Luisa. "La topografía de la ambigüedad (Buenos Aires en Borges, Bianco y Bioy Casares)." In her *Relecturas: Estudios de textos hispanoamericanos*, 139–154. Buenos Aires: Hachette, 1989.
Domínguez de Rodríguez Pasqués, Mignon. "El discurso fantasmal y la *mise en abyme* en *Sombras suele vestir* de José Bianco." In his *Estudios de narratología*, 99–122. Buenos Aires: Biblos, 1991.

Gai, Adam. "Lo fantástico y su sombra: Doble lectura de un texto de José Bianco." *Hispamérica* 34–35 (1983): 35–50.

Piña, Cristina, and Federico Peltzer. "Dos personajes solitarios en la novela argentina actual." *Revista universitaria de letras* 1.1 (1979): 80–98.

Prieto Taboada, Antonio. "Entrevista con José Bianco." *Hispamérica* 50 (1988): 73–86.

———. "El poder de la ambigüedad en *Sombras suele vestir* de José Bianco." *Revista iberoamericana* 125 (1983): 717–730.

Yúdice, George. "La voz del lector en *Sombras suele vestir*." *Punto de contacto* 1.3 (1976): 59–68.

Daniel Balderston

BLANCO, JOSÉ JOAQUÍN (Mexico; 1951)

An extraordinarily prolific writer whose works run the gamut from poetry to the essay, and from prose fiction to urban chronicles and biography, Blanco was born in Mexico City, where he continues to reside. He is an active contributor to various newspapers and periodicals, including *Revista de América* (Review of America); *La cultura en México* (Culture in Mexico), a supplement of the magazine *Siempre* (Always); *Unomásuno* (One Plus One); *La Jornada* (The Workday); *El Nacional* (The National); *Punto* (Period); and *Nexos* (Connections), of whose editorial board he is also a member. A number of these articles have been anthologized in volumes of his collected works. In addition, Blanco collaborated with director Paul Leduc to write the screenplay for the critically acclaimed film *Frida: naturaleza viva* (Frida), about the passions, both sentimental and artistic, of the Mexican artist Frida Kahlo.

Best known as a journalist whose weekly essays on themes related to urban life (condominiums, traffic, educational policy, the subway, public markets, police brutality, tourism, gay cruising) first appeared in the mid-1960s, Blanco (along with Carlos Monsiváis and others) is recognized as a seminal influence on the development of the *crónica* as a constant artistic presence in Mexican culture. He is also the author of three novels constructed around the image of the city as a landscape against which the individual components of the body politic—the middle classes, the marginalized or socially and sexually demonized, the economically and spiritually impoverished—try to survive on a daily basis in spite of acts of violence perpetrated against them by individuals, families and institutions. While not a constant in each and every text, Blanco does consider the issues surrounding the overt assumption of a homosexual identity in several of his literary essays, as well as in the novel *Las púberes canéforas* (The Pubescent Maidens; 1983). In each case, a rapacious, mercilessly threatening and clearly disillusioned Mexico in the 1980s is represented as the constant impediment to the expression of personal desires and the pursuit of gratification, public oratory on the need for tolerance notwithstanding. Fear and desperation are the forces motivating a society in crisis that preys on the others within itself to keep a fracturing social body patched together under the guise of a collective consensual identity.

Between 1973 and 1978, among his articles for *Siempre* Blanco included a series of written portraits of literary and cultural figures that either suggest or acknowledge gay identity. In Oscar Wilde's letters to his lover, for example, he finds a kind of forerunner of the contemporary repression of homosexuality, whether by totalitarian societies or by the hidden brutality of self-proclaimed democratic cultures that persecute their victims in equal fashion. Then, in the defiant banditry of Jean Genet's gay characters he identifies a counterparadise, an alternate world produced from the human debris of bourgeois heterosexual society. Indeed, Blanco seems to conclude with Genet that real dignity resides in the paradoxical equating of baseness and perfection; for them, the world of family, property, customs, morals and norms becomes the emblem of the grotesque. And subsequently, in Yukio Mishima's writings, Blanco revels in the absolute presence of the body and in its constituent parts as the site of the ultimate human consciousness of being alive. As an antidote to the anesthetized flesh of bourgeois civilization, he explores Mishima's emphasis on dirt, disease, violence, fever (body heat), death, and contagion to create an erotics of excess (akin to the atmosphere José Rafael Calva develops in *El jinete azul* [The Blue Horseman; 1985]).

If these articles suggest a general interest in cultures on the margin, in 1979 Blanco published ''Ojos que da pánico soñar'' (Eyes I Dare Not Meet in Dreams), which zeros in on the implications of professing a gay identity in his own country—not as a writer but in everyday life. Written as a piece of literary journalism in the first person—using both the singular *I* and the collective *we*—this essay addresses the reader directly as an implicated observer of (if not participant in) the many varieties of sexual behavior in the Mexican middle classes as well as the contradictions produced by the conjunction of sexual heresy and economic privilege. Blanco takes as his point of departure a phrase from T. S. Eliot—''The queer's gaze''—as an icon of the way straight society looks on its gay members: with a combination of fear and intrigue. This literary artifact—the look that both divides and unites erotically, depending on the point of view—is the key to his discussion of middle-class homosexuals' abandonment of sexual and political rebellion as social currency in favor of a comfortable co-optation by mass consumption into ''happy and harmless'' (Blanco, ''Ojos,'' 186), even conventional, citizens of the marketplace. While condemning gay men's sexuality, Mexican society is presented as looking the other way when it comes to gay men as consumers.

In 1983 Blanco united the genres of poetry, chronicle and prose narrative to form a bricolage novel whose underlying theme is urban violence, proposing to demythify homosexuals and the gay community as utopian exceptions to this overwhelmingly aggressive life. From sordid hotels to police stations, from ultramodern office buildings to nightclubs and bathhouses, *Las púberes canéforas* relentlessly roams the streets of Mexico City—referred to as cadavers by the characters—in search of victims and accomplices, persecution and brutality, to conclude that there is no social, sexual or political identity that can be offered as a refuge from reality.

Between the first chapter, in which Felipe escapes from his captors, who have dragged him to the outskirts of the city to kill him as an undesirable (read: homosexual), and the last pages outside the Jáuregui Baths, when La Gorda (a dentist whose exuberant language for describing his sexual encounters seems unnatural to friend and narrator Guillermo, who is in constant search of an appropriate and balanced style to tell his story) is accosted by undercover police agents and whisked away in an unmarked Volkswagen to certain death, *Las púberes canéforas* alternates desperate (and naïve) attempts to find an oasis of love with episodes of exploitation, fear and bodies as just another piece of merchandise for sale. Bureaucrat and would-be novelist Guillermo; his on-again, off-again young lover, Felipe, who dreams of success and upward mobility; and the lovers Claudia and Analía, who work as prostitutes, function as shifting centers around which multiple stories cohere.

These tales range from tragic encounters with wealthy "juniors" who brutally dominate either men or women they pay for sex, to "guarura boys" from the lower classes, who mimic the violence of the bourgeoisie, envious of their social and economic power; from carefully orchestrated masquerade parties in luxury apartments, to erotic liaisons in the backs of pickup trucks; and from the poetic idealization of sentiment (quotes from F. Scott Fitzgerald, Jaime Gil de Biedman, Quevedo, Sor Juana de la Cruz, Rubén Darío), to the images of the perfect body touted in popular culture and the media. Blanco's avowedly homosexual characters cross lines of class, ethnic origin and age to demolish any stereotyped notions of uniqueness or exceptionality in their attitudes toward others. That is, the gay community—those whose gaze "dare not be met in dreams"—appears as an assimilated part of the egocentric, self-serving society of the 1980s. Blanco's tacit assumption of homosexual identity (in its multiplicity of forms and practices) as a natural and intrinsic part of the larger community is tempered by his criticism directed at the latter group's complicity in the violent circumstances that frame contemporary urban life. Some gay men in the novel are victimized by a homophobic society; others fall victim to those whose sexual preference they share but whose economic means are unequal.

In several articles published in 1989 and 1990, Blanco once again examines the writings of foreign authors like the Greek poet Konstantinos Kavafis, in whose young male heroes he finds the embodiment of what will become a contemporary homosexual erotics of (poetic) form. In an essay from *Las intensidades corrosivas* (Corrosive Intensities; 1990), in particular, Blanco returns to Luis Zapata's revolutionary novel *El vampiro de la colonia Roma* (*Adonis García*; 1979) with a view toward considering what has happened to gay themes and the gay community in Mexico in the ten years since its first publication.

He recounts the obstacles faced by the author, the censorship of sales in spite of winning a literary prize, and the novel's conquest of readers by virtue of the quality of its prose. Blanco sees *El vampiro* as a wedge that, by its straightforward and honest narration of what was deemed "lo prohibido" (forbidden), opened up the literary marketplace to sexuality in general as a topic worthy of discourse beyond the realm of tabloids, caricatures, graffiti, and popular melodramas. Praising Zapata's bringing homosexual characters out of the literary ghetto, he simultaneously lauds him for not mythifying the image of protagonist Adonis García. Yet Blanco adds that the advent of the AIDS epidemic in the ensuing decade places *El vampiro* at another crossroads as well: that of a more innocent moment in social history that can now be viewed with nostalgia. This valuable essay is one of relatively few that address this historical perspective and place a filter over the ode to freedom and delight in life portrayed by Zapata's character, not in order to denigrate its vision but to renew its celebratory function in context at a time when death and melancholy prevail in so many relationships. He applauds *El vampiro* as a novel that has survived, not as a frozen monument but as a marker, a legacy of another era whose values merit another glance.

In his crossovers between literary journalism—the vivid chronicles of everyday life—and novelistic prose Blanco contributes a critical look at the official project of modernization in Mexico over the last few decades, and he contextualizes those who identify themselves as part of a homosexual community within this larger frame of reference. As John Brushwood and Sara Sefchovich have pointed out, the resulting texts are filled with a tone of disillusionment and self-criticism; the Mexican critics who have reviewed *Las púberes canéforas* seem to concur with this assessment while pointing out the value of his inclusion of a spectrum of gay characters in his narrative. Although a number of short reviews of his novels have appeared in the Mexican periodicals and journals in which he publishes, Blanco's writings have yet to be covered as a whole, especially outside Mexico. An English translation of "Ojos que da pánico soñar" ("Eyes I Dare Not Meet in Dreams"), considered by many a classic contemporary text on gay culture in Mexico, is included in an anthology of gay literature, *Gay Roots*, edited by Winston Leyland.

WORKS

"La carne se destruye en el desamor (Luis Zapata, *En jirones*)." *La Jornada*, Nov. 9, 1984, p. 20.

"¿Cuál literatura gay?" *Sábado*, supp. to *Unomásuno* 310 (Oct. 8, 1983): 11.

"Ensayando a Cavafis." *La jornada semanal* 5 (July 16, 1989): 43–44.

"Eyes I Dare Not Meet in Dreams." Trans. Edward A. Lacey. In *Gay Roots: Twenty Years of Gay Sunshine*, 291–296. Ed. Winston Leyland. San Francisco: Gay Sunshine Press, 1991.

"Genet: Si el mónstruo se vuelve narciso, ¿a quién le toca horrorizarse?" In José Joaquín

Blanco, *Retratos con paisaje: Ensayos de crítica (de "La cultura en México" en Siempre entre 1973–1978), 143–156*. Puebla, Mexico: Universidad Autónoma de Puebla, 1979.

"Gide: La instancia moralmente inspirada." In *Retratos con paisaje*, 95–124.

"Introduction." In Luis Zapata, *Adonis García: A Picaresque Novel*, 5–8. Trans. E. A. Lacey. San Francisco: Gay Sunshine Press, 1981.

"Mishima: Los beneficios del desastre." In *Retratos con paisaje*, 157–178.

"Ojos que da pánico soñar." In *Función de medianoche: Ensayos de literatura cotidiana*. Ed. José Joaquin Blanco, 181–190. Mexico City: Era, 1981.

Las púberes canéforas. Mexico City: Océano, 1983.

Review of *El vampiro de la colonia Roma* (Luis Zapata). *Unomásuno*, Mar. 15, 1979, p. 6.

"Wilde: El sentido moral de lo más trágico." In *Retratos con paisaje*, 27–30.

"Zapata: El vampiro en los años del SIDA." In José Joaquín Blanco, *Las intensidades corrosivas*, 187–193. Villahermosa, Mexico: Gobierno del Estado de Tabasco, 1990.

CRITICISM

Bermúdez, María Elvira. "La narrativa en 1983. La novela. (*Las púberes canéforas*)." *Revista mexicana de cultura* 45 (Jan. 1, 1984): 12.

———. "Novela de José Joaquín Blanco (*Las púberes canéforas*)." *Revista mexicana de cultura* 12 (May 15, 1983): 12.

Brushwood, John S. *La novela mexicana (1967–1982)*. Mexico City: Editorial Grijalbo, 1984.

Coccioli, Carlos. "Literatura de abyección (*Las púberes canéforas*)."*Excélsior*, Aug. 18, 1983, pp. 7A, 8A.

Cohen, Sandro. "Retratos vividos de blanco (*Las púberes canéforas*)." *Casa del tiempo* 34 (Oct. 1983): 48–49.

Coronado, Juan. "*Las púberes canéforas*." *Sábado*, supp. to *Unomásuno* 295 (June 25, 1983): 10.

González Rodríguez, Sergio. "*Las púberes canéforas* que estaban para mí." *Unomásuno*, July 30, 1983, p. 19.

Hernández Franco, Francisco. "José Joaquín Blanco, *Las púberes canéforas*." *La cultura en México de Siempre* 1105 (Aug. 17, 1983): 53–54.

Patán, Federico. Review of *Las púberes canéforas*. *Sábado*, supp. to *Unomásuno* 291 (June 4, 1983): 14.

Reyes, Juan José. "En torno a la homosexualidad (*Las púberes canéforas*)." *El semanario cultural de Novedades* 90 (Jan. 8, 1984): 3.

Schneider, Luis Mario. "El tema homosexual en la nueva narrativa mexicana." *Casa del tiempo* 5.49/50 (Feb.–Mar. 1985): 82–86.

Sefchovich, Sara. *México: país de ideas, país de novelas. Una sociología de la literatura mexicana*. Mexico City: Grijalbo, 1987.

Toledo, Alejandro. "Blanco en Blanco: *Las púberes canéforas*." *Casa del tiempo* 34 (Oct. 1983): 54–55.

Torres, Vicente F. "Gay Life (*Las púberes canéforas*)." *Sábado*, supp. to *Unomásuno* 293 (June 11, 1983): 12.

Trejo Fuentes, Ignacio. "Segunda novela de Blanco. *Las púberes canéforas.*" *Excélsior*, sec. "Cultura," June 12, 1983, p. 2.
Urrutia, Elena. "Deslumbres y sordideces (*Las púberes canéforas*)." *Unomásuno*, May 8, 1983, p. 17.

Claudia Schaefer-Rodríguez

BOHÓRQUEZ, ABIGAEL (Mexico; 1937) _____

Born in Caborca, in the state of Sonora, Bohórquez studied dramatic arts and dramatic composition in several state theater schools. During his long career in cultural activities connected with government institutions, he has founded and directed choral poetry and experimental theater groups, served as a contributor to Mexican newspapers and reviews and has written radio scripts.

Bohórquez's literary work has been primarily in poetry and drama. He has received national prizes, and his poetry has been included in several recent anthologies. Criticism on his work is still scant and limited in nature, mostly literary supplement reviews; there are also commentaries on individual poems and papers presented at scholarly meetings. *Cien comentarios después 1956–1991* (in press) is a collection of critical notes, and the present author has published a monograph on his poetry. In general terms, critics have focused on the aesthetic quality of his work and the power of his words. Yet despite the recognition he has received, he is little known in Mexican literary circles.

One can discern in Bohórquez's work a process of thematic and stylistic evolution, despite the fact that beginning with his first book, *Poesía i teatro* (Poetry and Theater; 1960), some of the features that became constants in his writing are apparent: the concentration on elements of daily domestic and provincial life, in order to give them an artistic elaboration that affords them a high level of transcendental meaning; the failure to idealize the homeland; and, above all, the song to love, already indicating that it is something other than pure and chaste love. In subsequent books, *Acta de confirmación* (Act of Confirmation; 1966; 2nd ed., 1969), *Canción de amor y muerte por Rubén Jaramillo y poemas civiles* (Song of Love and Death for Rubén Jaramillo and Polite Poems; 1967), and *Las amarras terrestres* (Terrestrial Ties; 1969), Bohórquez develops a playful poetry of desacralization, introducing neologisms and working with irony, one of his constant devices.

The labor of the poet in the face of social conflicts is already present in these early collections, and he went on to postulate a poetry of solidarity with the marginal, a poetry with a clear social function: the denunciation and protest of the exploitation of women, of the black man beaten in the street, of workers and students. In these works we find a clearly defined homosexual poetic voice, one that stands in direct relationship to Bohórquez's aesthetic project: poetry as liberating, as the unmasking of fallacies and oppression in a language that is free to explore all of its semantic possibilities. The office of poet is a permanent theme in Bohórquez's work: a constant search for the meanings of life, love, dead friends, the earth—without any sort of idealization and without being the mere reproduction of local speech within a provincial perspective. There is always an underlying humor, passion and even anger. Some of his poems are readings of other poems from world literature, an unending dialogue with other texts that are probed in depth in the poems on homosexual themes.

Homosexual love is a constant topic in Bohórquez's work, inseparable from a vision of the world grounded on an aesthetic of defiance and poetic subversion: homosexuality as a system of liberation, as a special sensibility for living, for being and for writing poetry. If it is true that beginning in the 1960s, one finds something like an opening or tolerance in Mexico toward manifestations of homosexuality, it is equally true that the moral state continues to be repressive and the social state continues to be extortionist, a view of things that underlies the book of poetry *Digo lo que amo* (I Say What I Love; 1976), whose title is a declaration, but not a confession, of love as erotic and is manifestly and openly provocative. This is not confessional poetry because as a whole it is a defiance of the scorn, the fallacy and the frivolity of a society ill with moral hypocrisy. Homosexuality functions as a sign of identity that seeks to base itself on a poetics of humor, parody, playfulness and at times outright scorn for hypocrisy.

Poesía en limpio 1979–1989 (Clean-Copy Poetry 1979–1989; 1990) again takes up the topic of homosexuality, which becomes a way of acceding to low-life hotels, edge-of-town haunts where love may be lived, a love that is shaped by the creaking of beds, sordid walls filled with graffiti, a love that discovers its pleasure in a masculine-defined body. These poems are nostalgic in tone, and there is a note of celebration, a high polysemous language of renewal.

In *PoesíDa* (PoetrAids; 1992), Bohórquez's most recent collection, terror becomes poetry in a gesture of solidarity with the persecuted, with those who have been marked and with the dead. The poetic voice moves between gravity and the need to recover the festive; it is always engaging in dialogue with the voices of literary tradition and the bolero as a culture of a machismo that is transformed into an appropriate vehicle for singing of homosexual love.

Eroticism in Bohórquez's work can be read as a permanent dialogue with the classical tradition of homosexual love seen as a game, as a constant dialogue with Virgil, Anacreon, the Aztec poet Nezahualcoyotl and the Bible. In this reappropriation of classical literary forms there is a transcendence of domesticity in order to attain a song of universal love. There are poems in which his burlesque and defiant stance is clear. It is in a mediation between the pornographic and stylized sexuality in which irony becomes his principal stylistic device, assuming the form of neologisms and phonetic derivations. Other texts are marked by the nostalgic tone of an intimate poetic speaker, one who is serious and overwhelmed in the face of the lack of love or abandonment.

Bohórquez's work summarizes a long tradition of erotic literature. It renews a language that had become worn down by the solemnity of the Romantics, and by making it do ludic service, the poet provides a notable transformation of the conventional forms of perception, re-creating with no sign of false modesty the "other" perspective that had been silenced through discreditation and persecution. His poems name the unnamed from Greek and Latin classics on down.

WORKS

Abigaeles, poeniñimos. Hermosillo, Mexico: Instituto Sonorense de Cultura, 1991.

Acta de confirmación. Mexico City: Alejandro Finisterre, 1966. 2nd ed., Mexico City: Arana, 1969.

Las amarras terrestres. Mexico City: Pájaro Cascabel Colección Estuario, 1969.

Canción de amor y muerte por Rubén Jaramillo y otros poemas civiles. Mexico City: Colección Parva OPIC, 1967.

Cien comentarios después (1956–1991). San Luis Río Colorado, Mexico: Sociedad de Escritores de San Luis Río Colorado (in press).

Destierro mayor. Mexico City: Federación Editorial Mexicana Biblioteca Selecta ALFEM, 1980.

Digo lo que amo. Mexico City: Federación Editorial Mexicana Colección Palabra Viva, 1976.

Memoria en la Alta Milpa. Mexico City: Federación Editorial Mexicana Colección Palabra Viva, 1975.

Poesía en limpio 1979–1989. Hermosillo, Mexico: Universidad de Sonora, 1990.

Poesía i teatro. Mexico City: Costa Amic, 1960.

PoesíDa. In press.

CRITICISM

Munguía Zatarain, Martha Elena. *Yo no estoy para rosas. La poesía en Sonora (1960–1975)*. Hermosillo, Mexico: Universidad de Sonora, 1989.

Martha Elena Munguía Zatarain

BORGES, JORGE LUIS (Argentina; 1899–1986) _____

Born in Buenos Aires to Jorge Guillermo Borges Haslam, a lawyer and professor of psychology, and Leonor Acevedo Suárez, descendant of an old Argentine family whose members had fought in the nineteenth-century independence and civil wars of the Río de la Plata, Borges grew up, with his sister, Norah, in a bilingual milieu under the tutelage of his paternal grandmother, Fanny Haslam. As a child he read works in English by Robert Louis Stevenson, Mark Twain and H. G. Wells, developing a profound interest in dictionaries and encyclopedias that would persist for the rest of his life. In 1909, a local newspaper, *El País* (The Country), published his first piece of writing, a translation of Oscar Wilde's "The Happy Prince."

Due to the increasing blindness of Borges's father, the family went to Europe;

they remained for four years in Geneva, where Borges attended the Lycée Jean Calvin. During this period, he learned French and read the modern classics. Borges also began the study of Latin and with the help of a dictionary learned German, translating Heinrich Heine's poems. He discovered contemporary expressionist poetry and was dazzled by German philosophers, particularly Arthur Schopenhauer and Friedrich Nietzsche.

When World War I ended, the family traveled in Spain, where Borges met several avant-garde writers and contributed to poetic publications. Before returning to Buenos Aires, he translated the German expressionists and met other prominent intellectuals. Back in Buenos Aires, he and a group of young poets produced *Prisma* (Prism), a "billboard review." Soon afterward, he founded *Proa* (Prow), a literary magazine. Both publications were intended to promulgate the avant-garde ideals that Borges had absorbed in Europe. This period also includes the beginning of Borges's friendship with Macedonio Fernández, whose intellectual influence Borges would recognize throughout his life. Borges began to participate in the intense intellectual life of Buenos Aires and to publish in the renowned review *Martín Fierro*, founded by Evar Méndez in 1924. During this time he formed many longtime friendships: with the Mexican writer Alfonso Reyes, while the latter was his country's ambassador in Argentina; Ricardo Güiraldes, who, with Victoria Ocampo, was the founder in 1931 of *Sur* (South), the most influential literary magazine of Latin America, in which Borges would publish for decades; and Adolfo Bioy Casares, a young writer who was not only a lifelong friend, but also an essential collaborator.

After a failed attempt to commit suicide, Borges underwent a series of transformative experiences in 1938: his father died in February, and consequently, Borges began to work as an assistant librarian in a neighborhood branch of the city library; and, in a moment of haste on Christmas Eve, he suffered an accident—a head wound—that kept him bedridden for weeks. Borges always attributed this circumstance, which brought him to death's door, to his decision to explore the narrative genre; he then produced his first fantastic short story, "Pierre Menard, autor del Quijote" (Pierre Menard, Author of the *Quixote*).

During the Peronist period (1946–1955), Borges was obliged to resign his position as librarian. In order to support himself, he decided to teach and lecture. After the fall of Perón's government in 1955, he became director of the National Library, was named member of the Argentine Academy of Letters and was appointed as professor of English literature at the University of Buenos Aires. Concurrently, Borges received an honorary doctorate from the University of Cuyo and the National Prize for literature. This delayed acknowledgment was accompanied by the worst form of punishment that a writer could receive: his doctors forbade him to read and write due to his increasing visual impairment.

Borges married Elsa Astete Millán, widow of Ricardo Albarracín Sarmiento, in 1967; they divorced three years later. In 1975, Borges's mother, who had been his diligent assistant after he became almost completely blind, died. In spite of his initial support for the right-wing military coup that interrupted the

Peronist government of María Estela Martínez de Perón in 1976, Borges four years later signed a "Solicitada sobre los desaparecidos" (Public demand regarding the disappeared), published in *Clarín* (Clarion), the most popular Argentine newspaper. In 1986, Borges married María Kodama, his former secretary and assistant. They took up residence in Geneva, where Borges died of cancer on June 14 of that year.

Borges's writings may be divided into three categories: poetry, essay and short story. With financial support from his father, in 1923 he published his first book of poems, *Fervor de Buenos Aires* (Fervor of Buenos Aires), with illustrations by his sister, Norah. This collection brought enthusiastic reviews. Two years later, *Luna de enfrente* (Moon Across the Way), another poetry book, appeared. In 1929 *Cuaderno San Martín* (San Martin Notebook) won him second prize in the annual Municipal Literary Contest of Buenos Aires. These three books were the basis for his reputation as a poet. However, Borges abandoned poetry almost entirely for years, returning to it only later, with different themes and forms.

During the 1920s, Borges wrote several books of essays for which he never authorized republication: *Inquisiciones* (Inquisitions; 1925), *El tamaño de mi esperanza* (The Size of My Hope; 1926) and *El idioma de los argentinos* (The Language of the Argentines; 1928). In 1930, he completed an unusual biography of a popular poet who had been a friend of his family, *Evaristo Carriego*. During the following years, he published two volumes of essays: *Discusión* (Discussion; 1932) and *Historia de la eternidad* (A History of Eternity; 1936).

In *Historia universal de la infamia* (A Universal History of Infamy; 1935), Borges collected several narrative pieces that had appeared in the weekly arts supplement of the newspaper *Crítica* (Critique). This book included the first short story written by Borges: "Hombre de la esquina rosada" (Street-Corner Man). During the next decade he dedicated himself entirely to developing the fiction that led him to be known worldwide. In 1942 he competed for the National Prize for Literature with *El jardín de los senderos que se bifurcan* (The Garden of the Forking Paths). When the prize was awarded to someone else, the magazine *Sur* organized a special issue entitled "Desagravio a Borges" (Vindication of Borges), to which major Hispanic writers and scholars contributed. Borges published *Ficciones* (Fictions) in 1944, a collection of short stories that incorporated the pieces presented in *Jardín*. The Sociedad Argentina de Escritores (Argentine Association of Writers) created a Prize of Honor for Borges. This decade was crowned with the publication of Borges's most celebrated book of fiction: *El Aleph* (The Aleph; 1949).

From then on, Borges became the giant of twentieth-century Argentine literature. In the 1950s he published a new book of essays, *Otras inquisiciones* (Other Inquisitions; 1952) and a compilation of brief pieces in prose and verse, *El hacedor* (The Maker; *Dreamtigers* in the English edition; 1960). At the same time, one of the major Buenos Aires publishing houses, Emecé, began issuing, under the direction of José Edmundo Clemente, Borges's *Obras completas* (Complete Works), which gave the writer the opportunity to make many alterations in the earlier books and to refuse to reprint the essays he had written in the 1920s. The first translation of a book by Borges, *Fictions*, was printed in Paris in 1951. One year later, Roger Caillois edited *Labyrinthes*, a compilation of writings in French translation.

After *El hacedor*, Borges published several important books of poems—*Elogio de la sombra* (In Praise of Darkness; 1969), *La rosa profunda* (The Profound Rose; 1975), *La moneda de hierro* (The Iron Coin; 1976), *Historia de la noche* (A History of the Night, 1977), *La cifra* (The Cipher; 1981) and *Los conjurados* (The Plotters; 1985); two collections of short stories, *El informe de Brodie* (Doctor Brodie's Report; 1970) and *El libro de arena* (The Book of Sand; 1975); and essays in collaboration with others and anthological selections of his previous work. By the mid-1970s Emecé had published a new edition of the *Obras completas* in a thick single volume, followed by a second volume of his *Obras completas en colaboración* (Complete Works in Collaboration; 1979), including only some of the books Borges wrote with other Argentine writers (Adolfo Bioy Casares, Betina Edelberg, Margarita Guerrero, Alicia Jurado, María Kodama and María Esther Vázquez).

In 1961, Borges shared the prestigious Prix Formentor with Samuel Beckett. This award marked the beginning of his international career. The clearest proof of his growing academic recognition is the string of honorary doctorates that Borges received from foreign universities: Oxford, Columbia, Michigan, the Sorbonne and Harvard, among many others. Although Borges was practically unknown in the Anglo-American world before the 1960s, the enthusiasm that he has aroused since then is immense. In 1962, two English collections of Borges's writings, *Ficciones* and *Labyrinths*, an anthology of short stories, essays and other pieces, were published in New York. European and American universities began to invite him to teach, and he traveled to various countries, lecturing. The diffusion of his writing was strengthened by the notes and commentaries that several intellectuals, none primarily involved in Hispanic studies, published during the 1960s, most notably those written by John Updike (1965) and George Steiner (1970) for *The New Yorker*, by Paul de Man (1964) for *The New York Review of Books* and by John Barth (1967) for *The Atlantic Monthly*. In 1970, *The New Yorker* printed an "Autobiographical Essay," which was included in the English edition of *El Aleph*, edited and translated by Norman Thomas di Giovanni.

It is obvious that, in old age, Borges had become a prominent figure, acclaimed by intellectuals all over the world, even though slanderers in his own country were legion. He was vehemently accused of being elitist because his political beliefs had swung from the philosophical anarchism of youth to the anti-Peronism of adulthood and finally back toward conservatism. Nevertheless, his alleged cultural elitism contrasted with the open attitude of his last years, which completely transformed his public image in Argentina: Borges agreed to countless radio and television interviews, thus inaugurating an unexpected channel of communication between him and his (future) readers. In this sense, besides the creative working, the published interviews, some of which are book length—Jean de Milleret (1967), Richard Burgin (1969), Antonio Carrizo (1983) and María Esther Vázquez (1984)—allow the reader to know personal aspects of his life, his opinions and ideas and, naturally, the image Borges sought to build of himself.

Although the bibliography on Borges is enormous, it is limited here to what has been written on sexually related topics and the various ways in which they are manifested in his works. Some occasional contributions to an understanding of this facet must be extracted from a reduced set of mainly psychoanalytical studies, which connect biographical information to textual peculiarities. Emir Rodríguez Monegal, the most meticulous and perceptive biographer of Borges, identified the origin of a latent oedipal conflict in the configuration of the writer's family. It is well known that Borges always rejected the psychoanalytical interpretation of his relationship to his parents, because he believed that Freud had constructed misleading and extreme simplifications of the complexities of human relations (Burgin 109). Beyond this opinion, Freudian readings cleared the way for studies that highlighted intriguing aspects of Borges's literary production. Apart from a literary biography by Rodríguez Monegal, intended to offer a narrative about the life of the writer that includes subtle readings of his texts, Didier Anzieu, a French psychoanalyst who based his analyses on Melanie Klein's and Jacques Lacan's theories, carried out a detailed examination of several short stories. More recently, an Argentine psychoanalyst, Julio Woscoboinik, published a book dedicated to reviewing the author's complete works from a similar point of view.

Put in a somewhat schematic way, the conflicting situation of Borges is revealed, in the first place, through the bilingual atmosphere of his childhood. On an unconscious level, the splitting of the original unity between mother and son into two different linguistic codes involves the presence of two mothers—the biological mother and the paternal grandmother—with two different bodies. In this peculiar configuration, the father comes to the surface as the center of domestic life, as a figure who regulates aspirations and the meaning of life for the child. According to Laura Silvestri, one of the aspects of the fantastic in Borges reveals autobiographical roots and concerns the conflict with the father, whence derives the writer's preference for the short story—a literary form the father had tried, unsuccessfully, to cultivate—and for a narrative technique that insistently reverts to the motif of the double. This duplicity incarnated in the pair pursuer/pursued is thus an unaware recourse to representation of both the hated father and the murderous son. The paternal meddling in Borges's life was so extreme that he even arranged the sexual initiation of his son with a prostitute in Geneva. Some textual evidences of this first experience, a traumatic one for the adolescent, may be traced in surprisingly late short stories like "El otro" (The Other) and "La memoria de Shakespeare" (Shakespeare's Memory).

In view of this panorama of complex relations and traumatic experiences, the little space left for the sexual dimension in Borges's writings is not surprising.

In the epilogue to *El libro de arena*, the writer declares that even though the topic of love is very common in his verses, it occurs only once in prose, the piece entitled "Ulrica." This is true, since motifs directly related to the erotic and/or the sexual appear only sparingly in Borges's prose pieces. There are allusions and references, but a plain treatment of the matter is completely absent. However, there is a series of texts in which sex plays a decisive role: basically "La secta del Fénix" (The Sect of the Phoenix), "La intrusa" (The Intruder), "Emma Zunz," and "Hombre de la esquina rosada."

In one of his most celebrated short stories, "Tlön, Uqbar, Orbis Tertius," Borges makes his real-life friend Bioy Casares into a literary character and has him repeat a sentence, supposedly quoted from an apocryphal encyclopedia: "Copulation and mirrors are abominable" (in English in the original). Many years before, a similar statement was used in "El tintorero enmascarado Hákim de Merv" (The Masked Dyer, Hakim of Merv), in *Historia universal de la infamia*. In both cases, the horror of sexual intercourse (or one of its consequences, paternity) arises from the fact that it multiplies individuals as mirrors do. This association may seem astonishing or even whimsical, since its final sense is to amaze the reader and metonymically to shift the attention from cause to effect: copulation may, in fact, turn out to be a way of propagating people— and perhaps that may be considered an abominable action—but this is not its only purpose. While not taking into consideration other aspects of the same phenomenon, what Borges denies is, doubtless, desire and sexual satisfaction. An outstanding and at the same time excessive example of this conception is "La secta del Fénix," a short story originally published in *Sur* (1952) and later included in *Ficciones*. Borges creates a fiction in which the existence of a pagan sect, which has been preserving a "secret" since the beginning of time, is postulated. Although the content of the secret is never made explicit, there is no doubt that it refers to the sexual act, which was confirmed by the author in an interview with Ronald Christ.

What has been said up to now corresponds to a universe of heterosexual relations. However, the arranging in terms of relations between men and women does not distinguish the fictional worlds created by Borges. For that matter, critics have had the chance to observe that in his writings, female characters are despised and denigrated figures, objects or goods that men can use, associated with danger and destruction, like La Lujanera in "Hombre de la esquina rosada" and several texts from *El informe de Brodie*: Juliana in "La intrusa," Serviliana in "El otro duelo" (The Other Duel) and Casilda in "Historia de Rosendo Juárez" (Rosendo's Tale). In Borges's literary production, dominated by male protagonists, there is only a small group of female characters, singularized by their social position and the relation that the narrator establishes with them: Beatriz Viterbo in "El Aleph," who, not being an indispensable character for the development of the plot, fulfills the need for evoking a frustrated love; Teodolina Villar in "El Zahir" (The Zahir); the Norwegian girl who mysteriously offers her body to a Colombian teacher in "Ulrica."

The only exception to the preponderance of male protagonists is "Emma Zunz," a short story published in *Sur* (1948) and included in *El Aleph*. Emma is a young woman who loses her virginity while elaborating an alibi to conceal a murder to avenge her father's death. In the culminating moment, while she is having her first sexual intercourse with a complete stranger, the narration is interrupted for some revealing reflections. The narrator includes a striking sentence, another example of the euphemisms that Borges employed whenever he wanted to avoid a straightforward mention of any form of sexual activity: "She thought (she was unable not to think) that her father had done to her mother the hideous thing that was being done to her now" (tr. Donald A. Yates, *Labyrinths*, 135). It is clear that, for the character and for the implied author as well, sexuality is possible only in a rape context. In spite of her fear and desperation, Emma Zunz goes ahead with her decision to sacrifice her virginity with no justification other than nourishing her hate.

Apart from the above-mentioned examples, Borges's works are oriented most of the time to a spectrum of human relationships dominated by male figures. In the frame of his homosocial fictions, the aversion to paternity leads to the consideration of the possibility of generating others without the participation of a woman, in the manner of the Greek myth of Pallas Athena, who sprang fully grown from the head of Zeus—according to mythology, the latter swallowed his feminine counterpart, Metis, out of fear that she might give birth to a son stronger than himself. In this regard, it is interesting to recall an answer Borges gave to Ronald Christ in relation to his collaboration with Adolfo Bioy Casares when shaping the fictitious H. Bustos Domecq, a pseudonym they used to publish *Seis problemas para don Isidro Parodi* (Six Problems for Don Isidro Parodi; 1942) and *Dos fantasías memorables* (Two Memorable Fictions; 1946). On that occasion, the writer said that while working together, they create a third person, different from each of them. Thus, on the basis of a description of a productive case of literary collaboration, it is possible to find, symbolically expressed, the creation of progeny from a purely intellectual effort.

An analogous concept is developed in texts like "El Golem" (The Golem), a poem included in *El otro, el mismo*, and "Las ruinas circulares" (The Circular Ruins), where the issue of procreation is embodied in the metaphor of dreaming: someone dreams that his act of dreaming confers existence on another individual. The situation becomes a nightmare when the dreamer discovers the possibility that someone else may be dreaming him. The last link in this chain of fixations lies in the radical fictionalizing of the author, who starts out as a protagonist of his own stories ("El Aleph," "El Zahir," "Borges y yo" [Borges and I] and "El otro").

Another facet of the homosocial dimension in Borges's writings can be seen in those texts that reveal a triangular relation. From the earliest period this narrative configuration seduced the writer. As a matter of fact, it is documented in the first short story he wrote, "Hombre de la esquina rosada," an expanded version of "Hombres pelearon" (Men Fought), an anecdote originally published in *El idioma de los argentinos* (1928). In the complex plot the motive for killing a man does not seem to be a compelling desire for a woman but the need to save the reputation of the neighborhood and to vindicate the injured pride of the murderer. In narratives like this, men kill each other because of values that embrace the defense of their ideals, the retaliation for previous deaths or even without apparent reasons. But, as Alicia Jurado observes, they never kill out of the rivalry between two men for a woman (108).

The most suggestive example of this kind of triangular configuration is "La intrusa" (1966), which can be interpreted as the triumph of brotherly love over any form of heterosexual attachment. The story is preceded by a reference to an apocryphal biblical passage (2 Kings 1:26), corresponding, in fact, to 2 Samuel 1:26, where David tells his friend: "I am distressed for thee, my brother Jonathan, very pleasant hast thou been unto me: thy love to me was wonderful, passing the love of women." The English version by di Giovanni corrects the reference and copies the last words of the quotation. It is not necessary to insist that this short story could be read either as a declaration of the superiority of fraternal affinity or as a devious rendering of homosexual passion. According to Silvestri, when the Argentine film director Carlos Christiansen released his adaptation of *La intrusa*, which was immediately censured by the authorities of the military government, Borges's reaction was one of indignation. Soon after, Borges published a note on censorship in which, although expressing his opposition to every form of totalitarianism, he stated it was acceptable in the case of the movie. The main problem, it seems, was that Christiansen depicted the two male characters as homosexuals. The anecdote proves that homosexuality was a troublesome realm for Borges to explore.

There is no question that "La intrusa" represents, subtly sexualized, the relationship between two brothers who reach their place of union in the body of the same woman. Although critics did not miss this point, most have been cautious not to project any particular sexual identity from it onto the life of the author. Silvestri, for instance, is hesitant to admit that homosexuality could have raised a profound conflict in Borges. Rodríguez Monegal, attending exclusively to the plot level, notices that "As is frequent in many stories by Borges, under a rigorous narrative of facts, it is possible to guess a darker story of latent homosexuality between the two brothers, the incestuous relation of two men through the body of the intruder that they shared during a certain time" (*Borges por él mismo*, 84). From a psychoanalytical perspective that moves onto the cultural dimension, Woscoboinik points out that the ambiguous situation of the man, who is empowered by his culture to possess a woman sexually but who cannot express his feelings and tenderness, in order to avoid being judged weak or womanly, may be considered either as the conceptual construction of a modern paradox or as the manifestation of "inner homosexual fantasies" (128). The relevance of this dimension is confirmed by one of Borges's characters, Rosendo Juárez, who establishes that "a man who thinks five minutes straight about a woman is no man, he's a queer" (*Doctor Brodie's Report*, 58).

In its double interpretive potentiality, "La intrusa" allows for a displacement from the homosocial to the homosexual pole of male relations. Homosexual-related topics were not easily dealt with by Borges, who tended to make negative statements about them in public. Because of this, it is interesting to rescue from oblivion the essay that he inserted at the beginning of the first printing of *Discusión* (1932), "Nuestras imposibilidades" (Our Impossibilities). In this piece, excluded from subsequent editions, the writer reflects on the distinctive traits of the citizen of Buenos Aires, the *porteño*. Among other things, Borges notices the existence of a double morality when judging (certain manifestations of) male homosexuality—he chooses the word "sodomy," which does not refer properly to the sexual identity of an individual but to a single sexual practice. According to this twofold morality, Argentineans were very tolerant with the active sodomite but despised the passive one. Borges does not delve deeply into details, but his accurate observation implies a preoccupation with inquiring into his own culture as a totality, including the encoding of sexual practices.

A last case is Borges's interest in a marginal figure, the *compadrito* (tough). In "Historia del tango" (A History of the Tango), a text added to the second edition of *Evaristo Carriego* (1955), he attested once more to his abiding curiosity about this character, the underworld of marginality from which he arises, and the tango, which is his most genuine form of expression. The universe of the tango was originally the brothels at the end of the nineteenth century, places visited often by men of every sort who were looking for women. This aspect underlines the heterosexual connotations of this social circuit. Nonetheless, the brothel was something other than a place to fulfill one's sexual fantasies. It was also a place of meeting and rivalry between rough individuals. The attraction that the writer felt for this traditional figure of Buenos Aires is documented in a drawing by him, known under the title "Compadrito de la edad de oro" (Tough of the Golden Age).

Woscoboinik makes useful comments upon the sexually ambiguous image of the *compadritos*. According to his approach, the drawing is built around two contradictory messages: the one transmitted by the face of the character that "shows a tough, challenging, arrogant expression, with an attentive and provocative glance, marked mustache and a clear scar"; and that of the body that suggests "elements of insecurity and sexual ambiguity," due to the roundness of its forms, in particular the hip, easily associated with the traditional image of a female body (120). A third aspect of the *compadrito*'s culture that Borges witnessed was the practice of tangoing in the streets by men alone, which he understood as a form of proving their ability to dance. The writer could not grasp—at least, he never showed evidence of any awareness of—the presence of a latent, barely repressed homosexual component in this kind of public exhibition. On the contrary, he insisted on the social prohibition that forbade "decent" women to participate in a dance that was considered immoral, in order to insist in the marginal origins of the tango.

These few examples show that not only in Borges's life, but also in the different worlds his imagination had built, sexuality is a difficult, if not an openly conflicting, aspect of human experience. In a profound sense, it seems obvious that the writer tried again and again to elide (the mention of) the sexual act and, because of that, to accept what Freudians call "the primal scene." Starting from the preceding observations and commentaries, it is legitimate to attempt a rereading of all of Borges's works in search of the many manifestations of a subject that ends up by shaping a painful, frustrated and ultimately atrocious version of this constituent of human life.

WORKS

Obras completas. 3 vols. Buenos Aires: Emecé, 1989.

MAJOR ENGLISH TRANSLATIONS

El Aleph (1949). Ed. and trans. Norman Thomas di Giovanni in collaboration with the author. New York: Dutton, 1970.
Atlas (1984). Trans. Antony Kerrigan under the same title. New York: Dutton, 1985.
Elogio de la sombra (1969). Trans. Norman Thomas di Giovanni as *In Praise of Darkness.* New York: Dutton, 1977.
Evaristo Carriego (1930). Trans. Norman Thomas di Giovanni, with the assistance of Susan Ashe, as *Evaristo Carriego. A Book About Old-Time Buenos Aires.* New York: Dutton, 1983.
Ficciones (1944). Trans. Anthony Kerrigan and others under the same title. New York: Grove Press, 1962.
El hacedor (1960). Trans. Mildred Boyer and Harold Morland as *Dreamtigers.* Austin: University of Texas Press, 1964.
Historia universal de la infamia (1935). Trans. Norman Thomas di Giovanni as *A Universal History of Infamy.* New York: Dutton, 1972.
El informe de Brodie (1970). Trans. Norman Thomas di Giovanni in collaboration with the author as *Doctor Brodie's Report.* New York: Dutton, 1972.
Labyrinths: Selected Stories and Other Writings. Ed. Donald A. Yates and James Irby. New York: New Directions, 1962.
El libro de arena (1975). Trans. Norman Thomas di Giovanni as *The Book of Sand.* New York: Dutton, 1977.
El oro de los tigres (1972). Trans. Alastair Reid as *The Gold of the Tigers: Selected Later Poems.* New York: Dutton, 1977.
Otras inquisiciones (1952). Trans. Ruth L. C. Simms as *Other Inquisitions, 1937–1952.* Austin: University of Texas Press, 1964.
A Personal Anthology. Ed. Anthony Kerrigan. New York: Grove Press, 1967.
Selected Poems 1923–1967. Trans. Norman Thomas di Giovanni and others. New York: Delacorte Press, 1972.

CRITICISM

Agheana, Ion T. *The Meaning of Experience in the Prose of Jorge Luis Borges.* New York: Peter Lang, 1988.

Aizenberg, Edna. *The Aleph Weaver: Biblical, Kabbalistic and Judaic Elements in Borges.* Potomac, Md.: Scripta Humanitatis, 1984.

————, ed. *Borges and His Successors: The Borgesian Impact on Literature and the Arts.* Columbia: University of Missouri Press, 1990.

Alazraki, Jaime. *La prosa narrativa de Jorge Luis Borges.* Madrid: Gredos, 1968. 3rd enl. ed., 1983.

————. *Versiones, inversiones, reversiones. El espejo como modelo estructural del relato en los cuentos de Jorge Luis Borges.* Madrid: Gredos, 1977.

————, ed. *Critical Essays on Jorge Luis Borges.* Boston: Hall, 1987.

————. *Jorge Luis Borges. El escritor y la crítica.* Madrid: Taurus, 1976. 3rd repr. 1986.

Anzieu, Didier. "Le Corps et le code dans les contes de J. L. Borges." *Nouvelle Revue de psychanalyse,* July–Aug. 1971, pp. 177–210. Repr. in his *Le Corps de l'oeuvre.* Paris: Gallimard, 1981. Spanish version as "El cuerpo y el código en los cuentos de J. L. Borges." *Revista de occidente* 143–144 (1975): 230–270.

Balderston, Daniel, comp. *The Literary Universe of Jorge Luis Borges: An Index to References and Allusions to Persons, Titles, and Places in His Writings.* Westport, Conn.: Greenwood Press, 1986.

Barnatán, Marcos Ricardo. *Conocer Borges y su obra.* Madrid: Dopesa, 1978.

Barrenechea, Ana María. *La expresión de la irrealidad en la obra de Borges.* Mexico City: Colegio de México, 1957. Translation Robert Lima as *Borges the Labyrinth Maker.* New York: New York University Press, 1965.

Barth, John. "The Literature of Exhaustion." *The Atlantic Monthly* 220 (Aug. 1967): 29–34.

————. "The Literature of Replenishment: Postmodernism and the Rebirth of the Novel." *The Atlantic Monthly* 245.1 (Sept. 1980): 65–71.

Bell-Villada, Gene H. *Borges and His Fiction: A Guide to His Mind and Art.* Chapel Hill: University of North Carolina Press, 1981.

Bloom, Harold, ed. *Jorge Luis Borges.* New York: Chelsea, 1986.

Blüher, Karl Alfred, and Alfonso de Toro, eds. *Jorge Luis Borges. Variaciones interpretativas sobre sus procedimientos literarios y bases epistemológicas.* Frankfurt: Vervuert, 1992.

Burgin, Richard. *Conversations with Jorge Luis Borges.* New York: Holt, Rinehart and Winston, 1969.

Carrizo, Antonio. *Borges, el memorioso: Conversaciones de Jorge Luis Borges con Antonio Carrizo.* Mexico: Fondo de Cultura Economica, 1982.

Charbonnier, Georges. *Entretiens avec Jorge Luis Borges.* Paris: Gallimard, 1967. Spanish trans. as *El escritor y su obra. Entrevistas de Georges Charbonnier con Jorge Luis Borges.* Mexico City: Siglo XXI, 1967.

Christ, Ronald. *The Narrow Act: Borges' Art of Allusion.* New York: New York University Press, 1969.

Genette, Gérard. "La Littérature selon Borges." In *Jorge Luis Borges,* 323–327. Paris: L'Herne, 1964.

————. Enl. version, "L'Utopie littéraire." In *Figures,* 123–132. Paris: Seuil, 1966.

Gutiérrez Girardot, Rafael. *Jorge Luis Borges. Ensayo de interpretación.* Madrid: Insula, 1959.

Jurado, Alicia. *Genio figura de Jorge Luis Borges,* 3rd ed. Buenos Aires: Editorial Universitaria de Buenos Aires, 1980.

Lindstrom, Naomi. *Jorge Luis Borges. A Study of the Short Fiction.* Boston: Twayne, 1990.

Matamoro, Blas. *Diccionario privado de Jorge Luis Borges.* Madrid: Altalena, 1980.

Milleret, Jean de. *Entretiens avec Jorge Luis Borges.* Paris: Pierre Belfond, 1967. Spanish trans. as *Entrevistas con Jorge Luis Borges.* Caracas: Monte Avila, 1971.

Molloy, Silvia. *Las letras de Borges.* Buenos Aires: Sudamericana, 1979.

Pérez, Alberto Julián. *Poética de la prosa de Jorge Luis Borges. Hacia una crítica bakhtiniana de la literatura.* Madrid: Gredos, 1986.

Prieto, Adolfo. *Borges y la nueva generación.* Buenos Aires: Letras Universitarias, 1954.

Rest, Jaime. *El laberinto del universo. Borges y el pensamiento nominalista.* Buenos Aires: Fausto, 1976.

Rivas, Jorge Andrés. *Alrededor de la obra de Jorge Luis Borges.* Santiago del Estero, Argentina: Dirección General de Cultura, 1980; Buenos Aires: Fernando García Gambeiro, 1984.

Rodríguez Monegal, Emir. *Borges par lui-même.* Paris: Seuil, 1970. Spanish trans. as *Borges por él mismo.* Barcelona: Laia, 1984.

———. *Jorge Luis Borges: A Literary Biography.* New York: E. P. Dutton, 1978. Trans. Homero Alsina Thevenet as *Borges. Una biografía literaria.* Mexico City: Fondo de Cultura Económica, 1987.

Rodríguez Monegal, Emir, and Alastair Reid, eds. *Borges: A Reader.* New York: E. P. Dutton, 1981.

Silvestri, Laura. "Borges y la pragmática de lo fantástico." *Jorge Luis Borges: Variaciones interpretativas sobre sus procedimientos literarios y bases epistemológicas,* pp. 49–66. Ed. Karl Alfred Blüher and Alfonso de Toro. Frankfurt: Vervuert, 1992.

Sosnowski, Saúl. *Borges y la cabala. La búsqueda del verbo.* Buenos Aires: Pardes, 1986. First ed., 1976.

Stabb, Martin S. *Borges Revisited.* Boston: Twayne, 1991. Originally *Jorge Luis Borges.* New York: Twayne, 1970.

Sturrock, John. *Paper Tigers. The Ideal Fictions of Jorge Luis Borges.* Oxford: Clarendon Press, 1977.

Updike, John. "Books: The Author as Librarian." *The New Yorker,* (Oct. 30, 1965): 223–246.

Vasquez, Maria Esther. *Borges, imagenes, memorias, diáglogos.* Caracas: Monte Avila Editores, 1977.

Wheelock, Carter. *The Mythmaker. A Study of Motif and Symbol in the Short Stories of Jorge Luis Borges.* Austin: University of Texas Press, 1969.

Woscoboinik, Julio. *El secreto de Borges. Indagación psicoanalítica de su obra.* Buenos Aires: Trieb, 1988.

Daniel Altamiranda

BORGHELLO, JOSÉ MARÍA (Argentina; 194?)

Born in Buenos Aires, Borghello, from the time he was two years old, lived in Mendoza, where he completed his secondary education. After writing his first

novel, *Que los niños huyan de mí* (Let the Children Run Away from Me; 1974),
he returned to Buenos Aires with a letter of introduction for Abelardo Arías,
also from Mendoza. Their meeting was the beginning of Borghello's deep
friendship with the author of *Alamos talados* (Felled Poplars; 1958), who gave
him literary advice and later introduced him to Poldy Bird, who published *Que
los niños* under her imprint, Ediciones Orión.

The novel deals with the life of Gustavo, who believes that children inhabit
a malignant universe tied to the forces of nature and that they dog his footsteps.
His paranoia impels him to pursue them obsessively, until he finally kills a boy
and throws his body down a sewer. The work, which has echoes of the Marquis
de Sade, Julien Green's tortured characters and the melancholy and decadent
world of Henri de Montherlant, is an unrestrained psychological inquiry into the
most forbidden territories of human thought, and its violence proposes the il-
lumination of the darkest corners of the unconscious. These scenes, which are
often harrowing for the reader, are combined with images of refined cruelty and
profound eroticism. As its two printings and the criticism on it indicate, the
novel was well received, although its presentation at the Feria del Libro (Book
Fair) in Mendoza was blocked by the organizers, who literally threw Borghello
out of the hall, alleging that "*Que los niños huyan de mí* was an immoral work
totally at odds with their Western and Christian principles."

Las razones del lobo (The Wolf's Reasons; 1974) is a volume of short stories
in which Borghello once again enters the dark zones of being, exploring his
fears and nightmares in a struggle with madness that poses a sarcastic, despairing
and subtle threat to the characters. The author included in this volume a story,
"La mirada del otro" (The Glance of the Other), in which there is the apparent
consummation of a homosexual relationship, although a deeper reading of the
text reveals that, as the title states, it is nothing more than a profound obsession
provoked by the solitude that drives the character to split and create an ideal I
to accompany him. Borghello's second book also had an enthusiastic reception.

Borghello required ten years to complete his third work, *Plaza de los lirios*
(Plaza of the Lilies; 1985). This ambitious novel, which carries the subtitle "*Una
particular relación, sin concesiones ni excusas* (A Private Story, Without Concessions or Excuses), is, in the words of the author, "undoubtedly a re-creation
of my own biography recast in the broad terms of fiction." Borghello moves
homosexual experience, which is usually played out against the backdrop of
large cities, to a rural Argentine setting—specifically, the province of Mendoza.
The novel also seeks to show in a parallel fashion the decadence of Argentina's
wealthy rural society and its confrontation with less powerful classes and with
the rising bourgeoisie on which it is ultimately forced to depend in order to
maintain a certain standing, or at least a certain brilliance. At the same time,
the novel casts light on what are perhaps the most marginal of gay demimondes,
the world of truckers' bars, slums and cockfight rings. This is a world inhabited
by individuals with noms de guerre like At Your Service, Immaculata, Pussy
Cat, Helen of Troy, the Countess, the Blue Angel and the Queen Mother. They

move in this world with almost complete liberty, speaking their own jargon and acknowledging each other in code because they know that they have been rejected "by the ranks of the normal people who make up society" (34).

This is a world very close to that of Jean Genet in *Diary of a Thief* and *Our Lady of the Flowers*. These characters, who always self-identify in the feminine, inhabit a dream realm that parallels the heterosexual world: engagement, virginity, homemaker, faithful wife, wedding gown. These are all elements that stand in opposition to the vision held by Flavio, the central character, who answers them by saying: "You could almost say you want that world with its principles, its limitations, and its resentments" (215). Flavio is a transitional character who navigates between two worlds, two periods, two opposing forms of thought, which for his "girlfriends" makes him a traumatized closet case. In his daily life, where everyone is aware of his homosexuality, he never ceases to be Flavio, but when he inhabits this other world, he becomes At Your Service. Yet he feels he does not belong to either world, and he is the most marginal of the marginal characters of the novel.

The title of the novel is taken from one of the places the members of the group frequent, a plaza that has seen better days and is no longer visited by decent people. This plaza in ruins is an obvious parallel to the decadent family mansion whose past splendors survive only in its inhabitants' memories. Flavio evinces a very complex personality based on his lack of definition, his individualism, his boundless egocentrism, his mystical features and above all, his prejudices that are part and parcel of the dying social class to which he belongs. The narrative of his complex and always unequal amorous relationships develops each of the characteristics mentioned. His final disappearance, which is also the beginning of the novel, is a metaphor for the extinction of those demimondes through which he moves.

Plaza de los lirios did not have the same success as Borghello's previous books, and it was virtually ignored by the media. The April 13, 1986, literary supplement of *La gaceta de Tucumán* (Tucumán Gazette) published a review signed by Clara María Murga that deals only with putative technical errors of the novel, at no point mentioning the moral, psychological or sociological values Borghello deals with. The book's slight commercial success is owed to the word of mouth that spread first within the Argentine gay community, then among others able to appreciate good literature, and the curious.

WORKS

Plaza de los lirios. Buenos Aires: Editorial Galerna, 1985.
Que los niños huyan de mí. Buenos Aires: Ediciones Orión, 1973.
Las razones del lobo. Buenos Aires: Ediciones Orión, 1974.
La salida y otros encierros. Buenos Aires: Editorial Galerna, 1992.

The quotes from Borghello are from my personal interview, Buenos Aires, August 8, 1989.

Osvaldo R. Sabino

BRUNET, MARTA (Chile; 1897–1967) _____

Brunet was one of the first Latin American women writers to deal with male homosexuality, in her novel *Amasijo* (Mixture; 1962), in which she utilizes psychoanalytical parameters to establish what is identified as the sexual deviance of its protagonist, Julián García, from his birth to his suicide. He is born after an accident in which his father is killed and his mother becomes an invalid. Brunet attributes García's homosexuality and his fascination with his mother's breasts to the fact that she breast-fed him long after he had ceased to be a baby. This, according to psychoanalysis, makes him a homosexual due to a fixation at the oral level. The mother desired a daughter, and when Julián was born, she treated him as a girl, letting his hair grow long, calling him "my little Goldilocks," and dressing him in pink. Thus, the psychoanalytical premise that the mother is responsible for the male child's sexual orientation is stressed.

Brunet shows her discomfort with the topic she has chosen in her treatment of Julián's emerging sexuality. She circumvents actual descriptions, referring instead to what she calls "the act" and avoiding the word *homosexual* throughout the text. Julián seduces a peasant boy, Florindo, whom he later abandons after helping him become an actor. The relationship between Florindo and Julián develops within parameters reminiscent of those through which females are socialized into accepting a passive, dependent role with regard to males. That is, women are always described as younger, less educated, lacking in economic power and social standing. This pattern is also found when homosexual relationships are described in many Latin American novels.

Julián suffers from self-destructive impulses motivated by his self-loathing because of his inability to father children to carry on the family name. He hangs himself on the stage where his latest successful play is being presented. This fatal ending is canonical in the sense that when dealing with homosexual characters, literary conventions indicate that they must die at the end of their stories, as do women—Emma Bovary, Anna Karenina, Nana—who transgress sociosexual norms. Brunet's novel is a good example of psychoanalytical homophobia as represented in a literary text, even though Kessel Schwartz has called it "a psychological study in depth of a homosexual" (249), adding that it "presents us with a textbook case of repression, shame and guilt" (250).

WORKS

Amasijo. Santiago, Chile: Editorial Impresora Zig-Zag, 1962.

CRITICISM

Schwartz, Kessel. "Homosexuality as a Theme in Representative Contemporary Spanish American Novels." *Kentucky Romance Quarterly* 22.2 (1975): 247–257.
Alfredo Villanueva

BULLRICH, SILVINA (Argentina; 1915) ─────────

Bullrich is the author of *Mal don* (Bad Deal; 1973), a novel with three narrative threads corresponding to the voices of its three protagonists: Diego, his sister Clara, and his friend Tommy. All grow up in the summer resort that gives its name to the novel, which is a reference to the distribution of marked cards in a card game. Bullrich adopts a deterministic stance with regard to her characters. Following parameters from nineteenth-century bourgeois ideology, she creates in Tommy a homosexual character reflecting prevailing cultural stereotypes. By means of a dialectical sleight of hand, she identifies marginal groups whose lack of control over their own sexuality relegates them to the category of the other; at the same time, their sexual appetites are mystified, thus justifying their persecution as a threat to normative bourgeois structures.

Bullrich makes Tommy the mouthpiece for the theory of putatively secret societies whose members are invisible but at the same time wield real power. The first of these is the homosexual minority in Argentinean society; Bullrich sets out to expose the homosexual freemasonry that, according to her, manipulates Argentine literary life. Diego believes that the choice of literature as a profession by a homosexual constitutes the best of luck. Moreover, the relationship between Tommy and Eduardo, his older, married, richer and socially prominent lover, follows a common pattern of female dependency. Tommy also feels the pressure to exhibit heterosexual behavior: being without a girlfriend makes one suspect. Such pressure reveals a cultural premise equating singleness with homosexuality; the homosexual is culturally obliged to form a heterosexual relationship through marriage. In a vicious circle, marriage makes him respectably invisible, masks his otherness and turns him into a threat to bourgeois morality. The theme of freemasonries is related to the theme of appearance vs. reality. Reality is a perception: one is what one appears to be. For both Tommy and Eduardo, bisexuality represents a compromise, a forced choice. Society demands marriage and procreation; once the norm has been satisfied, homosexuals may be allowed to pursue their heterodox drives. Latin American society, as described by Bullrich, grounds its code of conduct for males on the *appearance* of heterosexuality.

On the other hand, Bullrich proposes that apparently sexual categories are really localized within a power scheme. Thus Diego, who is heterosexual, comments that he was the French mistress of those economically emancipated females who could afford going to bed with a poor student. Tommy, as long as he utilizes his sexuality economically—that is, sells it—merely follows a pattern already established with respect to feminine sexuality. If this occurs within a heterosexual context—woman as merchandise—it is allowed. But when it occurs within a homosexual context—the male body as merchandise for other males—it goes against the Phallic Order shaping the hegemonic social infrastructure. Tommy has two options: to marry Clara or to find support in the homosexual freemasonry. Bullrich refuses to accept the possibility that Tommy may have sex with men for pleasure. Pleasure is the blind spot in her discourse.

Mal don offers still another version of the homosexual as the other, this time as the invisible threat to the social order, whose sexuality is tied to his drive for power and social control—all the more dangerous an enemy because he cannot be as readily identified as other marginalized groups. The homosexual as a scapegoat for social and cultural ills is a frequent theme in the Spanish American novel.

WORKS

Mal don. Buenos Aires: Emecé Editores, 1973.

Alfredo Villanueva

C

CALVA [PRATT], JOSÉ RAFAEL
(Mexico; 1953) ——————————————————————

Currently residing in Washington, D.C., where he directs a workshop on creative writing and conducts research on issues related to contemporary music, Calva was born in Mexico City and studied communications at the Universidad Iberoamericana. After participating in one of the university's literary workshops run by Marco Antonio Campos, he became a contributor to a number of journals dedicated to music, such as *Pauta* (Measure) and *Alta fidelidad* (High Fidelity). He publishes short fiction, articles on literature and book and film reviews in *La palabra y el hombre* (The Word and Mankind), *Tierra adentro* (Inland), *Vaso comunicante* (Communicating Vessel), and *Sábado* (Saturday), the weekly supplement of the newspaper *Unomásuno* (One plus one).

Primarily recognized as a writer of prose narratives, Calva published his first volume of stories, *Variaciones y fuga sobre la clase media* (Variations and Fugue on the Middle Class) in 1980. Orchestrated around a musical structure of point and counterpoint, these texts form a group of satirical tales about the dreams, ambitions, pretensions and delusions of those inhabitants of Mexico's capital who either aspire to the ranks of the middle class or who fall from grace in it. A mosaic of personality quirks, the effects of conspicuous consumption, extravagant lifestyles, false modesty and routine heterosexual encounters lacking intensity or passion, especially on the part of the woman (as in the story "Florentina"), this collection clearly established the tone of complacency and self satisfaction against which the novel *Utopía gay* (Gay Utopia) railed when it exploded on the literary scene in 1983.

It took Calva five years to find a publishing house in Mexico willing to accept the manuscript of his first novel, given its deliberate assumption of outlaw sexuality as the viable foundation for a future society, its carnivalesque transgression of moral (to say nothing of biological) laws and, perhaps most of all, its flaunting of erotic fantasy as a utopian haven from the rigid constraints—political, sexual, economic—of traditional Mexican (and Western) culture. In light of the heated polemic surrounding the publication of Luis Zapata's novel *El vampiro de la colonia Roma* in 1979 (published in English as *Adonis García*), such difficulties might almost be foreseen. But what of critic Luis Mario Schneider's assessment that what he terms "homosexual literature" (Schneider, 83) in Mexico has a certain historical tradition, that it begins neither with Zapata nor with Calva but instead with Miguel Barbachano Ponce in 1964, at least fifteen years earlier? Something different is happening in 1983, therefore, with *Utopía gay*, which, at least on the surface, does no more than reproduce a heterosexual union (even with child) in a union between two men. It might be the almost delirious philosophical passages, or the satirical reduction of entire systems of moral values to the level of the absurd or perhaps the fact that the avowedly homosexual protagonists, Carlos and Adrián, enjoy their relationship and are led neither to desperation nor to suicide (as is José Toledo in Barbachano Ponce's novel), but instead to a matter-of-fact celebration of it beyond the limits of the "possible" or the verisimilar (according to whom?), into the realm of utopia.

While David Foster has pointed out the novel's evident retake on the Christian story of the Immaculate Conception, one that sets up a cosmography of symbols and belief structures that form the basis of Western civilization, this might be examined in another mode. For Adrián's role as "padrimadre" (father–mother; 174) is not just to question the biological polarity of male/female by uniting the two in one body, or through the alternation of masculine and feminine adjectives in his interior monologues; nor is he interested in being a transvestite, though he admits having a passion for men's clothing (12) and laments the need to give it up during pregnancy. Rather, the assumption of Adrián's pregnancy makes evident the presence of sexual activity between himself and his lover; it is the public admission of a physical relationship (whether reproducing the norms of a heterosexual couple or not) that society is loath to recognize as a "natural" or desirable possibility. It is the visible contradiction of the "immaculate" part of the conception.

And what if two gay men dream the same dreams as a heterosexual couple— can Adrián's remarks about wanting his lover's child so badly that his wish came true (15) be interpreted as a closing of the socially imposed distance between gay and straight, parallel to the collapsing of male and female into one theoretically self-perpetuating biological being? Is this triumphal situation too transgressive—not estranged or alien enough—for heterosexual society to bear? Calva's attempt to address specific issues of homosexual identity during his official presentation of the novel to critics and the general public in June 1978 dissolved into what an anonymous reviewer termed a group therapy session (16) in which any crossovers between the self-identified heterosexual members of the audience and a generalized concept of homosexuality were essentially abrogated; to displace Carlos and Adrián's desires from the realm of the impossible is to postulate an alternative reality not far removed from the actual world— except, of course, for the "problematic" element of the two men themselves, whose love would then be "legitimated" by a scandalous proximity to the "norm."

Such a situation is ironic, given the fact that Adrián's pregnancy is the impetus for the couple's consideration of a "new" social order separate from the present one, freed from a class structure and in harmony with nature (thereby implying its own "naturalness"), one in which any hostility toward a child with two male parents would be nonexistent. Taking the biological impossibility as a premise, albeit outside the bounds of empirical logic, in his novel Calva still manages to pursue the construction of a family structure. Though projected toward the future and the erasure of all social and sexual stigmata from such a trinity of founding members, we are obliged to ask whether this vision of an alternative space proposes a substantially new concept, or whether it reproduces the demarcations of separate and essentially unequal spaces already present in Mexican society. In other words, the nightclubs, bars, discos, baths, and so on that function as sites of self-affirmation for marginal or alternative sexual identities may be conceived as models for Adrián's utopian civilization, their cue to him being the need to look elsewhere to "belong." These clearly demarcated zones of tolerance, the result of an official policy of liberal open-mindedness (called a "pose" by Carlos), segregate those considered socially and/or sexually unhealthy and deviant while not, at least overtly, persecuting them. Adrián's imagined paradise would establish a base from which to start anew, but what of the constant pressure from the rest of society, no member of which seems to survive intact by the end of the novel's biting attacks but which is not destroyed. In his attempt to wall others out, perhaps Adrián is walling himself into a permanent ghetto of "otherness."

Foster's discussion of Utopía gay stresses the power of utopian fantasy to criticize the shortcomings of the status quo, while Schneider's brief reflections on the novel underscore the main characters' alignment with a traditional family structure—father, mother, child—based on gendered divisions of labor and identity. Schneider finds the "normal vicissitudes" (86) of a heterosexual couple in Carlos and Adrián's relationship, down to the announcement of a pregnancy on the first page; for him, the literary elements of irony and satire are the tools used to combat discourses of exclusion by revealing their arbitrariness. In an essay on the Mexican novelists Luis Zapata and Calva, Claudia Schaefer-Rodríguez situates their texts within broader social and ideological frameworks to examine them in the light of the ambiguities produced by a "politics of tolerance" and the interplay between utopian and dystopian visions. Among the reviews of Utopía gay when it first appeared, one by Sandro Cohen stands out for its double-edged judgment. On the one hand, it praises the dialogue and literary techniques used by the author to turn society topsy-turvy and to question—with humor—unconscious assumptions about social and sexual conventions. On the other hand, Cohen goes on to assuage the "fears" of the reader who might be "shocked" by either the narrators of the novel or their demolition of the presuppositions of every inhabitant of Mexico City they come across, gay or straight. It is not for nothing that Cohen subtitles his essay "Don't Anyone Be Offended," for he assures us in his closing paragraphs that despite Carlos and Adrián's most fervent wishes, their utopia is still uninhabited.

If *Utopía gay* is a paean to the liberating possibilities of erotic (specifically homoerotic) fantasy with overtones of humor and sarcasm, then the novella *El jinete azul* (The Blue Horseman; 1985) is an ode to darker erotic desires tinged with a much more sensual, material and corporeal cast. Published shortly after Calva's first novel, this brief narrative sets the stage for its first-person tale of a search for sexual ecstasy by addressing the relativity of the term *sadism* and by vindicating its potential for undermining conventionalized forms of social violence by introducing the flesh of the human body as the vehicle for the ritual expression of violent passion as art.

Situated on the cutting edge of the surgical steel blade wielded by the surgeon/narrator to probe the depths of the bodies of young men he picks up on the streets of New York City, *El jinete azul* represents the essential commingling of violence and pleasure preserved at the orgasmic moment of the death of the victims. Instead of political violence, such as that perpetrated by nations in world wars, or the civil strife in Bangladesh or Biafra, or the decimation of entire populations in Hiroshima, Nagasaki or Vietnam (all of which he seems to equate with a masculine need to dominate and oppress), the narrator substitutes his own intense erotic rapture at the complete and "violent" possession of another body and spirit, following lengthy episodes of stalking his objects of desire in an urban world full of what he sees as "useless" and unfulfilling acts of violence.

Against a backdrop of classical music—Mozart's Requiem and *Don Giovanni*, for instance, as he dismembers the corpse of his latest lover—Keith Lawless tells the tale of creating a separate and purposefully "criminal" world for himself inside the darkened "cloister" of his apartment, from which he excludes any external interference, from the light of day to the need for clothing. Following the paths suggested by his readings of the Marquis de Sade, Thomas de Quincey, Edgar Allan Poe, Leopold von Sacher-Masoch, Albert Camus, Saint John of the Cross, and Jean Genet, the narrator describes his thoughts and activities as spiritual exercises leading to a kind of perverse perfection and purification. Since he believes the only real "perversity" exists in the consumer-oriented, processed food, prefabricated, homophobic prison of society outside his 42nd Street apartment, the narrator assumes his self-professed vampirism as an attempt at unity with his beloved in the pleasurable penetration of the phallic Toledo steel scalpel into Richard's chest. (This scene and others seem to be inspired almost directly by suggestive texts by the Marquis de Sade or Georges Bataille, with their ritualistic orgies of the flesh functioning as reaffirmations of the almost religious intensity of desire.)

By having ultimate control over the life and death of the young men, and by subsequently ingesting their flesh in an act reminiscent of sympathetic magic wherein they become part of his biological being, Lawless lays claim to his own desires at their moment of fruition and before they lose any of their intensity, rather than living at the mercy of those he denounces as the real devourers of human beings: wealthy men, such as his father, who have made their fortunes on the flesh and blood of masses of sacrificial victims. Death becomes an aesthetic moment chosen to preserve the peak of pleasure, beauty and youth. What the narrator does not count on, however, is the nostalgia for this particular lover, which leads him to the maximum expression of personal free will—to die in the same way as Richard and by the same knife (in the hands of a man as enamored of him as he was of the dead man), albeit in an almost romanticized effort to "join him" beyond good and evil.

It is obvious that what is at work in *El jinete azul* is more complex than a literal tale of anthropophagy, especially in the light of straight society's penchant for representing gay men as cannibalistic, self-consuming (whether by AIDS or by other virulent means), obsessive carriers of death and disease living in the endangered body politic. Calva's text places us squarely in the realm of figurative discourse that takes on the stereotypes judged to constitute a "homosexual identity" and carries them to extremes, in general terms much as *Utopía gay* does with a machista vision of homosexuality. But in this sexual and textual world, the negative becomes a natural virtue, and criminality—as Genet has suggested—transcends everyday reality to assume the role of a healthy transgressive identity going in the face of social conventions to establish, in its own way, an alternative "utopia" (which some might term a dystopia).

It is perhaps not surprising that no criticism has been published to date on this novella, given its use of sadomasochistic fantasy as the point of departure for a fairly lengthy disquisition on homoerotic desire and fulfillment. In a short essay written in 1992 for *Sábado* (Saturday), Calva states that Mexico and the United States (where he now resides) are fairly even with regard to the opportunities they offer for the expression of gay culture, with the exception of what he calls a subculture of sadomasochism that he finds "underdeveloped" (7) in Mexico. While not pretending to quantify or to qualify the existence or potential for such a subculture, it is evident that this variety of human response to sexual desires remains the least represented in Mexican public culture. *El jinete azul* goes a long way toward exploring such an erotic impulse and the motivations of the narrating subject. In the meantime, however, criticism has gravitated toward *Utopía gay*. Even book reviews of Calva's texts ceased to appear around the time of publication of *El jinete azul*.

WORKS

"Barbie va a la playa." *Sábado*, supp. to *Unomásuno*, July 25, 1992, p. 7.
El jinete azul. Mexico City: Katún, 1985.

Utopía gay. Mexico City: Oasis, 1983.

Variaciones y fuga sobre la clase media. Jalapa, Mexico: Universidad Veracruzana, 1980.

CRITICISM

Aguilera, Marco Tulio. "Alegato de José Rafael Calva, *Utopía gay*." *Excélsior*, sec. "Cultura," Apr. 17, 1983, p. 2.

Bermúdez, María Elvira. *"Utopía gay* descontaminar por la risa." *Revista mexicana de cultura* 16 (June 12, 1983): 10.

Cohen, Sandro. *"Utopía gay*: Que nadie se ofenda." *Casa del tiempo* 31–32 (July/Aug. 1983): 82–83.

Coronado, Juan. *"Utopía gay."* *Sábado*, supp. to *Unomásuno*, Aug. 6, 1983, p. 11.

Foster, David William. *Gay and Lesbian Themes in Latin American Writing*, 136–139. Austin: University of Texas Press, 1991.

"Fue presentado el libro *Utopía gay* de José Rafael Calva." *Unomásuno*, July 25, 1983, p. 16.

Katz, Alejandro. "Doble transgresión: La relación y la fantasía homosexual." *Sábado*, supp. to *Unomásuno*, Sept. 17, 1983, p. 10.

Reyes, Juan José. "Auténtica utopía." *El semanario cultural*, supp. to *Novedades* 61 (June 19, 1983): 3.

Schaefer-Rodríguez, Claudia. "The Power of Subversive Imagination: Homosexual Utopian Discourse in Contemporary Mexican Literature." *Latin American Literary Review* 33 (1989): 29–41.

Schneider, Luis Mario. "El tema homosexual en la nueva narrativa mexicana." *Casa del tiempo* 5.49–50 (Feb.–Mar. 1985): 82–86.

Toledo, Alejandro. "Escritura Calva en la novela gay." *Revista mexicana de cultura* 54 (Mar. 4, 1984): 11.

Trejo Fuentes, Ignacio. "A propósito de *Utopía gay*: La literatura homosexual." *Excélsior*, sec. "Cultura," July 31, 1983, p. 1; Aug. 1, 1983, p. 9.

Claudia Schaefer-Rodríguez

CAMINHA, ADOLFO (Brazil; 1867–1897) _____

Adolfo Caminha's *Bom-Crioulo* (published in English under the same title, which means "good nigger"; 1895), the first Brazilian naturalist novel to be conceived and written after the inauguration of the Republic, looks back in history. This technique of providing the historical background in which Amaro's story is embedded, besides situating him as a runaway slave, provides the story with a perspective that functions as both background and foreground for the development of the plot, and that operates on several levels within the narrative.

Once the first layer of the narrative is penetrated, *Bom-Crioulo* opens up as a meditation on Brazil as the place where the text was produced as the result of an intricate process of projection, compensation, repression and displacement. This omission of the external reality is an attempt to render that reality not as a commonsense external reality, nor even as a conventional historical narrative encountered in history books; rather, *Bom-Crioulo* is the rendering of the historical Real as a form of subtext. The rifts and discontinuities that constitute the text as a heterogeneous and multifaceted artifact ultimately represent the Real as an "absent cause." In other words, it does not matter that the text chooses to ignore the historical circumstances in which it was produced; what does matter is that they are ignored, because this omission points out the rifts and discontinuities.

Bom-Crioulo has traditionally been seen as a love story. However, to see it only as a story about homosexual love is to give the novel the character of a unitary, totalized universe, which impoverishes the work and denies its comprehensive discussion about the ideological constructs underlying the Brazilian life of the time.

The plot of the novel is seemingly very simple: a black sailor, Amaro (known as Bom-Crioulo), falls in love with a white cabin boy, Aleixo, and starts living this love on the ship where they work and in a rented room at the house of a Portuguese woman. This love is eventually transformed into crime when Bom-Crioulo finds out that Aleixo is having an affair with the woman. Bom-Crioulo then kills Aleixo and is taken to prison. In the last scenes of the novel, Bom-Crioulo is taken away by the police while the crowd looks at Aleixo's bloody corpse. On this level, it seems that the story does not present any novelty—there are countless stories of mad loves and passionate crimes. However, some more complex factors woven into the text transform this novel—only eighty pages long in the original version—into a very special case in Brazilian literature.

Although it might seem surprising that as early as 1893 a Brazilian novel deals with a love triangle involving homosexual love, the treatment of homosexual love is not a new subject in the Portuguese-language literature; it was the theme of *O barão de Lavos* (The Baron of Lavos), published in Portugal in 1891. However, *Bom-Crioulo* is the story of a homosexual love between a black man and a white man; more novel still, the black man is a former slave; and perhaps most novel of all, the woman, Carolina, is Portuguese. In the working out of this love story, several gender alignments and realignments are in operation, and they represent other levels of displacement that include class and race relations that, in their turn, point to even more complex ideological alignments.

Halfway through the novel, Bom-Crioulo goes back to his room in Carolina's house. The room, furnished by him and Aleixo, has a number of odd objects they have collected around the city. Bom-Crioulo lies down on the bed and starts inspecting the room. The fact that he has the emperor's picture in his room is no great surprise: both Amaro and Aleixo, being lower class, collect lithographs from magazines and plaster them on the walls of their little abode. However, the choice of a picture showing the emperor, an old patriarch, smiling indulgently points to other levels of significance. It is not clear at this point of the story if the emperor is still in power. The text says that Amaro escaped from the farm where he was a slave when he was eighteen, and he met Aleixo when he was thirty. In the twelve years of Amaro's life in the navy, the freedom of the slaves and the beginning of the Republic (1889) might have taken place, but the text makes no reference to such public affairs. The story—written in 1893—leaves this matter in suspense, as if the external political life, or any social life outside Amaro and Aleixo's relationship, does not have to be explicated. Since this is, after all, the story of a black man, why does the text choose to fall silent about these important details of Brazilian social life while clearly mentioning the highest figure—the emperor—who commands this life?

The text, by consciously avoiding such references, calls attention to the novel's special grammar; it proposes to re-create the outside world in a more intense and minute way, and the saturation of the sailors' lives with historical references would interfere with the intensity of the issues the text wants to discuss. Another reason is that the emperor, with the beard of a patriarch, functions as an organizing principle under which Bom-Crioulo and his story can take place. However, Bom-Crioulo goes beyond this point when he says that the emperor is "his man." Why does Bom-Crioulo choose to identify with a man who, obviously, was responsible for the continuation of the state of slavery into which many like him were born? And why stress the emperor's "benign" patriarchal mien?

In the novel, the mechanisms of law, taboo and censorship work themselves out in various ways. For Amaro, the Bom-Crioulo, his homosexuality is a given. He has completely assumed his sexual orientation and has found a partner, Aleixo. The beginnings of his life are dim in his memory, and in the text are organized around the fact that he was born a slave; even his examination for admission to the navy is a replay of the examination slave buyers gave to their prospective purchases. The fact of Bom-Crioulo's inescapable powerlessness extends itself to the very property of his body. As a slave, he does not have the right to possess anything. He is, instead, a thing possessed; as a sailor, although he has a small salary, he is the property of the navy. The only realm in which he has freedom is the choice of his sexual orientation.

It is, however, not a freedom that was given to him as his birthright. In the beginning of his life in the navy, Bom-Crioulo did not know he did not belong with the heterosexual group. His unawareness of his imminent homosexuality leads him to explore heterosexual life, in which he ends up a pitiful figure. Nevertheless, this sexual orientation may be a trope through which the text aligns itself politically, thus going beyond issues of sexuality itself, and it may be the reason for Bom-Crioulo's identification with the emperor. If there is a sense in which the emperor, and nobody else, represents Bom-Crioulo, it follows that Bom-Crioulo, and nobody else, represents the emperor. What does it mean to have a text in which the old imperial regime is figured in the form of a black homosexual who reveres the ruler? Amaro does not want to be involved in allegedly feminine intrigues and falsities, preferring the company of his navy colleagues. Besides expressing his preference for bonding with males, Amaro is expressing the need to be closer to the center of power. Being powerless, he wants at least to associate himself with the most powerful; better still, he wants to be close to the powerful who can be benign to him.

Women do not represent any source of power in a social environment where the main figure has a benign patriarchal smile as his principal asset. But in what sense does this patriarchal system represent Amaro's choice of sexual orientation and of a partner in Aleixo? More important, how are his choices reflected in the representation of a Brazilian society that had just emancipated itself from an imperial to a republican state? His love for the cabin boy gives Bom-Crioulo the first free impulses in his life. However, these free impulses, which lead him to free choices, work against his liberty. After twelve years in the navy, Bom-Crioulo wants to stay on land. However, it is not the trips, nor the dangers nor the sacrifices that tie Amaro to land: it is the need to be closer to Aleixo. At this point, the dismantling of the dichotomy farm/slavery–navy/freedom comes as the onset of Amaro's consciousness that what he believed to be freedom is only a yoke on his neck, an obstacle to the full expression of his affection for Aleixo. This love represents both his first free action and the beginning of his real slavery. Now he is flogged and continually punished; now he bullies his colleagues, criticizes the officers and challenges their orders. It is necessary for Amaro to be free in order to be born as a homosexual, which itself becomes another form of subjection. The moment he enters the free world is not, therefore, the moment he discovers his subjectivity; rather, it is the moment he discovers his sexual orientation, only to have it simultaneously transformed into the denial of this subjectivity.

It is significant that after Amaro escapes from the farm where he was kept as a slave, he spends a night in a cage before he is accepted into the navy. It is as if, to become a free citizen, he has to be born again. The cage is a womb from which he sees the wonders awaiting him outside: a free country where boats sail free, crisscrossing the river in all directions. His crossing of the boundary between his previous life as a slave and the new life of freedom gives him two things: possession of his own body and a new identity, a new name, Bom-Crioulo, the Good Black Man. The tension between the (homo)sexual body and the goodness implied in the name explains a novel like *Bom-Crioulo*, which can be properly understood only if it is considered as a trope for the struggle among various signifiers to become the master signifier of a nation in the process of being stabilized.

Slavery, which at the time of the publication of *Bom-Crioulo* had just been officially abolished by the Golden Law, comes back in full force. It is significant that Bom-Crioulo is not a mulatto; he is a full-blooded black. Moreover, besides being a black, he has an indefinite origin: nobody knows where he comes from. If nobody knows where he is from, he can be from anywhere and from everywhere. There is a sense in which Amaro, the Good Black Man, is the unknown Brazil that lurks behind every Brazilian's Brazil—a mysterious, uncomprehended, uncategorizable entity that needs to be made part of the nascent country.

To accomplish the inclusion and incorporation of Bom-Crioulo and of what he represents into a Brazilian nationality, accommodations, and even punishments, will be necessary. The deployment of force in the novel can be understood in two ways. First, the punishment given by men (represented by the navy) is more immediate, aimed at a more public system of humiliation: Caminha denounced the brutality and unfairness of public floggings the navy inflicted on its sailors. But the punishment administered by the woman, Carolina, is more private. Second, precisely because it is more immediate and more physical, the punishment inflicted by men is more superficial, less lasting: Bom-Crioulo has been whipped several times, yet continues to do the things that bring about his public punishment. The kind of punishment from Carolina not only is more private and more lasting, it is also more decisive. It is because of her transformation of Aleixo into a heterosexual that Amaro ends up killing the cabin boy, thus destroying the reason for his punishment. It is no coincidence, therefore, that the play Carolina attends before the last appearance of Bom-Crioulo is *The Fall of the Bastille:* Bom-Crioulo's fortress is destroyed at last. Carolina, or the power system she comes to represent, finally distributes "justice" by having Bom-Crioulo kill Aleixo and having Bom-Crioulo transformed into a being without reason or rights.

The mode of punishment that the navy employs—the public flogging of its sailors—belongs to the category of spectacle and aims primarily at disciplining through physical suffering. The punishment Carolina mediates—Bom-Crioulo's imprisonment—belongs to the economy of suspended rights: now Bom-Crioulo loses the liberty to come and go that he acquired when he left the farm; he is definitively separated from the object of his love and, more important, because he is separated from Aleixo, he is severed from his own subjectivity that was born as a result of his love for the cabin boy. In sum, without liberty, without Aleixo and without his subjectivity, Bom-Crioulo reverts to a purely animal level.

Therefore, in this novel that does not portray a conventional family structure, nor a stable social structure, the lawlessness is merely apparent. The structures of control are very much in place and exert their force in several ways. Still, an important question remains: What specific social conditions made possible the emergence of *Bom-Crioulo* in the Brazil of the end of the nineteenth century?

Bom-Crioulo, the text says, admires the emperor, calls him "his man" and abhors "the republicans" who criticize him. Later, Bom-Crioulo equates himself with the emperor by saying that he is as good as the emperor. From the point of view of the social and political formation the emperor represents—aristocratic, patriarchal—it would seem that the former slave has nothing to do with the structure of domination represented by the emperor. Yet, once he conquers Aleixo, Bom-Crioulo becomes a replica of the emperor: he rules over his charge, Aleixo, both as father and king and as a lover. The structure of domination reproduces itself endlessly, as in the phenomenon of the facing mirrors: even the seemingly least powerful person—Aleixo—provides a replica of the patriarchal system embodied in the emperor when he attempts to dominate Carolina.

It is as if, once fallen, the emperor rules more pervasively by having the power system he embodied reflect itself more decisively on several levels of society. Because Bom-Crioulo, a black homosexual, is shown as the emperor's great admirer, it seems that homosexuality is the figuration that the text proposes for the structure of power. Precisely because the word *homosexual* does not appear in the text, because the perpetration of this homosexual love is hidden under blankets or behind locked doors, it is more installed and more real, and can represent that which is not named: the Republic itself, already in existence when the novel was first published.

WORKS

Bom-Crioulo. Rio de Janeiro: Domingues de Magalhães, 1895. English version as *Bom-Crioulo: The Black Man and the Cabin Boy*. Trans. E. A. Lacey. San Francisco: Gay Sunshine Press, 1982.
Cartas literárias. Rio de Janeiro: Aldina, 1895.
Judite e lágrimas de um crente. Rio de Janeiro, 1887.
No país dos yankees. Rio de Janeiro, 1895.
A normalista. Rio de Janeiro: Magalhães, 1892.
A tentação. Rio de Janeiro: Lemmert, 1896.
Vôos incertos. Rio de Janeiro, 1886.

CRITICISM

Alcoforado, Maria Leticia Guedes. "*Bom-Crioulo* de Adolfo e a França." *Revista de letras* 28 (1988): 85–93.
Araripe Júnior, Tristão de Alencar. "*A normalista*, por Adolfo Caminha." In his *Obra crítica*, 2.319–328. Rio de Janeiro: Casa de Rui Barbosa, 1960.
Arruda, Breno. *Caminhos perdidos*, 99–120. Rio de Janeiro: Lux, 1924.
Broca, Brito. *Horas de leitura*, 231–236. Rio de Janeiro: Instituto Nacional do Livro, 1955.
Cavalcanti, Valdemar. "O enjeitado Adolfo Caminha." In *O romance brasileiro, de 1752 a 1930*, 179–190. Ed. Aurélio Buarque de Holanda. Rio de Janeiro: O Cruzeiro, 1952.
Dantas, Paulo. "Adolfo Caminha, escritor revolucionário." *Revista brasiliense* 8 (1956): 94–103.
Foster, David William. "Adolfo Caminha's *Bom-Crioulo*: A Founding Text of Brazilian Gay Literature." *Chasqui* 17.2 (1988): 13–23. Also in Foster's *Gay and Lesbian Themes in Latin American Writing*, 9–22. Austin: University of Texas Press, 1991.
Lopes Júnior, Francisco Caetano. "*Bom-Crioulo*: Between Love and Death." In *Proceedings of the Black Image in Latin American Culture Conference*, 230–240. Slippery Rock, Pa.: Slippery Rock University, 1989.
Montenegro, Abelardo F. *O romance cearense*, 70–76. Fortaleza, Brazil: Tipografía Royal, 1953.
Mota, Leonardo. *A padaria espiritual*, 132–138. Fortaleza, Brazil: Edésio, 1939.

Pereira, Lúcia Miguel. *Prosa de ficção, de 1879 a 1920*, 164–172. Rio de Janeiro: José Olympio, 1950.

Pessoa, Frota. "Adolfo Caminha." In his *Crítica e polêmica*, 215–233. Rio de Janeiro: Artur Gurgulino, 1902.

Ribeiro, João Felipe de Sabóia. *Alguns aspectos de Adolfo Caminha (à margem de sua obra e vida)*. Rio de Janeiro: Tuy, 1964.

———. *O romancista Adolfo Caminha, 1867–1967: Em comemoração de seu centenário*. Rio de Janeiro: Pongetti, 1967.

———. *Roteiro de Adolfo Caminha*. Rio de Janeiro: Livraria São José, 1957.

Sodré, Nelson Werneck. *O naturalismo no Brasil*, 191–195. Rio de Janeiro: Editora Civilização Brasileira, 1965.

Süssekind, Flora. *Tal Brasil, qual romance? Uma ideologia estética e sua história: O naturalismo*, 137–141. Rio de Janeiro: Achiamé, 1984.

Eva Paulino Bueno

CÁRDENAS, NANCY (Mexico; 1934) ——————

Cárdenas, a poet and playwright, was born in Parras, Coahuila. She studied literature in the graduate program at the Universidad Nacional Autónoma de México, then completed postgraduate studies in theater at Yale University. Cárdenas is well known in Mexico as a journalist and a theater director. In addition, she has worked as an actress, a translator and a teacher.

In 1988 Cárdenas coproduced and directed a play, *Sida, así es la vida* (AIDS, That's the Way Life Goes), by William Hoffman, about gay men and AIDS. She subsequently wrote the play *Sexualidades* (Sexualities), in which she presents four characters with different sexual orientations: one man is bisexual, another is gay, one woman is heterosexual, and the other woman chooses abstinence. In *Sexualidades II* she deals specifically with the experiences and issues of bisexual women. Cárdenas' poetry has appeared in Mexican newspapers and magazines.

"Cuaderno de amor y de desamor" (Notebook on Love and Nonlove; unpublished), as its title indicates, articulates a love discourse and a discourse on the lack of love or lost love. There are two moments in the poem (the entire book can be read as a long poem) that are rigorously synthesized in the use of the words *amor/desamor*. The poetic voice states clearly, from the first lines, the affective–erotic specificity of this poetic discourse; it is a poetic lesbian discourse. From the first lines the grammatical markers make clear that the subject is invoking a woman lover. The first pages of the book allude to a new genesis, a rereading of the foundational myth of the Western world. However, in Cárdenas's book the foundational heterosexual couple, Adam and Eve, has been replaced by two women who, alone and naked, will write their own story. The first three verses of the poem allude to the transformation of the myth of creation, and in these verses the temptations are the seductive powers of the other woman.

The poems of the first part of the book, dedicated to love as plentitude and to the joy of erotic and affective relationships between women, are in the tradition of Monique Wittig's *The Lesbian Body* (1975) in that they are a celebration of the lesbian body and, especially, the celebration of the beauty, the strength, and the youth of the lover. The poetic voice, through an invocatory tone, establishes a private discourse, a dialogue with the other woman, her lover. It is also a public discourse that asserts the legitimacy of lesbian love and lesbian identities. The relationship of the private and the public that is textualized through Cárdenas's poetic discourse is expressed in the two epigraphs of "Cuaderno de amor y de desamor." The first one, by the contemporary Mexican poet Xavier Villaurrutia, reads: "Dichoso amor el nuestro, que nada y nadie nombra" (How fortunate is our love, which names nothing and no one). The second, by the baroque Spanish dramatist Lope de Vega, asserts: "No hay cosa más pública que el amor" (Nothing is more public than love). The second epigraph refers to the public aspect of love in general, while the first alludes to the private or marginal space that gay and lesbian love occupies in a heterosexist society. Moreover, the two epigraphs allude to the public/private aspect of any literary discourse and, in particular, to the privacy of a poetic lesbian love discourse.

In Cárdenas's text there is a clear relationship between lesbian love discourse and poetic discourse. The desire and the need to write emerge from the encounters with her lover. Cárdenas is aware that her poetic lesbian discourse is a political act, and throughout the book there is the desire to proclaim and establish a lesbian poetic space from which the lesbian subject articulates her discourse. The celebratory tone of the first verses is transformed into an angry, vehement discourse on the lack of love. In this diatribe against her ex-lover the speaker creates an image of herself and of the other woman. The speaker blames the ex-lover and proclaims her own capacity to survive an uneasy relationship. The cruel ex-lover has two personalities and two gender identities: at one point she is referred to by the rhetorical question, Dr. Jekyll or Ms. Hyde? The speaker questions her ex-lover's feelings for her and attacks her inconsistencies.

In spite of the vehement expression of lack of love, there is a strong discourse throughout the text that claims and celebrates lesbianism as a possibility of life, and one of the instances of the love discourse is the possibility of positive and healthy relationships between women. Cárdenas's writing inscribes the need to challenge tradition and the stereotypes created by heterosexist culture and society. The poet transforms heterosexual cultural expressions in her poetic discourse by assimilating fragments of popular heterosexual love songs into the celebration of lesbian passion. The meanings of these cultural expressions, placed in the context of a poetic lesbian love discourse, are defied.

The cyclical structure of "Cuaderno de amor y de desamor," the articulation of one long poem of various repetitive motifs, gives the idea of a continuum, and it gives fluidity to the reading. Moreover, it textualizes the nonauthoritarian character of a lesbian discourse that goes against binary combinations and fixed roles prescribed by a heterosexist society. The lesbian love theme is recurrent in Cárdenas's book, and it has been an "eternal return" in her poetry since 1984. The poetic cycle culminates with the arrival of a new lesbian lover. The lines that opened the poetic discourse close it, suggesting that it is not an end but a new beginning.

WORKS

Anuario de poesía 1990. Mexico City: Consejo Nacional para la Cultura y las Artes, 1991.
"Cuaderno de amor y de desamor." Unpublished Ms.
"El día que pisamos la luna." Unpublished Ms.

CRITICISM

Ruiz Manjares, Patricia. "País que ataca a sus minorías, es un país emponzoñado por el fascismo." *Siempre* 1937 (Aug. 1990): 66–68.

                                                              Elena M. Martínez

CARDOSO, LÚCIO (Brazil; 1913–1968) ───────

Cardoso, one of the most important contemporary Brazilian authors, may be identified with the most avant-garde aspects of the novel in Brazil through his *Crônica da casa assassinada* (Chronicle of the Assassinated House; 1959). Brazilian literature (and, unfortunately, Spanish-language Latin American literature as well) manifests a strongly repressive nature, not to mention a strongly discriminatory one. Any work that might attempt to represent a sexuality that "dares not speak its name" must be banished from the canon, lie forgotten on the bookshelves and be summarily rejected by publishers. Yet despite this intense repression, Cardoso's novel is one of the works to overcome the protective barrier of the rigid moral values of the traditional Brazilian family.

Cardoso began as a writer with works of a regional character, like *Maleita* (1934). But this novel, as Alfredo Bosi has pointed out, suggests to the reader a "nightmarish atmosphere," a rhetoric that is hardly suitable to the conventional regionalist fiction produced in the period. *A luz no subsolo* (Underground Light; 1936) represents Cardoso's attempt to chart his own course with a more intimate tone that effectively evokes a tradition of the lyrical novel. His narrative may nourish itself on a Brazilian historical substratum, but Cardoso desconstructs it on the basis of a complex subjective perspective conveyed by a subject who undertakes a determined effort to understand his "difference."

Against the backdrop of the decadence of the agrarian and mining society of Brazil, Cardoso achieves a true masterpiece with *Crônica*. In an asphyxiating universe marked by pain, incest and deviant sexuality, a penetrating and strident narrative voice sets out to achieve a new profundity in the understanding of the convolutions of the Brazilian soul. For example, at no time does the narrator lose his specific focus as a Latin American—more specifically, as a Brazilian—in the process of grasping his universe. Difference, in every sense of the word, is the basic point of departure for a narrator who pursues one possible form of truth. The novel does not develop a monolithic line of understanding and reflection upon the facts presented. Rather, it elaborates a polyphony of focuses in which each one is part of a progressively evolving mosaic. Letters, diaries and confessions serve as building blocks in the novel; a single voice becomes meaningless, yielding to a choral narrative program. Moreover, and in consonance with the nature of the narrative voicing, the various narrators reject any psychoanalytical interpretation that is merely mechanical. Since incest and homosexuality are openly discussed, such an approach might seem to suggest itself. However, rather than pursuing any form of facile psychoanalysis, there is an attempt to understand human nature in its most basic dimensions, especially as regards sexuality of the character Timóteo, even if that sexuality may be considered deviant.

Timóteo is the novel's principal character, though the feminine figure of Nina is also the object of a profound examination with respect to the matter of difference. The process by which difference is represented, particularly as it centers on Timóteo, allows the reader to assess the close relationship between prose and poetry established throughout Cardoso's writing. At the same time the author presents us with André, heir of an orthodox Brazilian family who dresses as a woman—or, more accurately, who avails himself of his mother's faded clothes. André engages in a progressive deconstruction of the closely woven strictures that enclose the hallucinated atmosphere of the Brazilian family circle. Timóteo is and is not the symbol of a period that, like the family home, is disintegrating with an irreversible loss of social meaning. The central character therefore anticipates the androgynous figures that will be an integral part of our postmodern society, and any relation to Michael Jackson, Prince and others is no mere coincidence. Cardoso functions as something like a social antenna, in Ezra Pound's sense of the term, and he exhibits Timóteo as someone who, moving between hallucination and fantasy, between delirium and reality, attempts to grasp how differing sexual choices are formed and forged.

If on the one hand Timóteo could be considered a mad queen, which would be the cinematographic option for this work, on the other hand he could be seen as the locus of "indecidibility," to use a term coined by Jacques Derrida. Timóteo appears as the body of a man dressed in female clothing. Because he is so fat, his clothes begin to rip, revealing his flaw and his lack. The ridiculous and the grotesque in this situation function as metaphors for an individual who is incessantly searching for his identity. In the novel one is either a man or a woman, and the spaces in between can never be contemplated or allowed by the dominant society. Choice, if there were a choice, lies in these spaces in between, in the interstices that lead in many different directions. Indefinition is their nature, and this indefinition is what effectively strikes fear into the heart of a society of defined roles and sexualities that are more than just codified. *Crônica* quickly moves to articulate these interstices in an overwhelmingly repressive society, which makes Cardoso's novel an excellent founding text of Brazilian gay writing.

WORKS

Anfiteatro. Rio de Janeiro: Livraria Agir, 1946.
Céu escuro. Rio de Janeiro: Vamos Ler A Noite, 1940.
Crônica da casa assassinada. Rio de Janeiro: José Olympio, 1959.
O desconhecido. Rio de Janeiro: José Olympio, 1940.
Diário I. Rio de Janeiro: Elos, n.d.
Diário completo. Rio de Janeiro: José Olympio/INL, 1970.
Dias perdidos. Rio de Janeiro: José Olympio, 1943.
O enfeitiçado. Rio de Janeiro: José Olympio, 1954.
O escravo. Rio de Janeiro: Zélio Valverde, 1945.
História da lagoa grande. Pôrto Alegre: Globo, 1939.
Inácio. Rio de Janeiro: Ocidente, 1944.
A luz no subsolo. Rio de Janeiro: José Olympio, 1936.
Maleita. Rio de Janeiro: Schmidt, 1934.
Mãos vazias. Rio de Janeiro: José Olympio, 1938.
O mistério dos M M M. Rio de Janeiro: O Cruzeiro, 1962. In collaboration with João Condé.
Novas poesias. Rio de Janeiro: José Olympio, 1944.
Poemas inéditos. Preface and ed. Octávio de Faria. Rio de Janeiro: Nova Fronteira, 1982.
Poesias. Rio de Janeiro: José Olympio, 1941.
A professora Hilda. Rio de Janeiro: José Olympio, 1946.
Salgueiro. Rio de Janeiro: José Olympio, 1935.
Três histórias da cidade. Rio de Janeiro: Bloch, 1969.
Três histórias da província. Rio de Janeiro: Bloch, 1969.
O viajante. Ed. Octávio de Faria. Rio de Janeiro: José Olympio, 1973. Unfinished novel.

CRITICISM

Athayde, Tristão. *Estudos literários.* Rio de Janeiro: Aguilar, 1966.
Bosi, Alfredo. *História concisa da literatura brasileira.* 3rd ed. São Paulo: Cultrix, 1977.
Cardoso, Maria Helena. *Por onde andou meu coração.* Rio de Janeiro: José Olympio, 1968.
Carelli, Mário. *Corcel de fogo: Vida e obra de Lúcio Cardoso.* Rio de Janeiro: Editora Guanabara, 1988.
Coutinho, Edilberto. *Erotismo no romance brasileiro.* Rio de Janeiro: Nórdica, 1979.
Lopes, Francisco Caetano, Jr. "Uma subjetividade outra." In *Toward Socio-criticism*, 67–75. Ed. Roberto Reis. Tempe: Center for Latin American Studies, Arizona State University, 1991.
Reis, Roberto. *A permanência do círculo: Hierarquia no romance brasileiro.* Niterói, Brazil: EDUFF, 1987.

Santos, Hamílton dos. *Lúcio Cardoso—nem leviano nem grave*. São Paulo: Brasiliense, 1987.

Sodré, Nélson Werneck. *Orientações do pensamento brasileiro*. Rio de Janeiro: Casa Editoria Vecchi, 1942.

Francisco Caetano Lopes, Jr.

CASAL, JULIÁN DEL (Cuba; 1863–1893) _____

Pain and desolation mark all of Julián del Casal's writing. His poetry seems written in red; not the bloody red of a murder but the red of the laughing, coughing fit that ended his life, upon hearing a joke after dinner. He was born in Cuba on November 7, 1863. His mother died when he was five. After attempting a career in law, in 1888 Casal began contributing articles and poems to *La Habana elegante* (Elegant Havana). Later he also worked for *El Fígaro* (Figaro) and *El País* (The Country). During the last three years of his life, while suffering from tuberculosis, he wrote his three collections of poetry. He died on October 23, 1893.

His first collection, *Hojas al viento* (Leaves in the Wind), published in 1890, set the tormented and solitary tone of his poetry. In 1892, the violent *Nieve* (Snow) was published, perhaps the collection that is most identified with *modernismo* (modernism), the Spanish American melding of Parnassianism and symbolism. In it his interest in symbolist painting, the Japanese world, and Greek and Roman mythology is made clear. His last book, *Bustos y rimas* (Busts and Rhymes; 1893), includes a collection of short literary portraits of contemporary Havana personalities and a group of poems that continues his tradition of solitude, hopelessness and an obsession with sickness and the sick.

Casal is generally considered one of the first generation of modernist poets in Spanish America, although his despairing tone, drenched in blood and disgust, is unique among these poets. His prose—newspaper articles, some of them resembling short stories in structure—is full of scathing political and social criticism. His poetry, however, is extremely personal. Evidently influenced by Charles Baudelaire, Casal plunged into an introspective view of language and poetry, avoiding the egocentric style of José Martí (the major Cuban poet of the day) and other modernist writers, as well as any kind of civic poetry (dedications, tributes, eulogies).

Within his poetry a homosexual tone can be perceived. José Lezama Lima rightly said that "the sexual in Casal is peremptory and decisive" ("Julián del Casal" 75), although he never developed this statement to examine the specifically homosexual aspect of Casal's work. It is not the intention of this essay to "prove" the homosexuality of Julián del Casal—rather, it addresses not the man but the voice within his poems. There appears to be a tendency toward a homosexual imagination that is pertinent to Casal's view of woman and her image.

In "Rondeles" (Rondels), Casal mentions a secret, "la extraña cosa" (the strange thing; v. 7), "el secreto de mis males" (the secret of my ills; v. 15). It seems evident throughout his poetry that this secret is the reason, or at least part of the reason, that the poet swims in a sea of intranquillity and despair. The poetry's tendency toward the homosexual is always subtle and veiled, with nothing alluding explicitly to a gay topic. The reader must dig beneath the surface of the poems to unearth the fragments of a possible homosexual subject.

The only possible instance of overtly homoerotic imagery in Casal is his physical description of Prometheus in "Las oceánidas" (The Oceaniads). This passage is important because most modernist poetry revels in the representation of the woman's body, and also because the pain and joy of the prototypical rebel are inscribed in a man's—Prometheus's—body: desire is represented in male flesh.

Casal's poetry contains the repeated image of a man who rejects the social pleasures of life to immerse himself in either solitude or death, as in "El anhelo del monarca" (The Monarch's Wish) and "Bajorrelieve" (Bas-relief). In both poems, women as a sexual commodity or as a source of joy and happiness offer themselves to the reluctant man, usually in overtly erotic terms. Even though the plea of each of these women is only one of several rejected offers (money, honor), the woman's request is the last stated in both poems, just before the man's rejection of life and its pleasures. Heterosexual seduction is made central and is, at the same time, deliberately rejected.

"Páginas de vida" (Pages from Life), generally read as the farewell conversation between Casal and the famous modernist poet Rubén Darío, could also be viewed as the separation of two male lovers. This is perhaps the closest Casal came to portraying a homosexual relationship in his poetry. On a ship, one man talks to another about their mutual past (are they sailors? gentlemen traveling?). One man confesses to the other that he would wish to be with him, but that he cannot accept his ardent plea. The man listening comments at the end of the poem that he loses his calm every time he thinks of the other. The poem reveals an impossible love, perhaps because one of the men cannot bear to engage in a sexual act (the ardent plea) or because they are both afraid of this kind of relationship. Regardless of a passionate attraction, there is always a sense of remorse: no personal relationship in Casal's work is ever liberating. Casal dared to present this relationship but avoided an explicit seduction, a position that shows an author who cannot help writing about homosexuality but at the same time feels uncomfortable with it. Can the reading of a homosexual scene be reconciled with the established reading of the poem as Darío's farewell? Only if the reader accepts the notion that Casal was representing his literary relationship with Darío as if it were a homosexual relationship—a series of seductions that were never fully consummated.

But perhaps one can define the homosexual in Casal more carefully by looking at his representation of and relationship to women. An abrupt plunge into this subject can misread the way the poet sees woman, for there seems to be a dual image of her. One image fits within the category of the idealized woman, the marble statue that is all beautiful surface, the *art*ificial being, usually represented as a portrait, a plastic representation, as in "Camafeo" (Cameo) and "A Berta" (To Bertha): the typical modernist woman. The other type of woman is more a psychology than a physical representation. Even if some of them possess a marvelous beauty, Casal adds to them a personality with which he can identify, one that he finds both appealing and nonthreatening: "Ah, I always adore you as a brother," Casal concludes in "Virgen triste" (Sad Virgin), because she shares with him an eternal sadness and disenchantment with life. This brotherhood, however, does not dissolve the threat that he finds in a sexual attraction or encounter with a woman: woman is friend, but not lover. In "Esquivez" (Elusiveness) the poet plainly states that her enchantments have nothing to say to him and that he cannot offer her what she desires. In other, more desperate moments, Casal seems to realize this impossibility, but he excuses it by wallowing in self-contempt after telling a woman he cannot love her in spite of her beauty.

"A la castidad" (To Chastity) poses a series of conflicts in Casal's poetry that can work as a synthesis for the ideas this essay presents. From the very beginning Casal admits that he does not love Woman, that is, it is the *concept* of the woman that he does not love. But as the poet rejects the concept, the poem invokes a virtue, Chastity, that applies, through sexuality, both to Woman and to woman. Thus, while he explicitly rejects the beautiful modernist woman, he is also inherently putting aside the woman who could persuade him into a sexual relation. Casal invokes Chastity to protect himself from both types of women; he rejects the woman as a sexual subject. At the end, he asks Chastity for the calm of those who are pure of heart, the one thing that, in the rest of his poetry, he has convinced himself is impossible to reach. Uneasiness, the one trait permeating his poetry, reveals its homosexual component, along with his feelings toward woman.

WORKS

Hojas al viento: Havana: El Retiro, 1890.
The Poetry of Julián del Casal: A Critical Edition, 3 vols. Ed. Robert Jay Glickman. Gainesville: University Presses of Florida, 1976–77. [Contains both *Nieve* and *Bustos y rimas*.]

CRITICISM

González, Aníbal. "Arqueologías: Orígenes de la crónica modernista." In his *La crónica modernista hispanoamericana*, 108–120. Madrid: Porrúa Turanzas, 1983.
Lezama Lima, José. "Julián del Casal." In *Analecta de reloj*, in *Obras completas*, 265–99. Mexico City: Aguilar, 1977.

Vitier, Cintio. "Octava lección: Casal como antítesis de Martí." In his *Lo cubano en la poesía*, 242–268. Havana: Universidad Central de Las Villas, 1958.

Carmelo Esterrich

CHÁVEZ, DENISE (United States; 1948) _____

Born into a Mexicano family in Las Cruces, New Mexico, Chávez graduated in 1984 from the University of New Mexico with an M.A. in creative writing. A poet, playwright and fiction writer, she has taught in artist-in-residence programs, writers' workshops, universities and women's prisons. Her *Last of the Menu Girls* won the 1985 Puerto del Sol (Sun Port) fiction award, and her plays have been performed throughout the Southwest.

In a 1988 interview Chávez described herself as "a transmitter of the woman's voice, a voice that may or may not have been heard" (Eysturoy, 165), and in both "Novenas narratives y ofrendas nuevomexicanos" (New Mexican Novenas Narratives and Offerings) and *The Last of the Menu Girls*, she gives voice to a wide range of Chicana experiences. "Novenas Narratives" celebrates the diversity of Chicana experience in New Mexico. This play, a series of brief monologues representing Chicanas from a variety of age groups and economic backgrounds, includes the narrative of "a very tough bag-lady," an ex-convict who became a lesbian in prison. *The Last of the Menu Girls*, a first-person short-story cycle unified by its depiction of Rocío Esquibel, a New Mexican Chicana, consists of seven stories ranging in length from seven to fifty-one pages. Although the stories describe Rocío's childhood, adolescence and young adulthood, they are not arranged in chronological order; nor do they focus on plot development. Instead, they function as "scenes" describing Rocío's neighborhood, the significant people in her life and her changing roles as daughter, sister, niece, lover, neighbor and friend.

Chávez's work has received very little critical attention, and scholars have yet to examine the underlying lesbian themes. Debra Castillo provides the most comprehensive discussion of *Menu Girls* to date in her study of Latin American feminist literary criticism and women's bicultural texts. She explores Chávez's use of the subjunctive mood as a strategy for negotiating multiple cultures, languages and time periods. In his analysis of Chicano/a coming-of-age narratives and cultural resistance, Renato Rosaldo briefly describes Rocío's matriarchal lineage and suggests that her "bodily grace" and her adolescent sexuality enable her to "thrive in dangerous worlds." Yet Rosaldo's celebration of Rocío's "emerging sexuality" is problematic in light of Norma Alarcón's discussion of female subject formation and sexual identity. According to Alarcón, contemporary Chicana writers are exploring the "crisis of meaning" that occurs when female subjects refuse to speak in the culturally sanctioned positions of wife or mother; they have no place from which to speak and no alternate ways to represent—or even become—their gendered identity.

Chávez describes Rocío's "crisis of meaning" in "Shooting Stars" and "Space Is a Solid." In the first story Rocío narrates her unsuccessful search for an adequate model of womanhood. She explains that, unlike those women who could move "from girlhood to womanhood with ease," she found no models "womanly" enough to enable her to effect the transition. Each of the beautiful adolescent girls she describes is somehow "lacking," and Rocío concludes this account with an unspeakable longing, an "uncertain internal emptiness" (62). "Space Is a Solid" examines the consequences of Rocío's inability to take up her culturally sanctioned role as a "woman." Although she enters into a heterosexual relationship with Loudon, a self-obsessed university student, her feelings of homelessness and isolation—as well as her mental and physical exhaustion and her anorectic behavior—indicate her inability to fulfill the terms of Western culture's "heterosexual contract."

Rocío's "crisis of meaning" leads to a crisis of desire that both illustrates and extends Teresa de Lauretis's contention that Western culture provides no adequate representations of autonomous female sexuality. According to de Lauretis, this heterosexist, masculinist bias severely limits representations of "non-male-related sexual identities"; lesbian desire is desexualized and represented as a woman's narcissistic identification *with*, rather than sexual desire *for*, her mother or another woman (14). Yet Rocío's desire cannot be described as lesbian in either sense of the term. Although she thinks "about *loving* women" (her emphasis) and praises "[t]heir beauty and . . . their sure sweet clarity" (63), she can neither identify *with* them nor desire them sexually. Indeed, Rocío's desire is neither lesbian nor heterosexual.

Coupled with her inability to enter successfully into a heterosexual contract, Rocío's unrepresentable desire is even more devastating than de Lauretis's analysis suggests, for it problematizes all forms of female identification and desire. By thus depicting Rocío's inability to establish fulfilling relationships with others (either female *or* male), *Menu Girls* challenges existing definitions of gender and representations of female desire.

WORKS

The Last of the Menu Girls. Houston: Arte Público Press, 1986.
"Novenas narratives y ofrendas nuevomexicanos." In *Chicana Creativity and Criticism: Charting New Frontiers in American Literature*, 85–100. Ed. María Hererra-Sobek and Helena María Viramontes. Houston: Arte Público Press, 1988.

CRITICISM

Alarcón, Norma. "Making 'Familia' from Scratch: Split Subjectivities in the Work of Helena María Viramontes and Cherríe Moraga." In *Chicana Creativity and Criticism: Charting New Frontiers in American Literature*, 147–159. Ed. María Hererra-Sobek and Helena María Viramontes. Houston: Arte Público Press, 1988.

Castillo, Debra. *Talking Back: Toward a Latin American Feminist Literary Criticism.* Ithaca, N.Y.: Cornell University Press, 1992.

de Lauretis, Teresa. *Technologies of Gender: Essays on Theory, Film, and Fiction.* Bloomington: Indiana University Press, 1987.

Eysturoy, Annie O. "Denise Chávez." In *This Is About Vision: Interviews with Southwestern Writers*, 156–169. Ed. John T. Crawford, William Balassi and Annie O. Eysturoy. Albuquerque: University of New Mexico Press, 1990.

Rosaldo, Renato. "Fables of the Fallen Guy." In *Criticism in the Borderlands: Studies in Chicano Literature, Culture, and Ideology*, 84–93. Ed. Héctor Calderón, and José David Saldívar. Durham, N.C.: Duke University Press, 1991.

AnnLouise Keating

CHOCRÓN, ISAAC (Venezuela; 1930) _____

Isaac Chocrón was born in Maracay, Venezuela, on September 25, 1930, to Jewish immigrants. In 1939 the family moved to Caracas, where he and a friend, who later became fellow playwright Román Chalbaud, gave evidence of their theatrical inclinations at an early age by staging plays for neighbors and friends. Chocrón and his two siblings were raised by their father after their mother abandoned them in what constituted a major scandal at the time, an event that would surface in several of Chocrón's works. When Chocrón was fifteen, his father sent him to a military school in Bordentown, New Jersey, where his literary aspirations were encouraged.

Chocrón received a B.A. in comparative literature at Syracuse University and a master's degree in international studies at Columbia University. While pursuing graduate studies, he wrote his first novel, the now forgotten *Pasaje* (Passage). He returned to Caracas in 1956, to embark on a career with the Venezuelan State Department. This proved to be a turning point in Chocrón's life, surpassed only by his decision, several years later, to leave the financial security offered by his job as an economist and dedicate himself to professional writing and the theater.

His first play, *Mónica y el florentino* (Monica and the Florentine), premiered during the Primer Festival de Teatro Venezolano (First Venezuelan Theater Festival) in 1959. Since then, Chocrón has been writing plays continually, as well as five novels and several books of essays and theater criticism. Long regarded as one of Venezuela's top playwrights, a position he shares with his close friends and collaborators José Ignacio Cabrujas and Román Chalbaud, Chocrón has played a key role in the development of the Venezuelan theater. He was cofounder of the Nuevo Grupo (New Group), a theater group that revitalized the Venezuelan stage, and from 1984 to 1989 he was director of the National Theater Company. He has directed and translated several plays, and since 1978 he has taught drama at the Universidad Central de Venezuela and, more recently, at the Universidad Simón Bolívar. In addition to teaching, he lectures and has been a visiting professor at several universities in the United States.

Chocrón is an eclectic writer who often draws material from his background and personal experience. As a playwright he has evolved from conventional drama like *Mónica y el florentino* and *El quinto infierno* (The Fifth Hell) to experimentation with Brechtian techniques in *Asia y el Lejano Oriente* (Asia and the Far East) and theater of the absurd in *Amoroso* (Amorous). He added another dimension to his theater with *Simón*, a historical drama that examines the relationship of Simón Bolívar with his tutor, Simón Rodríguez.

Chocrón's first stage success was *Animales feroces* (Ferocious Animals; 1963), a play that uses nonlinear scenes to suggest a disorganized family album. The characters, members of a Jewish family, blame each other for their past failures and the suicide of a member of the younger generation. The play reflects one of Chocrón's most persistent themes: the unrelinquished and painful bondages that subjugate individuals to their biological families.

Asia y el Lejano Oriente (1966), considered Chocrón's most overt political statement (Monasterios, *Un enfoque*), deals with a group of people who sell their homeland to foreign investors. Its sixteen scenes include all the facets of a nation's inhabitants, from the local intelligentsia and government employees to petty thieves representing a nation consumed by materialism.

Chocrón consideres his next play, *Tric-Trac* (1967), a sequel to *Asia*. Totally experimental and devoid of a formal argument, the play calls for either a male or a female cast playing characters identified solely by numbers. These anonymous individuals, involved in a series of senseless games, are natural descendants of the characters in *Asia*. They are uprooted souls trying desperately to create a past and a culture for themselves (Monasterios, *Un enfoque*).

The idea that everything can be bought and sold is further developed in one of Chocrón's most amusing plays, *O.K.* (1969). The story centers on two mature women who share a younger lover until one of them decides to sell her rights over the man to her rival. Thus, not only nations but also personal relationships are subject to economic interests.

One of Chocrón's most controversial and successful plays, *La revolución* (The Revolution; 1972), deals with an aging transvestite and his manager/former lover who confront each other while preparing their act before the audience. These two figures emerge as opposite forces of marginality: authenticity versus evasion, submission versus rebellion, denial versus acceptance.

Chocrón has explored different narrative forms in his fiction: the epistolary novel in *Rómpase en caso de incendio* (Break in Case of Fire; 1975), the detective novel in *50 vacas gordas* (50 Fat Cows; 1982), and multiple narrators in *Pájaro de mar por tierra* (Bleached Seagull; 1972). His fiction is marked by the author's intervention, either as a character reconstructing through interviews the life of Miguel Antonio Casas, the protagonist of *Pájaro*, or collecting the letters left by Daniel Benabel in *Rómpase*. His fiction includes *Se ruega no tocar la carne por razones de higiene* (Please Don't Touch the Meat for Reasons of Hygiene; 1970), the story of two loners constantly looking for new sensations and experiences. Archaeologist N. L. Bofors and socialite Gloria Silva travel to rural Venezuela, but find themselves unable to communicate or relate to each other despite their common solitude and frustrations. This inability to communicate is the dominant trait of Mickey, the troubled protagonist of *Pájaro de mar por tierra*. After a series of unemotional relationships, Mickey disappears without any clear indication of his motives or whereabouts. Friends and relatives offer their stories of the young man, all giving a portrait of aloofness and self-centeredness.

Rómpase en caso de incendio follows the pilgrimage of Daniel Benabel from Caracas to Tangier, after the death of his wife and son in the Caracas earthquake, through a series of letters sent by Benabel. A man who has led a conventional life, Daniel finds freedom and self-fulfillment while coming to terms with his grief. In *50 vacas gordas* Chocrón parallels the life of Mercedes Alcántara, the protagonist, with the fifty years of economic prosperity enjoyed by Venezuela from the oil boom. In committing herself to identify the murderer of the crime she accidentally witnesses, Mercedes is able to transcend her dull existence and transform herself from a passive spectator to an active participant.

Chocrón's most recent novel, *Todo una dama* (A Real Lady; 1988) is a revealing, close look at the microcosmos of Latin American émigrés and diplomatic officers in Washington, D.C. The narration focuses on Alejandro Ponte Vecchio, a high-ranking Venezuelan diplomat known and respected for his good manners who conceals deep turmoil under an apparent tranquillity.

While Chocrón's drama has enjoyed wide critical attention, his fiction has been largely ignored. Several dissertations have been devoted totally or partially to his theater. Joyce Lee Durbin provides a comprehensive study of his drama with valuable insights into his themes and techniques. Milagro Larson concentrates on several plays to examine how Chocrón employs dramatic techniques to achieve different responses from his reader/audience. In Gleider Hernández-Almeida's comparative study, "Tres dramaturgos" (1978), Chocrón stands out as the foremost stylist of Venezuelan theater. Also focusing on his plays and on Chocrón as a transgressor is the 1991 study by Susana Rotker. Two valuable studies of his fiction are Edward H. Friedman's essays " 'Cherchez la femme' " (1987) and "Playing with Fire" (1988). Though focusing on specific novels, they provide an overall introduction to his work. Several interviews reveal his personal views on Latin American theater (Waldman) and his themes (Senkman). The most incisive interview is Miyó Vestrini's book-length *Isaac Chocrón frente al espejo* (Isaac Chocrón in Front of the Mirror; 1980), which affords a unique view of the author and his world.

Saúl Sosnowski's articles discuss Chocrón's Jewish background and how this is reflected in his work. Although some critics have addressed the presence of homosexuality in his plays, the discussion of this topic, with the exception of David Foster's analysis of *Pájaro de mar por tierra*, has not been extended to his fiction.

Chocrón is an early exponent of homosexual representation in Latin American literature. Aside from minor characters or incidents in his fiction, homosexuality occupies center stage in *Pájaro de mar por tierra* and *Todo una dama*. Though preceded by several novels of the 1960s, *Pájaro de mar por tierra* is a groundbreaking text as far as Latin American gay themes are concerned. Contrary to the regular treatment of homosexuals in twentieth-century Latin American fiction prior to the 1970s, *Pájaro* departs from the stereotypical screaming queen and sordid clichés. Here at last is a gay protagonist who looks and acts natural, a story that recognizes the existence of a gay subculture, even if that recognition gives prominence to the cruising and promiscuity of the gay world. As a victim of homophobic pressures arising from his own family setting, Mickey, the protagonist, never assumes his homosexual identity. Constantly drifting away from his homosexuality, in spite of an active gay life, he avoids and denies any gay perception of himself, thus excluding any sense of belonging. As Foster suggests, Mickey cannot relate to an exclusive heterosexual model nor to the stereotypical homosexual role.

Chocrón takes another look at denial in *Todo una dama*. Where Mickey experiences countless homosexual encounters, Alejandro Ponte Vecchio, the novel's protagonist, never satisfies his sexual attraction to his chauffeur. Far from assuming a gay identity, Ponte Vecchio adopts strategies to restrain his homosexuality. Realizing that any disclosure could jeopardize his bureaucratic position, he subjects himself to a conventional marriage and constant repression. Ironically, while he maintains a heterosexual image, people often refer to him as "todo una dama" (a real lady), due to his extreme politeness and good manners, without realizing the full implications of the attribution.

Bisexuality as a natural and suitable option surfaces unmistakably in *La máxima felicidad* (The Greatest Happiness; 1974) when Pablo and Leo, a homosexual couple, take as their common wife Perla, a prostitute Leo brings home. This unlikely trio not only accepts each other, but finds in their situation the perfect family arrangement. Even when Chocrón focuses on exclusive homosexuals, like Gabriel and Eloy in *La revolución*, he is more concerned with making a social comment than with reaffirming a gay identity. Friedman has commented ("'Cherchez la femme'") that homosexuality in *La revolución* is an analogy and not the object itself. Chocrón reflected in an interview (Vestrini) that he wrote the play in response to the crisis in social consciousness affecting Venezuela. In choosing two marginal characters who happen to be homosexuals, he condemns conformism and suggests that authentic outsiders like Gabriel are more apt to make radical changes in the establishment.

Chocrón has represented homosexuality in his work since the early 1970s. He has been responsible for honest portrayals of gay characters, individuals devoid of self-pity like Gabriel or self-assured like Juan David, the drama coach who befriends Mercedes in *50 vacas gordas*. Nevertheless, these and other gay characters are still marginal figures, and they are unable or unwilling to propose homosexuality as a legitimate option. In spite of recognizing homosexuality, it can be argued that Chocrón accommodates the subject within the mainstream discourse by rejecting the adoption of a satisfying gay life-style or assuming a truly contestatory position. Thus, homosexuality is often interpreted and regarded as another dimension of human sexuality.

WORKS

El acompañante. Caracas: Monte Avila, 1978.

Alfabeto para analfabetos. Caracas: Fundarte, 1980.

Amoroso o una mínima incandescencia. Caracas: Universidad Central de Venezuela, 1968.

Animales feroces. Caracas: Editora Grafos, 1963.

Asia y el Lejano Oriente; Tric-Trac. Mérida, Venezuela: Ediciones del Rectorado, Universidad de los Andes, 1967.

50 vacas gordas. Caracas: Monte Avila, 1982.

Clipper; Simón. Caracas: Alfadil, 1987.

Color natural. Photographs by Gaziano Gasparini; text by Isaac Chocrón. Caracas: Grupo Montana, 1969.

Doña Bárbara. Opera based on the novel by Rómulo Gallegos; music by Caroline Lloyd; libretto by Isaac Chocrón. Caracas: Instituto Nacional de Cultura y Bellas Artes, 1967.

Maracaibo 180. Maracaibo, Venezuela: Ediciones Centro de Bellas Artes, 1978.

La máxima felicidad. Caracas: Monte Avila, 1974.

Mesopotamia. Caracas: Editorial Ateneo de Caracas, 1980.

Mónica y el florentino. Caracas: Monte Avila, 1980.

Nueva crítica de teatro venezolano. Caracas: Fundarte, 1981.

El nuevo teatro venezolano. Caracas: Oficina Central de Información, 1966.

O.K. Caracas: Monte Avila, 1969.

Pájaro de mar por tierra. Caracas: Monte Avila, 1972.

Pasaje. Caracas: Ediciones Edime, 1956.

El quinto infierno. Caracas: Ediciones Zodíaco, 1961.

La revolución. Caracas: Editorial Tiempo Nuevo, 1972.

Rómpase en caso de incendio. Caracas: Monte Avila, 1975.

Se ruega no tocar la carne por razones de higiene. Caracas: Editorial Tiempo Nuevo, 1970.

Señales de tráfico. Caracas: Monte Avila, 1972.

Simón. Caracas: Alfadil, 1983.

Sueño y tragedia en el teatro norteamericano. Caracas: Alfadil, 1984.

El teatro de Sam Shepard: De imágenes a personajes. Caracas: Monte Avila, 1991.

Tendencias del teatro contemporáneo. Caracas: Monte Avila, 1973.

Todo una dama. Caracas: Alfadil, 1988.

Tres fechas claves en el teatro venezolano. Caracas: Fundarte, 1978.

Triángulo. Caracas: Editorial Tierra Firme, 1962.

CRITICISM

Azparren Jiménez, Leonardo. *El teatro venezolano y otros teatros*, 107–120. Caracas: Monte Avila, 1979.

Durbin, Joyce Lee. "La dramaturgia de Isaac Chocrón." Ph.D. diss., Texas Tech University, 1988.

Foster, David William. *Gay and Lesbian Themes in Latin American Writing*, 51–55. Austin: University of Texas Press, 1991.

Friedman, Edward H. "The Beast Within: The Rhetoric of Signification in Isaac Chocrón's *Animales feroces*." *Folios: Essays on Foreign Languages and Literatures* 17 (1987): 167–183.

———. " 'Cherchez la femme': El lector como detective en *50 vacas gordas* de Isaac Chocrón." *Discurso literario* 4.2 (1987): 647–656.

———. "Playing with Fire: The Search for Selfhood in Isaac Chocrón's *Rómpase en caso de incendio*." *Confluencia* 3.2 (1988): 27–37.

Hernández-Almeida, Gleider. "El Bolívar de Isaac Chocrón." *Confluencia* 3.2 (1988): 39–46.

———. "Isaac Chocrón: Lo histórico y lo antihistórico." In *Actas del IX Congreso de la Asociación internacional de hispanistas*. Frankfurt: Vervuert, 1989.

———. "Tres dramaturgos venezolanos de hoy: R. Chalbaud, J. I. Cabrujas, I. Chocrón." Ph.D. diss., University of Iowa, 1978.

Klein, Dennis. "The Theme of Alienation in the Theatre of Elisa Lerner and Isaac Chocrón." *Folio: Essays on Foreign Languages and Literatures* 17 (1987): 151–166.

Larson, Milagro. "Entrevista con Isaac Chocrón." *Confluencia* 6.2 (1991): 117–125.

Mannarino, Carmen. "Chocrón o la palabra intencionada." *Imagen* 100.78 (1991): 10–11.

Monasterios, Rubén. *Un enfoque crítico del teatro venezolano*, 92–96. Caracas: Monte Avila, 1975.

———. "*Tric-Trac*: Un reto a la imaginación." *Actual* 1 (1968): 194–203.

Moretta, Eugene L. "Spanish American Theatre of the 50's and 60's: Critical Perspectives on Role Playing." *Latin American Theatre Review* 13.3 (1980): 5–30.

Nigro, Kirsten F. "A Triple Insurgence: Isaac Chocrón's *La revolución*." *Bulletin of the Rocky Mountain Modern Language Association* 35.1 (1981): 47–53.

Rotker, Susana. *Isaac Chocrón y Elisa Lerner: Los transgresores de la literatura venezolana*. Caracas: Fundarte, 1991.

Senkman, Leonardo. "Entrevista a Isaac Chocrón: El misterio de la familia que heredamos." *Noah*. 1.1 (1987): 79–82.

Sosnowski, Saúl. "*Clipper* de Isaac Chocrón: Salida internacional." In *Ensayos sobre judaísmo latinoamericano*. Buenos Aires: Editorial Milá, 1990.

———. "Latin American Jewish Writers: A Bridge Towards History." *Prooftexts* 4.1 (1984): 71–92.

Suárez Radillo, Carlos M. *13 autores del nuevo teatro venezolano*, 178–181. Caracas: Monte Avila, 1971.

Vestrini, Miyó. *Isaac Chocrón frente al espejo*. Caracas: Editorial Ateneo de Caracas, 1980.

Waldman, Gloria. "An Interview with Isaac Chocrón." *Latin American Theatre Review* 11.1 (1977): 103–109.

Víctor F. Torres

COPI (Pseud. of Raúl Damonte; Argentina; 1941–1987)

In an unpublished autobiographical text, "Río de la Plata" (River Plate; 1984), Copi contrasts his maternal language, Argentine Spanish (*l'argentine*) with his *langue maîtresse* (*la française*: French, the "mistress language"). With the exception of three unpublished texts in Spanish ("Un ángel para la señora Lisca" [An Angel for Mrs. Lisca]; 1957); "La sombra de Wenceslao" [Wenceslao's Shadow]; 1983); "El cachafaz" [The Rogue]; 1983), Copi's entire oeuvre (eight novels, ten cartoon albums, ten plays) was written in French, although published Spanish versions (presumably executed by the author) exist for some of them. Although his family was sixth-generation Argentine, most of Copi's life was spent in exile. In 1945 his father (Raúl Damonte Taborda), a radical journalist and politician, was forced to flee with his family to Montevideo, Uruguay, with the advent of Peronism. In 1952 the family emigrated to Paris, returning to Uruguay and then to Buenos Aires in 1955. Copi's only real memories of Argentina were from age fifteen to twenty-two. In "Río de la Plata," he recalls his native country with mixed emotions:

I found myself, at the age of sixteen . . . in the immense city of Buenos Aires. . . . Having mastered the refinements of a *petit parisien*, I dedicated myself to sentimental adventures and social voyeurism. . . . How does one begin to speak about homosexuality in Argentina? . . . One is treated as an asexual by one's family during one's entire life. . . . Thanks to this tacit silence (everyone has something to hide), the homosexual finds a privileged place in his family during his youth. He's considered as the most talented and the one who has the most modern ideas. He dictates ideologies and fashions, counsels the young in matters of love, and puts up with the chattering of the old. . . .

Innocent Argentina! With the birth of the son of his father or sister, the homosexual must leave the family home, the new baby having already been installed in his ex-bachelor's room, now filled with children's toys. It's their tribal way of giving him leave. A tardy flight for a bird whose eccentricities and changes of humor are indulged only by his family. After having represented Hell, the family becomes Paradise Lost. Or a Hell Lost, but in any case Lost.

In the same autobiographical text, Copi wonders what his life might have been like had fate not placed him on vacation in Paris during the summer of 1963 when his father, forced to seek asylum in the Uruguayan embassy in Buenos Aires, cut off his allowance. Finding himself permanently exiled in Paris at the age of twenty-two, Copi set about reinventing his life. He would return to Argentina for only two short visits. The last, shortly before his death, was with his friend, the novelist Guy Hocquenghem, who would use the baroque world of Copi's family as the basis for key sections of his celebrated AIDS novel *Eve* (1987). All of Copi's works would remain banned in Argentina until

1984, after the return of constitutional democracy. Copi began by selling his sketches on the Pont des Arts, but he was soon drawing his famous *femme assise* (seated woman) for the *Nouvel Observateur*. His fame as a cartoonist grew quickly, and his drawings began to appear in *Charlie Hebdo*, *Hara Kiri*, and *Linus* (Italy). In the late 1970s he invented the character Libérett' for *Libération*. In later years, he drew for magazines as varied as *Gai pied* and *Paris Match*.

Copi's "Un ángel para la señora Lisca" had been produced in Buenos Aires when he was nineteen, but his emergence into the Parisian theatrical world happened almost by accident. Asked to write a sketch based upon his seated woman cartoon character, he ended up writing *Saint Geneviève dans sa baignoire* (St. Genevieve in Her Bath; 1966) and playing the title role himself under the direction of fellow Argentinean Jorge Lavelli, who would go on to direct five more of his plays. Copi recalls showing Lavelli the plays he had written in Argentina, only to be told that his kind of writing was no longer in vogue in France. "Thus I discovered the theater of the avante-garde and grafted myself onto it. It was a coincidence. It wasn't my tradition at all" (*Libération*, Dec. 15, 1987, 37). Lavelli commissioned Copi to write *La Journée d'une rêveuse* (A Dreamer's Day), a macabre play that proved a critical success. However, after being compared to August Strindberg, Copi found himself abandoned by many critics when he entered what he later termed his "drag queen" period. His next three major plays all produced, to his great delight, public scandals.

Eva Perón (1969), a not entirely unsympathetic but highly surrealistic version of the final hours of the woman whose husband had chased Copi's family into exile, provoked violent reaction in Argentina, where Copi's brothers had to go into hiding and where Copi himself was denounced in the newspapers as a "degenerate." The Paris production, directed by Alfredo Arias and starring Facundo Bo, playing Evita in drag, was interrupted by a gang of right-wing thugs, who proceeded to break all the sets and pour red paint on the cast members.

L'Homosexuel ou la difficulté de s'exprimer (The Homosexual, or the Difficulty of Expressing Oneself; 1971), directed by Lavelli and starring Copi as Madame Garbo, is quite easily the funniest (and perhaps most subversive) play Copi ever wrote. In it, Copi masters the tradition of classical French farce (the never-summoned doctor is named Feydeau) in one stroke and begins to move in the direction of the neoclassical form that he would master in his posthumously produced *Une Visite inopportune* (An Untimely Visit; 1988) and *Les Escaliers du Sacré-Coeur* (The Stairways of Sacré-Coeur; 1986). What Michel Cressole observes about *Une Visite inopportune*—"Classical unities, Molière-like *coups de théâtre* ... ferocious gay humor magnified in the style of the *Grand Siècle*" (*Libération*, Feb. 22, 1988, 40)—has its genesis in *L'Homosexuel*. Animating this hilarious but often sadistic farce about sex changes (and sexual roles) set in the wolf-infested Russian steppes is a near-perfect sense of timing, which more and more came to characterize Copi's art.

Loretta Strong (1973), a terrifying and not always immediately accessible monologue, again featured Copi, who appeared on stage stark naked except for high-heeled shoes and a coat of green paint. After a tour in Europe, the play opened in Washington, D.C., as a part of the French contribution to the American bicentennial celebrations. For many of his friends, Copi's most remarkable performance was in his *Le Frigo* (The Refrigerator; 1983), in which he played all six of the characters. His last performance was a public reading of his next-to-last play, *Les Escaliers du Sacré-Coeur*, in 1984.

Copi's critical success during his lifetime perhaps reached its apogee with the performance of his *La Nuit de madame Lucienne* (The Night of Madame Lucienne) at the Avignon Festival in 1985, with Maria Casarès in the role of Vicky Fantômas. But his greatest triumph was posthumous. Perhaps only Copi, writing for a Parisian audience, could have brought off a farce on the subject of AIDS. *Une Visite inopportune*, which won the Prix de la Critique Dramatique (Drama Critics Prize) for 1988, opens on the day that Cyrille, a famous Parisian actor, is celebrating the second anniversary of his AIDS diagnosis. His doctor, Professor Vertudeau—a genial lunatic whose hobbies including performing lobotomies on Sundays—calls in to check on his patient. "Nothing grave in the last few days?" he asks. "Only two heart attacks and a coma," replies Cyrille. "Very good indeed, much too good," observes the professor. "You should have been dead six months ago." Cyrille's nurse calls him the "Sarah Bernhardt of Public Assistance." Copi's hospitalizations, his friends recall, often turned into considerable *événements mondains* (social events). Jorge Lavelli, however, later admitted that he was at first shocked by the idea of beginning to rehearse *Une Visite* as Copi lay dying at the Hôpital Claude-Bernard. But Copi himself, Lavelli recalls, was "enormously amused" by his new text, and rehearsals went forward. The play opened to packed houses in February 1988, two months after Copi's death.

Attending Cyrille in *Une Visite* is his longtime admirer Hubert Dubonnet, who has come to show him aerial photographs of the mausoleum (equipped with television room and giraffe-skin chairs) that he is having constructed for him at Père Lachaise Cemetery. Enter two other characters: a handsome young journalist seeking a deathbed interview, who turns out to be Cyrille's disappointingly straight son, and a madcap diva, Regina Morti—all of whose lines are sung in Italian—who wants to marry Cyrille in order to play his mourning widow. A quarrel ensues as to who will have the rights to Cyrille's corpse. Regina Morti, having her own pantheon constructed in Genoa, proposes that Cyrille's remains be allowed to summer in Italy. Intractable, Hubert points out that it is "strictly illegal to send corpses on holiday, even within the Common Market."

Cyrille, who has been pursued for his entire career by hysterical female admirers, is horrified by the diva's proposal. "I can't possibly marry you," he tells Regina Morti. "I'm sorry to say I have AIDS." Going into a mad scene, the diva chokes on a chicken bone from a buffet catered by Fauchon. Mistaken for a lobotomy patient by the nurse, and stoned on Cyrille's opium, she is wheeled away into the operating room. Several scenes later, she returns equipped with an artificial brain of Professor Vertudeau's invention and sets into motion a final mad scene culminating in an outbreak of pistol fire. In the midst of it all, there arrives a giant sorbet covered with bees. Professor Vertudeau, dressed for the tropics, reappears on his way to found an AIDS mission in Africa.

Cyrille, dressed for the role of Hamlet, stages his own death before the enthralled assembly. But it is only acting. A deadly Aztec poison turns out to be nose drops. After the others depart, the play modulates into a lyrical denouement in which Cyrille and Hubert prepare to set off to read Lorca in the moonlight in a cherry orchard. But a fatal heart attack intervenes. In an ironic tribute to Lorca's "Llanto por la muerte de Ignacio Sánchez Mejías" (Lament for the Death of Ignacio Sánchez Mejías), Copi punctuates Cyrille's peaceful and untheatrical death with three lines of elegant simplicity:—"Hubert, quelle heure est-il?"—*Las cinco en punto de la tarde, señor.*—"C'est l'heure." (—Hubert, what time is it?—Precisely five o'clock in the afternoon, sir. —Then it's time. The reference is to Lorca's ephiphonemic use in his poems of the exact time of Ignacio Sánchez Mejías's death).

Copi's closest friend, Guy Hocquenghem, stated that Copi refused to see any subject—even AIDS—as taboo: "to laugh at everything . . . doesn't mean making fun of those who are ill; rather, it represents a victory over suffering and fear (*Une visite*, 62)." Nowhere is Copi's subversion of death and triumph of the imaginary more remarkable than in those lines in which Cyrille invokes the theater itself as a metaphor for the no-man's-land separating life from death:

As soon as we used to get to the final scenes, I was always impatient for the performance to end. I always wanted to throw off my character as quickly as possible. Once the curtain's fallen, before getting back to your dressing room, there's always an instant when you're no one. It's an unimaginable delight. I shall attempt to sneak into the beyond via one of those black holes. (62)

Any critical evaluation of Copi's theater is complicated by the fact that he created so many of his characters on stage. So, too, Copi's fiction is difficult to categorize because of the highly eccentric way in which he draws upon (and often distorts) details from his own life. In *La Vie est un tango* (Life Is a Tango; 1979), he creates a pseudohistorical novel from the rich vaults of his family history. In three of his novels, Copi himself is the protagonist. His last novel, *L'Internationale argentine* (The Argentine Internationale; 1988), a hilarious parody of Argentine cultural pretensions, mirrors a diplomatic world he knew firsthand. His first novel, *L'Uruguayen* (The Uruguayan; 1973), likewise contains many autobiographical elements. However, none of Copi's novels is autobiographical in any traditional sense. In *La Bal des folles* (The Queens' Ball; 1977), his most picaresque and perhaps most hilarious novel, he goes so far as to give his protagonist his own name, Raoul Damonte. He also causes his real-life publisher (Christian Bourgois) to perish in a fire in a notorious Parisian gay sauna.

And, at least so far as anyone knows, the real Copi never had an Italian lover who attempted a sex change in order to become a Carmelite nun.

Though they continue to have a considerable cult following among Parisian gays, Copi's novels have (at least in France) failed to receive the critical attention accorded his theater. Until his death, Copi was often dismissed by Parisian critics as a countercultural phenomenon. Since 1988, however, he has begun to be compared with Anton Artaud and Samuel Beckett. Critics have begun to find in his theater "the great themes of contemporary civilization: solitude, violence, the anguish of old age and death, *la difficulté d'être*" (the difficulty of being; Corvin, 205).

Nowhere in his oeuvre does Copi betray the slightest interest either in any gay political agenda or in a realistic depiction of the bourgeois or mainstream Parisian gay milieu. Indeed, whenever militant or bourgeois gay characters appear, they are held up to derision and often tortured or killed. In *La guerre des pédés* (The War of the Queers; 1982), a group of ferocious Brazilian transvestites wages a campaign of terror against the mustached clones who represent the militant side of the Parisian gay world. In *Les Escaliers du Sacré-Coeur*, a pretentious antique dealer known only as Pédé (Queer) is sodomized and robbed by two aging transvestites and killed no fewer than three times in the course of the play.

Les Escaliers du Sacré-Coeur, set in the vicinity of the notorious *pissotière* (public urinal) at the foot of the stairway leading up to Montmartre, is perhaps Copi's most magical and lyrical play. Staged posthumously and written in a verse worthy of his neoclassical models, *Les Escaliers* represents a remarkable fusion of farce, nostalgia for pre-1968 gay Paris, and classical form. Fifi and Mimi, two aging drag queens who have fled confinement to return to their old haunts, sodomize and murder an aging queen (Pédé), only to return in the second act as his servants, bearing him to cruise the *pissotière* in a sedan chair. Lou, an adolescent lesbian, is seduced by Ahmed, a young Arab, and returns to the scene nine months later to give birth to his child.

In a hilarious parody of classical recognition scenes, Pédé turns out to be Lou's long-lost father. Lou's mother, a society dowager, befriends Fifi and Mimi and proposes to take them to live in her villa in Nice. But Lou dies in childbirth and Ahmed dies of grief. Sapho (a young delinquent lesbian) and her band of "Saphettes" attempt to abscond with the baby, murder Pédé (for a third time), and are struck dead by a thunderbolt. The only survivors are Mimi and Fifi, who find a fortune in diamonds hidden on the bodies of the dead characters, adopt Lou's newborn (in order to teach him "tous les vices" [all the vices]), and end the play with a panegyric to Destiny.

Early in *L'Escalier*, Copi has Pédé pay a tribute to Blanche Du Bois: "Je ne faisais que passer" (I was only passing through). Like those of Tennessee Williams (whose plays he adored), Copi's strongest characters are women (or pseudo women): great ladies—Evita, Garbo (in *L'Homosexuel*)—drag queens, transsexuals. Through his heightened sense of the outrageous, Copi transforms the bleakest visions of reality into high farce. He always seeks to shock, but nearly always succeeds in transforming outrage and horror into delight.

As Guy Hocquenghem observes, "Copi's theater, like his drawings (if one looks at them closely), was always terrifying. Repeated murders, as in *Les Quatre Jumelles* (The Four Twins), infanticide in *La Tour de la Défense* (The Tower of La Défense), a disfigured monster turned murderess in *La Nuit de Madame Lucienne*, nothing less than so many nightmares on the stage. Yet these are nightmares in which anguish is suddenly destroyed by an outburst of laughter, by the joy of a gag. . . . A shudder dissolves into a spasm of hilarity" (81).

Fifi, at the end of *Les Escaliers du Sacré-Coeur*, perhaps best sums up Copi's art and imaginative gift: "L'illusion sera toujours / le plus naturel des vices" (Illusion will always be / the most natural of vices).

WORKS

The complete theater of Copi (with the exception of *Une Visite inopportune*) was edited by Christian Bourgois in the collection *10/18* (Paris: Union Générale d'Éditions, 1986). Vol. I (no. 1757): *La Journée d'une rêveuse* (1968); *Eva Perón* (1969); *L'Homosexuel ou la difficulté de s'exprimer* (1971); *Les Quatre Jumelles* (1973); *Loretta Strong* (1973). Vol. II (no. 1758): *La Pyramide* (1975); *La Tour de la Défense* (1978); *Le Frigo* (1983); *La nuit de Madame Lucienne* (1985); *Les Escaliers du Sacré-Coeur* (1986).

Le Bal des folles. Paris: Christian Bourgois, 1977.
La Cité des rats. Paris: Belfond, 1979.
La Guerre des pédés. Paris: Albin Michel, 1982.
L'internationale argentine. Paris: Belfond, 1988.
Une Langouste pour deux. Paris: Christian Bourgois, 1978.
Sainte Geneviève dans sa baignoire. 1966 (never published).
L'Uruguayen. Paris: Christian Bourgois, 1973.
La Vie est un tango. Paris: Hallier, 1979.
Virginia Woolf a encore frappé. Paris: Persona, 1983.
Une Visite inopportune. Paris: Christian Bourgois, 1988.

CRITICISM

Aira, César. *Copi*. Buenos Aires: Beatriz Viterbo Editora, 1991.
Corvin, Michel. "Copi." In *Dictionnaire encyclopédique du théâtre*, 205. Paris: Bordas, 1991.
Hocquenghem, Guy. "Copi soit-il." In Copi, *Une Visite inopportune*, 81–82.
Montaldo, Graciela. "Un argumento contraborgiano en la literatura argentina de los años '80: Sobre C. Aira, A. Laiseca y Copi. *Hispamérica* 19.55 (1990): 105–112.

David Wetsel

CORNEJO MURRIETA, GERARDO
(Mexico; 1939) _____

An examination of the literary production of Cornejo Murrieta reveals a significant deviation from its general genres, which include fiction, anthologies, criticism and cultural analysis. This significant exception is an example of gay writing. The text in question is the story "Por eso estoy aquí . . . " (That's Why I'm Here), which appears in his collection *El solar de los silencios* (The Ground of Silences; 1983); it is a story that to date has received little critical attention, despite its technical perfection and the manner in which it is reminiscent, in its literary re-creation of rural motifs, of the formal features and the content of texts by Edmundo Valadés, Juan Rulfo, and Martín Luis Guzmán.

It is important to note how *La sierra y el viento* (The Sierra and the Wind; 1977) has to a great extent overshadowed Cornejo's subsequent writing, perhaps because of the originality of its portrayal of the mythification and the fetishization of a nourishing ancestral land and its transforming agents, and the way in which its evokes urban horrors, the alienation and the uncertainty of the metropolis. Therefore the discovery of a text like "Por eso" is surprising.

The story is a metaphor of the arduous journey of a homosexual (or homophiliac, to use a more postmodern term) from his birth until his suicide. It is a journey grounded in a series of adversities and in the refusal of the "agent"— the main character—to accept his social surroundings. As an extended metaphor, the text focuses on an individual who destroys the wasteland he inhabits and from which he has arisen. What is most interesting about the story is its utilization of a sexual preference as a nonproductive or transcendentally nonproducing phenomenon in order to signal the failure of rural communities that are closely tied to the land. Thus, the metaphor becomes a paradox: the land is no longer fertile, but is only an indifferent spectator (in the sense of the rhetorical figure of prosopopoeia) of its own extinction through its faithfulness to the human machinations of destruction and self-destruction.

Cornejo's text centers on a family living in a mountain village that little by little becomes a desert. The men look for work and pretend, when they return sporadically from the outside, to have succeeded economically across the border in the United States. Meanwhile, it never rains, and the crops never flourish. The rural priest, during his erratic visits, preaches strict rules and proclaims castrating punishments. The women, who are numerous, wait tirelessly and with bated breath for the return of their men. All that are left are nervous virgins who console themselves in a play of masks.

Meanwhile, a father anxiously awaits a firstborn son, who turns out to be a daughter who dies from lack of care. He is "lucky" with his second child: a son—even though the mother dies in childbirth, as the village hag had predicted. In this atmosphere of infertility, the boy is smothered by maiden aunts who scrupulously devote themselves to undermining his wants and brutishly transfer their passions to the context of the church and to the obsessive care of the boy and his younger sister in an attempt to make them as alike as possible, which takes the emblematic form of dressing him as a girl when a photograph is to be taken.

Gradually, the boy makes himself up as a little girl and then as a woman, earning the intransigent disdain of his father. The latter dies, and the son is left as owner of his own restaurant until the appearance of a Guarijíu Indian, Timoteo, for whom he functions as father, brother and mother. In the face of the scorn of the villagers, he is finally left abandoned, overlooking a precipice. He throws himself over the precipice in order to emphasize the idea of death, as opposed to the continuity of life. With traces of fantastic literature, the text concludes with the metaphor of the search for the Father: ''It must have been at that moment, from the other side of reality, when he heard the clear cry of Timoteo: 'Father!' 'Father.' ''

Reality as it exists here, in the guise of daily social life embodied in the town, underscores how homosexuality or homoeroticism can only mean death as a consequence of the mismanagement of land and, ultimately, of life itself. In these terms, Cornejo's text is overwhelming for the pathos it evokes: it hinges on a sexual preference that is the result of specific social conditions in order to specify the death of a group of individuals, and in doing so, it is a text lacking in either humor or ludic catharsis. Cornejo goes well beyond Rulfo's texts, in the sense of the end of a species as seen in the delirious monologue of the main character. Homophilia here functions to underscore the loss of origins, of the land, and of life-giving water. There is no positing of a congenital homosexuality, but rather of an individual whose preference is a social product, a preference that turns bitter and self-destructive. There is a tragic allegory that is something like the final image of Radclyffe Hall's *Well of Loneliness*: not a path to homosexuality but an intranscendental splitting of life. It is a fugue toward nothingness, lacking mockery and humor, but one of an unusual resonance within Mexican regional writing.

WORKS

Al norte del milenio. Mexico City: Leega, 1989.

Cuéntame uno. Ed. Gerardo Cornejo Murrieta. Hermosillo, Mexico: Universidad de Sonora, 1985.

Las dualidades fecundas. Hermosillo, Mexico: Colegio de Sonora, 1986.

Inventario de voces. Ed. Gerardo Cornejo Murrieta. Hermosillo, Mexico: Universidad de Sonora, Instituto Sonorense de Cultura, Colegio de Sonora, 1992.

La sierra y el viento. Mexico City: Arte y Libros, 1977. 2nd ed., Sonora, Mexico: Gobierno del Estado de Sonora. 4th ed., Mexico City: Leega, 1990.

El solar de los silencios. Hermosillo, Mexico: Gobierno del Estado de Sonora, 1983.

CRITICISM

Van Horn, Karel. "*La sierra y el viento*: Del romance a la ironía." *Clit* 2–3 (1984–
     1985): 109–137.

                                                            Darío Galaviz Quezada

CORREAS, CARLOS (Argentina; 1931) _____

According to Oscar Terán, Correas's short story "La narración de la historia"
(The Narration of History), published in no. 14 of *Revista Centro* of the Centro
de Estudiantes de Filosofía y Letras of the Universidad de Buenos Aires (1959),
led to the closing of that journal by government authorities. Although Argentina
had returned to constitutional democracy following the ouster of Juan Perón in
1955, conservative forces, especially a reactionary Catholic hierarchy, which
had suffered considerable humiliation at the hands of the Peronist government,
asserted their authority over social morality as part of a program they felt would
restore decency to Argentine society. This same moralizing impulse provided
ideological underpinnings for the military coups of 1966 and 1976.

     "Narración" certainly had every reason to provoke moralistic outrage. In
addition to focusing on the cruising activities of a young university student, with
specific references to well-known public spaces for homosexual trysts, like the
bathrooms of the Constitución railroad station on the south side of the city,
Correas's story is explicit in its references to homoerotic acts. Eschewing the
coy euphemisms or the sudden shifts to ellipses of most precontemporary Western writing about homosexual encounters, "Narración" speaks of anal penetration, lingual stimulation, masturbation, and frottage, along with disarming
references to genital size: the "masculine" partner (*chongo* in Argentine Spanish) is only modestly endowed.

     But what makes Correas's story especially interesting, beyond the transcen-
dence of the conventions of reticence surrounding sexual dynamics still characterizing English-language models in the 1950s, is the correlation the story
makes between the interpersonal aspects of the homoerotic relationship and sociosexual politics in Argentina after Perón. Ernesto, the middle-class university
student, is the hunter; Mario, his impoverished and younger but aggressively
masculine pickup, is the hunted. Ernesto initially seems to be virtually a paradigmatic repressed petit bourgeois son, circumscribed more by vigilant maternal
love than by ogreish paternal authority, and he seeks sexual release in paradigmatic marginal spaces like public bathrooms, overgrown lots, and deserted sub-
urban streets. Mario initially appears as the swaggering exploiter of such needs,
confident in his power to stipulate the conditions of an encounter. However, as
the story progresses, it becomes apparent that Mario is desperately in need of a
protective figure, and as his guard quickly drops, he reveals an anxious tender-

ness that effectively androgynizes his macho pose. Ernesto, by contrast, is quick to seize on Mario's sudden weaknesses, takes his fill of Mario's willingness to give himself over to someone he believes will be a faithful lover, and then goes his contented way, able to sleep soundly for the first time in a long while. It is, of course, apparent that Mario will wait for him in vain, and Ernesto will move on to find a new adventure somewhere else.

Correas's story, then, becomes a historical allegory (hence the double play of the story's title) of the exploitation of a figure of the proletarian social classes, classes that had become remarginalized with the fall of Perón (a similar treatment is in Héctor Lastra's *La boca de la ballena* [The Whale's Mouth]). The latter half of the 1950s witnessed the reimposition of the prerogatives of a ruling oligarchy, with the universal reduplication of its morality and its technologies of social hegemony throughout the sectors of the bourgeoisie that supported it as a renunciation of Peronism. While a leftist position such as that represented by the *Revista Centro* was equally opposed to Peronist corporatism, it nevertheless felt the imperative to confront the assertion of a reigning hegemony of moral decency during the period, with the concomitant imperative to underscore the dimensions of hypocrisy present in the campaign of moral rectitude.

Correas, of course, does not view homosexual desire as such as a facet of social hypocrisy, in line with a view prevalent in the socialist and anarchist sectors in Latin America until the 1960s that homosexuality was part of the corruption by the dominant classes of the otherwise sexually hygienic (i.e., inherently heterosexual) proletariat. Because Mario's sexuality is present in a manner that breaks with the convention of the aggressive macho, Correas is able to suggest an important distinction between homosexuality as exploitation and homosexuality as a complex of desires that are as much social (the need for protection from a partner) as they are psychological and emotional (the need for trust, friendship and spiritual growth through a partner). Certainly this facet of "Narración," whereby the proletarian *pícaro* becomes an anguished quester and, on that basis, an abused victim, was just as scandalous to the censors as the story's erotic explicitness.

Correas's view of the social and moral hypocrisies of the post-Peronist period are reworked in his novel *Los reportajes de Félix Chaneton* (1984; see Foster 1991), where police corruption and civil rights abuses constitute a point of entry into an underworld created by decent society, as opposed to the prevailing image of a domain of social outcasts against which society can legitimately demand repressive protection. *Reportajes* assumes an autobiographical format, in which the narrative attempts of the title character at self-characterization in the modern period of social and moral instability are intersected with the problematics of sexual identity, both from the perspective of the exclusionary ideology of the dominant social system and from that of the sexual outcast who, by definition, transgresses that system, with all of the deleterious consequences such transgression inevitably implies.

WORKS

"La narración de la historia." *Revista Centro* 14 (1959): 6–18.
La operación Masotta (cuando la muerte también fracasa). Buenos Aires: Catálogos, 1991.
Los reportajes de Félix Chaneton. Buenos Aires: Celtia, 1984.

CRITICISM

Foster, David William. *Gay and Lesbian Themes in Latin American Writing*, 81–87. Austin: University of Texas Press, 1991.
Levinas, Juan Manuel. "Prólogo." In Correas, *Los reportajes de Félix Chaneton*, 11–13.
Terán, Oscar. *Nuestros años sesentas*, 168. Buenos Aires: Puntosur, 1991.

David William Foster

D

DAMATA, GASPARINO (Brazil; 1918–198?)

Damata, whose real name was Gasparino de Mata e Silva, was born in Catende, Pernambuco. After completing his secondary education, he worked as an interpreter on a U.S. base near Recife during World War II and then as a petty officer with the U.S. Transportation Corps on coastal voyages around Brazil and across the South Atlantic. After the war he became a professional journalist and served as the press attaché in the Brazilian embassy in Accra, Ghana, in the early 1960s. Later he led a bohemian existence in Rio de Janeiro, earning his living mainly by dealing in antiques and paintings. He died in the 1980s.

Damata published a novel and three collections of stories of his own and edited anthologies of gay fiction, gay poetry (in collaboration with the poet Walmir Ayala), and writings about the Lapa, the old bohemian area of Rio. Although a minor writer in strictly literary terms, Damata played an important role among the first generation of openly gay writers in Brazil. The anthologies of gay literature were pioneering enterprises in Brazil and served as the basis for the first anthology of Latin American gay literature translated into English, *Now the Volcano*, edited by Winston Leyland. The contacts created as a result of Leyland's visit to Brazil led to the creation of *Lampião*, the first major Brazilian gay newspaper, which appeared monthly from April 1978 to June 1981, of which Damata was one of the founders.

Homosexuality is a major theme in most of Damata's writings. In his first published work, the novel *Queda em Ascensão* (Fall in Ascension; 1951), an autobiographical novel set mainly on an American transport ship carrying supplies to Ascension Island, it forms the thinly disguised key to the climax of the story involving the friendship between the narrator—a Brazilian sailor—and an

American soldier. The short story "O capitão grego" (The Greek Captain),
published in the collection of sea stories *A sobra do mar* (The Remnants of the
Sea; 1955), deals with the ambiguous friendship among three young sailors who
are compelled to return to their ship and submit to the advances of the captain.

In Damata's last work, the collection of short stories titled *Os solteirões* (The
Confirmed Bachelors; 1976), male homosexuality forms the major theme and is
treated openly. The stories are set in Rio de Janeiro, mainly in the gay cruising
area in the city center around Cinelândia, and, as in Adolfo Caminha's *Bom-
Crioulo*, the city is a major presence in the book. Although published in 1976,
during the period of political liberalization, the stories are clearly set in the early
1960s, before the military dictatorship. Three of the stories deal with people's
attitude toward their own homosexuality, revealing a certain unease and defen-
siveness that also underlies the early works. The remaining five stories deal with
the alienation of city life and the power relationships between older, world-wise
homosexuals and the young men who provide sexual services in return for financial or emotional support. Two—"Paraíba" (Construction Worker) and
"Módulo lunar pouco feliz" (Unlucky Lunar Module)—are written as monologues by hustlers explaining and justifying their way of life, while the other
three are written from the point of view of the older men.

The most striking of these is the novella "O voluntário" (The Volunteer) in
which an army sergeant methodically seduces a young private and then loses
him through his possessiveness. The tough self-assurance of the sergeant and
the pliant though dignified attitude of the private make an interesting contrast
to the guilt and self-hatred of Dennis Murphy's American novel *The Sergeant*
(1958), on a similar theme. Power relations are equally evident in the story "A
desforra" (Revenge), in which a dentist humiliates a boy who has left him for
a woman. More moving is the story "Muro de silêncio" (Wall of Silence),
which tells of the last encounter between a middle-class gay man and a young
marine who has recently become a father; although submitting physically, the
marine remains unyielding in his private thoughts.

Damata describes an unattractive world in which predatory homosexual men
use their wealth, position and social skills to dominate poorer, often hungry
partners whose only assets are their youth, looks and virility. The young men
are anxious to preserve their heterosexual image by denying the homosexual
label. There is an equally unattractive streak of misogyny in the older characters,
yet their loneliness makes them vulnerable. The depressing picture is mitigated
by the neutral stance of the author, strong characterization, the lively colloquial
(some say ungrammatical) narrative style, the anticlimactic endings to the five
stories referred to above and the physical presence of the city of Rio. The
attitudes are those of a certain period (somewhat reminiscent of *The Boys in the
Band*, though less extreme). What comes across most strongly from these stories
and gives the book permanent value is the feel of a place and a time.

Damata was openly gay and a pioneering gay activist, but underlying his
writings are both a fascination with and an unease about homosexuality. He

depicts a world of power relations in which emotional relationships seem doomed to transience and failure. His works represent an observation of life rather than an idealized celebration, and are tinged with a disenchantment that stops short of pessimism. It is an uncomfortable picture, compellingly drawn.

WORKS

Antologia da Lapa. Rio de Janeiro: Leitura, 1965. 2nd ed. Rio de Janeiro: Codecri, 1978.
Caminhos da danação. N.p., n.d.
Histórias do amor maldito, comp. Gasparino Damata. Rio de Janeiro: Record, 1967.
Poemas do amor maldito. Ed. Gasparino Damata and Walmir Ayala. Brasília: Coordenada Editora de Brasília, 1969.
Queda em Ascensão: Romance. Rio de Janeiro: Edições O Cruzeiro, 1951.
"Revenge." In *Now the Volcano: An Anthology of Latin American Gay Literature,* 98–126. Ed. Winston Leyland. San Francisco: Gay Sunshine Press, 1979.
A sobra do mar. Rio de Janeiro: Ministério da Educação e Cultura, Serviço de Documentação, 1955.
Os solteirões. Rio de Janeiro: Pallas, 1976.
"Wall of Silence." In *Now the Volcano,* 127–144.
"The Volunteer: A Novella." In *My Deep Dark Pain Is Love: A Collection of Latin American Gay Fiction,* 171–224. Ed. Winston Leyland. San Francisco: Gay Sunshine Press, 1983.

Robert Howes

DANIEL, HERBERT (Brazil; 1946–1992) _____

Novelist, playwright, essayist and autobiographer, Herbert Daniel is best known for his unconventional writings on sexuality and his active support for AIDS campaigns. After founding two of the largest education and alliance centers for persons with HIV in Brazil, Daniel announced that he himself had HIV in January 1989. The disease took his life a few months before he could coordinate the Eighth International Conference on AIDS in Geneva.

While in medical school at Belo Horizonte in the late 1960s, Daniel discovered his passion for writing (initially drama) and socialism (especially Trotskyism). He headed several organizations that promoted an armed resistance to the bloody military dictatorship ruling the country since 1964. The years between 1969 and 1971 marked Daniel's largest contribution to the fragmented, yet highly repressed, guerrilla efforts to overthrow the illegitimate government. In order to free jailed fellow activists, Daniel assisted in the kidnapping of two ambassadors in Rio. In 1971, his photograph appeared on television and in newspapers throughout the country. Without a formal trial or a chance to present a defense, he was sentenced to death twice and to life in prison once. He was never apprehended, however. Also in 1971, Daniel met Cláudio Mesquita, a plastic artist who was to become his lifelong partner, and began an on-the-run existence. Nearly three years in hiding prepared him and Mesquita to leave the country with false documents. They fled to Argentina, then Chile. That was the beginning of seven years of exile abroad, approximately six of which they spent in France, after a few months in Portugal.

Possibly due to his open campaign for respect of different sexual orientations, including homosexuality, Daniel was never granted amnesty. His name alone was excluded from the Abertura (Opening), an amnesty process by which the military tried to gain ideological support and retain power when its social and economic programs failed. Daniel was also the object of ridicule—and his case became very popular—when Jô Soares, a nationally famous stand-up comedian, created the character Sebá, the Last Brazilian Exile in Paris. "It is much more shocking to be a gay person rather than the scapegoat of a dictatorship," Daniel declared in an interview ("O último," 25). Only after the statute of limitations expired in 1981 did he receive a passport and the right to reenter Brazil.

Daniel's style reveals significant influences from a variety of sources and employs several techniques: stream of consciousness, interior monologue, imaginary dialogues with split identities and surreal entities. A multitude of narrators and points of view are juxtaposed in the same narrative. Intertwining terse and verbose passages, Daniel uses fragmentations, graphic distortions and puns that make his narrative sound peculiar, uneven and almost neobaroque.

The underlining motif of Daniel's work is the conflicts and complexities of human sexuality, which take the form of an individual's painful search for understanding of its manifestations in verbal and body language and in social behavior. Daniel's approach to sexuality inevitably deals with self-criticism on the personal level and with unrestrained debate on the community level. Wide-ranging demystification becomes another central aim of his writings.

Passagem para o próximo sonho (Passage to the Next Dream; 1982), his first book-length text, is cataloged as "personal literature." Nevertheless, the author often subverts the author-narration-protagonist line of referentiality. He treats his own story as an invented one about a character not specifically himself. Daniel integrates dreams and symbolic ramifications that come to mind at the moment he writes. The work becomes a fertile combination of raw materials from his own life, without being an autobiographical novel. At times, the reader is baffled, since Daniel's story appears to take the shape of a labyrinth where many characters search for their abodes in their pasts, an effect produced by the use of various coded names alluding to the same person. Interestingly, in real life Daniel was forced to be Herbert, Marcelo, Beto, and many other "men" in order to survive as a guerrilla, escape the country, and obtain asylum. He spent eight years without an authentic identity document. In this respect, Daniel's writings contradict Daniel the narrator's notion that neither art nor life imitates the other. The problem with art, says Daniel (or one of the "narrator-characters" in *Passagem*), is its attempt to imitate life, which can be done only by inventions. The problem with life, in turn, is that people cannot give their lives the purposefulness typical of art or what is invented. Life and art, however, in these terms of personal identity, come very close to each other in Herbert Daniel's case.

Passagem is a unique piece of writing, a gathering of short stories and essays that explores the ideological battlefield of politics and the coming of age of someone who does not fit social expectations, except some of the expectations dictated by socialist groups. An appalling period of Brazilian history is discussed by Daniel, who had become one of the most influential writers of pamphlets and bylaws for the socialist militants. Massive repression propelled the "subversive" organizations to seek coherence and unity; yet internal intolerance and hazy objectives condemned them to weaken and divide into smaller groups, which in turn would weaken and divide, again and again, until all of them disappeared. In order to fit into the orthodoxy and sectarianism of such movements (as groups) and deserve his comrades' respect (as individuals), the prospective gay activist felt he had to "closet" himself again. He abstained from interpersonal sex for nearly seven years, from the age of twenty-one to twenty-eight.

One of the themes Daniel explores most fully in subsequent texts is the notion that part of the oppression of gays has to do with instilling in them a belief that they are "exceptional," a type of human predestined to be marginal (234). *Jacarés e lobisomens* (Dykes and Fags; 1983), a joint project with poet and critic Leila Míccolis, is both a valuable source of information on the history of gay movements and Brazilian and international periodicals that deal with gay and lesbian issues, and an astute argumentation on the complexities of guilt-free sexuality. Daniel addresses the language of intimate extortion through which people undertake to make gays and lesbians come out, "confess" or "bear witness" (26).

Daniel feels that having been a guerrilla and a gay does not give him special rights to speak in the name of a group of "perversive" or "perverted" people. His real-life experience provides him with the interest to write and the pleasure of learning while writing. This happens to be his choice not because he possesses any "confessional" and "sincere" truth to share (which would be nothing less than a gross error of egocentrism), but because sharing appears to be his vocation as a writer.

A point of confrontation in *Jacarés* is Daniel's distrust of the categories defined by conventional medicine, an attack fictionalized in *A fêmea sintética* (The Synthetic Female; 1983). The term *homosexual* and some of its derivations are creations of nineteenth-century psychiatry, and the lack of better terms is abiding. The terminology characterizes mainly a sexual action. Yet an act does not tell us much about the makeup of "homosexual desire." Daniel points out several aspects that underscore the imprecision of such a label. One of them argues that the object of desire is not always the object upon which an action is performed. Masturbation, bestiality and homosexuality, for instance, may be variations on or substitutions for a genital, heterosexual action. In his effort to understand *homosexuality* in dimensions that go beyond the meaning of a single term, Daniel conceives of it as a way of living one's desire, a process that depends on the individual's development. This process may breed various forms of volition that depend on sociohistorical forces that interact with one's perception of desire. To Daniel, *homosexuality* is ultimately an act of affected volition, rather than a "free discretion," the element that will cause an individual to live out, in different ways, his or her desire—either homosexually or heterosexually.

Another hybrid text, *Meu corpo daria um romance* (My Body Could Turn into a Novel; 1984), appears to be, in terms of format, Daniel's most ambitious project. It utilizes all of the discursive modes mentioned above. Daniel uses the concept *amalgam* to describe the text's composite and elliptical structure of memories, fictions and other fragments. His lengthiest piece is divided into eleven sections named for body parts and systems. Each of these segments represents one minute of an eleven-minute, late-night trip on a bus in the Copacabana section of Rio. Every segment repeats the two or three paragraphs that set up the bus scene in Part One: the male narrator is jeered by the bus riders. They are expressing a bigoted reaction to a kiss on the lips with which the narrator had said good-bye to his male lover before boarding the bus. Among the men calling the narrator-protagonist names are two youngsters from the Workers party, one of whom, ironically, wears a T-shirt that says SOLIDAR-NOSC, the name of the Solidarity party in Poland. The men's humiliating mockery leads the narrator to share a book-length reflection on the evolutions of his sexuality. The turmoil also inspires him to make a general statement about the human body as a point of psychological and political tension.

The narrative chronicles the narrator's past and present, from childhood in the early 1950s to his writing career in 1983. It sheds light on the teenager's adventures from bar to bar in the second half of the 1960s. It is an unfulfilled search for happy sex or for a truly loving encounter with "men who were like ladies." In the meantime, the youngster has matured enough to learn that the greatest barrier against him is his low self-esteem, his overwhelming opinion that he is ugly and obese. Better days await him, however. In his mid-thirties, the narrator not only has found a male partner truly capable of loving him and consoling him under any circumstances, but also been able to enjoy occasional and satisfying sex with women like Nina, whose conceptions about homosexuality become a thematic vein. Nina tells him that the increased number of homosexuals in the early 1980s runs parallel to other waves of liberalism, like the movement for the legalization of marijuana. The "gay fever," Nina contends, is a kind of protest against social evils of the times. Some individuals fed up with the system choose to show their disgust in that way. They end up influencing other people and thus creating a fad, a fashionable type of behavior: the gay behavior. For Daniel, however, if there is more homosexuality out there, then there is more of a search for pleasure in its own right.

Most of Daniel's learning has to do with behavior among male homosexuals. Within that world, he realizes, any ugliness may become a stigma; gays can be brutal when they reject one another. Feelings of unattractiveness often make him

hide from people but crave them at the same time. At an early stage of development he learns he can do well in heterosexual intercourse, but there is very
little pleasure in it compared to action with men. Most significantly, he knows
that fetishism of appearance is not simply a heterosexual male domain; women
and gay men also objectify the body. One of the most interesting features of
how Daniel perceives his own former sexual habits has to do with the discrep-
ancies between masturbatory fantasies and interpersonal actions. In the former
situation, he consistently dreamed of being penetrated by good-looking, insensitive young men, "plain dicks." While making love to flesh-and-blood men,
however, he himself would hold on to taboos held by men who would do nothing homosexual but penetrate: "no kissing on the lips, no touching the other
person's dick, and no messing with his own ass" (156). Daniel also learns that
the concern with such taboos needs to be part of a preliminary conversation
between two partners suddenly interested in each other. Who will be the active
partner and who will be passive? Daniel suspects that this questioning is universal; he knows it occurred in Brazil, Portugal and France in the 1960s and
1970s.

One of the most humorous pieces by Daniel serves to illustrate the heterogeneity within so-called homosexual and heterosexual categories. *As três moças
do sabonete* (The Three Women with the Bar of Soap; 1984) dramatizes fascinating crisscrossings in terms not only of sexual categories but also of age,
race and socioeconomics. Among the characters are three gay men who identify
themselves by use of women's clothing, hair styles and/or way of talking. One
character is convinced he is hermaphrodite by birth and says s/he longs to become thoroughly female. Fausto (or Tina)—a seventeen-year-old son of traditional landowning parents—changes his mind later in life about changing his
genitalia. The second character is rather authoritarian, wears female hair styles,
but dresses like a man. Luciano (Lulu), like Fausto, is white. He owns the small-
town beauty salon where José Barbosa (Zé), a black, muscular, semi-illiterate
man, works as the janitor. He, too, is effeminate in clothing and gesture. The
complexity of these characters within the symbolic manifestations of their sexual
orientation is best elaborated by two scenes. In the first, Valdirene (Direne), a
divorced woman who goes to bed with half the men in town, manages to seduce
Zé, after he has called her "bitch" and tried to stop her advances, by saying
he is a "lesbian." While they make love, Zé relates to her breasts as something
"as tasty as a prick." To Direne, Zé now is as good as a macho man. The scene
ends when, having reached orgasm, they share their confusion in regard to their
own gender as well as to that of the object of their sexual desires.

The other sequence that stands for a vast array of meaning involves the love
affair between Zé and Tiago, a young, white, middle-class guerrilla who has
just come out of the closet. To the great amazement of his straight friend Joïo,
Tiago has also, like Lulu and Tina, left behind the fear of being considered a
flaming faggot. Zé, who had always dreamed of meeting the perfect gentleman,
is interested in Tiago. But because he fears he will lose his job, he is willing

to give him up so that his boss, Lulu, also interested in Tiago, may "score" with him. Tiago, in turn, prefers Zé, to whom he is eager to give affection. Zé eventually becomes the first man Tiago ever kisses, which fills Tina and Lulu with jealousy. They attack Zé racially and morally, accusing him of not being a true fag but a fake one (just to keep the job at the salon), and of being a "lesbian," for making it with a queer.

Much as in *As três moças*, there seems to be an even blend of ludicrous and terrifying symbols in *Alegres e irresponsáveis abacaxis americanos* (Gay and Irresponsible American Pineapples; 1987), a novel on the myths and fears of AIDS, including the allusion in the title to gays from the United States. The connections between the epidemics, gays and prejudices, already discussed in *Jacarés*, become the center of *Alegres* and reappear in essay form both in *Vida antes da morte* (1989) and *AIDS, a terceira epidemia: Ensaios e tentativas* (1991). These last works dealing with the epidemics, especially *AIDS* (which he wrote with the American anthropologist Richard G. Parker), appear to call for solidarity with HIV carriers and to stress the necessity that we, as a society, now have for learning how to live with AIDS in private and social spheres.

WORKS

AIDS, a terceira epidemia: Ensaios e tentativas. São Paulo: Iglu, 1991. With Richard
     Parker.
Alegres e irresponsáveis abacaxis americanos. Rio de Janeiro: Espaço e Tempo, 1987.
A fêmea sintética. Rio de Janeiro: Codecri, 1983.
Jacarés e lobisomens: Dois ensaios sobre a homossexualidade. Rio de Janeiro: Achiamé,
     1983. With Leila Míccolis.
Meu corpo daria um romance. Rio de Janeiro: Rocco, 1984.
Passagem para o próximo sonho: Um possível romance autocrítico. Rio de Janeiro:
     Codecri, 1982.
As três moças do sabonete: Una apólogo sobre os anos Médici. Rio de Janeiro: Rocco,
     1984.
Vida antes da morte/Life After Death. Rio de Janeiro: Jaboti, 1989.

CRITICISM

"O adeus a um lutador." *Jornal do Brasil*, Mar. 31, 1992, p. 3.
"Herbert de Carvalho, o penúltimo exilado." *Pasquim* 643 (Oct. 22, 1981): 22–23.
"O memorialismo precoce acabou." *Pasquim* 703 (Dec. 16, 1982): 9–11.
"O último exilado." *Pasquim* 632 (Aug. 6, 1981): 25.

                                                                    Dário Borim, Jr.

DENEVI, MARCO (Argentina; 1922) ⸺⸺⸺⸺

Denevi, of Italian descent, was the youngest in a family of seven. He was born in Sáenz Peña, a suburb of Buenos Aires, where he lived for many years until he moved to Belgrano, closer to the downtown area. He attended law school but did not complete his studies. He held an administrative position until 1968, when he decided to dedicate himself to writing.

Denevi's writing career started in 1955 with the publication of his first literary creation and first novel, *Rosaura a las diez* (*Rosa at Ten O'Clock*). The book received the first prize in a contest sponsored by Editorial Kraft; it remains one of Argentina's best-sellers. Two years later, in collaboration with film director Mario Sofficci, Denevi adapted the novel into a movie that won the National Film Institute's first prize and the Critic's Award in Argentina in 1958 and was nominated at the Cannes Film Festival for best plot. In 1957 the play *Los expedientes* (The Expedients) won the National Prize for Comedy. In 1960 the novel *Ceremonia secreta* (*Secret Ceremony*) was awarded *Life* magazine's first prize for Latin American writers. From then on, Denevi's writing production increased, gaining local and international reputation and success.

Variety characterizes Denevi's output: novels, plays, essays, short stories, articles, screen or stage adaptation, even poetry. Commenting on this characteristic of his work, Denevi declared: "I tried to exhaust all the genres, as a kind of revenge" (Gálvez, 93).

A unifying element in Denevi's creations is that many main and secondary characters are insignificant in the eyes of society and history. These characters are "weak, loners or marginal" (Gálvez, 93), proclaimed failures and unnoticed shadows in the social order. Denevi's vision of his antiheroes is not one of empathy, which would provoke compassion in the reader. Echoing society's embarrassment, Denevi uses an irony that not only agrees with the view of history and the condemnation of the weak, but also allows him to avoid a sentimentalism that would encourage pity rather than interest.

Denevi's characters are antiheroes in the sense that they are the exact opposite of what is defined as exceptional and superior. Yet they represent a majority in society and in history, since they constitute the greatest number of the population. Through characters like Adalberto Pascumo in *Un pequeño café* (A Small Café; 1966) and Camilo Canegato in *Rosaura a las diez* (1955), Denevi gives a voice to the weak and the unfit. His selection of marginal characters reflects the reality of Argentine society and, unavoidably, of Latin American culture. Social misfits constitute a type that is regarded as being antiheroic. To portray marginality, Denevi uses a code based on physical appearance, public and private behavior, ethical values, social identification in the professional context and relation to the opposite sex—which often is female, since most of Denevi's figures of "weakness" are men. Given this circumstance, the homosexual man constitutes an ideal marginal character.

Homosexuality is neither a strong nor an omnipresent component in Denevi's work, although it appears frequently enough to deserve being addressed. It occurs occasionally and always in a marginal group. Denevi's attitude regarding homosexuality is not that of a militant or a defender, yet he is always unmistakably supportive. When he places homosexual characters in the spotlight, they are presented as they appear to the average "respectable" and "normal" member of the Argentine/Latin American population. They are the intriguing anomaly, annoying, shameful, entertaining and overly comical, but they never awaken any deep interest or respect. When Denevi presents homosexual characters in the context of the stereotypical average Argentine heterosexual groups, male or female, he locates them within this very social and cultural context.

In the novel *Los asesinos de los días de fiesta* (The Murderers of the Holidays; 1972), two of the main characters, Honorato and Patricio de la Escosura, are homosexual men. Through these two characters, Argentine men and Argentine women, as well as Argentine society as a whole, are portrayed by Denevi. The attitude of men toward male homosexuality is signified through stereotyped situations. The admission of Honorato as a member to the male group is granted through communion of interest in exhibited sexual acts when Honorato pays his dues by amusing the men with representations of sexual enjoyment or perversion. Pornography being an exclusively masculine domain in this society, and homosexuality being considered the exclusive domain of pornography, communication and acceptance occur within the irony and double meaning played by the author. Sex is also the exclusive domain of men, a reality that ironically unites homosexual and heterosexual men.

The division of this society into a male group and a female group does not seem to clearly generate a third group to which Honorato and Patricio de la Escosura would belong, for identifying and defining such a group as homosexual men would signify its acceptance and its respect. Maintaining a vague association with either of the two existing groups asserts that homosexuality is an anomaly, an error of choice, a psychological problem in need of being fixed. In Denevi's representation, because they do not fulfill their male role, homosexual men are rejected by women—whom, on the outside, they tend to resemble. However, they remain men, to the extent that the superiority of males over females, as a birthright, cannot be taken away. Homosexual men may be readmitted to the honored group as long as they share with heterosexual men what differentiates men from women: machismo. Men are suspicious of other men only when they do not communicate with them by using the proper social code, which consists mainly of being different from women and distancing themselves from them.

The evocation of homosexuality seems to be for Denevi more a means than an end. As through other marginal and unadmitted entities, the author observes and reveals the application of tacit or less tacit rules within the Argentine society specifically, and within the Latin American culture in general. The interest is in the reaction of the normality to the abnormality, of the moral to the immoral. By emphasizing the repercussion of a shock between established and rebel groups, Denevi reverses roles and ironically portrays the dominant normality as inferior and inadequate. He rewrites the conventional social code, thereby annulling it.

WORKS

Los asesinos de los días de fiesta. Buenos Aires: Emecé, 1972.

Ceremonia secreta. Buenos Aires: Calatayud, 1960. English version as *Secret Ceremony.*
     Trans. Harriet de Onís. New York: Time, 1961.

Los expedientes. Buenos Aires: Talia, 1957.

Obras completas. Buenos Aires: Corregidor, 1980.

Parque de diversiones. Buenos Aires: Emecé, 1970.

Un pequeño café. Buenos Aires: Calatayud, 1966.

Rosaura a las diez. Buenos Aires: G. Kraft, 1955. English version as *Rosa at Ten
     O'Clock.* Trans. Donald A. Yates. New York: Holt, Rinehart and Winston, 1964.

CRITICISM

Carranza, José María. "La crítica social en las fábulas de Marco Denevi." *Revista ib-
     eroamericana* 80 (1972): 477–494.

Gálvez, Raúl. *From the Ashen Land of the Virgin: Conversations with Bioy Casares,
     Borges, Denevi, Etchecopar, Ocampo, Orozco, Sabato in Argentina.* Oakville,
     N.Y.: Mosaic Press, 1989.

Revel Grove, Ivonne. *La realidad calidoscópica en la obra de Marco Denevi.* Mexico
     City: Costa Amic, 1974.

Yates, Donald. "Marco Denevi: An Argentine Anomaly." *University of Kentucky For-
     eign Language Quarterly* 9.3 (1962): 162–167.

                                                            Dominique M. Louisor-White

D'HALMAR, AUGUSTO (AUGUSTO THOMPSON; Chile; 1882–1950) ⸻

Winner of the first National Literature Prize awarded in his native country,
D'Halmar was the illegitimate child of a French sailor and an upper-middle-
class woman. A delicate child, he was nicknamed Margarita (Daisy) while attending school; he never completed his education because he would get sick
whenever tests were to be given. Luis Alberto Sánchez said of him, "Tall and
beautiful as an archangel, and homosexual as a Greek ephebe, he loved the sea
and adventure, oratory and the love that dares not speak its name" (17).

In 1902 D'Halmar published what has been called the first naturalist novel
in Chile, *Juana Lucero*, a story about the descent of a lower-class young girl
into prostitution and madness. In 1903, he founded a Tolstoyan colony that
failed, according to Ramón L. Acevedo, because of his "sickly dependence on
his grandmother." He formed a passionate friendship with another young writer,
Fernando Santiván, that went as far as the signing their literary production with
a joint name, Fernando D'Halmar or Augusto Santiván. Santiván's marriage to
D'Halmar's sister put an end to the friendship. These biographical details reap-

pear almost obsessively in D'Halmar's production: the quest for either a father or a friend who can serve as a double of the protagonist.

D'Halmar wrote a number of prose works dealing with homoerotic or homosexual relationships at a time when such a topic was not considered a fit literary subject. Of these, the most important is *La pasión y muerte del cura Deusto* (Passion and Death of Father Deusto; 1924), the story of the thwarted love affair between a Catholic priest from the north of Spain and a gypsy boy from Andalusia. Other major works dealing with libidinal relationships between older and younger men, presented as friendships within a father/son or master/servant configuration, are *Nirvana* (1920); *La sombra de humo en el espejo* (The Shadow of Smoke in the Mirror; 1924) and *Los alucinados* (The Hallucinated; 1935). The first two are autobiographical, dealing with D'Halmar's trips through the Orient, Egypt and India as a Chilean diplomat, and recounting his adventures with servant boys. The third consists of four short stories dealing with older male/younger male couples.

There are themes common to all of D'Halmar's homoerotic stories and novels. The relationships are all, with very few exceptions, doomed to failure and one of the two principal characters usually meets a tragic end, whether by suicide (Deusto) or through sickness (Zahir, Dariel, Pedro). In several instances, the younger man is the reincarnation of a woman the protagonist has loved and lost; in others, he is the incarnation of androgynous Mystery—that which lies beyond time and space and is signified by the figure of the Sphinx. Rarely does D'Halmar allow his characters full expression of their desires; only one, the gypsy boy in *Deusto*, dares give a name to his love for the priest, who rejects it and, while running away, dies under a train's wheels. Underlying the plots is a continuous questioning of man's relationships to the divine, nature and other men; the mechanisms of forgetting and remembrance; the elusiveness of desire; and man's ultimate aloneness. In spite of the place he occupies in the history of Chilean literature, D'Halmar's works are largely forgotten today; the most recent editions of his novels date from the 1960s.

WORKS

Los alucinados. Santiago, Chile: Ercilla, 1935.

Amor cara y cruz. Santiago, Chile: Ercilla, 1935.

Canciones con palabras. Santiago, Chile: Editorial del Pacífico, 1972.

Capitanes sin barco. Santiago, Chile: Ercilla, 1934.

Cristián y yo. Santiago, Chile: Nascimiento, 1946.

Gatita. Santiago, Chile: Imprenta Universitaria, 1917.

Juana Lucero. Santiago, Chile: Turin, 1902.

La lámpara en el molino. Santiago, Chile: Imprenta New York, 1914.

Mar. Santiago, Chile: Cruz del Sur, 1943.

Mi otro yo. Madrid: Editorial de la Novela Semanal, 1924.

Nirvana. Barcelona: Casa Maucci, 1920.

La pasión y muerte del cura Deusto. Madrid: Editorial Internacional, 1924.

La sombra de humo en el espejo. Madrid: Editorial Internacional, 1924.
Tríptico de pasión. Santiago, Chile: Ercilla, 1935.

CRITICISM

Acevedo, Ramón L. *Augusto D'Halmar: Novelista. Estudio de ''Pasión y muerte del cura Deusto.''* San Juan, P.R.: Editorial Universitaria, 1976.

Foster, David William. *Gay and Lesbian Themes in Latin American Writing*, 33–37. Austin: University of Texas Press, 1991.

Orlandi, Julio, and Alejandro Ramírez. *Augusto D'Halmar: Obra-estilo-técnica.* Santiago, Chile: Editorial del Pacífico, 1942.

Sánchez, Luis Alberto. *Historia comparada de las literaturas americanas.* Vol. IV: *Del vanguardismo a nuestros días.* Buenos Aires: Losada, 1976.

Alfredo Villanueva

DIACONÚ, ALINA (Argentina; 1945) ⸻

Diaconú was born and raised in Bucharest, Romania, where her father was a famous art critic and her mother a plastic artist. For political reasons her parents had to emigrate in 1959, and they chose Buenos Aires as their final destination. Although adaptation was not easy, Diaconú's efforts to integrate into her new society can be clearly observed in the fact that within only a few years she was among the outstanding writers of her generation in Argentina, and her work gained international recognition.

Her first novel, published in 1975, received excellent reviews. *La señora* (The Lady) is the story of a bourgeois woman who, in the midst of an existential crisis, allows her sexuality to flourish in an attempt to recapture the past and slow the loss of her youth. Although her second novel, *Buenas noches, profesor* (Good Evening, Professor; 1978) was awarded the *faja de honor* (sash of honor) of the Sociedad Argentina de Escritores (Argentine Society of Writers), the censors of the military junta deemed it immoral and ordered its confiscation soon after its publication. Nevertheless, the novel, which deals with the love between an older professor and an adolescent student, affirmed the literary qualities that Diaconú had revealed in her first work.

Enamorada del muro (Clinging Vine; 1981) presents, through the events during one week in the life of its protagonists, the ambiguities that besiege an aimless adolescent world, with its abrupt changes and its passing obsessions, examined in minute detail. The young protagonists, led by Bruma and King Kong, wander like lost and listless automata, set into motion by the ambivalence or dissatisfaction that grips them. *Enamorada* is probably the clearest description of the world of adolescents during the period of the military dictatorship in Argentina between 1976 and 1983.

Diaconú has stated that in her fourth novel, *Cama de ángeles* (Bed of Angels;

1983), "I have given birth to a monster, but it is a monster I love." She re-
creates the myth of the goddess Morgana, whom Hermaphoditus had disinterred,
in order to use it as the focal point of a relationship between the hermaphrodite
Angel-Angela (there is a play on the masculine and feminine forms of *angel*)
and Morgana, a diva in decline. The novel is narrated in the first person by the
hermaphrodite (who since the death of his mother lives alone, closed up in his
apartment). It is presented from the marginal perspective of a voluntary exile
that allows Diaconú, through her characters, to engage in a profound analysis
of reality versus appearances. The series of oppositions proposed by Angel-
Angela permeates the development of the story: masculine vs. feminine, I Angel
vs. I Angela, Morgana's decline vs. her glorious past, the superior vs. the me-
diocre, normal vs. abnormal, the quotidian vs. the extraordinary—all in the
context of observations concerning both the imperceptibility of trivialities and
the most profound questions of the spirit.

Morgana has reached such a point of confusion that she is unable to differ-
entiate between reality and the staged tragedies of her career. Angel-Angela, in
accord with the identity adopted for the moment and the masks used to establish
a distance from Morgana, describes the immense loneliness occasioned by his
physical condition and, in the end, the senselessness that surrounds him but that
is the only true meaning he has been able to find in his life. From his position
as narrator, Angel-Angela constantly seeks different ways to justify his condition, and he exhibits it more as a virtue than as an error of nature, seeing in
himself a new Tiresias. The most important thing for him about his life is the
juxtaposition of two possibilities, one that is congenital and one that is freely
chosen by him.

Morgana, as a consequence of her profession, also manifests an opposition
between appearances and reality, the element that provokes the hermaphrodite's
curiosity and his desire to penetrate the star's orbit, since from the outside he
has been unable to uncover her mysteries. The encounter between the two leads
to a journey during which their personalities will be laid bare. This journey is
both absurd and mythical, grotesque and meaningful. They enter into the dimensions of a real world that for them is populated by unknown and almost
infernal images. The catharsis of their adventure is the mythic journey, something similar to a voyage through the belly of the beast.

Although Diaconú draws neither psychological nor sociological conclusions,
she maintains a balance that is sufficient to make her characters and their story
profoundly credible. She is basically concerned with the aesthetics of her story,
and she attempts to present the central question with the greatest artistic skill
possible, along with a mixture of humor and irony, two elements that figure
prominently in her characterization of the inner world of the hermaphrodite. As
Diaconú says, "A work should basically be a question and not an answer. I do
not want to provide solutions because I don't have any." The situation described
in the novel is irresolvable. The end of the narration closes a circle that represents and inevitably returns to the beginning.

The many allusions in Diaconú's novels to Argentine historical events, some direct and others oblique, make this novel a symbolic collage, and Morgana and Angel-Angela and their worlds constitute a powerful metaphor of the decline of the country as seen from the perspective of the last year of what propelled it into chaos, the Process of National Reorganization by which the military sought to restructure the country.

WORKS

Buenas noches, profesor. Buenos Aires: Ediciones Corregidor, 1978.
Cama de ángeles. Buenos Aires: Emecé, 1983.
Enamorada del muro. Buenos Aires: Ediciones Corregidor, 1981.
Los ojos azules. Buenos Aires: Editorial Fraterna, 1986.
El penúltimo viaje. Buenos Aires: Javier Vergara Editor, 1989.
La señora. Buenos Aires: Rodolfo Alonso Editor, 1975.
Quotes by Diaconú are from my personal interviews with her in Buenos Aires in 1984, 1986, and 1990.

Osvaldo R. Sabino

DIEZ CANSECO, JOSÉ (Peru; 1904) _____

Diez Canseco's 1934 novel, *Duque* (Duke), deals with the corruption of the higher classes in Peruvian society through the trope of homosexual deviance. It has become a commonplace to attribute sexual intolerance to the politics of the Right. Diez Canseco's text shows how the political Left also operates from paradigms of sexual conduct first laid out by the European bourgeoisie according to parameters of correctness/incorrectness. Virility came to be defined as the abandonment of sexual passion and the sublimation of sensuality through the development of a national and social leadership. Sexual lack of control was seen as subverting the social order and posing a danger for state security. Two strategies became operational: on the one hand, a total desexualization of the social body (always identified as the masculine body) was preferred; and on the other, rules were created to place individual sexuality at the service of the state. This occurred in revolutionary movements as well. Thus, from very early on, the Russian Revolution abandoned its policies concerning sexual freedoms, and the French Communist party preached racial salvation through the family, condemning abortion and sterilization as bourgeois practices. In Latin America, João Trevisan and Allen Young have explored the homophobia of the Left in Brasil and Cuba. The antibourgeois Latin American novel reflects these ideological developments.

Diez Canseco utilizes the trope of aberrant sexual conduct on the part of Teddy Crownshild Soto Menor and his lover and future father-in-law, Carlos Astorga, to signify bourgeois moral decadence and to depict homosexuals as having a great deal of invisible social and economic power. Teddy and Carlos belong to the upper middle class. Their world is ruled by a homosexual free-masonry described in hierarchical and economic terms—sex between upper-class males and their servants, valets and chauffeurs. Diez Canseco includes heterosexual sex and lesbian scenes as well, intending to show that the upper bourgeoisie has always abused sexuality. In a short chapter about the ideological framework of the novel, it becomes evident that the concept of the social phi-losopher Max Simon Nordau of "degeneration" is still current. When one of Teddy's friends expresses the view that homosexuality is, after all, a different kind of beauty, the author feels compelled to footnote the comment, dissociating himself from it. The only open homosexual, Pedro, is portrayed as a piggish buffoon. Astorga seduces Teddy through discourse, referring to "Socrates, Plato, Wilde, Verlaine, Michelangelo, Shakespeare, Poe, all the damned apologists of the dirty vice." Teddy breaks with Astorga after watching himself in a mirror as they make love and vows never to return to "that dirty lair where the filthy sodomitic demon awaited him." *Duque* represents a current in Peruvian narra-tive that stigmatizes homosexuality from the parameters of leftist ideology.

WORKS

Duque. Lima: Biblioteca Peruana, 1973.

CRITICISM

Escajadillo, Tomás G. "Estudio preliminar." In José Diez Canseco, *Estampas mulatas*, 7–53. Lima: Universo, 1973.
González Dittone, Enrique, and Rafael Salmón de la Jara. "Perfil humano de José Diez Canseco." In José Diez Canseco, *Susy*, 11–34. Lima: Renée de Diez Canseco, 1979.
Trevisan, João, trans. *Perverts in Paradise.* London: GMP Publishers, 1986. Trans. of *Devassos no paraiso.*
Villanueva-Collado, Alfredo. "Meta(homo)sexualidad e ideología en dos novelas anti-burquesas peruanas." *Confluencia* 7.2 (1992): 55–63.
Young, Allen. *Gays Under the Cuban Revolution.* San Francisco: Gay Fox Press, 1981.

Alfredo Villanueva

DONOSO, JOSÉ (Chile; 1925) ——————————

Donoso, born in Santiago, Chile, studied at the University of Chile and at Prince-ton University. He has taught English literature at the Universidad Católica in Chile and has been a visiting professor at the writers' workshop of the University of Iowa. He also has taught at Princeton University and Dartmouth College.

Donoso currently lives in Chile, where he teaches and participates in academic and journalistic activities. He often travels to foreign universities.

The novel *Coronación* (Coronation; 1958) centers on Doña Elisa, an old woman who from her bed controls her closed world and all the people around her. In spite of her age and her senility, as the novel progresses, this old princess becomes more sane in comparison with the rest of the residents of her mansion. The other characters live in her shadow; they steal from each other, hate each other, abuse each other and love one another in a constant game of reality and fiction within the fiction of the narrative. In this way the narrative takes on the dramatic dimensions of lunacy in which envy and repression emerge, and hidden passions and solitude appear.

The most important element of the text is the behavior of people around Doña Elisa. She is enveloped in two worlds: her own, which includes her grandson Andrés, and the world of the servants. Fifty-four-year-old Andrés is single and has taken upon himself the care of his grandmother. She symbolizes Andrés's complete lack of freedom and experience, his indecisiveness and his fear of any type of risk.

The attraction and desire that Andrés feels toward Estela, the young servant girl, is nothing more than Doña Elisa's fantastic and demented jealousy that is transformed into her grandson's daydreams. Andrés does not remember any activity in his life that has broken the rules dictated by a social class that is decaying from lack of heirs and from the destructive effects of a class of servants and workers who live, fornicate, proliferate and take risks that incessantly threaten the existence of the ruling class.

Even though the text does not offer clear evidence of Andrés's homosexuality, the reader must look for an interpretation of the gaps that are hidden behind the text. Andrés has been castrated by his grandmother and by a society in which sexual roles are well defined. He does not fit into the social context of his friends, like Carlos, the doctor, who are married and have lovers. With other men, mostly his age, Andrés discusses authors and French biographies such as one dealing with Marie Antoinette, queen of France. A homosexual characterization potentially exists, but no open discussion nor development is given because Andrés cuts off all communication that could lead to this unmentionable topic. The narrative silence corresponds to the rules and regulations imposed by the culture because this subject is one that must be avoided out of fear of shame. Within the culture, homosexuality is mentioned only when used against an individual or a group for political reasons or for defamation.

In *Este domingo* (This Sunday; 1966), the main character is a child who, by means of dramatized games, acts out the absurdities of the adult world. The narrator takes on the voices of the grandfather, Alvaro; his wife, Chepa; and one of the grandsons who tries to understand the activities of the adults. The novel can be understood through a situational game that follows the psychological lines of the characters. Chepa is attracted to Maya, a prisoner she helped free. She replaces her husband, whom she treats like a brother, and her grown children with him. At the same time Alvaro has replaced the many women of his sexual fantasies with Violeta, his mother's maid. The grandchildren replace the adult absurdity with games that imitate the adult world by means of good and bad characters who constantly fight for power.

The novel is built on obsessions and substitutions that gradually take on reality. Chepa, left alone by her children and sexually abandoned by her husband, allows herself to be drawn to Maya. She visits him in jail, then helps free him and sets him up in the outside world. The maternal and sexual obsession that she feels toward Maya is centered on the mole near his lip. She is also attracted to his rough hands. This mole is also the point of attraction for Alvaro, who has gradually lost his masculine appearance and is, according to his grandchildren, turning into a doll. Alvaro is superficially repulsed by Maya's mole, but this feeling takes on different meanings to the point of becoming an obsession that both attracts and dominates. The mole that is a symbol of grotesque masculine beauty for Maya is, for Alvaro, a symbol of death and of his loss of virility and power. He can longer control Chepa, nor can he control Violeta, because she too is now under Maya's power. Although homosexuality does not explicitly exist in the text, the reader doubts the repulsion/attraction that Alvaro feels toward Maya. The feeling within the text is one of claustrophobia and must remain so in order to avoid any type of discussion of sexual satisfaction or dissatisfaction. The text permits this freedom only within the children's games, which are no more than parodies, stated in innocent or comic tones, of what the children have seen or heard.

Within *El lugar sin límites* (*Hell Has No Limits*; 1966/1971), homosexuality appears both as an object and as an element in a system of political power that is manipulated by Don Alejo, landowner of the region and the heir to the land grants (*encomiendas*) that have been in his family since the Spanish colonization. He owns both large tracts of land and the entire town where the novel takes place. The meeting place for all the characters and the central focus of the narrative is the town brothel and bar, which is run by Japonesa Grande (Big Japanese Woman). Manuela, a homosexual drag queen, arrives here to act one evening and becomes the star of the show. The men in the town solicit "her" each night; they have fun with her and also ridicule her. The star's happiness is linked to her acceptance, but her triumph fades and she gradually becomes an object of abuse at the end of each performance. Japonesa Grande bets Don Alejo that she can convince Manuela to make love to her. She succeeds, and as a result of the bet they become the owners of the property that the brothel stands on. An additional product of this bet is Japonesita (Little Woman Japanese), who becomes the owner of the brothel when her mother dies.

As Manuela grows old and mentally relives her days of splendor, the town becomes more and more isolated from all forms of civilization and communication. Both Japonesita and her father, Manuela, are in love with Pancho, a truck driver who is Don Alejo's godson and protégé. Pancho's arrival excites both father and daughter, but especially Manuela, who decides to get her red

Spanish flamenco dress out of the trunk so that she can dance and sing for him. Manuela regains her charms and at the same time breaks with the daily routine that is suffocating her. She seduces Pancho, kissing him and dancing for him; they then dance together until his brother-in-law discovers them. Pancho denies the facts and hits Manuela to show his hatred of queers. His problem is that any form of secrecy has been removed, and he must reveal himself to society. He will not accept the accusation that he is gay for fear of being judged.

Many readers sense that Pancho does not accept himself, though the text does not clearly say so. Nevertheless, Pancho does not publicly accept his sexuality with another member of his family present in the bar. On the other hand, it is clear that Pancho accepts and responds to Manuela's caresses privately, when he is excited by the dance and the darkness that separates them from the socially acceptable heterosexual world outside. Fear that his secret will become known forces Pancho, at his brother-in-law's insistence, to physically punish Manuela. In doing so, he unintentionally kills her. In this way the drag queen is victim of both the system and her own honesty. Manuela is accepted in the town by her equals, the women, who consider her one of them. She is the star that fades and eventually dies; both heroine and victim who finally escapes the destruction of the town. Pancho is left with his guilt and society's stigma.

The theme of lesbianism appears in *El obsceno pájaro de la noche* (The Obscene Bird of Night; 1970), beneath the mask of a children's game played by seven old women and Iris Mateluna, the only adolescent in the Rinconada nursing home. In their games, dramatized in the secrecy of the basement, Damiana plays the role of Iris's baby. Iris, in her role as mother, must feed Damiana and clean her sexual organs, which provokes laughter among the other old women. All of this activity must be hidden from the other members of society in the nursing home/orphanage. El Mudito, a character who goes through different transformations and has various names throughout the novel, is related to the loss of masculinity. He becomes the seventh old woman in the group. The old women castrate him and turn him into one of them. This game of dramatizations and changes, personification within the narrative, allows for an escape from the adult world and into solitude. The homosexual character does not exist within the text, but appears through the dramatizations that include homosexual activities. Thus sexual tendencies that do not correspond to the established norm are hidden behind the mask of a game.

Homosexual behavior is also evident in *Casa de campo* (Country House; 1978), in which one of the adolescent characters takes control of games that are a projection of the adult world. The child actors identify with the roles they play in the dramatized games, and they generally seek the role that best fits their personality. Juvenal is the homosexual who assigns the roles and has power over the other actors. Celeste, his mother, recognizes his sexual "deviance" because of his fixation on women's makeup and other activities generally regarded as feminine. Juvenal is extremely devoted to his mother. He manipulates her just as he manipulates and attracts his family when he plays the piano during their nightly gatherings. Like Manuela in *El lugar sin límites*, Juvenal openly declares his homosexuality to his social group. When he catches his cousins Justiniano and Higinio mutually masturbating, he says that he does not want them to touch each other, adding that he is the only faggot in the family (154). He tells his cousins that the difference between masturbating each other and being fags who dress up like marquises and roll their eyes while playing the piano, like him, is very minimal.

The difference between Manuela and Juvenal, both openly gay characters, lies in the fact that Juvenal holds power and dominates the group. He does not allow himself to become the victim of a system; he takes advantage of it. Nevertheless, Juvenal's open homosexuality is a subject the adults never mention. Only Celeste lets the reader know that she recognizes Juvenal's sexual tendencies, but does not discuss them.

La misteriosa desaparición de la marquesita de Loria (The Mysterious Disappearance of the Marquise of Loria; 1980) presents a lesbian relationship between two adults, Tere Castillo and Casilda. Casilda is the mother-in-law of the main character, Blanca, a Nicaraguan living in Madrid. Casilda and Tere Castillo are, at the same time, lovers of the Count of Almanza. The novel first recounts the escapades of Blanca as frustrated wife and then lover. Her private life with her husband and her secret life with her lover, a painter, are depicted. The novel becomes more and more pornographic as the secret becomes more exposed. The protagonist finds herself in a sexual act along with Tere Castillo and Almanza. In another situation, open lesbianism is seen within a closed and secretive context. Here lesbianism is not a game nor a dramatization, as it was in *El obsceno pájaro de la noche*, but a preference within a group who accept it as civilized behavior. This group has a different concept of what is permitted within society, and the orgy is the way of going against the established norms of society, even though the truth never leaves the group. Later in the novel, the narrator describes Casilda's attempt to seduce Blanca, her daughter-in-law. Casilda suggests that they and Tere Castillo go to Paris together. Casilda tries to legalize what is secret by stating that current moral standards are more flexible than before. The narrator does not offer an opinion and allows the characters to reveal their ideas regarding sexual behavior through the dialogue.

In *El jardín de al lado* (The Garden Next Door; 1981) homosexuality is insinuated by the attraction the main character feels toward the younger characters on whom he spies. The main character and narrator is an exiled writer who lives in Sitges, a beach resort that attracts European tourists and is known for its sexual freedom. Julio, the writer, is attracted to Bijou, the son of exiled Chileans who live in France. Nevertheless, when he feels that he is identifying with homosexuals, he becomes upset and confesses that in spite of his liberal posture, he fears the criticism of society that still declares all homosexual relationships "acts of sin" (79). Bijou frequents gay bars, and he has direct contacts in the gay world. What the narrator fears most is the close tie between his son, Patrick, who lives in Marrakesh, and Bijou. The proximity of the beautiful adolescent makes him uncomfortable, but the attraction that he feels for him is not really sexual; rather, it is a desire to become him and adopt his values and appetites. The same thing happens when the narrator watches the couple next door while they dance and enjoy themselves. His attraction is obsessive, and behind the mask of the attraction that he feels for their beauty and youth he hides an envy that covers his desire to possess and be possessed.

Bijou is a freethinker who must survive. The characters who know him in the gay world say that he is not a queer, but that sometimes will go with an old queen who is willing to pay him, then go to a bar to pick up women to cleanse himself. The text presents not homosexuality but sexual freedom—an availability to sexual pleasure without discrimination between male and female partners. Thus the purely homosexual activity does not play a role within this context or is avoided by the narrative voice for fear of criticism.

Finally, one can observe that any sexual activity that does not correspond to what is permitted by the establishment takes the form of a game, the theater or a show, and hides behind the idea of sexual diversity. The characters in general reject homosexual activity and thus mask it. Manuela, the drag queen in *El lugar sin límites*, suffers punishment and death; Juvenal in *Casa de campo*, on the other hand, is known to be gay by those within a group that he dominates. This group does not identify with what is acceptable and not acceptable in the adult world. Homosexuality is presented in Donoso's works, but no direct narrative opinion discusses the problem and reaches a defensive stance.

WORKS

Casa de campo. Barcelona: Seix Barral, 1978.
Coronación. Santiago, Chile: Zig-Zag, 1958.
Este domingo. Santiago, Chile: Zig-Zag, 1966.
El jardín de al lado. Barcelona: Seix Barral, 1981.
El lugar sin límites. Mexico City: Joaquín Mortiz, 1971.
La misteriosa desaparición de la marquesita de Loria. Barcelona: Seix Barral, 1980.
El obsceno pájaro de la noche. Barcelona: Seix Barral, 1970.

CRITICISM

Calderón, Héctor. "Ideology and Sexuality, Male and Female in *El obsceno pájaro de la noche*." *Ideologies and Literature* 5.1 (1985): 31–50.
Gutiérrez Mouat, Ricardo. *José Donoso: Impostura e impostación*. Gaithersburg, Md.: Hispamérica, 1983.
Kostopulos-Cooperman, Celeste. "Man's Search for Liberty and Authenticity in the Fictional Microcosm of José Donoso—an Existential." In *The Creative Process in the Works of José Donoso*. Ed. Guillermo I. Castillo-Feliú. Rock Hill, S.C.: Winthrop Studies on Major Modern Writers, 1982: 67–76.

Swanson, Philip. "Structure and Meaning in *La misteriosa desaparición de la marquesita de Loria.*" *Bulletin of Hispanic Studies* 63 (1986): 247–256.

Urraca, Beatriz. "El concepto de personaje en *Casa de campo*: Entre la tradición y la innovación." *Revista chilena de literatura* 31 (1988): 105–124.

A. Alejandro Bernal

E

EIELSON, JORGE EDUARDO (Peru; 1924)

Eielson, born in Lima, is a plastic artist who writes poetry and works as a performance artist. His moving back and forth between painting and literature demonstrates an experimental stance that defies classifications, although he is better known for his written work. His early poetry is marked by the reading of the Spanish mystics and a deep awareness of the catastrophe of World War II. On a trip to Europe he devoted himself exclusively to painting while in Paris. After a crisis of expression Eielson produced poems, reminiscent of the great Peruvian poet César Vallejo (1892–1938), in "Habitación en Roma" (A Room in Rome; in *Poesía escrita*), that perhaps best represent his quest for the body and his sense of the apprenticeship of life. The exploration of the word in the visual and sculptural aspects of poems in "Temas y variaciones" (Themes and Variations; in *Poesía escrita*), and "Canto visible" (Visible Song; in *Poesía escrita*) among other experimental texts, also leads to silence and mistrust of language. Eielson has progressively displaced the word as an autonomous object, converting it into an instrument for revealing the wonder and horror of human existence.

In *El cuerpo de Giula-no* (Giulia-no's Body; 1971), where the focus is on the metamorphosis of writing, the transvestism of the narrator in an imaginary game of masks that extends from Venice to a beach in Lima. The characters change their roles with respect to the dominant gender paradigm, and actually change their biological sex. Giulia, the narrator's lover, a model-prostitute, photographer-priestess-mother-innocent-perverse, is also Giula-no (Giulia plus *ano* [anus]), a beautiful, fat, adolescent ice-cream vendor. The rituals of sex are undertaken by these figures through their indeterminate desire, free of the dominant models.

Taking as a basis a poem that he had rewritten on various occasions, Eielson composed over a period starting in the 1960s a narrative on the Peruvian sea, *Primera muerte de María* (María's First Death; 1988). One of its features is the endowment of the Peruvian characters with the language and sensuality of ancestral traditions. In a parody of biblical narratives, Eielson intercalates an autobiographical diary in which he relates some of his artistic obsessions with a description of Lima in its death throes. The characters exchange colors and masks related to popular Catholic rituals, yet their carnal desires are never repressed. Pedro, a friend of the fisherman José, earns a living sodomizing a young man of the upper class. Described against the backdrop of a corrupt society and the abuse of power, these characters embody the basic themes in Eielson's poetry and visual arts: death and desolation.

Eielson has written texts about pre-Columbian art, an aspect of his work that he calls "Paisaje infinito de la costa del Perú" (the endless landscape of the Peruvian coast). His happenings have included a performance party in the moving car of a subway train in Paris involving unknown participants, an experience that confirms his idea of art as a living organism. Perhaps the most significant example of his vision of the human body is *Noche oscura del cuerpo* (Dark Night of the Body; 1983), a series of fourteen poems based on a trope taken from Saint John of the Cross and focusing on the loving, divided, multiplied body. In them masturbation, defecation, self-contemplation and lamentation are reference points for the exploration of a plural *I* that is unattainable and irrepressive.

WORKS

"Cámara luciente." *Kuntur. Perú en la cultura* 5 (1987): 42–45.
El cuerpo de Giula-no. Mexico City: Joaquín Mortiz, 1971.
Mutatis mutandis. Lima: La Rama Florida, 1967.
Noche oscura del cuerpo. Bilingual ed.; French version by Claude Couffon. Paris: Altaforte, 1983. Complete version, Lima: Jaime Campodónico. Editor/Colección del Sol Blanco, 1989.
Poesía escrita. 2nd ed., rev. and enl. Mexico City: Vuelta, 1989. Contains all of Eielson's published poetry, plus previously unpublished and scattered material.
Primera muerte de María. Mexico City: Fondo de Cultura Económica, 1988.

CRITICISM

Canfield, Martha L. "Lazos de color—nudos de luz: Jorge Eduardo Eielson: Pintor y poeta." *Inti* 34–35 (1991–92): 187–192.
Chirinos, Eduardo, and Jannine Montauban. "Un místico en la noche oscura." In E. Chirinos, *El techo de la ballena. Aproximaciones a la poesía peruana e hispanoamericana contemporánea*, 59–68. Lima: PUCP, 1991.
Cobo Borda, Juan Gustavo. "J. E. Eielson: *El cuerpo de Giula-no*." In his *La otra*

literatura latinoamericana, 43–46. Bogotá: El Ancora/Procultura/Cocultura, 1982.

Forgues, Roland. "Un doloroso adiós. Entrevista a Jorge Eduardo Eielson." In his *Palabra viva*, 2.81–93. Lima: Studium, 1988.

Higgins, James. "Two Poet-Novelists of Perú." In *Hispanic Studies in Honour of Geoffrey Ribbans*. Ed. Ann L. Mackenzie and Dorothy S. Severin, 289–296. Liverpool: Liverpool University Press, 1992.

Oquendo, Abelardo. "Eielson: Remontando poesía de papel." *Hueso húmero* 10 (1985): 3–10.

Oviedo, José Miguel. "Jorge Eduardo Eielson o el abismo de la negación." *Cuadernos hispanoamericanos* 417 (1985): 1991–1996.

Reisz de Rivarola, Susana. "De la elegía latina a la *Poesía escrita* de Jorge Eduardo Eielson o Mar de amor nuevamente entonado." *Sur* (Buenos Aires) 350–51 (1982): 173–186.

Urvanivia Bertarelli, Eduardo. "Los 'Reinos' de Jorge Eduardo Eielson." *Revista de crítica literaria latinoamericana* 13 (1981): 71–79.

Zapata, Miguel Ángel. "Matriz musical de Jorge Eduardo Eielson (entrevista y selección de poemas)." *Inti* 26–27 (1987–1988): 93–114.

Roberto J. Forns-Broggi

ETTEDGUI, MARCO ANTONIO
(Venezuela; 1958–1981) ⎯⎯⎯⎯⎯⎯⎯⎯⎯⎯⎯⎯

A writer, journalist, art critic and performance artist, Ettedgui between 1975 and 1978 acted in plays by Lope de Vega, Bertolt Brecht, Henrik Ibsen and Venezuela's Román Chalbaud. In 1979 he became interested in writing, directing and performing in spectacles combining poetry, theater and painting. He also lectured on the avant-garde theater and began working for the newspapers *El Universal* and *El Carabobeño*, and publishing articles about dance in *Sunshine* magazine. In 1980 and 1981 he was involved in a series of events focusing on the role of literature and art in mass communication. One of them, titled "Conductas científicas" (Scientific Behaviors), was based on *Dial a Poem* by John Giorno. He also performed in garages, where he staged a series of happenings called "Arteología" (Artology), in which he integrated his poetry into the body experience by mixing texts with acting while taking a bath or brushing his teeth. And in public spaces such as the National Art Gallery, the Museum of Contemporary Art, and the Rajatabla Theater in Caracas, he celebrated social events like his birthday, Valentine's Day, a Dada evening, and his hospitalization for the removal of a kidney stone. In September 1981 Ettedgui, acting in the play *Eclipse en la casa grande* (Eclipse in the Big House), was accidentally shot to death on stage when an actress fired a prop gun that, unknown to anyone, contained an iron bar.

In spite of his youth, Ettedgui left an abundant body of work in poetry, theater and conceptual art. *Ettedgui: Arte información para la comunidad* includes a selection of his texts with introductory essays by Juan Calzadilla (theater), Elsa Flores (conceptual art) and Alejandro Varderi (poetry), as well as photographs by Julio Vengoechea documenting his happenings. Most of his work, however, remains unpublished.

Ettedgui's pieces were conceived with a clear sense of breaking the boundaries between low and high art from a homoerotic perspective. Drawing on surrealism and dadaism, his poetry and theater plays favor a rhizomatic structure that opens language toward a semiotic plurality, with desire and pleasure as the driving forces. They favor multiple levels of meaning in conformance with Baudrillard's map of decomposed fragments in a postmodern pastiche—eclecticism without hierarchy, so to speak, enabling the ensemble of apparently contradictory references. In this sense, his book *Tacón agudo* (Sharp Heel; 1980) brings to the center what had been left at the margins of Latin American culture, the existence of a sophisticated urban homosexual culture often blended into mainstream society: a conversation about female attire between two transvestites, a priest, a dwarf and a soldier in a gay bar or the recycling of cultural artifacts (television, beauty contests, Spanish pop singers, American cars) by a metropolitan housewife, a taxi driver and a student becomes a piece of a fragmented landscape often obliterated by society and the subject of intervention by the mechanisms of power.

To the extent that Ettedgui's texts are the poetical and critical frame of his bodily experiences, it is not surprising that in his performances he brought together on stage ignored minorities and the symbols of power and nostalgia in a postindustrial society. Ettedgui read as he drank rum against a backdrop of television sets, computers, and altars filled with Catholic and popular imagery, dancing to Caribbean rhythms and escorted by transvestites, homosexuals, lesbians, and drug addicts. The audience little by little invaded the stage, and the events ended with a techno-retro-kitsch party. The public readings and performances in which Ettedgui engaged in scatological acts and masturbation with animals became a success, shaking passivity and transgressing desire. Ettedgui, however, did not conceive his works with an intention of *épater le bourgeois* but, rather, with the purpose of "changing the private behavior of the spectator," as he wrote in the text for his event *Feliz cumpleaños, Marco Antonio* (Happy Birthday, Marco Antonio; 1980), a spectator living in a Latin American city and, therefore, shifting continually from the sublime to the grotesque. Thus, Ettedgui's work becomes an allegory for cultural, social and sexual anxiety in an urban setting that the author attempts to soothe with his sense of humor and his own behavior, totally freed from political, social and moral restraints.

Two of Ettedgui's plays, *El error* (The Error; 1981) and *Sanitario para caballeros* (Men's Room; 1981) treat several issues related to certain poems and events. *El error* deals with Susana and Ana María, lovers haunted by the phantom of Ana María's deformed baby, whom Susana killed, that is transposed into a doll that they show to people and that Ana María uses for masturbation in her attempt to exorcise her guilt. *Sanitario para caballeros* details the sexual experiences of a go-go boy who also works in the bathroom of a bar and the misogyny of a physics professor, who is engaged in a monologue about the role of science in the theory of mass communication. Drawing on the avant-garde theater and the deep psychological profiles of Ingmar Bergman's characters, Ettedgui undertakes the decanonization of culture and the delegitimation of social values in an increasingly conservative community. Thus, his main achievement, in view of the shortness of his productive period, to draw attention to the conventions of Venezuelan society, characterized by its lack of memory and the quickness to erase all traces of physical and intellectual disturbance.

WORKS

Ettedgui, arte información para la comunidad. Ed. Alejandro Varderi, Juan Calzadilla and Elsa Flores. Caracas: Oxígeno, 1985.

Alejandro Varderi

F

FERNÁNDEZ-FRAGOSO, VÍCTOR
(Puerto Rico; 1944–1982)

Born in San Juan, Fragoso arrived in New York City in 1965. After receiving his Ph.D. from the University of Connecticut with a dissertation on the Dominican poet Pedro Mir, he worked for the Puerto Rican Traveling Theater in New York City. During the 1970s he was very active in the Hispanic theater there, and put together three theatrical pieces based on the poems of the Puerto Rican Julia de Burgos, the Dominican Pedro Mir and the Chilean Pablo Neruda. He also wrote original plays. In Puerto Rico, he published poetry in *Zona carga y descarga* (Loading and Unloading Zone), one of the most important literary magazines of the 1970s, and *Claridad* (Clarity), the most important pro-independence newspaper. In New York City, Fragoso founded a literary group and editorial project called La Nueva Sangre (New Blood). He wrote seven books of poetry, only two of which have been published. At the time of his death, he was an associate professor at Rutgers University, which created the Víctor Fragoso Scholarship for students of literature and theater. He is the first known Puerto Rican poet to die of AIDS.

Fragoso produced the first two books of poetry by a Puerto Rican that explicitly textualize homosexuality, *El reino de la espiga. Canto al coraje de Walt y Federico* (The Realm of the Ear of Grain. Song to the Courage of Walt and Federico; 1973) and *Ser islas/Being Islands* (1976). As is true of most of the Puerto Rican gay and lesbian writers who textualize issues related to their sexuality, the poems of Fragoso deal with the personal and the political. Of course, in gay and lesbian poetry produced in a sexist, homophobic society (as is the case with women's writing), the personal is the political and vice versa. For Fragoso and for the majority of Puerto Rican gay and lesbian writers, the political includes the status of Puerto Rico vis-à-vis the United States. The political independence of Puerto Rico and the political freedom of the homosexual person, as well as the personal freedom of every Puerto Rican and every human being on the planet, are closely linked. In *Ser islas* this interrelation is the basis for the central metaphor of a universe of islands, each one different but all part of the bigger island Earth/Humanity. What matters is the freedom to be different, which is the most universal of human rights. Herein lies the heroism of each person and the heroism of the lyric subject in Fragoso's poems. *El reino de la espiga* and *Ser islas* form a political and philosophical, as well as a personal, autobiography.

The more intimate—and shorter—poems of Fragoso deal with love, loneliness and sex. The background in many of them is gay post-Stonewall New York City. Instead of using an explicit language, Fragoso chooses ambiguity and a metaphorical language (probably because of his admiration for Federico García Lorca). But more important than the subject matter and the images is the resulting homosexualization of reality (love, sex, the night, a door): for example, the doors, keys and keyholes in poem 13; the narrow streets in poems 22 and 18; the wind in poem 19; the thread in poem 14, all in *El reino de la espiga*. A superb example of homosexualization of reality occurs in one of the first poems in *Ser islas*: "dressed in stars on his forehead." At the end of this short poem, the "beautiful young man" and the lyric speaker ejaculate, and so does the night.

WORKS

La expresión teatral de la comunidad puertorriqueña en Nueva York. New York: Centro de Estudios Puertorriqueños, 1975.
El reino de la espiga. New York: Nueva Sangre, 1973.
Ser islas/Being Islands. Trans. Paul Orbuch. New York: El Libro Viaje, 1976.

CRITICISM

Barradas, Efraín. "Fragoso, Víctor, *Ser islas/Being Islands*." *Sin nombre* 9.4 (1979): 91–93.
———. "Fragoso, Víctor, *El reino de la espiga: Canto al coraje de Walt y Federico*." *Ventana* 12 (Apr.–May 1975): 35–40.
Droz, Vanessa. "Testimonio de la labor literaria de Víctor Fragoso." *El Mundo*, Feb. 11, 1982, p. 6–B.
———. "Víctor Fragoso, inédito." *El Mundo*, Oct. 3, 1982, p. 7–B.
Martínez-Capó, Juan. "La escena literaria. Víctor Fragoso, *El reino de la espiga: Canto al coraje de Walt y Federico*." *El Mundo (Puerto Rico ilustrado)*, Mar. 16, 1975, p. 10.
———. "Libros de Puerto Rico. Víctor Fragoso, *Ser islas-Being Islands*." *El Mundo (Puerto Rico ilustrado)*, Aug. 28, 1977, p. 9–B.
Rodríguez-Matos, Carlos A. "Actos de amor: Introducción al estudio de la poesía puer-

torriqueña homosexual y lesbiana/Acts of Love.'' *Desde este lado* 1.2 (Fall 1990): 21–33. Trans. William Mena.

————. ''Apuntes para un acercamiento a la poesía puertorriqueña contemporánea: 1962–1986.'' *Revista del Instituto de cultura puertorriqueña* 94 (Oct.–Dec. 1986): 45–55.

Carlos A. Rodríguez-Matos

FOGUET, HUGO (Argentina; 1923–1985) —————

Foguet was born and died in Tucumán, but his life as a merchant seaman took him all over the world, which accounts for the enormous quantity of cultural references in his works, supported by innumerable and varied readings. Like any author who may be described as coming from the ''interior'' of the country or as producing ''regional literature,'' he published a series of texts that slowly began to be considered a part of Argentine literature, as least as it is identified by Buenos Aires. From the volume of stories *Hay una isla para usted* (There's an Island Just for You; 1963) to the novel *Frente al mar de Timor* (Facing the Timor Sea; 1976), his books do not go beyond the limits of the Tucumán community or the endogamic force of a writing that gradually begins to overflow the narrow confines of provincial practices. With the novel *Pretérito perfecto* (Past Perfect; 1983), the book of poems *Naufragios* (Shipwrecks; 1985) and the posthumous stories of *Convergencias* (Convergences; 1986), Foguet achieved national and international recognition.

Both Foguet's poetry and his fiction focus on the intersection between power and sexuality, historicity and sexual division, temporality and racism, classist rituals and textual cannibalisms, all undermined by the construction and deconstruction of nationality. In *Naufragios*, for example, the ''Meditación de Martín Lutero en el w.c.'' (Martin Luther's Bathroom Mediation) unquestionably refers to Walt Whitman, via Federico García Lorca's *Poeta en Nueva York* (Poet in New York). By the same token, other texts—especially the ones grouped together under the title ''En el Canal'' (In the Canal)—are based on metaphors in which history manifests itself in terms of living and insistent strata of successive and simultaneously polyphonic temporalities, preserving through words the tortuous traces of colonialization and the forced capitalism in the Southern Cone. However, the foundation of Foguet's writing is not the condition of the mestizo but a metaphor of incest as the experience of the same copulating with the same in the framework of a narcissistic familiarity (nationality) understood within the liberal framework of the bourgeoisie. Utopia, in his writing, lies in androgyny or hermaphroditism, which is the basis of the allegory of Tiresias, with his successive experiences of man and woman, or of men appropriating the power of women to construct the canons of divinity.

Foguet's writing cannot achieve Otherness. It describes difference and allows for the repressed to emerge; it raises aesthetically what had been excluded and despised by the official history of Argentine culture, which is not a textual corpus of the "interior" (which would be its least important feature) but a model of cultural production. The zone of textual production in Foguet is, therefore, sameness, even in the unfolding of all of the possible plays on oppositional binarism. The key to these binarisms is what is nonbinary, noncorrelative about sex and desire. For this reason the utopia is androgynous, a locus where the two sexes can cohabit peacefully and where the law of genital exclusivity is unconstitutional, where desire can reproduce itself as a consequence of the immediacy of the other gender. The other utopia, which is probably more synthetic, is that of the hermaphrodite, capable of reacting with his "double" body to every sexual opportunity.

For Foguet, the world reveals a dispersion of genders, races, classes and texts, which history combines capriciously but repetitively. There is no such thing as the production of knowledge, but rather an experience of castration in the face of the orientation of desire that makes of the other an appendix of the same, lost in an earlier time, yet now (at the time of the writing) plausibly recoverable in a frenzy outside the law (and therefore outside gender, race, sex and class), attainable only via a terrorist act or at least one that is violent and even self-destructive.

Foguet writes what may be considered an inversion of the erotic novel of the nineteenth century, particularly those that constitute an intersection between eroticism and nationalism; the result is a carnivalized view of modernization and modernisms. Therefore, one cannot speak in terms of a polyphonic novel that, through a collage of numerous sources (Foguet's vast reading), forms a network of truth; rather, it is an ironic and monologic view that looks toward difference without actually attaining it, thereby characterizing it in terms of degradation, decadence, apocalypse, the end of the world, without ever transcending the narcissistic limits of the subject and without escaping from the paternal law of pleasure.

Pretérito perfecto narrates a correlative process. On the one hand, it details the construction of an Argentine national tradition based on successive exclusions relating to sex, race, religion and class. That construct is embodied in the paradoxical figure of Clara Matilde, the aging representative of the national bourgeoisie, who is the victim of the policelike interrogation of the historian Furcade. On the other hand, the novel describes the emergence of all the elements that have been excluded by this construct and the ways in which they manifest themselves, beginning with early-twentieth-century populist movements and midcentury Peronism, which lead to successive outbursts of social repression that leave behind the bodies of the dead, the disappeared and the despairing.

Through a recounting of Clara's memory, based on gossip, and the no less self-interested articles drawn from newspapers (the stuff of official history), the novel marshals a series of characters and narrators. These include Clara's daughter, Celita Sorensen, "the androgynous Grace," who is always portrayed clad in worn jeans: she is the focal point for a problematics of sexuality in the novel, a little boy with a vagina, suggestive of the image of the hermaphrodite. By contrast, Solanita is the woman with the phallus, perfect, divine, always unpredictable. Both women succumb to the allure of Surya, the black, the exotic, the spurious, the raunchy, the definitive macho. They come together in Surya, and through him the family's lineage will be reduced to the impotent reality of the mestizo body.

In contrast to Surya, Gabriel Iturri is the homosexual boy–man. He goes from the provincial town of Yerba Buena to Paris, where he is consecrated by the kisses of Marcel Proust, next to whom he is buried. Then there is Rachel del Busto Beausergent, the eternal woman of eternal desire, before whom the entire family succumbs. Rachel and Surya, by exposing the separation of the androgynous, enter into the desiring and metonymic vertigo of the demands of the other. They are the ones who have need of the other, and they seek desperately to return to an original androgyny, going against society's customs, conventions, principles and rules. They are desire incarnate, bodies torn by castration. Gabriel and Rachel are capable of giving up everything, and they lay bare the basic lack at the heart of the family, the political and vital weakening of the patriarchy.

Finally, there is Patricio Santillán, the matron with a penis, the homosexual, enormous and exhuberant, in his aura of French manners and Greco-Latin bearing. He is barely able to sublimate desire in ceremonial masturbations of a grand style that shades off into decadence on the shores of the Río de la Plata. The other characters embody the emergence of bisexuality, with all of its charms and its dangers to the illusion of a unified and regulated national identity. This problematical nationality may still be milked for profit by the dissatisfied European. An example of this is the episode concerning Imelda Lazarte, a prostitute from the slums of Tucumán to whom the Virgin appears and who foresees the end of the world. She is killed by the military but immortalized in a popular myth in a sequence of events that, according to Foguet (although it is certainly apocryphal) was used by Federico Fellini in a film.

Pretérito perfecto, as a text that functions on two levels in a Proustian attempt to reconstruct time while demonstrating its irreparable loss, examines the lethal result of modernization in a Borgean process that subsumes all of Western culture, fragmenting and abolishing the underpinnings of its meaning. This narration, which is nostalgic (what is lost forever) and apocalyptic (the future as already abolished) is superseded in *Convergencias*, the title story of which portrays the possibility of realizing a repressed homosexual desire in the now classic Freudian ceremony involving dreaming and the body of a woman.

A Brazilian brothel provides the setting for a narrator/character (everything here is replicated and doubled) to attain the otherness of sex and time via the body of Adessabeba. Lying next to her triggers dispersed memory that comes together in a shared historical homosocial experience; temporal planes converge, along with desire that, at the moment of greatest frenzy, includes João, who is

described as a Greek combination of ambiguity and beauty, the masculine counterpart to Adessabeba. João sought to find himself on the *Hermaphrodite*, a ghost
ship employed in the slave trade. His meeting with Adessabeba occasions other
meetings, infinite previous encounters in other languages, leading him to witness
a scene in the cabin of the boat where he is engaged in the "indescribable act
of perverting a boy." This instant, like a violent and sadistic crystallization of
rape and torture, constitutes a broad, transnational allegory of political violence
grounded in sexual violence, one that is not exclusively Argentinean, through
which homosexuality reclaims its right to a place in a hermaphrodite or androgynous utopia (Adessabeba–João), albeit one that is always a failure.

Homosexuality appears as the always excluded but tenacious other that underlies and sustains heterosexual representation. Yet this lack seems to be what
spurs desire without achieving its satisfaction, thereby leading to a violence now
directed toward the subject itself. Such a narrative arrangement allows one to
perceive the framing of a perverse cultural dynamic (one that is perhaps modern,
perhaps postmodern) through which "going beyond" what is permitted in order
to reveal the "other face" of heterosexuality implies recognizing how one is
both victim and victimizer of a will to pleasure that is oriented to and subjected
to the pleasure of the Other—that enslaving system, that cultural machine of
capitalism, that ghost ship that always comes into view in order to legitimate
repression and homophobia.

WORKS

Convergencias. Buenos Aires: Ada Korn Editores, 1986.
Frente al mar de Timor. Buenos Aires: Granica, 1976.
Hay una isla para usted, y otro cuentos. Tucumán: Consejo Provincial de Difusión
    Cultural, 1963.
Naufragios. Buenos Aires: El Imaginero, 1985.
Pretérito perfecto. Buenos Aires: Editorial Legasa, 1983.

Gustavo Geirola

G

GABEIRA, FERNANDO PAULO NAGLE (Brazil; 1941)

Journalist, essayist, autobiographer and novelist, Fernando Gabeira is best known by the public and literary critics for his three-volume autobiography, which appeared between 1979 and 1981. It chronicles his personal and intellectual growth from guerrilla activism against the Brazilian military dictatorship in the 1960s to his return to Brazil in 1979, after nine years in exile in Chile, Algeria, Cuba and various European countries.

The trilogy and its predecessor, a 1980 book version of a polemical Paris interview with the political tabloid *Pasquim* (Broadside), have aroused both contempt and excitement. "There is a puerile attraction to the interviewee," argues Robert Krueger, whose irony and dissatisfaction target Gabeira "as a sexy, intellectual, romantic, contemplative, somewhat repentant *ex-guerrilheiro*" (177). Even though one of Gabeira's objectives is "to smash the idol of the romantic mystical macho myth of the Latin American *guerrilheiro*," as Krueger puts it, "he embodies it." Failing to discern the unique power of Gabeira's storytelling, Krueger states that the Brazilian author's "reactionary" perspective on the past is nostalgic, self-centered, heavily psychological and subjective.

Gabeira's work has also received much better reception. The first volume of his autobiography, *O que é isso, companheiro?* (What's This, Pal?; 1st ed. 1979), won the Jaboti, an important Brazilian literary award, in 1981. The three volumes remained on top of the best-seller list of the popular magazine *Veja* (Look) for several years. Silviano Santiago is one of the first critics to call attention to the extraordinary quality of this narrative, even though he justifiably attacks Gabeira's lesser talent in *Hóspede da utopia* (Guest in Utopia; 1981). For Santiago, the novel's flaw emerges at the outset: a note by Gabeira warns the reader that characterization in the following narrative complies with some real-life characters' consent (''Pizza'').

Davi Arrigucci, Jr., also candid about Gabeira's shortcomings and strengths, relates the similarities between Gabeira's award-winning book and Graciliano Ramos's classic *Memórias do cárcere* (Jail Memoirs; 1953). In both autobiographies, the course of historical facts and the journey of individual existences merge. They result in careful narratives embellished by convincing self-scrutiny and imaginary contours.

In Gabeira, a trustworthy center of consciousness is in charge of sharing a remarkable, nearly epiphanic series of experiences. His writing conveys a sense of self that ''narrates and reveals itself even within its human vulnerability, even within its sexual ambivalence, without seeking subterfuges'' (Arrigucci, 131). Gabeira rejects an earlier pretense to revolutionary heroism. His interest, ten years after the utopia of an armed socialist revolution, switches from verbose political theories to the politics of common deeds and desire. A more mature Gabeira focuses on ''pragmatic issues of everyday life and supports the emergence of groups such as women, blacks, and homosexuals, which have been marginalized from traditional debates on class struggle'' (Arrigucci, 136). Gabeira's utmost effort is to bring happiness to people via their social and interpersonal relationships.

In close harmony with the themes of his writings, Gabeira has been engaged in campaigns for a wide range of causes, most of them concerned with the environment, women's self-determination, death and starvation in the backlands, sexual liberation and an integral sense of democracy. This political orientation has nothing to do with seizing the power of the state. As developed in later works, mainly *Diário da crise* (Diary of the Crisis; 1984) and *Diário da salvação do mundo* (Diary of the Salvation of the World; 1987), this sense of democracy must address issues such as eating habits, public transportation, domestic relations, birth control, freedom of expression and representation for minorities and disenfranchised groups.

With his ''alternative'' agenda, Gabeira does not forgo either irreverence or self-criticism. He openly criticizes not only his own previous illusions and misconceptions about Cuba and proletarian revolutions but also his unavoidable measure of conceit. He is also concerned with the past and present mistakes of the Neanderthal Left (as he puts it), whose revolutionary effort, besides other contradictions, usually ignores the basic questions of machismo. Gabeira challenges authoritarian and capitalist technocrats, who continue to twist and turn the press and decision-making processes in Brazil by violent repression and hypocritical ideologies of order and progress.

Despite his defeat in two campaigns for public office (the final vote for state governor of Rio de Janeiro in 1986 and the primaries for vice president of Brazil in 1989), Gabeira has achieved some of his sociopolitical goals. Besides spreading polemical, innovative views through fiction and nonfiction works, he has stirred unprecedented debate, in both conservative and progressive media, concerning the legalization of abortion and marijuana, the benefits of women's collectives and child-care support and respect for every person's sexual orientation.

Gabeira's writing suggests how nontraditional sexual orientation is often considered a form of exoticism. During his first year in Brazil after exile, Gabeira was invited to give speeches around the country. Despite a loud and festive reception in Rio de Janeiro, typical of one for national heroes like soccer champions, he may have looked and sounded like an extraterrestrial to many Brazilians—and to himself, a renewed notion of Brazil must have acquired the shape of a different planet. In *Entradas e bandeiras* (Portals and Flags; 1981), the third volume of his autobiography, he says that after a panel discussion in Aracaju, a local newspaper described him as "physically fragile, and therefore maybe he was homosexual" (118). In Curitiba, a homeless gay man in his early thirties caught the lecturer's attention. When Gabeira gave him some money, the man took it and returned Gabeira's smile. "He felt I belonged to a friendly tribe," says the narrator (138). Gabeira later learned that everyone in town knew this outcast, especially after someone paid the homeless man to kiss a politician in the streets during rush hour, in order to humiliate the politician.

One of the first Brazilian gay/lesbian newspapers, *Lampião* (Street Light), published an interview with Gabeira that provoked mixed reactions. Some friends appreciated the sincerity of his account of major personal changes; they even acknowledged their belief it would help them reconsider their own machismo. Others did not accept those changes. "They accepted me as a guerrilla, but not as a homosexual," Gabeira stated. Curiosity about his sexuality rose to such a height that even people in the street would ask him whether he was or was not a homosexual: "If I said I was a homosexual, I'd be lying. If I said I wasn't, I'd be lying too." The narrator in *Entradas* adds that "the classification they used could only allow us to lie. To start saying the truth meant, above all, to lie" (99).

Gabeira realized he had very little in common with many leftists years before the ban against him was lifted. With the members of the Brazilian Committee for Amnesty International in Sweden, for instance, he had little to share but memories of their struggle in Brazil and the desire to go home. In *Crepúsculo do macho* (Twilight of the Macho; 1980), the second volume of his autobiography, the narrator recalls Gabeira's premonitions: "In the beginning, we will hesitate to join in, a little surprised by what we see, but we will soon find our own crowd and forget the dark ages in exile." Gabeira pledged alliance with the minorities on the committee, the blacks and the homosexuals, and said to the other militants: "There will be one Brazil for you and another for us" (213).

The narrator in *Crepúsculo* argues that Joseph, one of his best Brazilian friends on the committee, made him come to understand homosexuality better in its complexity and within its limits. Gabeira then came to grips with homosexuals' views about patriarchal society and the way in which homosexuality could be explained only by taking patriarchy as a starting point. Joseph had moved to Sweden after falling victim in Goiás to the dominant myth that people of the same sex cannot love each other. Gabeira, though, wondered if Joseph were not living a symmetrical counterpart of this myth in Europe: "the assumption that love was possible only between people of the same sex . . . " (*Crepúsculo*, 215). In 1978, immediately after such realizations, Gabeira met Karin, a Swedish sociologist with whom he instantly fell in love. The romance obviously undermined Joseph's assumptions.

The narrator in *Crepúsculo* informs us that the Parisian branch of the Brazilian Committee for Amnesty was no less bigoted. It refused a generous offer by Les Étoiles, a pop music group formed by black homosexuals who were successful in France and wanted to raise money for Amnesty International. The committee declined to accept their help simply because the artists were homosexuals.

A forum was scheduled on the final decision and the issue of homosexuality itself. Gabeira started to voice his suspicions regarding the direction several members who opposed the resolution were taking: "perhaps there was no room for debate" (*Crepúsculo*, 233). He questioned the way the members approached their act of censorship: the overall defensive tone, the appeal to academically recognized categories and lists of gay celebrities, as well as the extensive Marxist–Leninist digressions on homosexuality. Before Gabeira realized he was partly mistaken, he cited Joseph's short statement on the question: "Homosexuality is to look and click; if it doesn't click, no need to debate." Within the same viewpoint, Gabeira added, "The kings in ancient times who accepted gays as artists in their courts were more enlightened than the leftists, who turned down a gay [musical]" (234).

The narrator in *Crepúsculo* looks back and acknowledges Gabeira's mistake: the debate with the Amnesty Committee was a success, after all. Many leftists confessed that such talks helped them erase what remained of their prejudices. The members of the committee redefined their position on the question of homosexuality. A group of women, called Círculo (Circle), developed new concepts and shared experiences that could help them fight machismo upon returning to Brazil. The narrator confesses that at the time he himself had been dealing with an unexpected sense of guilt, narcissism and doubt about what the members would say about him, since he had started to practice ballet.

Gabeira's ambivalent understanding of sexuality had emerged much earlier, however. In *O que é isso, companheiro?*, an anecdote from his 1970 jail experience illustrates this point. Political activists and prisoners of other types, like thieves and rapists, were crowded into the same cells. Many of those individuals had done nothing to justify their being in custody. Police detectives were expected to make a daily quota of arrests, explains the narrator. They would go out in the streets, hunting for unprotected people like homosexuals living in poverty, mentally ill vagrants or individuals who happened not to be carrying their worker's identification card, a document meant to prove to the police that a person was not a "vagabond."

Even though most social groups there helped each other while ignoring gays, the imprisoned leftists, in general, expressed their solidarity with the homosexuals. The presence of gay men was particularly absurd, since they were arbitrarily jailed in order for them to do the cleaning and to deliver goods within the police station.

Gabeira was not totally like his comrades. On the one hand, they all agreed that the gay men were terribly abused, yet managed to bring some real joy to an otherwise miserable place. From the hallways, gay men blew kisses to the other inmates and expected some in return. Public decorum prohibited the leftists from blowing kisses back, however. "All we could do was to protest when cops brought in these men and exposed their breasts which had been enlarged by hormones. It was like showing off an animal or a piece of merchandise" (*O que*, 243). On the other hand, the text reveals Gabeira's feelings of "ambivalence," as he puts it, toward that human display. With one eye, he would feel indignant and disgusted; with the other, he was definitely curious and excited. Addressing his comrades, "who might have gone on to become respectful fathers and political leaders," the narrator confesses ten years later, "You should not think that my interest was piqued because they looked like women. Marlene had no breasts, and she was the one who attracted me the most" (243).

Indeed, the issue of Gabeira's masculinity became an obsession of the Brazilian press after 1979. Many people seemed scandalized by his habit of wearing a *tanga*, a string-like bikini bottom. Reporters often asked him to elaborate on the question of his masculinity. Questioned by *Última hora* (Final Hour), a Rio de Janeiro newspaper, he replied that he wouldn't defend his "masculinity" by resorting to the old liberal argument that alleges that no one should meddle in other people's private matters. Instead, he charged that "my masculinity is a problem for *Última hora*, not me" (*Entradas*, 85–86).

Regarding the issue of masculinity, the narrator in *Entradas* comments on one of a series of articles Gabeira wrote just after his arrival in Brazil in 1979. A freelance journalist, Gabeira investigated the killing of Ângela Diniz, a member of the jet set, by her jealous lover, who could not accept the fact that she spent time with a German woman who was sexually interested in her. Gabeira ended up writing a book on the case. *Sinais de vida no planeta Minas* (Signs of Life on the Planet Minas; 1982) intertwines Diniz's story with those of other women from the state of Minas Gerais, historical figures who also faced taboos and opposed men's wishes; the trial of Diniz's lover was shown live on television. Apparently a large fraction of Brazilian society—men and women—favored his acquittal. "It was a national *mise-en-scène* to glorify machismo," the narrator states in *Entradas*. At the door of the courthouse, the killer was cheered by the crowds, an event that summoned up "a key question of our culture" (89).

There is further evidence that Gabeira's autobiography does not lack in tension between what used to be and what his frame of mind is at the moment he writes. Masculinity, with which he was not too concerned when he spoke with *Última hora*, certainly involved different expectations for him during childhood. As a child Gabeira would masturbate with other boys. They proclaimed that they were the biggest machos and that they would "eat" all the men hometown folk identified as *veados* (faggots). Nevertheless, the narrator's voice of recollection in *Entradas* does not sound condescending, repentant, or glorifying. It sounds affectionate or endearing, for example, when Gabeira mentions a councilman, a renowned gay man, who rented a hotel room for his adventures. The important man, wearing tie and suit, knelt down and kissed Gabeira and the other boys quite noisily while bathing them in the bathtub. The narrator goes on to equate the councilman's care with Gabeira's grandmother's cheering as she gave him a daily bath.

The narrator understands that the boys with active roles in the homosexual relationships he describes were losing their innocence after some time, and the *veados* turned out to be intelligent and critical people questioning the boys' refusal to exchange roles. When those topics emerged, "We discretely started to get away. That was the beginning of repression for us" (*Entradas*, 102).

Eventually, repression became the primary target of Gabeira's discourse. One of his greatest accomplishments in life, the narrator writes in *Entradas*, was to stop fearing male friendships: "The limits are always fluid, but almost every honest person knows he or she can love another person of the same sex." Gabeira's irony hence makes him wonder: "Wouldn't men have some sort of radar to control the maximum speed of their sentiments if they were to find themselves falling for other men? And what fuels this radar beyond repression?" (99).

WORKS

Carta sobre a anistia: A entrevista do Pasquim, conversação sobre 1968. Rio de Janeiro: Codecri, 1980.

O crepúsculo do macho: Depoimento. Rio de Janeiro: Codecri, 1980.

Diário da crise. Rio de Janeiro: Rocco, 1984.

Diário da salvação do mundo. Rio de Janeiro: Espaço e Tempo, 1987.

Entradas e bandeiras: Depoimentos. Rio de Janeiro: Codecri, 1981.

Goiânia, rua 57: O nuclear na terra do Sol. Rio de Janeiro: Guanabara, 1987.

Hóspede da utopia. Rio de Janeiro: Nova Fronteira, 1981.

Nós que amávamos tanto a revolução: Diálogo Gabeira–Cohn Bendit. Rio de Janeiro: Rocco, 1985.

O que é isso, companheiro? 2nd ed. Rio de Janeiro: Codecri, 1982. Also as *Les Guerrilleros sont fatigués; témoignage*. Trans. Anne Rumeau. Paris: A. M. Metaille, 1980.

Partido Verde: Propostas de ecología política. Rio de Janeiro: Anima, 1986.

Sinais de vida no planeta Minas. Rio de Janeiro: Nova Fronteira, 1982.

Vida alternativa: Uma revolução do dia-a-dia. Pôrto Alegre: L & PM, 1985.

CRITICISM

Arrigucci, Davi, Jr. "Gabeira em dois tempos." In his *Enigma e comentário: Ensaios sobre literatura e experiência*, 119–140. São Paulo: Companhia das Letras, 1987.

Figueiredo, Vera Follain de. "Nos trilhos da memória; Uma leitura da obra de Gabeira." *O eixo e a roda* 6 (July 1988): 263–274.

Krueger, Robert. "Abertura/Apertura: A Political Review of Recent Brazilian Writings." In *The Discourse of Power: Culture, Hegemony and the Authoritarian State in Latin America*, 172–193. Ed. Neil Larsen. Minneapolis: Institute for Study of Ideologies and Literature, 1983.

Malard, Letícia. "Análise contrastiva de *O que é isso, companheiro?*, de Fernando Gabeira, e *Reflexos do baile*, de Antônio Callado." In *O eixo e a roda*, 75–120. Belo Horizonte: Faculdade de Letras da Universidade Federal de Minas Gerais, 1982.

Santiago, Silviano. "Alegria e poder." In *Nas malhas da letra: Ensaios*, 11–23. São Paulo: Companhia das Letras, 1989.

———. "Pizza, tevê e utopia." *Leia livros*, Nov. 1981, n.p.

———. "Prosa literária atual no Brasil." In his *Nas malhas da letra: Ensaios*, 24–37.

Viana, Dulce Maria. "O narcisismo da memória." *ULULA: Graduate Studies in Romance Languages* 1 (1984): 73–80.

Dário Borim, Jr.

GAMBARO, GRISELDA (Argentina; 1928)

Gambaro, born in Buenos Aires, is recognized as one of Latin America's most talented dramatists, as well as the best-known female playwright in Argentina. She also has written a number of short novels and stories. In 1963, Gambaro received the Argentine National Endowment for the Arts Award, which allowed her to publish *Madrigal en ciudad* (Madrigal in the City; 1963), a collection of three novellas. The following year, she won the Emecé Publisher's Prize for the collection of short stories and novellas in *El desatino* (Folly; 1966). Her novel *Una felicidad con menos pena* (A Happiness with Less Suffering; 1968) won an honorable mention from Sudamericana Publishers in 1967; the play *El campo* (The Camp; 1967) premiered in 1968 and won first prizes from the city of Buenos Aires, the magazine *Talía*, the municipal radio station of Buenos Aires, and the Asociación Argentores (Argentina's equivalent of Equity). In 1976 she again won the Premio Argentores for the play *Sucede lo que pasa* (What Happens Is What Happens; premiered 1976). Other works by Gambaro include *Las paredes* (The Walls; premiered 1966), *Los siameses* (The Siamese Twins; premiered 1967), *Información para extranjeros* (Information for Foreigners; 1972), *Nada que ver con otra historia* (Nothing to Do with Another Story; 1972), *Decir sí* (Saying Yes; 1978), *Dios no nos quiere contentos* (God Doesn't Want Us to Be Happy; 1979), *Ganarse la muerte* (Earning Death; 1976), *La malasangre* (Bad Blood; premiered 1982) and *Lo impenetrable* (The Impenetrable Madame X; 1984). Her plays have been staged in New York by the Spanish Theater Repertory Company and by several university groups. Her drama also has been performed in Italy, France, Germany, Venezuela, Uruguay and Mexico.

On the back cover of *Lo impenetrable*, Gambaro explains the impulse that led her to write a work that she identifies as "so out of character for me." It began, she says, as "a joke reflecting back on itself," a change of pace from the dark dramas she produced in Argentina in the 1960s and 1970s. It soon became obvious to Gambaro, however, that she could not write "according to the canons of the genre"; therefore, she decided to create a parody, a "remake" of traditional erotic texts in which she could humorously treat some of the themes and conventions associated with that kind of writing. Without a doubt, *Lo impenetrable* is a humorous work, but it is also a profoundly disturbing one, for as it deconstructs and destabilizes the literary traditions surrounding erotic fiction, it also decenters many of our commonly held notions about sexual identity and desire.

As the title indicates, *Lo impenetrable* deals with the issue of penetration as a source of sexual pleasure for the female, and it examines the role the penis plays in the gratification of a woman's sexual needs. Madame X, the central character of the novel, believes that she must be penetrated by a man in order to achieve sexual satisfaction, despite the fact that she and her maid, Marie, engage in lesbian activities that appear to bring her to climax on a fairly regular basis. Madame X dismisses her relationship with Marie as unimportant and unfulfilling, and continues to seek the elusive penis, embodied in the person of Jonathan, the alleged gentleman who admires her from afar and promises in numerous love letters to impale her on his "erect mast." Most of the action of the novel revolves around Madame X's unsuccessful attempts to connect with Jonathan and to be penetrated by him. However, each attempted assignation leads the young man closer to death as he experiences uncontrollable and massive ejaculations at the mere sight of his would-be mistress. He finds that the phallus, literally and figuratively, is a weight too heavy for him to bear. At the novel's end, he dies at Madame X's feet, leaving her frustrated and complaining that he has neglected his duty to her. He replies, "It doesn't matter. . . . The impenetrable is the source of all pleasure, because there is no pleasure without the unknown" (148).

Jonathan's words echo Jacques Lacan's conceptualization of Desire: it is that which lies outside language, unknowable and unspoken, unrecognized and displaced in a metonymic series of substitutes for the ultimate transcendental signifier that escapes definition. Madame X's behavior in the novel indicates that while she may not understand the theory behind Jonathan's words or agree with him on the conscious level, she nevertheless lives her life in accordance with the principle he has laid out before her. Time after time, her desire to be penetrated by Jonathan's penis is deflected and transferred to Marie, who stands in for the missing phallus and assumes its role. But because Madame X senses that there is something lacking in a lesbian encounter, she shifts her desire back to Jonathan, only to have it slip back to Marie once again. Jonathan's death puts a temporary kink in the chain of movement, but it is immediately set in motion again as a new gentleman appears on the scene, and the process begins again.

Although the relationship Madame X has developed with Marie is clearly the primary one in her life, and the one that brings her the most physical pleasure, she rejects it as untenable because it does not center on the act of penile penetration. She constantly turns away from the known element in search of the unknown, in the belief that what she has never experienced (penetration by a male) must be more pleasurable than what she has enjoyed in the past (clitoral stimulation by a woman).

While Jonathan's perpetually erect penis and frequent ejaculations make it clear that he is not impotent, his inability to channel his sexual energy into its putatively normal outlet makes him, in essence, a useless tool as far as Madame X is concerned. He cannot satisfy her or meet her demands for sex; therefore, whatever power and authority the phallus would normally hold over the female is negated, and the penis, which functions as a symbol for phallic power, is exposed as a fraud. The demands placed on the penis by the female clearly have a castrating effect on the male; the more she desires his organ, the less he is able to meet her needs. When Jonathan dies, Madame X transfers her attention to another man, but there is little in the novel to suggest that she will be more successful with a new suitor. The fact that the novel ends as it begins establishes a circular pattern, which can be read as a sign that Madame X is destined to repeat the same mistakes as long as she continues to associate feminine desire with penetration. Ultimately, *Lo impenetrable* reconfigures the penis as a source of feminine *dis*pleasure (or frustration), and it presents an ironic reversal of one of the basic premises of erotic fiction. In this way, Gambaro parodies not only the conventions of the genre but also the excessive importance attached to the penis in that kind of writing. By extension, the notion of phallic power is undermined, and the penis becomes the butt of the joke.

Recent studies of female sexuality, specifically those carried out by Shere Hite, suggest that the vast majority of women do not achieve orgasm solely on the basis of penile penetration. Hite suggests that women are taught to value the penis and to regard the desire for penetration as the natural expression of female sexuality, since heterosexuality is deeply ingrained and intercourse is regarded as the dominant paradigm for all sexual relationships. Ironically, however, her findings show that intercourse produces fewer orgasms in women than does lesbian activity. She posits that women who are involved in lesbian relationships rely more heavily on clitoral stimulation and overall body sensuality than do heterosexual couples. But because Freudian sexual models have been upheld as the norm throughout most of the twentieth century, women are taught to feel an aversion for same-sex relationships and to privilege the masculine over the feminine. Hite's findings go against the grain of traditional, male-biased erotica, which perpetuates the myth that women are pleasured by the penis. Similarly, Gambaro's *Lo impenetrable* reveals the penetration myth to be a hoax and reconfirms, in the pathetic comedy of Madame X, the self-destructive pattern set in motion when a woman buys into the system and denies her sexual needs on the basis of socially constructed ideals.

The metafictional elements in the novel call attention to the fact that erotica is often formula fiction, but they also point to ways in which the formula can be altered. The narrator offers many suggestions and observations about the writing of erotic texts throughout the novel and provides an appendix summarizing these guidelines. The overt narratorial comment acts as an internal self-reflecting mirror, which signals the duplicitous nature of the novel to the reader. It becomes clear that we are dealing with a parody of erotic fiction rather than a work of erotic fiction as such when we realize that the text does not necessarily conform to its own set of rules. It may be farfetched to read *Lo impenetrable* as a new model for erotic fiction; but it must certainly be read as a deconstruction of old models. Madame X proves that her course of action will lead to continued frustration; only Marie offers the possibility of change, for she is the one character in the text who seems most in touch with her sexual nature. The narrator's closing remark, that Marie might be the protagonist of a future novel, opens the doors to conjecture about how feminine desire in erotic fiction could be reworked and presented in other ways. What form that expression will take remains to be seen.

Homosexuality plays an insignificant role in Gambaro's theatrical pieces, but it is nevertheless a latent force in plays like *Los siameses* (1967) and *El campo* (1967). Diana Taylor has noted the eroticized violence at work in these dramas. The tensions between Lorenzo and Ignacio, who may or may not be Siamese twins, have sexual undertones, most notably in the scene where Lorenzo spies on Ignacio's lovemaking, identifying with him to the extent that he is no longer clearly able to distinguish between self and other. He is envious of Ignacio's virility, which stands in marked contrast to his own impotence. This leads him to prove his sexual prowess, but, as Taylor notes, he is doomed to fail because "he feels nothing but contempt and repulsion for women" (115). The relationship between Martín and Franco in *El campo* is similar in the positioning of the female character, Emma, as the sex toy that is part of the game played by the males. Franco is grossly exhibitionistic in his fetishized Gestapo uniform. He mixes sex, violence and humiliation in a titillating way as he pushes Emma into Martín's arms, setting himself up as a "sadistic spectator" (Taylor, 126). Sexual perversion does not reside in the act between the confused Martín and the desperate Emma, however; it is focused on the pleasure Franco derives through voyeuristic activity and through his love of control and domination. The sadomasochistic character of the relationship between Franco and the others is one of the central focuses of the play. While not exclusively homosexual, the military outfit, leather boots and whip that make up Franco's outfit have clear links to the leather bars frequented by one well-defined segment of the gay male population.

WORKS

Decir sí. In *Hispamérica* 7.21 (1978): 75–82.
El campo. Buenos Aires: Insurrexit, 1967.
El desatino. Buenos Aires: Emecé, 1965.

Dios no nos quiere contentos. Buenos Aires: Editorial Lumen, 1979.
Una felicidad con menos pena. Buenos Aires: Editorial Sudamericana, 1968.
Ganarse las muerte. Buenos Aires: Ediciones de la Flor, 1976.
Lo impenetrable. Buenos Aires: Torres Aguero Editor, 1984.
Información para extranjeros. In *Teatro 2.* Buenos Aires: Ediciones de la Flor, 1987.
Madrigal en ciudad. Buenos Aires: Goyanarte, 1963.
La malasangre. In *Teatro 1.* Buenos Aires: Ediciones de la Flor, 1984.
Nada que ver con otra historia. In *Teatro.* Ed. Miguel Angel Giella, Peter Roster and
        Leandro Urbina. Ottawa: Girol, 1983.
Las paredes. In *Teatro.* Barcelona: Editorial Argonauta, 1979.
Los siameses. Buenos Aires: Insurrexit, 1967.
Sucede lo que pasa. In *Teatro 2.* Buenos Aires: Ediciones de la Flor, 1987.

CRITICISM

Foster, David William. "Pornography and the Feminine Erotic: Griselda Gambaro's *Lo
        impenetrable.*" *Monographic Review/Revista monográfica* 7 (1991): 284–296.
Hite, Shere. *The Hite Report. A Nationwide Study on Female Sexuality.* New York:
        Macmillan, 1976.
————. *Women and Love. A Cultural Revolution in Progress.* New York: Knopf, 1987.
Mitchell, Juliet, and Jacqueline Rose. *Feminine Sexuality: Jacques Lacan and the École
        Freudienne.* New York: W. W. Norton, 1982.
Taylor, Diana. *Theatre of Crisis. Drama and Politics in Latin America,* 96–147. Lex-
        ington: University Press of Kentucky, 1990.

                                                                        Cynthia Duncan

GARCÍA RAMIS, MAGALI (Puerto Rico; 1946)

Homosexuality does not appear in García Ramis's early collection of short stories, *La familia de todos nosotros* (All Our Family; 1976) or in her more recent
essays collected in *El tramo ancla* (The Anchor Leg; 1991). Nevertheless, many
of these texts begin an exploration of Puerto Rican girlhood, a theme that becomes intertwined with an idealization of the homosexual and the marginal that
reaches its fullest development in the novel *Felices días, tío Sergio* (Happy
Days, Uncle Sergio; 1986).

   Girlhood begins at home, and García Ramis, like other Latin American
women writers, tells stories about female enclaves. Hers are extended families
made up of formidable aunts, grandmothers and seemingly weak mothers, set
apart by their high-walled houses and by narrow-minded views that divide the
world into Good (the Catholic church, Europe and the United States, white
people and the military) and Bad (atheists and Protestants, new African nations,
the mambo and Puerto Rican nationalists). Not only does García Ramis not
celebrate this private world of women, she situates it within the economic elite

and lays bare her characters' Eurocentric, racist and sexist values. Moreover, she gives her girl protagonists/narrators the task of escaping from the female-dominated family through all that it holds most contemptible: gender rebellion and nationalist politics.

Conservative relatives have the primary responsibility of imparting gendered identity to the young of the household. While for the girl this process seems to consist mainly of admonitions to be obedient and to stay within the confines of the home, the sternest warnings are associated with sexuality. Convinced that female nature is essentially asexual, her mother and aunts uphold bourgeois patriarchal demands for female chastity; teach the girl that she is a "pure lily" who must protect herself from men, who are naturally sexual ("carry a wolf around inside them"); and stress her difference from maids, mulattoes and vice-ridden women whose apparently uncontrolled sexual behavior is equated with racial, political and class deviance. So while the girl can possibly negotiate some freedom of movement and expression in childhood—as when Lidia of *Felices días* chooses the active role of chimpanzee over that of domestic Jane during Tarzan games—the full force of the limitations placed on the bourgeois female, as well as the misogyny implicit in her family's sexual morality, hits at puberty. It is when vigilance over her behavior increases that she becomes estranged from male playmates, who are encouraged to "take to the streets," and, most important, she becomes alienated from her own sexualized body and desire, which are labeled as either nonexistent or evil.

Since most adult female characters in García Ramis's work do not question the social, economic or political systems in which they are enmeshed, they cannot help the girl to escape. This role is given to certain male relatives: members of the family who have sufficient contact with the girl yet somehow stand apart from the domination and aggression that is equated with masculinity. In the title story of *La familia de todos nosotros* and "Todos los domingos" (Every Sunday), this is an older cousin who shares the girl's somewhat feminine pursuits and for whom the girl experiences her first crush. This male figure is more developed in *Felices días*, where the uncle, Sergio, embodies both the allure of adult male sexuality and a challenge to a gender/sex system that separates men into "wolves" and women into "lilies." On an extended visit from New York, Sergio immediately sets himself off as different from other men: he allies himself with children, reads poetry, talks of art, shows tenderness and even cries. He is, as the narrator Lidia reveals at the end of the story, "most probably a homosexual." Although there are a few discreet hints that this may be true, Sergio's sexual desires are not as important as the use of homosexuality to symbolize a rejection of, and possible freedom from, normative masculine mores, as well as to underscore the relationship between gender/sexuality rebellion and progressive politics.

Sergio returns to a bourgeois island culture that maintains clear boundaries between the masculine and the feminine, and between a European or Anglophile "us" and a racially mixed, barbarous "them." Schoolboys police one another with taunts of *pato* (faggot) and *mujercita* (little woman); girls take care to avoid the color purple or lavender scent to prove they have no mulatto tastes; adults exile effeminate boys to the United States or threaten them with severe beatings. Nevertheless, the vehemence of this social control suggests fear that these boundaries between masculinity and femininity, white and black, are far more flexible and shifting than is comfortable or necessary to maintain the status of the island bourgeoisie. Thus, the sexually ambiguous Sergio—he is both male and womanly, a member of the family and a nationalist—represents the crossing and blurring of boundaries that enclose fixed identities and the power relations they entail. The homosexual is not just situated at the margin: he (García Ramis does not explore what position the lesbian might have) opens up rigidly protected categories and thereby serves as a catalyst for change on many levels.

Although Sergio returns to New York and dies young, he has guided his niece Lidia out of the maternal home and into a diverse and nationalist Puerto Rico. As she falls in love with him and keeps his memory, she learns both to reject the asexual femininity demanded by her family and to embrace a larger family that includes all of her country's men and women. As a marginal, opposition figure, the homosexual Sergio not only challenges normative masculinity but also appears to give birth to the new woman.

WORKS

"Cuando canten 'Maestra vida.' " In *Apalabramiento: Cuentos puertorriqueños de hoy*, 131–139. Ed. Efraín Barradas. Hanover, N.H.: Ediciones del Norte, 1983.
La familia de todos nosotros. San Juan: Instituto de Cultura Puertorriqueña, 1976.
Felices días, tío Sergio. Río Piedras, P.R.: Editorial Antillana, 1986.
Seven essays in *El tramo ancla: Ensayos puertorriqueños de hoy*, 45–78. Ed. Ana Lydia Vega. Río Piedras: Editorial de la Universidad de Puerto Rico, 1991.

CRITICISM

Colón, Eliseo. "*Felices días, tío Sergio*." *La torre* 1.1 (Jan.–Mar. 1987): 165–170.
Figueroa, Alvin Joaquín. "Feminismo, homosexualidad e identidad política: El lenguaje del otro en *Felices días, tío Sergio*." *La torre* 5.20 (1991): 499–505.
López, Ivette. "Minute and Fragrant Memories: *Happy Days, Uncle Sergio*, by Magali García Ramis." In *Splintering Darkness: Latin American Women in Search of Themselves*, 111–122. Ed. Lucía Guerra Cunningham. Pittsburgh: Latin American Literary Review Press, 1990.

Mary Jane Treacy

GIORDANO, ENRIQUE A. (Chile; 1946) _____

El mapa de Amsterdam (The Map of Amsterdam; 1985) was published in Santiago, Chile, in January 1985, during the military regime of General Augusto

Pinochet. Although the book was not officially censored, only individuals with contacts among the underground cultural media of Santiago were able to read and appreciate this fascinating piece of gay poetry. *Mapa* is supposedly a lost manuscript rescued by Madela, a fictional female friend of Alejandro (who is the voice, protagonist and writer in the text), and is sent to Enrique Giordano, who publishes it. Within this fictional frame, the poem tells the story of Alejandro's homosexual affairs, using a tragic "soap opera tone" without necessarily falling into camp or kitsch. It is an operatic text in which many voices converge into one: Alejandro's tale of exile, solitude and deception. Divided into three parts ("The Map," "Intermap," and "Countermap") and two epilogues ("Pre-epilogue," and "Epilogue"), this poetic discourse oscillates between poetry and narration without being a poem in prose or poetic prose. It is a unique and androgynous text replete with erotic zones that allow the exploration of the sites of a textual body. *Mapa* is a "complete version" of a male body and its process of identification with the reader and the text, according to Giordano in the letter to the editors about the possibilities for its publication:

Dear Sirs:

I don't know how this manuscript will strike you . . . I have quite some doubts concerning Alejandro's poetry. His texts seem more like soap operas to me. And there are details that disturb me. . . . Nevertheless, I like the manuscript and identify with it completely. (Heller, 37)

In his book *The Articulate Flesh: Male Homo-Eroticism and Modern Poetry* (1987), Gregory Woods explains the link between the male body and what he calls the "articulate flesh" in homoerotic modern poetry. Woods argues that homoerotic poetry is part of the mainstream of poetic writing, not distinct and differentiated within it. A critic who ignores the sexual orientation of a lyric voice, in particular in a love poem, Woods risks overlooking the significance of the poetry itself. In his own words:

Eros pitches his house in the human body. It is here that all declarations of love, poetic or otherwise, have their origin; and it is hither that, even after their dizziest flights of spirituality, they must return. The verbal flourish of erotic candour—the song or sonnet, graffito or billet doux—is an echo of the body's signs, an articulation of the flesh. (1)

The section "Entremapa" (Intermap) will illustrate how the erotic zones of the map present the notion of a male body that both suffers and experiences pleasure. Only pleasure can redeem it. This poem avails itself of an intense tone in which the lyric voice identifies himself as homosexual. A quotation from the mainstream Peruvian poet César Vallejo (the second most important poet in Latin America after Chile's Pablo Neruda) is used in this section of the poem: "This evening it's raining like never before; and, heart, I don't feel like living." Vallejo's lines here explain the position of Alejandro, the poem's main character, vis-à-vis Patricio and their relationship with their shared exile. While Alejandro is absent from Chile, traveling, Patricio remains in inner exile: they have lost the space that they once shared. Throughout the poem, Alejandro, the voice speaking, is identified by two letters that serve as a frame for the text: one from an Argentine friend, Madela, and the other from the "author," the poet and scholar Enrique Giordano. The lyric voice has no spatial dimension in the small town of the province in which he dreams with his early lover, Miguel, of fancy trips through maps, or in Philadelphia with his American lover, Michael.

There is a cartographic sense in which *Mapa* becomes part of a paradigm that can be called a "gay topography of pain" to the extent that there is no place for the character's gayness in that world: Lilian Uribe identifies the main "semantic field" of the poem as a center of pain for all things lost and remembered by the speaker (89). However, the illusion of oral sex at the end of the "Entremapa" section recaptures that "garden" the lyric voice never had.

WORKS

El mapa de Amsterdam. Santiago, Chile: Libros del Maitén, 1985. Trans. Benjamin Heller as "The Map of Amsterdam." Unpublished.

CRITICISM

Quiñones, Juanita. "Acercamiento a la deconstrucción de la metáfora en *El mapa de Amsterdam*, de Enrique Giordano." *Extremos líricos del Caribe a la Araucana* 3–4 (1987): 79–88.
Uribe, Lilian. "La diseminación del plano real en *El mapa de Amsterdam.*" *Extremos líricos del Caribe a la Araucana* 3–4 (1987): 89–100.
Woods, Gregory. *Articulate Flesh: Male Homo-eroticism and Modern Poetry.* New Haven: Yale University Press, 1987.

Daniel Torres

GOMBROWICZ, WITOLD (Poland, 1904– France, 1969) _____

Gombrowicz was, strictly speaking, neither Latin American nor gay. Born in Poland, he found himself in Argentina at the outbreak of World War II and remained there until 1963, when he returned to Europe (but not to Poland). Although he lived in poverty and obscurity for much of his life, he is now acknowledged as one of the most innovative writers of the century. A man of rare literary and philosophical insight, Gombrowicz examines, in his novels, plays and diaries, such fundamental problems of identity as sexuality and nationality.

Shaped by the experience of exile, his views on nationality are especially acute. Poland is, as he writes in *A Kind of Testament* (1968), a country of "weakened forms," a "minor" nation whose claims on the individual must be resisted. Driven by the "demon of symmetry" and analogy that characterizes his work, Gombrowicz assimilates Argentina to Poland. Neither nation, he argues, fits comfortably into Europe or America; neither is self-confidently "superior." Facing "the reality of inferiority," he advocates distance, inversion and degradation, strategies that anticipate Gianni Vattimo's weak thought. The strength of Gombrowicz's own thought lies in its rigorous assumption of a peculiar type of weakness: "abnormal, twisted, degenerate, abominable and solitary" (*Testament*, 37). Despite the parallels to Franz Kafka and Samuel Beckett, few modern writers are as resolute about locating authenticity in lowness, truth in dissent and freedom in displacement. "Anyone [Polish or Argentine] who attaches importance to his spiritual development, must," Gombrowicz declares, "regard Poland or the Argentine as an obstacle, almost as an enemy. That is the only way to feel *really* free" (*Testament*, 57). Far from finding freedom within a particular national space, Gombrowicz seeks it elsewhere: not in an impossible beyond (he remains concerned with both Polish and Argentine culture) but in a powerfully tense in-between.

For Gombrowicz, in-betweenness (his term) is more than an intellectual abstraction; it marks him not only nationally but also sexually. Not exactly hetero-, homo-, or bi-, Gombrowicz eschews classification: being, for him, is not reducible to sexuality. This does not mean that he is "in touch" with himself; in fact, he describes himself as "always 'between' and never 'in,' . . . like a shade, a chimera." Against this ghostliness he pits not merely health and vigor but also disease and dissipation: "It was reality for which I searched in the simplicity and the brute health of the lowest social classes. . . . But I also looked for that reality inside myself, in those vague intestinal areas, deserted, peripheral, inhuman, where anomalies flourish together with Formlessness, Disease, Abjection. . . . Man's reality is the reality both of health and disease" (*Testament*, 41). Gombrowicz's in-between, precisely because it is neither comfortable nor stable, is thus the site of what is most human: creativity, critique, passion and desire.

The belief that desire is indefinite and undefinable is expressed in his first, and perhaps most famous, novel. *Ferdydurke* (1937) is a tragicomic tale that holds that "it is a false assumption that man should be definite" (86). After all, "The things we think, feel, and say today will necessarily seem foolish to our grandchildren" (86). *Ferdydurke*—the title is universally meaningless—addresses the folly of *fixing* meaning: "Man [must] realize that he is not expressing himself in harmony with his true nature, but in an artificial manner painfully inflicted on him from outside" (86). With this realization comes the fear of dispossession "because we shall discover that [our personalities] do not completely belong to us. And instead of bellowing and shouting: I believe this, I feel that, I am this, I stand for that, we shall say more humbly: In me there is a belief, a feeling, a thought'' (86). This latter formulation (in which the subject is ''inhabited''), derived from Friedrich Nietzsche and Sigmund Freud, underscores the highly intersubjective nature of Gombrowicz's individual. His true and authentic ''man'' (his language and ideas are often quite masculinist) is no more an island than he is a plaything of the collective. Refusing the programs of Sartrean existentialism, Marxism–Leninism, and Catholicism, Gombrowicz delineates a self whose measure lies in what he calls the interhuman.

The notion of the interhuman, generous and cruel, further complicates the definition of desire. While Gombrowicz's novels and diaries are replete with homosexual signs, and while he himself acknowledges homosexual experiences, he hardly yields a clear erotic portrait. For instance, in *Ferdydurke*, when the subject of homosexuality is made explicit, it is promptly dismissed, not because it is immoral and disturbing, but because it is not disturbing enough. Within an enlightened world of tolerance and progress, it becomes known, domestic, proper, even artistically urbane. Against this reassuring but false definition of desire, Gombrowicz places ''fra . . . ternization,'' a ''private, physical, corporeal equality,'' which cannot be seamlessly articulated (hence the ellipses). ''Fra . . . ternization'' resembles the ''extreme'' homosexuality that Gombrowicz relates in his *Diary* (1957–1969; quotes that follow are from Vol. I, 142). ''Frenetic to the point of madness,'' this sexuality bears a truth and authenticity that Gombrowicz cannot fully discuss. ''Much time will pass,'' he says, ''before it will be possible to talk, let alone write about this.'' What he does write about is the ''fury of 'manly' men'' that, though cursed and feared by society, is found among ''the healthiest and most ordinary boys from the lower classes.'' An allusion to his early years in the ''lower depths'' of Buenos Aires, this sense of vitality in corruption and creativity in vice is explored in *Trans-Atlantyk* (1952), Gombrowicz's only novel set in Argentina and the one most ''extremely'' engaged with homosexuality. Here, in an allegorical battle between ''abnormal, perhaps . . . limitless liberty'' and ''fidelity to the past,'' a *puto* (male hustler; faggot) struggles to win a young man away from his father. Gombrowicz's tendency to depict ''true'' homosexuality as a putative vice that liberates is problematic; but it is crucial to his uniquely ironic romanticization of raw physicality and restive form.

Form is the central term in Gombrowicz's lexicon. Fraught with contradiction, form makes us false and inauthentic, deforms us and yet is necessary to our existence; it is what we least desire (it is a ''painfully external imposition'') and what we most desire (desire itself, as lack, is a form of formlessness). Gombrowicz's inquiry into form, problematizing the ''will to identity'' and exposing the lightness of being (Milan Kundera is indebted to him), makes suspect any attempt to determine the nature of individual sexual desire. Indeed, he often seems more concerned about a ubiquitous, if unacknowledged, perversity across lines of gender, age, class, intelligence, belief and orientation. In *Pornografia* (1960), two aging men desire not so much masculinity or femininity per se as ''immaturity.'' Gombrowicz describes this as an impulse toward ''undervalue,'' by which he means a desire for the insufficiency, inferiority and imperfection of youth. He contrasts these vibrant "undervalues" with the staid and serious "values" of maturity. Thus, the two protagonists desire the young boy, Karol, but only insofar as his youthfulness can be deployed alongside that of the young girl, Henia. As with so much of Gombrowicz, it is difficult to read this dynamic as gay.

In *Cosmos* (1965), the difficulty is even greater, for the object of the narrator's obsession is embodied in the fantastically interconnected mouths of two women from different social classes, Lena and Katasia (mouths, knees, rumps, faces and other fetishized body parts abound in all the novels and plays). Male-to-male desire is more fitful and centers on a curious onanistic bond between Lena's father and the narrator, Witold, and an equally curious semiological bond between Witold and Fuchs, his partner in deciphering a swarm of signs. From a sparrow on a wire to a crack in a wall to a deformed lip, these signs are joined in a rush of meaning, dangerous and seductive. Highlighting the pitfalls of interpretation, *Cosmos* can serve as a cautionary tale for those who would take the signs of the author's life—his marriage, like Borges's, at the end of his life; his "collaborative" friendships; his infatuation with so-called degradation and abnormality; his often haughty defense of the underside—as the truth of his authentic self. Witold Gombrowicz and his writings are partly, but only partly, what we make of them.

WORKS (Date of first Polish publication given in parentheses)

Cosmos (1965). Trans. Eric Mosbacher. London: MacGibbon & Kee, 1967.*

Diary (1957–1969), 3 vols. Trans. Lillian Vallee. Evanston, Ill.: Northwestern University Press, 1988–1993.

Ferdydurke (1937). Trans. Eric Mosbacher. London: MacGibbon & Kee, 1961. Trans. into Spanish with the collaboration of Virgilio Piñera and Humberto Rodríguez Tomeu as *Ferdydurke*. Buenos Aires: Argos, 1947.*

A Kind of Testament (1968). Trans. Alastair Hamilton. London: Calder & Boyars, 1973.

The Marriage (1953). Trans. Louis Iribarne. New York: Grove Press, 1969.

Operetta (1966). Trans. Louis Iribarne. London: Calder & Boyars, 1971.

Pornografia (1960). Trans. Alastair Hamilton. London: Calder & Boyars, 1966.*

Possessed: Or the Secret of Myslotch. Trans. J. A. Underwood. London: Marion Boyars, 1980. First published as *The Enchanted* (1937) under the pseudonym Nienaski.

Princess Ivona (1935). Trans. Krystyna Griffith-Jones. London: Calder & Boyars, 1969.

Trans-Atlantyk (1952). Spanish version as *Transatlántico*. Trans. Kazimierz Piekarec y Sergio Pitol. Barcelona: Barral Editores, 1971. French version as *Transatlantique*. Trans. Constantin Jelenski and Geneviève Serreau. Paris: Denoël, 1976.

Cosmos, Ferdydurke and *Pornografia* published in one volume—New York: Grove Press, 1978. Quotations in this essay are from this book.

CRITICISM

Balderston, Daniel. "Estética de la deformación en Gombrowicz y Piñera." *Explicación de textos literarios* 19.2 (1990–1991): 1–7.

Boyers, Robert. "Gombrowicz and *Ferdydurke*: The Tyranny of Form." *Centennial Review* 14 (1970): 284–312.

Brodsky, David. "Gombrowicz's Spatial Poetics." In *Proceedings of the XIIth Congress of the International Comparative Literature Association*, 2.277–282. Munich: Iudicium, 1990.

Carcassonne, Manuel, et al. *Gombrowicz, vingt ans après*. Paris: Christian Bourgois, 1989.

DeRoux, Dominique. *Gombrowicz*. Paris: Christian Bourgois, 1971.

Georgin, Rosine. *Gombrowicz*. Lausanne: Éditions l'Age d'Homme, 1977.

Goldmann, Lucien. "The Theatre of Gombrowicz." *Tulane Drama Review* 14 (1970): 102–112.

Gombrowicz, Rita. *Gombrowicz en Argentine: Témoignages et documents 1939–1963*. Paris: Denoël, 1984.

Matamoro, Blas. "La Argentina de Gombrowicz." *Cuadernos hispanoamericanos* 469–470 (1989): 271–279.

Szacki, Jerzy. "Gombrowicz's Anti-Philosophy." *Polish Perspectives* 31.1 (1988): 70–73.

Thompson, Ewa M. *Witold Gombrowicz*. Boston: Twayne Publishers, 1979.

Van Buuren, Maarten. "Witold Gombrowicz et le grotesque." *Littérature* 48 (1982): 57–73.

Bradley Epps

GUDIÑO KIEFFER, EDUARDO
(Argentina; 1935) ──────────────────────

Guidiño Kieffer was born in the town of Esperanza. Although trained as a lawyer, he has devoted himself to journalism, translation and fiction writing. He has published over a dozen books, including novels and short stories. His narrative ranges from the experimental and magic realism to social realism and satire. Guidiño Kieffer's best-known work is a neopicaresque novel, *Guía de pecadores* (Guide for Sinners; 1972). Written in a very colloquial Buenos Aires vernacular, it explores, in a series of interlaced vignettes, the lives of the poor, the derelict and the oppressed in the underworld and lower middle class of Buenos Aires. Newspaper headlines and captions, as well as epigraphs from Golden Age picaresque novels, are part of the collagelike structure of the novel, which seeks to reveal the absurdity and grotesqueness of contemporary urban experience in a tone that is somewhat reminiscent of the works of social realist painters like the American Paul Cadmus or writers like John Rechy. Gay characters and the gay experience are only part of this view of the marginal aspects of society.

A section of this novel, "Rara avis in terra" (Rare Bird on Earth) was included in *Calamus*, an international anthology of male homosexuality in twentieth-century literature, alongside works by Konstantinos Kavafis, Federico García Lorca, E. M. Forster, Jean Genet, and Allen Ginsberg. Gudiño Kieffer's selection presents, in the form of an interior monologue, the pride, creativity, even genius—as well as anxiety, heartbreak and loneliness—of a bald female impersonator whose highly ritual striptease act is performed to the music of Bach's choral prelude "Jesus, Joy of Man's Desiring."

Besides this extraordinary novel, the rest of Gudiño Kieffer's work, although it reveals a very open attitude toward sexuality and "deviant" human behavior, does not deal with gay characters and themes except in a tangential manner. Another novel, *Medias negras, peluca rubia* (Black Stockings, Blond Wig; 1979), narrates the life of identical male twins. It merges a homoerotic undertone and incidents with other types of erotic manifestations like heterosexual love and love for the mother or an animal. Some minor gay characters appear in it, but they are presented in a stereotypical and somewhat unsympathetic manner (as are most characters in the novel) and do not really illuminate or present new insights into the gay experience.

In general, the work of Gudiño Kieffer may be characterized as based on a panerotic vision that allows for all forms of sexual manifestations, not only human but also animal, magical and mythical. In the title story of *La hora de María y el pájaro de oro* (Mary's Hour and the Gold Bird; 1975), the sun at noon, the gold bird and a human character are blended into a myth of rape. In the same book, a selection titled "Delfín" (Dolphin) narrates the "extraordinary tale of the love of a dolphin for a boy" in which dolphins are described as "voluptuous and inclined to love" (15–16). In this vision, then, the homoerotic experience appears as a manifestation of a larger, perhaps universal, force, which may appear as both noble and degenerate. Gudiño Kieffer's satiric mode appears to emphasize the latter.

WORKS

Carta abierta a Buenos Aires violento. Buenos Aires: Emecé, 1970.
Fabulario. Buenos Aires: Losada, 1969.
Guía de pecadores. Buenos Aires: Losada, 1972.
La hora de María y pájaro de oro. Buenos Aires: Losada, 1975.
Jaque a Pa y Ma. Buenos Aires: Emecé, 1982.
Magia blanca. Buenos Aires: Emecé, 1986.
Medias negras, peluca rubia. Buenos Aires: Emecé, 1979.
No son tan Buenos tus Aires. Buenos Aires: Emecé, 1983.
Nombres de mujer. Buenos Aires: Emecé, 1988.
Para comerte mejor. 2nd ed. Buenos Aires: Losada, 1969.
Será por eso que la quiero tanto. Buenos Aires: Emecé, 1973.
"A Sinner's Guide Book." Trans. Ronald Christ and Gregory Kolovakos. In *Calamus. Male Homosexuality in Twentieth-Century Literature*, 408–414. Ed. David Galloway and Christian Sabisch. New York: Quill, 1982.
¿Somos? Buenos Aires: Emecé, 1982.
Ta te tías y otros juegos. Buenos Aires: Emecé, 1980.
¿Y qué querés que te diga? Buenos Aires: Editorial de Belgrano, 1983.

Didier T. Jaén

GÜIRALDES, RICARDO (Argentina; 1886–1927)

The oldest member of the Generation of 1922, Güiraldes superficially appears to be a cosmopolitan oligarch escaped from a fin-de-siècle novel: suave, worldly, vastly wealthy, as at home in the salons of Paris as in his suite at the Hotel Majestic on Buenos Aires's elegant Avenida de Mayo. Yet there was another side to Güiraldes: mystical, intellectually curious, aesthetically engaged and, mostly important, enthralled with the life of the gaucho he observed on the family *estancia* (cattle ranch) at San Antonio de Areco in the province of Buenos Aires.

Güiraldes married Adelina del Carril in 1913, and there is no evidence to suggest he engaged in bisexual experimentation either as a youth or in his manhood. Yet, had such experimentation taken place, it would not be particularly surprising. He was, after all, a young man who had indulged in the pleasures of the Place Pigalle, who in his grand tour of 1910–1912 smoked hashish in Ceylon; who, in both Buenos Aires and Paris, ran with a fast and bohemian crowd that included such figures as Valéry Larbaud, Paul Valéry and André Gide. Beyond this, Güiraldes's spiritual restlessness led him toward Eastern religions, particularly Hinduism, which took a rather benign view of sexual variation (compared with the Catholicism of early-twentieth-century Argentina).

Such speculations, however, are in many ways beside the point, in that Güiraldes's contribution to a so-called gay literature is more covert than overt, centered not on the homosexual per se but on what Leslie Fiedler defined as the homoerotic. And just as Fiedler's essay "Come Back to the Raft, Huck Honey" (which evolved into the more general *Love and Death in the American Novel* [1960]) was both revolutionary and scandalous in its reading of *Huckleberry Finn* (and, by extension, all of *Huck*'s innumerable literary offspring), so a consideration of the homoerotic elements in Güiraldes's major work, the novel *Don Segundo Sombra* (1926), evokes a similar discomfort.

That *Don Segundo Sombra* evinces a powerful homoerotic strain should be expected. As climax and closure of what the Argentine literary tradition calls *la gauchesca*—a cultural production based on highly ideologized versions of the role of the gaucho in Argentine social history—the novel exhibits various elements that characterized the genre from its inception in José Hernández's pseudo epic *Martín Fierro* (1872, 1879), of which intense male bonding is one. In a nation with a preponderantly male population, one in thrall to the cult of friendship, it is unsurprising that such a thread runs through the novel.

Don Segundo Sombra, at its heart, is a profoundly misogynistic book. The only redeemable female characters are the long-lost mother of the protagonist, Fabio Cáceres; the kindly and asexual *curandera* (folk healer); and Aurora, the girl whom Fabio does little more than rape before he takes to life on the cattle trail. Otherwise, women are a source of conflict: petty, scheming, hopelessly attached to the town and the Liberal scheme that will ultimately destroy the gaucho world. During his courtship of Paula on Don Candelario's *estancia*, Fabio says, "I dreamt they dropped me in a hole, like an ironwood post, and stamped down the earth till my ribs cracked and I couldn't breathe (488). The analogue of heterosexual romance is burial alive.

In contrast, life on the pampas is innocent, masculine and free. It is the place where relationships are purest, deepest and least vexed, a place characterized by labor that is both intensely physical and strongly libidinal in its emphasis on conquest: roping, riding and breaking horses. All this is conducted, of course, with the phallic hardware of gaucho life: the lasso, the whip, the omnipresent knife. On occasion, the subliminal sexual charge bubbles to the surface. In chapter IV, at the end of a mock duel between Goyo and Horacio, Goyo, who has lost, remarks, "You're hard to take." Horacio replies, "What? Did your sister tell you?" (364). The analogy of duel and sexual activity is even more strongly evoked in the knife fight between Fabio and his rival for Paula's affection, Numa, in chapter X. After Fabio slashes his opponent across the forehead, "Numa dropped his knife to the floor and stood there, his legs spread and his head low, frozen with fear" (499). The posture of defeat leaves little to the imagination.

The strongest homoerotic allusions emerge in connection with Fabio's relationships with Patrocinio Salvatierra and Don Segundo. In the former instance, in a scene of almost too obvious oedipal significance, Patrocinio and Fabio go to the crab beds to kill the rogue bull that has gored Fabio's horse, Comadreja. As they confront the bull, Fabio declares, "Out of the will to murder that we shared was born a strong sentiment of friendship. Two men enduring danger together come out of it intimates, like a couple after an embrace" (438).

Don Segundo meanwhile is the man Fabio runs away from home to join. The young boy's relationship to him is characterized by humility, passivity and deference to the individual Fabio refers to as "mi hombre" (my man). Don Segundo masters him again and again, often with the threat of physical violence. Even near the novel's conclusion, when Fabio's inheritance is announced and he realizes that if he accepts it, he will lose the idyllic world he has enjoyed, he relinquishes his own desires at Don Segundo's command: "I realized any resistance on my part would be met with a blow, and that pleased me in a way that perhaps other people wouldn't understand. For Don Segundo, I was still that little *guacho*" (487).

These sentiments reveal the core of homoeroticism's function in the novel. *Don Segundo Sombra* postulates an eternal, male, adolescent world in which time is suspended. As long as this suspension is maintained, Fabio may remain a gaucho, and the gauchos themselves may escape the inevitable domestication and extinction that history has in store for them. As the novel's conclusion demonstrates, Güiraldes realized that such a resistance was doomed.

WORKS

Don Segundo Sombra. Buenos Aires: Editorial Proa, 1926. English version as *Don Segundo Sombra: Shadows on the Pampas*. Trans. Harriet de Onís. New York: Farrar & Reinhart, 1935. Quotations are cited from *Obras completas*. Buenos Aires: Emecé, 1962.

CRITICISM

Ara, Guillermo. *Richard Güiraldes*. Buenos Aires: Editorial "La Mondrágora," 1961.

Bordelois, Ivonne. *Genio y figura de Ricardo Güiraldes*. Buenos Aires: Editorial Universitaria de Buenos Aires, 1967.

Curet de De Anda, Miriam. *El sistema expresivo de Ricardo Güiraldes*. Río Piedras: Editorial Universitaria, Universidad de Puerto Rico, 1976.

Donahue, John. *"Don Segundo Sombra" y "El Virginiano": Gaucho y cow-boy*. Madrid: Pliegos, 1987.

Ghiano, Juan Carlos. *Ricardo Güiraldes*. Buenos Aires: Editorial Pleamar, 1966.

Leland, Christopher T. *The Last Happy Men: The Generation of 1922, Fiction and the Argentine Reality*, esp. 119–147. Syracuse, N.Y.: Syracuse University Press, 1986.

Romano, Eduardo. *Análisis de "Don Segundo Sombra."* Buenos Aires: Centro Editor de América Latina, 1967.

Christopher Towne Leland

GUMIEL, PABLO (Bolivia; dates unknown) _____

The case of Pablo Gumiel is representative of the limits and problems that homosexuality has experienced in becoming an open subject in Bolivian society. Gumiel published only one short narrative, *Erebo* (1955), the first Bolivian contemporary text that openly treats homosexuality. Erebo, according to the etymology of the name, is a very dark place (Erebus) situated between Hades and Earth. The effect of the narrative is similarly dark and foreboding. The protagonist, Jacob, recounts his life as a long passage through darkness. His sense of discontent begins with the realization that his sexual orientation is toward the same gender and ends with his death.

Erebo exhibits some of the themes that were part of a late Romantic tradition in Latin America that emphasized sentimentalism. The first of these themes is the social rejection of someone with different characteristics. Second, the protagonist internalizes the sense of alienation as part of his own psychology. Jacob thinks of himself as *anómalo* (abnormal) and as someone punished by god. The third element of this tradition is an idealized treatment of the relationship between Jacob and his lover. The most interesting feature of the book is the way in which the story is narrated. The reader learns about Jacob's life through a conversation in a hotel room in a small town near La Paz. There Jacob and his lover (a man called ''he'') are together for the last time. After having broken off the relationship sometime before, this is a moment of reconciliation. In this room they review a letter, an intimate confession of Jacob's life, that he had sent to his lover before their meeting.

In a sense the whole story is confined to this letter. The letter is Jacob's life, and it is also Jacob's death, because immediately after reading it, both characters die. The letter, written in a confessional tone, addresses how terrible life has been for Jacob. From the jokes and rejection he suffered while at school, until his adulthood, when he is forced to look for sexual partners among the lowest classes of society, Jacob is an outcast and a very solitary person. Some facts have marked his life with a tragic twist—for instance, his first love committed suicide while still a schoolboy. Jacob is accused of having caused the suicide, but he feels that society forced his lover to take his life. This is also a prediction of his own death, because he feels that society, by denying him a space to fulfill his sexual needs, is pushing him toward death. After reading the letter, both characters, without any further explanation, seem to understand that there is no hope of happiness for them in this world and proceed to kill themselves.

Jacob's letter depicts his life as being as dark as Erebus. By contrast, he is represented as a very light person. From his physical attributes (white and blond) to his artistic sensibility, he is described as a fragile and delicate person. He represents innocence, and because of this, his love shines against the dark background of an evil society. The tragedy of his life comes from this society, which is incapable of granting him a place. The basic structure of the book is the confrontation between darkness and light, with the victory of darkness. This portrait undoubtedly is very simplistic, and the easy sentimentality of the narration shows only black and white figures, good characters and a bad society, while failing to touch the more complex issues of homosexuality in a given social context. The narrator idealizes himself, and therefore homosexuality, making homosexuals victims of Bolivian society without trying to understand the causes of this conflict.

However, the book has special value because it is the first literary text that openly treats homosexuality in Bolivia, and it does so from the perspective of the homosexual individual. The difficulty of writing such a work is apparent from the shadow surrounding the identity of the author. No literary history contains any reference to him, nor do dictionaries of Bolivian literature mention him or his work. Moreover, little is known about Gumiel within cultural and intellectual circles in La Paz. This suggests that perhaps Pablo Gumiel is a pseudonym and demonstrates how difficult it is publicly to raise the subject of homosexuality in Bolivia. Gay and lesbian experience is a reality on all levels of Bolivian society, but is something about which one never speaks, much less writes.

WORKS

Erebo. La Paz: Ediciones Isla, 1955.

Leonardo García-Pabón

H

HERNÁNDEZ, JOSÉ (Argentina; 1824–1886)

Hernández, the author of the gaucho epic *Martín Fierro* (first part 1872; second part 1879) is undoubtedly an emblematic author of Argentine literature. Literary criticism and cultural writing in general have constructed around his person and his work a series of putatively national and spiritual values relating to Argentine identity. At the same time, these studies have established the canonical character of a literary genre known as the gauchesque.

Hernández's work reveals the political emblematization of the gaucho, transformed into the sign of both machismo and a national identity. *Martín Fierro* lays bare socioeconomic controversies through a series of binary situations that are basic to Argentine historical development: countryside/city, barbarism/civilization, province/Buenos Aires, native/immigrant. The two parts into which the poem is divided (''The Gaucho Martín Fierro'' and ''The Return of Martín Fierro'') allow for the comprehension in a single text of the various reaccommodations that the movement from one binary pole to the other implies.

Despite the polemics the poem has provoked in academic circles and beyond, there is still no ideological study, either partial or global, of Hernández's poem that is not based on premises that have already been canonized or thematized by Argentine culture. This is important to the extent that *Martín Fierro* and other texts that deal with the theme of the gaucho have been projected into popular culture. One of these unconsidered aspects turns on the homosocial problematics (recognized, for example, in the case of the tango), especially when it overlies a homoerotic dimension. Such an approach would unquestionably spark a series of readings with the potential to move examination of the poem in fresh critical directions.

An examination of the most authoritative critical sources reveals how Ezequiel Martínez Estrada and Jorge Luis Borges, and even a recent anthology of eroticism in Argentine literature (Herrera), are unable to recognize any element of the homoerotic in *Martín Fierro*. Yet Josefina Ludmer has demonstrated the dynamics of these texts when forced to confront the presence of difference and otherness. It is possible to define the gaucho, she says, only on the basis of a series of systematic exclusions. The gaucho and his masculinity are principally the consequence of an operation of exclusion and feminization of the immigrant. But this list could be extended to include other disjunctions like the sexual (women), the political (the Native Americans), the racial (blacks), the social (the representatives of the urban order).

Italians and Spaniards (almost always identified by pejorative words in Argentine culture) are presented in terms of a process of feminization: they are cowardly, incapable of fighting with a knife or of undertaking a heroic task, tied to work and domestic tasks and completely lacking any knowledge about activities related to the raising of cattle. The immigrant is always on the side of the powerful and collaborates with the forces of oppression. The gaucho also identifies himself via mirror imaging, in terms of another gaucho. This is one point of entry into the homosocial under the guise of friendship (an issue that cuts across multiple sectors and practices of Argentine culture), a feature that has been identified by critical commentary without being pushed to its ultimate consequences. To admit the other as an equal implies a narcissistic dimension in the order of identifications. Identification supposes the choice of an erotic object based on a discriminating restriction that, when it becomes an aggressive expulsion, assumes the form of xenophobia, racism, machismo and homophobia (for example, the gaucho calls immigrants *maricas*, or pansies). By contrast, Martín Fierro's buddy Cruz represents what cannot ever be recovered; the family order (houses, wife and sons) constitutes a global sign on the level of property: they are the gaucho's capital and, as such, can be lost and recovered, replaced or supplemented. As a consequence, in Fierro's famous advice to his and Cruz's sons, the alleged knowledge attained via experience and the imposition of the state portrays a petit bourgeois and masculine order. These words of advice are intended to guarantee the efficacy of the union among men.

For this reason woman is not even considered in the order of legality. In only one stanza (II.4757–4762) is she admitted as an unnecessary possibility and as a domain of absolute danger. In any event, like the immigrant, woman fulfills an intermediary role in order to permit every possible relationship (love/hate) among men. She causes men to move in an erotic dimension masked as challenge and duel: the black woman in the seventh canto of the first part motivates the knife fight between Martín Fierro and her black companion, which allows for the challenging of racial difference and its homophobic correlate (the black man is first a bull and then a newborn tigress). The scene with the *terne* (gaucho slang for someone who is valiant) supposes a reference to the sexual utilization of the protagonist's sister, via the play between brother-in-law and sister. The white woman held captive by the Indians at the outset of the second part of the poem is the point of departure in the sequence of actions that lead to Cruz's death. Martín Fierro and Cruz have run away from civilization to live among the Indians; there Cruz dies of a plague for which the white men and the captive woman are held responsible. Fierro must seek his revenge against the Indians and return to civilization, with the submission to the law that such a return implies. The duel with the Indian is based on the specular quality of fascination ("He looked at me and I looked at him"; II.1156) and is developed on the basis of a masculine amorous interplay proposed as the alternative between life and death, passive and active, below and above, knifed and knifing.

These duels, based on an initial identification involving a lethal outcome, serve to eliminate racial and sociopolitical differences, and are counterbalanced by the story of the relationship between Fierro and Cruz. The duel between Fierro and Cruz ends in friendship, a sublimated way of proposing their teaming up, crossing the frontier into the utopia of illegal barbarism, where they will establish a homoerotic hearth and home.

From the outset, the seduction of the one by the other allows Fierro to save his life from the military police hounding him and Cruz to sever, in an act of betrayal (he is the police sergeant), his ties to authority (which we learn had taken his wife from him). Thus emerges the possibility of "living together" (II.408) among the Indians, where they can "hide there/our poor situation/alleviating with our union/that harsh captivity" (II.415–418). There is a crescendo of weeping and wailing, prayers and the use of diminutives, all in the context of the roles of marital imagination. Cruz dies in Fierro's arms, entrusting to the latter "his baby boy." Fierro prays to Jesus and faints, only later weeping over Cruz's grave. "Deprived of so many goods" (II.967), the gaucho does not know what to do with his life. Immediately, the moans of the captive white woman provide a new amorous challenge, in which his final destiny (with the murder of her son by the Indians along the way) will be his return and subjection to official culture (not, it must be stressed, with the woman in heterosexual companionship by his side). This means subjecting himself to the universality of the law, renouncing paternity (the separation of Cruz from his newfound sons and from Cruz's son, cast to the four winds in the geometrical form of a cross, as Cruz's name [cruz=cross] prefigures), all based on the secret oath taken by all never to reveal their true identities. All this demonstrates adherence to an ideology of the weak and the loss of identity under the guise of changed names.

This fraternity of the marginal, based on a supposed wisdom in the face of brutal history, will guarantee the union of men who have been feminized, in terms of gaucho cultural postulates, by the law, left with no choice but to assume their castration through an illusion of the macho, as much racist as it is xenophobic. The entire theological order of honor, the love between men, submission, pacificism and renunciation will undeniably exercise a subsequent impact on the allegedly countercultural ideologies of subaltern sectors of Argentine society.

If *Martín Fierro* is the paradigm of Argentine national identity, the consideration of these homoerotic matrixes requires their appropriate historicization. Thus one can see a line of research inquiry that extends from the rape of the political adversary in Esteban Echeverría's "El matadero" (The Slaughterhouse; ca. 1839), considered a founding text of Argentine fiction, to Borges's stories; included as well is the feminization of the rebel (identified as subversive) via torture in the literature relating to military barbarism during recent dictatorships.

WORKS

El gaucho Martín Fierro. Contiene al final una interesante memoria sobre el camino transandino. Buenos Aires: Imprenta de la Pampa, 1872.
La vuelta de Martín Fierro. Buenos Aires: Librería del Plata, 1879.

CRITICISM

Borges, Jorge Luis. *El "Martín Fierro."* Buenos Aires: Columba, 1953.
Herrera, Francisco. *Antología del erotismo en la literatura argentina.* Buenos Aires: Editorial Fraterna, 1990.
Ludmer, Josefina. *El género gauchesco: Un tratado sobre la patria.* Buenos Aires: Sudamericana, 1988.
Lugones, Leopoldo. *El payador.* Buenos Aires: Otero, 1916.
Martínez Estrada, Ezequiel. *Muerte y transfiguración de Martín Fierro.* Mexico City: Fondo de Cultura Económica, 1948.
Unamuno, Miguel de. "El gaucho Martín Fierro: Poema popular gauchesco de don José Hernández." *Revista española* 1.1 (1894): 5–22. Also in his *Obras completas*, 8.47–63. Madrid: Afrodisio Aguado, 1958.
Viñas, David. "José Hernández, del indio al trabajo y a la conversión (1872–1879)." In his *Indios, ejército y frontera*, 159–164. Mexico City: Siglo XXI, 1982.

Gustavo Geirola

HERNÁNDEZ, JUAN JOSÉ (Argentina; 1932)

Hernández was born in Tucumán (according to some sources, in 1940); he moved to Buenos Aires when he was a young man, and he still lives there. He has written both poetry and prose. His writing includes the novel *La ciudad de los sueños* (The City of Dreams; 1971), but his best work has been in the short story, distinguished by two collections: *El inocente* (The Innocent; 1965) and *La favorita* (The Favored Woman; 1977). He has won many prizes and has been praised by Latin American writers like Gabriel García Márquez and Tomás Eloy Martínez. He has included his own stories in several anthologies, and his *Cuentos* (Stories; 1986) contains a complete bibliographic listing of his works, including translations into other languages; it is the only one to include a previously unpublished story, "Sacristán" (Sexton). To date, Hernández's writings have not received the academic attention to which their widespread publication would seem to entitle them. There are only two brief notes by major critics focusing on themes, without attempting to characterize the complex structures of his stories. Alejandra Pizarnik and Daniel Moyano do not refer to childhood and the intimate relations (national, and therefore political) in stories like "El sucesor" (The Heir) and "La favorita" between childhood and perversion and transgression. Moyano is careful to discuss the sociological debate over so-called provincial or regional writing, over a fictional and local-color folklore, on the one hand, and the imitation of a cosmopolitan literature centered in Buenos Aires, on the other, with all of the weight of writers like Jorge Luis Borges and Julio Cortázar. According to Moyano, this juncture is not resolved by a turn to the sort of Latin Americanness represented by the new Latin American narrative of the 1960s and 1970s and by authors like the Mexican Juan Rulfo. He goes on to underscore the presence, in the origins of Hernández's texts, of the grandmother—the Chieftess Mother, as she is called in "La inquilina" (The Boarder), one of Hernández's stories that deals with matriarchal power and how it structures provincial cultural horizons.

Despite the extensive enumeration of the themes in his works, nowhere does Hernández refer explicitly to the link between the body and sexuality dealt with in so many dimensions by the stories, one of which involves the gay.

A categoric exile in Hernández's poetry, which refers repeatedly to nostalgia for an unrecoverable land (the mother, the childhood, the patios and the siestas of provincial life), invites us to contemplate an idyllically Proustian construction of the past or the Bovarian complaint about the present (Fleming), where mirrors reflect another, the "deceitful image" or "I my own enemy." A narcissistic configuration runs from the maternal bosom to the uprooted present that structures a defining equation between desire and the other: "Thirst, my body, the world." This pleasureful setting, where one would "be eternally/color, pulp, delight," is disturbed by a presence that, based on delights that parallel the maternal ones, impedes the return to the "lost hearth," thanks to the "dark angel—splendid skin/and branches to afflict my blood" or the "angel of my secret," which also is dark-skinned. The semantic relations between childhood and the angel, based on this narcissistic formation of the I in its homoerotic mirroring and its sexual ambiguity, make up the productive center of Hernández's best stories, as can be seen in "Princesa" (Princess), dedicated to Alejandra Pizarnik.

The close link between the child and the angel has multiple variations in Hernández's fiction. If some of his texts link it to homoeroticism and even to something that is explicitly homosexual, others use the child as a subaltern figure on which desire can be practiced and that can be utilized as a substitute for a missing object of desire. Angel and child share the way in which they give themselves over to the sex of the other or participate in sexuality without fixed generic markers. In other cases, the angel and/or children are markers via which socioeconomic and cultural differences are revealed, as in "Como si estuvieras jugando" (As Though You Were Playing), "Julián," and "Reinas" (Queens). Or they may directly constitute the allegorization of the allegedly "innocent" that bursts forth in a political context that is supposedly adult—"Así es mamá" (That's How Momma Is)—as well as in the representation of dark-skinned northerners, noisy hordes of Peronist sympathizers who advance on Buenos Aires dreaming of social vindication. *La ciudad de los sueños* is the space envisioned in remote provincial corners that, like the figure of the omnivorous mother, "must go forth in order to save herself," since "the complex and contradictory relationship between the province and Buenos Aires [is viewed as a] need to sever ties and abandon rural origins despite the impossibility of ever forgetting completely" (Amar Sánchez, 926). If the urban (either provincial or big-city) is discernible in a binarism of visible/invisible that allows for transvestism, the latter is not the same thing in both settings.

If the anonymity of Buenos Aires allows the canceling out of the past, there is neither clothing nor mimicry capable of concealing one's family origin in a small provincial town, which is the setting for the best of Hernández's stories. Therefore the facade of decency is constructed at the expense of children ("La señorita Estrella" [Miss Star]) or the sacrifice of adults who are "different" (widows, homosexuals, the deformed), which includes being at the mercy of clever grandmothers capable of legalizing transgressions within the parameters of the law. For instance, the grandmother in "La inquilina" legalizes the extramarital relations of her grandson when she incorporates the other woman by renting her a room. In "Como si estuvieras jugando," the grandmother utilizes her granddaughter to escape from poverty through simulated begging, a sinister symbol of class self-exploitation. Playing—which in general presupposes the victimization or infantilization of a third party—or the mask (both obsessively theatrical) provides for the precarious satisfaction of desire, especially for the homosexual man or the lesbian.

In "Anita," a story that is marvelously gay despite its inclusion in official secondary-school textbooks in Argentina, two boys unwittingly construct a love story using a spider. In "El disfraz" (The Mask), a female dwarf overcomes her strong feelings toward a woman friend by fulfilling her love for the latter through use of a mask of the woman that allows her access to the friend's ex-lover in a ceremony of "seductions and the sweetly dirty." "La señorita Estrella," undoubtedly one of Hernández's most powerful texts, also turns on dramatic scenes and cross-dressing in the fulfillment of lesbian desire. Its power resides not only in the victimization of the figure of the paralyzed father who functions as a spectator, but also in the replacement of the female friend by a male child who is just as nice. The incestuous desire of a brother can attain, as in "El inocente," spheres of glorious pleasure when he returns his sister to the past and together they bring about the sacrifice of a crippled neighbor child by playing a game that makes murder look like an accident. Incest can, as in "El viajero" (The Traveler), be the basis for a family triangle filled with mirror images and pleasure-giving negotiations: the brother, who decides to leave because he is dissatisfied with the husband his sister has chosen, ends up caressing the body of his brother-in-law with the latter's silent consent. In other cases, the child makes use of powers over adults in an act of terrorist violence, as in "Venganza" (Revenge) and "El ahijado" (The Godson), in which the child gets away with murdering his aunt thanks to a death certificate provided by the doctor. These are acts of violence whose wellspring is the family itself.

The homosocial basis of play and the machismo of what is decent, as can amply be seen in "La reunión" (The Reunion), in "Tenorios" (Seducers), and in the pact between men so magnificently described in "Las dalias" (The Dahlias), would seem to portray in Hernández's stories a family violence and a sociocultural corruption produced by the positions of an infrastructural matriarchy and a symbolic patriarchy. This contradiction is developed in a setting limited to the endogamic space of the province and, without the characters realizing it, is exorcisable only through exile or submission, the latter in the pleasureful devouring of the son by the mother, with the son wallowing in his status as a favored slave and the stunting dissolution of his subjectivity as he is turned into an "angel of the Lord."

WORKS

La ciudad de los sueños. Buenos Aires: Editorial Sudamericana, 1971.
Claridad vencida. Buenos Aires: Burnichon Editor, 1957.
Cuentos. Rosario, Argentina: Alción Coquena Editora, 1986.
La favorita. Caracas: Monte Avila Editores, 1977.
El inocente. Buenos Aires: Editorial Sudamericana, 1965.
Negada permanencia y La siesta y la naranja. Buenos Aires: Ediciones Botella al Mar, 1952.
Otro verano. Buenos Aires: Editorial Sudamericana, 1966.

CRITICISM

Amar Sánchez, Ana María. "Juan José Hernández: La constitución de un nuevo referente." *Revista iberoamericana* 125 (1983): 919–927.
Fleming, Leonor. "Una literatura del interior: El noroeste argentino." *Cuadernos hispanoamericanos* 408 (1984): 132–145.
Moyano, Daniel. "Prólogo: Los exilios de Juan José Hernández." Juan José Hernández, *"La señorita Estrella" y otros cuentos*, i–v. Buenos Aires: Centro Editor de América Latina, 1982.
Pizarnik, Alejandra. "Conversación con Juan José Hernández." In Juan José Hernández, *Cuentos*, 7–9. Rosario, Argentina: Alción Coquena Editora, 1986.

Gustavo Geirola

J

JUANA INÉS DE LA CRUZ (Mexico; 1648?–1695)

An illegitimate child of a Spanish captain, Pedro Manuel de Asbaje y Vargas Machuca, and Isabel Ramírez de Santillana, Juana Ramírez was born in San Miguel de Neplanta, probably in 1648. In accordance with the information provided by the writer herself in a celebrated autobiographical text, the *Respuesta a Sor Filotea de la Cruz* (Reply to Sister Philotea of the Cross), she learned to read at the age of three, deceiving the teacher of her sister in order to be allowed to attend classes at the local primary school. Her calling for studying was so intense that when she found out about the university in the capital city of the viceroyalty of New Spain, she conceived the idea of attending dressed as a man. This was an astounding possibility, in view of the cultural parameters of the period. For that reason, Juana had to resign herself to reading and learning on her own in the library of her maternal grandfather, Pedro Ramírez, in Panoayán. She gave early evidence of her literary vocation with a poetic composition, a *loa* (poem of praise) to the Blessed Sacrament, that has been lost.

Soon after, Juana moved to Mexico City, where she lived with relatives of her mother. When she was fourteen years old, Doña Leonor Carreto, Marquise de Mancera and the vicereine, invited her to reside at court because of her admiration for the knowledge and extraordinary creative powers of the young prodigy. In that refined atmosphere, Juana had numerous opportunities to display her unusual intellectual abilities in front of the illustrious scholars of the age and to recite her poetry at courtly celebrations.

In 1667 Juana entered the aristocratic Carmelite convent in Mexico City. Because of health problems, she left a few months later. She ultimately made her profession with the religious name of Sor Juana Inés de la Cruz in the convent of Saint Jerome, where she remained for the rest of her life. When her patrons, the Marquis de Mancera and his wife, returned to Spain, the new viceroy, Archbishop Payo Enríquez de Ribera, favored her with his esteem and affection. The cathedrals of Mexico City, Puebla and Oaxaca commissioned her to compose *villancicos* (Christmas carols about themes taken from the New Testament and the popular Christian tradition). Her religious poetry includes sonnets and *romances* (Spanish octosyllabic ballads).

In 1680, when the Marquis of la Laguna and his wife, the Countess of Paredes, arrived with a triumphal arch, Sor Juana composed *Neptuno alegórico* (Allegorical Neptune). At this time, she had become a renowned public figure. In 1683, following the dramatic pattern of the Spanish cloak-and-dagger comedy, she wrote *Los empeños de una casa* (Household Intrigue). At the request of the Countess of Paredes, she composed her finest one-act religious play, *El divino Narciso* (Divine Narcissus), an allegorical piece first performed in 1687. Her dramatic production is completed by twelve *loas*—brief dramatic preludes in verse—two allegorical *autos* (religious mystery/miracle plays)—*El mártir del Sacramento, San Hermenegildo* (St. Hermenegildo, the Sacrament's Martyr) and *El cetro de José* (Joseph's Scepter)—and a comedy in collaboration with Juan de Guevara, *Amor es más laberinto* (Love Is the Great Labyrinth). In all of them, Sor Juana evidences a complete assimilation of the seventeenth-century Hispanic dramatic tradition, in the style of the playwright Pedro Calderón de la Barca.

The last known dated work by Sor Juana is *Respuesta*, signed in 1691, the self-defense that is one of the most remarkable cultural documents from the Latin American colonial period. During her last years, after having disposed of her personal library under orders from her confessor, Sor Juana devoted herself to the religious life. She died in Mexico City during the cholera epidemic of 1695.

Two volumes of her writings were printed in her lifetime, a rare privilege few contemporary poets could enjoy: *Inundación castálida de la única poetisa, musa décima* (Castalian Flood of the Unique Poetess, the Tenth Muse; 1689) and *Segundo volumen de las obras de Sor Juana Inés de la Cruz* (Second Volume of the Works by Sister Juana Inés de la Cruz; 1692). These were followed by a third volume, *Fama y obras póstumas del Fénix de México* (Fame and Posthumous Writings of the Mexican Phoenix; 1700), which includes the first biography of the writer, the "Aprobación" (Censor's Approval) by Diego Calleja.

Sor Juana's personal lyric poetry contributed the most to the consolidation of her reputation as a poet. One part consists of occasional pieces written for court and church that represent the major part of her poetic production. These poems reveal her unique capacity to deal with the varied codes and literary traditions that dominated the Spanish Golden Age. A second group is the philosophical poems, in which the sonnet form prevails; an outstanding example is "Este que ves, engaño colorido" (This Colorful Deception That You See). The topics in

the philosophical and moral poems are typical of baroque literature: the deception of the senses, the brevity of human life and beauty and the unavoidable
destiny of being nothing but dust. This category includes a renowned satirical
poem, "Hombres necios que acusáis" (Injudicious Men Who Accuse), and *redondillas* (a type of quatrain) that denounce the hypocritical behavior of men.
The theme, which is part of a long pastoral tradition of invectives against abuse,
was illustrated by Sor Juana in terms of the business of daily life. This poem,
articulated as a succession of indisputable arguments, has attracted many feminist readings of it as an inspired manifesto of women's rights.

Sor Juana's love poetry provoked myriad discussions and conjectures about
possible love affairs during her stay at court. She lyrically explored one of the
most popular subjects among her contemporaries, that of lovelorn individuals
involved in triangular relations, in sonnets like "Feliciano me adora y le abor-
rezco" (Feliciano Adores Me, and I Detest Him). In general, the poet exalted
women's fidelity, underscoring the expression of feelings like jealousy and loneliness due to the absence of the beloved, and grief for love lost. Among many
other pieces that deserve attention are the sonnets "Detente, sombra, de mi bien
esquivo" (Halt, Shadow of My Elusive Love) and "Al que ingrato me deja
busco amante" (I Lovingly Seek the One Who Ungratefully Despises Me), and
the *redondillas* "En que describe racionalmente los efectos irracionales del
amor" (In Which the Poet Rationally Describes the Irrational Effects of Love).
The question is whether those poems correspond to personal experiences, re-
membrances of youth, or whether they are literary entertainments. A considerable number were written at the request of others. For this reason, it is
unnecessary to attempt to discover behind each poem a particular anecdote the
available historical documents do not record.

The most ambitious work by Sor Juana is the philosophical poem titled *Primero sueño* (First Dream; 1685–1690?), in which the poet describes the intellectual adventures of the soul, freed from the body when dreaming, as it seeks
to reach the prime mover and a full understanding of the universe. The poet
followed the formal tendencies that the Spanish master of baroque poetry, Luis
de Góngora y Argote, had established with his *Soledades* (*Solitudes*; 1612–
1613). In a poem of 965 lines Sor Juana introduces learned words and neologisms, mythological allusions and an astounding syntactic intricacy that make
the text a paradigmatic example of euphuistic difficulty. With regard to the
intellectual content of the poem, critics have noted the influence of the writings
of the German Jesuit Athanasius Kircher, who had imposed an orthodox version
of Renaissance Platonic hermeticism.

Sor Juana wrote a kind of theological treatise, *Crisis sobre un sermón* (Critique on a Sermon; 1690), to refute the ideas of the Portuguese Jesuit Antônio
Vieira, considered to be the best preacher of the period. The bishop of Puebla,
Manuel Fernández de Santa Cruz, published the text without the nun's permission, under the title *Carta atenagórica* (Athenian Letter). The bishop attached
a letter of his own, signed with the pseudonym "Sor Filotea de la Cruz," in

which he recommended that the nun abandon secular topics and dedicate herself entirely to religious ones. Sor Juana's text was harshly criticized by almost every man of distinction, for it was inconceivable that a woman would devote herself to such a serious topic, reserved for men. Sor Juana answered the attacks with her *Respuesta a sor Filotea*, in which she gave details about her precocious intellectual vocation, building a narrative of her life, defined by the constant passion for learning. In the last resort, it is her right to seek knowledge that Sor Juana defended so vigorously. She insisted that her calling to literature and her thirst for knowledge were innate qualities and, therefore, she should not be judged for them. In straightforward disagreement with the common sense of her time, Sor Juana maintained that knowledge was not only licit for women but also extremely useful for them.

In addition, the *Respuesta* is the best place to find a reasonable explanation for one of the more persistent debates surrounding the figure of the Mexican nun: why, being a cultivated, intelligent and beautiful woman, did she decide to live a cloistered life? Several arguments had been advanced since her literary rehabilitation in the first decades of the twentieth century. The different opinions may be summarized in two arguments: the sociological one, according to which her illegitimate origin would have prevented her from aspiring to an honorable marriage; and the psychological one, which assumes an unidentified amorous deception in her youth, one that marked her life decisively. The critic with the best explanation for the question is the Nobel Prize winner Octavio Paz, who, in his *Sor Juana Inés de la Cruz o las trampas de la fe* (*Sor Juana; or the Traps of Faith*; 1988), considers that it is in the childhood of Sor Juana— characterized by the absence of her biological father, the uncertain bond between her mother and her stepfather and the positive relation with her maternal grandfather—that one finds the path the poet followed: the renunciation of married life, the confinement to the cell/library during her adulthood, her rebellion against the authorities and even the plot of the *Primero sueño*.

In the cultural context of the seventeenth century, there were only two respectable life paths for a woman: marriage or the convent. In the *Respuesta a Sor Filotea*, Sor Juana acknowledged her total negation of the first option as the main reason for taking the habit. Although an orthodox Christian, Sor Juana lacked a profound religious inclination. She simply wanted to live alone, to spend her time reading and learning and to avoid any mandatory occupation that would impede her study.

Leaving to one side these biographical mysteries, which fade with an accurate historical perspective, it is necessary to consider the rumors concerning Sor Juana's sexual identity, unquestionably the most persistent and insidious ones in Latin American literary history. Even those who abstain from facing the lesbian preference attributed to her cannot avoid including more or less veiled allusions to such a troublesome matter. That explains why expressions like ''gossip and suppositions'' and ''curious and superfluous interpretations'' abound in the numerous biographies and commentaries on the poet and her works. Under such a circumstance, the tone of fervent vindication through which critics try to defend her against the accusation of having been an "example of dangerous deviancy" is understandable.

Beyond suppositions and conjectures, the only textual evidence that can be adduced consists of Sor Juana's statements about her repulsion for matrimony and the courtly poems she wrote, in which, besides a masterful use of the rhetoric of love, she registers her personal relationship with the viceroy, the Marquis of Mancera, and his wife, Leonor Carreto, and later with the Marquis of la Laguna and especially his wife, the Countess of Paredes. To the latter the poet addressed a great number of lines, under the literary nicknames Fili, Lisi, and Lísida, that include her more audacious poems. On some occasions, especially when the poet revealed her affection to the countess, the language she used allowed for some suspicion. If it is acceptable that the rhetoric of friendship recalls that of love, or that it is in fact the same, then those poems speak of faithfulness, feelings and passions with no ulterior significance. Thus, it is surprising that the first editor of the *Inundación castálida* inserted an explanatory note at the head of the first poem dedicated to the countess: "Either the gratitude of being favored and applauded, or the awareness she had of the eminent natural gifts that Heaven gave to the vicereine, or that secret influence . . . of humors or of stars, which is called sympathy, or all these together provoked in the poet a love for her Excellency with *an ardor so pure* such as the reader will see in the context of all the book" (Romance 16, *Obras completas*, 1.48; emphasis added).

The fact that the editor felt the need to remove any possible shadow of doubt surrounding the relationship between the two women is by its very nature suggestive. Likewise, the epigraphs added to Sor Juana's courtly poetical compositions, although they insist on emphasizing the decency of the writer's emotions—as in the case of the sonnet "Detente sombra de mi bien esquivo," whose epigraph reads: "Which restrains a fantasy contenting it with decent love"—show a tendency to impose a biographical pattern on her writings (Luciani). The poet herself asserted that her love was a spiritual one. If one interprets friendship as a platonic feeling of attraction between persons of the same sex, then the expressions that Sor Juana used in poems like this can be read as manifestations of such a feeling. In addition, it is necessary to take into account how the themes Sor Juana displayed in her love poetry correspond to an already lengthy literary tradition, that of Provençal courtly love. The most unusual fact in this case is that a woman would make use of these standardized forms of expression of affectivity and gratitude and, even more, that she would sign them.

Despite the argumentative subtleties of Sor Juana's defenders, who endeavor to affirm the "normalcy" of her feelings, the controversy rises again and again with lines like the following: "I have no idea about that;/I only know that I came here [to the convent]/so nobody could verify/whether I am a woman" ("Romance en respuesta a un caballero del Perú, que le envió unos barros diciéndole que se volviese hombre" [In Reply to a Gentleman from Peru, Who Sent Her Some Flower Vases, Asking Her to Become a Man]; Romance 48, *Obras completas*, 1.136–139). Specialized criticism has never satisfactorily worked out problematical passages like this, in which intricate variations of human relationships are implied.

Sor Juana stands out in the cultural milieu of her time because of her vindication of women, a manifestation *avant la lettre* of feminist concerns that only centuries later would become a part of modern discourse and practices. Current criticism has fluctuated between an accurate understanding of the grounds of those arguments that support the thesis of a secret sexual identity through malicious gossip—the refusal to accept that a woman, whether in the seventeenth century or now, could reach the high intellectual and creative level she did—and an outspoken exaltation of her lesbianism. Margo Glantz has been inclined to consider Sor Juana as an instance of the "indefinite and perfect" genre of androgyny that "fits her better in its alchemical connotation than in the non-verifiable one of homosexuality with which she is usually charged, with all the derogatory force that the figure of lesbianism usually implies" (123). On the other hand, there are those who aspire to mark Sor Juana's writings as the origin of Latin American lesbian poetry, secularly restricted by cultural standards that forbade the writer to acknowledge the true nature of her/his love in public (Bautista). However, when assessing Sor Juana's literary production, it is of no importance whether the real person was a lesbian or not. What really matters is that, in spite of the extreme limitations of her time and society, she managed to communicate her elusive feelings with sensitivity and talent and to provide a testimony of resistance to male prerogatives.

WORKS

The Dream. Partially trans. Gilbert F. Cunningham. In "Sor Juana's *Sueño*: A Fragment in English Verse." *Modern Language Notes* 83.2 (1968): 253–261.

Inundación castálida. Ed. Georgina Sabat-Rivers. Madrid: Castalia, 1982.

Obras completas, 4 vols. Ed. Alfonso Méndez Plancarte and Alberto G. Salceda. Mexico City: Fondo de Cultura Económica, 1951–1957.

A Woman of Genius: The Intellectual Autobiography of Sor Juana Inés de la Cruz. English trans. of *Respuesta a Sor Filotea* by Margaret Sayers Peden. Salisbury, Conn.: Lime Rock Press, 1982.

CRITICISM

Alfau de Solalinde, Jesusa. *El barroco en la vida de Sor Juana*. Mexico City: Instituto de Estudios y Documentos Históricos, 1981.

Arenal, Electa. "Sor Juana Inés de la Cruz: Speaking the Mother Tongue." *University of Dayton Review* 16.2 (1983): 93–105.

Bautista, Juan Carlos. "La sonrisa de Sor Juana." *Fem* 14.95 (1990): 13–16.

Bénassy-Berling, Marie-Cécile. *Humanisme et religion chez Sor Juana Inés de la Cruz:*

La femme et la culture au XVIIe siècle. Paris: Publications de la Sorbonne, Éditions Hispaniques, 1982. Spanish trans. as *Humanismo y religión en Sor Juana Inés de la Cruz*. Mexico City: Universidad Nacional Autónoma de México, 1984.

Chávez, Ezequiel A. *Sor Juana Inés de la Cruz. Ensayo de psicología*. Barcelona: Araluce, 1931.

Flynn, Gerard C. *Sor Juana Inés de la Cruz*. New York: Twayne, 1971.

Galaviz, Juan M. *Sor Juana Inés de la Cruz*. Madrid: Historia 16/Quorum, 1987.

Glantz, Margo. "Las hijas de la Malinche." In *Literatura mexicana hoy. Del 68 al ocaso de la revolución*, 121–129. Ed. Karl Kohut. Frankfurt: Vervuert Verlag, 1991.

Jiménez Rueda, Julio. *Sor Juana Inés de la Cruz en su época (1651–1695)*. Mexico City: Porrúa, 1951.

Leiva, Raúl. *Introducción a Sor Juana Inés de la Cruz. Sueño y realidad*. Mexico City: Universidad Nacional Autónoma de México, 1975.

Luciani, Frederick. "Sor Juana Inés de la Cruz: Epígrafe, epíteto, epígono." *Revista iberoamericana* 132–133 (1985): 777–783.

Pascual Buxó, José. *Góngora en la poesía novohispana*. Mexico City: Universidad Nacional Autónoma de México, 1960.

Paz, Octavio. *Sor Juana Inés de la Cruz o las trampas de la fe*. Mexico City: Fondo de Cultura Económica, 1982. English version by Margaret Sayers Peden as *Sor Juana; or the Traps of Faith*. Cambridge, Mass.: Harvard University Press, 1988.

Peña, Margarita. *Sor Juana Inés de la Cruz a la luz de la "Respuesta a sor Filotea."* Salamanca, Spain: Colegio de España, 1983.

Perelmuter Pérez, Rosa. *Noche intelectual: La oscuridad idiomática en el "Primero sueño."* Mexico City: Universidad Nacional Autónoma de México, 1982.

Pfandl, Ludwig. *Sor Juana Inés de la Cruz, la décima musa de México. Su vida, su poesía, su psique*. Trans. from the German by Juan Antonio Ortega y Medina. Mexico City: Universidad Nacional Autónoma de México, 1963.

Sabat-Rivers, Georgina. *El "Sueño" de Sor Juana Inés de la Cruz: Tradiciones literarias y originalidad*. London: Tamesis, 1977.

Schons, Dorothy. "Some Obscure Points in the Life of Sor Juana Inés de la Cruz." *Modern Philology* 24 (1926): 141–162.

Xiráu, Ramón. *Genio y figura de Sor Juana Inés de la Cruz*. Buenos Aires: EUDEBA, 1967.

Daniel Altamiranda

L

LEVI CALDERÓN, SARA (Mexico; 1942) _____

Levi Calderón was born in Mexico City to a Jewish family of considerable wealth. After earning a graduate degree in sociology, marrying and having two children, she came out as a lesbian and began a career as a writer. She currently is living in the San Francisco area while working on a sequel to her first novel.

Dos mujeres (*The Two Mujeres*; 1990), Levi Calderón's one published novel to date, has been a best-seller in Mexico since its appearance, in spite of her family's attempts to thwart sales by purchasing and storing copies of the book. Valeria, the autobiographical narrator of this often lyrical text, relates her story of coming out, the slow and deliberate emergence from social and familial compulsions to conform to traditional heterosexual gender roles, as well as to the cultural attitudes and values of her upper-class Jewish heritage.

The first of three clusters of chapters into which the novel is divided chronicles the growing passion between Genovesa, a struggling young artist, and Valeria, a sociologist/writer. The narrative opens with a divorced, almost thirty-nine-year-old Valeria experimenting with new friendships, especially with women, that scandalize her two sons, who claim no longer to recognize their mother (at least as they wish her to be). Emotion-laden dialogues between the two women and Valeria's numerous interior monologues reflect her increasing feelings of physical attraction toward the other woman and her inability (as yet) to find concrete ways to express these feelings because her parents, former husband and children have all censured them as abnormal. In scene after scene, in front of her mirrored reflection, Valeria tries to assess who she is and what she wants to be; her frequent bouts of tears are the result of this tortured process toward a final triumphant recognition that she can no longer hide or constantly deny her desire for another woman as she reveals in detail the sensations she experiences from head to toe.

From dreams and fantasies, followed by a dark tunnel of despair and repression, Valeria and Genovesa move closer to each other as they are physically intimate during a long weekend in the picturesque artists' colony of San Miguel Allende, an intimacy postponed after constant interruptions of previous attempts at what has been called "el encuentro de dos epidermis" (the encounter of two epidermises; Anhalt, 12). Valeria is held hostage for these acts by the revenge of her family members, who steal her diary and threaten to restrict her activity by economic means, beginning with closing her bank account and canceling her American Express card. First in New York City, then back in Mexico, the two women confront the internal and external impediments to their physical and psychological fulfillment as gay women on a narrative trail that leads to a false ending in which Valeria and Genovesa separate. As each flees from the other, from her own longings and from an overt acceptance of a lesbian identity, Valeria resolves to document this process in writing, a decision that leads to the construction of the novel in the hands of the reader.

The second section picks up Valeria's life story from childhood to the final point of reconnection with Genovesa, thereby negating and reversing the rupture of the first portion of the text. Against a backdrop of popular culture (the development of the radio and cinema industry in Mexico, references to the feminine myths promoted by women's magazines and the latest fashions from Hollywood) and imprecise echoes of historical events like World War II, Valeria recounts the early explorations of her sexuality with male classmates in a Jewish-run private school. When her brother Efraín, harbinger of future male companions and self-appointed representative of inherited values to be upheld, plays the role of policeman and reports her "reputation" to her father, she is ferociously beaten, a measure intended to correct her behavior. Such "educative" punishment appears later, in her marriage to Luis. However, Valeria's reaction is to construct a private fantasy world as an alternative to the family structure that attempts to modify her appearance, demeanor and choice of partners to conform to a more traditional (heterosexual) model of a young woman of their class and social standing.

Despite the ritualistic application of makeup and perfume, the attendance at sweet sixteen parties and a command performance as the central figure in a lavish wedding ceremony—or perhaps owing to all of these masquerades—Valeria remains unhappy, unsatisfied and alienated from her body. Many sessions of psychoanalysis later, following the displacement of her nascent desires onto the male analyst as a substitute for the woman she really seeks, she is "reborn." Not independent of social pressures, but now acutely aware of her rejection of ready-made categories of identity, Valeria decides to finish her university education and to liberate herself from the bonds of the accusations of her mother, father, brother and sons, all of whom have punished her physically and emotionally for her sexual transgressions, which they see as personal offenses. She chooses self-imposed exile, and flees abroad to seek pleasure in the arms of both men and women.

The last section of the novel brings Genovesa back for a passionate reunion. Their experiences of separation and experimentation—from marriage, to trysts with South American revolutionaries, to erotic encounters with the wives of friends—have brought them back together in a happy ending: relaxing in the nude on a beach in the Greek islands, Valeria and Genovesa savor the (ironic) news that Valeria's manuscript—the novel of their life together and apart—has been accepted for publication in, of all places, Mexico.

While no critical analysis of Levi Calderón's writing has yet been published, aside from brief book reviews by Nedda de Anhalt and Elena Martínez, this novel's contribution to Latin American literature undeniably deserves more detailed attention. In its foregrounding of issues of lesbian identity in contemporary Mexican society, *Dos mujeres* addresses the relative (and in some cases absolute) absence of gay women from cultural representations of all types. Though not the singular issue around which this narrative is woven, the construction and profession of lesbian identities are certainly the most dominant characteristics of a text that also considers crucial factors of identity like class, ethnic origins and age. Of particular note is the novel's situating the discussion of lesbian sexuality in the privileged bodies of upper-class women, who have the freedom and means to respond to societal ambivalence and/or persecution with "exiles" of various types: summer homes, beach retreats, ashrams, prolonged trips abroad, apartments in the United States and so on. The acquisition and availability of these privileged spaces would appear to put into question the invisible or outsider status of the two women under consideration—a status not automatically conferred to begin with—whose lives do not converge with the experiences of lesbians of other social or economic classes, who lack the luxury to choose among the alternatives presented in this text, or even the opportunity to produce a discourse on their sexuality.

In other words, while rigidly defined gender categories are placed in question by the characters in the novel, even as they assume fairly traditional active/passive roles in their erotic life, the class hierarchy never comes under scrutiny, and the contradictions that arise—when Valeria's male servant dies, she steadfastly refuses to take over his chores around the house so as not to descend into the ranks of the lower classes to serve her sons, although it was evidently proper for him to have done so—are resolved by Valeria's recourse to the very sources of financial security and patriarchal power that imposed the restrictions she has come to detest. First, Valeria relies on the family's wealth to maintain herself and her lover; she then converts the lived experience of rejection into a publishable story whose market value will potentially afford her a continuity of the economic comfort to which she is accustomed. As a work of literature, the two women's bodies acquire a value as symbolic capital that they are stripped of in real life as flesh-and-blood members of society.

Sexual desire rooted in opposition to the heterosexual norm is blamed for

Valeria's father's heart attack and declining health (the ultimate breakdown of the pivotal figure of the patriarch), but it is only in the novel she writes that Valeria is vanquished by death, a sad figure broken and deserted by all. Her choice to alter this ending and opt for exile instead (by tearing up this part of the manuscript) defies such a tragic outcome. But at a time when Mexican culture boasts of an exemplary official tolerance of all types of political as well as sexual activity, one might wonder about the contradictory messages embodied in this text.

WORKS

Dos mujeres. Mexico City: Editorial Diana, 1990. English version as *The Two Mujeres.* Trans. Gina Kaufer. San Francisco: Aunt Lute Books, 1991.

CRITICISM

Anhalt, Nedda G. de. "Caleidoscopio erótico." *Sábado*, supp. to *Unomásuno* 683 (Nov. 3, 1990): 12–13.
Martínez, Elena M. Review of *Dos mujeres* (Sara Levi Calderón) and *Amora* (Rosamaría Roffiel). *Letras femeninas* 18.1–2 (Spring–Autumn 1992): 175–179.

Claudia Schaefer-Rodríguez

LEZAMA LIMA, JOSÉ (Cuba; 1912–1976)

Lezama Lima was born to a bourgeois family in Havana. His father, an officer in the Cuban National Army, died when his son was eight years old. From an early age, the boy suffered from asthma. In 1918, the family moved to the United States.

Lezama Lima studied law at the University of Havana. Soon after graduating, he decided to abandon the profession. His literary career had begun during his university days with contributions to several Cuban cultural magazines: *Verbum* (1937), *Espuela de plata* (Silver Spur; 1939–1941) and *Nadie parecía* (It Seemed like Nobody; 1942–1944). During this period, he initiated a friendship with the Spanish poet Juan Ramón Jiménez. Lezama was the founder and editor of the renowned *Orígenes* (Origins; 1944–1956), one of Latin America's most important vanguard literary reviews. *Orígenes*, a platform for the divulgence of modernist ideas in the Hispanic world, managed to publish forty issues, among which the one dedicated to José Martí's centennial (1953) stands out. Poets like Cintio Vitier, painters and sculptors like René Portocarrero, and thinkers like María Zambrano were members of the *Orígenes* group. They supported the values of Catholicism and a philosophical and critical perspective that was profoundly Neoplatonic.

When Lezama was twenty-one years old, he wrote a long poem titled "Muerte de Narciso" (Death of Narcissus), which was published in 1937. Books of his poems subsequently appeared at four-year intervals: *Enemigo rumor* (Enemy Rumor; 1941), *Aventuras sigilosas* (Secret Adventures; 1945), and *La fijeza* (Constancy; 1949). It was possible to identify the influence of Paul Valéry, Paul Claudel, and T. S. Eliot in Lezama's poetry, but certain elements of its impenetrableness can be traced to the great poets of the Spanish baroque period, in particular Luis de Góngora.

After the triumph of the Cuban Revolution in 1959, Lezama Lima published *Dador* (Giver; 1960). His initial adherence to the revolutionary program brought him an appointment as director of the Department of Literature and Publications of the Cuban National Council of Culture in 1960. The next year, he was elected vice president of UNEAC, the National Union of Cuban Writers and Artists. As a part of his public activity, Lezama compiled the monumental three-volume *Antología de la poesía cubana* (Anthology of Cuban Poetry; 1965). The 1960s were a pivotal period in Lezama's personal and professional life. His mother died in 1964, and few months later he decided to marry María Luisa Bautista.

With the original publication of *Paradiso* in 1966, Lezama became one of the major Latin American novelists of the twentieth century. In 1972, he received Spain's Maldoror Prize for his collection of poems, *Poesía completa* (Complete Poetry), a delayed recognition of his vast poetic production. Lezama Lima died in Havana in 1976. A book of poetry, *Fragmentos a su imán* (Fragments for His Magnet) and an incomplete novel, *Oppiano Licario*, appeared in 1977.

Critics have pointed out that organicity and coherence are distinctive qualities of Lezama Lima's writings. These two features increase the effects of the cultivated difficulty in his work, a difficulty whose most consistent manifestation is verbal obscurity. These characteristics are not a result of chance or the author's whim, since Lezama developed a complex poetic system based on the image as a privileged form of knowledge. According to Lezama, it is a matter of looking for the absolute and the comprehension of the world beyond appearances. Such thinking reveals that the writer is confident in the existence of a reality hidden behind the appearances of the physical world. Consequently, a constant feature in his essays is the search for concealed connections and unexpected linkings that move away from the linearity of rationalistic thought. Lezama strives to found a new causality, grounded on pure speculation, in which historical and fictitious characters, literary texts, and artistic works drawn from varied cultures fuse freely. Consequently, his dissatisfaction with rationalism does not lead to a celebration of irrationality, but to the laborious building of an alternative rationality with a poetic basis.

Lezama Lima uses the expression "Eros relacionable" (relatable Eros) to describe an almost mystical way of understanding invisible unity. The textual correlative of this idea emerges in his poetry, which propounds to the reader an aesthetic experience that surpasses the simple comprehension of meaning. The essay "Las imágenes posibles" (Possible Images; 1948) is a key text for delving into Lezama's creative system. In it, the image is presented "as an absolute, the image that recognizes itself as image, the image as the last among the possible versions of history" (*Confluencias* [Confluences]; 1988, 300). From this conception of the world as image, Lezama derived a theory of culture, a somewhat poetical history of civilization, in "Las eras imaginarias" (The Imaginary Eras; 1958). Throughout his intellectual life, Lezama applied his categories to the study of the Egyptian, Chinese and Greek cultures. Reechoing the same conceptual schema, he wrote the celebrated essays of *La expresión americana* (The American Expression; 1957).

The merits of Lezama Lima as a poet and as an essayist are beyond question. Nevertheless, his international recognition is based on his narrative works, especially *Paradiso*. The formative experiences of José Cemí, from the age of five until the end of his adolescence, when he attains a poetic knowledge of the world, are reported in this novel. *Paradiso* has been defined as a bildungsroman (Fazzolari), although it goes far beyond the parameters of a purely narrative family chronicle to become a compendium of all the topics in Lezama Lima's poetry. The narrative also covers the ideas and insights on literary and cultural subjects that Lezama displayed in his essays. The Argentine writer Julio Cortázar, one of the earliest commentators on the novel, considered *Paradiso* to be a "novel, which is also a Hermetic treatise, a Poetics and the poetry that arises from it" (138).

Because of the large number of correspondences between the writer's personal life and the events portrayed in the novel, the autobiographical nature of *Paradiso* has repeatedly been suggested. The father's death early in the protagonist's life, the asthma and physical weakness of José Cemí, and the mother's command that he become the historian of the family are only a few of the elements that have been highlighted. According to Raymond Souza, *Paradiso* should be considered either "an autobiographical novel or a fictionalized autobiography" (88). Nevertheless, it is not an autobiography but an incorporation of personal experiences and their reworking into a fictitious aesthetic unity. The first seven chapters are devoted to reporting the main character's family story: the absorption of an ancestral mythology in the vein of James Joyce and Marcel Proust. The second part, chapters 8 to 11, concerns the schooldays of José Cemí and his philosophical and sexual initiation, in which his friends Fronesis and Foción play a major role. Chapter 12 is a sort of intermezzo formed by four parallel stories that apparently are unrelated to the rest of the novel: the heroic feat of Atrius Flaminius when invading Greece; the different ways of perceiving an object—a Danish jar—that is broken, or not, by a child; the nocturnal incident of a man who is visited by the invisible; and the cataleptic condition that a musical critic attains to defeat time. All these correspond, according to the writer, to José's dreams. The last part of the novel, chapters 13 and 14, develops the figure of the enigmatic Oppiano Licario, who appeared sporadically in the first part (chapters 5–7). If it is possible to read the novel as the description of a growing process, one that leads the character to the profound apprehension of creativity, the tripartition indicated above corresponds to three significant stages in José Cemí's life: (1) family influence, (2) the quasi-philosophical discussions with his friends in adolescence and (3) the half-veiled presence of Oppiano Licario, who becomes the final guide in Cemí's formation.

In the earliest stage, two males of the family are the main influence. The paternal figure is introduced as an insuperable model. Over and over again, the differences that separate father and son are underlined by the narrator's voice. These differences signal a basic opposition between strength and weakness that corresponds to the topical confrontation of arms and letters in the literary realm. Father and son connect with each other in an uncertain way. However, the relationship is presented not in terms of a generational conflict but as a mutual dependence. For the child, the Colonel's death means a cosmic emptiness, the disappearance of the family center and the material impossibility of rebelling against his power. On the other hand, Uncle Alberto fulfills many important functions in the novel's plot. Because of him, Cemí's father, José Eugenio, met his wife-to-be, Alberto's sister. He is also the one who initiates young Cemí into the exploration of language and its expressive possibilities. In fact, the text of a letter containing a curious catalog of fish species that Alberto sends from abroad becomes a major event for the child. The reading of this letter provokes a deep reaction in José, as if an entrance to an unknown world, full of promises, would open up to his innocent eyes. Alberto's letter, then, stimulates José Cemí's imagination after the death of his father and after the first contact with his putative father, Oppiano Licario.

Critics have indicated two major literary antecedents for the novel. First, its title unquestionably alludes to the final section of Dante Alighieri's great religious epic, *The Divine Comedy*. Gustavo Pérez Firmat, who has studied this connection in detail, states that the link between the two texts includes not only the configuration of the relationships among the characters but also the reelaboration of several symbolic elements. Second, Gustavo Pellón notices that echoes of André Gide's *Corydon* (1924), a panegyric of homosexuality in the form of a novel, appear in the dialogues about this matter in chapter 9. Lezama's vast erudition, in which information on classic mythology, Oriental religions, painting, music and literature come together, amazed the readers of *Paradiso*. Another remarkable property of this novel is its personal, obscure and occasionally unintelligible language. Even the speech of the characters is constructed with no apparent criterion of realistic portrayal. What is said is not an imitation of everyday language, but instead an intricate re-creation, with the same artistic peculiarities and the same richness of imagery, of the narrator's discourse. Proliferation, a rhetorical procedure related to *amplificatio*, whose textual sign is the repeated use of prosopopoeias, circumlocutions, periphrases and apostrophes, is one of the baroque techniques Lezama uses in his works.

The scandal resulting from the meticulous and forthright descriptions of erotic behavior of some of the characters was one of the factors that influenced the early diffusion of the novel, which was promptly translated into Italian (1971), French (1971), and English (1974). The novel seemingly exhibits every form of sociosexual conduct: heterosexual and homosexual relations, incest and adultery, voyeurism and sadomasochism. The sexual content of the novel inspires contradictory interpretations. The homosexual subject in *Paradiso* provoked a polemic between the Peruvian writer Mario Vargas Llosa and the critic Emir Rodríguez Monegal. Pérez Firmat thinks that "Cemí's attainment of paradise entails a concomitant affirmation of his homosexuality" (247). He takes into consideration the pattern that, according to received psychoanalysis, defines masculine homosexuality as "the result of a child's fixation on the mother coupled with a fear of an authoritarian or aloof father" (252). Relying on this, on the absence of heterosexual relations in Cemí's life and on the fact that during his schooldays he had been a witness and a mute accessory to several sexual initiation rituals where exhibitionism and voyeurism were involved, Pérez Firmat concludes that José Cemí is undoubtedly a homosexual. Although the topic receives a detailed treatment, the supposed homosexual component of the main character is in no way made explicit in the narrative. However, one must agree with Pérez Firmat that "Throughout the novel homosexuality is equated with descent" (253). But Enrique Lihn, in an article exposing the negative value attached in the novel to homosexuality, states that it is necessary to admit that "the *valuational discourse of Paradiso* (which is only a part of the novel) and the plot (Foción's fate among others) condemn and punish homosexuality, they perhaps attempt to exorcise it, they oppose to it 'a category superior to sex,' Cemí's perfect and creative androgyny" (16–17).

In *Paradiso* sexuality is presented as a part of life, which does not mean that all its manifestations are equally accepted. In fact, on many occasions the narrator refers to certain sexual practices as perversions or deviances. In the fictitious world of Lezama Lima, sexuality is a force that can destroy the individual and, consequently, one that must be kept under control. Thus, even though *Paradiso* may be understood as an exploration of human sexual behavior (Souza), it does not assert any particular sexual code other than heterosexual practices.

In chapter 8, the child José Cemí witnesses phallic rituals. The first of them is officiated by the amply endowed Falarruque; the second, by Leregas, a student from the countryside. The descriptions of virile members, which make evident an obsession with their form and their extraordinary dimensions, are full of images whose grandiloquence mingles with a burlesque tone. Verbal proliferation becomes a poetic homology of the exacerbated sexuality of both characters, while their exhibitionism results in social punishment. Falarruque loses his privileged position as warden of the schoolyard, and Leregas is expelled from school for his impudence during geography class. The story of these two secondary characters does not end here. Falarruque has a series of sexual adventures with a number of women and men that occupies a long chapter section. At the end of this sequence, the narrator establishes a principle of social behavior that seems omnipresent in Lezama Lima's universe: sexual indefinition as a distinctive factor in adolescence.

The second part of chapter 8, corresponding to the vacation period, is devoted to the story of Godofredo, nicknamed the Devil, whose perversion is voyeurism. This anecdote, told by Fronesis, is intertwined with that of Father Eufrasio, a priest whose sexual deviance leads him to attempt copulation without pleasure and without bodily contact with the other. Chapter 9 concerns the beginning of José Cemí's university studies. This part is interesting for the information provided concerning Cemí's readings—the Roman historian Suetonius, the German writer Johann Wolfgang von Goethe, and Miguel de Cervantes's *Don Quixote*—and his opinions on Hispanic criticism, including a brief exposition on ''the true relations between Góngora and the Count of Villamediana.'' The chapter also introduces a new secondary character, an athlete whose public demeanor is distinguished by his contempt for and continuous aggression toward homosexuals. Despite his macho attitude, he is discovered having sexual intercourse with Leregas in a basement.

A connection between sodomitic activities and a spatial descent is notable. The punishment for the Albornoz–Leregas affair is the expulsion of both men. The scandal occasioned by the circulation of the news among the students gives rise to a discussion, a sort of Platonic dialogue, that occupies the rest of the chapter and part of the following one. The only defender of homosexuality is Foción, whose soul is tormented by the passion he feels for Fronesis, a strong emotion that will not cease to be purely spiritual. As far as Fronesis is concerned, sexual deviance is the expression of an ancestral memory. Since the remembrance of such a legendary age is preserved during childhood, he holds that children who do not evolve as adolescents and then as adults remain fixed in this period forever, and as a consequence they will always be attracted to individuals of the same sex.

Foción holds, on the contrary, the unexceptionality of homosexual conduct. Quoting Saint Jerome, he accepts the existence of an androgynous state previous to the creation of women. Foción's self-justifying argument is based on the belief that during a primeval stage, humankind was androgynous, gender differentiation being a later phenomenon strengthened by social custom. Through examples drawn from history, he underlines the predominance of homosexual practices in primitive societies, which leads him to conclude that their characterization as exceptional, deviant, or sick activities must be a recent development. The discussion between Foción and Fronesis is interrupted by the arrival of the latter's girlfriend, Lucía. When they leave, Cemí, who has been silent during the dispute, begins to talk about the topic. His thesis adopts as a starting point St. Thomas Aquinas's observation that ''unnatural'' sin is a form not of malice but of bestialism.

Acccording to these theoretical exchanges, sexuality appears hazardous. In chapter 10, the narrator describes the first sexual intercourse between Fronesis and Lucía, which is successful only after using an ''amulet,'' a shirt with a hole he needs in order to be able to penetrate her, thereby exorcising the psychological phantom of losing the penis. Fronesis, terrified of the female genitals, manages to overcome his initial disability in order to have sexual intercourse with Lucía, hiding her sex. Foción has a busy sexual life that includes a red-haired young man who is dangerous and mentally unbalanced. At this point, a symbolic parallel between the two stories becomes clear: Foción, accepting once and for all the loss of Fronesis as a probable sexual partner, has drawn a black circle on his chest to shoot himself accurately. The mark on the chest and the hole in his friend's shirt function as a bridge that couples them on the metonymic level.

Finally, the characters whose sexual activities are described in the novel work as models or alternatives for sexual development with whom Cemí establishes an acquaintance. His learning, however, is not represented as a direct experience, with the exception of a short encounter with Grace Ginsley on a Florida beach, but as the result of conversational, discursive experiences. In fact, Pellón maintains that "Homosexuality and other sexual deviations offer Cemí the knowledge of good and evil and a form of immortality, which is understood as an eternal cycle of destruction and creation" (43).

Before examining *Oppiano Licario*, a novel that Lezama left unfinished, it will be worthwhile to rescue from oblivion one of the earlier narrative pieces by the author. "Fugados" (Escapees) was published as a short story in the magazine *Grafos* in 1936. Under the guise of an insignificant anecdote—two students, instead of attending classes, spend the day at the beach—the narrative depicts the inner realm of the younger character, Luis Keeler, who goes from the exultancy provoked by Armando Sotomayor's unexpected invitation to intense despair when Armando leaves him alone, without explanation, to stay with another boy. Even though there is no explicit reference to a sexual content, it is clear that the gamut of Luis's feelings, romantically associated with the progress of the day and the difference states of the sea, corresponds to the dynamics of attraction between individuals of the same sex prior to any sociocultural codification of affectivity.

Oppiano Licario, whose original title was *Inferno* (Hell; cf. Ortega; Pelegrín), is a continuation of and a complement to *Paradiso*. Unlike the latter, *Oppiano Licario* is set not in America but in Europe and Africa, and the axis of the search for the absolute is no longer José Cemí but Fronesis, who seeks his biological mother—his origin—and manifests his sexual drives—his true self. In the process of becoming the protagonist, Fronesis is magnified as the object of desire for others. From the beginning of the novel, he exerts an attraction so powerful that those he does not accept are led to try to destroy him. In chapter 1, for instance, Palmiro enters Fronesis's room to kill him with a knife. In the darkness, the aggressor does not realize his victim is not there, and attacks the pillows on the bed. Later the Moorish Cidi Galeb—who frequently visits the decadent artists Champollion and Margaret, with whom Fronesis becomes acquainted in France—is so obsessed with Fronesis that, devoid of any trace of self-respect, he gets drunk, insults the man he loves, and causes of all sorts of jealousies and quarrels. The two characters form a binary opposition in which the noble, sublime and spiritual in Fronesis contrast with the low, stingy and corporeal in Galeb.

In chapter 3 Galeb and Fronesis spend the night together in the same bed. Knowing the secret desire of Galeb, Fronesis allows him to touch his body. When Galeb begins to go too far, Fronesis leaves the room. As Pelegrín notes, "The innocence of Fronesis, no matter what Lezama says, may be considered the height of perversity vis-à-vis his homosexual friend" (144). After leaving his bedmate, Fronesis compares Galeb and his old friend Foción. The contrast between them leads Fronesis to a fundamental discovery: rejecting Galeb, an immediate opportunity, opened the door to the complete acceptance of Foción. In metaphorical terms, the union between them, though they are separated by the ocean, is consummated during Fronesis's masturbation at the end of the chapter. Thus, one of the governing principles of Lezama's fictional world reappears, applied to human relations: the renunciation of the real, immediate and present, in order to embrace the remote and evoked (the image). In the last resort, Fronesis's complete acceptance of Foción may be understood as the recognition of a hidden part of himself, which starts the healing of the search for his authentic self.

The novel also represents the social acceptance of homosexuality, albeit only under certain conditions. Toward the end of *Paradiso*, Doctor Ricardo Fronesis had taken part in a vehement discussion with Foción in order to protect his son from what he considered the imminent risk of their friendship. According to the information given, Doctor Fronesis had been pursued by the homosexual love of Sergei Diaghilev, a famous Russian choreographer. This youthful experience was the root of his homophobic attitude. During his conversation with Foción, in addition to this personal reason, Doctor Fronesis cited public opinion, which had been critical of the relation between the two young men. In *Oppiano Licario*, Foción is the protagonist of a heroic, although ineffectual, action. He throws himself into the sea as a symbolic approximation to the beloved. In chapter 9, the narrator refers to this contact with water as if it were an erotic affair. Once again, the descent from the greatest joy into the depths of misery is at stake here. Foción is attacked by a shark, which rips off one of his arms. The blood lost is so life-threatening that he requires a transfusion. Paradoxically, Doctor Fronesis offers his own blood to save him. It is obvious that this sequence is intended to represent a physical union between enemies through the mixture of blood.

Since the novel was left unfinished, it is impossible to discern the outcomes of these narrative threads and, consequently, the ultimate outlines of homosexuality, not in the American Heaven of adolescence but in the European Hell of adulthood. Readers will never know, for instance, whether Galeb would assault Fronesis in retaliation for his rejection, nor whether the relationship between Fronesis and Foción, consummated in France thanks to financial assistance from

Doctor Ricardo Fronesis, would evolve to any particular point. What is beyond question is that the narrator's perspective is always critical: he denounces the "vicious zones" of Galeb's personality in the same way he had maintained in *Paradiso* that Foción was a sick man who believed that normalcy was an illness.

WORKS

Antología de la poesía cubana. Havana: Consejo Nacional de Cultura, 1965.
Confluencias. Selección de ensayos. Havana: Letras Cubanas, 1988.
Cuentos. Havana: Letras Cubanas, 1987.
Fragmentos a su imán. Havana: Arte y Literatura, 1977.
Obras completas, 2 vols. Mexico City: Aguilar, 1975–1977. *Fragmentos a su imán* and *Oppiano Licario* are not included.
Oppiano Licario. Mexico City: Era, 1977.
Paradiso. Mexico City: Era, 1968. Ed. prepared by Julio Cortázar and Carlos Monsiváis.
    Paradiso. Critical ed. coordinated by Cintio Vitier. Mexico City: Secretaria de Educación Pública, 1988. English trans. under the same title by Gregory Rabassa. Austin: University of Texas Press, 1988.
Poesía completa. Havana: Instituto del Libro, 1970.

CRITICISM

Alvarez Bravo, Armando. *Lezama Lima*. Buenos Aires: Jorge Alvarez, 1968.
Camacho-Gingerich, Alina. *La cosmovisión poética de José Lezama Lima en 'Paradiso' y 'Oppiano Licario.'* Miami: Ediciones Universal, 1990.
Cortázar, Julio. "Para llegar a Lezama Lima." *Unión* 5.4 (1966): 36–60. Also in his *La vuelta al día en ochenta mundos*, 135–155. Mexico City: Siglo XXI, 1967.
Fazzolari, Margarita Junco. *'Paradiso' y el sistema poético de Lezama Lima*. Buenos Aires: Fernando García Gambeiro, 1979.
Lihn, Enrique. "*Paradiso*, novela y homosexualidad." *Hispamérica* 8 (1979): 3–21.
Matamoro, Blas. "*Oppiano Licario*: Seis modelos en busca de una síntesis." *Texto crítico* 5 (1979): 112–125.
Ortega, Julio. "De *Paradiso* a *Oppiano Licario*: Morfología de la excepción." In Lezama Lima, *Paradiso*, 682–696. 1988.
Pelegrín, Benito. "Espejo, doble, homólogo y homosexualidad en *Oppiano Licario* de José Lezama Lima." In Centre de Recherches Latino Americaines, Université de Poitiers, *Coloquio internacional. Escritura y sexualidad en la literatura hispanoamericana*, 129–154. Madrid: Fundamentos, 1990.
Pellón, Gustavo. *José Lezama Lima's Joyful Visions. A Study of "Paradiso" and Other Prose Works*. Austin: University of Texas Press, 1989.
Pérez Firmat, Gustavo. "Descent into *Paradiso*: A Study of Heaven and Homosexuality." *Hispania* 59 (1976): 247–257.
Rodríguez Monegal, Emir. "*Paradiso* en su contexto." *Mundo nuevo* 24 (1968): 40–44. Also in his *Narradores de esta América*, 130–155. Montevideo: Alfa, 1974.
Ruiz Barrionuevo, Carmen. *El 'Paradiso' de Lezama Lima*. Madrid: Insula, 1980.
Sarduy, Severo. "El heredero." *Filología* 24 (1989): 275–285. Also in Lezama Lima, *Paradiso*, 275–285. 1988.

Simón Martínez, Pedro, ed. *Recopilación de textos sobre José Lezama Lima*. Havana: Casa de las Américas, 1970.

Souza, Raymond D. *The Poetic Fiction of José Lezama Lima*. Columbia: University of Missouri Press, 1983.

Ulloa, Justo C., ed. *José Lezama Lima: Textos críticos*. Miami: Ediciones Universal, 1979.

Vizcaíno, Cristina, and Eugenio Suárez Galbán, eds. *Coloquio internacional sobre la obra de José Lezama Lima*. Madrid: Fundamentos, 1984.

Waller, Claudia Joan. "José Lezama Lima's *Paradiso*: The Theme of Light and the Resurrection." *Hispania* 53 (1973): 275–282.

Daniel Altamiranda

M

MANRIQUE ARDILA, JAIME (Colombia; 1949)

Manrique Ardila, born in Barranquilla, currently resides in New York City. He holds a B.A. in English literature from the University of South Florida. He also participated in the Spanish Workshop at Columbia University in 1977 under the direction of Manuel Puig. Manrique has taught literature and writing at the New School for Social Research and Parsons School of Design. He received the Colombian National Poetry Award Eduardo Cote Lamus in 1975 for his poetry collection *Los adoradores de la luna* (The Moon Worshipers), and he has been writer in residence at several creative writing workshops in both the United States and Colombia. Both Manrique's poetry and his narratives have been translated into English.

From his first narrative, *El cadáver de papá* (Dad's Corpse; 1978; rev. ed., 1980) to his novel in progress, ''Twilight at the Equator: A Journey,'' Manrique deals almost exclusively with two themes. One, that of sexual orientation, has become much more apparent in his most recent novels. The other, that of Colombia's destruction due to drug-related violence, has remained a constant throughout his narratives.

El cadáver de papá, Manrique's first long narrative, introduces the reader to Santiago, who will reappear in each of his following narratives. In this first novel, the main character seems lost in a sea of events that he has caused. He is the illegitimate son of a wealthy man who has only recently, and very superficially, accepted him. In the opening pages he kills his dying father and experiences a sexual release in doing so. He also dresses as a flapper, wearing his dead sister's clothes on the last night of carnival. He watches, dressed in drag, while a group of drunken young men gang-rape his unconscious father-in-law. The father-in-law was knocked unconscious by Santiago himself during a struggle while the father-in-law was attempting to rape the disguised Santiago. These two episodes, coupled with the disappearance of Santiago's father's corpse from the funeral home, point to the direct assault that the author is making on the established patriarchal order. This assault must be violent, and it must break all societal rules. Santiago is an outsider and has never experienced any type of acceptance from a patriarchal figure. By ejaculating while smothering his dying father and fighting off his father-in-law while dressed as a woman, he links sexual pleasure and power to the destruction of gender-specific roles and authoritarian figures.

Colombian Gold (1983) borrows heavily from *El cadáver de papá*; in fact, the same episodes are used. The only change is that Santiago rapes his father-in-law. In the end he reluctantly accepts the leadership of a revolutionary group after he is betrayed by his father and father-in-law's class. Once again, the few sexual scenes serve to highlight Santiago's assault on and destruction of a patriarchal order. In these first two novels same-sex relations are seen as violent acts that challenge and destroy the established societal code. In both cases Santiago must attempt to destroy authority figures because he has never been accepted by them nor by the social class they represent. In both novels there is a noticeable element of homoeroticism among the male characters. The constant repression and violence that pervade society prevent any type of opening up of one character to another.

Latin Moon in Manhattan (1992) gives the reader a completely different Santiago. In this novel, the main character is openly gay and must constantly deal with his mother's attempts to marry him off to the lesbian daughter of a cocaine kingpin. Santiago also must face his childhood friend's death from AIDS and the nightly attempts at seduction from a flasher whose apartment is directly across the alley from his. Gone is the violence of the first two novels, and in its stead is a sense of humor that allows the reader to share in the travails of a gay Latino with one foot in Manhattan and the other in the Colombian barrio of Queens. Although the drug culture's hold on Colombians living in the United States is present, the novel is concerned much more with Santiago's desire to maintain his gay identity and at the same time to satisfy his family and the demands placed upon him by Colombian cultural traditions. He juggles two cultural traditions, gay-Manhattan and Colombian-Queens, and manages to blend and separate both so that the reader gets a true sense of the problematics of a gay Latino in the United States.

The novel in progress, ''Twilight at the Equator: A Journey,'' opens with Santiago fearing his own death. He has just survived a severe case of pneumonia and has been brought face to face with the reality of AIDS. Although he tested HIV-negative, he suffers from survivor's syndrome and falls into a deep, self-reflective depression. His brush with death allows him to remember his friends Reinaldo Arenas and Manuel Puig, both recently dead. The reflection and search for answers push Santiago to leave New York and return to Colombia on a visit that deepens his knowledge and understanding of himself. Once again he has a strong, positive gay identity and must balance it with the concepts of masculinity established in Hispanic culture. The novel is a journey that begins in a hospital room in New York, travels to Puig's last home in Cuernavaca, Mexico, and goes on to the isolated regions of Colombia where the narrator traces his origins and visits his two grandmothers, one black and the other white. "Twilight" appears to be a journey of self-examination in which the narrator analyzes himself in order to sort out the positive and negative aspects of both cultures and to come closer to the Colombian culture of his youth. In Manrique's last two novels, the gay identity of the main characters is taken as a matter of fact, with no negative connotations. The violence associated with the same-sex relations of the first two novels is gone. The last two novels present a main character who, although slightly neurotic, is secure in his sexuality and at ease in the cultures of the United States and of Colombia.

The ease of living in both cultures almost simultaneously is also apparent in Manrique's short story "The Day Carmen Maura Kissed Me." Here the narrator highlights an episode in which Carmen Maura, for a number of years the lead star in Pedro Almodóvar's outrageous postmodern films, has a Coca Cola with his heterosexual transvestite friend, Luis/Luisa, at New York's Algonquin Hotel. The narrator is openly gay, and Luis/Luisa is relieved to have escaped Colombia with his life. The violence had erupted into the middle class, and he could no longer go about his day-to-day activities without receiving constant threats. Although he is not gay, his difference is viewed as unacceptable in Colombia, and he must escape to protect himself and his girlfriend. Manrique thus harkens back to the violence evident in his earlier novels and shows that although Santiago, his favorite main character, may have changed, Colombia has not.

WORKS

El cadáver de papá. Rev. ed. Bogotá: Plaza y Janes, 1980. Orig. 1978.
Colombian Gold: A Novel of Power and Corruption. New York: Clarkson N. Potter, 1983.
"The Day Carmen Maura Kissed Me." *Christopher Street* 142 (Jan. 1990): 24–27.
Latin Moon in Manhattan. New York: St. Martin's Press, 1992.

                                                                Steven M. DuPouy

MARAT, ABNIEL (Puerto Rico; 1958) _____

Playwright, actor and poet, Marat—or Morales—was born in Carolina in 1958. He studied theater, history and literature at the University of Puerto Rico, and holds a B.A. from Boricua College in New York City. Marat has lived on the mainland since 1986, and is a librarian at Cornell Medical College.

At the beginning of the 1980s, Marat was one of the most promising young playwrights in Puerto Rico. Between 1982 and 1984, three of his one-act plays, all dealing with homosexuality, were staged at the theater of the University of Puerto Rico and at the Café-Teatro La Tea in Old San Juan. Like many of his poems, they defend the right of homosexuals to live (and love) in freedom. The title of his only book of poetry published to date characterizes the subject of his poems: *Poemas de un homosexual revolucionario*. This "revolutionary homosexual—also the implied playwright of *Dios en el "Playgirl" de noviembre*, "The Story of the Madman Who Became Sane," and "Nocturne on the Sex of the Unicorns"—is a Puerto Rican nationalist who, like Víctor F. Fragoso in *El reino de la espiga* (The Realm of the Grain of Corn), associates the (revolutionary) task of liberating Puerto Rico from the United States (and from capitalism, sexism, classism, racism) with the (equally revolutionary) task of freeing the homosexual from a sexist, homophobic society. The political destiny of the homosexual and of the island are one and the same. (This allegorical fusion is at the center of Luzma Umpierre's "The Mar/Garita Poem," from *The Margarita Poems* [1987]).

The colonized island that became the "ay-land" (*ay* = pain) in Reynaldo Marcos Padua's novel *Welcome to the Ay-land of the Piña Colada* (1985), is also the I-land of the oppressed homosexual/Puerto Rican. In Marat's plays, the man who is killed by his homosexual lover for not being loyal to their relationship bears the name of the man considered to be the great traitor of Puerto Rican nationalism and its leader, Pedro Albizu Campos, Luis Muñoz Marín. The two most influential Puerto Rican playwrights, René Marqués and Luis Rafael Sánchez, have re-presented the treason of Muñoz Marín in *La muerte no entrará en palacio* (Death Will Not Enter the Palace; 1957) and *La pasión según Antígona Pérez* (The Passion According to Antígona Pérez; 1968), respectively. Against the figure of Muñoz Marín the speaking subject of *Poemas de un homosexual revolucionario* (Poems of a Revolutionary Homosexual; 1985) defines his identity: "I/Abniel Marat/Puerto Rican/Homosexual/Poeta:/the Universe introduced itself into my mouth/and I spit on you with stars of living rebellions/Judas/dog/traitor/May you burn in hell!" (6–7). From this perspective, and guided by Walt Whitman, Federico García Lorca, Pablo Neruda, and other poets, Marat has gone on to write poems about homosexual love, Puerto Rican nationalism, Spanish America, the environment, oriental mysticism, AIDS, and other subjects, in an ever-inclusive thematics that is always sung by the Puerto Rican homosexual voice sustained throughout at least six plays and seven books of poetry.

WORKS

Dios en el "Playgirl" de noviembre. Río Piedras, P.R.: Edil, 1986.
Materia prima (obra poética completa). Río Piedras, P.R.: Edil, 1993.
Poemas de un homosexual revolucionario. San Juan: Gallo Galante, 1985.
"Tres lirios de cala/Three Calla Lilies." Unpublished; three one-act plays.

CRITICISM

Figueroa-Chapel, Rafael. "Crítica de teatro. *Nocturno en el sexo de los unicornios*, de Abniel Morales." *El mundo*, Aug. 1, 1982, p. 7-B.
Rivera de Alvarez, Josefina. *Literatura puertorriqueña: Su proceso en el tiempo*, 917. Madrid: Partenón, 1983.
Rodríguez, Carlos A. "Apuntes para un acercamiento a la poesía puertorriqueña contemporánea: 1962–1986." *Revista del Instituto de cultura puertorriqueña* 94 (Oct.–Dec. 1986): 45–55.

Carlos A. Rodríguez-Matos

MATOS-CINTRÓN, NEMIR (Puerto Rico; 1949)

Matos-Cintrón was born in Santurce. She holds a B.A. from the University of Puerto Rico and has worked as a television scriptwriter. She is currently writing a script for a full-length film on people dealing with AIDS and a book of poems in homage to friends who have died of AIDS. She teaches at Sacred Heart University, Fairfield, Conn. Matos-Cintrón has published poems and prose in several periodicals in Puerto Rico, where she gives frequent public readings of her poetry. Her poems have appeared in important anthologies of contemporary Puerto Rican poetry.

Matos-Cintrón was the first Puerto Rican poet to textualize lesbianism openly. This poetization of the lesbian is elaborated within the two thematic fields of the political and the personal. The political refers to the feminist views of women and of the world; to sociopolitical issues like the Vietnam War, socioeconomic classes and the Native American nations that frequently appear in social or protest poetry of the 1960s and 1970s; and to the Puerto Rican nationalist agenda. The personal refers to lesbian love and sex. As in the case of Víctor Fragoso, the emancipation of the individual and the emancipation of groups, societies and nations are intrinsically intertwined. One of the poetical strategies for the development of the political agenda is an inventory of female myths of oppressed or disappeared cultures like the Taínos of the Caribbean islands and the Yoruba people who were brought to the Caribbean as slaves. This inventory is completed with Puerto Rican nationalist women, whom Matos-Cintrón calls "earth women" ("Canto a las mujeres tierra" [Song to the Earth Mothers] in *Las mujeres*) and who are the opposite of the bodyless/soulless women of patriarchal, capitalist societies ("Me robaron el cuerpo" [They Stole My Body], in *Las mujeres*).

The explicit, colloquial language of sex is a poetic strategy in which the political (feminist and lesbian) agenda and the personal (love, sex) coincide. Women, as the title of *Las mujeres no hablan así* (That's Not the Way Women Talk; 1981) states, are not supposed to talk in such an open and defiant way about politics and sex, particularly sex among women. In the poem "Vuelo en las aletas de tu crica en pleamar" (I Fly on the Wings of Your Cunt at High Tide), Matos-Cintrón not only defies sexist and partriarchal norms, but also class and elitist norms, because even some liberated women, among them feminists and lesbians, do not dare to use colloquialisms considered too vulgar (so called *malas palabras* [dirty words], like *crica*, that refer to the genitalia). As the titles of her two published books suggest, the female, feminist, lesbian, Puerto Rican nationalist lyric subject of *A través del aire y del fuego, pero no del cristal* (Through Air and Fire, but Not Glass) and *Las mujeres no hablan así* refuses to talk the classist, sexist language of the patriarch and rejects the images of the feminine that it has imposed on women throughout centuries of oppression. Matos-Cintrón proposes the new woman, the queer woman delivered to her through Yoruba mythology and through nationalist Puerto Rican herstory.

WORKS

A través del aire y del fuego, pero no del cristal. Río Piedras; P.R.: Atabex, 1981.
"Ante el vacio" (p. 198), "Antipoema" (p. 199), "Atabex" (196), "Canto a chango" (p. 195), "Esta noche" (p. 197), "Este poema" (p. 197), "Hace tres días" (p. 198), "Me robaron el cuerpo" (p. 195), "Nombres" (p. 200), "Soy olvido" (p. 201), "Todo conspira" (p. 201), "Tu ausencia" (p. 197), "Veterano" (p. 200). In *De lengua, razón y cuerpo: Nueve poetas contemporáneas puertorriqueñas*, 193–199. Ed. Aurea María Sotomayor. San Juan: Instituto de Cultura Puertorriqueña, 1987.
Las mujeres no hablan así. Río Piedras, P.R.: Atabex, 1981.
———., and Yolanda V. Fundadora. "Carta abierta a Manuel Ramos Otero (El Chú) en respuesta al artículo 'La luna ultrajada': 'Somos folkloristas y tradicionalistas.' " *Claridad*, Feb. 19, 1982, p. 11.

CRITICISM

Echeandía, Servando. "Sobre Nemir Matos." *Reintegro* 3.1 (1983): 12–13.
Ramos-Otero, Manuel. "La luna ultrajada." *Claridad*, Feb. 5, 1982, pp. 8–11.
Sotomayor, Aurea María, ed. *De lengua, razón cuerpo: Nueve poetas contemporáneas puertorriqueñas*, 54–57. San Juan: Instituto de Cultura Puertorriqueña, 1987.

Carlos A. Rodríguez-Matos

MATTOSO, GLAUCO (pseud. of Pedro José Ferreira da Silva; Brazil; 1951)

Mattoso suffers from glaucoma, which has led him to abandon his profession of librarian. His first name is an assumed reference to his eye problems. His distinctive persona in photographs and drawn images is thick glasses, accompanied by leather clothing, jackboots, and a skinhead haircut. Mattoso's persona is a public sign of his commitment to an explicit, in-your-face representation of various forms of sexuality considered deviant less for their antiheterosexist and homoerotic dimensions than for their defiance of middle-class hygiene and its most recent manifestation, safe sex.

Mattoso is the author of several books of poetry that are marked more by verbal and graphic images of an exaggerated masculinity calculated to swamp the prevailing belief, in a country like Brazil, that homosexuality means limp-wristed faggotry than they are by good writing. Clearly inspired by the concrete poetry movement in Brazil of the 1950s and 1960s, books like *Línguas na papa* (Tongues on the Cock; 1982), *Memórias de um pueteiro: As melhores gozações de Glauco Mattoso* (Recollections of a Whorehouse [?]: The Best Tidbits of Glauco Mattoso; 1982) and *Limeiriques & outros debiques glauquianos* (Limericks and Other Glauquian Morsels; 1989) are characterized both by ingeniously outrageous graphics and by impressive verbal acrobatics, which makes for a challenging task in translating his texts: *pueteiro* is clearly derived from *puteiro* (brothel), which is in turn derived from *puta* (whore), while *línguas na papa* is a trope extracted from *papas na língua*: *falar sem papas na língua* means not to beat around the bush. In the original metaphor *papa* means potato, but in Mattoso's trope it has its vulgar sexual meaning, cock. Mattoso's dedication to often complicated and multilingual wordplay in his texts serves to unpack conventional sexual meanings through various forms of troping (with all of the unsubtlety associated with limericking and other broad forms of wordplay), as well as to naturalize unconventional sexual metaphors, especially those he associates with the representation of "dirty sex" (including sadomasochism) and its challenges to a bland and ultimately antierotic conventional sexuality.

Rockabillyrics (1988) is a series of Brazilian song lyrics, with an underlying erotic content, based on the American rockabilly tradition. This work demonstrates Mattoso's interest in American cultural sources, already evident in the U.S. English-based wordplay in his erotic poetry and in his incorporation of extensive American material in his quasi-sociological treatise *O calvário dos carecas: Histórias do trote estudantil* (The Calvary of the Pledges: Tales of Student Fraternities; 1985), which develops the views that Anglo-American and Brazilian academic fraternities are veiled manifestations of homoeroticism, with the notable naturalization of practices that echo conventional society's rejection of deviant dirty sex. Mattoso's use of English-language sources and his careful documentation of them reveals his training in library science.

Mattoso's most ambitious work brings together his analysis of so-called dirty sex and the judicious use of bibliographic sources. *Manual de pedólatra amador: Aventuras & leituras de um tarado por pés* (Manual of the Amateur Foot Fetishist: Adventures and Readings of Someone Really into Feet; 1986) is loosely structured as the autobiography of the narrator, who describes his discovery, through the initiation rites of an academic fraternity, that he is a foot fetishist. His sexual explorations and development, both heterosexual and homosexual, turn on the increasingly metonymic displacement of sexual possibilities, especially those of the allegedly dirty variety, toward the foot—dirty or clean, shod or bare—and include the establishment of a professional practice based on the manipulation of the foot to cure illness and disease, with the added dimension of the erotic possibilities of that manipulation (at least for the attending professional). In part a send-up of Western-style sex manuals and first-person "sentimental education" narratives, Mattoso's work is most productively read as part of his larger literary project of naturalizing the supposedly outer fringes of erotic experience and, in the process, underscoring the hypocrisies and ideological slippages of heterosexism. Thus, one of the virtues attributed to foot fetishes is a range of intensely erotic experiences that all fall within the range of safe sex, since the *Manual* poses the rhetorical question of how many people have contracted AIDS through pedal manipulation. With the graphic artist Marcetti, Mattoso has produced a comic book version of the *Manual, As aventuras de Glaucomix, o pedólatra* (The Adventures of Glaucomix, the Foot Lover; 1990).

Mattoso was involved with Brazil's famous gay-rights journal of the 1970s, *Lampião* (Lantern/Streetlight), and he has published his own broadsheets, *Jornal Dobradil* (1977–1981) and *Revista dedo mingo* (Little Finger Review; 1982). In typical Mattoso fashion, *Jornal Dobradil* involves a wordplay: it is a trope of *Jornal do Brasil* (Journal of Brazil), the Rio de Janeiro daily that is considered one of most influential media forms of the hegemonic bourgeoisie: good taste, solid values, expository objectivity and liberal good conscience.

WORKS

As aventuras de Glaucomix o pedólatra. São Paulo: Quadrinhos Abriu Quadrinhos Fechou, 1990.

O calvário dos carecas: História do trote estudantil. São Paulo: EMW Editores, 1985.

Dicionarinho do palavrão & correlatos, inglês-português, português-inglês. 2nd ed. Rio de Janeiro: Editora Record, 1991.

Limeiriques & outros debiques glauquianos. São Paulo: Edições Dubloso, 1989.

Línguas na papa: Uma salda dos mais insípidos aos mais picantes; poemas. São Paulo: Pindaiba, 1982.

Manual do pedólatra amador: Aventuras & leituras de um tarado por pés. São Paulo: Editora Expressão, 1986.

Memórias de um pueteiro: As melhores gozações de Glauco Mattoso. 2nd ed. Rio de Janeiro: Edições Trote, 1982.

O que é poesia marginal. 2nd ed. São Paulo: Brasiliense, 1982.

O que é tortura. São Paulo: Brasiliense, 1984.

Queda de braço: Uma antologia do conto marginal. Rio de Janeiro: Club dos Amigos de Marsaninho, 1977.

Rockabillyrics. São Paulo: Olavobras, 1988.

CRITICISM

Foster, David William. "Sexual Theory in the Tropics: Glauco Mattoso's *Manual do pedólatra amador*." In his *Essays on Latin American Cultural Diversity*. Albuquerque: University of New Mexico Press, 1993.
Parker, Richard G. *Bodies, Pleasures, and Passions: Sexual Culture in Contemporary Brazil*. Boston: Beacon Press, 1990.

David William Foster

MENA-SANTIAGO, WILLIAM MANUEL (Puerto Rico; 1954) ⸻⸻⸻⸻⸻⸻

Mena-Santiago, poet and social and political activist, was born in Juana Díaz. He holds a master's degree in social psychology from Pennsylvania State University, where he is completing a Ph.D. in early childhood education. He is director of a counseling program for drug and alcohol addicts in the Latino community of North Philadelphia. Mena-Santiago is active in the movement for the release of the Puerto Rican political prisoners in the United States and is a member of the Partido Mundo Obrero (Working World party), U.S. Hands Off Cuba Coalition and other political organizations. He also is a contributor to *Workers World Newspaper*. His poetry has appeared in magazines and anthologies in Puerto Rico and the United States, and his first collection of poems, *Las voces idas* (The Departed Voices; 1987), was considered one of the year's best by the Instituto de Literatura de Puerto Rico (Puerto Rican Institute of Literature). He has several manuscripts ready for publication, one of them dealing with AIDS. Mena-Santiago gives frequent public readings of his poetry.

The speaking subject of Mena-Santiago's poems has the assertive, optimistic and caring tone found in the poetry of some of his favorite political poets, Miguel Hernández (Spain), Pablo Neruda (Chile), Roque Dalton (El Salvador), and Juan Antonio Corretjer (Puerto Rico). But a good dose of irony, which holds in check the forbidden forces of nostalgia and pessimism that may accompany self-absorption, results in a very personal voice. In one poem, "Soy uno de los vivos" (I'm One of the Living), he defines himself as a "poeta cojonudo y tierno" (a tender poet with balls). Like some of his "forbidden poets," as he calls the aforementioned and other communist poets like César Vallejo (Peru) in many of their political poems, Mena-Santiago favors a direct and precise language, generally with an ironic twist.

Mena-Santiago's poetry is in constant movement. "Fui yo, yo lo hice" (It Was Me, I Did It) represents the urgent masturbatory movement of the hand. In *Las voces idas*, the theme of love is never focused on for long. The gender of the love object remains neuter, as in the first poems of many homosexual and lesbian poets. No openly homosexual speaking subject (or object of desire) can be discerned in Mena-Santiago's poetry. In a poem where love is the main subject, it still remains genderless (''Unnamed Lover''). The poet refers to the past ''joy'' and its continued importance ''now,'' evoking what a play currently being staged in Puerto Rico calls *Love in the Time of AIDS*. The speaking subject receives a joyous revelation: the subject to whom love matters so much is a person with AIDS. Facing disease and death, he assumes the assertiveness, vitality, immediacy, precision, defiance and irony characteristic of Mena-Santiago's poetry. Mena-Santiago seems to be committed to writing most of the poems that deal with the experience of AIDS in English. The PWA (person with AIDS) who speaks in Mena's poems remains as defiant as ever in his rejection of the facile pity of the stranger.

WORKS

Las voces idas. Ponce, P.R.: n.p., 1987.

Various poems. In *Poesía joven de Puerto Rico*, 79–84. Ed. Manuel de la Puebla. Río Piedras, P.R.: Mairena, 1981.

Various poems. *Antología de poesía puertorriqueña 1983*, 76. Ed. Marcos Reyes-Dávila and Manuel de la Puebla. Río Piedras, P.R.: Mairena, 1983.

Various poems. In ''Los límites del silencio/Shouting in a Whisper. Latino Poetry in Philadelphia: An Anthology.'' Ed. Frances Negrón-Muntaner. Unpublished.

Various poems. In Carlos A. Rodríguez-Matos. ''Retazos: Poesía del sida en lengua hispana.'' *Sidahora* 13 (Winter 1992): 21–27, 55.

Carlos A. Rodríguez-Matos

MISTRAL, GABRIELA (pseud. of Lucila Godoy Alcayaga; Chile; 1889–1957) ⸺⸺⸺⸺⸺

Even though Mistral scholarship includes some 100 books and hundreds of articles in which a biographical approach is the rule, scholars until recently have been reluctant to situate Mistral's erotic representations of women within a lesbian matrix. That reluctance reflects the hegemonic heterosexuality of the Latin American critical establishments and the political circumstances of Mistral's continuing monumentalization. Her public image as a rustic, saintly schoolteacher who becomes a Madonna-like figure and eventually a regal Nobel queen begins in the fascination of male critics with a handful of so-called love poems, written early in her career, interpreted as statements of devotion to and longing for a dead (male) lover. That interpretation goes on to regard the poet's lullabies and school-based work as expressing a frustrated desire to bear children. The idea of the ''symbolic mother'' projects onto Mistral's work and life a pattern of desire–longing–frustration–renunciation–transcendence in order to enforce a rigid division of sex roles that has ''successfully written her lesbianism out of existence'' (Molloy, 116). For the ongoing development of an explicitly feminist consciousness, it is important to investigate components of that censorship, and to consider the possibility that Mistral was complicit in the repressive versions of femininity that her texts have been called to serve. This manner of analyzing the canonized figure of Gabriela Mistral is vital to understanding how women as historical, speaking subjects intersect with Woman as a social construction in Latin America.

A reader-oriented rather than an author-oriented perspective informs recent feminist interpretation of Mistral's work as a site for exploring multiple, coexisting identities in women, identities that the Chilean Raquel Olea and Argentine Sylvia Molloy link with the "unspeakable" identity of the lesbian. The association of lesbian identity with the "unspeakable" is corroborated in one of the psychological or zoomorphic fables of Arévalo Martínez: the male narrator–protagonist of his story "La signatura de la esfinge" (The Mark of the Sphinx) presents an account of the hidden identity of "Elena," a mysterious female character whose reputation and past correspond in many details to the real-life Gabriela Mistral. The story is structured to explain that the "unspeakable accusation" that she is "a masculine woman" misrepresents her "true nature" as "a lion" whose unhappiness stems from never having met a worthy mate, one as strong and regal as herself. Arévalo Martínez's story, with its cover of fiction, is unique in recording what Mistral's contemporaries thought and spoke about, but kept from print.

Some might object that it is limiting and limited to regard Mistral's representation of women as reflecting a lesbian sensibility, yet no perspective could be more restrictive and exclusionary than the ahistorical mode of symbolic motherhood that dominated Mistral criticism for some fifty years (beginning with the "Palabras preliminares" [Opening Words] introduction to her first volume of poetry, *Desolación*). One of Mistral's most sensible critics, her longtime friend Palma Guillén, has summarized the great themes of Mistral's poetry: love, suffering, desire, the mysteries of death, Nature's beauty and mystery as a permanent yet passing phenomenon; childhood and the adult woman's relation with it being her most original theme" (Guillén, 1973, xiii). Present in all of these is the theme of love and desire among women, collectively and individually.

A wider conceptualization of Mistral, one in which "there is no reason to continue hiding that she had lesbian relationships," would make the poet more relevant, more interesting to people today (Olea, cited in Lazarotti, 31). Apparently we are not so far from the first two decades of the twentieth century, when the national press attacked women's reading groups as "descabelladas locuras innaturales" (unnatural madness; cited in Kirkwood). Latin Americanists familiar with the extraordinary range of her work claim to be ready to reject Mistral's kitschy canonization as "spiritual mother," but it seems that until some literary detective appears with documentary "smoking-vibrator proof" of the subject's lesbianism, few will posit in print what virtually all concede in private. It is certain that the poet's friendships with women were at the center of her daily life, and that her emotional intimacy with women sustained her through her deepest crises (invidious attacks in Chile, her mother's death, the suspension of her pay that left her fundless in Europe, her adopted son's apparent suicide in Brazil).

Gabriela Mistral's life can be divided into three eras. The first (1889–1920) is her residence in a variety of provincial towns and cities in Chile, and her rise in that country's educational establishment. Despite her lack of any academic degree, she moved from teacher's assistant to headmistress of Chile's most prestigious public school in fifteen years, an advancement tied to the expansion of the Chilean educational system and to her prolific record of publication. The Chilean period ends with her participation in the educational reform program of José Vasconcelos in postrevolutionary Mexico (1920–1922). This first stay in Mexico was followed by residence primarily in Europe, but also in Latin America, as Mistral worked for various international organizations. During this second period (1925–1940) she earned her living primarily through journalism, and in a consular post mandated by a special act of the Chilean legislature in 1933. The rise of fascism, the Spanish Civil War and hostilities leading to World War II in Europe contributed to her return to Latin America in 1938, when the publishing house Sur, directed by the Argentine Victoria Ocampo, printed *Tala* (Felling of Trees), Mistral's second major volume of verse. Mistral was living in Brazil when she became the first Latin American to receive the Nobel Prize for literature (1945). During her final years (1945–1957) she was working simultaneously on two books of poetry, an extension of her volume *Lagar* (Wine Press; 1954) and the posthumously published *Poema de Chile* (Poem of Chile; 1967) while she lived in Mexico, California, Italy and New York; in 1954 she made a brief visit to Chile. On her death in 1957, Chilean president Carlos Ibáñez declared three days of official mourning.

To date there is no comprehensive biography of Gabriela Mistral; her public recognition subordinated much of her life and ''character'' to a preexisting code of saintliness. Qualities specifically associated with sanctity in women—personal modesty, secret suffering, a gift for prayer, concern for less fortunate others, the purification of debilitating sexuality, leading to renunciation and self-abnegation—are presented to explain the subject's eccentricity and to reinforce the stereotype of Chilean femininity (coquettish, yet devoted to home and family) that Mistral's figure flatly contradicts. Accounts of Mistral's public figure therefore employ the conventions of hagiography to explain the subject's rejection of marriage, her bearing no children, her continual, restless wandering and her supposed obliviousness to money and personal appearance. We need to sort out the circumstances linking her with an exemplary femininity, and to identify components that the homages suppress because ''la idea de mujer infértil, solterona y lesbiana no resulta atractiva'' (the idea of the infertile woman, a spinster and a lesbian, is unattractive; Olea, cited in Lanzarotti, 31).

The hagiography most amply covers her early years in Chile, from her birth in 1889 as Lucila Godoy Alcayaga, in the provincial town of Vicuña, some 400 kilometers north of the capital. Her father was an unemployed schoolteacher and former seminarian, Jerónimo Godoy, who had been married for a year to Petronila Alcayaga, thirteen years his senior, who had a teenage daughter, Emelina, from an earlier relationship. The apocryphal genealogies all center on the supposedly indelible influence of this father, whom the poet scarcely knew, since he abandoned his wife and daughter when she was three years old. His erratic employment as a schoolteacher, his penchant for composing and singing verses, the trees he planted and his bohemian character are all invoked to account for his daughter's (otherwise inexplicable) wandering, writing and interest in the natural world. That same hagiography that avers the father's absence forever marked his daughter makes the women who lived with her (her mother, her half sister, her grandmother, the sculptor Laura Rodig, the educator and diplomat Palma Guillén, the educator Consuelo Saleva, the writer Doris Dana) into faceless models of devotion, self-sacrifice and charitableness drawn from the same code of female sanctity that characterizes Mistral-as-monument.

As backdrop to the monument we have numerous lyrical descriptions of Mistral's childhood milieu in the Valle de Elqui, an agricultural and mining area located on the edge of the desert north of Santiago, that turn that area into a quasi-biblical locale and that state her origins as reflecting an idealized, mythical past for the nation. In the accounts of Mistral's difficulties during her years of erratic formal schooling and then in her teaching career, the principal theme is that of perseverance in battles with the devil (close-minded clergy, incompetent teachers, uncomprehending and jealous supervisors). The successful outcome of the battles establishes the pattern for years to come: a clear-seeing and forward-thinking man intervening on her behalf provides disinterested encouragement that affirms the subject's dedication to teaching and her own dark awareness of her fate.

In contrast to the hagiography, the record of Gabriela Mistral's publications, appearing from 1905 on, show her particular interest in short, meditative prose pieces on social topics as well as the intimist essays that were common at the time. Of particular note are her reflections, while yet a teenager, on female friendship, women's education and the revolution in Russia. She wrote for provincial newspapers in Vicuña, Coquimbo, and Antofagasta. Her base of readers expanded with her transfer to teach in the city of Los Andes, just a few hours from Santiago.

The regular transfers from one school to another, reflecting her rise in the educational establishment, were a direct consequence of Mistral's publications. Beginning about 1912, she was publishing in Theosophical Society magazines, literary journals throughout Chile and periodicals read by schoolteachers. Her national reputation dates from 1914, when her "Sonetos de la muerte" ("Sonnets on Death") took first prize in a literary contest in Santiago. In 1917 fifty-five items by Mistral were included in a series of schooltexts, edited by Manuel Guzmán Maturana, that were distributed throughout Chile and other Latin American nations. The texts included prose poems or parables and didactic verse. In her earliest journalism, and especially from 1918, when she went to live and work in Punta Arenas, the southernmost city in Chile, Mistral was deeply concerned with social and economic injustice—a concern that she, like many of her female contemporaries, justified as an extension of the schoolteacher's role.

Although Mistral's career as a school employee lasted only from 1905 to 1925, the Liceo de Niñas, the state-sponsored girls' school, was crucial to legitimating her presence in the public sphere: in its all-female world and in the primarily female world of the normal schools, Mistral and her female contemporaries were figures of absolute and unquestioned authority. Women also enjoyed each other's company while furthering their individual and collective interests in groups such as the Women's Reading Circles, the Women's Club, and the Professional Women's Association: the women's political action campaigns of the 1930s and 1940s began in these groups (Kirkwood; Meza). The similarities and differences between Mistral and the women of the associations are instructive. Although the associations were formed by and for married women, urban women, their political philosophy, like Mistral's, sought to reform or humanize the state through the enactment of protective laws preventing the exploitation of women and children. Also like her female contemporaries, Mistral regarded education as the single greatest factor in improving the conditions of absolute dependency in which women (and consequently many children) lived.

Mistral's possible complicity in the construction of her public image could be traced to a rhetorical stance that she shared with other Chilean protofeminists in the first quarter of the twentieth century: positing woman as a center of moral righteousness by invoking the existing code of female sanctity offered a means of countering informal and institutional misogyny. The desexualized figure of the saintly rural schoolteacher enabled Mistral to express alienation and outrage at a culture that registered woman solely in terms of the ability to arouse male desire. The quasi-parental, semireligious figure of the schoolteacher led to Mistral's becoming a register for the construction of woman within the discourse of nationhood in Chile, for the religious idealism attributed to the teacher answered the secular state's need to bolster its authority.

Mistral was living in Mexico when *Desolación* (Desolation), her first volume of poetry, was published (1922), bearing a prologue (probably written by Federico de Onís) that represented the poet as an unknown rustic. This characterization, combined with the fictions of the poet's personal modesty and devotion to children, enduringly established the terms of Gabriela Mistral's fame. Although she was indeed known and recognized among educators, her characterization as unknown played down the possibility of any threat to the status quo. It was in this context that her praisers and promoters described her in terms overtly intended to recall the Virgin Mary, and her male contemporaries honored and recommended her aesthetic with the understanding that it was particularly suited to women readers. Notwithstanding their enthusiasm, Federico de Onís, Pedro Prado, and Paul Valéry praised her work for its moral code without adopting in their own writing what they professed to admire in hers.

More than any other aspect of Mistral's lifelong production, a single group of less than two dozen short, lyric poems (out of some 120 items in *Desolación*) has constituted the base for the narrative construction of her life that has continued up to the present day. Drawing from the group of poems subtitled "Dolor" (Pain), which are dedicated "a su sombra" (to his shadow), that pseudobiographical narrative reads the poems as a *historieta*, a soap-operatic account of how the poet, an innocent country girl, is betrayed by a young man, first after he degrades their chaste love by engaging in a consensual physical relationship with another woman, and subsequently when he kills himself in despair over what he has become.

It is impossible to underestimate the impact, extension and durability of the soap-opera narrative that, as Palma Guillén (1973) observes, derives from male fantasy (x). This soap-opera narrative holds that the anger and bitterness of *Desolación* arises from the poet's frustrated longing for womanly fulfillment, since the suicide of this young man to whom she is eternally pledged denies her the (male) child for whom she longs. Here the clichés of feminine sanctity enter to counter the image of a barren old maid with no sexual interest in men. To account for the various positive depictions of rural women in the countryside, which stand in contrast to the poet's first-person allusions to suffering and a generalized, unspecified desire, the conventional interpretation stipulates that Mistral's social consciousness is an attempt to transcend the visceral pain, "the melancholy sting of infertility" (Díaz Arrieta). The evidence of Mistral's early journalism contradicts, however, the notion that frustrated desire dating from the 1909 suicide of her real-life acquaintance, Romelio Ureta, precipitated a turn to writing on behalf of children and mothers.

The prose poems of *Desolación* present a consciously elaborated statement of the poet's aesthetic and moral intentions that in no way corresponds to either the simplified soap-opera narrative or to its supposed consequence of quasi-maternal renunciation. Describing the confluence of desire and pain, these prose poems depict a variety of situations that pose the origins of speech in the quality of woundedness. Suffering is key to the ability to apprehend beauty. Whether male or female, artists are a special caste whose immersion in the life of the imagination is a sensory experience vastly superior to heterosexual desire, which the poet describes as grotesque.

The prose poems of *Desolación*, which are people with the walking, talking wounded, recall the centrality of suffering of lesbian characters in fiction such as Radclyffe Hall's *The Well of Loneliness* (1928) and Djuna Barnes's *Nightwood* (1936), both of which represent lesbians as misunderstood outsiders. The speakers or characters in the aesthetic universe of Mistral's prose and narrative poetry represent a consciousness set apart from that of ordinary human beings. As in *Nightwood* and as in the work of the poet H.D., the narrating or speaking voice is situated outside, looking in on, witnessing scenes of passion and betrayal. This stance, which critic Alberto Sandoval Sánchez and others in the feminist collection *Una palabra cómplice* (A Complicitous Word) describe as voyeurism, emphasizes the speaker's or speakers' conscious psychic distance and dissimilarity from those who are watched. In the prose of *Desolación*, Mistral projects human consciousness onto the olive grove, the rose, the tree or the mud, illustrating a third perspective in which the projection of desire on a specific individual is the harbinger of betrayal. Others in the generation of Chilean writers to which Gabriela Mistral belonged similarly anthropomorphized the natural world (Villegas). She differs from them in her concentration on suffering, a theme that begins in *Desolación* and is constant throughout her work: that no love between man and woman can be satisfied, and that carnal desire is synonymous with pain.

The series "Poemas de las madres" (Poems of the Mothers) hints at the possibility of erotic satisfaction. Rather than the generalized pantheism so often attributed to Mistral, these prose poems individually and as a group propose a specifically female sensory experience of infinite sweetness that the poet associates with a creativity antithetical to the patriarchal family, marriage and heterosexuality. These and others of Mistral's prose parables use the veiled language of semimystical speech for its similarity to the language of love, without patriarchal heterosexuality's threat of male violence and demand for sexual favors. Here Mistral again shares with her contemporaries an interest in theosophy and spiritualism as an arena for philosophical conjecture independent of the entrenched conservatism of the church (Rama).

Multiple references to suffering and the intimate wound are the most definitive aspect of Mistral's poetic production (Concha). To take these as symptomatic of female jealousy toward the philandering male lover, with feelings of guilt and betrayal intervening consequent to his suicide, would reduce the poet's multiple expressions of rage, in *Desolación* and later works, to individual frustration. This interpretation fails to account for the poet's ongoing preoccupation with femininity as a visceral experience of blood and breast, entrails, flesh, bone and milk. Mistral's vehement insistence on desire as a wound, when joined, in *Desolación*, with her concentrated attention to the physical traces of that wound in specifically feminine self-representations, recalls definitions of the lesbian by theoretical writers like Catherine Stimpson and Adrienne Rich.

When Mistral evokes the body of the mother, she is at her most utopian, constructing an autonomous female and ultimately lesbian identity (cf. Monique Wittig). Mistral's seeming preoccupation with the theme of motherhood, her evocations of gestation and the mother-infant relation show her claiming those aspects of the female body that least interested male writers of her day. Celebrating maternity is a pretext for an eroticism at once concentrated on the female yet utterly devoid of masculine influence. This emphasis on the female body continues in her major aesthetic statements after *Desolación*, in the introduction to *Lecturas para mujeres* (Readings for Women; 1924) and in "Colofón con cara de excusa" (Shame-Faced Colophon; printed in the 1945 edition of *Ternura* [Tenderness]). As in her "Recuerdo de la madre ausente" (Memory of the Absent Mother; 1923 [Bahamonde points out an earlier version published in

Antofagasta in 1911]) and in many of her lullabies, the female body is a source of women's authority as namers, readers, singers and tellers of subversive tales.

Subsequent to *Desolación* the verses that Mistral chose for *Ternura* (1925, 1945) continue to assert as primary the physical experience of woman as depicted from a female subjectivity. While the poems of *Ternura* (the most widely reprinted of Mistral's volumes) are in some sense directed toward children, we must observe the truism that children do not buy books. This supposed writing for children presents a sensibility that is at times erotic (in the lullabies) and at times political (in the rondas), and in "Colofón," Mistral explicitly states that her lullabies are intended, first and foremost, for the use of other Latin American women.

For all the panegyrics about Mistral's character, we know too little about the day-to-day details of her life from the time she took up residence in France (in 1925) to shortly before she was awarded the Nobel Prize in 1945. Her correspondence and publications prior to 1920 give an idea of her life in Chile. Palma Guillén, whom Vasconcelos designated to assist Mistral on her arrival in Mexico, seems a reliable source: she includes dates and places and gives an overall sketch of Mistral's activities from 1920 to 1922, as she traveled through Mexico, setting up rural schools and libraries and compiling *Lecturas para mujeres*. Guillén avoids the impressionism of other contemporary accounts of Mistral's activities, and she declares her solidarity with Mistral against a relentlessly hostile world.

Leaving Mexico following the furor that Guillén describes in the preface to *Lecturas para mujeres*, Mistral traveled to Europe. On her return to Chile in 1925, she resigned her position in the school system, having served her twenty years. At that point she may have intended to set up a school in La Serena, where her sister and mother lived, but when she was called to work in Europe with the League of Intellectual Cooperation of the League of Nations, her departure was definitive: after 1925, she returned to Chile for only two very brief visits.

Documents from the years of Mistral's residence and travel in Europe and the Americas could present a source rich in possibility, when pieced together as a narrative record, of a Latin American woman who built a life beyond the familial boundaries that have defined the lives of the vast majority of women. Her extensive correspondence is of particular interest; Rosario Hiriart's edition of Mistral's letters to Cuban writer Lydia Cabrera is a fine example. Her letters deal primarily with the failing health of their mutual friend Teresa de la Parra, a Venezuelan writer who was Cabrera's inseparable companion. In contrast to Mistral's published correspondence with famous men—Mexican writer Alfonso Reyes, the Costa Rican publisher García Monje and Chilean novelist Eduardo Barrios—the letters to Lydia Cabrera present the poet's unstinting adoration of the dying Teresa de la Parra. Absent from the letters to Cabrera are the feelings of mistrust and betrayal that appear in Mistral's correspondence with other writers, who published or permitted third parties to publish her letters without her consent, with consequences occasionally disastrous to Mistral. Cabrera knew to protect that trust, but not others: Mistral's attempts to maintain a friendship with Cabrera were strained by her bitter disappointment with the Cuban-born writer's upper-class milieu of society ladies and her failure to answer Mistral's letters.

Present-day readers tempted to discern in Mistral's correspondence some truer version of the self will find that the self depicted therein is as wittingly constructed as in any of her poetry or journalism, as the edition of Mistral's so-called love letters, primarily to Chilean poet Manuel Magallanes Moure, written from about 1914 to 1921, so strongly indicates. The mistitled *Cartas de amor de Gabriela Mistral* (Gabriela Mistral's Love Letters; 1978), dating from the period when the poet was composing *Desolación* (1914–1921), offer a variety of self-representations—poor but honorable country girl, shy poetess, distant intellectual, stood-up date, to name just a few—that all lead away from physical intimacy with the male addressees. What is valuable in these letters is their evidence of the varieties of pose that Mistral adopted. They reinforce a theme deduced from careful studies of poems for which multiple drafts are extant: that the author deliberately constructed a single love biomythology (Scarpa). The internal evidence of the drafts, paired with the external evidence of the personal correspondence, indicates the fictivity of the autobiography of *Desolación*. The poetic representation of a single love therein is a unifying element permitting an extended commentary on desire, suffering and death, viewed from a perspective resolutely outside and beyond heterosexual engagement.

An important event in Mistral's life was the special act of the Chilean legislature that in 1933 made her consul for life, with the right to choose her residence. Initially she went to live in Naples, but either her antifascism or her gender made her unacceptable to the Italian authorities. Her residence in Madrid ended with the publication in Chile of a private letter criticizing Spain's people and politics. Following a move to Lisbon, the disastrous impact of the Spanish Civil War in the Basque country prompted the 1938 publication of *Tala*. Victoria Ocampo's subsidizing of the enterprise and Palma Guillén's editing of the volume, which Mistral dedicated to her "and in her, to the piety of the Mexican woman," provide a strong contrast to the circumstances surrounding Columbia University's Instituto de las Españas' publication of *Desolación* sixteen years earlier, where Mistral appeared under the auspices and through the agency of men: Pedro Aguirre Cerda, Eduardo Barrios and Federico de Onís.

Mistral's later poems, from *Tala* on, constitute the center of Sylvia Molloy's brilliant lesbian reading of the Chilean poet's work. Like the Chilean feminist Raquel Olea, Molloy regards as paramount the undoing of Mistral's image as poet of sentimentalized maternity and "faux naif ditties" for children. Molloy's radical rereading proceeds from matricide as it is represented in Mistral's poem "Electra en la niebla" (Electra in the Mist; undated but certainly written after 1938). Molloy's analysis would lead to a totally new interpretation of Mistral's innovations in *Tala* as well as in *Lagar* (1954), for the theme of the mother's death and the situation of being haunted by her ghost are similarly present in

"La fuga" (The Flight) and "La otra" (The Other Woman), the prefatory poems of *Tala* and *Lagar*, respectively. Like "Electra," "La fuga" shows the poet as wanderer, in exile from patriarchy.

In *Tala* the death of the mother becomes the occasion for a series of "nocturnos" (nocturnes, night poems) dealing with death, and of graveside meditations. The last of these, "Lápida final" (Final Gravestone), ranges over the body of the dead mother, putting the memory of breasts, eyes, lap and hand in the context of a "vast and holy symphony" of old mothers. Mistral's notes published as an appendix to *Tala* suggest that the last poem of the series, a *plegaria* (supplication), "redeems the series as a whole," which she sees as representing the "fruits of pain." Where earlier interpretations have settled on the image of the pious, suffering daughter, Molloy explores the consequences of a matricide that situates the speaker outside of patriarchy. That theme of matricide, linked to the poet's self-representation as a wanderer, establishes the condition of exile and haunted return from which the poet speaks, not just in *Tala* but in nearly all of the later work. Thus in *Tala*, Mistral's later project of creating a consciously female-written poetry proceeds from the necessity of escaping or abandoning the physical world: poem after poem moves past a range of female ghosts into a dream world of liberatory solitude.

The last volume that Mistral published in her lifetime, *Lagar* was barely noted when it first appeared in 1954, coinciding with her final visit to Chile. The numerous homages published at the time of that visit and following her death in 1957 concentrate on relating the pre–1938 poetry to Mistral's public figure. Prior to the advent of feminist criticism in Chile, critics who mentioned *Lagar* at all generally described it as willfully hermetic and excessively difficult. Interpretations of *Lagar* in the earlier mold of Mistral's personal piety, spiritually and vague philosophical leanings are, for the most part, inadequately theorized, or follow ideological convenience. The tragic self-representations of *Lagar*, particularly in the very powerful series "Locas mujeres" (Crazy Women), are very different from the didactic, strongly narrative romance of *Poema de Chile* (Poem of Chile, 1967). Yet both are premised on speech that begins with a shedding of identity and loss of self that is the basis for Mistral's stance as a prophet of destruction in *Lagar* or ecological doom in *Poema de Chile*.

While the figure of Gabriela Mistral was adapted to a range of political exigencies during her lifetime, with her death in 1957 her image became a fixture in public art. The "floating Gabriela" that appears on Chilean stamps, murals, banknotes and photo homages is a disembodied head in profile or a transparent, tutelary spirit superimposed over or against that of an adult woman with one or more children. In the appropriation of her figure for explicitly political, nationalistic purposes, Mistral becomes a site for positing a timeless, inborn identity— national, racial, sexual, with the specific image being a function of the target constituency. In contrast to the somewhat youthful, populist image of the saintly schoolteacher, regimes seeking to shore up their prestige abroad invoked her as "Latin America's cultural ambassador, the Nobel Queen." In more unstable or transitional regimes she is especially liable to appear as a Chilean Horatia Alger, a loyal traveler who roamed the word while remaining mindful of her origins. In these depictions of the schoolteacher, the ambassador-queen and the loyal citizen-at-large (all reified in the verses and minibiography that some four generations of Chilean schoolchildren have been assigned to memorize) "Gabriela Mistral" is "almost a synonym for sexual ambiguity, with her cropped hair, her long robes, and her seldom shaving" (Bianchi). That sexual ambiguity is less an acknowledgment of lesbian possibility than a negotiated space in which the desexed queen, a female man, mediates between the state and Woman as producer of future citizens (Pratt).

The secularized Madonna grew less attractive with age. Some ten years after a death that otherwise sober chronologies describe as an apotheosis, critics published evidence of her paranoia and suggested that she was arteriosclerotic (Díaz Arrieta, C. Alegría). In the later 1970s several volumes of Mistral's prose were published, less because Gabriela Mistral was popular than because the rightwing dictatorship sought in her a safe contrast to the political inconvenience of Chile's other Nobel laureate, Pablo Neruda, who was affiliated with the Communist party. By the 1980s, cultural critics seeking to escape the percieved limitations of the poetess were turning to the rich, complex body of Mistral's prose. With the turn toward her prose the cult of Gabriela Mistral may be coming full circle, moving away from the point of antithesis and returning her to a changed pantheon. Successful assertions of Mistral's indigenous roots (C. Alegría; Guzmán) and her complex political and class allegiances (F. Alegría; Concha) replaced earlier characterizations of Mistral as a remote "descendant of conquistadors" (Díaz Arrieta). Some seemingly strange political pronouncements of her later years have been read as her shrewd manipulation of her image as a distracted old lady (Schopf; Calderón; F. Alegría). Such explorations of ideological issues in Mistral's intellectual development establish a precedent for the questioning of sexual identity in her public figure. Just as it took critics and historians with allegiances and identifications marginal to those of Chile's cultural status quo during the Pinochet era to pinpoint Mistral's mestizo roots, so it will take a feminist criticism, likewise working from a consciously minority or dissenting perspective, to challenge the tendency to locate Mistral in relation to a male desire that is patently irrelevant to her stated primary interests and to her positing a specifically female subjectivity.

If Gabriela Mistral was complicit win the state-sponsored monumentalization of her figure, such strategies of accommodation would be a means of coping with her vulnerability as a self-educated, lower-middle-class woman from the provinces who lacked family or marital advantages. The complex and contradictory relationship between Gabriela Mistral and the Chilean government did not end with her retirement from the public schools. In her decades of service representing Chile and/or Latin America in various international organizations and in her intracontinental lecture tours, newspapers and local intellectuals greeted her as a semiofficial speaker on behalf of education. Yet the categories of normal schoolteacher and lyric poet that permitted her access to literary life scarcely correspond to the identity as a rural Latin American woman that she emphasized after she left Chile. In the end she was an autodidact rather than a normal schoolteacher, and her writing career was as anchored in journalism as in the lyric.

Rather than seeking to uncover a hidden or private Mistral, we need to interrelate the diplomat and this woman who witnessed firsthand some extraordinary and important transitions in the intellectual history of Latin America, and to correlate these with the woman who joked, drank scotch and smoked cigarettes endlessly, who raised an adopted child from infancy and prescribed herbal cures to the leading intellectuals of her day. The perpetual identification with outsiders, exiles, who are acutely aware of being different and who are ill at ease with the world that surrounds them is a feature of her work that is congruent with what may be called a lesbian sensibility, for it is evident in the work of professed lesbian or bisexual women writers of her time. However difficult a positive identification of Gabriela Mistral, the public figure, as a lesbian, we must work to include lesbian possibility in the literary interpretation of her work and within the social history of early-twentieth-century Latin America. In doing so, the case of Gabriela Mistral, both as a cultural text and as a producer of texts, offers an invaluable and inviting point of departure for understanding the forms and figuration of sexual identity.

WORKS

Antología. Santiago, Chile: Zig-Zag, 1940, 1982.

Cartas de amor de Gabriela Mistral. Comp. Sergio Fernandez Larraín. Santiago, Chile: Andrés Bello, 1978.

Croquis mexicanos. Comp. Alfonso Calderón. Santiago, Chile: Editorial Nascimento, 1979.

Desolación. New York: Instituto de las Españas, 1922. Various subsequent editions.

Elogio de las cosas de la tierra. Comp. Roque Esteban Scarpa. Santiago, Chile: Andrés Bello, 1979.

Epistolario. Cartas a Eugenio Labarca (1915–1916). Santiago, Chile: Ediciones Anales de la Universidad de Chile, 1957.

Epistolario de Gabriela Mistral y Eduardo Barrios. Ed. Luis Vargas Saavedra. Santiago: Centro de Estudios de Literatura Chilena, Pontifícia Universidad Católica de Chile, 1988.

Gabriela anda por el mundo. Comp. Roque Esteban Scarpa. Santiago, Chile: Andrés Bello, 1978.

Gabriela Mistral y Joaquín García Monje: Una correspondencia inédita. Magda Arce and Eugenio García Carrillo. Santiago, Chile: Andrés Bello, 1989.

Gabriela piensa en . . . . Comp. Roque Esteban Scarpa. Santiago, Chile: Andrés Bello, 1978.

Grandeza de los oficios. Comp. Roque Esteban Scarpa. Santiago, Chile: Andrés Bello, 1979.

Lagar: Poemas. Santiago, Chile: Editorial del Pacífico, 1954.
Lagar II. Santiago, Chile: Ediciones de la Dirección de Bibliotecas, Archivos y Museos, 1991.
Lecturas para mujeres. 5th ed. Mexico City: Porrúa, 1967, 1976. Orig. 1924.
Magisterio y niño. Comp. Roque Esteban Scarpa. Santiago, Chile: Andrés Bello, 1979.
Materia: Prosa inédita. Comp. Alfonso Calderón. Santiago, Chile: Editorial Universitaria, 1978.
Motivos de San Francisco. Comp. César Diaz-Muñoz Cormatches. Santiago, Chile: Editorial de Pacífico, 1965.
Poema de Chile. Text rev. Doris Dana. Santiago, Chile: Editorial Pomaire, 1967.
Poesías completas. Comp. Margaret Bates and Gabriela Mistral. 4th ed. Madrid: Aguilar, 1976. Orig. 1958.
Prosa religiosa de Gabriela Mistral. Comp. Luis Vargas Saavedra. Santiago, Chile: Andrés Bello, 1978.
Recados contando a Chile. Comp. Alfonso M. Escudero. Santiago, Chile: Editorial de Pacífico, 1957.
Recados para América: Textos de Gabriela Mistral. Ed. Mario Céspedes G. Santiago, Chile: *Revista pluma y pincel*/Instituto de Ciencias Alejandro Lipschutz, 1978.
Reino: Poesía dispersa e inedita, en verso y prosa. Comp. Gaston von dem Bussche. Valparaíso, Chile: Ediciones Universidad de Valparaíso, Universidad Católica de Valparaíso, 1983.
Selected Poems of Gabriela Mistral. Trans. and ed. Doris Dana. Baltimore: Johns Hopkins University Press, 1971.
Selected Poems of Gabriela Mistral. Trans. Langston Hughes. Bloomington: Indiana University Press, 1957.
Siete cartas de Gabriela Mistral a Lydia Cabrera. Ed. Rosario Hiriart. Miami: Peninsular Printing, 1980.
Tala. Buenos Aires: Editorial Sur, 1938. Also Santiago, Chile: Andrés Bello, 1979.
Tan de Usted. Epistolario de Gabriela Mistral con Alfonso Reyes. Ed. Luis Vargas Saavedra. Santiago, Chile: Hachette/Ediciones Universidad Católica de Chile, 1990.
Ternura. 4th ed. Buenos Aires: Espasa-Calpé, 1946; 2nd ed., 1945.

CRITICISM

Acta literaria: Seminario La obra de Gabriela Mistral. no. 14. Concepción, Chile: Departamento de Español, Universidad de Concepción, 1989.
Alegría, Ciro. *Gabriela Mistral íntima.* Lima: Editorial Universo, 1968.
Alegría, Fernando. "Aspectos ideológicos de los *Recados* de Gabriela Mistral." In *Gabriela Mistral*, 70–79. Ed. Humberto Díaz-Casanueva et al.
———. "Gabriela Mistral's Ideology." In *Women in Hispanic Literature: Icons and Fallen Idols*, 215–226. Ed. Beth Miller. Berkeley: University of California Press, 1985.
———. *Genio y figura de Gabriela Mistral.* Buenos Aires: Editorial Universitaria, 1966.
Bahamonde, Mario. *Gabriela Mistral en Antofagasta: Años de forja y valentía.* Santiago, Chile: Editorial Nascimento, 1980.
Bianchi, Soledad. "Ni santa ni divina." *Apsi* 418 (1992): 11–12.

Busshe, Gaston von dem. *Visión de una poesía*. Santiago: Anales de la Universidad de Chile, 1957.

Calderón, Alfonso. "Esta vez que la Mistral volvió a Chile." *Ateneo* (1989): 459–460.

Catalog of the Gabriela Mistral Collection. New York: Barnard College Library, 1979.

Concha, Jaime. *Gabriela Mistral*. Madrid: Tauro, 1983.

Dana, Doris. *Index to Gabriela Mistral Papers on Microfilm 1912–1957*. Washington, D.C.: Organization of American States, 1982.

Daydí-Tolson, Santiago. *El último viaje de Gabriela Mistral*. Santiago, Chile: Editorial Aconcagua, 1989.

Díaz Arrieta, Hernán. (pseud. "Alone"). *Gabriela Mistral, premio nobel 1945*. Santiago, Chile: Editorial Nascimento, 1946.

———. "Gabriela Mistral." In his *Los cuatro grandes de la literatura chilena durante el siglo XX*, 120–171. Santiago, Chile: Editorial Nascimento, 1962.

Díaz Casanueva, Humberto, et al., eds. *Gabriela Mistral*. Jalapa, Mexico: Universidad Veracruzana, 1982.

Escudero, Alfonso M. *Las prosas de Gabriela Mistral: Fichas de contribución a su inventario*. 2nd ed. Santiago: Anales de la Universidad de Chile, 1957.

Fariña, Soledad, et al. *Lecturas de mujeres Taller Literatura La Morada*. Santiago, Chile: Cuadernos de La Morada, Centro de Análisis y Difusión a la Condición de la Mujer, 1989.

———. Una palabra cómplice: Encuentro con Gabriela Mistral. Santiago, Chile: Isis Internacional, 1990.

Figueroa, Virgilio. *La divina Gabriela*. Santiago, Chile: Impresor El Esfuerzo, 1935.

Gazarian-Gautier, Marie-Lise. *Gabriela Mistral, the Teacher from the Valley of Elqui*. Chicago: Franciscan Herald, 1975. Orig. published in Spanish.

Guillén de Nicolau, Palma. "Gabriela Mistral 1922–1924." In Mistral, *Lecturas para mujeres*, vii–xii. 5th ed.

———. "Introducción." In Gabriela Mistral, *Desolación, Ternura, Tala, Lagar*, ix–xlviii. Mexico City: Porrúa, 1973.

Guzmán, Jorge. "Gabriela Mistral: 'Por hambre de su carne.' In his *Diferencias latino-americanas*, 13–77. Santiago: Centro de Estudios Humanísticos de la Universidad de Chile, 1984.

Homenaje a Gabriela Mistral. Santiago: Anales de la Universidad de Chile, 1957.

Jiménez, Onilda. *La crítica literaria en la obra de Gabriela Mistral*. Miami: Ediciones Universal, 1982.

Jorquera Toro, Betty. *Compendio bibliográfico de Gabriela Mistral*. Vicuña, Chile: Mueso-Biblioteca Gabriela Mistral, 1985.

Kirkwood, Julietta. "Feminismo y participación política." In *La otra mitad de Chile*, 13–42.

———. *Ser política en Chile: Las feministas y los partidos*. Santiago, Chile: FLASCO, 1986.

Ladrón de Guevara, Matilde. *La rebelde Gabriela*. Santiago, Chile: Empresa Editoria Araucaria, 1984.

Lanzarotti, Claudia. "Sospechosa para todos." *Apsi* 418 (1992):30–33.

Marchant, Patricio. *Sobre árboles y madres—poesía chilena*. Santiago, Chile: Sociedad Editora Lead, 1984.

Meza, M. Angélica, ed. *La otra mitad de Chile.* Santiago, Chile: Centro de Estudios Sociales, 1985.

Molloy, Sylvia. "Female Textual Identities: The Strategies of Self-Figuration." In *Women's Writing in Latin America: An Anthology,* 107–124. Ed. Sara Castro-Klarén, Sylvia Molloy and Beatriz Sarlo. Boulder, Colo.: Westview Press, 1991.

Pinilla, Norberto. *Biografía de Gabriela Mistral.* Santiago, Chile: Editorial Tegualda, 1945.

Pratt, Mary Louise. "Women, Literature, and National Brotherhood." In *Women, Culture and Politics in Latin America. Seminar on Feminism and Culture in Latin America,* 48–73. Berkeley: University of California Press, 1990.

Rama, Ángel. *La ciudad letrada.* Hanover, N.H.: Ediciones del Norte, 1984.

Rodríguez Fernández, Mario. "Gabriela Mistral: La antimalinche." *Atenea* 459–460 (1989): 131–139.

Rodig, Laura. "Presencia de Gabriela Mistral: Notas para un cuaderno de memorias." In *Homenaje a Gabriela Mistral,* 282–292.

Samatán, María Elena. *Gabriela Mistral, campesina del Valle de Elqui.* Buenos Aires: Instituto Amigos del Libro Argentino, 1969.

Santa Cruz, Lucía, Teresa Pereira, Isabel Zegers and Valeria Maino. *Tres ensayos sobre la mujer chilena: Siglos XVIII–XIX–XX.* Santiago, Chile: Editorial Universitaria, 1978.

Santelices E., Isauro. *Mi encuentro con Gabriela Mistral, 1912–1957.* Santiago, Chile: Editorial del Pacífico, 1972.

Scarpa, Roque Esteban. *La desterrada en su patria (Gabriela Mistral en Magallanes: 1918–1920).* Santiago, Chile: Editorial Nascimento, 1977.

———. *Una mujer nada de tonta.* Santiago: Fondo Andrés Bello/Editorial de la Universidad Católica de Chile, 1976.

Schopf, Federico. "Reconocimiento de Gabriela Mistral." *Eco* 248 (1982): 152–171.

Silva Castro, Raúl. *Estudios sobre Gabriela Mistral. Precedido de una biografía.* Santiago, Chile: Zig-Zag, 1935.

———. *Producción de Gabriela Mistral de 1912 a 1918.* Santiago: Anales de la Universidad de Chile, 1957.

———, ed. *Retratos literarios.* Santiago, Chile: Ediciones Ercilla, 1932.

Taylor, Martin C. *Sensibilidad religiosa de Gabriela Mistral.* Spanish trans. by Pilar García Noreña. Madrid: Gredos, 1975.

Teitelboim, Volodia. *Gabriela Mistral pública secreta.* Santiago, Chile: Ediciones BAT, 1991.

Torres Rioseco, Arturo. *Gabriela Mistral. Una profunda amistad, un dulce recuerdo.* Valencia, Spain: Editorial Castalia, 1962.

Vargas, Saavedra, Luis. "Cartas de Gabriela Mistral." *Revista Mapocho* (Santiago) 23 (1970): 19–29.

———. "Hispanismo y antihispanismo en Gabriela Mistral." *Revista Mapocho* (Santiago) 22 (1970): 5–24.

———. *El otro suicidio de Gabriela Mistral.* Santiago: Ediciones Universidad Católica de Chile, 1985.

Villegas Morales, Juan. *Estudios sobre la poesía chilena.* Santiago, Chile: Editorial Nascimento, 1980.

Elizabeth Rosa Horan

MOHR, NICHOLASA (United States; 1938)

Nicholasa Mohr is the most significant Nuyorican (Puerto Rican born in New York) writer whose work focuses on the Puerto Rican metropolitan experience. Her books, which reflect the varied ethnic experience of the city, emphasize the communal nature of the Nuyorican, traveling between two cultures, island and mainland, psychologically, spiritually and physically.

A distinguished teacher, lecturer and visual artist whose experience includes study at Pratt, the Art Students League, the New School for Social Research and the Taller de Gráfica Popular (Popular Graphics Workshop), Mohr was born in New York City, the youngest of eight children and the only daughter of the Golpe family; the family later moved to the Bronx, where she spent her formative years. The death of her father when she was eight and of her mother while she was in junior high matured the young woman, who was then forced to live with relatives. She attended a trade school, majoring in fashion illustration; as a child of a poor family, she was initially not encouraged to attend college. An early teenage marriage failed; later, while studying at the New School, Mohr met her husband Irwin, now deceased. They had two children, Jason and David, and lived in Teaneck, New Jersey, in an old house; the attic was her print studio. Much of her early print work and printing was marked by numbers, letters, words and phrases—a kind of early graffiti. They attracted the attention of publishers, who approached her to describe her experiences and to depict the Puerto Rican New York experience in a novelistic way. Writing in English, she published her first novel, *Nilda*, in 1975; *El Bronx Remembered: A Novella and Stories*, in 1975; *In Nueva York*, in 1977; *Felita*, in 1979; *Rituals of Survival: A Woman's Portfolio*, in 1985 and *Going Home*, in 1986. Mohr currently teaches creative writing, lectures and is preparing several novels.

Nilda is an adolescent bildungsroman of a young Nuyorican girl during World War II. Marked by autobiographic elements, it describes family circumstances, social conflicts and the strong sustaining presence of her mother. *El Bronx Remembered*, set in the 1950s, consists of eleven short stories of social and neighborhood changes—the first presence of drugs in "Tell the Truth . . . "; the aging Jewish bachelor now surrounded by Puerto Rican families, in "Mr. Mendelsohn"; the differential status accorded on the island and on the mainland in "Uncle Claudio"; the new ethnic group, gypsies, in "A Lesson in Fortune Telling"; and Pentecostal churches in "Love with Aleluya" and the novella "Herman and Alice."

In Nueva York depicts a community on the Lower East Side of Manhattan, "Losaida." In this collection of eight short stories, community life centers on Rudi's luncheonette and its neighborhood customers, who are revealed in their emotional variants. "Lali" concerns a young woman brought from the island to marry the older owner; "The Robbery" shows conflicts within the community when two adolescents die in a frustrated attempted burglary; "I Never Even Seen My Father" records the conversations of two high school friends—Lillian, a college student, and Yolanda, a drug user—as their lives change. "The Perfect Little Flower Girl" demonstrates love and ingenuity in the gay and lesbian community.

Felita and *Going Home* are works aimed at an elementary school audience. Both reflect prejudice and its manifestations on the streets of New York and in Puerto Rico, and the values of support, particularly in the grandmother and other members of the extended family.

In six short stories, *Rituals of Survival: A Woman's Portfolio* profiles Nuyorican women of different classes, ages, and social backgrounds as they make self-affirming choices in the city. Carmela in "A Time with a Future" chooses independent living as a senior citizen; Lucia, a tuberculosis patient on Ward's Island, suffers a relapse and dies on her twentieth birthday, remembering the tranquil waters of her Puerto Rican childhood. Amy in "A Thanksgiving Celebration" imaginatively retreats into her grandmother's storytelling to prepare a special meal for her children under penurious conditions. Virginia, a lesbian in "Brief Miracle," attempts to play a straight role and fulfill family expectations.

Mohr's publications mark her as the most important female writer on the Nuyorican literary scene. Her short stories reveal a multifaceted, variegated and often fragmented community differentiated in class, economic status, gender and education. Critical reviews cite Mohr's diversity of experience and her willingness to explore nontraditional topics in a traditional literary form and in English.

Gay and lesbian topics appear in Mohr's work as part of community life. The individuals and their stories are simple extensions of the everyday interactions of city dwellers. Mutual support in time of emotional and economic stress is often cited. "The Perfect Little Flower Girl" (*In Nueva York*) is told by an omniscient author. However, through the eyes of Raquel Martínez, the protagonist, it is about how neighbors should exist. Her neighbors, a gay couple, Johnny Bermúdez and Sebastián Randazzo, must confront Johnny's draft notice for service in Vietnam and Sebastián's poor health. An arranged marriage with a partner in a lesbian couple will guarantee income for sickly Sebastián while Johnny is in the military. A church wedding and appropriate reception will formalize the arrangement; societal acceptance is assumed when Raquel plans the reception and permits her youngest daughter to be the little flower girl. Treated with realism and affection, with the appropriate song by Hilda, the flower girl—"You've Got a Friend"—community is affirmed.

In *El Bronx Remembered*, the novella "Herman and Alice" relates the loneliness of Herman, an aging, professional, closeted gay man after the breakup with his lover, the "arranged marriage" that solves the problem of Alice's teenage pregnancy, Herman's desire for affection and Alice's inability to relate to motherhood and Herman, a homosexual. Mohr directly approaches themes of isolation, the difficulty of relationships between coworkers, the guilt and alienation from family of urban gay males and the abusive treatment they sometimes receive from those they attempt to befriend.

"A Brief Miracle," in *Rituals of Survival: A Woman's Portfolio*, has a lesbian protagonist. Virginia, a somewhat stereotyped adolescent, falls in love with her high school English teacher and flees with her across the country. In the ensuing years, the relationship crumbles but the friendship remains, and Virginia has been unsuccessfully involved in a number of relationships, both male and female. Uncertain of her future, after an absence of ten years (and now twenty-six), she returns home as a handsome, well-dressed woman, and befriends a single father—neither of them has lived happily ever after thus far. Virginia, in search of "something steady and real," moves in with Mateo and attempts to resolve ten years of child abuse, abandonment and poor living conditions for him and his two children. Her parents hope for a Catholic marriage and a prodigal daughter's return. Virginia, however, discovers deception in the straight world—a partner who values bars and buddies over a relationship, children who lie and play hooky from school and dissatisfaction with her adopted lifestyle. Roots and belonging are not here. She flees back to her former lover, seeking a refuge from the failed attempt at inauthenticity, and the comfort of the familiar and the real.

In "The Perfect Little Flower Girl," "A Brief Miracle" and "Herman and Alice," Mohr represents gays and lesbians as universal characters, ordinary individuals with the concerns of intimacy, support and community in Latino New York. Her character development is dynamic and verisimilar; her settings are realistic; and the conflicts are authentic. Gay and lesbian characters are figures in the panoramic murals of urban Nuyorican life. Mohr's contribution is their representation and their presence in the panorama; typically, their absence is noteworthy.

WORKS

El Bronx Remembered: A Novella and Stories. New York: Harper, 1975.
Felita. New York: Dial, 1979.
Going Home. New York: Dial, 1986.
In Nueva York. New York: Dial, 1977.
Nilda: A Novel. New York: Harper, 1975.
Rituals of Survival: A Woman's Portfolio. Houston: Arte Público, 1985.
Something About the Author: Autobiography Series. Detroit: Gale, 1989.

CRITICISM

Blicksilver, Edith. *The Ethnic American Woman: Problems, Protests and Lifestyles.* Dubuque, Iowa: Kendall Hall, 1978.

———. *Hispanic Writers*. Detroit: Gale, 1991.

Turner, Faythe, ed. *Puerto Rican Writers at Home in the USA: An Anthology*. Seattle: Open Hand, 1991.

John C. Miller

MOLLOY, SYLVIA (Argentina; 1938) —————

Literary critic, professor and novelist, Molloy was born in Buenos Aires. Since completing her doctorate in literature at the Sorbonne, she has taught Latin American literature at Vassar College, Princeton University and Yale University. As of 1994 she is Albert Schweitzer professor in the humanities at New York University.

En breve cárcel (*Certificate of Absence*; 1981), one of the first lesbian Spanish American novels, tells the story of a woman writer who commits herself to write about her love affair with a woman. The plot of the novel is double, articulating both the story of the love affair and the process of writing about it. The narrator articulates not only her affair with Vera, her former lover, but also memories of her childhood, aspects of her relationships with her family and her dreams. At the beginning of the novel, the protagonist, secluded in an empty room that was the scene of her love affairs, starts writing. Through the process of writing, she attempts to come to terms with the loss of her lover. She tries to bring back to her memory the feelings of the affair and to exocrise them. This text, born out of an act of separation—the breakup of the lovers—is a cathartic exercise written to recover the lost lover through the writing process and to purge the author of the feelings for her lover. That double purpose of the act of writing is synthesized, with the rigor that characterizes Molloy's writing, in the words *figar/olvidar* (to shape/to forget).

The novel elaborates an interesting connection between tradition and singularity, writing and reading. Molloy's novel belongs to the literary traditions of the French *nouveau roman* (new novel) and the Río de la Plata. Most of the critics who have studied the novel have focused on its formal aspects, and few have homed in on the novel's lesbianism. Perhaps this is because in *En breve cárcel* the lesbian identity of the protagonist–writer, and the identities of her lovers, is not problematized. Although in the novel the space of the lesbian desire seems to be marginal—a small rented room—lesbian existence, lesbian identities and lesbian lives are at the center of the text.

The singularity of Molloy's novel is that it is based on the protagonist's reading of lesbian relationships, in contrast to the traditional (heterosexual) literary discourse that reads female experiences only in terms of their relationship to men. The nameless protagonist engages in a process of reading her life through the relationship with others, all of them, except her father, women (her mother, her sister, her aunt and her lovers). Thus, the novel is a lesbian novel not only in the strict sense that defines lesbianism in terms of a sexual connection and erotic bonding among women, but also in the sense that the novel privileges the emotional ties among women. That is, in the sense that *lesbian* has been defined by Lillian Faderman in *Surpassing the Love of Men: Romantic Friendship and Love Between Women from the Renaissance to the Present*: sexual contact may be a part of the privileged relationship between women to a greater or lesser degree, or it may be entirely absent.

Tradition and singularity, and reading and writing, are intertwined in *En breve cárcel*. There the process of reading and writing takes place in a game of forgetting the (lesbian) love story and remembering it. The first term, *forgetting*, connotes abandonment and lack of feeling, while the second, *remembering*, connotes establishment, affirmation, reassurance. The woman writer (like the character Funes the Memorius in Jorge Luis Borges's famous story) cannot forget. Reading a text always implies a process of remembering and forgetting, since a book is like a tissue with multiple connections and references. Hence, the process of reading her lesbian relationships is conditioned by what she as a reader remembers, and what she forgets. This text, like any literary text, is founded on a tradition and at the same time proposes a transgression of that tradition. *En breve cárcel* is a narcissistic novel in the sense that the woman writer, through the exploration of her relationships with women, begins a process of self-analysis. The other woman, her former lover, offers her the dimension of dialogue for her self-analysis. The novel is also narcissistic in the sense that it reflects upon the process of its own writing. One could say that as a narcissistic, self-reflexive or "metafictional" novel, *En breve cárcel* allows the exploration of fiction through its writing. The exercise of writing as a narcissistic act is synthesized in the conjunction and repetition of *ritos/espejos enfrentados/infancia* (rituals/facing mirrors/childhood). The protagonist–writer examines her own image through the examination of the other women (her sister, her lovers) and through her own writing.

There are several references to mirrors, and the protagonist's gesture of writing implies her examination through the process of looking at her relationships with other women. The many allusions to the gaze and to the act of looking recall Narcissus looking at himself in the water. Even the name of one character is an allusion to the act of looking or seeing: Vera, with an implication of the Spanish verb *ver* (to see). Furthermore, the protagonist–writer compares Vera to Narcissus. The references to "endless board game" synthesizes the game of glances, a metaphor for looking at herself and seeing herself through the image of the other, and stresses the communication and identification between lesbian lovers.

The repetition of the word *mask* in *En breve cárcel* implies the duplicity of the process of writing, as well as the splitting of the protagonist's identity. The mask permits a transformation, the possibility of being someone else. It allows the woman writer of the novel to annihilate the I and reaffirm the dialogue between the I and the she (that is, the other woman, the former lover). Moreover, the mask serves to ensure the privacy of a lesbian amorous discourse in a repressive society. Symbolically, the lesbian writer writes from a decentralized, intermediary, undefined space. In *En breve cárcel* the protagonist faces the problem of many lesbian writers who write from the marginal space that the heterosexual literary tradition has assigned to lesbian writing and representation. The representation of the physical and the geographical space is interesting in the novel, especially the representation of the room where the protagonist writes, which is a rented space, a transitory place, a room of casual encounters, the site of love affairs and breakups. The room, the topos of the prison house of love and the prison house of literature (Foster), is also a metaphor of the space of the erotic lesbian desire.

Lesbianism seems to be limited to the space of the rented room. The physical limitations of the room, described as small and dark, intensify the sensation of entrapment, and help the reader to visualize the private character of the story that is narrated. However, by telling her (lesbian) love story, the protagonist, writing from the isolation of her room, feels she is able to go beyond her seclusion. There are few references to geographical spaces in the novel. The woman writer and the reader are confined to the limitations of the room where she writes. However, at a certain point the fact that the woman is in exile is mentioned; she is from Buenos Aires and lives now in the United States. Exile has been used in lesbian literature as a metaphor for the marginality of lesbians in society, the experience of an outsider. That is, exile is a representation of the ex-centric space lesbians occupy in a heterosexist society.

En breve cárcel, like psychoanalytical practice, provides an intermediary space to represent the forgotten (lesbian) love stories and to attempt the search for a coherent history. Freudian theory presents narrative issues, and psychoanalysis works with stories that are characterized by silences, fragmentation and gaps. The novel is characterized by its fragmentation and rupture, which are textualized at the level of the articulation of the story and at the level of linguistic constructions. The narrator insists on the ambiguous condition of the story and the ambiguity of language.

The narrator of *En breve cárcel* oscillates between order and disorder, violating boundaries and restrictions. Throughout the text the desire to establish narrative order is present but impossible. Furthermore, the narrator insists that she is not interested in writing realistic literature. She rejects the idea that the novel she is writing could see the reality as an object. The language of the novel is a map of the protagonist–writer's amorous failures. The text introduces a defamiliarization with language, and the author explores and exploits the different connotations of words, playing with the expressive possibilities of opposites and oxymoronic constructions to express what a referential language cannot express. The novel privileges the indeterminacy of meanings. The protagonist–writer does not want to reduce the meanings of language and of her story by being precise. The consciousness of the self and the examination of a life from a particular moment is one of the features that *En breve cárcel* shares with autobiography. The novel, like many lesbian texts, is characterized by a confessional tone—the need to confess and to reflect the inner world. The woman writer, as a lesbian writer, attempts to give voice to her particular situation through the process of writing.

Although *En breve cárcel* has some features of autobiographical discourse, it is not an autobiography, since autobiography implies a complete and coherent discourse whose parts have been submitted to a specific arrangement to create uniformity. Rather, one of the most remarkable textual features of *En breve cárcel* is its fragmentation. The text is written from a state of violence, the violence produced by the separation of the lovers and the violent acts that have occurred in the protagonist's life. She states that she wants to write an autobiography and mentions the Mexican poet Sor Juana Inés de la Cruz, but later she rectifies this position. The body of the protagonist, as the text itself, appears fragmented by and subjected to violence. The woman cannot find a complete image of self through her narration, and when she looks at herself in mirrors, she can see only parts of her body, or her body as a site of violence. There are many references to the unevenness and the layers of the protagonist's skin, pointing to the Barthesian literary conception of a text: a tissue of multiple connections and fragments.

The text is composed as a mosaic in which dreams provide important insights. The oneiric space functions as an *espejo enfrentado* (facing mirror). There are many dreams, one of which has a special significance and shows the relationship of writing to the character's sexual orientation. It is the dream in which the protagonist's father calls her and asks her to visit Ephesus and gaze on the goddess of fecundity. When the writer wakes up, she realizes that she prefers another goddess—Diana, the huntress, who represents a pattern of violence and rupture that is textualized at the level of the enunciation and of the enunciated. It refers to the way the anecdote is arranged and to the lesbian meanings that are articulated. Diana, the huntress, represents the detachment of the protagonist—and ultimately Molloy—from the heterosexual meanings and literary tradition. The goddess of violence functions as a voice that reclaims a lesbian existence and the right to a lesbian space within the literary tradition.

WORKS

En breve cárcel. Barcelona: Seix Barral, 1981. Trans. Daniel Balderston with the author as *Certificate of Absence*. Austin: University of Texas Press, 1989.

CRITICISM

Foster, David William. *Gay and Lesbian Themes in Latin American Writing*, 110–114. Austin: University of Texas Press, 1991.
García Pinto, Magdalena. "La escritura de la pasión y la pasión de la escritura." *Revista iberoamericana* 132–133 (1985): 687–696.
Kaminsky, Amy. "Sylvia Molloy's Lesbian Cartographies. Body, Text, and Geography."

In *Reading the Body Politic. Feminist Criticism and Latin American Women Writers*, 96–114. Ed. Amy K. Kaminsky. Minneapolis: University of Minnesota Press, 1993.

Martínez, Elena M. "*En breve cárcel*: La escritura/lectura del (de lo) otro en los textos de Onetti y Molloy." *Revista iberoamericana* 151 (1990): 523–532.

Elena M. Martínez

MONSIVÁIS, CARLOS (Mexico; 1938) _____

Anthologist and journalist, Monsiváis is best known as a writer of chronicles and an essayist, mixing both genres in order to describe and explain the complexity of contemporary Mexican society, especially that of Mexico City and its surrounding areas. He produces an analytical discourse characterized as alternative because he focuses on the collective problems and cultural expressions of society at large, as well as on marginal and minority sectors like gangs, feminists, independent labor unions and opposition groups that usually do not have access to, yet are, misrepresented or not, portrayed by the dominant mass media.

Within these parameters, Monsiváis acknowledges his gay identity, although it is not at the center of his chronicles. However, in some of his works he incorporates matters valuing the creative capacity and the intellectual and artistic talent of homosexuals, such as the famous popular singer Juan Gabriel and the controversial poet Salvador Novo. In this way he criticizes a patriarchal and homophobic society that tends to ignore, to view with prejudice and to harass the Mexican gay community and its manifestations. Hence, Monsiváis exposes and denounces the marginalization, limited possibilities, and suffering of this minority group, which has struggled to be accepted in a political process that enjoys his support and participation.

In his chronicles, Monsiváis generally examines social phenomena within their historic context, resulting in a diachronic perspective that significantly surpasses simple and enumerative description, as well as a pamphleteering and doctrinaire vision. He reinforces his style and critical capacity by applying different theories of interpretation, mixing their conceptual terminology with Mexican popular dialect and introducing a variety of literary and technical resources. In this way, the human and colloquial atmosphere, the play on words, the combinations and intertextuality, the plumbing of individual and collective psychology produce a rich expression and increase alternative messages. At the same time that Monsiváis's chronicles oppose any form of tendentious manipulation and the sort of ephemeral and superficial messages produced by the dominant mass media, Monsiváis questions the ideology and false morality of the oligarchy when he includes, reproduces and gives considerable space to oppressed voices, popular demands and protests in their dialectical and irreverent forms of speech. Furthermore, he investigates origins, causes and variations in social contradictions, as well as the lives of those the dominant system seeks to hide, to distort or to silence.

Consequently, Monsiváis's chronicle–essay is not an ordinary register of marginalized and popular culture, but contains an analytical discourse that is profound, incisive, ironic, humorous and easily accessible, one that attracts all types of readers, from the expert to the layman. Monsiváis himself demonstrates an active concern to ensure the extensive distribution of his works through alternative, academic and even commercial and government presses, and he supports the social and political demands of marginal and minority sectors. Such a praxis, and his interest in distributing his chronicles in as broad a fashion as possible, fulfill the function of his alternative discourse: he presents an interpretation of social conflicts and cultural expressions in a unique style that evokes alternative actions in Mexico and assures his primary goal in writing: a chronicle that reflects the voice of popular readers who are capable of capturing, meditating on and transforming the oppressive reality they inhabit.

Monsiváis's works include *Días de guardar* (Holy Days of Obligation; 1971), an examination of how being Mexican constitutes a process, especially in Mexico City and its surroundings, grounded in a specific social and historical context. It is a classic because of its interpretation of major holidays, events and social phenomena of the 1960s. Monsiváis writes a sociological and literary analysis on a variety of topics, descriptions, situations and famous personalities. This first collection already displays his ironical, incisive and humorous style, a combination of colloquial and conceptual terminology and an understanding of Mexican collective psychology and its mythology. Monsiváis also exposes and denounces intervention and manipulation by the dominant oligarchy, which represses and impedes liberation or transformation movements like the student revolt of 1968. Moreover, he recovers the barrio's myths, joys and misfortunes, attempting to characterize and explain the collective will in its condition as victim of marginalization and silence.

Escenas de pudor y liviandad (Scenes of Modesty and Lewdness; 1988) examines a world of popular spectacle, recognizing the valuable role and social function of mass idols, nightclubs, discotheques, bars and dance palaces that feature music ranging from boleros to punk, expressing the feelings and likes of a society that is less prejudiced. In this way, he identifies a type of sociological barometer regarding customs that in the past were practiced only by the marginalized but now belong to large sectors of society.

Monsiváis the anthologist, armed with a selective criterion favoring popular culture and social criticism, in *A ustedes les consta* (For Your Information; 1980) rescues the most important Mexican chronicle writers of the nineteenth and twentieth centuries who were ignored or minimized by official discourse. He emphasizes, in light of his criteria, promoting the forgotten chronicles that helped build the Mexican literary and popular identity and in part were a vehicle of protest and denunciation.

WORKS

A ustedes les consta. Mexico City: Era, 1980.

Amor perdido. Mexico City: Era, 1978.

El crimen en el cine. Mexico City: Secretaría de Gobernación, 1977.

Del difícil matrimonio entre cultura y medios masivos. Hermosillo, Mexico: Papeles de Lupe Fusiles, 1984.

Días de guardar. Mexico City: Era, 1971.

Entrada libre. Mexico City: Era, 1987.

Escenas de pudor y liviandad. Mexico City: Grijalbo, 1988.

Nuevo catecismo para indios remisos. Mexico City: Siglo XXI, 1982.

CRITICISM

Blanco, José Joaquín. "*Días de guardar* diez años después." *Nexos* 4.45 (1981): 43–50.

Castañón, Adolfo. "Un hombre llamado ciudad." *Vuelta* 14.163 (1990): 19–22.

Cossío, María Eugenia. "El diálogo sin fin de Monsiváis." *Hispanic Journal* 5.2 (1984): 137–143.

Domínguez Michael, Christopher. "Carlos Monsiváis en sus cincuenta años." *Proceso*, Apr. 4, 1988, pp. 58–59.

García Flores, Margarita. "Carlos Monsiváis. El gran púas de la cultura mexicana es un gato tierno y trabajador." In her *Cartas marcadas*, 309–321. Mexico City: Universidad Nacional Autónoma de México, 1979.

Urrelo, Antonio. "*Amor perdido*: Inversión de la dicotomía y montaje de sus mecanismos." In his *Verosimilitud y estrategia textual en el ensayo hispanoamericano*, 112–132. Mexico City: Premià, 1986.

Manuel Murrieta Saldívar

MONTAÑO, LUIS (Luis Rascon Montaño; Mexico; 1954–1985) _____

César Avilés has asserted that Montaño's *Brenda Berenice o el diario de una loca* (Brenda Berenice or the Diary of a Queen; 1985) is "a compendium of gay terminology and expression that projects a character and situations of real weight and life-like dimensions" (44). Such a characterization is useful in specifying how the fundamental aspects of this novel concern language in general and three particular aspects of language to which the text gives special prominence: (1) the production of language; (2) the delimitation of speech; and (3) the conversational character of the work on the basis of the genre that underlies it.

These three aspects serve to outline the textual dynamics of *Brenda Berenice* as the verbal construction of a contradictory gay identity, one that is in permanent crisis and whose constitutive basis is an artistic work. Thus, the verbal apparatus is sustained by a literary process larger than mere linguistic production, a specific manner of speech and one genre. The literary processes involved here subtly manifest the oppressive features of a determinate sexual practice, its struggle against the dominant and restrictive sexual ideology that it fragments and its criticism of a putative human liberty. It is in the end a subalternative text in the face of an institutional literature recognized as morally and aesthetically valid.

Brenda Berenice is the story, told in flashback via a disjointed chronology, of the salient features of a self-assumed congenital homosexual, from his childhood in the north of Mexico (Montaño was from the northern Sonoran town of Cananea) to his residence in Mexico City. He knows from the earliest stages of his consciousness that he is different (and scorned because of it), despite his initial attempts to incorporate himself into the majority of his companions at school. But that ceases to motivate his process of individuation, since the contemplation of the sexual exploits of another homosexual assures that his salvation lies in running away with his first lover, a doctor serving a mandatory tour of social service in the town. He follows the doctor to Mexico City, where he experiences anonymity and the integration into the marginal world of prostitutes, queers, literary studies and fashion design, in order to create his own language, his own vision and understanding of the world and his own identity.

In contrast to established linguistic practices that rely on clichés and worn modes of expression in conformance with a law of least effort, *Brenda Berenice* organizes a personal, alternative dictionary that expands on entries in the standard dictionaries at hand. Throughout there is a display of terminological innovation that adheres to the basic morphosyntactic rules of Spanish while providing for new formations that are both intelligible and original. Thus the narrator is a producer of new communicative forms because this is his obligation, and he has the ability, the desire and the knowledge to do so. This implies a series of verbal elements that give meaning to the world while making the particular textual universe in which they are found unique and nontransferable, with an appeal to the concept of literary autonomy without promoting unintelligibility.

That social groups have a tendency to produce specialized forms of speech (slang, argot, jargon) is a correlative of resistance to the dominant class, a resistance that serves as a form of sanction. Resistance is here the mark of the need both to survive and to thrive. In order for marginal groups to produce a new discourse within relatively limited syntactic, grammatical and phonetic confines, they must turn to the resources provided by wit, imagination and play, carnivalizing language in a project of intrinsic ephemerality. Recognition of that discourse by the academy or other social groups implies its disappearance as an alternative, bringing with it the requirement that words and expressions be replaced by something new. Specific speech implies the maintenance of a specific identity and collaboration in the integration of a specific personality and its concrete practices.

The diary is the form Montaño uses for the integration of these processes, a diary whose features inscribe it in the tradition of the picaresque narrative. Although the voice of this text lacks an antagonistic counterpart (such as one would find in a dialogue-based novel) in terms of plot development or interpersonal conflicts on the levels of overall plot and specific incidents, an antagonistic dimension exists on another level: the protagonist is his own antagonist. To the extent that he elaborates the portrayal of a contradictory personality, it makes sense that in the face of an aggressive social reality, he seeks refuge in his own speech and in a realm of play, and that in the face of a scorn that would seek to eliminate him, he seeks a form of recovery. He loses Iván, his first lover, at a party he himself has organized; he abandons his love in San Francisco because an economic emergency calls him back to Mexico; he maintains his ties to his family through letters to his mother, to which she never replies with more than a line; he is over and over again the victim of misfortune (jail, mockery, beatings) because of an apparent instability that makes him vulnerable.

The diary, with undated divisions into days, seems to have been written in a single night, and ends with "Good night. Yours." We never learn Brenda's age; we never know how old he was when he left his hometown, when he arrived in Mexico City or when the events described took place. Atemporality, therefore, seems to bespeak the eternal nature of his case, with the impression that much more than a specific movement or a specific criticism of concrete sexual practices is at issue. Homosexuality transcends historical confines and becomes an eternal question. This is not without a paradoxical quality for the detailed description of incidents and any pleasure to be derived from the passing ridicule, in vignette fashion, of the individuals involved. The protagonist is characterized by a singular mediocrity. The atemporality, or at least the chronological non-specificity, of what is recounted also signals how the voice of the protagonist, with constant reference to ellipses and information deficit, assumes prior knowledge. His interlocutor—himself, the diary or the reader—already knows what he is talking about, is already an accomplice in a dirty and sinful conversation that is nevertheless entertaining and a catharsis for all involved. Rather than making use of a gender identity that will function as a narrative vehicle, the author repeatedly addresses the diary as a captive interlocutor; yet it is the captive reader who is at issue, whether himself also a homosexual or an unrepentant sympathizer.

Montaño also wrote theater, but there is no evidence of its having been produced. He lived in Hermosillo, Sonora, and studied literature. His character, Brenda Berenice, represents a particular homosexual matrix that has not been sufficiently explored, one characterized by the self-incorporation of multiple models, which can be seen in the way the novel presents him as an overwhelming presence. Brenda speaks, feels, observes, expresses opinions, pronounces judgments and articulates a personal position vis-à-vis a dizzying array of personalities drawn from every imaginable realm of life, both Mexican and international. Literary and historical models, the movies and radio all play a role in determining the conduct of the protagonist, constituting references to an extra-textual mode of being for quotidian homosexuality.

Gender crisis and the particular crisis of speech and linguistic production in the context of creating and narrating an identity do not overlook the fact that a choice is made from what abounds in mass media in order to undertake an integration of identity. Thus it is significant that model homosexual personages like Oscar Wilde and Alexander the Great are not cited: identity is explicitly integrated by reference to disperse and multiple temperaments and personalities. *Brenda Berenice o el diario de una loca* may not be a great novel, but it has undeniable freshness and humorous ingenuity in the way it provides space for rethinking concrete literary and sexual practices of difference.

WORKS

Brenda Berenice o el diario de una loca. Mexico City: Domés, 1985.

CRITICISM

Avilés, César. "Ubicación de *Brenda Berenice o el diario de una loca* dentro de la tradición literaria." In *Memoria. XII Coloquio de las literaturas regionales*, 39–46. Hermosillo, Mexico: Universidad de Sonora, 1992.

Darío Galaviz Quezada

MONTEFLORES, CARMEN DE (Puerto Rico; 1933) ⸺⸺⸺⸺⸺⸺⸺⸺⸺⸺⸺⸺

Born to a Spanish father and a Puerto Rican mother, Carmen de Monteflores left Puerto Rico at the age of sixteen to study art at Wellesley College. After receiving her B.A. in 1953, she studied sculpture in Paris and painting in the United States. She continued her work as an artist while raising five children in Montana. After moving to California with her family, Monteflores stopped painting, began writing poetry and entered graduate school, where she studied clinical psychology. In 1978 she completed her Ph.D. and is currently a practicing psychotherapist in Berkeley.

Singing Softly/Cantando bajito (1989), Monteflores's first novel, depicts three generations of Puerto Rican women and their ability to survive despite the racism, sexism, classism and other forms of oppression they experience. In this bilingual novel, Monteflores draws on autobiographical material to imaginatively re-create the life of her grandmother in the protagonist, Pilar, the daughter of a black mother and white father. Narrated from the perspective of the granddaughter, Meli, *Cantando bajito* utilizes a nonlinear narrative and shifting points of view to draw a complex picture of Pilar as daughter, lover, mother, widow, *abuelita* and friend. The novel contains overlapping stories, including Meli's ambivalence concerning her Puerto Rican heritage; the racism and classism Pilar experiences in her common-law marriage with Juan, an upper-class, white-skinned Puerto Rican; intergenerational conflicts between mothers and daughters; and the relationship between Pilar and Seña Alba, the black midwife feared by other members of the community.

In "Invisible Audiences," a personal narrative based on a presentation at OUT Write 90, a U.S. national lesbian and gay writers conference, Monteflores positions herself as a Puerto Rican lesbian writer and explores the ways her ethnicity, sexuality, family background and gender influence her work. She adopts metaphors of hiding and "coming out" to examine issues related to secrecy and self-censorship, including her fears in promoting herself as a lesbian writer, her desire to reach an extensive (white, heterosexual, middle-class) readership and her reluctance to reveal family secrets. In addition to describing the conflicts she experienced while writing *Cantando bajito*, Monteflores reflects on the ways writing the novel transformed her by compelling her to acknowledge and examine her own racism and heterosexism, as well as her responsibilities as a daughter.

Although Monteflores's work has not received critical attention, her self-defined position as a lesbian writer and her depictions of relationships between women in *Cantando bajito* raise provocative questions concerning lesbian writing. According to conventional definitions, the novel cannot be considered a lesbian text. As Monteflores herself notes in "Invisible Audiences," *Cantando bajito* does not contain explicitly lesbian material; indeed, the novel does not explore sexual relationships between women. However, by emphasizing that the novel's original audience was the lesbian feminist community; by publishing with a predominantly lesbian press; by identifying herself as lesbian in the novel's bio; and by promoting the book as a lesbian, Monteflores introduces what Judith Mayne calls "lesbian codes" and a "lesbian inflection" into readings of the text.

Rather than a full-blown critique of heterosexuality, the lesbian inflection is more ambivalent, for it simultaneously affirms and resists the sexual fictions of patriarchal culture. We see this ironic stance most clearly in the novel's female friendships, especially in the enigmatic relationship between Pilar and Seña Alba. By exploring Seña Alba's protective, nonpossessive love for Pilar and Pilar's inexplicable, only partially acknowledged feelings for the black midwife, Monteflores subtly challenges the assumed "naturalness" of heterosexual relationships. She creates a lesbian subtext that destabilizes, without entirely overturning, the novel's heterosexual matrix.

WORKS

"Invisible Audiences." *Out/Look* 3 (1990): 65–68.
Singing Softly/Cantando bajito. San Francisco: Spinsters/Aunt Lute, 1989.

CRITICISM

Mayne, Judith. "Lesbian Looks. Dorothy Arzner and Female Authorship." In *How Do I Look? Queer Film and Video*, 103–135. Ed. Bad Objects-Choice. Seattle: Bay Press, 1991.

AnnLouise Keating

MONTENEGRO, CARLOS (Cuba; 1900) ⸻

At a very early age, Montenegro joined the navy and was imprisoned at nineteen for having killed a man in a brawl. While in prison, he wrote a series of short stories that led Cuban intellectuals to wage a successful campaign for his release. Once out, he wrote *Hombres sin mujer* (Men Without Women; 1935), a novel based on his experiences in prison.

Hombres sin mujer is unusual in Latin American literature for its depiction of a homosexual relationship between a black and a white, in terms very similar to Adolfo Caminha's *Bom-Crioulo* (1895). In both novels a black male, described in terms of his superior physical form and outwardly masculine behavior, falls in love with an adolescent, blond, blue-eyed male, fifteen to eighteen years old. The courtship is restrained, in each case involving an episode where the black male suffers extreme physical punishment for having protected the white adolescent from harm at the hands of macho males. Both novels end with the white boy's death at the hand of the black male because of jealousy, a third character having intervened to cause a rift in the relationship. Each killer loses his life as well; thus, both novels have the predictable unhappy ending for homosexual relationships that has acquired canonical status in Western literature.

There is an easily recognizable model for this type of plot: Shakespeare's account of the relationship between the Moor of Venice, Othello, and his beautiful, adolescent, white wife, Desdemona. Thus, one may venture the hypothesis that in relationships between whites and members of any other racial group, the expected outcome is rupture, separation and personal tragedy for both partners, or at least for the nonwhite partner (David Hwang's *M. Butterfly* is a good example from another genre), irrespective of the gender of the individuals concerned. One may generalize even further and hypothesize that relationships with individuals perceived in terms of their threatening otherness will be depicted as ultimately tragic.

At the same time, *Hombres sin mujer* offers an excellent description of the codes governing macho maleness. Macho males will use weaker or younger males for sexual purposes without losing their masculinity as long as they are not emotionally involved. Impassiveness is a marker of maleness; feeling is a marker of weakness (femaleness). Even violence is to be dissociated from emotion. The macho code also deals with language use: macho men do not talk unnecessarily; queers do. Desire expressed as possession and possessiveness, and the perception of the other as sexual property, are acceptable; passion, which is characterized by a loss of self-control, and thereby associated with women, is not.

Against this background Montenegro brilliantly subverts dominant discourse by making the particular relationship between Pascasio, the black man, and Andresito, the white adolescent, transcend the naturalist constraints of the plot and achieve tragic status. Such subversion is achieved not only by openly documenting the change Pascasio undergoes because of his love for Andresito, but also through the trope of Christian sacrifice. Pascasio suffers a brutal beating while hanging by his wrists after having roughed up the prison warden who wants Andresito; Montenegro openly compares him to ''a black Christ'' and the suspension to a crucifixion. Andresito, meanwhile, has decided to give himself to the warden in order to free Pascasio. Pascasio finds out, surprises them together once he is freed, and in a fit of jealousy kills the boy. Immediately afterward, he cuts off the hand with which he struck his lover and bleeds to death in the arms of a weeping, older prisoner.

This is not naturalism; in fact, it resembles the tragic sequence at the end of many a romantic opera: betrayal, murder, madness, suicide. Pascasio, as a character, is elevated to the stature of a black tragic hero; Andresito is the tragic victim. *Hombres sin mujer* shows the tension between the naturalist discourse embodied in the obsessive theme of male sexuality and the romantic discourse embodied in the main characters' development toward death through sacrifice. Montenegro allows the reader a glimpse into a world where passion, tenderness and homosexuality are not incompatible, a truly remarkable achievement.

WORKS

Hombres sin mujer. Mexico City: Editorial Oasis, 1981. Orig. 1935.

CRITICISM

Pujals, Enrique J. *La obra narrativa de Carlos Montenegro.* Miami: Ediciones Universal, 1980.

Alfredo Villanueva

MONTERO, MAYRA (Cuba; 1952) ⎯⎯⎯⎯⎯⎯

Within a seemingly traditional narration—extracted, perhaps, from her journalistic background—Montero writes with fluid versatility, producing works that range from the historical to the pornographic. She was born in Havana, and moved when she was eight to Puerto Rico, where she still resides. She has worked as a journalist in Puerto Rico and as a correspondent throughout Central America and the Caribbean. Her first published work, *Veintitrés y una tortuga*

(Twenty-three and One Turtle; 1981), is a collection of short stories that fit beautifully within the classical definition of the genre: they are brief, detailed narrations written around single events. Their topics are diverse, from the death of tightrope walker Karl Wallenda, told alternately from the point of view of a paranoid clown and of a child, to the effects of exile on a couple's daily routine. With her first novel, *La trenza de la hermosa luna* (The Beautiful Moon's Tress; 1987), Montero put to use her research on voodoo in a historical novel set during the last days of Jean Claude ("Baby Doc") Duvalier's regime in Haiti. Her second novel, *La última noche que pasé contigo* (The Last Night I Spent with You; 1991), was published in a collection of erotic literature. A graphically erotic novel that explores the sexual crises of a middle-aged couple on a Caribbean cruise, *La última noche* also addresses lesbian relationships among three women. In a style that mixes journalistic documentation and literary prose, her third novel, *Del rojo de su sombra* (Of the Red of His Shadow; 1992), deals with the Haitian minorities in the northern Dominican Republic. The novel examines the Gagá, a socioreligious cult, and its celebration of Holy Week, along with the love and deep hatred between two of its leaders, a man and a woman.

Except for reviews of her work in several newspapers, Montero's work has not received attention from North American Hispanists. Her literary endeavors and her treatment of gays and lesbians, however, are of great importance to an understanding of her writing within the context of Caribbean Spanish literature.

"Halloween en Leonardo's" (Halloween at Leonardo's), a story from *Veintitrés*, establishes the approach Montero will use for her portrayal of gay characters in her writing. The story tells of the possibly fatal attack on Melo Saldaña by his lover's former lover, Cuqui Navarro, during a Halloween party at Leonardo's a famous disco of the 1970s in Puerto Rico. Montero is very careful in revealing their gay status, always disclosing it without any sort of homophobic or scandalous narration: gayness is taken by the female narrator as a matter of course. The story does not mean to reveal the violence and irrationality of gays in general, but to portray impulsive behavior in these specific characters. The costumes that the men wear to the party reveal their attitude toward their own gayness: Cuqui is a flamboyant Dracula with feathered fans and a golden cape who offers a feather to Melo's lover, Roquito Sánchez, the feather being an overtly gay symbol in Puerto Rican culture. Cuqui's forward gesture seems to correspond to his open jealousy of the couple. Melo is a skeleton, a costume in which he feels thoroughly uncomfortable; he is constantly adjusting the "bones" painted on his body stocking. Whether this discomfort is an uneasiness about being gay, or simply about Roquito's former lover being at the party, is never certain, but this tension seems to be what causes the fight between Cuqui and Melo, with Cuqui finally breaking a bottle on the back of Melo's head.

In terms of narrative, the case is much more complex in *La última noche que pasé contigo*, even though the relaxed attitude toward gay characters is maintained throughout. The lesbian nature of the love triangle is never foregrounded until the end of the novel. This does not mean that the women are relegated to the background; they are actually the generating focus of all the sexual adventures in the story. The novel deals with the middle-age sexual crisis of a couple on a Caribbean cruise. The narration alternates between Fernando and Celia, interrupted by a series of love letters written by a certain Abel to Angela. The bulk of the novel is dedicated to the extramarital sexual experiences that Fernando and Celia have had in their lives, but the connection of their love affairs to the letters is not clear until the last section of the novel, when we realize that Fernando's grandmother was Angela, and Abel was a pseudonym for Angela's female lover, Marina, who eventually abandoned Angela for a zoologist named Julieta, who happens to be Fernando's lover on the cruise ship (something that Fernando does not realize until the very end of the novel). The love of these three women has marked Fernando deeply. When he was a child, he carried the letters between Marina and his grandmother, and in a way the women's relationship was a model for his subsequent loves. Similarities abound in both the lesbians' and in Fernando and Julieta's relationship: Napoleon's Josephine is the metaphor with which Marina evokes Angela's image, and Fernando recalls Julieta when he stares at a painting of a naked black man embracing Josephine with his snake-like penis. The passion that Angela develops for the sexual acts of animals (Julieta is conducting research on that topic, and Marina writes to Angela about it) also stays with Fernando throughout his life.

The novel's erotic scenes are detailed and unabashed. However, the lesbian relationship is not part of this pornographic narration. There is much erotic imagery in the letters, but the violence present in the heterosexual acts is altogether absent in the lesbian narration. The lesbian love affair is surrounded, and in fact defined, by the passionate lyrics of boleros, including the title of the novel. Fernando and Celia, before they were married, used to listen to Angela read the letters aloud. In a way, it is as if Fernando (and perhaps even Celia) is trying, unsuccessfully, to re-create the tender and passionate love that radiates from those letters, but what comes out of his attempt is a desperate, false copy of Angela and Marina's affair. It is curious that Fernando creates a difference between Angela's love and the sexual acts of lesbians in general. At one point in the novel, he fantasizes with Julieta about her having sex with a woman, unaware that she is the woman who took Marina away from his grandmother. Fernando's vision is violent and sadistic: he, the man, looks upon the scene, orders what to do, how to do it and when to do it. Fernando becomes the controller of the sexual scene, and the lesbians must obey his commands. This is radically different from the lesbian love affair in the letters: Fernando's fantasy is graphic and explicit, while the lesbian letters are suggestive without ceasing to be erotic. Fernando's lesbian concept, in fact, is rendered false by the world that Angela and Marina create for themselves through the letters.

Throughout her work, Montero never uses generic types; her characters are individual and unique. The portrayals of Marina and Angela, and even of Cuqui and Melo, are not stereotypes but unique characters. What is refreshing in Montero's writing is her lack of interest in forcing a social issue into her narration, projecting instead her fascination with both gay and straight characters.

WORKS

Del rojo de su sombra. Barcelona: Tusquets, 1992.
La trenza de la hermosa luna. Barcelona: Anagrama, 1987.
La última noche que pasé contigo. Barcelona: Tusquets, 1991.
Veintitrés y una tortuga. San Juan, P.R.: Instituto de Cultura Puertorriqueña, 1981.

Carmelo Esterrich

MORAGA, CHERRÍE (United States; 1952)

Cherríe Moraga was born in Whittier, California. She is one of three children of the marriage between a first generation Mexican-American, Elvira Moraga (born in California in 1914) and a Canadian-American, Joseph Lawrence, who was born in San Francisco in 1926. Coming of age during the Chicano movement (mid-1960s through early 1970s) and the emergence of the feminist and gay and lesbian movements, she was part of the first generation of Chicanos who attended universities in comparatively large numbers. She has a B.A. in English literature (1974) and an M.A. in creative writing from San Francisco State University (1980). She currently lives in San Francisco and teaches writing in Chicano studies at the University of California at Berkeley. As an originally working-class and college-educated light-skinned Chicana lesbian, the tensions between race, culture, class, gender and sexual orientation have generated a rich set of themes and political concerns that have made her creative work essential for the exploration of identity, difference and social transformation in contemporary culture.

Winner of the Before Columbus Book Award for 1986, the groundbreaking *This Bridge Called My Back* (1983), edited with Gloria Anzaldúa, was Moraga's first published book. As in other efforts in which Moraga has collaborated, the book is an anthology (a collective rather than an individual endeavor) that brings together diverse texts (poems, short stories, personal narratives and essays) by nonwhite women. Subtitled *Writings by Radical Women of Color*, the book seeks to produce the spiritual and theoretical base for a different feminism through intense and sometimes painful dialogue. Considered a best-seller by independent press standards (there is also a Spanish-language edition published in 1988), this book's publication was made possible by, and coincided with, the increased need of women of color to open up forums that acknowledged and transformed homophobia, sexism and racism in the movements that had nurtured many of its contributors. These critiques produced the context for the articulation of a new subject position that was both interpellated and silenced within these movements (civil rights and feminism).

Articulating a discourse of simultaneous affinity and difference within a new imagined community of women of color, Moraga's image of "The Welder," a poem included in the collection, synthesizes the proposed new political project. The voices of Latina, Black, Asian and Native American women spoke from a similar space (since they were silenced and othered by hegemonic racist and sexist discourses), but were nevertheless also historically and culturally specific. The recognition of strategic affinity produced a narrative I that often slipped into a "we" (and vice versa), in an attempt to represent political solidarity aimed at social transformation in a common project. For Chicana critic Norma Alarcón (1990), it is precisely the redefinition of the knowing subject (the narrative I) that is one of the most important contributions of *This Bridge* to international feminism, although its token recognition has not transformed the hegemonic discourses of feminism still centered on an individualist conception of the subject.

Apart from her role as editor, Moraga has published several texts that share at least one basic premise, regardless of genre: the need for coalition among oppressed peoples, particularly women. At the center of her texts is a deep-felt desire to connect with women as political agents and to reconnect symbolically with significant women in her personal life, most notably her mother. An example of this is the poem "Half-Breed," in which gender identifications supersede those based exclusively on race. However, in Moraga's work, identification and the sometimes immobilizing recognition of difference go hand in hand. The multiple instances of separation among women (along class, race, sexual orientation, and familial axes), and the overcoming of the pain produced by these, are central to Moraga's narrative of social change, since dialogue must be used to assure that differences do not remain obstacles in coalition-building and communication.

In "La güera" (The Light-Skinned Woman), the narrative voice (self) critically explores the contradictions of being a light-skinned Chicana and the need to identify with a community of Chicano/as. As in many other texts by Moraga, writing becomes both a problematical and a privileged space for reconciliation with the mother and with culture. The essay begins with an epigraph by Emma Goldman that underlines the need to make the experiences of others part of "our" own experience, in order to eliminate the oppression of all. This epigraph condenses another of the central premises of Moraga's texts. Since identity is virtually impossible because difference can always be claimed on multiple grounds, it is crucial for both political and subjective gain that the oppressions of others be made part of our own by reading or inscribing our oppressions into those of others. By following the epigraph with the telling of her mother's story and her capacity for storytelling, the text attempts to narrow the gaps between the narrative voice (well educated) and the mother (illiterate) while still claiming a kinship.

The affinity desired by the text is based on Moraga's ability to identify with the mother's oppressions as a poor, brown and heterosexual woman through Moraga's simultaneous experiences of marginalization and empowerment as an educated, light-skinned lesbian. Given the relative privilege afforded to light-skinned, English-speaking and educated people in both American and Chicano societies, Moraga has repeatedly pointed out that it has been primarily through experiencing desire within homophobic social structures that she has been enabled to connect with others, including her own oppressed culture. Yet, in contrast with most identity-based politics, where hierarchies are strictly established to determine the allegedly most important struggles, Moraga points to the danger of ranking oppressions and the need to name the supposed enemies within. The ignoring of the effects of dominant ideologies on specific oppressed groups and the interpellation of all subjects to ideologies of racism, homophobia and sexism is for Moraga as dangerous as the structures themselves. With this double emphasis, she has helped to deconstruct the notion of people of color and women as victims, and has pointed to the complexities of constructing an inclusive discourse of social empowerment that takes the contradictions of the subject into account.

The second book on which Moraga collaborated was the anthology *Cuentos: Stories by Latinas* (1983), edited with Alma Gómez and Mariana Romo-Carmona. In the preface to this work, the editors point out the multiple contradictions embedded in the project of writing short stories in the context of the United States. As with African-American feminists, the oral storytelling tradition is invoked as the direct antecedent for women's ability and desire to write stories. However, the editors acknowledge that the need to write the stories stems from the diasporic nature of migrant cultures, where the storytellers are displaced and their importance diminished in the cultures of origin. In this sense, writing the stories (rather than telling them within community settings) transforms the stories significantly. One of the most important of these transformations is the mediation of the publishing industry, which makes the stories unavailable to significant sectors of the community they are assumed to interpellate. This gap emphasizes the multiple constructions and subjectivity positions always present (in both oral and literate social contexts) in all communities. Thus, the community articulated by Moraga, Romo and Gómez is symbolically nurtured by the mothers (as producers of unwritten stories), but is addressed to the daughters, who are likely to identify as feminists and are U.S.-born and literate. The proposed discourse also privileges women's experiences in opposition to the historically sexist representational practices of other groups with access to writing, mainly men, and defends literary discourse as a space for claiming identity and community rather than assimilation. However, the resistance to assimilation is already partially articulated from within, and the articulation of a position against this process must be read as strategic rather than descriptive of a sociocultural context to which the writers transparently belong.

Loving in the War Years: Lo que nunca pasó por sus labios (1983; the subtitle means "What Never Passed Her Lips"), Moraga's first individual book, is a combination of poetry, essays and short stories encompassing seven years of writing. The title, like the introduction, points to the cultural tensions that inform this book. Linguistically articulated and inscribed in the page, this text is about resistance and coming to voice and body with as few compromises as possible. The book's structure suggests a journey of empowerment for a specifically Chicana lesbian body/voice; the fundamental site of transformation is within, in the capacity to love one another and the reconciliation of subject to maternal culture through language. Although racial politics is still very much present in this book ("I wrote this book because we are losing ourselves to the gavacho" (iii; *gavacho* means honkie), there is a discursive emphasis on the subject's intimacy as the necessary base for any significant project of transformation. Love and desire, two supposedly intimate and individual feelings, become the driving force of any form of broad-based feminist and lesbian activism.

Moraga's deceptively simple proposal in *Loving in the War Years*—that Chicanas must learn to love each other—is in fact a call for fundamental transformations in Chicano culture. Loving themselves as Chicanas and one another as lesbians has been made difficult not by the limitations of specific subjects but by a culture in which male representations of women and male mediations of women's relationships (with the complicity of some women) have culminated in a deep-seated mistrust rather than solidarity among women. In this sense, women and lesbians are living during the war years when loving one another is an act of resistance.

One very understudied element in this book is the representation of the father, since it is in this text more than any other that identifications with the mother become further problematized through the father's representation. Moraga's articulation of desire (for other women and social change) is partially based on the difficult but central identification with the mother, even when the mother is a source of rejection, Anglo-ization and sexist ideologies. The father, absent in most cases, is described as queer, and this queerness refers to both race and femininity. What the narrative voice ultimately detests (apart from his whiteness) is not the father's masculinity but his "lack" of manhood; his potential homosexuality. The narrative voice—a female voice—thus articulates a desire to fill the position of the father as a real man in relation to the mother and, through her knowledge of female desire, to be able to satisfy the mother sexually.

This text is also key in the concatenation of texts in the book, since it produces the site for the putative origin of lesbian desire. In the following text in the book, a poem titled "La dulce culpa" (Sweet Guilt), the lyric voice rhetorically asks, "What kind of lover have you made me, mother?" Because of the father's inability to be a man, the daughter feels compelled to fill the void in a provocative shift of sexual imaginary. Unlike the male Mexican and Chicano texts that define the woman as a hole and absence, the representation of the father in the text is the absence that the daughter feels capable of filling and, at least textually, half fills. The daughter's text, since it acts out the desire, would reenact the

rejection of the daughter by the mother. It attempts to repair the damage produced by the father's lack of desire—an erotic proposal that can never materi-
alize—and marks the textual body of the daughter and the possibilities of sexual
pleasure.

Another text that further complicates the origin of lesbian desire as the filling
of the male position in regard to the mother is "The Slow Dance," a poignant
exploration of the fluidity of desire. In this short voyeuristic story, the narrator
constructs a space from which she acts out (but does not perform) conflicting
identifications with a butch/femme couple dancing. The text thus becomes the
site where desire is appeased but not fully experienced. The admiration of the
butch's control of the situation (Elena) results in an identification with her,
although the possibility of being seduced is not discarded. What determines the
direction of the subject's desire is ultimately the body of the mother in need of
seduction. Thus, the daughter learns how to hold and handle a woman, almost
in preparation to hold the first (and ultimately the only) object of her desire, the
mother. Yet as the images of the two women return, the narrative voice wishes
to dance with Elena, the woman in control, but she is unable to do so because
she is dancing with someone else. Feminized by her inability to provide for the
mother, the only desire possible is that of the voyeur, since the narrative voice
is used to not having her (culturally tabooed) desires fulfilled. The ambiguities
of this text suggest that the frustration of not having the mother simultaneously
produces a subject who wants to be the seducer (the position of the man) and
the seduced (through identification with the mother), in a continuous oscillation
where identity is always slipping.

While the early sections of the book concentrate on the foundation of lesbian
desire in relation to the incapacity of the father and the daughter's need to please
the mother, the middle sections contain several texts that problematize language
and race, as well as a set of poems that can be read allegorically as narratives
of community and connection. The texts relating to language are emblematic of
the contradictions embedded in reclaiming another desire through language. In
"It's the Poverty," the inhabiting of language is represented as a risk. To engage
with the symbolic entails dangers to the project of knitting a woman's community, since the access to and exercise of language entail the loss of the maternal body and the inscription of unbridgeable differences with the mother
culture. The specific mechanism through which this loss is effected is the appropriation of the master's words by the formerly subaltern voice.

A second poem that builds upon the perceived dangers in using language as
a strategy to heal, privileging the body as the space for transformation, is "You
Call It Amputation." This poem also questions the class bias inherent in assuming that writing (the symbolic) can bring back what has been lost or mutilated
by history (marked on the body). In an oppositional dialogue with Virginia
Woolf (one of the foremost representatives of an individually middle-class-
centered feminist discourse), Moraga effectively contests the assumption that
writing (and particularly literature) can make whole what the many manifesta-

tions of violence have inscribed in a body. This position does not mean, however, that language is unimportant in the difficult discursive political task of building a Chicana feminist community. However, language is always double-edged, due to its capacity to separate and frame the poetic voice away from the mother, culminating in the opposite aim of the feminism Moraga defends: the discursive bonding of all women.

The final essay in *Loving in the War Years*, "A Long Line of Vendidas" (the Spanish word, marked for the feminine, means sellouts), is a deconstruction of the myth of La Malinche, a frequent exercise by Chicana writers since the 1980s (La Malinche—or Doña Marina, as the Spanish renamed her—served as a translator for Cortés and was also his mistress). The essay intertwines cultural myth and personal biography on various levels, and is nurtured by, but seeks to destroy symbolically, the experiences that the narrator relates in most texts included in the book. One of the central elements of the essay is the cultural contradiction of the narrative voice, which identifies with the mother on the basis of their shared experience of gender oppression, but realizes the mother's role (in a metaphoric sense) in perpetuating a lack of solidarity among women. This contradiction leads the narrative voice to explore the origin of this disempowering practice among women that Moraga sees as stemming from Mexican mythology, to be played out in Mexican and Chicano families, including her own, to this day.

The identification of women with men's interests against each other's is rooted in the need to gain male approval and avoid the stigma placed on women by the dominant cultural discourse as unreliable and potential traitors. Moraga invites the reader to reframe the myth of La Malinche and to focus not on her relationship with Cortés, but on her relationship to her mother and the latter's decision to sell out her daughter. Although Moraga questions the original version of the story as told by the Spanish soldier Bernal Díaz de Castillo in his *Historia verdadera de la conquista de la nueva España* (True History of the Conquest of Mexico; 1568), she maintains that even if we were to accept the myth as truth, the mother's behavior is consistent with the Mexican cultural imperative whereby it is a wife's duty to put men first. Thus, the mother, and not the culture, is really a *vendida* for selling out her daughter, since she is doing what the culture dictates as appropriate behavior for women. However, as is made clear by the potential polysemy of the term *vendida*, coming from a long line of sellouts could be read at least in two ways: as being sold and as selling out other women. The long line of *vendidas* includes the mother who sells the daughter, the daughter who is sold and the community of women who are objects to be treated as tokens of exchange. At the same time, the *vendida* is categorized as a traitor through her sexuality if she is sexual with the white man she was sold to or with a woman who, by virtue of being a lesbian, is assumed to have been corrupted by allegedly foreign influences.

These sexual transgressions have in common the rejection of the Chicano/Mexican male's prerogative to control the sexuality of what he views as his women. Moraga thus proposes feminism and lesbianism as two necessary practices in the questioning of Malinche's myth and its underpinnings, yet she explicitly rejects lesbian separatism as a political alternative, since it does not take into account the need for women of color to participate in and transform the ethnic communities to which they belong. In more personal terms, this agenda means reconnecting to a broader, culturally affirming discourse; other women of color and feminists. This three-pronged strategy and set of needs are also represented in the last poem of the book, "Querida compañera" (Beloved [Female] Companion). This last poem is written mostly in domestic language (a sign of having arrived at a new definition of community), and it effectively uses the double meaning of *lengua* in Spanish—language and tongue—to represent the intertwined nature of speech and desire in articulating a political framework for lesbian feminists of color.

Giving up the Ghost (1986), Moraga's first play, is credited with breaking a twenty-year silence of Chicana lesbians in the history of Chicano theater (Yarbro-Bejarano, 1988). Various important motifs previously explored come to play in this text, including the love of the mother as the locus of desire and conflict. The title of the play seems also to encompass a typical feature of Moraga's work: polysemy. The ghosts in the play are multiple: patriarchy, internalized sexism, heterosexism, blurred gender identifications, multiple linguistic landscapes, cultural contradictions, anger and impossible desires. In a more literal sense, the ghost may refer both to Amalia's need to invoke her dead former male lover in order to be able to make love to Marisa and to Marisa's ghosts, along with her secrets and unresolved pain.

The strategy of including both a heterosexual and a lesbian, and further blurring the first's sexual identity through her intimacy with Marisa, reaffirms the project of finding common spaces in which women can communicate and heal. This insistence is reinforced in the text as it represents the lives of both women as constrained by the same structures. Corky's image of her own subjectivity and consequent social shaping of desires are mediated by popular movies, where the privileged position is occupied by male and culturally hegemonic characters that Corky seeks to emulate as a way of gaining representational empowerment. However, there is ambivalence in the treatment of these tensions. On the one hand, Corky seeks empowerment through male white identifications; on the other, she is interpellated by a female subjectivity that locates her disempowerment within her own body.

These tensions are not, however, clear-cut dichotomies, and the text seeks multiple ways of organizing them in order to open up spaces for lesbian desire and women's solidarities. However, the insistence on the materiality of the symbolic—womens' bodies as structured absences—is stressed in key sections of the play like Corky's rape story. The rape occurs in a Catholic school, and the rapist is a Mexican man who allegedly looks like her father. The rapist speaks Spanish, and Corky finds herself obeying him even when she knows that she will be violated. The reasons for acquiescing are painful: the fact that he is speaking Spanish commands a cultural passivity; the fact that he looks familiar suggests the universality of the law of the father. These various cultural discourses coalesce to prevent Corky from resisting. Once the rape is over, she shares with only one girl who does not support her. What is left is a sense of erasure in which her subjectivity lacks representability: her vagina and her cultural power are identical in their impossibility to signify. They are holes.

Writing, as well as building coalitions, is a function of desire in Moraga's texts. In *Giving up the Ghost*, Marisa is represented as a writer, and it is through writing that the pain can be addressed, since once it is shared, it becomes part of the social text and is not exclusively the subject's. Thus, two sites of empowerment are needed: the word and the body. Through writing, there is access to political subjectivity and power; through the body, to memories and pleasures. And in both cases, as suggested by the ambiguities of sexuality/gender and the necessary strategy of switching codes, the process of community-building is never free from tensions, nor is it a definitive utopia. It is a constant struggle to define spaces for dialogue and multiplying the possibilities of exchange for women's solidarities. In sum, as is suggested by the poem "La ofrenda" (The Offering; 1991), the intricate connections between writing, desire, reclaiming the body and reknitting the family coalesce in a new meaning: writing is an offering to the memory or the life of someone who could not write, but wrote on our bodies.

However, even when writing makes an experience available to multiple readers, this does not mean that it removes the pain of memory and text. The trust accorded to smell over writing or language is linked to the premise of the body as surface not to be seen (the sense of sight is deprivileged), but to be experienced in its pleasures and/or pains. As in *Giving up the Ghost*, there is great ambivalence concerning sexuality as the butch, Tiny, is seduced by Lola in what is, in effect, a silencing strategy. As Lola penetrates Tiny, she asks her not to speak and instead speaks for her. However, through the sexual exchange with a figurative sister, Lola can have access to a desire that does not oppress her, but gives her back a body alienated by male-centered notions of women's desires. The loss of Tiny to breast cancer can only partially be salvaged by the text, which functions as a material inscription for the narrator's desire/pain for a lost body.

Moraga speaks to the fluidities and contradictions of women's desires in political and intimate spaces with a courage that never allows for simple answers. The invocation of the mother's voice and body is ultimately a claim for roots and an affirmation of a women's culture of resistance that has been appropriated and mediated by the daughters, who, in the name of the mother, have created a context for an imaginary community of women bent on transforming the cultures that have insisted on silencing them.

WORKS

Cuentos: Stories by Latinas. New York: Kitchen Table Press, 1983. Ed. with Alma Gómez and Mariana Romo-Carmona.

Giving up the Ghost. Los Angeles: West End Press, 1986.
"Half Breed." In *Chicana Lesbians: The Girls Our Mothers Warned Us About*, 95. Ed. Carla Trujillo. Berkeley: Third Woman Press, 1991.
Loving in the War Years. Boston: South End Press, 1983.
"La ofrenda." In *Chicana Lesbians: The Girls Our Mothers Warned Us About*, 3–9.
This Bridge Called My Back: Writings by Radical Women of Color. New York: Kitchen Table Press, 1983. Ed. with Gloria Anzaldúa. Spanish version as *Esta [sic] puente, mi espalda: Voces de mujeres tercermundistas en los Estados Unidos.* Trans. Ana Castillo and Norma Alarcón. San Francisco: ISM Press, 1988. Ed. with Ana Castillo.

CRITICISM

Alarcón, Norma. "Interview with Cherríe Moraga." *Third Woman* 3 (1986): 127–134.
———. "Making Familia from Scratch: Split Subjectivities in the Work of Helena Viramontes and Cherríe Moraga." In *Chicana Creativity and Criticism: Charting New Frontiers in American Literature*, 147–159. Ed. Tey Diana Rebolledo. Houston: Arte Público Press, 1988.
———. "The Theoretical Subject(s) of *This Bridge Called My Back* and Anglo-American Feminism." In *Making Face, Making Soul: Haciendo Cara*, 356–369. Ed. Gloria Anzaldúa. San Francisco: Aunt Lute Foundation, 1990.
Estévez Sánchez, Martha. "Setting the Context: Gender, Ethnicity and Silences in Contemporary Chicana Poetry." In *Contemporary Chicano Poetry: A Critical Approach to an Emerging Literature*, 1–23. Ed. Martha Estévez Sánchez. Berkeley: University of California Press, 1985.
Herrera-Sobeck, María. "The Politics of Rape: Sexual Transgression in Chicana Fiction." In *Chicana Creativity and Criticism*, 177–181.
Quintanales, Mirtha N. "*Loving in the War Years*: An Interview with Cherríe Moraga." *Off Our Backs* 14.12 (Jan. 1985): 12–13.
Saldívar-Hull, Sonia. "Feminism on the Border: From Gender Politics to Geopolitics." In *Criticism in the Borderlands: Studies in Chicano Literature, Culture and Ideology*, 203–220. Ed. Héctor Calderón, and José David Saldívar. Durham, N.C.: Duke University Press, 1991.
Saporta Sternbach, Nancy. "A Deep Racial Memory of Love: The Chicana Feminism of Cherríe Moraga." In *Breaking Boundaries: Latina Writings and Critical Readings*, 48–61. Ed. Asunción Horno-Delgado, Eliana Ortega, Nina M. Scott and Nancy Saporta Sternbach. Amherst: University of Massachusetts Press, 1989.
Umpierre, Luz María. "With Cherríe Moraga." *Americas Review* 14 (1986): 54–67.
Yarbro-Bejarano, Yvonne. "Cherríe Moraga." In *Chicano Writers: First Series*. Ed. Francisco A. Lomelí and Carl Shirley. Detroit: Bruccoli Clark Layman/Gale Research.
———. "Cherríe Moraga's *Giving up the Ghost*: The Representation of Female Desire." *Third Woman* 3 (1986): 113–120.
———. "Chicana Literature from a Chicana Feminist Perspective." In *Chicana Creativity and Criticism*, 129–138.

Frances Negrón-Muntaner

MORO, CÉSAR (Peru; 1903–1956) _____

Moro, born in Lima, was a painter and poet who wrote primarily in French. His only book of poems in Spanish, *La tortuga ecuestre* (The Equestrian Turtle; 1957), was published posthumously. It became one of the emblematic texts of the latter generations of Spanish-Americans, representing the culmination of the strictly surrealist phase in Moro's creation. It remains one of the most beautiful works of passionate love written in any language. The poems illuminate the various dimensions of human love, *amour fou* (passionate love) and sublime love, all of which may be considered among the few things, along with poetry and freedom, that save man from despair.

There is no narration by the poetic I, nor is there any development of feelings in the poems. Instead, they reveal the torment and surprise that repeatedly produce a presence/absence of the subject/object of secret love and the endless metamorphosis that this entails. Even the least adept reader is able to ascertain that the "you" to whom the discourse is directed is undoubtedly masculine.

In 1925 Moro left Peru to live in Paris. He was an established artist, having produced paintings and sketches, but his driving ambition was to become a great ballet dancer. At the time, he had written very few poems. In 1926 and 1927, he participated in two expositions, one in Paris and the other in Brussels. Soon financial difficulties forced him to reduce his art activities and to give up his dreams of the ballet.

In 1929, Moro met the famous surrealists Paul Eluard and André Breton, and he became attracted to the surrealist movement, convinced that this was the only effort of the day attempted to bring human existence to its maximum level of incandescence. Soon thereafter, he began to write poetry at a frenzied pace. At the same time, he chose French as his poetic language, a choice to which he remained loyal even after he returned to South America, with the single exception of *La tortuga ecuestre*.

In its most prestigious period the Paris group generally condemned homosexuality, as well as onanism, copophagia, zoofilia and exhibitionism. Moro attended the gatherings presided over by Breton and participated in experimental sessions (which later served as the underpinnings of the periodical *Le Surréalisme au service de la revolution* [Surrealism in the Service of Revolution]), but he always maintained a reserved front, refusing to accept dogma or doctrines. During that time, Moro had many relationships with White Russians, who were numerous in the French capital; his great love during those years was a former cadet at the Czarist Academy of St. Petersburg named Lev (or León). Moro always kept his photo of Lev; even in his last house in Peru, Lev's photo was at the head of his bed, next to those of Antonio, the inspiration for *La tortuga encuestre*, as well as those of Antonio's son, Jorgito, and of his great friends from Paris and Mexico: Simon and Henry Janot, Xavier Villarrutia, Agustín Lazo, Remedios Varo, Alice Rahon, Wolfgang Paalen, Leonora Carrington.

Issue 5 of *Le Surréalisme au service de la révolution* (May 1933) includes a poem by Moro, *Renommée de l'amour* (The Fame of Love), dedicated to "the only love without pain without fortune without return." At the end of 1936, Moro gathered a collection of his French poems since 1930, with the idea of publishing them, but the project was never realized. In 1987, André Coyné edited a collection of Moro's poetry dating back to 1930 with the ironic title *A l'Occasion du nouvel an* (On the Occasion of the New Year), the irony being that the poems were published in March, and their contents offer nothing celebratory. These poems make evident the convolutions that love always produced in Moro, for whom love could quickly burst into hatred, changing in a moment and demonstrating a desire to destroy itself as something classifiable as abominable.

Among the poems written after *Renommée de l'amour* that were not included in *Ces Poèmes* (These Poems; 1987), a poem that begins "Guarde moi vite dans ton coeur" (Keep Me Alive in Your Heart) constitutes the only example of erotic poetry; it evokes the lover as the father, with his hairy chest, his quivering testicles, his legs like the columns of a church, his stream of sperm, rubbing one's eyes, rubbing one's body, and filling one's mouth.

Upon returning to Lima in 1934, Moro resolved to shake up his "sad and provincial" hometown by staging a series of happenings that would simultaneously express the two feelings that surrealism instilled in him: existential despair and hope. In 1935, the first Surrealist Exposition in South America embroiled Moro in a bitter debate with the Chilean poet Vicente Huidobro (who also wrote in French); his attacks on the latter's poetry earned him Huidobro's explicit homophobic scorn. In April or May of 1938 Moro, who had moved to Mexico, where he would live for ten years, met Antonio, a boy who was about to enroll in the Military College of Tacuba. At the end of May, Moro wrote the first verses of what became *La tortuga ecuestre*. Immediately he realized that his new love went beyond those he had previously experienced and that, in one way or another, this love was going to mark the rest of his life. He promptly abandoned French and began to write in Spanish. It took him until July 1939 to complete the book. Filled with gods and beasts, the poems find their unity in the intensity of a passion both carnal and cosmic, a passion that brings with it revelations and cataclysms.

In January 1939, Moro started a book of letters that did not get beyond the seventh letter, written in November. These letters, which were left unpublished when he died, help one to understand the stages of his passion, from its most fervent moment to the time it began slowly to dissipate. In 1940, Moro prepared an edition of *La tortuga ecuestre* for which a subscription notice was sent out. The edition ultimately failed, and the only thing that came of it were three poems published in 1944, in number 15 of *El hijo pródigo* (Prodigal Son), dedicated to A. A. M., Antonio's initials. *Lettre d'amour* (Love Letter), a long French poem published in December 1942, constitutes the conclusion of what may be termed the "Antonio cycle" in Moro's work. He and Antonio never broke off their relationship completely. They continued to exchange letters until mid-1955, but Antonio was no longer the star "that darkened the day and lit up the night."

Moro resumed writing poetry in French in 1940. Love continued to be the principal source of his inspiration, although his expression became increasingly baroque. His last book of poems, written after his return to Lima (1949–1950), is titled *Amour à mort* (Love Until Death, 1990).

When he turned away from surrealism, Moro began to read Marcel Proust, for whom he soon formed an unceasing admiration. He wrote two rather lengthy texts defending Proust against André Gide, whom he considered ingenuous and falsely objective. Moro never stopped emphasizing that it was impossible to deny Proust's homosexuality. What fascinated Moro in Proust's work was that everything was said, better than any work before or after it, without the appearance of proselytizing and without sacrificing the magic of dreams to the often implacable rigor of his analysis of passion.

WORKS

Amour à mort et autres poèmes. Ed. André Coyné. Paris, 1990.

Los anteojos de azufre. Ed. André Coyné. Lima, 1958.

Ces Poèmes . . . . Trans. A. Rojas. Madrid: A. Coyné, 1987.

Couleur de bas rêves tête de nègre. Lisbon: E. A. Westphalen, 1983.

Obra poética. Ed. Ricardo Silva Santisteban. Lima: Instituto Nacional de Cultura, 1980.

La tortuga ecuestre y otros poemas, 1924–1949. Ed. André Coyné. Lima: Ediciones Tigrondine, 1957. Also as *La tortuga ecuestre y otros textos.* Ed. Julio Ortega. Caracas: Monte Avila, 1976.

Vida de poeta. Lisbon: E. A. Westphalen, 1983.

CRITICISM

Coyné, André. *César Moro.* Lima: Torres Aguirre, 1956.

———. "Moro entre otros y en sus días." *Cuadernos hispanoamericanos* 448 (1987): 73–89.

———. "Moro una edición y varias discrepancias." *Hueso húmero* 10 (1981): 148–170.

———. "No en vano nacido, César Moro." *Eco* 243 (1982): 287–306.

Escobar, Alberto. "La escritura de Moro; César Moro, el pintor." In his *El imaginario nacional,* 26–36. Lima: Instituto de Estudios Peruanos, 1989.

Ferrari, Américo. "César Moro y la libertad de la palabra: Tres bosquejos." In his *Los sonidos del silencio: Poetas peruanos en el siglo XX,* 51–60. Lima: Mosca Azul, 1990.

Higgins, James. "César Moro." In his *The Poets in Peru: Alienation and the Quest for a Super-Reality,* 122–144. Liverpool: Francis Cairns, 1982.

Ortega, Julio. "César Moro." In his *Figuración de la persona,* 117–128. Barcelona: Edhasa, 1971.

Paoli, Roberto. "La lengua escandalosa de César Moro." In his *Estudios sobre literatura peruana contemporanea*, 131–138. Florence: Stampa Editoriale Parenti, 1985.

Sobrevilla, David. "Surrealismo, homosexualidad y poesía." In his *Avatares del surrealismo*, 167–188. Lima: Instituto Francés de Estudios Andinos, Pontificia Universidad Católica del Perú, 1992.

Westphalen, Emilio Adolfo. "Digresión sobre surrealismo y sobre César Moro entre los surrealistas." In *Avatares del surrealismo*, 203–216.

André Coyné

MUJICA LAINEZ, MANUEL (Argentina; 1910–1984)

On September 11, 1910, the year in which Argentina celebrated its centennial, Manuel Mujica Lainez was born in Buenos Aires. He was born into a society that was already beginning its decline, a factor that was later reflected in all of his literary production. Between 1923 and 1926, the entire family—Manuel Mujica Farías, Lucía Lainez Varela, and their two children, Manuel (Manucho) and Roberto (Buby), three years younger than his brother—lived in Europe. In Pairs, Mujica Lainez studied at the École Descartes and stayed for eight months in England. This trip to Europe greatly influenced him; the exposure to European culture at so young an age awakened in him a love of "la historia que no se aprende en los textos sino frente a los monumentos, a los palacios, en los museos" (history that can't be learned from books, but by visiting monuments, palaces, and museums; Carsuzán, 47). Upon his return to Argentina, Mujica Lainez finished high school and attended the University of Buenos Aires, where he studied law for two years.

In 1932, Mujica Lainez began working for the newspaper *La Nación* in Buenos Aires, where he remained until his retirement in 1969. His tenure at the prestigious Buenos Aires newspaper was instrumental in his formation as a writer. He recognized the impact of his career at *La Nación*, not only because of the discipline he developed as a journalist but also because *La Nación* afforded him the opportunity to meet some of the foremost intellectuals of his day, including Eduardo Mallea, Leopoldo Lugones, Leonidas de Vedia, Alvaro Melián Lafinur, Adolfo Mitre and Alberto Gerchunoff.

In 1936, Mujica Lainez published his first book, *Glosas castellanas* (Castilian Glosses), beginning a varied and distinguished career that produced approximately forty titles, including translations (Shakespeare, Molière, Racine, Dante, Longfellow) and personal correspondence. In addition, he supplied the text for a series of photography books. Over the course of his lifetime, Mujica Lainez wrote numerous articles, short stories and poems, some of which were never published; others were published separately in various print media, many unfortunately are now unavailable.

One of the most influential periods in Mujica Lainez's life was the years between 1937 and 1946, when he worked at the National Museum of Decorative Arts. His experiences there, along with his numerous trips abroad, had a profound influence on his aesthetic and cultural development. During this period Mujica Lainez developed what later became one of the marks of his works: a fascination with objects. He conceived of inanimate objects as having a secret "life" of their own, imperceptible to human beings.

Mujica Lainez received numerous prizes and distinctions during his lifetime, including the Premio de Honor (Prize of Honor) from the Sociedad Argentina de Escritores (SADE; Argentine Writer's Society), the Premio Nacional de Literatura (National Prize for Literature), and the Premio Kennedy (Kennedy Prize). In addition, he held numerous prestigious offices, including secretary and vice president of SADE. In 1956, he was named a member of the Academia Argentina de Letras (Argentine Academy of Letters) and the Melville Society. In 1959, he was elected to the Academia Argentina de Bellas Artes (Argentine Academy of Fine Arts). Mujica Lainez was honored by other countries as well. The French government named him an official of the Order of Arts and Letters in 1964 and awarded him the Cross of the Legion of Honor in 1982. His works also earned him the Italian title of Knight of the Order of Merit in 1967. On March 28, 1984, Mujica Lainez was named *ciudadano ilustre de Buenos Aires* (Illustrious Citizen of Buenos Aires). He accepted this award less than a month before his death in Córdoba (Argentina), on April 21.

Aquí vivieron (Here Is Where They Lived; 1949) and *Misteriosa Buenos Aires* (Mysterious Buenos Aires; 1950) stand out among Mujica Lainez's collections of short stories. In both works, he uses a technique common to many of his novels: allusion to real people and historical events. This contributes to the richness of the narrative by adding a dimension of verisimilitude. His novelistic production can be divided into two groups. The first set of novels has been called the "saga de la sociedad porteña" (saga of Buenos Aires society), a portrait of Buenos Aires from the end of the nineteenth century to the first half of the twentieth. Mujica Lainez based this series of works largely on the testimony of members of his own family who had experienced the opulence of an era now long gone. *La casa* (The House; 1954), *Invitados en El Paraíso* (Visitors in Paradise; 1957), *Los cisnes* (The Swans; 1977) and *El gran teatro* (The Great Theater; 1979) are among this group of works.

The novels of historical re-creation, notably those that might be called Mujica Lainez's major trilogy, form the second group. These consist of *Bomarzo* (1962), *El unicornio* (*The Wandering Unicorn*; 1965) and *El laberinto* (The Labyrinth; 1974), which take place in Renaissance Italy, medieval France, and baroque Spain, respectively. All of Mujica Lainez's works share a common theme: a strong preoccupation with beauty for its own sake. This idea traces its roots to the widely held nineteenth-century concept of art for art's sake. His novels strongly advocate the idea that authentic and lasting beauty cannot be derived from the present time, the here and now, but must be attributed to "the more fascinating past," as affirmed by the talking house, Mujica Lainez's voice in the novel *La casa*.

Mujica Lainez's work is characterized by an elegance of style and a scrupulous attention to language. Its most recurrent themes include the idealization of the past, the existence of art for its own sake, the importance of objects and the re-creation of a decadent, vanished aristocracy. Other frequent topics include the search for an unattainable love relationship, one through which a human being might achieve salvation; the desire for immortality; and the presence of incorporeal beings, whose voices join with those of objects, which are inanimate only in appearance. Unfortunately, to date Mujica Lainez's works have not received the recognition they deserve, in spite of their being some of the most original writings in contemporary Latin American fiction.

Referring to his novel *Sergio* (1976), Mujica Lainez declared, "Por primera vez me atreví a contar más abiertamente una historia homosexual" (For the first time I have dared to openly tell a story about homosexuals; Vázquez 118). It may amaze modern readers that Mujica Lainez did not "openly" deal with the theme of homosexuality until he was sixty-six years old; however, in the context of the times, such a reticence is not surprising. He belonged to a society that was traditionally machista; in addition, in the circles in which he moved—the intellectual world of the upper middle class in Buenos Aires—the theme of homosexuality was treated through allusion or euphemism, or else completely ignored. Any other attitude toward this subject would have been considered either unacceptably daring or an indication of extremely bad taste. This sociohistorical context makes clear why Mujica Lainez carefully avoided expressing any opinions about homosexuality: it is treated, along with the notion of prostitution, as an ancient phenomenon, almost as old as the human race itself. While the lack of overt support for, or appreciation of, homosexuality is noteworthy, so is the fact that Mujica Lainez never treats it negatively. This is not at all surprising, because in spite of the writer's discretion, he openly acknowledged his own homosexuality and provided clear indications regarding his sexual preference in *Cecil*, an autobiographical novel published in 1972. That Mujica Lainez goes no further than simply depicting homosexuality should not be minimized, however. Indeed, in comparison with the attitudes of his contemporaries (Roberto Arlt, for example), it is clear that he takes a much more positive stance in his writings than his colleagues, even though in his works he never goes so far as to openly defend a homosexual lifestyle.

Homosexuals, masculine as well as feminine, appear even in his early writings. Among the secondary characters are Lord Gerald Dunstanville and Sir Clarence Trelawny, both from the story "Memorias de Pablo y Virginia" (Memories of Pablo and Virginia, in *Misteriosa Buenos Aires*). Homosexuals also figure in *Crónicas reales* (Royal Chronicles; 1967), *El viaje de los siete demonios* (The Journey of the Seven Demons; 1974) and the stories of the collection *Un novelista en el museo del Prado* (A Novelist in the Prado Museum; 1984).

Major homosexual characters in Mujica Lainez's prose include figures in two stories from *Aquí vivieron*: Miguel, secretly in love with his cousin Ignacio, in "El cofre" (The Coffer); and Francisco Montalvo and Teresa Rey, a married couple who are profoundly affected by a visit from the mysterious and sexually ambiguous Mrs. Foster in "La viajera" (The Traveler). Other homosexual figures are Juan Cordero, a disciple of Felipe Arias de Mansilla in "Las ropas del maestro" (The Teacher's Clothes), and Ofelia, the housekeeper in "El salón dorado" (The Golden Parlor), from *Misteriosa Buenos Aires*. There is also a hidden dimension of homoeroticism between Gustavo and the narrator in *Los ídolos* (The Idols; 1953), and between Ginés de Silva and Gerineldo de Rivera in *El laberinto*. In *La casa*, the homosexual characters increase in number: Tristán and Francis, two youths who died as adolescents and whom the author seems to have immortalized in their ephebic splendor; Paco, the extravagant uncle who is depicted briefly in a tumultuous scene with his valet, Hans; Francis's nanny; and Zulema, the maid—the two women openly portrayed as lesbians. Other figures who appear in *Invitados en El Paraíso, Bomarzo, Los cisnes, El gran teatro* and *El escarabajo* (The Scarab; 1982) complete the list. In spite of the presence of homosexuals in these works, the theme of homosexuality is more explicitly treated in *El unicornio, Sergio* and *El retrato amarillo* (The Yellow Portrait; 1956).

El unicornio, narrated in the first person by Melusina, one of the immortal Fates, uses the theme of sex change to imbue the story with clear homosexual connotations. She asks her mother, also one of the Fates, to give her "a young, beautiful body" (155). The protagonist could never have imagined that her mother's vengeance would have led the older woman to transform her daughter into a handsome youth, doomed to live consumed by a secret love. A gallery of ambiguous situations and figures marks the narrative: the carriage of the supposed ten bridesmaids (in reality, young men disguised as women); Aiol's sister, Azelaís, who is disturbingly androgynous; Aymé, the lord of Castel-Rousillon, passionately in love with Aiol; and Onfroi IV, the king of Torón, with his court of pages and eunuchs. In *Sergio*, Mujica Lainez uses the protagonist's attraction to the siblings Juan and Soledad Malthus to justify the inclusion of the homosexual theme. Sergio first becomes aware of the pair by looking at their photographs; later he meets them. At the beginning of the narration, Sergio cannot admit to himself that Juan interests him; however, the love between the two youths ultimately triumphs at the bloody conclusion of the work, which reflects the turbulent climate of Argentina in the second half of the 1970s.

It is important to realize that the evasive techniques employed by Mujica Lainez (the idea of sex change or the "confusion" that Sergio feels when looking at the photographs of Juan and Soledad Malthus) represent two opposing perspectives. On the one hand, such an indirect treatment of the theme can be viewed as a concession to the strict conventions of the times. On the other hand, it represents a strategy intentionally employed by the author, cognizant that the only way to treat this theme was to minimize its visibility. Mujica Lainez opted for the use of allegory, thus permitting another reading of the text; this alternative reading draws its strength from what is not said. A similar process of allegorization is apparent in *El retrato amarillo*, a little-known work that has a particularly interesting background. At the beginning of the 1950s, Mujica Lainez conceived an idea for a novel that would take place in El Tigre, a resort area in the province of Buenos Aires. He was enthusiastic about the work; however, after talking with his wife about the project and showing her his manuscript in progress, she advised him to abandon it. Her objections were based on its controversial theme, a posture hardly surprising in view of the times. Thus, *El retrato amarillo* was not published until 1956, in the third issue (September–October) of the now defunct magazine *Ficción*, and was not republished until 1987, when it was printed privately by the Amigos de Mujica Lainez (Friends of Mujica Lainez).

Although originally planned as a novel, *El retrato amarillo*, because of its length, is really a novella. The protagonist is Miguel, a young man on the verge of adolescence who lives with his widowed mother. In their home, the memory of the boy's deceased father seems to take on a tangible presence. Mujica Lainez creates a dichotomy between the ghostly paternal figure and the boy's hopeless attempts to remember him clearly. For reasons Miguel is never able to discern, a well-hidden secret surrounds his father, complicating the youth's attempts to explore the deceased's memory. Even the mention of his father seems to reopen the family's wounds, causing Miguel's relatives suddenly to become reticent. The key to the mystery is an old photograph that gives the novel its title, a portrait of Miguel's father and his close friend, Max van Arenbergh. Although not expressly stated in the text, it is hinted that the secret involves a homosexual relationship between the two men. Simultaneously portrayed as a protagonist and a victim, Miguel's character is one of the most successful aspects of the work: his internal conflicts, his extreme sensibility, and his acute loneliness make him a kindred spirit of other Mujica Lainez figures, especially the tormented Francis of *La casa*.

A literary work often acts as a mirror in which the author's personal experiences are reflected; this is particularly true of homosexual authors, as can be seen in the works of Marcel Proust, André Gide, Arthur Rimbaud, Paul Verlaine, Oscar Wilde, Walt Whitman, James Baldwin, Truman Capote, Yukio Mishima, Luis Cernuda, Federico García Lorca, Manuel Puig and Abelardo Arias. Mujica Lainez is no exception, and it is therefore possible to find significant indications of his homosexuality in his fiction. *El retrato amarillo* provides the reader with convincing evidence of the unmistakable importance of the ghostly father as a pivotal influence on the novel's development. In addition, while there is ample documentation regarding the impact of the author's mother and three maiden aunts on his maturation, little has been said about his father, who died in 1939.

The older man's role and the part he played in the formation of the writer's personality can be viewed as one of example by absence. Manuel Mujica Farías was a typical socialite who, in the early years of the century, paid as much attention to his social obligations as to his professional responsibilities, and he did not hesitate to leave the upbringing of his children to his wife. It is thus inevitable that Mujica Lainez's father would be reflected in several characters— for example, Duke Pier Francesco Orsini's father in *Bomarzo* and the deceased senator whose memory is evoked by his widow, Clara, in *La casa*. However, it is only in *El retrato amarillo* that the paternal character takes on true importance, for the first and only time in Mujica Lainez's work, as Miguel struggles to recover his father's image in a pathetic attempt to affirm his own identity. The work is unfinished; it is therefore impossible to predict how Miguel's personality would have evolved. However, it is not unreasonable to assume that Mujica Lainez's upbringing in an almost exclusively female environment had a decisive influence on the development of the writer's homosexuality.

There are still other autobiographical indications in Mujica Lainez's fiction that are relevant to this discussion. During their stay in London, Manuel and his brother Roberto had a private tutor, John Light. Years later, the writer alluded to his relationship with Light as one in which he had learned "muchas cosas malas de él" (many bad things from him), while admitting that there had also been "cosas buenas" (good things; Vázquez, 22). It appears that the sexual initiation of the adolescent Mujica Lainez was one of those "bad things" (Villordo, 1991, 61). In light of the above comments, the following sentences referring to Tony, one of the characters in *Invitados en El Paraíso*, has an autobiographical subtext: "En París descubrió un mundo: los museos, el teatro, el ballet. Descubrió que tenía gusto; que discernía los objetos hermosos y extraños. *Se descubrió a sí mismo. Tuvo por primera vez atisbos más claros de lo que se escondía en su interior, en lo más secreto*" (In Paris, he discovered a new world: the museums, the theaters, the ballet. He discovered that he had good taste; that he could discern strange and beautiful objects. *He discovered himself. For the first time he had clearer insight into what he was keeping inside himself, in the most secret core of his being* [106; emphasis added]). Within this context, it is most suggestive that one of the characters who tries to seduce Sergio in the novel of the same name, is an Englishman named Jerome Light.

Without being overly crude or explicit, homosexuality is a constant theme in Mujica Lainez's narration. His works are marked by a notable preponderance of male characters over female protagonists; these figures find themselves in a variety of intriguing situations. Some are extremely conflictive (*El retrato amarillo*, *La casa*, *Sergio*, *El unicornio*); others are less so, due to their implicit ironic tone (*Crónicas reales*, *El viaje de los siete demonios*, *Los cisnes*). Yet, regardless of the particular characteristics of each work, all of Mujica Lainez's fiction is indelibly marked by the profound comprehension of one who speaks sincerely from personal experience.

WORKS

Aquí vivieron: Historias de una quinta de San Isidro: 1583–1924. Buenos Aires: Editorial Sudamericana, 1949.

Bomarzo. Buenos Aires: Editorial Sudamericana, 1962. English trans. Gregory Rabassa. New York: Simon and Schuster, 1969.

Bomarzo, cantata. Verona, Italy: Plain Wrapper Press, 1981. Bilingual ed.

Bomarzo, opera. New York: Boosey and Hawkes, 1967. Bilingual ed.

El brazalete y otros cuentos. Buenos Aires: Editorial Sudamericana, 1978.

Canto a Buenos Aires. Buenos Aires: Editorial Guillermo Kraft, 1943.

La casa. Buenos Aires: Editorial Sudamericana, 1954.

Cecil. Buenos Aires: Editorial Sudamericana, 1972.

Los cisnes. Buenos Aires: Editorial Sudamericana, 1977.

Crónicas reales. Buenos Aires: Editorial Sudamericana, 1967.

Cuentos inéditos. Buenos Aires: Planeta, 1993.

De milagros y de melancolías. Buenos Aires: Editorial Sudamericana, 1968.

Don Galaz de Buenos Aires. Buenos Aires: Francisco Colombo, 1938.

El escarabajo. Barcelona: Plaza y Janés, 1982.

Estampas de Buenos Aires. Buenos Aires: Editorial Sudamericana, 1946.

Glosas castellanas. Buenos Aires: Librería y Editorial "La Facultad," 1936.

El gran teatro. Buenos Aires: Editorial Sudamericana, 1979.

Los ídolos. Buenos Aires: Editorial Sudamericana, 1953.

Invitados en El Paraíso. Buenos Aires: Editorial Sudamericana, 1957.

El laberinto. Buenos Aires: Editorial Sudamericana, 1974.

Miguel Cané (padre): Un romántico porteño. Buenos Aires: C.E.P.A., 1942.

Misteriosa Buenos Aires. Buenos Aires: Editorial Sudamericana, 1950.

Un novelista en el museo del Prado. Buenos Aires: Editorial Sudamericana, 1984. Barcelona: Seix Barral, 1984.

Páginas de Manuel Mujica Lainez seleccionadas por el autor. Buenos Aires: Editorial Celtia, 1982.

Placeres y fatigas de los viajes: Crónicas andariegas, 2 vols. Buenos Aires: Editorial Sudamericana, 1983–1984.

Los porteños. Buenos Aires: Ediciones Librería "La Ciudad," 1979.

El retrato amarillo. Buenos Aires: Amigos de Mujica Lainez, 1987. Orig. *Ficción* 3 (Sept.–Oct. 1956): 11–62.

Sergio. Buenos Aires: Editorial Sudamericana, 1976.

El unicornio. Buenos Aires: Editorial Sudamericana, 1965. Trans. by Mary Filton as *The Wandering Unicorn.* New York: Taplinger, 1983.

El viaje de los siete demonios. Buenos Aires: Editorial Sudamericana, 1974.

Los viajeros. Buenos Aires: Editorial Sudamericana, 1955.

Vida de Anastasio el Pollo (Estanislao del Campo). Buenos Aires: Emecé Editores, 1948.

Vida de Aniceto el Gallo (Hilario Ascasubi). Buenos Aires: Emecé Editores, 1943.

In 1978, Editorial Sudamericana began publishing the complete works of Mujica Lainez. At the present time (1993), five volumes have appeared. The last volume, which consists of Mujica Lainez's work up to and including *Invitados en el Paraíso*, appeared in 1983.

CRITICISM

Carsuzán, María Emma. "Estudio preliminar." In Manuel Mujica Lainez, *Manuel Mujica Laniez*, 7–56. Buenos Aires: Ediciones Culturales Argentinas, 1962.

Castellanos, Carmelina de. *Tres nombres en la novela argentina*, 14–24. Santa Fe, Argentina: Ediciones Colmegna, 1967.

Craig, Herbert. "Proust y Mujica Lainez: La memoria asociativa." *Cuadernos hispanoamericanos* 409 (July 1984): 101–106.

Cruz, Jorge. *Genio y figura de Manuel Mujica Lainez*. Buenos Aires: Eudeba, 1978.

Font, Eduardo. *Realidad y fantasía en la narrativa de Manuel Mujica Lainez (1949–1962)*. Madrid: Ediciones José Porrúa Turanzas, 1976.

Ghiano, Juan Carlos. "Mujica Lainez, cuentista de Buenos Aires." In Manuel Mujica Lainez, *Cuentos de Buenos Aires (antología)*. 4th ed. Buenos Aires: Huemul, 1978.

Matamoro, Blas. "El crepúsculo de los señores." In his *Oligarquía y literatura*, 273–302. Buenos Aires: Ediciones del Sol, 1975.

Piña, Cristina. "Los indicadores ideológicos en la obra de Manuel Mujica Lainez." *Revista de literaturas modernas*, annex 5 (1989): 81–92.

Ruiz, Díaz, Adolfo. "Para una lectura de Manuel Mujica Lainez." *Academia* 15 (1987), 249–264.

Schanzer, George O. "De la gloria de don Ramiro al desengaño de don Ginés." In *Romance Literary Studies: Homage to Harvey L. Johnson*, 133–140. Ed. Marie A. Wellington and Martha O'Nan. Potomac, Md.: José Porrúa Turanzas, 1979.

———. "Mujica Lainez, cronista anacrónico." In *Actas del Sexto Congreso internacional de hispanistas*, 677–680. Toronto: Department of Spanish and Portuguese, University of Toronto, 1980.

———. *The Persistence of Human Passions: Manuel Mujica Lainez's Satirical Neo-Modernism*. London: Tamesis Books, 1986.

Sorkunde Vidal, Frances. *La narrativa de Mujica Lainez*. Bilbao, Spain: Servicio Editorial, Universidad del País Vasco, 1986.

Sur 358–359 (1986): entire issue.

Tacconi de Gómez, María del Carmen. *Mito y símbolo en la narrativa de Manuel Mujica Lainez*. Tucumán, Argentina: Universidad Nacional de Tucumán, 1989.

Vázquez, María Esther. *El mundo de Manuel Mujica Lainez*. Buenos Aires: Editorial de Belgrano, 1983.

Villena, Luis Antonio de. "El país Mujica Lainez." In Manuel Mujica Lainez, *Antología general e introducción a la obra de Manuel Mujica Lainez*, 9–33. Madrid: Ediciones Felmar, 1976.

Villordo, Oscar Hermes. "Estudio preliminar." In Mujica Lainez, *Páginas de Manuel Mujica Lainez seleccionadas por el autor*, 11–36.

———. *Manucho: Una vida de Mujica Lainez*. Buenos Aires: Planeta, 1991.

———. "Nuevo estudio preliminar." In Manuel Mujica Lainez, *Cuentos de Buenos Aires (antología)*, 5–37. 7th ed. Buenos Aires: Huemul, 1984.

Ángel Puente Guerra

MUÑOZ, MIGUEL ELÍAS (Cuba; 1954) _____

Muñoz was born in Ciego de Avila (Camagüey) to a family of peasants and merchants. Early in the 1960s, his father made plans to emigrate to the United States, but political reasons delayed the departure until 1968, when thirteen-year-old Miguel and his younger brother, Jorge, were permitted to leave for Madrid, separate from their parents, who had permission to emigrate to the United States. They were taken in by their father's cousin until their parents could complete the necessary paperwork for their sons to join them. The family had settled in Gardena, a suburb of Los Angeles, because relatives lived there. In the fall of 1969, Miguel enrolled in Leuzinger High School. He later completed his B.A. in Spanish at California State University, Dominguez Hills. On graduation, Muñoz received a Del Amo Foundation scholarship to study in Madrid at the Universidad Complutense. He then returned to graduate studies at the University of California, Irvine, site of the many adventures of "Landi" in *Los viajes de Orlando Cachumbambe* (Orlando Cachumbambe's Adventures; 1984). After receiving his doctorate in Spanish, Muñoz became an assistant professor of Latin American literature at Wichita State University in Kansas. Although he loved teaching, he returned to California and full-time writing. Sexuality in literature—gender roles and gender identity—is a concern in his works; Muñoz writes texts that denounce and attack those traditional structures.

In *Los viajes*, stereotypical patterns of the Hispanic male are noted when high school students join a volunteer brigade of cane workers in Cuba. A sick student is described as suffering from acute laziness and chronic queerness. There are the rumors that circulate among the group about a homosexual who lets himself be "done" by other members of the group. And there is a description of the shame the protagonist feels when faced with his own nudity and that of fifty other boys. This novel reveals little atypical of the traditional biographic heterosexual format.

In contrast, Muñoz's second novel, *Crazy Love* (1989), reflects the sexual exploration of a bisexual U.S. Cuban rock musician in Los Angeles whose crossover dreams traverse borders of ethnicity, sexual identity and family values. In English and using a variety of literary forms—letters from his youngest sister, interior monologue and traditional narrative—Muñoz profiles the rise of Nito (Julianito) as a rock musician from a garage band to a crossover group with an Anglo lead singer and writer, Erica, who becomes his lover.

Julian's sexual education begins in Cuba with initiation/rape by the neighbor's children and Catholic images of hell associated with sexuality. His father exhibits macho behavior with demonstrative displays of his erection and constant questions about his son's genitals. Masturbation leads to faggotry, according to popular statements; hormone shots are contemplated to cure Julian's artistic tendencies. Julian's sexual education includes seduction by the village priest and forced sexual servicing of a male cousin, who discovers Julian engaged in sexual exploration with his sister.

When Julian arrives at college and forms his rock group, he and another musician, Lucho, become lovers, much to the disgust of another group member, Joe. Julian later seduces Amanda, a Salvadoran refugee, and spends a year in Spain denying her existence. The casting couch and a handsome male agent, Lee, who successfully produces his first commercial record, attract Julian. Sexual exploration continues to be detailed in such incidents as a three-way with a "groupie." The U.S. Cuban family is concerned about the loss of its son to the American dream; his loss is freedom in the United States from the Cuban ethos. "Step 3," the third part of the novel, reflects the international rock scene and transitions: Julian, the pretty boy posing on the Spanish steps, constant group arguments, a love triangle—Julian, Lucho, and their manager (parallel with the Beatles and Brian Epstein)—the Cuban slang of sexual double entendres (*choteo*), rock figures like Tina Turner and Boy George.

Contentiousness results in the final crossover—or is it a final prostitution? Julian shares a house with his grandmother, a bed with Erica, and the musical world with a new group, Erica and the LA Scene. Top booking has been lost. He is faced with the crisis of authenticity while he identifies with Aureliano Buendía of Gabriel García Márquez's *One Hundred Years of Solitude*: life, girlfriend, and musical choice to be made in this exploration of sexuality and ethnicity.

In 1989, Muñoz published two collections of poetry, *No fue posible el sol* (The Sun Was Not Possible) and *En estas tierras/In This Land*. Muñoz has stated that he can write poetry only in Spanish; the translations in the latter are by Miguel Gallegos and Karen Christian. Of the four parts of *En estas tierras*, only "Estados alterados/Altered States" is relevant here. In the often coded use of the second-person-singular pronoun *tú* without further delineation, the love object can be the same or the opposite sex. "Entre comillas" (Between Quotation Marks) uses the vocabulary of concealment and the gay/lesbian world to carry its message. "Beauty Queen" is a similar way to describe "las caderas y *el bulto* en la pista de luces" (hips and basket [male crotch] on the lighted dance floor), while "S and M" uses sexual power to describe racial tensions between Puerto Ricans and Jews. "Black Dandy" through physicality, perfumes and sensuality portrays a gay queen in California. The poems "Promesas de San Valentín" (Valentine Promises) and "Creyente renegado" (Renegade Believer) use the pronoun *tú* in an ambiguous manner with wordplay focusing on *rey* (king) and *reina* (queen) in the former. In general, *En estas tierras/In This Land* reveals the opening to same-sex love relationships while focusing on exile, adaptation and reflection on the diverse elements of U.S. society.

No fue posible el sol is a collection of poems written in Spanish that is divided into two sections, "Raro espejismo" (Unusual Mirror Image) and "Los vaticinios" (Forecasts). In the former is a series of poems that, seen in their totality, appear to define a gay relationship. Once again the lover, *tú*, is not gender-identified. However, in "Una época más" (One More Time) the verse "Cuestiono haberme inventado otra familia (sin niños)" (I wonder about having invented another family [without children]) seems to represent a same-sex relationship. In a similar way, in "Te busco en México" (I'll Look for You in Mexico), the key line seems to be the millions of "At your services" men receive. "Él no es él" (He Is Not He) deals with illness and death and could possibly represent AIDS, a theme that appeared two years later in Muñoz's novel *The Greatest Performance* (1991). The poems "Tus pesadillas" (Your Nightmares) and "En tu cuarto" (In Your Bedroom) once again use the intimate *tú* without specifying gender, but dealing with friendship, identity and authenticity.

In general, the second part of the collection, "Los vaticinios" describes other aspects of U.S. culture, from Disney World and The Gallery in Los Angeles to news items and Oliver North. "Jugarretas" (Games) includes a gay couple, Peter and Carlos. But self-referencing the text seems clearest in the last poem "Faltaba" (All I Needed), in which Muñoz presents as his general worldview "Faltaba decir, honestamente, lo que he dicho" (All I needed was to say, honestly, what I have said), the repeated rhetorical question of authenticity.

The Greatest Performance, in alternate chapters related by the two protagonists, narrates the coming of age of Rosita, a lesbian, and Mario, a gay man who dies of AIDS; their island experience; exile in Madrid and California; family values; and emergent individuality. The novel is noteworthy in its direct treatment of gay and lesbian sexuality and life-styles.

Mario's early experiences in Cuba reflect the early awakenings of the macho and the *mariposa* (butterfly, a Spanish metaphor equivalent to fairy) and Rosa's intense female friendships of early childhood. Mario's father recognizes his son's orientation, rejects him and attempts to beat him into being straight. Rosita experiences the sexual advances of the uncle to whose protection she and her brother are entrusted in Madrid. Both characters allow themselves self-definition in California. Dialogue, monologue directed toward the reader, feverous dreams and sexual encounters are interwoven until the last chapter, when Mario and Rosita are joined together: "After searching Heaven and Earth for a true love, for a generous homeland, for a family who wouldn't abuse or condemn us, for a body who wouldn't betray our truest secrets, we found each other: a refuge, a song, a story to share" (149).

The work of Muñoz demonstrates the linguistic and ideological evolution of thematic content, from the political to the intimate, from Chicano power and Hispanic racism, to AIDS and homosexuality, gay and lesbian. His first novel, written in Spanish, approaches differentness; *The Greatest Performance* encapsulates it. The three novels move from assured heterosexuality to bisexuality to homosexuality, as they go from Spanish to English. Muñoz's poetry, written in Spanish, includes gay content as a portrait of a relationship, a social environment and love poems. Neither his thematic content nor his foci are unidimensional.

In his work Muñoz represents the evolving writer, both linguistically and thematically, in both prose and poetry. As a U.S. Cuban, raised in California, he has observed societal changes, the sexual revolution and AIDS, and he is an important voice in multicultural Hispanic literature of the United States.

WORKS

Crazy Love. Houston: Arte Público Press, 1989.
En estas tierras/In This Land. Tempe, Ariz.: Bilingual Press/Editorial Bilingüe, 1989.
The Greatest Performance. Houston: Arte Público Press, 1991.
Los viajes de Orlando Cachumbambe. Miami: Editorial Universal, 1984.
No fue posible el sol. Madrid: Editorial Betanía, 1989.

CRITICISM

Bracho, Richard. "Neither Here nor There." *Bay Area Reporter*, Aug. 15, 1991, pp. 29, 40.
Filbin, Thomas. Review of *The Greatest Performance. Contemporary Fiction* 12.1 (Spring 1992): 135–136.
McLellan, Dennis. "Latinos Have a Story to Tell." *Los Angeles Times*, Dec. 27, 1991, pp. E1, E3.
Rivero, Eliana. "(Re) Writing Sugarcane Memories: Cuban Americas and Literature: *Paradise Lost or Gained?*" In *The Literature of Hispanic Exile*, 164–182. Ed. Fernando Alegría and Jorge Ruffinelli. Houston: Arte Público Press, 1990.
Vásquez, Mary Seale. "Family, Generation and Gender in Two Novels of Cuban Exile: Into the Mainstream." *Bilingual Review/Revista Bilingüe* (forthcoming).
Velez, Lydia. "Separación y búsqueda como opción social en las novelas de Elías Miguel Muñoz." *The Americas Review* 18.1 (Spring 1990): 86–91.

John C. Miller

N

NÁJERA, FRANCISCO (Guatemala; 1945)

Considered one of the most distinguished poets of contemporary Guatemala, Nájera has published twelve books in verse as well as poetic prose. *El sueño de Dios* (The Dream of God; 1987) won second place in the short narrative category at the 1987 Certamen Permanente Centroamericano en Guatemala (Permanent Central American Contest in Guatemala). In addition, *sujeto de la letra a* (subject to the letter a; 1991) was awarded second place at the Concurso de Poesía 1990 (1990 Poetry Contest) sponsored by the Institute of Latin American Writers of New York.

Homoeroticism is articulated in diverse ways throughout Nájera's work. Besides poems or narratives in which the poetic voice, self-defined as masculine, expresses an erotic relationship with another man, there are those in a voice that does not identify its gender and that, generally, uses the third person to describe erotic relationships between women as well as between couples and a third person. In the first category are the poem "Con la libertad del amor" (With the Liberty of Love; 1987) and two poems from *Los cómplices* (The Accomplices; 1988), "Incomprensible como su pecho o tu espalda" (Incomprehensible Like His Chest or Your Back) and "Las tres monedas del marinero" (The Sailor's Three Coins). All the poems from the book *Canto de María* (Song of Mary; 1989) belong to the second category. Homoerotic allusions can also be found in the remainder of Nájera's works, but these mainly chronicle heterosexual relationships.

Georges Bataille's ideas on eroticism serve to formulate a discourse on homoerotic as well as heterosexual writings that explains why expressions of homoeroticism have been based on heterosexual models. In Nájera's work we see this interchangeability in the notion that the erotic object is a body independent from its gender. As a result, his works present few glimpses of the characters' faces, while providing explicit details of their bodies.

Bataille's ideas, as well as those of other French theorists like Roland Barthes and Jacques Lacan, are used to develop a sort of poetic in *Servidumbre de lo carnal* (Servitude of the Carnal; 1986). Dante Liano has said of this book, "The sustained tone of the composition, the original quality of the images, the knowledge of rhythm, the freshness of expression . . . make us suspect a very special literary talent" (57). One of the most interesting aspects of *Servidumbre* is the suggestion of a very close relationship between writing and eroticism. In the same manner in which, as Bataille states, there occurs an exaltation of life in eroticism that approximates the limits of death, a search for the dissolution of the I to achieve the continuity of the self, so writing originates within the same exalted state and through the discontinuous fusion attempts to achieve a continuity in which one is flung toward ectasy and death: "It is this void—so furiously wished for by whoever may have written the text—which drives us to such a frantic state, to such inconceivable violence, that only the annulment of all limits—of consciousness itself—can satisfy the writer" (*Servidumbre de lo carnal*, 4).

The erotic relationship that seeks the dissolution of the I and the discontinuance of time and space in order thus to abolish the limits that separate lovers, is the theme in the series of poems that constitute the section "Con la libertad del amor," from the book of the same title, which narrates one night of love between a man and an adolescent. In lines written in an intimate tone not found in the rest of Nájera's poetry, the poetic subject openly describes the sexual encounter and declares his love for the youth. This poem demonstrates one characteristic of Nájera's work: what is culturally defined as masculine or feminine is not deconstructed, and distinctions between the sexes are maintained. In this way, in the works that describe the relationship between two men, there is no feminization; rather, both members of the couple are represented following masculine models. This also indicates that a heterosexual perspective is not adopted in order to present the relationship. What does exist is the intention to assign privilege to one of the two, a possible reflection of Bataille's influence. In "Con la libertad del amor," the man (who tells the story in the first person) plays the dominant role in the erotic relationship (as in Bataille's theory), and the possession of the adolescent's body has for him a meaning absent for the adolescent: the recovery of youth. On the other hand, the man appropriates the body and the voice of the youth in such a way that the reader may recognize the youth only through the man's discourse.

The attempt to transcend an immediate reality that imposes limits through the denial of the categories of time and space is repeated in "Las tres monedas del marinero," which narrates the encounter between a man and a sailor in a relationship apparently motivated by money. The coin, however, is a symbol of the lack of identity. In this narrative, profoundly reminiscent of Jorge Luis Borges, the denial of identity is used to suggest that both characters in the story are repeated infinitely and repeat their erotic ritual, but find only loneliness throughout their search. The narrative structure of this story is emblematic of what is sought in *Los cómplices*: long sentences that are reiterated in a hallucinating circularity attempt to communicate to the reader the character's loneliness, while at the same time they make the reader an accomplice in the search. On the other hand, the homoerotic relationship is defined here by a certain narcissism, the reflection in the other that always returns the self's image: "The man, on his knees, recognizes himself in the sailor and recovers old afternoons in sad hotels, nights of sheets and bodies smelling smoke and sweat, of paradises and secret ceremonies in which the lovers are reflected like silent nude mirrors." Narcissism leads him to loneliness.

Loneliness and emptiness are central themes of "Incomprensible, como su pecho o tu espalda." In this poem the poetic subject adopts a "you" form that describes to us the encounter between a man lying face down on the rug and the body that penetrates him. In spite of the surrender, it is not possible to recover the other: "His body is shaken, and with his moans he would like to recover you, reach you now as you perfectly escape, but . . . his desire is only the reflection of your emptiness."

Canto de María attempts to accomplish the transgression that, according to Bataille, characterizes all of the erotic. The protagonists of these poems are biblical figures who exhaust the combinatory possibilities of the erotic act: in the section "Poemas de David" (Poems of David) the sexual relationship between King Saul and David is described; "Arca de la alianza" (Ark of the Covenant) marks the sexual alliance between Saul, David and Bathsheba; "Loores de María" (Praises of Mary) celebrates the encounter between Mary and her cousin Elizabeth; and "Misterios golosos" (Sweet Mysteries) delights in Mary's, Bathsheba's and Joseph's sexual appetites.

In the book's introduction, through a new reading of the Christian myth of the Fall, what constitutes the restructured axis of the different sections appears as the celebration of erotic desire. Eve is not deceived by the serpent, but bites the apple to satisfy her desire; Adam is not Eve's victim but her accomplice. Since Christianity has condemned not only all relationships that do not follow the heterosexual model, but also the erotic in general, *Canto de María* is situated in a space of prohibition in order to go beyond the transgression. In a ludic tone that confers great singularity to this selection of poems, revealing close ties between games and eroticism, the characters in the poems exist in the biblical territory to celebrate the encounter of their bodies and the satisfaction of erotic desire. In this way, as in all of Nájera's poetry, the body's pleasure is recovered, and body and text embrace to demonstrate that, in the long run, they are one and the same.

WORKS

Canto de María. Guatemala City: Impresos D&M, 1989.
Carne de seres que al encontrarse pierden la razón. Guatemala City: Impresos D&M, 1987.
Los cómplices. Guatemala City: Impresos D&M, 1988.
Con la libertad del amor. Guatemala City: Impresos D&M, 1987.
En el espejo de la mirada. Guatemala City: Impresos D&M, 1990.
Nuestro canto. Guatemala City: Impresos D&M, 1986.
Poemas de amor y otras mentiras. Guatemala City: Impresos D&M, 1991.
El río de los fragmentos. Guatemala City: Impresos D&M, 1992.
Servidumbre de lo carnal. Guatemala City: Impresos D&M, 1986.
Su cuerpo, las palabras. Guatemala City: Impresos D&M, 1990.
El sueño de Dios. Guatemala City: Impresos D&M, 1987.
sujeto de la letra a. Guatemala City: Impresos D&M, 1991.

CRITICISM

Liano, Dante. *Rassegna Iberistica* 27 (1986): 56–57.

Ana Sierra

NANDINO, ELÍAS (Mexico; 1900–1993) ───────

Elías Nandino was born in Cocula, Jalisco, in 1900—not in 1903, as most biographies erroneously state. He studied in Cocula and Guadalajara, and later moved to Mexico City, where he graduated as a surgeon in 1930. He began writing poetry at the age of seventeen, influenced by Manuel M. Flores and Manuel Acuña. Two years later, he published his first poems in *Bohemia* in Guadalajara. In 1924, he wrote *Canciones* (Songs), a collection of poems that was not published until 1947 (in *Poesía*); *Color de ausencia* (Color of Absence) was published in 1932. His life was marked by the symbiotic relationship he established between his career as a surgeon and his poetic vocation. During his years at the medical school of the Universidad Nacional de México, he created a journal called *Allis Vivere* in which he and fellow residents could publish their sonnets and epigrams. This publication led him to a meeting with two eminent members of the literary group called Los Contemporáneos (The Contemporaries), which was prominent between 1928 and 1931: Xavier Villaurrutia and Salvador Novo. Although some critics associated Nandino with the Grupo Jalisciense (Jalisco Group), headed by Alfonso Gutiérrez Hermosillo, his style and the themes privileged in his poems were closer to those of the Contemporáneos.

Medicine exerted a vigorous influence on Nandino, who as a result wrote his famous *Nocturnos* (Nocturnes; 1955–1960). Although open about his homosexuality, Nandino maintained a standard of discretion that allowed him to pursue his career as a respected surgeon. He was section head at the Juárez Hospital

and at the penitentiary, an experience that profoundly marked him and his poetry. Many people, marginalized because of their sexual behaviors and/or preferences, came to Nandino with their medical problems. This prompted him later
to specialize in proctology.

In 1937, Nandino taught literature in the Escuela Normal para Maestros
(Teachers Normal School). In 1956, he and Alfredo Hurtado, founded the review
Estaciones (Stations), a literary journal that invited plurality (it ceased in 1960).
Nandino published young nonconformist writers who tended to be ostracized
by leading literary figures like Alfonso Reyes and Octavio Paz. From 1960 to
1964, he directed the artistic journal *Cuadernos de bellas artes* (Fine Arts Note-
books), published by the Instituto Nacional de Bellas Artes (National Institute
of Fine Arts). In 1979 Nandino won the prestigious Premio Nacional de Poesía
(National Poetry Prize). In 1982, he received the Premio Jalisco (Jalisco Prize)
and the Premio Nacional de Ciencias y Artes en Lingüística y Literatura (National Sciences and Arts Prize in Linguistics and Literature). Today, a number
of important Mexican presses, such as Fondo de Cultura Económica, are reviv-
ing his works by republishing most of his poems. He died in 1993.

His friendship with Gilberto Owen, Jorge Cuesta, Salvador Novo and particularly with Xavier Villaurrutia energized Nandino's writing, and in 1937 he
published *Sonetos* (Sonnets), which established him as an original poet. With
this publication, Nandino acknowledged the romantic influence of Mexican poets Salvador Díaz Mirón, Manuel José Othón, and Luis Urbina, and of the
Spanish poet Juan Ramón Jiménez. From *Eco* (Echo; 1934) to *Río de sombra*
(River of Shadow; 1935) and *Prismas de sangre* (Blood Prisms; 1945), love
and eroticism, but also self-doubt and skepticism about social, moral and religious institutions, permeated Nandino's poetry. *Nocturnos* treats interrelated
themes present in earlier works: death/life, solitude–absence/presence, God–re-
ligious/negation of God and religion, injustice and hatred, solidarity, language
and poetic writing. As the title of his collection suggests, his *Nocturnos* were
written at night, a time propitious for versifying about collective and personal
solitude. Although enciphered, his verses are never bound by rigid versification
or by rhetorical aestheticism as they endlessly question the mysteries of daily
life. Throughout his work, Nandino wishes to reconcile body and soul, which
explains the recurrent imagery of fragmentation and the anatomical metaphors
that speak for his passionate allegiance to corporeal life. The poetry from *Eternidad de polvo* (Eternity of Dust; 1970) to *Erotismo al rojo blanco* (White Heat
Eroticism; 1982) provides a space for Nandino to relinquish hermeticism and
clarify the charged sexuality of his earlier verses. He writes freely about his
homosexuality, as he comes to realize that physical degeneration resulting from
aging is far more worrisome and limiting than social and moral conventions.

By and large, academic criticism has dismissed Nandino as a peripheral figure.
His works are included in numerous anthologies, and his name is mentioned in
studies on the Contemporáneos. But his poetry has not been, until recently, the
object of close analysis. Nonetheless, his works have been widely reviewed in

Mexico, and the *Diccionario de escritores mexicanos, siglo XX* (Dictionary of Mexican Writers, Twentieth Century) provides an excellent bibliographical source for the reviews published in Spanish. Seeking to unravel Nandino's cryptic verses, Alfredo Hurtado, David Arce and Frank Dauster were among the first critics (in the late 1950s/early 1960s) to produce extended studies on the aesthetic value of his poetry. They examined the dual presence of romanticism and symbolism in his poems, his refinement of the lyrical form (the sonnet), his place among the Contemporáneos, and themes like human suffering, poetry as a tool for transforming reality, religion, death, love and eroticism. The 1980s opened the door to more challenging analysis. Of particular interest are recent introductions or forewords to republished anthologies of Nandino's works. Sandro Cohen reasserts Nandino's importance and examines how Contemporáneos like Villaurrutia were swayed by their friendship with Nandino and their work thereby transfigured. His reading of Nandino's desperate necessity to see God, to return to primitive adoration similar to the pre-Abrahamic rejection of God as an abstraction, sheds light on the link between religion and blasphemy in his verses.

Carlos Monsiváis's contribution is by far the most innovative. For him, Nandino's poetry is also an ideological and political statement denouncing sexual heterodoxy. A chronological study of Nandino's works allows him to point out the increasing unveiling of sexuality and sexual preference manifest in Nandino since *Cerca de lo lejos* (Near to Far Away; 1979). Monsiváis questions the circumscribing definition of eroticism implied by most essays dealing with the sexualization of Nandino's poetry, and prefers to emphasize the notion of erotic dissidence. Finally, no less important is Nandino's biography, written in the first-person singular by Enrique Aguilar and published in 1986. In this book, Nandino lays bare the most intimate details of his life, linking them to his poetry. It is the voice of a lucid man who wishes to be outrageous and provocative in order to erode the mystique around sexuality and to support the next generations of gay writers.

Critics often mention eroticism in Nandino, but few are willing to shed light on the concept of the erotic and what it implies in his poetry. Georges Bataille's study on eroticism allows us to bring forth the underlying relations between Christian theology, the notions of sin, prohibition, transgression and life/death, and the erotic in Nandino's work. His religious upbringing (he was an altar boy and attended Catholic school for many years) greatly influenced his life, his sexuality and his literary production. In his biography Nandino explains that "the priests initiated [him] into homosexuality and opened for him the roads to pleasure." Contradictions in his religious faith troubled Nandino, but he nonetheless tried to remain true to himself and to his desires without completely rejecting it. He manipulated the contradictions, the rules and laws on which this system of belief is built, in order to lead what is viewed in Mexico as the unorthodox life of a homosexual.

The notion of sin is a constant presence in Nandino's verses. The dictionary of the Spanish Royal Academy defines sin as a voluntary transgression of religious laws and precepts. The particular sins Nandino commits are the sin of the flesh and the act of sodomy described as an act that goes against nature. But he exploits the fact that we all live in sin, and that prohibition invites transgression, which in turn leads to confession and to absolution. Rather than trying to find a cure for what, as a physician and as a poet, he considers to be a perfectly normal organic state, Nandino chooses to live with the guilt weighed on him since the day of his birth. He sees eroticism as a game between transgression and prohibition, and considers transgression as the essential condition for what Bataille calls ''general stability and preservation of life.'' Nandino considers that in Villaurrutia's poetry ''the theme of death is the product of his existential angst caused by his homosexuality.''

To a certain extent this is also true of Nandino, for whom death is the ''rhetorical motive'' through which he expresses the doubts and repentance caused by his transgressive sexuality. However, what distinguishes him from Villaurrutia and other members of the Contemporáneos is the extent to which he cannot dissociate life from death. As a surgeon, he saw death as a reality every day. Moreover, although the ultimate meaning of eroticism is death, Nandino conceives of it in terms of what could be compared to Aztec human sacrifice, in which ''the one who is sacrificed grants life to death, and death is a sign of life, an unlimited overture.'' His carnal life has kept him singularly earthbound, and his noncompliance has sustained the discursive revelation of transgression manifest in his poetry. Paraphrasing Bataille, one could say that for Nandino, eroticism and poetry both lead to eternity, to death and, through death, to continuity.

Another significant characteristic of Nandino's poetry is that the codified and self-censored language used to portray his sexual encounters produces verses that have been read reductively as erotic, thereby glossing over the important issue of sexual preference. In Enrique Aguilar's *Elías Nandino. Una vida no/velada*, Nandino makes clear that his poetry is not simply sexualized but homosexualized. He cannot conceive his homosexuality in any other way than by assuming the active role of phallic penetration with men who are anally virgin. He vehemently rejects the feminine, which he associates with passivity, weakness and lack of skill. Consequently, the ''penile receptacle'' of his penetration can only be the anus of a ''real macho.'' In his collection of poems *Eco*, drawings of fragmented bodies illustrate his verses. The fragmentation is undoubtedly the reflection of his feeling of alienation and the division between body and mind, between his desires and desires that are socially constructed. However, what is striking is the constant presence of the image of the phallus, his seeming to favor the phallus as an ''erotogenic zone.'' This could in part explain the fact that his works attracted predominantly essentialist criticism that bound eroticism with heterosexuality. Strong masculinity within homosexuality seems to have been mainstreamed in Mexican gay literature, which leads us to ask whether for Nandino this model is a way to justify or to alleviate his sense of guilt, a way to rescue his manhood, his strength and his resilience, which dominant ideologies would otherwise consider to be endangered. Perhaps this sexual acting out of masculinity is the "authentic" product of Nandino's eroticization of masculine power; and if this is so, one could speculate on how different this eroticization is from the imposed and predetermined eroticism defining and coercing the heterosexual world. Or perhaps this type of object choice is simply narcissism. At times Nandino seems to engage in such eroticization in order to have the privilege of subverting masculine power. This hypothesis only begins to answer these questions, and it is likely to raise new ones.

WORKS

Cerca de lo lejos (1972–1978). Mexico City: Fondo de Cultura Económica, 1979.
Color de ausencia. Mexico City: n.p., 1932.
Conversación con el mar. 2nd ed. Guadalajara: Cuarto Menguante, 1982. Orig. 1948. Also as *Conversación con el mar y otros poemas*. Mexico City: Delegación Cuauhtémoc, 1986.
Eco. Mexico City: Imprenta Mundial, 1934.
Erotismo al rojo blanco. Mexico City: Editorial Domés, 1982.
Espejo de mi muerte. Mexico City: Manuel Altolaguirre, 1945.
Eternidad de polvo. Mexico City: Joaquín Mortiz, 1970. 2nd ed. Guadalajara: Departamento de Bellas Artes del Gobierno de Jalisco, 1981.
Naufragio de la duda. Mexico City: Nueva Voz, 1950.
Nocturna palabra. Mexico City: Fondo de Cultura Económica, 1960. 2nd ed. Mexico City: Universidad Nacional Autónoma de México, 1976.
Nocturna suma. Mexico City: Tezontle, 1955. 2nd ed. Mexico City: Editorial Katún, 1982.
Nocturno amor. Mexico City: Cuadernos del Unicornio, 1958.
Nocturno día. Mexico City: Ediciones Estaciones, 1959.
Nocturnos intemporales. Mexico City: Universidad Nacional Autónoma de México, 1990.
Poemas árboles. Mexico City: Ediciones del Norte, 1938.
Poesía. Mexico City: privately published, 1947–1948. Includes *Canciones* (1924), *Nudo de sombras* (1941), *Prismas de sangre* (1945), *Conversación con mi muerte* (1947).
Prismas de sangre, Conversación con el mar y otros poemas. Mexico City: Editorial Agata, 1945/1991.
Río de sombra. Mexico City: Imprenta Mundial, 1935.
Sonetos. Mexico City: privately published, 1937. Mexico City: México Nuevo, 1939. Mexico City: Editorial Katún, 1983. 2nd ed. Mexico City: Editorial Agata, 1991.

CRITICISM

For works of criticism published before the 1960s, see *Diccionario de escritores Mexicanos, Siglo XX*.
Aguilar, Enrique. *Elías Nandino. Una vida no/velada*. Mexico City: Grijalbo, 1986.

Bataille, Georges. *L'erotisme*. Paris: Editions de Lunuit, 1957.

Cohen, Sandro. "Elías Nandino en el balance." In Elías Nandino, *Antología poética 1924–1982*, 11–26. Mexico City: Editorial Domés, 1982.

Espinasa, José María. "Prólogo." In Nandino, *Nocturnos intemporales*, 5–8.

Esquinca, Jorge. "Prólogo." In Elías Nandino, *Costumbres de morir a diario*, 9–11. Guadalajara: Departamento de Bellas Artes, 1982.

————. "Prólogo." In Nandino, *Prismas de sangre, Conversación al mar y otros poemas*, 9–11.

Monsiváis, Carlos. "De los poderes menguantes y las recuperaciones irónicas." In Nandino, *Erotismo al rojo blanco*, iii–xii.

Villaurrutia, Xavier, "Prólogo." In Elías Nandino, *Costumbres de morir a diario*, 11–14. Guadalajara: Departamento de Bellas Artes, 1982.

————. "Prólogo." In Nandino, *Eco*, 7–9. Mexico City: Editorial Katún, 1982.

Marina Pérez de Mendiola

NAVA, MICHAEL (United States; 1954) ————

Born in Stockton, California, Michael Nava is the second of six children. His great-grandparents came to the United States during the Mexican Revolution and settled in Sacramento. Nava attended Sacramento's Norte del Rio High School, where he was captain of the debate team and was elected president of the student body. He earned an undergraduate history degree at Colorado College and won a fellowship to Buenos Aires, where he spent a year studying the poetry of the Nicaraguan modernist Rubén Darío. While enrolled in the Stanford Law School, Nava wrote his first novel. As a lawyer he has worked for the city attorney of Los Angeles and at present is a research attorney for an appellate court judge in that city.

Nava's career as a novelist began with *The Little Death* (1986), a mystery narrated in the first person by Henry Rios, a burned-out lawyer who has abandoned his practice to solve a murder. The novel is punctuated with law jargon so exasperating to the mother of the dead man that she says, "I cannot follow you when you start quoting the law at me." Rios is brought into the world of the rich when he falls in love with Hugh Paris, thus the title of this book (French for orgasm, "the little death"). The title of Nava's second novel, *Goldenboy* (1988), refers to two characters in the book: a teenager who dies before the story begins and a lowlife who preys on young gays. Henry Rios, again the narrator, is asked to defend Jim Pears, who is accused of murdering Brian Fox. In this novel Rios finds love, and an added dimension to the tension comes with Larry Ross, a friend dying of AIDS. In *How Town* (1990), Nava's third novel, Rios is living comfortably with his young lover, who is diagnosed HIV positive and appears only at the beginning and the end of the novel. The story concerns a heterosexual accused of pedophilia. Assisting Rios on the case are Terry Ormes, a woman who first appeared in *Little Death*, and Freeman Vidor, a black private investigator who first appeared in *Goldenboy*. In Nava's most recent novel, *The Hidden Law* (1992), Rios takes on the defense of a young Chicano, Michael Ruiz, accused of killing a Chicano politician. The boy attempts to cover for the actual murderers, out of a naïve deference to his girlfriend, and it takes much work on the part of Rios to bring the facts to light. A new love enters Rios's life as an earlier one fades, and Rios finds a surrogate son in his straight client Michael Ruiz.

Nava has been received well by critics. According to Clair Peterson, "Where many California thriller writers tend to reach for fevered images and cinematic melodrama, Nava sticks with a gut-level integrity that may heighten reality but never overlooks it (60)." Victor Zonana has written appreciatively of Henry Rios: "A kinder, gentler Philip Marlowe, the perfect mystery protagonist for the multicultural and multiracial Los Angeles of the 90's" (E1). What is most attractive about the Rios character is his vulnerability, his weaknesses for work, alcohol and love. Julie Reynolds notes that Rios has "circumnavigated the emotional block often enough." Tom Nolan has praised the craft of Nava's plots: "Puzzle pieces fall into place without too much fuss" (A11). John Preston particularly likes the finale in *How Town*, a novel he describes as "one of the best gay-themed detective novels yet written" (63). Preston finds in the finale an element of genuine surprise for the reader, not a trick contrived to wrap loose ends together. The character of Henry Rios has been singled out by Larry Romans for special tribute because in one novel, *How Town*, Nava puts Rios into the position of defending an accused child molester. Taking such risks with a main character, forcing him to fancy-dance around unpopular topics, makes Nava a novelist unafraid of controversy. Nava has won two literary awards from Lambda Rising for *Goldenboy* and one award, "best gay mystery of the year," for *How Town*.

The gay love themes that permeate Nava's fiction begin with his first novel, although in that story Rios's relationship with Hugh Paris is ruptured by the latter's death. A more satisfying involvement comes in the second novel, not only because the lover endures, but also because Nava seems more comfortable writing about the gay subculture in California. In *The Little Death* Rios is not as absorbed in being gay as he is in *Goldenboy*. This second novel contains some touching gay love scenes, and the sexual maturity of the narrator helps give stability to the plot. Readers are not so apt to worry about Rios's ability to find love and can concentrate on his ability to solve a crime. The second novel also introduces a lesbian relationship that by novel's end is quite unsatisfying: one of the lesbians becomes cold; the other, hostile. In *How Town* there is some nasty homophobia from a policeman who was molested as a child, providing an opportunity for eloquence on toleration of sexual preference.

The Rios character in all the novels is a thinly disguised picture of Nava himself: both are lawyers, both work in California, both are gay, both are Hispanic. The main character strengthens with each successive novel. In the first, Rios is struggling to find himself: an overworked lawyer, a gay man without a lover. In the second novel, he succeeds in love; in the third novel, he can accept his lover's sickness; and in the fourth novel, he can accept his lover's decision to leave. What makes this last acceptance doubly moving is that the young lover moves in with a man also diagnosed HIV positive. Nava has attributed his interest in writing gay mysteries to his respect for the stories of Joseph Hansen, but Nava has bettered his mentor in one way: Nava's prose style is more elegant, more satisfying, than Hansen's ever is.

WORKS

Goldenboy. Boston: Alyson Publications, 1988.
The Hidden Law. New York: Harper Collins, 1992.
How Town. New York: Harper & Row, 1990.
The Little Death. Boston: Alyson Publications, 1986.

CRITICISM

Hopbell, Phillip. "Lawyer's Moonlighting a Mystery." *Lambda Rising* 1.5 (1987): 1, 8.
Nolan, Tom. Review of *How Town*. *Wall Street Journal*, May 11, 1990; p. A11.
Peterson, Clair. "Enter Goldenboy." *The Advocate*, Oct. 10, 1988, pp. 60–61.
Preston, John. Review of *How Town*. *Outweek*, Aug. 1, 1990; p. 63.
Reynolds, Julie. "Terror, Ennui and Sleaze." *Los Angeles Daily Journal* 30 May 1990: 7.
Romans, Larry. "Whodunnit?" *Dare*, Oct. 19, 1990; pp. 9, 14.
Smalling, Allen. "The Mysteries of Writer Michael Nava." *Outlines*, June 1990; p. 35.
Zonana, Victor F. "Poetic Justice." *Los Angeles Times*, May 6, 1990; pp. E1, E13.

George Klawitter

NEGRÓN-MUNTANER, FRANCES
(Puerto Rico; 1966) ⸻

Poet, critic, free-lance reporter and film/video director, Negrón-Muntaner was born in Santurce. In 1986 she moved to Philadelphia, where she came in close contact with the Latino, mainly Puerto Rican, community. She has a B.A. in anthropology from Temple University, and is enrolled in the Ph.D. program in comparative literature at Rutgers University.

Negrón-Muntaner has published poems and essays in periodicals in Puerto Rico and the United States, such as *Mairena, Conditions, The Painted Bride Quarterly* and *Centro*. She is a founder and editor of *Desde este lado* (From This Side), and she directed the first video ever made by a Puerto Rican on the subject of AIDS, *Eso no me pasa a mí/That Does Not Happen to Me*. Negrón-Muntaner has completed an anthology of Latino poets in Philadelphia, *Los límites del silencio/Shouting in a Whisper*. She is writing a book about the gay movement in Puerto Rico and is preparing her second book of poetry, "El púrpura se ilumina" (The Brightness of Purple), for publication. Her first book, *Anatomía de una sonrisa* (Anatomy of a Smile), will be published by the Instituto de Cultura Puertorriqueña (Institute of Puerto Rican Culture) in San Juan.

The thematic range of Negrón-Muntaner's poetry, from *Anatomía* (which is the basis of this commentary, unless otherwise specified) to "El púrpura se ilumina" to her most recent single poems, is becoming more and more inclusive, paralleling the all-encompassing Puerto Rican revolutionary homosexual speaking subject of Abniel Marat's poetry: the (divided) self, love, (lesbian) sex, sexism, feminism, classism, racism, ethnicity, exile, AIDS and all that pertains to the realms of the personal and the political, on the basis of the conviction that everything is germane to literature. Her poems challenge the classification of high or low poetry; it is a matter of emphasis, she says in "bodypolitics," a poem about AIDS: "between the beautiful and the ugly/a question of accent/between great and poor poetry/a matter of rhythm and politics" ("Los límites").

This defiant attitude, a constant throughout Negrón-Muntaner's texts, is in part a result of the speaking subject delineated from the very beginning in *Anatomía*: the body of a lesbian/Puerto Rican/poet constructing line by line, verse by verse, her freedom, freeing herself/itself from the "official story" of the "patriarchal fantasy" according to which the young woman is a princess waiting to be rescued by a man. Instead of the prince, it is the woman, or her leftover body, who returns to save herself from the comatose state of the anorectic princess; to save her "hunger of life" by virtue of her healed wounds, some of which smile ("prefacio" [preface]). Eventually the body becomes free, alive and smiles/writes "the anatomy of a smile" that is the book.

In her journey to freedom, the lesbian speaking subject loves other women, not only physically and anatomically, but also physiologically: "Digesting my food in your stomach and accumulating the bestiary of fats in the dusty walls of your interior that is mine now (that's love)" ("First Love"). But hers is a guerrilla journey in which love is like a mirage. ("viaje" [journey]).

WORKS

Anatomía de una sonrisa: Poemas anoréxicos/Anorexic Poems: Anatomy of a Smile. Trans. Isabel Vázquel-Maldonado. San Juan: Instituto de Cultura Puertorriqueña, in press.

"Echoing Stonewall and Other Dilemmas: The Organizational Beginnings of a Gay and Lesbian Agenda in Puerto Rico, 1972–1977." *Centro* 4.1 (Winter 1991–1992): 76–95; and 4.2 (Spring 1992): 98–115.

"Insider/Outsider: Making Films in the Puerto Rican Community." *Centro* 3.1 (Winter 1990–1991): 81–85.

Los límites del silencio/Shouting in a Whisper (Latino Poets in Philadelphia). Santiago, Chile: Cuarto Proprio, 1994.

"El púrpura se ilumina." Unpublished MS.
"Sobre la generación soterrada." *Claridad (en rojo)*, Sept. 11, 1987, p. 25.

CRITICISM

Acevedeo, Rafael. "Anatomía de un prólogo." In Negrón-Muntaner, *Anatomía de una sonrisa. Poemas anoréxicos/Anorexic Poems.*
Albaladejo, Luis Raúl. "La generación soterrada." *Claridad (en rojo)*, July 10, 1987, p. 14.
Cancel, Mario R. "Mayagüez y la llamada Generación del '80." *Claridad (en rojo)*, Jan. 12, 1989, p. 20.
Jiménez Benítez, Adolfo E. "La poesía puertorriqueña de los ochenta." *Claridad (en rojo)*, Jan. 12, 1989, p. 22.
Jiménez Corretjer, Zoé. "Poetas de la 'última' generación." *Claridad (en rojo)*, Dec. 2, 1988, p. 22.
Rodríguez Matos, Carlos. "Los poetas en los límites del silencio." In Negrón-Muntaner, "Los límites del silencio."

Carlos A. Rodríguez-Matos

NOVO, SALVADOR (Mexico; 1904–1974) _____

Novo started his career as a poet at an early age; *Poemas de adolescencia* (Adolescent Poems; 1918–1920) is his first book. In it are two poems that deserve special attention: the sonnet "A Xavier Villaurrutia" (To Xavier Villaurrutia), a love poem, is a symbolist exercise in which Novo presents himself and Villaurrutia as proud sinners. It feminizes Villaurrutia and develops an aporia when the poem reveals the silence in which the souls of the poet and his friend are immersed. Yet at the conclusion of the poem, the poet screams to Villaurrutia that he must suffer, cry and love. The second poem is "Oración" (Prayer), in which the poet problematizes the transition from boyhood to manhood. *Nuevo amor* (New Love; 1933) is considered one of the best books of poetry written in Spanish and a key text to understanding the Mexican avant-garde. The poems are written in the epicene genre, bringing the hetero/homo opposition to the point of collapse. At the same time they try to recuperate love into the masculine domain, as in "Tú, yo mismo" (You, I Myself). A masculine eroticism appears in poems like "Este perfume intenso de tu carne" (The Intense Perfume of Your Flesh) and "Junto a tu cuerpo" (Close to Your Body), not just because the images are masculine but also because of the lack of the traditional feminine images associated with eroticism since the Renaissance. The *Romance de Angelillo y Adela* (Ballad of Angelillo and Adela; 1933) creates a very difficult balance between irony and the beauty of a love story in the Andalusian manner, like Federico García Lorca's ballads in the *Romancero gitano* (Book of Gypsy Ballads; 1928). The text comes close to becoming a poetic joke, but the high quality of the poetry maintains the central conceit. *Poemas proletarios* (Proletarian Poems; 1934) is written in an antiheroic mode. The individual poems revindicate the virile values of the revolution, and they even attack the machismo of the army (e.g., "Roberto, el subteniente" [Roberto, the Sublieutenant]) or the ignorance of the soldiers ("Bernardo, el soldado" [Bernardo, the Soldier]). In *Never Easy* (1935), poem VIII is an erotic poem like the ones in *Nuevo amor*.

Sátira. El libro ca . . . (Satire. The Son of a . . . Book) represents the triumph of the baroque in Novo's poetry and of the aesthetics of meanness: poetry as a weapon to hurt the other, to damage his reputation, status, prestige or position. The prologue is a sonnet in which Novo satirizes his own body and his life as a writer. It may very well help to study the aporia created between the public character and symbolic figure, Salvador Novo, the conservative essayist and highly honored member of the Mexican Establishment, and Novo's last image as an old man in wigs, with plucked eyebrows and heavy makeup: a magnificent writer and reactionary tart. The first part, "La diegada (1826)," is a collection of poems against his political and intellectual enemy, the painter Diego Rivera, who is presented, among other insults, as a cuckold (an excuse to develop a rich imagery related to bulls, bullfights, horns, etc.). One of the best is "La diestra mano sin querer se ha herido" (The Right Hand Has Been Hurt by Chance). Communism and the Mexican revolution are also targets of Novo's attacks. The skillful use of imagery related to human and animal feces (baroque scatology) is worth noting. The second part, "Salutaciones" (Salutations) is a series of dialogues to his decadent phallus. Poems like "En este comienzo de año" (At the Beginning of This New Year), "1959," "Misiva a Salvador" (Letter to Salvador) and "1960" are also written in the neobaroque tradition. The third part is "Este fácil soneto cotidiano" (This Easy Everyday Sonnet), made up of scatological poems about bureaucrats, artists and intellectuals. The most interesting is the one dedicated to Tristán Marof, a Bolivian Communist lecturer, author of "Literatos afeminados" (Effeminate Literati), an example of gay bashing from the 1930s. In this poem the use of the baroque hyperbole is perfect. There are also poems dedicated to venereal diseases. The fourth part, "Y he de concluir, soneto, y contenerte . . . " (And I Have to Conclude, Sonnet, and Restrain You . . .), a collection of poems about himself, in which he matches the poetic force of his first love poems, only to destroy the poetic illusion with an ironic force in the last lines.

The play *Cuauhtémoc* tells the story of Mexico's conquest. The construction of gender is very illuminating. Cuauhtémoc always addresses Hernán Cortés as Malinche (Cortés's female Indian interpreter), whom tradition views as a traitress, thereby denying this new feminine couple their symbolic parenthood of Mexico. Cuauhtémoc becomes Mexico's father and mother. In the introduction to *La guerra de las gordas* (The War of the Fat Ladies, 1963), Cuauhtémoc had already been characterized as "Omega of the Indigenous World" (10). In the play *El sofá* (The Sofa; 1969), when Consuelo—the daughter—wants to continue the family tradition of being a tailor, her request is denied. Although the purpose of the play is to ridicule the American tourist, it is also a portrayal of a dysfunctional Mexican family. The play *El tercer Fausto* (The Third Faust) is an openly gay drama: Alberto sells his soul to the devil to become a woman in order to conquer the love of Armando. Once Alberto becomes Ella (She), he finds out that Armando was already in love with him. It is a very naïve composition, aimed to be a scandal in the Mexico of the 1950s, but it received no attention because of the bad quality of the production.

El joven (The Young Man; 1923/1933) is a short work of outstanding quality, a Proustian exercise in which a young man wanders around the brand-new big city that is becoming the Mexico City of the 1920s. *Nueva grandeza mexicana* (New Mexican Grandeur; 1946) is a modern chronicle of Mexico City that has been exceptionally influential because of its exposure of Mexican popular culture. *La vida en México en el período presidencial de Avila Camacho* (Life in Mexico During the Presidency of Avila Camacho; 1965) is the second volume of Novo's collection of newspaper articles on literature of manners, literary criticism, gossip, society columns, politics, humor and popular culture. In *Cocina mexicana o historia gastronómica de la ciudad de México* (Mexican Cuisine or Gastronomic History of Mexico City; 1967) Novo adopts the masculine point of view of the historian or the chronicler instead of revindicating other possibilities like the point of view of the cook (Novo was an excellent one) or the chronotrope of the kitchen. "Memoirs," Novo's erotic memoirs, present in an explicit manner the underground gay life of Mexico City. *Letras vencidas* (Defeated Words; 1962) is a collection of articles dealing with the literary criticism of Novo's late work; as the title indicates, these texts present a moment of pessimism, although at the same time he is at the peak of public and official fame and recognition. *Las locas, el sexo y los burdeles* (Flaming Queens, Sex and Brothels; 1979) promises more than it delivers.

Novo wrote the script of *El signo de la muerte* (The Sign of Death; 1936), one of the first movies by Cantinflas, as well as numerous other movie scripts. *El signo* is the only film in which Cantinflas appears as a transvestite. The last scene, a fight between seminaked Aztec warriors and policemen, resembles a dream in an avant-garde movie instead of conventional slapstick.

WORKS

Cocina mexicana o historia gastronómica de la ciudad de México. Mexico City: Porrúa, 1967.

Diálogos. Mexico City: Los Textos de la Capilla, 1956. Contains *El joven II*; *Adán y Eva*; *El tercer Fausto*; *La güera y la estrella*; *Sor Juana y Pita*; *Malinche y Carlota*; *Diego y Betty*; *Cuauhtémoc*; *Eulalia*.

La guerra de las gordas. Mexico City: Fondo de Cultura Económica, 1963.

El joven. Mexico City: Imprenta Mundial México, 1933.

Letras vencidas. Jalapa, Mexico: Universidad Veracruzana, 1962.

Las locas, el sexo y los burdeles. Mexico City: Diana, 1979.

"Memoir." Trans. Erskine Lane. In *Now the Volcano: An Anthology of Latin American*

Gay Literature, 11–47. Ed. Winston Leyland. San Francisco: Gay Sunshine Press, 1979.

Nueva grandeza mexicana. Mexico City: Era, 1967. Orig. 1946.

Poesía. Mexico City: Fondo de Cultura Económica, 1961. Contains *Poemas de adolescencia; XX poemas; Espejo; Nuevo amor; Seamen Rhymes; Romance de Angelillo y Adela; Poemas proletarios; Never Ever; Frida Kahlo; Florido Laude; Decimos: "Nuestra tierra"; Sonetos.*

Sátira El libro ca . . . . Mexico City: Diana, 1978.

El sofa. In Salvador Nova, *Ticitezcatl* [plays]. Jalapa: Universidad Veracruzana, 1966.

La vida en México en el período presidencial de Avila Camacho. Mexico City: Empresas Editoriales, 1965.

CRITICISM

Blanco, José Joaquín. "La crítica de Novo." In his *La paja en el ojo. Ensayos de crítica*, 92–105. Puebla: Universidad Autónoma de Puebla, 1980.

González Mateos, Adriana. "Novo amor: Una sátira." In *Multiplicación de los contemporáneos: Ensayos sobre la generación*, 149–165. Ed. Sergio Fernández. Mexico City: Universidad Nacional Autónoma de México, 1988.

Monsiváis, Carlos. "Salvador Novo. Los que tenemos unas manos que no nos pertenecen." In his *Amor perdido*, 265–296. Mexico City: Era, 1988.

Salvador A. Oropesa

O

OBEJAS, ARCHY (Cuba; ca. 1950) _____

Obejas writes fiction, poetry, theater and journalism. Although not widely published, she writes in Spanish and English, and has been included in publications that focus on Latina literature in the United States, like *Woman of Her Word* and *Third Woman*; in well-established journals like *Bilingual Review* and *Revista chicano-riqueña*; in nonmainstream publications—supported mainly by lesbian and gay organizations—*Discontents, Common Lives/Lesbian Lives* and *Antigonish Review*; and in many journals and collections of radical gay and lesbian fiction and poetry. Obejas's articles have appeared in *Chicago Reader, Chicago Tribune, The Advocate, Windy City Times, High Performance, Chicago Reporter, The Catalyst, Chicago Magazine, Chicago Sun-Times, Hispanic Magazine* and *La Raza*. Her poetry and fiction are published in *The Best of Helicone Nine, 1979–1989, West Side Stories, Abraxas, Antigonish Review, Beloit Poetry Journal, Bilingual Review, Common Lives/Lesbian Lives, Qrhyme Poetry Review, Conditions, Ikon, Interstate, Phoebe/George Mason University Review, Rambunctious Review, Revista chicano-riqueña, Sing, Heavenly Muse!, Sinister Wisdom* and many others. She coproduced and cowrote the first television sitcom by, for, and about U.S. Hispanics, *Aquí me quedo* (I'm Staying Right Here), a one-hour pilot on WBBS-TV in Chicago (October 1985). She wrote, produced, and directed *Brisas de Marianao* (Marianao Breezes), a one-act tragicomedy, for Latino Chicago Theater at the University of Illinois at Chicago (June 1984).

At present Obejas is the director of a writing workshop for talented high-school students, with an emphasis on minority recruitment, at Roosevelt University, Chicago. She also teaches poetry at Columbia College in Chicago. As an active journalist and writer, she has won awards: Peter Lisagor Exemplary Journalism Award; artist-in-residence at Yaddo, Saratoga Springs, New York;

National Endowment for the Arts creative writing fellowship in poetry; and artist-in-residence for the Ragdale Foundation. She frequently lectures on diversity and poetry, most recently on lesbians and gay men in the multi-cultural mainstream, as part of the faculty lecture series at the Art Institute of Chicago.

In a seminal study on Cuban-American women writers, Eliana Rivero cites Obejas as undergoing the transition from immigrant to ethnic, and shaping the body of marginalized discourse in American literature in the process. Because she has lived in the United States, Obejas exposes the oppression of the dominant Anglo culture, as well as of her own cultural tradition, in her writings. Besides the discourse of biculturalism, her literature incorporates that of sexual identity, adding sexual preference to the categories of exile, immigrant and ethnic.

Although Obejas has been included in publications and collections that deal with biculturalism and marginality, I know of no instance in which her sexual orientation is mentioned. Given the present climate of exclusion in literary and academic arenas, her confrontational attempt not to mask her sexual identity with the issue of cultural ambivalence has kept her out of mainstream publications. Since Obejas has not published a complete book, one can hardly accuse those publications of being biased; however, the silence regarding such a text does confirm that we as literary critics are indeed heterosexual readers. In fact, much of what Obejas has written integrates the lesbian vision as simply one more aspect of her Latina identity, a vision that bridges the division between herself as a Latina lesbian and her identity as an American ethnic. Thus, in order to understand her writing, we need to overcome the heterosexual prejudice that is often brought to a homosexual text.

A tenor of Obejas's poetry and fiction is the presence of an open sexual preference that challenges heterosexuality. In her poem "Guests," for example, she subverts the "straight" stance. To highlight only this poet's bicultural identity and ignore the homosexuality that informs her discourse is to allow a bias to misread a very good author. This is not to claim that Obejas's texts do not attack the forces oppressing the Latina; on the contrary, her affirmation of her lesbianism connects the discourse of homosexuality to that of biculturalism. Her poetry and prose go beyond bicultural identity to include gender, race, violence and the AIDS crisis. Both English and Spanish poems invade the oppressing forces to voice her sexual persona as part of her biculturalism, evincing a writing that is more than the effort to bind identity to nationality alone. As she puts it: "These are familiar lives in foreign languages" ("Lifes").

In Obejas's writings, the female subject's object of desire is a female body. This homoerotic attraction defines a world felt, experienced and lived from a lesbian standpoint without any traces of the other. Her endeavor voices the dignity of the homosexual. Several recent stories concern a lesbian journalist between love affairs who wanders around Chicago's gay community. In one story, she works for an avant-garde journal whose editor—with *womn pwr* license plates—torments her for exposing activists who play politics with the

AIDS epidemic. In another story, a neurotic lesbian invests the narration with the pathos of a lost love through minor traffic accidents. In another, a gay couple is brutally exposed to the cruelty that looms in their own relationship. Obejas's homosexual narrative does not reveal an ideal world in which gays live happily. In it, a broken romance serves as a metaphor to build identity. Her characters fight a battle between desires and the lack of role models that expose lovers to desperation. From this permanent broken romance—most of her recent stories deal with the heartbreak of lesbian and gay love—Obejas views a hostile world that impedes her grasp of the humanity of others she encounters.

In the same way, the poetic voice is that of a lesbian in the act of naming her world: "[We are n]ewborns on the birthing table" ("Reunion"). This new birth represents a break with heterosexual love myths. As the lesbian experiences "love," she becomes aware that this feeling destroyed her mother and, therefore, strives to create a different concept of coupledom. In the poem "Sunday," the rejection of love is connected to the destruction caused by heterosexual love. The homosexual must abolish the definition of a world centered on ineffectual constructs from the heterosexual world. Her claim that the pain caused by love is intrinsic to the heterosexual relationship points to an enterprise that targets the eradication of utopianism. It is with gays that a love modeled after the heterosexual idea of future has to be eliminated:

Personally, I'd prefer to evolve beyond the concept of lovers, of couples, of love. The future is moot then; the future has no choice but to be now. It strikes me as the most revolutionary lesbian/feminist thing to do. Forget hunger, equality, environmentally correct garbage bags, let's work to eliminate heartbreak instead. Love, coupledom, the right person—they're as anachronistic and elusive as Puerto Rican independence: Everybody's for it, but no one's quite sure what it means or how to get it. ("La obsesión," 6)

Here, the narrator has realized that the rhetoric of idealistic love prescribed for the heterosexual happy ending is the root of much of the homosexual couple's existence. Hence, in the name of the future, the homosexual revolution has to liberate a heterosexual world that accepts a painful existence.

WORKS

"The Escape." In *Nosotras: Latina Literature Today*, 44–48, Ed. María del Carmen
        Boza, Beverly Silva and Carmen Valle. Binghamton, N.Y.: Bilingual Press, 1986.
"Guests, After Langston Hughes." *Xtra/CWR* 2 (Spring 1991): 5.
"Lifes." In *The Poetry Connection: Chicago Dial-a-Poem 1981–1991*. Chicago: Chicago
        Council on Fine Arts, 1991.
"The Neighborhood." *Qrhyme Poetry Review* 2.1 (Summer 1991): 36.
"La obsesión." 1992. Unpublished MS.
"Reunion." *Qrhyme Poetry Review* 2.1 (Summer 1991): 37.

CRITICISM

Rivero, Eliana. "Cubanos y cubanoamericanos: Perfil y presencia en los Estados Unidos." *Discurso literario* 7.1 (1989): 81–101.

———. "From Immigrants to Ethnics: Cuban Women Writers in the U.S." In *Breaking Boundaries. Latina Writings and Critical Readings*, 189–200. Ed. Asunción Horno-Degaldo et al. Amherst: University of Massachusetts Press, 1989.

Vigil, Evangelina, ed. *Woman of Her Word: Hispanic Women Write. Revista chicano-riqueña* 9.3–4 (Fall 1983).

Librada Hernández

OLMOS, CARLOS (Mexico; 1947) ⸻

Born in Chiapas, Olmos began in the professional theater in 1972 with the farce *Juegos fatuos* (Fatuous Games), and is now considered one of the important recent voices in Mexico. His theatrical production (principally farces and full-length pieces) has received prizes in Mexico and recognition abroad. His most recent work is *El eclipse* (The Eclipse; 1990), which has had numerous performances in Mexico City and elsewhere in Mexico, and is outstanding for its sharp perceptions concerning cultural conflicts in that country.

Homophilia is a recurring theme in three of his works, although in one of them, *El brillo de la ausencia* (The Glow of Absence; 1982), it is dealt with only obliquely. Nevertheless, even this treatment is noteworthy for what it has to say about the attitude of the Mexican Left toward so-called erotic minorities. This attitude oscillates between support for minorities because it is the prestigious thing to do and scorn because there is not a serious struggle; it is important to note that at the present moment homophilia is absent from Mexico's political agenda.

Notwithstanding such an exclusion (and perhaps owing to it), the theme has assumed a growing presence in the country's cultural production, almost always as part of a struggle between two moral codes. *El presente perfecto* (Present Perfect; 1982) and *El eclipse* exemplify this point. In the first play, two characters, Gabriel (a former student) and Alba (his former teacher), confront each other along a psychological and political axis. In the past, Alba falls in love with Gabriel after discovering the close friendship and sexual attraction between Gabriel and another young man. Alba finds a kindred spirit in Gabriel and believes him to be a man capable of giving and receiving pleasure. Nevertheless, she exercises an influence on the love between the two boys, first by turning them in and then by attempting to win Gabriel's love for herself, guided by her firm belief that the relationship between the two boys is incorrect. In the present, each leads his/her own quiet married life, devoid of passion. Gabriel, who is the more powerful, now manipulates a group of young men in a decision that affects his former teacher, with the goal of achieving his political objectives. He has learned the lesson well, even if the memory of his young love still lives within him.

What catches the reader's attention in *El presente perfecto* is the absence of a gay stereotype (a term that is inapplicable to Gabriel) or any ardent erotic details. Rather, homophilia appears in the play as a sensibility, a caring that does not exclude the possibility of the sexual and a manifestation of a capacity to give and receive pleasure. Homophilia is not a nucleus of identity—even though it alludes to a difference, it does not seem to be lived as an essence— nor is it even a major concern, although it does become the possibility of being the object of aggression or "corrective" intention. *El eclipse* reveals the same treatment of homophilia.

In two acts *El eclipse* focuses on the conflict between six individuals over- whelmed by social, family and personal factors in a small port on the coast of the state of Chiapas in southern Mexico. It is a village with an impoverished economy that contrasts with the wealth of people from the outside. The family faces the need to emigrate to find a better life, to the detriment of bonds of affection for the place where they have invested their hopes and their efforts. They are marked by the death of the male head of the family, fractured in their moral unity, and pressured by an offer from foreign investors to buy their prop- erty. All six are to a greater or lesser degree bearers of two codes that do battle for cultural hegemony. The grandmother and mother represent a traditional vi- sion of sexual roles, the tie between parents and children, religion, sexual pleas- ure and maternity. The aunt is a repressed old maid (who had been left pregnant by an American minister) who, in her search for peace, converts to a religion that forbids her to celebrate with her family or to salute the flag and sing the national anthem (in a country of revolutionary nationalism!). The sister is a carefree young woman filled with TV culture, profoundly hedonistic and ac- cepting of her own sexual desires and those of her brother. Gerardo, the pro- tagonist, is a grade-school teacher who is described as having the sensitivity of a poet. He struggles between the loyalty he owes his family and its moral code and the one he owes his own most intimate needs and desires, which includes his relationship with Mario. The sixth person, Mario, is from Mexico City, pretending to be in town to photograph the eclipse, he enters into the bosom of the family, which owns the small inn where he stays, in search of Gerardo, whom he had met in a male bar and with whom he had gone to a hotel.

Gerardo decides, during the eclipse, be faithful to his impulses which take the form of a prolonged kiss given to Mario. His mother discovers them, and Gerardo flees with Mario to escape his mother's sad and confused reaction. In the end, all that is left is the hope that they will be together in an imprecise future. Gerardo therefore emerges as the best synthesis of a moral conflict that overwhelms the family, and the cosmic disorder signaled by the title of the play is a correlative of a disorder in values: the darkness in the middle of the day is the agony of one spiritual world and the establishment of another.

But what is homophilic in *El eclipse* is more than Gerardo's struggle to live his gayness; it is the struggle to make an affirmation of the individual and of a new moral order. This of course does not imply that homophilia is only incidental, something scandalous introduced to attract the audience. On the contrary, it is a central element, since it serves to question the naturalness of basic social institutions: heterosexuality and sexual roles. By the same token, it affirms the independence of the values held by the children in the face of their parents, their pleasure and sexual desire in the face of Christian asceticism, and their drives in the face of reason. As a consequence, Gerardo's decision, rather than corresponding to gay liberation and coming from someone who denies any belief in eternity or future happiness, appears as self-fulfillment, an act of fidelity to his personal will, as he calls it—or, in a Nietzschean sense, to his self-glorification.

Other significant dimensions of Olmos's treatment of homophilia may be summarized as follows: First, as in *El presente perfecto*, the homophilic person situates himself in a nonmetropolitan space. Second, his story is part of a generalized suffering and oppression. That is, the character is not the only one who is marginal; rather, he lives in the midst of marginal individuals. Moreover, homophilia is not the only basis of his conflict, since his job as a grade-school teacher puts him in an economically precarious position, as he himself states it: a marginality among marginals and as part of other marginations, all of which surely places his homophilia in a proper dimension. Third, the characters are typically masculine in their behavior, as are the great majority of persons who participate in homoerotic contacts, with the exception of classic stereotypes like the effeminate and the transvestite. What is interesting here is the rupture implied in the supposed naturalness of the man–masculinity–heterosexuality that is so convenient to hegemonic discourse. Fourth, homophilia is not only a strictly carnal relationship between two men but also a friendship and companionship based on a shared sensibility—in short, a phenomenon of love. The friendship is evident in shared beers, cigarettes, conversations, reactions and concerns. The details of bodily contact are limited to a hand that rests on the other man's leg (something possible among friends in Mexico), hand contact and a kiss and reference to a hotel.

Homophilia is not an identity deriving from the possession of a significant difference, even if the feeling of being different is present. It is not an essence that is culturally created, nor is it something natural, nor even a circumstance of erotic exclusivity: both Gabriel in *El presente perfecto* and Mario in *El eclipse* are married. The only reference to a putatively gay community that might evoke their relationship to a collective identity is given by their going together to a bar. The fact that it is called a male bar and that the main character has gone there to find something different, and out of a desire to forget the death of his father, significantly colors such an evocation. Moreover, there is no term in the play to mark the relationship between the characters or the erotic-affective desires of each of them, as either gay or homosexual. This conceptual vacuum might seem suspicious and not verisimilar, and could be attributed to the author's ideology. Without denying the latter as probable, the negation of identity in this way as a reality—although not one that includes everybody—would seem to reflect this apparent vacuum. What remains to be researched are the representational types that allow for such erotic-affective experiences to be grasped. In Olmos's works these experiences would seem to be the logical consequence of a close friendship—indeed a radical view in a country where friendship seems to be as sacred as matrimony.

In general, such an approach to homophobia must be viewed as particularly productive from the point of view of its exposition before a virtually prejudiced public, since it creates greater opportunities for the establishment of an identification with the character of the play and, therefore, a greater possibility for establishing lines of understanding between an audience and a phenomenon traditionally considered to be alien. *El eclipse*, then, speaks of a convulsed Mexican provincial setting, one that is quite the opposite of national myths of gentle rural societies. Underlying the work are reference to the deepest economic crisis the country has faced since the Revolution of 1910: scandalous political and administrative corruption, a hegemonic grip on mass culture, the end of populist, protectionist, and welfare governments and the beginning of a privatizing and denationalizing economic project open to international capital: These are all phenomena that have led to the sundering of the Mexican social fabric.

Gentle rural society no longer exists in Mexico. The national project is now present only in political speeches completely lacking in credibility. The countryside has ceased to be the guardian of tradition; it can only serve as the stage for a reaccommodation of civil society and a moral tradition that collapses under the weight of its inability to satisfy individual desires and the affective needs as part of a cultural front that would emphasize self-glorification and pleasure. The latter would include a homophilia that has begun to speak its name outside Mexico City, not with militant acts and identity campaigns but in the form of a struggle for a self-acceptance of sensibility, as a self-affirmation.

WORKS

El eclipse. Mexico City: Universidad Nacional Autónoma de México, 1990.
Teatro. Jalapa, Mexico: Universidad Veracruzana, 1983. Includes *Lenguas muertas, El presente perfecto, La rosa de oro*, and *El brillo de la ausencia*.

Guillermo Núñez Noriega

ORTIZ TAYLOR, SHEILA (United States; 1939) _____

Chicana writer Sheila Ortiz Taylor was born in Los Angeles. She completed the Ph.D. in English literature at UCLA in 1973 and currently teaches literature and

creative writing in the English department at Florida State University in Talla-
hassee. Her major creative works are three novels—*Faultline* (1982), *Spring
Forward/Fall Back* (1985), and *Southbound* (1990), and a collection of poetry,
Slow Dancing at Miss Polly's (1989).

One of the most important contributions of Ortiz Taylor's fiction and poetry
to a discussion of gay/lesbian issues in literature is the manner in which her
works problematize rigid identity categories. As a self-identified lesbian of Chicana background, Ortiz Taylor is associated simultaneously with several communities. Her works are populated by multifaceted characters who evolve
constantly and for whom traditional classifications of gender, sexual orientation
and ethnicity have little relevance. Through her writing she challenges such
classifications and acknowledges the dynamic nature of identity.

In Ortiz Taylor's first novel, *Faultline*, protagonist Arden Benbow is a divorced lesbian mother of six who is struggling to win custody of her children.
The novel comprises a series of narratives about Arden by her friends, family
and acquaintances, interspersed with Arden's own commentary. The story of
Arden's youth, marriage and subsequent relationship with the wife of her husband's best friend unfolds through the accounts of these "character witnesses."
Her former husband, the man who supplies her with feed for her 300 rabbits,
her live-in nanny (a black drag queen), an elderly former showgirl who owns a
trailer park in Mexico, the social worker sent to investigate Arden's suitability
as a mother and a variety of other characters provide testimony.

In this novel, the motif of the "faultline" has significance beyond its literal
connotation as a geological phenomenon. According to Arden, an earthquake
produced by a shift along the San Andreas Fault is partially responsible for
bringing her and her lover, Alice, together, for it was during the chaos following
the tremor that the two women discovered they have fallen in love. On a more
symbolic level, the recurrence of the faultline motif serves to underscore the
view of identity—as fluid and subject to perpetual shifting—that the novel suggests.

In Ortiz Taylor's second novel, *Spring Forward/Fall Back*, connections between the lives of the novel's lesbian characters are forged through the interweaving of dispersed narrative threads. The novel, which spans a period of ten
years, begins in the Catalina Island town of Avalon, home to protagonist Elizabeth. The first of the text's three parts, "Spring Forward," takes place the
summer after Elizabeth graduates from high school. It is a summer of awakening
and change, for she discovers that her beloved English teacher is an active
member of Avalon's lesbian community. Later, Elizabeth makes the difficult
decision to leave the island to attend college along with her best friend, Grace.

In the second section of the novel, "Fall Back," the action shifts to Santa
Monica, where twenty-nine-year-old Marcie Tyson decides to leave her husband
and buys a home for herself and her unborn child. Like Elizabeth, Marcie is
introduced to, and later welcomed into, a gay/lesbian community whose center
is a bar called the Daily Planet. The novel's final part, "Equinox," brings to-

gether the two previous narratives after ten years have elapsed. When Elizabeth and Marcie meet at the Daily Planet, the relationship between Elizabeth and Grace, who have been lovers since college, is waning; Marcie's relationship with her female partner is also ending. Throughout *Spring Forward/Fall Back*, relationships are constantly forming, changing and dissolving; the novel suggests that such movement and the unconventional family structures it produces are liberating for those involved.

In *Southbound*, the sequel to *Faultline*, the unity of Arden Benbow's family—her lover, Alice, six children, black drag queen–nanny Topaz Wilson, 300 rabbits—is challenged when Arden reluctantly seeks a teaching position and must face the prospect of leaving Los Angeles. Arden survives a series of calamities on the way to interview at the Modern Language Association convention and is offered a teaching position at a college in Florida. After she accepts the job, Arden sets out for Florida with Topaz to find a house for the family, and the adventures of "Operation Southbound" begin.

The final chapters of *Southbound* take on the tone of a hilarious thriller as Arden and Topaz discover that they have become innocent pawns in a smuggling operation run by Arden's stepfather. As in Ortiz Taylor's previous novels, the unreliability of appearances is underscored, and at one point Arden claims that her own identity seems to have "the texture and substance of Play Doh" (121). Her reminiscences about her childhood among her Spanish-speaking, tortilla-making great-aunts bring Arden's Chicana heritage to the foreground; this heritage and her roles as mother, lesbian, poet and teacher are among the multiple facets of the protagonist's identity. The novel has frequent unanticipated plot twists and offers surprising revelations about the characters. The ending of *Southbound* is open, yet optimistic. All of Ortiz Taylor's novels, in fact, place the unpredictability of people and life in a favorable light.

Unique characters and everyday incidents are portrayed with gentle humor in *Slow Dancing at Miss Polly's*; while the themes of memory and the trials of daily existence recur in many poems, each one can be read as a self-contained vignette. The collection is divided into three parts: "Album," "Dyke Patrol" and "Sunday Morning." In "Album," Ortiz Taylor's persona captures imaginative images of her mother, father and an uncle who committed suicide; of herself as a free-spirited young girl; of the aging owner of a Puerto Rican guest house; of the friendly residents of a trailer park near her childhood home. The speaker describes these people as if looking at their photographs, filling in poetry where her memory leaves a blank. The poems convey a sense of the passage of time: her mother and father have grown old and died; the Airstream trailers have been replaced by luxury double-wide mobile homes; she now observes the world through the lens of adulthood.

The poems of "Dyke Patrol" focus on the speaker's relationships with former lovers and other lesbians and offer a humorous retrospective of events leading to her divorce. In "Sunday Morning" the intimacy and comfort of life with her partner are translated into poetic images. In the poems of this final part of *Slow*

Dancing at Miss Polly's, the motif of crafting—houses, meals, art, relationships—and the related theme of naming as a means of constructing identity are developed. The section begins and ends with poems about an individual's many "selves." In "Naming," the speaker compares a person's many selves to a waiter's stack of plates; these selves are marked by the nicknames one has earned. The final poem, "Sunday Morning," similarly celebrates the coexistence of very different identities within one individual.

Critics of Chicano/a literature generally have not included Ortiz Taylor's works in their studies, in part because her writing foregrounds lesbian identity while traditional signs of Chicano cultural identity are less prominent. It should be noted, however, that in *Southbound* Chicano culture plays a more significant role than in the two previous novels. The very existence of Ortiz Taylor's writing bears witness to the difficulty of assigning a single, monolithic identity to any individual, and her texts clearly advocate a view of gender, sexuality and ethnicity based on perpetual movement between possible identities. In each of the three novels discussed here, various supposedly heterosexual characters acknowledge and act upon their attraction for a person of the same sex. These eruptions of homosexuality destabilize exclusive definitions of sexual orientation and suggest that there is truth beyond the obvious homophobia in Elizabeth's stepfather's comment that "[y]ou could be standing right next to one and never know it" (*Spring Forward/Fall Back*, 191).

Ortiz Taylor's works depict an ideal society unfettered by restrictive gender roles, not unlike the utopia envisioned in Manuel Puig's *Kiss of the Spider Woman* (1976). The families that function most successfully in *Faultline, Spring Forward/ Fall Back*, and *Southbound* are "frontier families" whose adult members move between parental roles and whose children are offered an array of unconventional gender role models. The opinion promoted by Arden Benbow's former husband (and circulating in society in general)—that *lesbian mother* is an oxymoron and contrary to nature—is refuted by these families in which traditional patriarchal hierarchy has been dissolved. Ortiz Taylor's writing champions the undermining of oppressive hegemonic institutions and celebrates shifting, ever-changing identities. Her texts are testimonials to the existence of a subjectivity that rejects the constraints of a permanent, exclusive status as female, or lesbian or Chicana. Ortiz Taylor's fiction and poetry thus counter critics' tendency to ghettoize writers. By problematizing gender and ethnicity, her works challenge the notion of identity as fixed and limited.

WORKS

Faultline. Tallahassee, Fla.: Naiad Press, 1982.
Slow Dancing at Miss Polly's. Tallahassee, Fla.: Naiad Press, 1989.
Southbound. Tallahassee, Fla.: Naiad Press, 1990.
Spring Forward/Fall Back. Tallahassee, Fla.: Naiad Press, 1985.

CRITICISM

Bruce-Novoa, Juan. "Homosexuality and the Chicano Novel." *Confluencia* 2.1 (Fall 1986): 69–77.

————. "Sheila Ortiz Taylor's *Faultline*: A Third-Woman Utopia." *Confluencia* 6.2 (Spring 1991): 75–87.

Christian, Karen. "Will the 'Real Chicano' Please Stand Up? The Challenge of John Rechy and Sheila Ortiz Taylor to Chicano Essentialism." *Americas Review* 20.2 (Summer 1992): 89–104.

Karen S. Christian

P

PAZ, SENEL (Cuba; 1950)

Paz is representative of a new generation of Cuban writers whose work has been actively promoted on the island since the creation in 1979 of the Ministry of Culture. Born and raised in the rural province of Las Villas, Paz obtained wide recognition as a writer in 1979 when he was awarded the Premio David (David Prize) for his collection of short stories, *El niño aquel* (That Boy, 1980). In 1983 he published his first novel, *Un rey en el jardín* (A King in the Garden), which was awarded the Premio de la Crítica (Critic's Prize) as one of the ten best books of the year.

Both *El niño aquel* and *Un rey en el jardín* use a first-person confessional tone to articulate Cuban rural life. However, this testimonial perspective—paradigmatic of Cuban revolutionary literature—is more reflective and personal, preferring to examine the smaller and more intimate details of everyday rural life instead of the larger sociopolitical structures. Efraín Barradas has written that while Paz's first two texts are imaginative and unconventionally fantastic, they nonetheless are testimonies of a young boy who, while not participating actively in the revolutionary struggle, witnessed this important historical event.

"Como un escolar sencillo" (Like a Simple Schoolboy) and "No le digas que la quieres" (Don't Tell Her You Love Her) are passages from a novel in progress that have appeared in print. In these two pieces, the protagonist from the first two books reappears as a young man growing up within the Revolution. "No le digas que la quieres" relates the protagonist's love affair with his girlfriend and how they finally began having sex. It is a sensitive and moving story of love and respect that challenges the machismo of traditional Cuban society, in which men reduce the sexual act to a game of power.

In 1991 Paz published *El lobo, el bosque y el hombre nuevo* (The Wolf, the

Forest and the New Man), a story about the friendship between an openly gay
man and a straight Communist activist. *El lobo* received the prestigious international Juan Rulfo Award that same year. Prior to the publication of this long
story, none of the author's texts had dealt with homosexual themes or presented
a homosexual sensibility. Many see *El lobo, el bosque y el hombre nuevo* as a
sign of the regime's openness in relation to gays and lesbians; the early homophobic policies of the Revolution that resulted, for instance, in the creation
of the reeducation camps in the late 1960s are now seen by many as a thing of
the past. Queers for Cuba, a San Francisco gay organization in support of Cuba,
reports that when Paz's story was made into a play, it sold out to mixed audiences in Havana. In addition, a film version, directed by Tomás Gutiérrez Alea,
one of Cuba's most distinguished directors, is currently being made. On the
other side of the debate, José María Espinasa, although recognizing Paz's talent
as a narrator, does not see *El lobo, el bosque y el hombre nuevo* as a softening
of the Revolution's stance toward homosexuals. For him the text signals more
a defensive attitude by the regime to the issue of homosexuality than a concrete
example of openness. According to Espinasa, sexual repression (above all of a
homophobic nature) is a continuing problem in Cuba, and it will remain so until
Cuba's leaders manage to create an imaginative political way out of the critical
situation on the island.

El lobo, el bosque y el hombre nuevo* utilizes a confessional mode, used by
Paz in his other texts, to tell the story of Diego and David's friendship. David,
heterosexual, a lover of literature and an enthusiastic supporter of the Revolution, recounts how he first met the openly gay Diego and how their friendship,
despite David's homophobic attitude, developed. What brings the men together
is their mutual love and respect for literature. They meet at the ice cream parlor
Coppelia, a notorious homosexual cruising area in Havana. In 1961 the Revolution's Operation 3P, a roundup of prostitutes, pimps and pederasts to "solve
the problem of homosexuality," raided Coppelia in what has humorously and
pathetically been called "la cacería de locas" (faggot hunting). The author's
selection of this site for David and Diego's initial meeting is not gratuitous, nor
is his mentioning in the story of the reeducation camps and the celebrated author
José Lezama Lima, whose openly homosexual scenes in *Paradiso* caused much
controversy among the revolutionary cultural policymakers. It is as if by finally
writing about these things, Paz wanted to exorcise the Revolution's past indis-
cretions in regard to homosexuality.

In the story Diego identifies three models of male homosexual life: the so-
called homosexuals, men who like men but who can restrain their desire (also
in this category he includes men whose social and political positions stop them
from acting on their homosexual feelings); the *maricones* (queers), men who
simply cannot control themselves at the sight of a man's penis; and the *locas*
(queens), men who first and foremost are motivated by and for the male sexual
organ and spend (waste) all of their time pursuing it—the worst of them, ac-

cording to Diego, are the *locas de carroza* (flaming queens), who have no tact and are totally flighty and empty. While initially calling himself a *maricón*, Diego later identifies himself as homosexual. For as Diego sees it, the homosexual can control himself and is thus able to concentrate on his work and on nobler endeavors.

Diego's three models reveal the extent to which this story continues within the Revolution's Manichaean and moralistic division of the world into good and evil, with no middle ground. Diego's *maricones* and *locas* are identified as the Bad Homosexuals in contrast to the political engagement of the Good Homosexual. This Manichaeism neutralizes any internal heterogeneity: the homosexual will be accepted as long as he sides with the internal homogenization of the Revolution. Otherwise he will be stigmatized and silenced. In the story the narrator praises Diego's revolutionary attributes as if he were trying to compensate for, or make the reader forgive, his homosexuality. (At one point in the story Diego makes the case that he is just as patriotic and stable as anyone, and that if it came to choosing between having sex with a man or being a good Cuban, he would choose being a good Cuban.)

El lobo, el bosque y el hombre nuevo romanticizes the gay–straight friendship and desexualizes the homosexual, thus allowing him to fit comfortably within the revolutionary social structure that supports a value system grounded in uniformity. Throughout the story Diego never oversteps the limits that have been imposed on him: "Nuestra amistad ha sido correcta" (Our friendship has been correct). In the end Diego decides to leave the island. But before leaving, he advises David that the Revolution needs to soften its stance toward homosexuals, not to continue to punish them for their sexual-object choices. He hopes that David, a new breed of *hombre nuevo* (new man, a direct reference to Che Guevara's idealized new man), will inspire others to be more accepting of homosexuals.

While the representation of homosexuality in *El lobo, el bosque y el hombre nuevo* appears at first glance to be a significant development in Cuban revolutionary letters, which has traditionally silenced homosexual desire and discourse, Diego in fact is not allowed to tell his own story in his own words and through his own voice. His voice is mediated, rearticulated, filtered through David's authoritative (revolutionary) discourse. In the end this romanticized friendship, structured around a simplistic narrative device of sentimentality, does not challenge the revolutionary establishment's paradigm of power, nor does the story challenge the ordinary reader to confront his or her attitudes toward homosexuals outside of the literary space.

WORKS

"Como un escolar sencillo." *Areíto* 35 (1984): 44–46.
El lobo, el bosque y el hombre nuevo. Havana: Edición Homenaje, 1991.

El niño aquel. Havana: Unión Nacional de Escritores y Artistas de Cuba, 1980.
"No le digas que la quieres." *Casa de las Américas* 142 (1984): 148–154.
Un rey en el jardín. Havana: Editorial Letras Cubanas, 1983.

CRITICISM

Barradas, Efraín. Review of *Un rey en el jardín. Hispamérica* 39 (1984): 120–122.
————. "*Un rey en el jardín*: Verosimilitud, historia y estilo." *Casa de las Américas*
     149 (Mar.–Apr. 1985): 148–54.
Bejel, Emilio. "Entrevista a Senel Paz." *Hispamérica* 52 (1989): 49–58.
Espinasa, José María. "Una de Cuba por las que van de arena." *La jornada*, Sunday
     supp. (Mexico City), Feb. 2, 1992, pp. 23–27.
López, Iraida. "Tres preguntas a Senel Paz." *Areíto* 35 (1984): 42–44.
Muñoz, Elías Miguel. "Senel Paz." In *Dictionary of Twentieth-Century Cuban Litera-
     ture*, 349–351. Ed. Julio A. Martínez. Westport, Conn.: Greenwood Press, 1990.
Resik, Magda. "Escribir es una suerte de naufragio: Habla Senel Paz del cine, de la
     crítica y de la literatura." *La gaceta de Cuba*, Sept.–Oct. 1992, pp. 14–18.

                                                              Francisco Soto

PELLEGRINI, RENATO (Argentina; 193?)

Pellegrini was born in Villa María, a town in the province of Córdoba. At the
age of sixteen, after dropping out of high school, he falsified his documents and
ran off to Buenos Aires "because life in a small town is always suffocating."
Upon his arrival in the capital, he moved into one of the many cheap boarding-
houses along the Avenida de Mayo. He subsequently got work as a salesman
in a store where he also had a room in which to sleep. He became infected with
lice and ended up spending two months in a hospital. This real-life experience
is included in his first novel, *Siranger* (1957)—according to Abelardo Arias,
"It was Renato Pellegrini who introduced crabs into Argentine literature." Pellegrini worked for the Tirso publishing firm and was employed by Fabricaciones
Militares (Military Manufacturing) in Campana; he also traveled extensively
throughout Argentina during this period.

    Soon after Pellegrini's arrival in Buenos Aires, when he was only seventeen
years old, he met the writer Abelardo Arias, with whom he maintained a deep
friendship. Tirso was Arias's own publishing house, and he used it to bring to
the Argentine public works by European homosexuals like Roger Peyrefitte,
Carlo Coccioli, Henri de Montherlant, Julien Green, Albert Simoniun, and André
Gide. Pellegrini was hired by Arias as his editor; according to Pellegrini, the
latter "Frenchified him" and convinced him to travel to Paris, where he came
into close contact with existentialist groups. Upon his return to Buenos Aires,
encouraged by Arias and Manual Mujica Lainez, he began writing *Siranger*, the
first of his two novels.

Pellegrini's biography contains no prizes nor official honors. Quite to the contrary, *Siranger* resulted in his being denied the *faja de honor* (sash of honor) awarded by the Sociedad Argentina de Escritores (Argentine Society of Writers), even though it had been designated for him; he was also denied the prize given by the publishing house Editorial Kraft. Something similar occurred with *Asfalto* (Asphalt; 1964). The 1964 jury of the Festival Literario de Necochea (Necochea Literary Festival), consisting of Silvinia Bullrich, Jorge Masciangoli, and Arias, among others, could not bring itself to award him a prize. The novel also was banned by the censors and the case ended up before the Argentine Supreme Court. According to Pellegrini, the awards he can remember are in the nature of the recognition he received from Marta Lynch when she stated publicly at the Necochea Festival that "the best prize for *Asfalto* is that it made them so afraid of it they ended up banning it," as well as the words of Juan Jacobo Bajarlía, who as his defense lawyer stated, "Pellegrini was urinating on all the Buenos Aires moralists."

The most notable features of Pellegrini's narrative include the descriptive economy of the existentialists, mixed with clear neonaturalist touches that constantly evoke specific Argentine literary traditions, especially the work of Roberto Arlt. Manuel Mujica Lainez, with whom the writer at one time had a very close friendship, used to say that he "could not conceive of writing that way."

Siranger was written during 1955; following the misunderstandings involving the Editorial Kraft prize, it was published by Tirso in 1957. It is the first Argentine novel that, despite the fact that the majority of critics have chosen to ignore it, openly presents the theme of homosexuality. The work was presented to the public in a formal ceremony by the author's closest friends, Abelardo Arias and Mujica Lainez, and it enjoyed an excellent critical reception. The novel is divided into three parts. The first two focus on a series of homoerotic relations dominated by the main character, Gerardo Leni, and the friend who takes him in after his arrival in Buenos Aires, Jorge Retio. Also dealt with are the constant attempts by both men to hide or ignore their true inclinations and feelings. Without much success, Gerardo attempts to maintain relations with several women, among them Iris Day, a nightclub singer who is unsuccessful in her efforts to seduce him.

In the third part, after Gerardo discovers Jorge in bed with a twelve-year-old boy, a homosexual theme is most openly developed. After Gerardo's discovery, Jorge brutally attempts to possess Gerardo. The latter resists, suppressing his true feelings and acting horrified at his friend's advances. Jorge embarrassedly asks his friend to forgive him, saying, "It's not my fault I'm this way. It's something stronger than me" (156). Jorge ends up in jail for pederasty, although Gerardo is unaware of the real reason and thinks he is responsible for Jorge's being in jail. Thanks to a new job, Gerardo is able to lead a more comfortably dissipated life with new friends. His love life with women goes from bad to worse, and his unsatisfied and impossible relationship with Iris ends when the latter, feeling rejected, commits suicide. Gerardo thereupon receives a note from

Jorge in which he announces his release from prison and his plan to visit him, saying, "Don't attempt to run away—it won't work" (149). Gerardo, frantic because he realizes that he has betrayed not only his friend but himself as well, throws himself in front of a train. At the last moment he realizes that Jorge, who had been following him, throws himself on top of him in a vain attempt to save him. Both are crushed by the engine.

"When I published my second novel, *Asfalto*, in 1964, in which the discreet and guilt-ridden relations of *Siranger* became no longer either discreet or guilt-ridden, the critical and legal situation had deteriorated completely, and I felt myself very isolated." Mujica Lainez wrote a prologue for *Asfalto*, although at the last minute he refused to sign it with his own name. Arias promised to present the book formally, but in the face of the controversies it provoked, he begged off the very afternoon of the event. In the end Pedro Orgambide did the honors. The only review was one that Adolfo Mitre published in the newspaper *La Nación* (The Nation). The magazine *Gente* (People) published an interview with Pellegrini in its first issue. A few days afterward, in one of her typical gestures of solidarity, María Angélica Bosco warned Pellegrini that, on the basis of a complaint made by the Postal Service, a judge, in accord with the obscenity provisions of the Penal Code, had ordered his arrest and the confiscation of the entire edition of *Asfalto*. Defended by Juan Jacobo Bajarlía, Pellegrini was twice found not guilty. But when the case reached the Supreme Court, he lost by a 2–1 decision and received a suspended two-month sentence. The case received extensive coverage in the press, and in the end the police canceled the order to confiscate copies of the book.

Although neither the themes nor the characters in *Asfalto* are significantly different from those in *Siranger*, the view of sexuality is completely opposite from that in the earlier novel. In *Siranger* the discovery of same-sex attraction is presented under a burden of guilt and shame that can only culminate in suicide. But *Asfalto*, although some of the sexual situations are presented with elements of violence and even aberration (seduction under the guise of protection, rape and male prostitution), shows a completely difference face. Eduardo Ales is a young provincial who, like Gerardo Leni, abandons his studies at the age of sixteen and runs away to Buenos Aires. After several disastrous liaisons he meets Ricardo Cabral, a provincial congressman who lost his seat after being exposed as a pederast. Cabral has been in jail, and upon his release has sought refuge in this grandmother's house in Buenos Aires. Cabral, who is perhaps too much like Jorge Retio, takes Eduardo in and gets him a job in the bookstore of a homosexual friend. Except for Julia, a young woman who lives upstairs and who falls in love with Eduardo, all of the characters in the novel are homosexuals completely devoid of guilt or shame for their condition. Eduardo's short romance with Julia triggers his final understanding that, like those around him, he can experience his sexuality freely.

Asfalto includes not only repeated explanations of homosexuality and the dark underworld in which it was forced to move in the 1950s, but also numerous scientific allusions and even a catalog of homosexuals throughout history, none of which had been mentioned in Argentine literature. Unfortunately, the legal cases, censorship, the confiscation of *Asfalto* and critical silence have resulted in the suspension of Pellegrini's writing. The jacket flap of *Asfalto* announces as forthcoming *La columna* (The Column) and *Fauna* (Fawn), but they never appeared. Since the banning of *Asfalto* in the 1960s, Pellegrini has lived in a town near Buenos Aires, completely divorced from the capital's literary world.

WORKS

Asfalto. Buenos Aires: Ediciones Tirso, 1964.
Literatura tabú: Del marqués de Sade a La Historia de O *(ensayos)*. Buenos Aires: Ediciones Tirso, 1959.
Poemas lejanos. Buenos Aires: Ediciones Tirso, 1960.
Siranger. Buenos Aires: Ediciones Tirso, 1957.

The quotations from Pellegrini and Arias are based on my personal interview in Buenos Aires, Aug. 18, 1989.

Osvaldo R. Sabino

PEÑA, TERRI DE LA (United States; 1947) _____

A life-long resident of Santa Monica, California, Terri de la Peña was born to a Mexican immigrant mother and a fourth-generation Mexican-American father. Her short stories have won several awards, and she received the 1992 Chicano/ Latino Literary Award for *Territories*, a collection of short stories. The most comprehensive account of her life can be found in "Good-Bye Ricky Ricardo; Hello Lesbianism," Peña's coming-out story. In this autobiographical narrative, Peña recounts her childhood sense of "differentness" and outlines the ways traditional Chicano mores, the Catholic Church, and her own desire to be a good Chicana daughter compelled her to repress her lesbianism until her mid-thirties. As she describes her family's gradual acceptance of her lesbianism and her first adult (Anglo) lover, Peña challenges both the conventional stories of lesbian daughters rejected by their families and stereotypes concerning Chicano *familia*. "Good-Bye Ricky Ricardo" also charts Peña's coming out as a writer; through-out the narrative she interweaves her growing confidence in her sexual identity with her increasingly successful efforts to become a published (lesbian) author.

Like her coming-out story, Terri de la Peña's fiction examines Chicana lesbian–feminists' attempts to integrate their ethnic and sexual identities. Her short stories employ realistic settings, characters and dialogue to depict these women's experiences: their double invisibility in "Labrys"; their attempts to establish cross-cultural romantic relationships in "Sequences" and "Blue"; the cultural misunderstandings that often arise between Chicana lesbians and their Anglo lovers in "Beyond El Camino Real" and "Desert Quartet"; and the simultaneous sexual and cultural bonding that can occur between Chicana lesbians in "La Maya," "Mariposa" and "Mujeres morenas."

Margins, Peña's first novel and one of the first Chicana lesbian novels to be published in the United States, incorporates many of the themes found in her shorter works. The novel focuses on Verónica Meléndez, a young Southern California Chicana lesbian–feminist and aspiring writer, as she comes to terms with the death of her first lover, a Chicana childhood friend; becomes sexually involved with a male-identified white woman and a Chicana-Tejana lesbian; enters a multicultural lesbian community; and gradually reveals her sexual identity to her family. By juxtaposing Verónica's coming out as a lesbian with her coming out as a writer, Peña explores a wide variety of issues, including homophobia, sexism and internalized racism in the Chicano community; Catholicism's heterosexist patriarchal dogma; and stereotypical images of Chicanas' sexuality. By placing her protagonist in a multicultural lesbian community and by emphasizing Verónica's unproblematic acceptance of her lesbianism, Peña counters heterosexist misconceptions concerning the "unnaturalness" of lesbianism.

Although Peña's work has yet to receive critical attention, her portrayal of Chicana lesbian–feminists' experiences in contemporary U.S. cultures provides an important corrective to what Bonnie Zimmerman describes as the "static and potentially entrapping" views of (white, middle-class) lesbian identity found in much twentieth-century U.S. lesbian literature (*The Safe Sea of Women*, 25). Like many Anglo lesbian texts, Peña's fiction is designed to appeal to a wide readership. She utilizes many of the literary conventions—including constructions of lesbian identity, romantic-sexual relationships and Lesbian Nation—found in mainstream Anglo lesbian fiction. Yet these themes have further implications in Peña's Chicana-centered works. In "La Maya," "Mariposa," "Mujeres morenas," and *Margins*, for example, the protagonists' (re)discovery of their Mexican Indian spiritual-cultural heritage parallels their sexual relationships with dark-skinned Chicanas or *mexicanas*. By thus associating physical desire with her protagonists' desire to reclaim their cultural roots, Peña expands conventional (Anglo) descriptions of lesbian identity formation.

Similarly, by exploring the diversity among U.S. lesbians, Peña problematizes facile concepts of a monolithic, all-embracing Lesbian Nation and illustrates Cherríe Moraga's assertion that the lesbian of color's "very presence violates the ranking and abstraction of oppressions" (*Loving in the War Years*, 53). Whereas the majority of Anglo lesbian texts focus primarily on the dominant culture's sexism and homophobia, Peña's works depict the linguistic and cultural isolation Chicana lesbians often experience in Anglo lesbian communities. Like Peña herself, many of her protagonists are self-supporting urban Chicanas who attempt to negotiate between traditional Chicano culture, the larger, Anglo society and lesbian communities. By thus positioning her Chicana lesbians on the borders of multiple worlds, she explores diverse, overlapping forms of oppression.

If, as Zimmerman asserts, U.S. lesbian fiction "has helped shape a lesbian consciousness, community, and culture from the movement's beginning" (*The Safe Sea of Women*, 2), Peña's work plays an important role in *re*shaping contemporary U.S. lesbian–feminist community. By illustrating contemporary U.S. lesbians' diverse cultural, economic and regional backgrounds, her fiction challenges earlier (mis)conceptions of a monolithic (Anglo) lesbian movement.

WORKS

"Beyond El Camino Real." In *Chicana Lesbians: The Girls Our Mothers Warned Us About*, 85–94. Ed. Carla Trujillo. Berkeley, Calif.: Third Woman Press, 1991.

"Blue." In *Riding Desire*, 149–153. Ed. Tee Corinne. Austin, Tex.: Banned Books, 1991.

"Desert Quartet." In *Lesbian Love Stories*, 2.154–161. Ed. Irene Zahava. Freedom, Calif.: Crossing Press, 1991.

"Good-Bye Ricky Ricardo; Hello Lesbianism." In *The Original Coming out Stories*, 223–233. 2nd Ed. Julia Penelope and Susan Wolfe. Freedom, Calif.: Crossing Press, 1989.

"La Maya." In *Intricate Passions: A Collection of Erotic Short Fiction*, 1–10. Ed. Tee Corinne. Austin, Tex.: Banned Books, 1989.

Margins. Seattle: Seal Press, 1992.

"Labrys." In *Word of Mouth: Short-Short Stories by Women*, 31–33. Ed. Irene Zahava. Freedom, Calif.: Crossing Press, 1990.

"Mariposa." In *Lesbian Bedtime Stories*, 2.7–17. Ed. Terry Woodrow. Little River, Calif.: Tough Dove Books, 1990.

"Mujeres morenas." In *Lesbian Love Stories*, 2.85–93. Ed. Irene Zahava. Freedom, Calif.: Crossing Press, 1991.

"Sequences." In *Finding the Lesbians: Personal Accounts from Around the World*, 162–171. Ed. Julia Penelope and Sarah Valentine. Freedom, Calif.: Crossing Press, 1990.

AnnLouise Keating

PENTEADO, DARCY (Brazil; 1926–1987) _____

Darcy Penteado was born in São Roque, in the state of São Paulo. He made his name as a stage designer, book illustrator, painter and society portraitist, leading the life-style of a successful middle-class professional. He was one of the founding members of the editorial board of *Lampião*, Brazil's first regular gay newspaper, and became a high-profile spokesman for the Brazilian lesbian and gay movement in the late 1970s and 1980s.

Penteado turned to literature relatively late in life, publishing three collections of stories, a novel and a book of childhood recollections. His first book of stories, *A meta* (The Goal; 1976), which deals openly with various aspects of the gay male life-style and acknowledges Penteado's own homosexuality, was the subject of critical comment and newspaper gossip because of his social prominence. His literary production covers the brief period of sexual freedom and creativity between the rise of the gay liberation movement and the onset of the AIDS epidemic. In Brazil this corresponded to the period of political liberation and intellectual optimism that followed the worst excesses of the military dictatorship of the early 1970s. Penteado's stories about gay life are generally lighthearted and optimistic, with a positive message and an ironical or humorous twist. Some are little more than extended and sometimes banal anecdotes, but the more successful show a sustained fantastic imagination, such as "Conto de fadas número dois" (Fairy Tale Number Two), in which a queen's tomb becomes first a tourist attraction and then a place of religious pilgrimage, and "Jarbas, o imaginoso" (Jarbas the Imaginative), in which a young gay man creates a series of fantasies for the amusement of his older lovers. The best of these stories is the delightful "Bofe a prazo fixo" (Part-time Hustler), in which a young factory worker earns enough money from an intense sexual relationship with a rich homosexual to marry, maintaining a nonsexual friendship after his marriage and inviting the homosexual to become his child's godfather.

Another group of stories is more realistic, dealing with the emotional states and life-style of an experienced gay cattle rancher in "Capim australiano, ou o amor para toda a vida" (Australian Grass, or A Love to Last a Lifetime), a closeted married gay who resorts to a transvestite prostitute as a compromise solution to his sexual problems in "Engrenagens" (Gearings) and a delinquent hustler in "Reginaldo." The two most striking stories of this group, both published in *A meta*, have an element of social criticism. The title story describes the painful emotions and recollections set off in a prosperous homosexual architect by the sight of a crippled black man; they range from guilt to compassion, fear of appearing ridiculous and finally a suicidal joy. In "A carreira de um libertino paulistano, ou a semana perfeita de um senhor homossexual, de boa colocação social" (The Career of a São Paulo Libertine, or the Perfect Week of a Homosexual Gentleman, of Good Social Standing), Penteado details the self-indulgent concerns of an affluent gay engineer as he prepares for a fancy-dress party and a water-skiing weekend, and engages in casual sex while his German lover is away. After attending an upper-class party where there is delicious food, elegant clothes, expensive jewelry and fatuous conversation, the engineer picks up a hungry, unemployed Northeasterner and takes a perverse pleasure in beating down his price and then obliging him to take the passive sexual role. The story is recounted deadpan, with no overt comment or attempt at irony by the author, thus increasing the impact of the satire.

Less successful artistically, though interesting politically, are Penteado's portrayals of utopian gay relationships. In the novella "Espartanos" (Spartans), he paints an idyllic picture of three generations of masculine gay men who ignore social conventions and personal jealousies, living together harmoniously in a fulfilling three-way relationship. In his novel *Nivaldo e Jerônimo*, Penteado brings in other social and historical themes, setting the novel against the background of the military repression of the early 1970s and the guerrilla movement in the Araguaia area of the interior. It tells the story of the love between an attractive, apolitical young man and an older, committed left-wing militant who goes off to fight as a rural guerrilla. The novel is essentially a *roman à these*, an interesting attempt to bridge the gap between gender and class politics, between the newly formulated demands for personal and emotional liberation of gay men and the rigid convictions of the older left-wing ideologies. Neither of these two works succeeds completely in a literary sense. The idealized relationship between the men in "Espartanos," with its absence of conflict, lacks tension, while it is difficult to believe that a committed guerrilla such as Jerônimo would fall so deeply in love with an apolitical youth who eventually drifts into drugs, prostitution and transvestism. The novel has two alternative endings, which highlights the frequent artistic weakness in Penteado: his chronic inability to find endings that develop naturally out of the plots of his stories. Despite these defects, however, both works are well written, coherent and courageous in their deliberate intention to show a positive alternative to the many writings that depict gay relations in a negative light.

WORKS

"Australian Grass, or A Love to Last a Lifetime." In *My Deep Dark Pain Is Love: A Collection of Latin American Gay Fiction*, 225–240. Ed. Winston Leyland. San Francisco: Gay Sunshine Press, 1983.

Crescilda, e os espartanos. São Paulo: Edições Símbolo, 1977.

"Jarbas the Imaginative." In *Now the Volcano: An Anthology of Latin American Gay Literature*, 247–233. Ed. Winston Leyland. San Francisco: Gay Sunshine Press, 1979.

Menino insone: Uma narrativa fragmentada em contos e crônicas, 1964–1982. São Paulo: Editora Soma, 1983.

A meta. São Paulo: Edições Símbolo, 1976, 2nd ed., 1977.

Nivaldo e Jerônimo. Rio de Janeiro: Codecri, 1981.

"Part-time Hustler." In *My Deep Dark Pain Is Love*, 241–244.

"Snow White Revisited." In *Now the Volcano*, 237–245.

Teoremambo: Delito delirante para coro e orquestra. São Paulo: Livraria Cultura Editora, 1979.

CRITICISM

Foster, David William. *Gay and Lesbian Themes in Latin American Writing*, 76–80. Austin: University of Texas Press, 1991.

Robert Howes

PERI ROSSI, CRISTINA (Uruguay; 1941) _____

Born in Montevideo, Peri Rossi studied literature at the Instituto de Profesores Artigas and taught in various high schools and in the university of that city. She also contributed extensively to the famous cultural weekly *Marcha* (March). Her fiction has received some of the most important prizes in Uruguay, such as the 1968 Premio de los Jóvenes de Arca (Arca Publishers Prize for Young Writers) for the stories *Los museos abandonados* (The Abandoned Museums) and the 1969 Premio Biblioteca de Marcha (Marcha Library Prize) for the novel *El libro de mis primos* (My Cousins' Book). She was active in the left-wing Frente Amplio (Broad Front) coalition, and left the country before the 1973 military coup, taking up residence in 1972 in Barcelona. In 1975 the military junta denied her a passport, and she took Spanish citizenship.

While in Spain, Peri Rossi received the 1973 Premio Inventarios Provisionales (Provisional Inventories Prize) for her book of poems *Diáspora* (Diaspora), the 1975 Premio Palma de Mallorca de Poesía (Palma de Mallorca Poetry Prize), the 1976 Premio Narrativa Inédita Benito Pérez Galdós (Benito Pérez Galdós Prize for Unpublished Fiction) for *La rebelión de los niños* (The Revolt of the Children) and the 1983 Premio Puerta de Oro (Golden Door Prize) for her short story "El ángel caído" (The Fallen Angel), which is included in *Una pasión prohibida* (A Forbidden Passion; 1986). She received a writers award in 1977–1978 from the Fundación Juan March (Juan March Foundation), and she spent 1981 in Berlin as a writer in residence at the Deutscher Akademischer Aus-tauschdients (German Academic Exchange Service). She currently resides in Spain, where she works as a journalist and translator.

Her writing includes the collections of short stories *Viviendo* (Living; 1963), *Los museos abandonados* (1968), *Indicios pánicos* (Indexes of Panic; 1970), *La tarde del dinosaurio* (Afternoon of the Dinosaur; 1976), *La rebelión de los niños* (1982), *El museo de los esfuerzos inútiles* (The Museum of Useless Efforts; 1983), *Una pasión prohibida* (1986) and *Cosmoagonías* (Cosmoagonies; 1988); the novels *El libro de mis primos* (1969), *La nave de los locos* (Ship of Fools; 1984), *Solitario de amor* (Love Solitaire; 1988) and *La última noche de Dostoievski* (Dostoyevski's Last Night; 1992); The books of poetry *Evohé* (1971), *Descripción de un naufragio* (Description of a Shipwreck; 1975), *Diáspora* (1976), *Lingüística general (*General Linguistics; 1979), Europa después de la lluvia* (Europe After the Rain; 1987) and *Babel bárbara* (Barbarous Babel; 1991); and the essays of *Fantasías eróticas* (Erotic Fantasies; 1991).

In all of Peri Rossi's writing, both her fiction and her poetry, there is a sustained rejection of the heterosexual as the only form of sexual encounter. While this proposition is present throughout her work, in some works a ho-mosexual perspective is more openly present. These works include her poetry as a whole (with the exception of *Europa después de la lluvia*) several short stories, the novel *La nave de los locos* and the essays of *Fantasías eróticas*.

Although homoeroticism is one theme among many in Peri Rossi's poetry, in *Evohé* it is the sustaining motif. The collection opens with a quote from Sappho, and the poetry of the collection can best be described as sapphic in that woman becomes the materialization of the desire of the lyric speaker. Some of the poems focus on the sacred nature of lesbian love and compare the body of the woman to a temple and the act of love to prayer. "Evohé" is the cry of the bacchants—as it expressed in Euripides's play *The Bacchants*—the celebrants in the rites honoring Bacchus. The bacchic rites may originally have been religious, but they subsequently became profane. This orgiastic, bacchanalian spirit dominates many poems in the book, particularly those describing feminine orgasm.

In *Descripción de un naufragio*, the woman's body is identified with marine geography, and the lyric speaker describes in sensual terms the curves, hollows and damp zones of the female body. Sexual encounters become approaches to "her deep, pink groin" (65), and Peri Rossi's book transforms woman into a paradigm of the beloved subject, the only being capable of arousing passion.

Diáspora engages in occasional forays into an extremely baroque language in the attempt to suggest a high degree of eroticism via the repetition of certain phonemes, and one poem makes explicit reference to the beauty of female homosexuality, which emerges as nothing less than a declaration of principles; female masturbation is also poeticized.

Lingüística general makes specific mention of the subversion of social conventions established by political power, the church and medicine implied by love between women, and there is a harsh criticism of social norms in regards to sexual roles. *Babel bárbara* continues the line of her earlier books in specifying the amorous passion woman awakens in the lyric speaker. Babel represents the universal woman; it is ambiguity, the confusion of languages and sexes through which the poetic voice constantly manifests her love. The myth of the origin of languages is correlated in the book with that of the origin of woman, in order to speak the history of an amorous passion.

In Peri Rossi's fiction, a story like "El baile" (The Ball), included in *Viviendo*, narrates the mutual attraction between a provincial girl, Silvia, and an actress who comes to perform in Silvia's hometown. The actress makes use of a Harlequin disguise at a masked ball to express her love for Silvia beneath a masculine identity. Silvia falls in love with her, thinking she is a man. But the attraction for the actress lies beneath the surface, an attraction Silvia felt the first time she saw her act on the stage.

"Gambito de reina" (Queen's Gambit), from *La tarde del dinosaurio*, is an ambiguous story that resists an easy interpretation. Alejandra wishes she had been born a man, and there is a parallelism established between the life of the characters and the life of bees in a hive. Alejandra is compared to a queen bee, and her homosexual relations with Mnasidika, the "Ephebus little girl" (123) are described.

In another story, "La rebelión de los niños," included in the book of the same name, the boy narrator adds to his collage, made on a chair, the photograph of two lesbians kissing each other and touching each other's breasts—which, according to him, incites one's emotions rather than one's instincts, which is what the magazine's publisher probably intended. There is also a mention of how his brother needs to become informed before choosing his sexuality, which means that sexuality is a choice and not the imposition of biology.

The final chapter of the novel *La nave de los locos* contains a "porno-sexy" lesbian spectacle between two women who imitate Marlene Dietrich and Dolores del Rio (although one of them might be a transvestite). "El testigo" (The Witness), in the anthology *Cuentos eróticos* (Erotic Stories; 1988), narrates the amorous relations between a lesbian and her various lovers, to which her son is witness. The boy, in love with one of his mother's female lovers, ends up raping both women.

Peri Rossi's essays in *Fantasías eróticas* also include views on lesbianism and male homosexuality. "Nochevieja en el Daniel's" (New Year's Eve in Daniel's) describes a lesbian bar in Barcelona where on the last night of 1989 two Italian women appear who are a perfect example of lesbians who imitate heterosexual conduct. In "Entre la ficción y la realidad" (Between Fiction and Reality) some stories of gays, lesbians and tranvestites are mentioned. In chapter 6, she describes the gay fantasy of St. Sebastian's martyrdom and its relation to sadomasochism. In Peri Rossi's opinion, this fantasy marks the enormous difference between masculine homosexuality and lesbianism, to the extent that the latter rejects the link between eroticism and violence: lesbians have never taken as their own either sadomasochistic paraphernalia or its aesthetics. "La ambigüedad erótica" (Erotic Ambiguity) speaks of tranvestites.

Peri Rossi's writing as a whole asserts the need for the individual to assume sexual identity as something separate from both biological and social impositions. She states in "Del libro de la memoria" (From the Book of Memory), part of an unpublished book, that "Sexual identification is always a mistake, since identity is something others give to us" (78). In this sense, the episode from *La nave de los locos* involving the lesbian spectacle of Marlene Dietrich and Dolores del Rio imitators is quite telling in several respects: a multiple mirror image is produced in the main character, Lucía, who imitates Charlotte Rampling, who imitated Helmut Berger, who in turn imitated Marlene Dietrich—with all of them, man and women, imitating an ambiguous, androgynous model. On the other hand, the other character is unidentified and could just as well be a man disguised as a woman or a woman or a transvestite (which is also an ambiguous figure). What is significant is that it is "someone who had decided to be what he wanted to be and not someone with an already determined being" (191). The fundamental proposition here involves the preeminence of will and desire in the face of biological determination and social imposition.

Lucía's vision imitating Marlene Dietrich, roughed and dressed as a man wearing earrings, produces an authentic revelation for Equis (X), the central character of the novel, who feels himself subjugated by ambiguity. What Equis sees is a "beautiful Ephebus" (195). He discovers "two simultaneous worlds, two distinct callings, two messages, two forms of dress, two perceptions, two discourses" (195), which are inseparably bound together. It is for Peri Rossi the lesbian model of ambiguity, of uncertainty or sexual duplicity, which is what can also be discerned in the Babel of *Babel bárbara*.

Homosexual theory appears to be divided between those who adduce essentialist or natural principles in the creation of the homosexual subject, which would support the idea of a universal gay or lesbian identity, and more recent hypotheses that discard essentialism in order to understand that the homosexual subject is a discursive product, the result of a multiplicity of discourses. In this sense, Peri Rossi subscribes to Michel Foucault's theoretical attempts to deessentialize sexuality and to historicize homosexuality. Peri Rossi's works reveal her rejection of essentialist ideas with respect to any sexual typology, whether heterosexual, homosexual or bisexual.

In another fragment *La nave de los locos*, two characters conclude that the attribution of a sexual identity is neurotic, and in *Fantasías eróticas*, Peri Rossi speaks of how imaginary construction, the ability to fantasize, is absolutely imperative for any erotic life. She asserts that one reveals more about what one is through desire than through what one is; and, referring to a lesbian couple in which one member is dressed as a man, she speaks of the fiction of being someone else, of choosing sex as one chooses the color of a piece of clothing. Peri Rossi, who has openly acknowledged her homosexual orientation, commented in a 1978 interview with John F. Deredita that political revolution must go hand in hand with sexual revolution, referring specifically to the problem of minority sexual tendencies, feminist issues and the struggle against both institutionalized and veiled machismo. "Revolution must out of necessity pass through sexual liberty" (136); otherwise, many reactionary sexual attitudes will continue to prevail. In her story "El testigo," one can see how masculine domination ends up in violence against the lesbian couple. The son of one of them, jealous of his mother's lover, bursts in on the two of them and assaults them sexually—forcing them to kiss and fondle each other, and violently penetrating one of them—thereby imposing the law of physical force, macho law. As he leaves his mother's room, he tells her "Don't worry about me. I'm now a real man. Just what this house was lacking" (152). With this he announces that any accord among the three of them is over. As a man, he understands that any relation between women is incomplete and that a man is required to normalize the situation, in order for things to go as they should.

Masculine power is exercised through the phallus-as-whip, which fulfills the function of an instrument of punishment as an attribute of masculinity that allows the boy to threaten the two women. Against this aggression of masculine power via the phallus Peri Rossi legitimates the subversion of lesbian love, which may also include religious irreverence. Women do not need the phallus to obtain pleasure, and a feminine character in *La nave de los locos* explains how she finds a certain harmony in impotence. In these terms Peri Rossi's writing is, in general terms, characterized by the sustained denunciation of any form of domination and by the attempt to achieve human liberation from established norms—social, political and sexual. In this context one must understand her defense of lesbian love as the possibility of choosing one's own sexual identity, as part of the exercise of liberty in the face of accepted norms of social behavior.

WORKS

Babel bárbara. Barcelona: Lumen, 1991.
"Del libro de la memoria." *Quimera* 100 (1990): 76–79.
Descripción de un naufragio. Barcelona: Lumen, 1975.
Diáspora. Barcelona: Lumen, 1976.
Evohé. Montevideo: Girón, 1971.
Fantasías eróticas. Madrid: Ediciones Temas de Hoy, 1991.
Lingüística general. Valencia, Spain: Prometeo, 1979.
La nave de los locos. Barcelona: Seix-Barral, 1984.
La rebelión de los niños. Barcelona: Seix-Barral, 1988.
La tarde del dinosaurio. Barcelona: Plaza y Janés, 1985.
"El testigo." In *Cuentos eróticos*, 141–152. Barcelona: Grijalbo, 1988.
Viviendo. Montevideo: Alfa, 1963.

CRITICISM

Brena, Tomás G. "Cristina Peri Rossi." In his *Exploración estética: Estudio de doce poetas de Uruguay y uno de Argentina*, 463–484. Montevideo: Impresora Record, 1974.
Deredita, John F. "Desde la diáspora: Entrevista con Cristina Peri Rossi." *Texto crítico* 9 (Jan./Apr. 1978): 131–142.
Kantaris, Elia. "The Politics of Desire: Alienation and Identity in the Work of Marta Traba and Cristina Peri Rossi." *Forum for Modern Language Studies* 25.3 (July 1989): 248–264.
Mora, Gabriela. "Cristina Peri Rossi." In *Spanish American Women Writers: A Bio-Bibliographical Source Book*, 436–445. Ed. Diane E. Marting. Westport, Conn.: Greenwood Press, 1990.
———. "Peri Rossi: *La nave de los locos* y la búsqueda de la armonía." *Nuevo texto crítico* 1.2 (1988): 343–352.
Narváez, Carlos Raúl. "La poética del texto sin fronteras: *Descripción de un naufragio, Diáspora, Lingüística general*, de Cristina Peri Rossi." *Intí* 28 (Autumn 1988): 75–88.
Olivera-Williams, María Rosa. "*La nave de los locos* de Cristina Peri Rossi." *Revista de crítica literaria latinoamericana* 7.23 (1986): 81–89.

Rodríguez, Mercedes M. de. "Oneiric Riddles in Peri Rossi's *La nave de los locos*." In *Romance Languages Annual 1989*, 521–527. Ed. Ben Lawton and Anthony Tamburri. West Lafayette, Ind.: Purdue Research Foundation, 1990.

Verani, Hugo. "La historia como metáfora: *La nave de los locos* de Cristina Peri Rossi." *La torre* 4.13 (1990): 79–92.

———. "La rebelión del cuerpo y el lenguaje." *Revista de la Universidad de México* 37.11 (Mar. 1982): 19–22.

Carmen Domínguez

PERLONGHER, NÉSTOR (Argentina; 1949–1992)

Perlongher published poems, translations and literary criticism in various international publications. His works include the books of poems *Austria-Hungría* (1980), *Alambres* (Wires; 1987), *Hule* (Rubber; 1989), and *Parque Lezama* (Lezama Park; 1990). He also published two books of essays with a strong sociological emphasis: *O negócio do miché: Prostituição viril em São Paulo* (Male Hooker Trade: Male Prostitution in São Paulo; 1987) and *El fantasma del SIDA* (The AIDS Phantom; 1988).

Austria-Hungría includes one of Perlongher's best poems in terms of homosexual or, as he preferred, perverse writing (personal interview, São Paulo, Summer 1991): "¿Por qué seremos tan hermosas?" (Why Are We Girls So Pretty?). This poem is based on a ludic rhetoric in something like a dramatic monologue of a paradigmatic screaming queen in which readers recognize each other and even laugh. It is an extreme example of a subculture or counterculture of pathos when it is assumed, yet there is always the suspicion that, to some degree, the center is to be found in the margins.

The pride of pain turns sour in a tone that is apparently festive; it decreases where laughter turns sweet and sour, yet remains realistic. "The empire of *Austria-Hungría* is a disputed empire. A world that is falling apart, a tardy, impossible project of unity. A search for integrity . . . ." This jacket blurb conditions a reading of the political aspects of the nonrealization of a utopia, with all the tensions that it implies. It is interesting to note that in the self-acceptance of a marginal subculture, which has now come out of the closet, by the lyric voice in *Austria-Hungría*, there is a poetic project: to unveil another voice, another pain, another way of being.

This project can be seen in Perlongher's other books of poems, *Alambres, Hule* and *Parque Lezama*: when the homosexual or perverse voice emerges, there is always an affirmation of a voice that is traditionally marginalized. The poem "Miché" (Male Hooker, from *Alambres*) illustrates the poetic fascination that could well be the work of the sociologist of *O negócio do miché*. Parallel to "¿Por qué seremos tan hermosas?" in the profusion of a quasi-neobaroque and ornamented language, this poem shows the oscillation between the masculine/feminine of the homosexual *miché* subject (the female/male tranvestite), the fetishism for certain objects and the sensuality of the chaotic enumerations.

In Perlongher the lyric gay speaker reproduces the melodramatic discourse of characters in novels like Manuel Puig's *El beso de la mujer araña* (*Kiss of the Spider Woman*; 1976), but Perlongher shows the pathetic and human side of these characters. We could say that in the elaboration of a homoerotic *ars poetica*, Perlongher literally passes the microphone to a marginalized voice in order to make it the center of his poetic discourse.

WORKS

Alambres. Buenos Aires: Último Reino, 1987.
Austria-Hungría. Buenos Aires: Último Reino, 1980.
El fantasma del SIDA. Buenos Aires: Puntosur, 1988.
Hule. Buenos Aires: Último Reino, 1989.
O negócio do miché: Prostituição viril em São Paulo. São Paulo: Brasiliense, 1987.
Parque Lezama. Buenos Aires: Sudamericana, 1990.

CRITICISM

Kamenzain, Tamara. "El escudo de la muerte: De Lamborghini a Perlongher." *Rio de la Plata: Culturas* 7 (1988): 115–120.
Zapata, Miguel Ángel. "Néstor Perlongher: La parodia diluyente." Intí: Revista de literatura hispánica 26–27 (1987–1988): 285–297.

Daniel Torres

PIÑERA, VIRGILIO (Cuba; 1912–1979) _____

Piñera was born in the colonial city of Cárdenas. From 1924 to 1937 his family lived in Camagüey, where he finished his secondary studies. He moved to the capital to study at the University of Havana, but failed to obtain his degree because he did not defend his insightful doctoral thesis on the poet Gertrudis Gómez de Avellaneda. The Cuban capital was an exciting and stimulating city for a young intellectual from the provinces. Of even greater impact was Piñera's association with José Lezama Lima and the group of poets connected with the magazine *Orígenes* (Origins; 1944–1956), to which he contributed sporadically for many years.

Disenchanted with the lack of opportunities for writers in Cuba, Piñera accepted a post in Buenos Aires in 1946. For the next twelve years, except for brief visits to Cuba, he lived in self-imposed exile. It proved to be a period of intense production. In addition to several short stories and essays that appeared in the Argentine magazine *Sur* (South), he published two notable works of fiction during this time: his most perplexing and complex novel, *La carne de René* (René's Flesh; 1953), and his masterful collection of stories, *Cuentos fríos* (Cold Tales; 1956). He returned to Cuba in 1958 to coedit José Rodríguez Fcó's aggressive new journal *Ciclón* (Cyclone; 1955–1958).

Piñera is recognized as one of the earliest exponents of the theater of the absurd, as well as its first practitioner in Latin America. Although infrequently mentioned as a novelist, he also cultivated this genre. In his three novels he explores the absurd and fantastic nature of everyday reality. Piñera's poetry includes *Las furias* (Furies; 1941), a volume that contains some of the most somber verses ever written in Cuba. With the publication of *La isla en peso* (The Island in Balance; 1942) Piñera found his own voice.

From its very beginning Piñera's work ran against the current of Cuban literature, which had a strong realist tradition. Piñera emerged as a member of a tiny minority of Cuban writers who were committed to vanguard tenets. A despairing vision of the individual's existence coupled with absurd techniques in both theater and narrative, depersonalized characters, shockingly grotesque themes and imagery, black humor, the predominance of trivial and irrational elements, the inversion of the putatively normal or natural order of things and the use of objective language epitomize Piñera's literature. If readers of Piñera's texts feel tempted to put them down, it is because they are reacting to the author's brutal treatment of reality and to his representation of the world as absurd and irrational, a place almost literally upside down, too sinister to warrant further study. Piñera's intent is to challenge the reader, to uproot preconceived notions of literature, and to demolish traditional expectations, only to replace them with duplicity, uncertainty and ambiguity. The irreverent mocking of all things, including the most taboo and sacred subjects—a manifestation of absurd and grotesque humor—is present in Piñera's theater and in his short stories; it is a form of skepticism associated with the characteristics of *choteo* (a particularly irreverent and rebellious attitude against all matters of seriousness and authority). For Piñera, *choteo* is an intrinsic part of the Cuban character and language. Thus, by extolling the familiar and specific language of the popular sectors of Cuban society, he makes possible the degradation of bourgeois values. *Choteo* in Piñera's work affirms his preoccupation with the forgotten lower classes and with the desire to recognize their contribution to the Cuban identity.

At a time when the subject of sexuality in literature was a taboo, it should not be surprising that its treatment in Piñera's writing is mostly symbolic, clandestinely embedded in carefully constructed images. The human body and its needs, as well as man's sometimes agonizing dependence on both, are always present in his work. What strikes Piñera's readers, however, apart from the absurd and grotesque nature of his vision, are the disquieting metaphors that reveal a subversive order struggling to surface. In this new order that calls for the reader's acceptance of an abnormal, irrational, grotesque and absurd perspective, we find the revelation of the homophobic and homosexual dimension in Piñera's work. Often revealed by the presence of fantastic elements and transfigured as a result of a process of internalized abstraction (from literal to figurative), the homosexual dimension is always linked to the energy and the imagination of the artistic spirit.

Among taboos connected to the homosexual perspective in Piñera's work is that of anthropophagy, a subject that is the focus of the short story "La carne" (Meat), in which self-consumption is the solution to the unavailability of meat, and in the drama *El flaco y el gordo* (The Skinny Man and the Fat Man; 1959): after the skinny patient eats his fat hospital companion, thus becoming the fat man, a new cycle begins at the end of the play with the arrival of a skinny man as his roommate. In both of these works, a semantic game is played between the two meanings of *carne* (as meat and flesh). This ambiguity is explored in greater depth in the novel *La carne de René*, in which Piñera offers what is undoubtedly his most personal testimony regarding homosexual panic.

Piñera's grotesque descriptions of homosexuals often seem to condemn the nature of homosexuality. Nevertheless, the split personality of the closeted homosexual and the divided psyche of the double reveal his perception of homosexuality as a long and painful struggle for self-acceptance and individual expression. Piñera equates aspects of everyday reality with abnormal, irrational and grotesque elements. In many of his stories and in his novels, perhaps more so than his theater, the convergence of these elements leads to and makes possible the eruption of the fantastic order. The grotesque distorts, inverts, degrades; the fantastic exalts, liberates and creates. Subversively contained in absurd and grotesque aspects of reality, the fantastic dimension struggles to the surface. The homosexual world in Piñera's literature, in a similar manner, is latently, surreptitiously present. This means that homosexuality is bound to the creative process represented by both the grotesque and the fantastic. The absurd and the grotesque catalyze the appearance of the creative spirit personified by the homosexual and represented by the fantastic. Inversion and distortion (doubled and mirrored images) are the representation of the writing process, a disfigured rendition of our physical reality transfigured and made magical by the genius of the artist. The ambiguity in Piñera's work regarding homosexuality is an expression of what this distortion represents, which is the essence of literature.

Piñera's enthusiasm for the Cuban Revolution was dashed as early as 1961, when he was briefly incarcerated as a homosexual. This experience resulted in many years of living in fear and silence. After the condemnation of his work because of his sexual preference and the subversive nature of his short novel *Presiones y diamantes* (Pressures and Diamonds; 1967), he died in Havana in 1979, in virtual obscurity. The fear and despair expressed in Piñera's late work is unmistakable. Sexuality, art and death are perceived as the only forms of liberation, the ultimate escape from a panic that splits one's personality. Living far removed from society and from active participation in his country's intellectual life was Piñera's only choice during his last years. Even without hope of having his work published, he continued writing. Most of his work from this period reveals man's condition as an unsuspecting victim, condemned to a cavernous existence and kept alive by a powerful and consuming darkness.

WORKS

Una broma colosal. Havana: Unión, 1988.

La carne de René. Madrid: Alfaguara, 1985.

Cuentos. Madrid: Alfaguara, 1990.

Cuentos fríos. Buenos Aires: Losada, 1956. English version as *Cold Tales.* Trans. Mark Schafer. Hygiene, Colo.: Eridanos Press, 1988.

El conflicto. Havana: Espuela de Plata, 1942.

Dos viejos pánicos. Havana: Casa de las Américas, 1968.

El que vino a salvarme. Buenos Aires: Sudamericana, 1970.

Un fogonazo. Havana: Letras Cubanas, 1987.

Las furias. Havana: Espuela de Plata, 1941.

La isla en peso. Havana: Espuela de Plata, 1942.

Muecas para escribientes. Havana: Letras Cubanas, 1987.

Pequeñas maniobras. Havana: Ediciones R., 1963.

Poesía y prosa. Havana: Orígenes, 1944.

Presiones y diamantes. Havana: Ediciones Unión, 1967.

Teatro completo. Havana: Ediciones R., 1960.

Teatro de la crueldad. Havana: Instituto del Libro, 1967.

Teatro del absurdo. Havana: Instituto del Libro, 1967.

El teatro y su doble. Havana: Instituto del Libro, 1969.

CRITICISM

Aguilú, Raquel. *Los textos dramáticos de Virgilio Piñera y el teatro del absurdo.* Madrid: Pliegos, 1988.

Arenas, Reinaldo. "*La isla en peso* con todas sus cucarachas." *Mariel* 1.2 (1983): 21.

Arrufat, Antón. "Virgilio Piñera o los riesgos de la imaginación." *Unión* 2 (1987): 145–150.

Balderston, Daniel. "Lo grotesco en Piñera: Lectura de 'El álbum.'" *Texto crítico* 34–35 (1986): 174–178.

Carrió Mendía, Raquel. "Estudio en blanco y negro: Teatro de Virgilio Piñera." *Revista iberoamericana* 152–153 (1990): 871–880.

Chichester, Ana García. "Superando el caos: Estado actual de la crítica sobre la narrativa de Virgilio Piñera." *Revista interamericana de bibliografía* 42.1 (1992): 132–147.

Espinosa Domínguez, Carlos. "El poder mágico de los bifes: La estancia argentina de Virgilio Piñera." *Cuadernos hispanoamericanos* 471 (1989): 73–88.

Fernández Ferrer, Antonio. "El <disparate claro> en Cortázar y Piñera." *Revista iberomericana* 159 (1992): 423–436.

Gilgen, Read Grant. "Virgilio Piñera and the Short Story of the Absurd." *Hispania* 63.2 (1980): 348–355.

González-Cruz, Luis F. "Arte y situación de Virgilio Piñera." *Caribe* 2 (1977): 79–86.

Ibieta, Gabriella. "Funciones del doble en la narrativa de Virgilio Piñera." *Revista iberoamericana* 152–153 (1990): 975–991.

Koch, Dolores M. "Virgilio Piñera, cuentista." *Linden Lane Magazine* 1.4 (1982): 14–15.

———. "Virgilio Piñera y el neo-barroco." *Hispamérica* 37 (1984): 81–86.

López-Ramírez, Tomás. "Virgilio Piñera y el compromiso del absurdo." *Areíto* 34.9 (1983): 38–40.

Matas, Julio. "Infiernos fríos de Virgilio Piñera." *Linden Lane Magazine* 1.4 (1982): 22–25.

Méndez y Soto, Ernesto. "Piñera y el tema del absurdo." *Cuadernos hispanoamericanos* 299 (1973): 448–453.

Morello-Frosch, Marta. "La anatomía: Mundo fantástico de Virgilio Piñera." *Hispamérica* 23–24 (1979): 19–34.

Narváez, Carlos R. "Lo fantástico en cuatro relatos de Virgilio Piñera." *Románica* 13 (1976): 77–86.

Ortega, Julio. "*El que vino a salvarme* de Virgilio Piñera." In his *Relato de la utopía: Notas sobre la narrativa cubana de la Revolución*, 99–113. Barcelona: La Gaya Ciencia, 1973.

Rodríguez Feó, José. "Una alegoría de la carne." In his *Notas críticas*, 165–167. Havana: Union de Escritores y Artistas de Cuba.

———. "Hablando de Piñera." In *Notas críticas*, 41–52. Havana: Unión, 1962.

Torres, Carmen L. *La cuentística de Virgilio Piñera: Estrategias humorísticas*. Madrid: Pliegos, 1989.

Ana García Chichester

PIZARNIK, ALEJANDRA (Argentina; 1936–1972)

Pizarnik was born in Buenos Aires to a Jewish family that had immigrated from Eastern Europe. Her being a first-generation Argentine, according to her biographer, Cristina Piña, may have contributed to the awareness of being an alien, a characteristic that appears in almost every piece of her literary creation. In 1954 she began to study philosophy at the University of Buenos Aires, but soon switched to literature. At the same time she attended the school of journalism. In 1955 Pizarnik started painting under the direction of the well-known Uruguayan artist Juan Batlle Planas, an activity that greatly influenced her idea of the visual appearance of the poem. During the same year, she translated, in collaboration with Juan Jacobo Bajarlía, selections from the French writers Paul Eluard and André Breton. Soon after, she became a member of the avant-garde group Poesía de Buenos Aires (Poetry of Buenos Aires) and a frequent visitor at one of the cultural centers of the period, the home of the poet Oliverio Girondo and his wife, Norah Lange.

   In 1960 Pizarnik moved to Paris, where she lived for four years. During her stay in the French capital, she wrote for literary magazines like *Les Lettres nouvelles* (New Letters), *Nouvelle Revue française* (New French Review) and *Mito* (Myth). She translated Antonin Artaud, Henri Michaux, Léopold Sedar Senghor, Aimé Césaire and Yves Bonnefoy into Spanish and took classes, though not systematically, on the history of religion and contemporary French literature at the Sorbonne. The Argentine novelist Julio Cortázar and the Mexican poet Octavio Paz were among her friends and supporters. Pizarnik's European experience seems to have been decisive not only in terms of her private life, but also for the shaping of an innovative aesthetics. When she returned to Buenos Aires, she was no longer an experimental writer in search of her own voice, but a mature poet who had given form to a special and distinctive poetics. In 1966 Pizarnik received the Buenos Aires First Prize for Poetry. Two years later, she was awarded a Guggenheim fellowship, and a Fulbright scholarship in 1971. These were days of public recognition and, paradoxically, of increasing anxiety and desolation. After trying to take her life several times, she was committed to a psychiatric clinic. Finally, during a weekend leave, she killed herself with a drug overdose on September 25, 1972.

Pizarnik's poetry is part of the modern literary tradition of Gérard de Nerval, Charles Baudelaire, Arthur Rimbaud, Isidore Ducasse (who wrote under the name of Comte de Lautrémont), and Antonin Artaud—a tradition in which the aesthetic conceptualization of poetry as a supreme and transcendent act implies an ethics. In fact, as Piña points out, her literary aesthetics led Pizarnik to shape her life according to the set of features traditionally attributed to the myth of the *poète maudit*. Deeply influenced by the surrealist poets, Pizarnik's perception of the poetic goes further than the physical writing of a poem and has to do with her entire life.

There have been several attempts to organize Pizarnik's heterogeneous work. Alejandro Fontenla, who concentrated his research on the poetic writings, proposed two periods. Although the themes developed in both of them are the same—childhood, the creative act, death, the night—Fontenla realizes that in Pizarnik's last two books, poetic and human experiences are plumbed to almost unimaginable depths. Moreover, a formal contrast is perceptible, since in the earlier books Pizarnik employs assorted metrical structures but in each case accepts the limits imposed by the idea of verse, while in the later books she experiments with a form of lyrical prose in which the logic of delirium, with its constructive principle based on phonic and semantic associations, prevails. Starting from the notion of the obscene, understood etymologically as concerning the irrepresentable, Cristina Piña prefers to point out two perspectives rather than two periods. In one portion of Pizarnik's texts, mainly the prose works, the obscene reveals itself directly. In the poems, by contrast, this category appears as the purely unspeakable, as an absence or a camouflage.

Pizarnik's literary production has at least two aspects: a public one, which consists of the seven poetry books she published during her lifetime, and a private one that is known through the posthumous edition of the *Textos de sombra* (Texts of Shadow 1982); and selected fragments of her diaries. A key text like *The Bloody Countess* must be considered separately because of its relationship to both facets. The poems, whether in verse or poetic prose, reveal a tragic and disturbing side of her creativity and personality. Her other texts, mainly obscene, reveal a joyful, witty and childlike temperament. The roots of this duality are probably connected with her complex personality. In the synthetic formulation provided by her biographer, Alejandra was ''an agonic creature, metaphysically unsheltered, fascinated by death, and on the verge of crucial experiences in life and, simultaneously, an almost wild woman because of her corrosive and charming wielding of humor'' (*Alejandra Pizarnik*, 57).

Pizarnik's first book, *La tierra más ajena* (The Most Alien Land; 1955) is a collection of her ''prehistoric poems.'' Although Pizarnik rejected this first work when she became a mature poet, it is a valuable document for tracing the influences and thematic interests of her formative years. The freedom of images and the use of enumeration as a constructive principle indicate the pervasive presence of surrealism. The poems are associated with the dominant tendencies of poetry in the first half of the twentieth century: the inclusion of elements extracted from the most immediate and antipoetic aspects of daily life and the construction of an urban atmosphere.

During the period when Pizarnik was linked to the literary group that supported the magazine *Poesía Buenos Aires* (Poetry Buenos Aires)—principally Raúl Gustavo Aguirre, Elizabeth Azcona Cranwell and Edgar Bayley—she published two books: *La última inocencia* (The Last Innocence; 1956) and *Las aventuras perdidas* (The Lost Adventures; 1958). In both, she provides a unique inflection for her personal themes; death, exposure, the night, the division of one's subjectivity. The idea of poetry as a way out of the ''horror of civilization'' is introduced in *La última inocencia*, where death emerges as an uncertain poetic symbol, the cause of the uppermost fear and yet also a captivating and mysterious object. *Las aventuras perdidas* is dominated by childhood conceived as a place for pure naiveté and plenitude.

The poems included in *Árbol de Diana* (Diana's Tree; 1962), *Los trabajos y las noches* (Works and Nights; 1965) and *Extracción de la piedra de locura* (Extraction of the Stone of Madness; 1968) were written during Pizarnik's French period. At that time, she was so fascinated by Valentine Penrose's book *Erzébet Báthory, la comtesse sanglante* (Erzébet Báthory, the Bloody Countess), that she decided to re-create the historical figure of the Hungarian countess in what became one of the most puzzling books of Argentine literature. *La condesa sangrienta* (*The Bloody Countess*), a difficult-to-classify text, was published for the first time in the Mexican journal *Diálogos* (Dialogues) in 1965 and reprinted in book form in 1971 and 1976.

In 1971 Pizarnik published her last collection of poems, *El infierno musical* (The Musical Hell), which included pieces already printed in *Nombres y figuras* (Names and Figures; 1969). Apart from the above-mentioned books, Pizarnik produced several critical pieces, short stories, poems and a theatrical piece entitled *Los poseídos entre lilas* (The Possessed Among Lilacs), some of them published in American and European magazines and journals. They were brought together by Olga Orozco and Ana Becciú in *Textos de sombra y últimos poemas* (Texts of Shadow and Last Poems; 1982).

The bibliography of Pizarnik's work, although important, is not extensive. The earliest commentaries were reviews of some of her books, such as the one that Enrique Pezzoni devoted to *Los trabajos y las noches* in the literary magazine *Sur* (South), and biographical sketches and evocations written on the occasion of her death. Among the latter, an article by Juan Gustavo Cobo Borda (1972) is an outstanding presentation of the poet. An early methodological approach to Pizarnik's poetry is David Lagmanovich's paper (1978). In 1981 Cristina Piña published a book-length study, *La palabra como destino* (The Word as Destiny), in which suicide is analyzed as a "governing force in the poetry of Alejandra present at the deepest level of her writing, beyond any coincidence with reality" (10–11).

The diffusion of Pizarnik's writings in the English-speaking world began in the early 1980s with the anthology of Latin American women poets entitled *Open to the Sun* (edited by N. Jacquez Wiesser; 1979); four poems in prose with a brief introduction note by Susan Pensak appeared in *13th Moon* (1980), a periodical devoted to writing by women. Pensak also translated an interview with the poet by Martha I. Moia originally printed in 1972. Frank Graziano has edited an excellent anthology of prose and poetry, translated by Suzanne Jill Levine, María Rosa Fort and Graziano, with an excellent foreword and notes.

Criticism has examined several traditional and current issues in the corpus of Pizarnik's work. Francisco Lasarte studies the relationship to surrealism in one of the most thoughtful articles published on Pizarnik's poetry. Thorpe Running considers that the matrix or central core of Pizarnik's published work is the idea of "absence," around which every other element of her poetics—repetition, death, childhood—acquires its specific meaning. The Confessional tone is the focus of Robert E. DiAntonio, who thinks that "Pizarnik's poetics form part of an agonizing voyage of self-discovery, both for the poetess and for the reader" (52). Alicia Borinsky surveys the problem of voice and poetic technique, taking as a starting point two posthumous publications, the anthology *El deseo de la palabra* (The Desire for the Word; 1975) and *Textos de sombra*. Delfina Muschietti makes good use of feminist and poststructuralist ideas in a reading of Pizarnik's last production, concluding that her texts "speak about an experience in a foundational manner for Argentine poetry; that of the constitution of the subject-woman in our culture" (232). The lesbian dimension of Pizarnik's personal experience had not been considered until the publication of Cristina Piña's biography in 1991, a well-written piece by one of the best-informed scholars of Pizarnik. The literary manifestations of homosexual concerns were explored by David William Foster in his studies on *The Bloody Countess* (1991; forthcoming) and the exhaustive analysis of the representation of the body in the poetry of Pizarnik (forthcoming).

Although there is no doubt about the sexual identity of Alejandra Pizarnik, it is quite surprising that, beyond oblique remarks, the subject and the repercussions of her lesbianism in her writing have not been investigated in depth. It is possible to suggest several explanations for this lack of attention. The sociocultural milieu in which Pizarnik was raised and educated, and in which she developed her literary activity—Buenos Aires in the 1950s and 1960s—was not openly supportive of anything other than heterosexuality. Foster states that the poet "wrote at a time when lesbian identity as such could not be forthrightly articulated," her poetry "is characterized by both an evasiveness as to the gender identity of the poetic voice and its addressee and by the adoption of a conventional, normalized female/male discourse of love" ("Representation," 4).

This assertion leads to a second reason: the problem of Pizarnik's own vacillations as someone who seems to have experienced her sexuality as problematic throughout her life. In this regard, Piña emphasizes the consequences of the troublesome relationship Pizarnik had with her parents and the impossibility of emotional maturity and the attainment of a stable sexual identity with a peaceful acceptance of her body and her sexuality. She tended to fall in love with older men or to enjoy their company. This was a constant constituent of Pizarnik's relationships during adolescence. According to Piña, such an attraction corresponds to her relationship with the paternal figure and her elaboration of the Oedipus complex (*Alejandra Pizarnik*, 68). Only during her stay in France and the final years in Argentina is there evidence of her sexual intimacy with women. Yet, Piña finds it inappropriate to extract from the writings actual aspects of Pizarnik's sexual behavior regarding the fluctuating choice of heterosexual and homosexual partners and with reference to her erotic freedom toward the end of her life.

Finally, it is not clear whether this intimate conflict—which can be claimed to explain eccentric aspects of her behavior, like the decision to take the night as her appropriate realm, her refusal to work and the use of stimulants—may be used as the basis for interpretation. Is writing overdetermined by the sexual orientation of the writer? How does this bio/sociopsychological constituent of one's personality determine the choice of themes and their intellectual treatment? What scriptural marks should be isolated on the surface of someone's writing in order to evaluate the degree to which sexuality is a relevant factor in literary research? Obviously these questions go beyond the treatment of the production of a particular writer. Thus the procedure adopted here will be to survey Pizarnik's entire production, pointing out the appearance of sexually related topics.

The first thing that attracts the reader's attention is that, with two exceptions, the texts Pizarnik chose to publish do not contain obvious hints of her sexual orientation. On the contrary, a considerable part of her poetry is articulated through the conventional discourse of love poetry. In several poems of *La última inocencia*, the poetic voice splits in two. The poet addresses herself, calls herself by her own name, in order to delineate the absence of the lover, as in "La enamorada" (Woman in Love). Beyond ay inviting biographical conclusion, it is worthwhile to observe that the rhetoric of love imposes the presentation of a heterosexual couple in the lyrical sphere, although it is emptied of all sexual connotations. The poetic voice establishes a dialogue with itself in which the other, the beloved, is referred to through the continual use of the masculine form *amado*. Clearly, this does not require that the real referent correspond to a male individual, since this sort of epithet may be used to refer to a woman as the masculine, active member of the couple.

Pizarnik's tragic conception of love permeates her writing. A popular poem, "Cenizas" (Ashes) from *Las aventuras perdidas*, recounts a love story in two moments, that of recalling and that of loneliness. Once again, the reference demands a heterosexual couple clearly identified by the grammatical gender: the poet feels *sola* (alone, feminine) and speaks to her *amado* (beloved, masculine). Similar linguistic markers direct the reading of many other texts in this collection: "La danza immóvil" (The Motionless Dance), "Exilio" (Exile), "El ausente" (The Absent One), "Desde esta orilla" (From This Shore). This is truly problematic when rendering an English version of her poetry, particularly the adjectives and pronouns.

Another significant text of *La última inocencia* is "Solamente" (Only), where the poet states that she understands the "truth," something that explodes in her desires and every other substantial manifestation of her being. Nowhere does this truth receive an outspoken content because it appears to be a secret verity. In such a case, the poem becomes enigmatic and could be deciphered as a declaration of acceptance of the poet's most private sexual drives or anything else. It is not a case of defining a precise and unique meaning, but of observing the use of vagueness, which allows a reading of the poem as an oblique allusion to sexuality. The consequences of ambiguity are increased when different levels of reference merge. A case in point is the poem "Tiempo" (Time), also from *Las aventuras perdidas*. While DiAntonio acknowledges "moments of erotic epiphany" (50) in this piece, Borinsky, reading it in a quite different way, considers that the writer eludes the autobiographical component in her work by means of an intensification of the internal glance, in such a way that childhood would be a dissolving origin, a dragging force toward her other edge.

The love motif is almost entirely absent from *Árbol de Diana*. It appears only in a frequently anthologized poem, "Sólo la sed" (Only the Thirst), where the cliché "amor mío" (my love), referring to the poet's feelings, is a way of alluding to the beloved without specifying gender. An especially confidential and intense exploration of romantic and erotic topics is found in *Los trabajos y las noches*, a collection divided into three sections. The opening piece, "Poema" (Poem), presents the theme of the other—*tú* (you)—as someone whom the poet loves but also as part of a two-person whole, a "we," the source of contentment and the possibility of sharing the deepest experiences, life itself. In "Revelaciones" (Revelations) the lover's body is the paramount object of desire and, indeed, something the poet has possessed.

It is revealing to observe that the masculine adjective *amado* is combined, metonymically, with the body of the lover and not with the lover him/herself, allowing for ambivalence. "En tu aniversario" (On your Birthday), "Destrucciones" (Destructions), "Amantes" (Lovers) and "Reconocimiento" (Recognition) also employ this vagueness, where discriminating gender markers are avoided. However, in "Tu voz" (Your Voice) there is no question about the masculine condition of the alluded voice. Aside from the use of a masculine adjective in the first line, the rest of the text, devoid of corroborating indications, does not allow us to state that the poem describes a heterosexual relationship. The closing poem of the first part, "Sentido de su ausencia" (Meaning of His/Her Absence), one of the most frequently quoted of Pizarnik's poems, illustrates the obstacles to translation. Since the third-person possessive pronoun in Spanish is not marked for the gender of the possessor (but rather for the gender of what is possessed), the English version (because English marks the gender of the possessor) necessarily has to clarify the reference by deciding for either the masculine or the feminine. Graziano opts for "his" in his translation. This is only one example that represents a generalized problem. Graziano takes note of a related problem where ambiguity of gender is troublesome when pronouns are excluded in the original: "Since English requires pronouns where Spanish does not, we were occasionally obliged to make gender assumptions based upon whatever textual evidence presented itself, thus suffering the loss of the original's ambiguity" (5).

In the last section of *Los trabajos y las noches*, the subject matter changes completely. Access to the innovative poetic world, even more private and difficult to grasp, is achieved here. The language is transformed into a nonrational system of communication. It is the emergence of an inner voice, partially articulated, in which the logic and grammatical connectors are replaced by the extended use of juxtaposition. In *Extracción de la piedra de la locura*, topics related to human attraction are barely present. In "Escrito en el Escorial" (Written at the Escorial), "El sol, el poema" (The Sun, the Poem) and "Estar" (Being), the poetic voice recovers the traditional tonality of the old Spanish *cantiga de amigo* (lover's song). An extreme manifestation of this recovering is the direct quotation in "El sueño de la muerte o el lugar de los cuerpos poéticos" (The Death Dream or the Place of the Poetical Bodies). But the seduction of love in its most physical aspect appears sporadically. In "Como agua sobre una piedra" (Like Water on a Stone) a subtle image suggests an abrupt interruption of the sexual act, like a snapshot that transforms the climax in a moment of complete fusion. In addition to these isolated examples, a certain sublimating pressure placed by the rhetoric of love on physical contact is at work in this book as well as in *El infierno musical*.

During her French period, Pizarnik's literary imagination was seduced by the gruesome story of Erzébet Báthory, a noblewoman who tortured and killed over six hundred young women in sexual rituals associated with the search for eternal youth. *La condesa sangrienta* is presented as a commentary on Valentine Penrose's text, a set of brief notes or vignettes, that induces a meditation not only on the historic individual but, more significant, on human nature. In the prologue, Pizarnik recognizes Penrose's merits in presenting a form of beauty that does not correspond to the one traditionally promoted by the official culture of all "civilized" societies: "The sexual perversion and the insanity of the Countess Báthory are so patent that Valentine Penrose overlooks them in order to focus exclusively on the convulsive beauty of the character" (9–10). Retaining this strategy of suspending ethical and psychological considerations, Pizarnik's creativity goes beyond mere commentary to display a tableau of mainly descriptive vignettes, written in a highly lyrical prose.

Despite this narrative stance, *Condesa* is in no way a novelistic presentation of Báthory's activities. The textual articulation depends, then, on the arrangement of the episodes and not on the intricacy of the plot, so that the image of the central character is delineated through partial insights. The three introductory pieces, "La virgen de hierro" (The Iron Virgin), "Muerte por agua" (Death by Water) and "La jaula mortal" (The Lethal Cage), are meticulous expositions of the sophisticated instruments of torture and varied forms of torment the servants of the countess use to fulfill her sadistic fantasies. This initial subset is especially meaningful. Although the rest of the sections introduce personal remarks as well as speculative considerations, the prevailing tone of the beginning conditions the reading of the whole. It determines the interpretation of torture as a displaced form of rape in a ritualistic situation. The narrator's use of the present tense, the insistence on certain details—the hieratical attitude of the countess, who attends ceremonial sessions of torture and death wearing white clothes, the change of the color of those clothes as they soak up the blood of her victims—and a pictorial language through which the most horrifying images are created, contribute to the representation of the ritual.

In the fourth vignette, the narrator renounces an exclusively expository tone in order to add subjective remarks, conclusions that seek to explain different sides of the horrible eroticism of the countess. Later, in "El espejo de la melancolía" (The Mirror of Melancholy), the lesbian component of her personality is defined in plain language: "No one was ever able to confirm the truth of the rumors about the countess's homosexuality. We will never know whether she ignored the tendency or, on the contrary, admitted it as a right she accorded herself along with all the other rights" (Suzanne Jill Levine's translation in Graziano, 100).

Several other features stand out. There is a component of cruel irony that has gone unnoticed by commentators. In "The Iron Virgin," for instance, the innocence traditionally attributed to a virgin is brought into play, contrasting with the brutality of the instrument of torment described. The mechanical virgin extracts the blood of young women in a deadly embrace. Virginity, youth, an embrace are, in cultural terms, affirmative signs, which are articulated here in a destructive combination. Another feature of the text is a persistent voyeurism. Over and over again, the narrator introduces statements like "La condesa, sentada en su trono, contempla" (The countess, sitting on her throne, watches; 15) or "La condesa contempla desde el interior de la carroza" (The countess observes this from inside her coach; 20). The contemplation of the suffering of others is a key element for the depiction of the perverse sexuality of the countess, who occasionally handles torture instruments herself. Voyeurism also has a second structural function. As Foster has pointed out on several occasions, this expository procedure is not just a literary representation of an alternative form of sexuality but also a manner of introducing the reader in the text as a voyeur (*Gay and Lesbian Themes*; "Of Power and Virgins").

Finally, being an austere and puzzlingly beautiful presentation of sadistic depravity, *Condesa* supposes a particular interest in topics related to sexuality that had already emerged in Pizarnik's public behavior, transmuted as a colloquial obscene humor (Piña, *Alejandra Pizarnik*). Humor, however, has no place in this book because the fascination with death runs parallel to that with sex. This connection is explicit. In fact, the narrator observes that "If the sexual act implies a sort of death, Erzébet Báthory was in need of the visible, elemental, vulgar death in order to be able to die, in turn, by the figurative death that is orgasm" (Piña, *Alejandra Pizarnik*, 31). The interweaving of sex and death, connected as it is with power, generates an almost unmanageable universe, with a distinctly destructive character. In sum, the central attempt of *Condesa* is to denounce the misuse of unlimited power rather than to legitimate homosexuality as an alternative manifestation of eroticism.

The rest of Pizarnik's literary production was published in a compilation prepared by Olga Orozco and Ana Becciú. This volume poses at least two theoretical problems. The first involves ethical concerns when an editor presents texts that the author decided not to publish in book form, like the poems of the 1963–1968 period and the dramatic version of *Los poseídos entre lilas*. The second has to do with the aesthetic complications raised by considering the strict intellectual method to which Pizarnik subjected her creative impulses. A consequence of her extensive reworking of the texts is that nobody can be sure whether the unpublished pieces should be considered finished products. Leaving these problems aside, it is worthwhile to examine in some detail a prose text included in *Textos de sombra*. "Violario" (On Rape) is the description of an experience from adolescence (it is impossible to tell if this corresponds to an actual event or not) that evokes lesbian rape. Even though the facts—during a funeral a woman embraces her from behind—may be interpreted in a nonsexual way, the idea of having been abused, inscribed at least in Pizarnik's poetic imagination, is revealing. A pivotal factor in "Violario" is the presence of a dead man who becomes a silent representation of Death and appears in close association with an unwanted sexual incident. Susan Pensak translated this text into English, although her rendition is not completely satisfactory, since there is a confusion with verbal endings, due to the particular use of the second-person-singular form in Buenos Aires Spanish. As a result, what is a command ("Look at the flowers. . . . Keep looking at the flowers"; my translation) that justifies the final decision of not writing any other poem with flowers, becomes an almost trivial assertive statement: ''I looked at the flowers. . . . I continued looking at the flowers'' (Pensak's translation, 60).

From the list of examples already cited, which could be easily extended by taking into account several pieces from ''La bucanera de Pernambuco o Hilda la polígrafa'' (The Lady Buccaneer from Pernambuco or Hilda the Polygraph), it is evident that themes related to sexuality do not have a privileged position in Pizarnik's works. The manifestations of human attraction, whether heterosexual or homosexual, are the expression of a subjectivity in permanent conflict. Rather than a communication of actual experiences, Pizarnik displays an inner exploration of her own phantoms through a challenging treatment of language.

WORKS

Alejandra Pizarnik, a Profile. Ed. and trans. Frank Graziano. Durango, Colo.: Logbridge-Rhodes, 1987.

Árbol de Diana. Buenos Aires: Sur, 1962. Also Buenos Aires: Botella al Mar, 1988.

La condesa sangrienta. Buenos Aires: López Crespo, 1971. Also 1976. English trans. as *The Bloody Countess* in *Other Fires: Short Fiction by Latin American Women*. Ed. Alberto Manguel. New York: Clarkson N. Potter, 1986.

El deseo de la palabra. Barcelona: Barral, 1975.

Extracción de la piedra de locura. Buenos Aires: Sudamericana, 1968.

El infierno musical. Buenos Aires: Siglo XXI, 1971.

Nombres y figuras. Barcelona: La Esquina, 1969.

Obras completas. Poesía y prosa. Buenos Aires: Corregidor, 1990. Despite its title, this volume does not include Pizarnik's three first books.

Poemas. Buenos Aires: Centro Editor de América Latina, 1982.

Textos de sombra y últimos poemas. Ed. Olga Orozco and Ana Becciú. Buenos Aires: Sudamericana, 1982.

La tierra más ajena. Buenos Aires: Botella al Mar, 1955.

Los trabajos y las noches. Buenos Aires: Sudamericana, 1965.

La última inocencia y Las aventuras perdidas. Buenos Aires: Botella al Mar, 1976.

CRITICISM

Borinsky, Alicia. ''Muñecas reemplazables.'' *Río de la Plata: Culturas* 7 (1988): 41–48.

Camara, Isabel. ''Literatura o la política del juego en Alejandra Pizarnik.'' *Revista iberoamericana* 132–133 (1985): 581–589.

Caulfield, Carlota. ''Entre la poesía y la pintura: Elementos surrealistas en *Extracción de la piedra de locura* y *El infierno musical* de Alejandra Pizarnik.'' *Chasqui* 21.1 (1992): 3–10.

Cobo Borda, Juan Gustavo. ''Alejandra Pizarnik: La pequeña sonámbula.'' *Eco* 26.1 (1972): 40–64.

DiAntonio, Robert E. ''On Seeing Things Darkly in the Poetry of Alejandra Pizarnik: Confessional Poetics or Aesthetic Metaphor?'' *Confluencia* 2 (1987): 47–52.

Fontenla, Alejandro. ''Prólogo.'' In Pizarnik, *Poemas*, i–viii.

Foster, David William. *Gay and Lesbian Themes in Latin American Writing*, 97–102. Austin: University of Texas Press, 1991.

———. "Of Power and Virgins: Alejandra Pizarnik's *La condesa sangrienta*." Forthcoming.

———. "The Representation of the Body in the Poetry of Alejandra Pizarnik." Forthcoming in *Hispanic Review*.

Lagmanovich, David. "La poesía de Alejandra Pizarnik." In *XVII Congreso del Instituto internacional de literatura iberoamericana*, 885–895. Madrid: Cultura Hispánica, 1978.

Lasarte, Francisco. "Más allá de surrealismo: La poesía de Alejandra Pizarnik." *Revista iberoamericana* 125 (1983): 867–877.

Moia, Martha I. "Some Keys to Alejandra Pizarnik." *Sulfur* 8 (1983): 97–101. Trans. Susan Pensak.

Muschietti, Delfina. "Alejandra Pizarnik: La niña asesinada." *Filología* 24 (1989): 231–241.

Pensak, Susan. "Alejandra Pizarnik (Argentina, 1936–1972)." *13th Moon* 5 (1980): 55–74.

Pezzoni, Enrique. "Alejandra Pizarnik: La poesía como destino." *Sur* 297 (1965): 101–104. Also in his *El texto y sus voces*, 156–161. Buenos Aires: Sudamericana, 1986.

Piña, Cristina. *Alejandra Pizarnik*. Buenos Aires: Planeta, 1991.

———. *La palabra como destino. Un acercamiento a la poesía de Alejandra Pizarnik*. Buenos Aires: Botella al Mar, 1981.

———. "La palabra obscena." *Cuadernos hispanoamericanos. Los complementarios* 5 (1990): 17–38.

Running, Thorpe. "The Poetry of Alejandra Pizarnik." *Chasqui* 14.2–3 (1985): 45–55.

Soncini, Anna. "Itinerario de la palabra en el silencio." *Cuadernos hispanoamericanos. Los complementarios* 5 (1990): 7–15.

Daniel Altamiranda

PORTILLO TRAMBLEY, ESTELA
(United States; 1936) _____

Estela Portillo Trambley was born in El Paso to Frank Portillo and Delfina Fierro. In 1953 she married Robert Trambley. After earning a B.A. (1957) and an M.A. in English literature (1977) from the University of Texas, El Paso, Portillo Trambley began her career as a teacher of English and later as chair of the English department at Technical High School in El Paso. In 1969–1970 she produced her own radio talk show, which she has described as "very political" (Bruce-Novoa, 166), followed in 1971–1972 by "Cumbres" (Peaks), an all-Spanish television show on culture and the fine arts. Her literary production began to take shape between 1970 and 1975, when Portillo Trambley became a resident dramatist at El Paso Community College, where she founded the Chicano Theater group. Her first play, *The Day of the Swallows* (1971), is considered by Juan Bruce-Novoa to be a precursor of a Chicano theater of professionalism, as the individual dramatist moves away from the collective creation of local groups like the Teatro Campesino (Peasant Theater).

After receiving the Quinto Sol Award in 1973 from the University of California at Berkeley's Chicano Publishing House, Portillo Trambley's literary work, prose and poetry gained major national recognition. Her radio drama "The Burning" was staged at the Western Public Radio Workshop in September 1983; *Puente Negro* won the Second Annual Women's Plays competition at St. Edward's University at Austin in 1984; and *Blacklight* won second prize in 1985 in the New York Shakespeare Festival's Hispanic American playwrights' competition.

Reacting to her critics' labeling her a women's liberationist, Portillo Trambley has accepted her preference for women characters: "For a woman it's difficult to write male characters. So I decided to write about women" (Bruce-Novoa, 167). Her work shows this tendency toward women characters, most of them Mexicans or Chicanas of various social backgrounds, who confront society's biased gender divisions; the latter include physical aggression sanctioned by the institution of marriage—even rape, looked upon by men as a natural form of their society-given control over women. Two major examples of her feminist interest in documenting women's experience stand out: *Trini*, a novel of a Mexican Indian girl who, despite having been raped at an early age, turns her life around with the aid of her philosophical search for love; and the play *Sor Juana*, a historical re-creation of the seventeenth-century Mexican nun Sor Juana Inés de la Cruz's struggle to integrate her feminist self and her mystical being.

Perhaps Portillo Trambley's open feminist activism has prevented her acceptance by Chicano men, as she pointed out: "It's going to take a lot of conditioning before men say that I am a Chicano writer and that I write as well as the men" (Bruce-Novoa, 171). Nonetheless, Portillo Trambley can be viewed as a precursor of the strong feminist Chicano movement of the 1980s. In fact, her play *The Day of the Swallows* was seen initially as a lesbian text: "The plot is about lesbians; I knew nothing about them, but I was going to sell it" (Bruce-Novoa, 170). Despite the economic exploitation of a lesbian plot and the clear defiance of the heterosexual-male-dominated Chicano canon, this play, along with John Rechy's novel *City of Night* (1963), initiates lesbian/homosexual characters into Chicano literature. In the line of the traditional Hispanic theater, *The Day of the Swallows* is a tightly constructed play that draws its lesbian thematic center from its emphasis on the soothing feminine powers of Mother Earth. The cult of the goddess is represented by a main character, Doña Josefa, a middle-aged woman who, hurt by men, turns to nature for refuge and makes her home, facing a peaceful lake, a true feminine *locus amoenus*. Well-liked and respected by women for her social commitment to the oppressed (for example, she takes a boy away from an abusive alcoholic father), she finds her life turned around when she rescues a young woman from prostitution and eventually falls in love with her. After a year of secrecy, the women are discovered in their lovemaking by David, Doña Josefa's adopted child; Doña Josefa brutally kills him by cutting out his tongue. The news that her lover had planned to marry a young Indian man causes Doña Josefa to commit suicide by throwing herself into the lake, home of her supernatural *duendes*, spirits of light that had guided her life of good deeds.

Portillo Trambley is a clear precursor of postmodernist Chicana literature in showing an early rejection of assimilation into the male-oriented mainstream culture. Her female characters recognize that such an assimilation would annihilate the feminine creative self. Her work resists chronological label, since it predates the feminist social agenda for the improvement of women's and their children's civil rights, and it pioneers an exploration of the deeper meanings of the feminine experience, which includes lesbianism. Not a lesbian manifesto by today's literary standards, *The Day of the Swallows*'s lesbian love and sexual pleasure (although not the central point of the play) provide powerful theatrical sociopoetic symbolism of the lesbian experience.

WORKS

"The Burning." In *Images of Women in Literature*, 421–580. Ed. Mary Anne Ferguson. Boston: University of Massachusetts Press, 1986.

Chicanas en literatura y arte. Berkeley, Calif.: Quinto Sol, 1974.

The Day of the Swallows. In *Contemporary Chicano Theater: An Anthology*, 204–245. Ed. Roberto J. Garza. Notre Dame, Ind.: University of Notre Dame Press, 1976. Also *We Are Chicanos*, 224–271. Ed. Philip D. Ortego. New York: Washington Square Press, 1973. Also in *El Espejo—The Mirror: Selected Chicano Literature*, 150–193. Ed. Octavio Ignacio Romano V. and Herminio Ríos C. Berkeley, Calif.: Quinto Sol, 1972.

Impressions. Berkeley, Calif.: El Espejo//Quinto Sol, 1971.

Rain of Scorpions and Other Writings. Berkeley, Calif.: Tonatiuh International, 1975.

Sor Juana and Other Plays. Ypsilanti, Mich.: Bilingual Press/Editorial Bilingüe, 1983.

Trini. Binghamton, N.Y.: Bilingual Press/Editorial Bilingüe, 1986.

"Women of the Earth." Master's thesis, University of Texas–El Paso, 1977.

CRITICISM

Bruce-Novoa, Juan. "Estela Portillo." In his *Chicano Authors: Inquiry by Interview*, 163–181. Austin: University of Texas Press, 1980.

Cárdenas, Lupe. "Los personajes femeninos en *The Day of the Swallows* de Estela Portillo-Trambley." In *Mujer y literatura mexicana y chicana: Culturas en contacto*, 293–297. Ed. Aralia López González, Amelia Malazamba and Elena Urrutia. Mexico City: Colegio de México, 1990.

Castellano, Olivia. "Of Clarity and the Moon." *De colores* 3.3 (1977): 25–29.

Castro, Ginette. "Memorie ethnique et religion dans *Rain of Scorpions*." In her *Le Facteur religieux en Amérique du Nord*, 307–324. Talence, France: Centre de Recherches Amérique Anglophone, Maison des Sciences de l'Homme d'Aquitaine, 1986.

Dewey, Janice. "Doña Josefa: Bloodpulse of Transition and Change." In *Breaking Boundaries: Latina Writings and Critical Readings*, 30–47. Ed. Asunción Horno Delgado, Eliana Ortega, Nina M. Scott and Nancy Saporta Sternbach. Amherst: University of Massachusetts Press, 1989.

Herrera-Sobek, María. "La unidad del hombre y el cosmos: Reafirmación del proceso vital en Estela Portillo Trambley." *La palabra* 4–5.1–2 (Spring–Autumn 1982–1983): 127–141.

Martínez, Eliud. "Personal Vision in the Short Stories of Estela Portillo Trambley." In *Beyond Stereotypes: The Critical Analysis of Chicana Literature*, 71–90. Ed. María Herrera-Sobek. Binghamton, NY: Bilingual Press/Editorial Bilingüe, 1985.

Meier, Matt S. *Mexican American Biographies: A Historical Dictionary, 1836–1987*, 179–180. Westport, Conn.: Greenwood Press, 1988.

Miguélez, Armando. "Aproximaciones al nuevo teatro chicano de autor único." *Explicación de textos literarios* 15.2 (1986–1987): 8–18.

Parotti, Philip. "Nature and Symbol in Estela Portillo's 'The Paris Gown.' " *Studies in Short Fiction* 24.4 (Fall 1987): 417–424.

Rodríguez, Alfonso. "Tragic Vision in Estela Portillo's *The Day of the Swallows*." *De colores* 5.1–2 (1980): 152–158.

Ryan, Bryan. *Hispanic Writers*, 377–379. Detroit: Gale Research, 1991.

Schiavone, James David. "Distinct Voices in the Chicano Short Story: Anaya's Outreach, Portillo Trambley's Outcry, Rosaura Sánchez's Outrage." *The Americas Review* 16.2 (Summer 1988): 68–81.

Vallejo, Tomás. "Estela Portillo Trambley's Fictive Search for Paradise." *Frontiers: a Journal of Women Studies* 5.2 (Summer 1990): 54–58.

Vargas, Margarita. "Lo apolíneo y lo dionisiaco: Hacia una semiótica en *Sor Juana* y *The Day of the Swallows* de Estela Portillo Trambley." *Gestos* 5.9 (April 1990): 91–98.

Vowell, Faye Nell. "A Melus Interview: Estela Portillo Trambley." *Melus* 9.4 (Winter 1982): 59–66.

Rafael Ocasio

PUIG, MANUEL (Argentina; 1932–1990) —————

Puig was born in General Villegas, a small pampas town in Argentina, where he had his first glimpse of machismo and its oppressive authority. His experiences growing up in General Villegas were eventually depicted in his first novel, *La traición de Rita Hayworth (Betrayed by Rita Hayworth*; 1968). Like Puig, the protagonist, Toto, is fascinated with Hollywood movies. Toto is a sensitive young man who cannot accept the macho role assigned to him; he is a budding artist who feels betrayed not only by the great star of the novel's title—that is, by the Hollywood icon—but also by his father and the patriarchal order that he represents.

Puig's life was marked by self-exile and constant traveling. At the age of fourteen he left his home town and moved to Buenos Aires to attend a boarding school. After several career moves—architecture, philosophy, the military—

Puig traveled to Italy in 1955 to study at Cinecittà. His film studies in Rome proved to be enriching, but Puig's moviemaking dreams were thwarted by the neorealist school that dominated the Italian film scene at the time. He wanted to tell stories in the fashion of the American directors he had come to admire, but Hollywood was a dirty word at Cinecittà. The dogmatic neorealist agenda came to represent, for Puig, one more manifestation of the authoritative mentality he had known in General Villegas. Neorealists, in his opinion, were not exciting storytellers.

Puig left Italy and lived for some time in Stockholm and London. Driven by his passion for film, he returned to Argentina in 1960 to work as an assistant director. He stayed for three years and then moved to New York City, where he found employment as a flight attendant for Air France. In his spare time he was writing screenplays that—he later admitted to friends and interviewers— were basically remakes of Hollywood film classics. His first novel, in fact, was written originally as a film script.

Puig's travels nourished his fiction. While living in Mexico he worked on *Pubis angelical (Pubis Angelical*; 1979), which takes place in a Mexican hospital. His New York sojourn led to *Eternal Curse on the Reader of These Pages*, which he wrote in English and then translated into Spanish as *Maldición eterna a quien lea estas páginas*; 1980). Both *Sangre de amor correspondido (Blood of Requited Love*; 1982) and Puig's last novel, *Cae la noche tropical (Tropical Night Falling*; 1988), are set in Brazil, where the writer spent a great deal of time. Puig was living in Cuernavaca, Mexico, when he died of a heart attack after gall bladder surgery. At the time of his death he was working on a screenplay based on the life of Antonio Vivaldi.

Manuel Puig had a talent for capturing the voices and melodramatic themes of popular culture. He incorporated in his work mass-media constructs like the dime novel (*folletín* in Spanish), the detective novel, Hollywood movies and radio serials. His novels, however, recontextualize those mass-media products in such a way as to render them artistic and literary. Puig's writing has elicited numerous articles and several books, and has found its way into Hollywood through the film version of *El beso de la mujer araña (Kiss of the Spider Woman*; 1976), directed by Héctor Babenco (1985). Puig also reached a wide international audience through the many productions of his theatrical version of the novel. He has won praise from both highly specialized critics and mainstream readers worldwide.

Many of Puig's characters define their needs and aspirations around movie plots and Hollywood stars. Molina, in *El beso de la mujer araña*, narrates several movies to his cellmate Valentín and emulates the leading ladies in those narratives. In *Pubis angelical*, the protagonist, Ana, dreams of a famous Viennese actress who was employed and exploited by American film studios. Gladys, one of the main characters in *The Buenos Aires Affair* (1973), watches movie classics on the ''Late Late Show,'' and excerpts from these melodramas are cited as epigraphs at the beginning of each chapter of the novel. The parodied

movies underscore Hollywood's predominant role in the shaping of contemporary society and its pervasive presence in Latin American culture. But, most
important, the narrated and cited films are passageways into the characters'
subconscious lives. The implied reader of Puig's texts functions as a sort of
voyeur of those cinematic tales; a silent—but creative—observer of the characters' breakdowns and triumphs; a witness to their sexual fantasies and their
quest for happiness.

Puig's first novel, *La traición de Rita Hayworth*, depicts and denounces a
society in which most relationships are based on power hierarchies and gender
roles are assigned within an ambience of violence and rape. At the school described in this biographical work, the younger students are assaulted and sexually abused by the older ones. In the broader community beyond the school, it
is women who suffer assault and eventual betrayal by men. *Boquitas pintadas*
(*Heartbreak Tango*; 1969), Puig's second novel, focuses on the life of a wom-
anizer, Juan Carlos Echepare. Through this Don Juan type the theme of machismo is further explored. The female characters dream of living like
melodrama heroines. As they emulate the pastiche figures in those hackneyed
love stories, they unveil the pain and frustration they feel, their dissatisfaction
with the limiting roles—wife, mother, whore—they are expected to fulfill.

Three of Puig's novels offer exciting possibilities for the discussion of a gay
subjectivity: *The Buenos Aires Affair, El beso de la mujer araña*, and *Pubis
angelical*. By exploring sexuality in contexts that demystify and problematize
its previously spoken truths, these books suggest that much of what we understand to be natural in sexuality is in fact learned. The novels propose that social
mechanisms not only repress or prohibit certain forms of gender performance,
but produce and channel sexuality itself. Sexual liberation—Puig seems to be
saying in these books—must begin in a subversion of the very material of
gender: language.

The Buenos Aires Affair, Puig's third novel, presents the first explicit depiction of a homosexual act in his oeuvre. Leo, the protagonist, is a sadistic man
obsessed with his penis. He is genitally superendowed, but can perform sexually
only when he is inflicting pain on his partner. As soon as his partner stops
resisting him and begins to welcome his penetration, Leo loses interest and his
erection. Early in the novel, Leo follows a vagrant gay man from the bus to an
alley, and he lets this stranger perform fellatio on him. Excited by the man's
solicitous nature, Leo demands to possess him. But the man refuses to let Leo
penetrate him, claiming that he is much too big. Leo forces him, and they
struggle; Leo then hits the man with a brick when he tries to escape, leaving
him unconscious and perhaps dead. Leo is haunted by this crime. His overwhelming feelings of remorse and fear eventually lead to his death.

More than addressing a gay problematic, *The Buenos Aires Affair* seeks to
explore the pathologies inscribed in the language of psychoanalysis. The novel
deconstructs the Freudian case history in order to show its manipulative sym-
bology, its male-heterosexual ideological agenda. The novel does not concern

itself with homosexuality per se, but with sexualities, both Leo's and Gladys's, that transgress most taboos: sadism, masochism, zoophilia, necrophilia, among others. Because of his sexual complexity, his so-called illnesses and perversions, Leo deviates from all the forms of gender conduct and performance Freud defined as normal. The novel thus presents a parallel between the orderly, closed world of the detective novel (which it parodies), the romanticized, unrealistic world of Hollywood classics (which it cites) and the world of putatively normal sexuality that Freudian psychoanalysis authorized and sanctioned as scientific truth.

The Buenos Aires Affair is an exciting and complex tour de force depicting sexual fantasies—the inner workings of the master/slave relationship—but it is far from being a celebration of gay themes, as Puig's next novel, *El beso de la mujer araña*, is. *El beso de la mujer araña* is Puig's most important legacy to the development of a gay subjectivity in contemporary Latin American fiction. Borrowing from Herbert Marcuse's post-Freudian *Eros and Civilization* (1962), this fourth novel presents a passionate defense of a polymorphous, perverse and total form of sexuality. The text proposes a new sexual order and underlines the homosexual's role in anticipating this order. It presents, as well, the utopian vision of a world without sexual barriers and oppressive gender fictions.

Two men are in jail for crimes against society: Valentín is a political activist; Molina, a corruptor of minors. Throughout the novel, Molina narrates to Valentín his personal versions of several Hollywood movies. These tales are heavily encoded with allusions to the relationship that will emerge between the two prisoners and elicit discussions about masculinity and femininity. Molina identifies with women. This identification—Molina's mimicked damsels, femmes fatales and bourgeois ladies—allows Puig to expose and denounce the brainwashing suffered by women in a patriarchal society. But Molina's character serves yet another function: by assuming the sexuality and desire of a woman, this queen commits a crime against culture. Molina is literally outside the written heterosexist law.

Valentín cuts to the core of Molina's passive, female-identified homosexual identity; he tries to make him understand that in order for Molina to be a true woman, if that is what he wants, he does not have to humiliate himself or feel inferior; being macho does not give one special privileges or rights over others. But in spite of his sermons on equality, Valentín has imposed within the cell a dictatorial system not very different from the system that tortured and incarcerated him. He has become Molina's oppressor. Eventually, Molina helps Valentín nurture a gentler, more feminine side of himself, and the two prisoners become friends and lovers. Ironically, the cell is both a trap and a private, liberating space where the characters can speak and act freely, creating their own rules and narrating their own endings.

In addition to the story of Molina and Valentín, *El beso de la mujer araña* offers the reader a long essay that summarizes the work of Freud and Marcuse, among others. This scientific text, in the guise of footnotes, focuses primarily

on the history of homosexuality. The novelistic text could be read as a fictionalization, within the space of the novel, of the hypotheses advanced in the footnotes, that is, as verification of the theory. As the dialogue between these two
apparently disparate discourses—science and fiction—develops, a message is
gradually and forcefully articulated. Puig's novel advocates the resurrection of
an original impulse: the impulse to enjoy the body in its totality, to conceive of
sexuality as an end in itself, free from the stigma of family and the procreation
of children.

El beso de la mujer araña envisions a society where relationships are not
based on hierarchies, where machismo is no longer a cultural obligation and
where oppressive systems of authority are disarmed. The footnotes suggest that
this society will be possible only when every man liberates the woman within
him. At the end of the novel, this utopian world is represented as a primordial
island in Valentín's short but happy dream. It is important that Valentín be the
one to imagine this utopia. He is supposedly a straight man who ends up accepting and assuming his innate homosexuality, a political activist who attains
a deep and transforming understanding of his feminine side and his gay self.
Valentín is able to liberate and love Molina, the woman trapped in the recesses
of his psyche, the woman whom society, with its surveillance, has managed to
repress.

The futuristic world that appears in *Pubis angelical*, Puig's next novel, is the
antithesis of the utopia envisioned in *El beso de la mujer araña*. But the voice
that delivers this science-fiction nightmare is infused with the same passionate
rejection of patriarchy that characterized the preceding work. In the future society of the Polar Era, young women are forced into institutionalized prostitution, required to fulfill male fantasies. Earth has survived a catastrophe and
continues to perpetuate the macho values of a previous era. However, the foundations of this masculine order are beginning to crumble. The rulers—all heterosexual men—are making desperate attempts to stay in control; their
supremacy, however, is only a simulacrum. They are waging war against wom-
ankind because they have realized that women are capable of seizing power.
Ana, the protagonist, has much in common with other characters in Puig's novels: with Mita, the frustrated wife in *La traición de Rita Hayworth*; with Gladys,
the submissive and masochistic artist in *The Buenos Aires Affair*, even with
Molina. But Ana, in contrast, manages to detect the strategies of the phallocentric system of thought that enslaves her. She learns to read men. Unlike Molina,
Ana is empowered by her sexual fantasies, and she openly denounces the way
men have deceived her. Like Valentín, she realizes that the superior being she
has been searching for lives inside her, and she finds strength and peace in this
realization.

Although each of Puig's novels is unique in form, most of them tell the same
tale. He brilliantly narrates the story of lonely individuals who seek a special
friend in a world defined by betrayal and mistrust. Betrayal, a recurring theme
in Puig's writings, lurks in the Hollywood movies that Molina narrates; in the

surveilling eyes of the angels in *Pubis angelical*. It is betrayal by an oppressive patriarchal god in *Sangre de amor correspondido*, betrayal by culture disguised and accepted as nature and by language plagued with stereotypes and homophobia.

Puig's exiled characters find themselves inhabiting a funhouse of language where fantasies abound, where truth is elusive and definitive versions of reality are never authorized. Gender identity, for these people, is always in the process of being defined, ever changing. They dare to speak and incarnate the language of sex; they confess their innermost secrets and tell their stories as they set out to find the perfect lover. Happiness is nowhere in sight, yet they manage to create, within themselves, a short but happy dream.

WORKS

Bajo un manto de estrellas/El beso de la mujer araña. Barcelona: Seix Barral, 1983. English version of *Bajo* as *Under a Mantle of Stars*. Trans. Ronald Christ. New York: Lumen Books, 1989. English version of dramatic adaptation of *Beso* as *Kiss of the Spider Woman*. Trans. Michael Feingold. In *DramaContemporary: Latin America*, 19–61. Ed. Marion Peter Holt and George W. Woodyard. New York: P.A.G. Publications, 1985.

El beso de la mujer araña. Barcelona: Seix Barral, 1976. English version as *Kiss of the Spider Woman*. Trans. Thomas Colchie. New York: Knopf, 1979.

Boquitas pintadas. Buenos Aires: Editorial Sudamericana, 1969. English version as *Heartbreak Tango*. Trans. Suzanne Jill Levine. New York: Dutton, 1973.

The Buenos Aires Affair. Buenos Aires: Editorial Sudamericana, 1973. English version as *The Buenos Aires Affair*. Trans. Suzanne Jill Levine. New York: Dutton, 1976.

Cae la noche tropical. Barcelona: Seix Barral, 1988. English version as *Tropical Night Falling*. Trans. Suzanne Jill Levine. New York: Simon and Schuster, 1991.

La cara del villano. Recuerdo de Tijuana. Barcelona: Seix Barral, 1985.

Maldición eterna a quien lea estas páginas. Barcelona: Seix Barral, 1980. English version as *Eternal Curse on the Reader of These Pages*. Trans. Manuel Puig. New York: Random House, 1982.

Mystery of the Rose Bouquet. Trans. Allan Baker. London: Faber and Faber, 1988.

Pubis angelical. Barcelona: Seix Barral, 1979. English version as *Pubis Angelical*. Trans. Elena Brunet. New York: Vintage/Aventura, 1986.

Sangre de amor correspondido. Barcelona: Seix Barral, 1982. English version as *Blood of Requited Love*. Trans. Jan Grayson. New York: Vintage, 1984.

La traición de Rita Hayworth. Buenos Aires: Editorial Jorge Alvarez, 1968. English version as *Betrayed by Rita Hayworth*. Trans. Suzanne Jill Levine. New York: Dutton, 1971.

"Vivaldi: A Screenplay (Excerpt)." *Review of Contemporary Fiction* 11.3 (Fall 1991): 177–181.

CRITICISM

Barraza, Eduardo. "El beso de la mujer araña: Elocución y diseño." *Estudios filológicos* 23 (1988): 25–34.

Boling, Becky. "*El beso de la mujer araña*: or Whose Story Is This?" *Gestos* 3.5 (Apr. 1988): 85–93.

Bost, David H. "Telling Tales in Manuel Puig's *El beso de la mujer araña.*" *South Atlantic Review* 54.2 (May 1989): 93–106.

Campos, René Alberto. *Espejos: La textura cinemática en La traición de Rita Hayworth.* Madrid: Pliegos, 1985.

Cheever, Leonard A. "Lacan, Argentine Politics, and Science Fiction in Manuel Puig's *Pubis Angelical.*" *South Central Review* 5.1 (Spring 1988): 61–74.

Christ, Ronald. "Interview with Manuel Puig." *Christopher Street* 3.9 (Apr. 1979): 25–31.

Conniff, Brian. "The Learned Executioner and the Chick from Suburbia: *Kiss of the Spider Woman* as Prison Literature." *Review of Contemporary Fiction* 11.3 (Fall 1991): 228–238.

Corbatta, Jorgelina. *Mito personal y mitos colectivos en las novelas de Manuel Puig.* Madrid: Orígenes, 1988.

Epple, Juan Armando. "*The Buenos Aires Affair* y la estructura de la novela policíaca." *La palabra y el hombre* 18 (Apr.–June 1976): 43–59.

Hernández-Novas, Raúl. "El reto de la mujer araña." *Casa de las Américas* 184 (July–Sept. 1991): 70–76.

Kerr, Lucille. *Suspended Fictions: Reading Novels by Manuel Puig.* Urbana: University of Illinois Press, 1987.

Labani, Jo. "Voyeurism and Narrative Pleasure in Manuel Puig's *The Buenos Aires Affair.*" *Romance Studies* 19 (Winter 1991): 105–116.

Levine, Suzanne Jill. "Manuel Puig Exits Laughing." *Review of Contemporary Fiction* 11.3 (Fall 1991): 189–196.

Lewis, Bart L. "*Pubis angelical:* La mujer codificada." *Revista iberoamericana* 123–124 (Apr.–Sept. 1983): 531–540.

Madrid, Lelia M. "La diferencia, la semejanza: La visión de lo femenino en *El beso de la mujer araña* de Manuel Puig." *Revista canadiense de estudios hispánicos* 14.3 (Spring 1990): 567–572.

McCracken, Ellen. "Manuel Puig's *Heartbreak Tango*: Women and Mass Culture." *Latin American Literary Review* 18 (Spring 1981): 27–35.

Merrim, Stephanie. "For a New (Psychological) Novel in the Works of Manuel Puig." *Novel* 17.2 (Winter 1984): 141–157.

Muñoz, Elías Miguel. *El discurso utópico de la sexualidad en Manuel Puig.* Madrid: Pliegos, 1987.

Ostergaard, Anne-Grethe. "Dynamics of Fiction in *El beso de la mujer araña.*" *Latin American Theatre Review* 19.1 (1985): 5–12.

Solotorevsky, Myrna. "El cliché en *Pubis angelical y Boquitas pintadas*: Desgaste y creatividad." *Hispamérica* 38 (Aug. 1984): 3–18.

Stavans, Ilan. "Good–Bye to M.P." *Review of Contemporary Fiction* 11.3 (Fall 1991): 159–164.

Tittler, Jonathan. "Order, Chaos, and Re-Order: The Novels of Manuel Puig." *Kentucky Romance Quarterly* 30.2 (1983): 187–201.

Zimmerman, Shari A. "*Kiss of the Spider Woman* and the Web of Gender." *Pacific Coast Philology* 23 (Nov. 1988): 106–113.

Elías Miguel Muñoz

R

RAMOS OTERO, MANUEL (Puerto Rico; 1948–1990) _____

Ramos Otero could be considered the author who literally took Puerto Rican contemporary homosexual literature out of the closet. His narrative—*Concierto de un metal para un recuerdo y otras orgías de soledad* (Concert of One Brass Instrument for a Memory and Other Orgies of Loneliness; 1971), *El cuento de la mujer del mar* (The Story of the Woman from the Sea: 1979), *Página en blanco y staccato* (A Blank Page and Staccato; 1987)—and his poetry—*El libro de la muerte* (The Book of Death; 1985) and the posthumous *Invitación al polvo* (Invitation to Dust; 1991)—constitute one of the first openly homoerotic Caribbean literary discourses, especially with respect to a writing that frames an oscillation between the masculine and the feminine.

In *El libro de la muerte*, the speaker explicitly declares himself a homosexual voice. The homoerotic relation between two or more men is established in the field of a discursive analysis that allows for the reading of a voice that is different from the feminine or the masculine. In Ramos Otero the positions change, and decadence is in opposition to plenitude, to the deviation of another way of being and the guilt of another form of redemption. Three zones are elaborated. The first is "Fuegos fúnebres" (Funeral Fires), poems in which one can hear the voices of a few characters represented by a transgendered or illusionist lyric speaker who crosses masculine and feminine attributes. The second zone includes epitaphs to homosexual writers like Federico García Lorca, Oscar Wilde, Tennessee Williams, Yukio Mishima, Charles Rimbaud, Paul Verlaine, José Lezama Lima, Fernando Pessoa, Joris Karl Huysmans, Konstantinos Petrou Kavafis and René Marqués.

The third zone, the epilogue, inscribes a phrase that glosses and rewrites the famous verse of the Mexican nun Sor Juana Inés de la Cruz—concerning stupid macho men who without reason accuse women of being what they, stupid men, provoke in them—and modifies it to refer to fags. It is a key phrase to understanding queerness as it is expressed by Ramos Otero in his poetic discourse. These verses are based on a feeling shared with the feminine: the object of desire is a man. It is necessary to clarify that the absolutism by which masculine and feminine reciprocal relationships are allegedly the only normal sexual relationships possible is restrictive, because for the feminine the object of desire is not exclusively the masculine and vice versa. That is why readings like this one attempt to establish other margins that would not exclude other tendencies. "Fuegos fúnebres" focuses on a parade of characters who declare an androgyny where the genres are fused, and when the enigmatic Puerto Rican Marina Arzola (1939–1976) is mentioned in one of the poems, she is described as having both male and female characteristics. Her capacity to be a rather marvelous woman, tied to the textual ambiguity of gender, confirms how she exhibits characteristics in which the categories of masculine and feminine are fused harmoniously and almost imperceptibly.

In another poem a sailor, Gilbert Robbins, dresses as a woman and lives as though he were other individuals; his funeral is characterized by the presence of both feminine and masculine religious icons. Details like the spangled dress and the ostrich fan illustrate how the feminine attributes border on drag, producing the fascination of the illusionist that makes us think he is someone else. It is the capacity to turn into a woman and to experience a metamorphosis. Here homosexual writing meets the feminine, to the extent that both the woman and the homosexual have been relegated to the margins. The feminine and the homosexual meet, not in the terms of the ridicule directed against the queen but in a gesture of a solidarity based on how both exist on the fringes of society. This is how the space of the subculture and the counterculture, in which the affirmation of this other way of being is situated, is that of the tension with official culture in a tacit but direct questioning of the crisis of obsolete values.

Independently of the fact that Ramos Otero eventually became the homosexual voice of a particular form of writing, there are still matters open to question. First, if one belongs to a subculture or counterculture within the official culture (establishing new closets or spaces with closed doors), does this writing attempt to create its space within that language and that speech? Second, even though Ramos Otero approaches the feminine with, for example, elements like the spangled dress and the ostrich fan, are these two objects intrinsically feminine, and if so, why are they? Third, is the homosexual relationship and the homoerotic in poetry something that necessarily excludes heterosexuality and heteroerotism?

In the remainder of his work Ramos Otero states violently and through a carefully elaborated language the necessary deconstruction of gender for creating a true sexual liberty. The short stories in *Concierto de un metal para un recuerdo y otras orgías de soledad*, for example, illustrate the beginnings of this homoerotic preoccupation that is pursued in *La novelabingo* (Bingonovel; 1976), in which there is a dominant identification between the homosexual and the feminine as related paradigms.

Another characteristic feature is the jaundiced view with which Ramos Otero at times attacks the status quo. His posthumous work *Invitación al polvo* directly addresses the AIDS crisis. The beginning of the poem "Nobleza de sangre" (Nobility of Blood) shows this preoccupation by formulating an accusation against the hypocritical religious attitude concerning the plague by thanking God for sending AIDS. Apart from the identification between the homosexual and the feminine as related phenomena and the jaundiced view mentioned above, Ramos Otero uses a discourse that could be described as vile while endowing it with poetic status. The lyric speaker experiments with the baroque sources of the love poem, recontextualizing the lyric and sublime into the limits of the vile. It is a reading that codifies the sensual and sexual possibilities of the metaphysical sonnet as one of the greatest institutions of Hispanic poetry. Ramos Otero seeks to scandalize in order to liberate, and he attacks established institutions that fail to include the homosexual as a human possibility, with a view to establishing the homoerotic as an integral part of Puerto Rican and Hispanic American culture and literature.

WORKS

Concierto de un metal para un recuerdo y otras orgías de soledad. San Juan, P.R.: Cultural, 1971.
El cuento de la mujer del mar. Río Piedras, P.R.: Huracán, 1979.
Invitación al polvo. Río Piedras, P.R.: Plaza Mayor, 1991.
El libro de la muerte. Río Piedras, P.R.: Cultural, 1985.
La novelabingo. New York: Libro Viaje, 1976.
Página en blanco y staccato. Madrid: Playor, 1987.

CRITICISM

Barradas, Efraín. Review of *Concierto de un metal para un recuerdo y otras orgías de soledad. Sin nombre* 3 (1972): 108–110.
Costa, Marithelma. "Entrevista: Manuel Ramos Otero." *Hispamérica* 59 (1991): 59–67.
Ferré, Rosario. "Ramos Otero o la locura versus la libertad." *El mundo* (San Juan, P.R.), July 12, 1977, p. 16A.
Gelpí-Pérez, Juan G. "Desorden frente a purismo: La nueva narrativa frente a René Marqués." In *Literature in Transition: The Many Voices of the Caribbean Area; a Symposium,* 177–187. Ed. Rose S. Minc. Gaithersburg, Md./Upper Montclair, N.J.: Hispamérica, 1982.
"Interview with Manuel Ramos Otero." *The Dispatch: Newsletter of the Center for American Studies, Columbia University* 5.1 (Fall 1986): 14–16.
Martínez, Jan. "Manuel Ramos Otero o los espejos de Mahoma." *El reportero,* Nov. 10, 1985, pp. 52–53.
Mohr, Nicholasa. "Puerto Rican Writers in the United States/Puerto Rican Writers in

Puerto Rico: A Separation Beyond Language.'' *The Americas Review* 15.2 (Summer 1987): 87–92.

Montero, Oscar. Review of *El cuento de la mujer del mar. Sin nombre* 7 (1980): 65–69.

Mullen, Edward. ''Interpreting Puerto Rico's Cultural Myths: Rosario Ferré and Manuel Ramos Otero.'' *The Americas Review* 17.3–4 (Fall–Winter 1989): 88–97.

Pina-Rosales, Gerardo. ''Mejor la destrucción, el fuego: Manuel Ramos Otero (1948–1990): In Memoriam.'' *Nuez: Revista de arte* 3.7 (1991): 9–10.

Review of *La novelabingo. El mundo* (San Juan, P.R., May 29, 1977, p. 16A).

Rodríguez, Jorge. ''El amor entre dos hombres es como el amor entre dos espejos.'' *El reportero* (San Juan, P.R.), Jan. 16, 1987, pp. 17–19.

Rodríguez de Laguna, Asela. ''Balance novelístico del trienio 1976–1978: Conjunción de signos tradicionales y rebeldes en Puerto Rico.'' *Hispamérica* 23–24 (1979): 133–142.

Daniel Torres

RECHY, JOHN (United States; 1934) ⸺⸺⸺

Rechy is a Chicano or (as they say in Texas) a Mexican American writer who was born and who grew up in El Paso. His parents, Roberto Sixto Rechy and Guadalupe Flores, were of Mexican and Scottish descent. Spanish is his native language, and he did not learn to speak English until he went to school. He received a B.A. degree from Texas Western College and later attended the New School for Social Research in New York City. His published writings are in English, and he is considered one of the most important American gay novelists. The author of nine novels and a book-length essay, Rechy has also produced plays and numerous magazine articles, essays and some translations from Spanish. His first novel, *City of Night* (1963), was an international best-seller, translated into a dozen languages. Two other novels also made the best-seller list, *Numbers* (1967) and *Bodies and Souls* (1983). Several of his books—*City of Night, Numbers, This Day's Death* (1969), *The Sexual Outlaw* (1977) and *Rushes* (1979)—center on gay topics; but all his works usually include some gay characters and related themes. From El Paso, Rechy moved on to live briefly in New York, Los Angeles, San Francisco, New Orleans and Chicago, cities that provided the background for his first novel. He finally settled in Los Angeles, where he teaches literature and film courses in the graduate writing program at the University of Southern California.

City of Night is a first-person narrative of the adventures, across the United States, of a young male hustler. He journeys from El Paso to New York, Los Angeles, Hollywood, San Francisco, Chicago—all meccas of homosexual life—and ends in New Orleans for Mardi Gras. When the novel first appeared, it was not clear to most critics and the general reading public that this was the work of a Chicano author. Now it seems inevitable that, because of the somewhat autobiographical nature of the novel, we should visualize its protagonist/narrator as Chicano, although this is not made apparent in the novel. Nonetheless, its not-so-thoroughly-assimilated hero may be seen to trace the steps of that large portion of the Chicano population that follows the urban streets, rather than the agricultural paths of the land. Doubly marginalized, the wandering hero makes his country in the nether lands of the cities of night.

The title and epigraph of the novel refer to a late Romantic poem, "The City of Dreadful Night," published in 1874 by James Thompson. The city described in the poem with images of night and darkness, of death, gloom and desolation, is an allegorical dwelling for those who, having lost all hope or faith, find no solace in the world. In Rechy's novel, through the hero's adventures, a kaleidoscopic view of homosexual America—with all its little tragedies, black humor and frenzied restlessness—is presented to the reader. It is a series of fragments that are complete in themselves. One of these, originally titled "The Fabulous Wedding of Miss Destiny," won the 1961 Longview Foundation fiction prize for short story. The fragments are held together by the lens through which we look: the point of view of the narrator, who is a participant and not simply an observer. He is afflicted with the same condition as the world that he observes, not just by his sexual inclination but by his relentless search for an elusive and mysterious satisfaction, and by his view of things: humorous and devastatingly bitter, colorful, yet obscure, indifferent and desperately entrapped or immersed in its own vision. The novel could be considered picaresque by its structure as well as by the somber tone of its humor.

City is unified by a theme that permeates all of Rechy's works: the loss of salvation and the search for a substitute. At the beginning of the book, the narrator (as a child) is faced with the finality of the death of his pet dog and the loss of innocence in the realization that dogs don't go to Heaven. By the end of the chapter, the theme of the loss of salvation is transferred to the main character and becomes the motive for the search. The phrase "substitute for salvation" appears in most of Rechy's works. Rechy himself explains it thus:

I mean the phrase in a very religious sense, that we are raised to expect that love, kindness prevails and that there will be indeed salvation; if you live well you will be rewarded— all that bullshit. Then we discover an existential void; that there is no such thing. And part of the contemporary neurosis, the existential nightmare, is based on the fact that we try to substitute for that; some people by trying to make a lot of money; other people by acting compulsively in other areas—in sex, for instance. There is simply no substitute for that promise which was made and unfulfilled. Once you withdraw that promise, there is nothing to take its place. (Leyland, 2.255)

This theme applies to the character's obsessive search and, by extension, to the world in which he moves. At the same time, the search constitutes a form of cosmic rebellion and damnation. After the long search through cities and lives, the story ends back where it started, in El Paso.

Rechy's second novel, *Numbers*, continues the theme of the relentless search and, although less clearly, the deep existential undertones of *City of Night*. In this novel, the main character, Johnny Rio, who has been a hustler in Los Angeles, drives back to that city after a self-imposed exile of three years. Now his purpose is to prove himself more handsome and desirable than ever, to conquer the sex jungle, then to leave. He has allotted himself ten days in California and set an arbitrary figure of thirty conquests. After cruising various areas of the city, he selects Griffith Park. Here he achieves his goal, each of the thirty encounters recounted in detail for the reader. Now Johnny is ready to leave, but on the way out, he turns his car once more into the park. By the end of the book the conquests total thirty-seven.

Rio, immersed in the apparently meaningless obsession of the addicted, seems desperately bent on a compulsive course, driven by a force that precedes and undermines conscious decision. Even more, in an obscure way, the search negates consciousness, the awareness of death and meaninglessness. The numerical search gives temporary structure to the void. Here is how the author explains the character:

I think that Johnny Rio in *Numbers* is a real existential creature trying to thwart the certain knowledge of doom by collecting and counting sex acts. *Numbers* is a very misunderstood book.... The reaction to it was outrage—but it's not a pornographic book. It's a book about a nightmare, about someone trying to avoid death. It's a beautifully structured book.... Unfortunately, it is flawed; it is the one book of mine that I would like to rewrite some day, I hope.... I would like the thing to move relentlessly as a sexual horror story, an existential nightmare, and I think it slows down.... It's a very literal book. After several years of relative "seclusion" in El Paso after the publication of *City of Night*, I came back to Los Angeles and discovered Griffith Park. I found myself out of control and courting sexual encounters. You may be surprised to learn that years later I came back to break Johnny Rio's record and yet Johnny Rio was based on myself. (Leyland, 2.256)

After the frantic and obsessive sex hunt of the main characters in Rechy's first two novels, *This Day's Death* has the quality of a slow-motion nightmare. Two intertwined events, one in El Paso (the slow death of the protagonist's mother), the other in Los Angeles (an agonizingly long, drawn-out trial on sex perversion charges) painfully grind down the main character, Jim Girard, and force him to grope through deeply hidden layers of his consciousness as he drives back and forth from one city to the other.

Girard, drowning in his mother's obsessive love for him, begins to view her death-in-life as her ultimate weapon in the war to possess him. When the battle is joined, he must come to terms with his past, his feelings of love–hate, not only in relation to his mother but in all his relationships. In this conflict between the mother's possessive love and her son's (and daughter's) fight for liberation, the Chicano background of the character is more evident than in previous works. Only that background explains the tormented love–hate dilemma, in the character's head, in relation to the mother.

In the other nightmare, although the alleged homosexual encounter (in Griffith Park) of which Girard is accused (and could have happened) never occurred, he is found guilty. The verdict forces him to accept his latent homosexual inclinations. All his projects for a future heterosexual life as a lawyer are destroyed by the stroke of the pen of a particularly insensitive judge, acting as a God of fate. The novel is thus an indictment of the judicial system, including police, lawyer and judge.

Though intertwined, the two stories could be separate, and in fact they are maintained that way by the character's necessity to keep secret his legal–sexual trouble. But separate they would be less powerful, and it is the intertwining of the two anguishes and the need for a double life that give intensity to both. At the same time, this helps to underscore the indictment not only of the judicial system but also of a society that criminalizes an otherwise harmless act and, therefore, provides the opportunity for the system to corrupt itself into a travesty of justice. The troubles Jim Girard encounters are not only those of an innocent heterosexual man who is accused of a homosexual act he did not commit but also, and at the same time, those of a homosexual who could have committed, and later does commit, the act Girard is wrongly accused of. This subtle fusion of two characters (two destinies) is one of the most interesting aspects of the novel. Thus the point of justice in question becomes not whether the act was committed, but whether in justice that act should be judged.

Two subsequent novels, *The Vampires* (1971) and *The Fourth Angel* (1972), no longer center on the homosexual world, yet still deal with the world of the social/sexual outsider. The first is a sexual fantasy dealing with the battle between purity and evil; the other, a story of adolescents coming of age in El Paso during the 1960s. A 1986 play, *Tigers Wild* (a quote from Blake), is based on the second of these novels.

In 1976 Rechy received a grant from the National Endowment for the Humanities. He then wrote his next book, which constituted another significant departure, although one that remains faithful to the themes of his previous works. In *The Sexual Outlaw: a Documentary. A Non-fictional Account, with Commentaries, of Three Days and Nights in the Sexual Underground* (1977), Rechy temporarily abandons the pretense of the fictional mode to engage in what can be considered testimonial literature. The accounting of events, the obsessive search for promiscuous sexual encounters, is reminiscent of *Numbers*, and one of the motivating factors seems to be the same: the main character's need to reaffirm for himself, over and over, his undiminished sexual attractiveness to others. But added to this—by interweaving commentaries, interviews and newspaper clippings—is the view of the gay person as sexual outlaw and rebel. Public homosexual encounters and behavior, in this perspective, constitute a form of defiance and rebellion against repressive authorities in a society that makes a crime out of sexual encounters between consenting adults, a point that was initially made in *This Day's Death*. More interestingly, the book illustrates the split of the author between writer and character: while the protagonist's motivation is still an obscure force or desire, the writer, as intellectual master-mind, adds social awareness and commitment.

The form and style of the book constitute the main departures for Rechy, as he describes it in the foreword to the 1984 edition:

I conceived this book as a "prose documentary." The stark style I attempted—different from that of all my other books—and its "black-and-white" imagery are intended to suggest a documentary film. The "essays" function as the "voice-overs" and speak at times in affirmation of Jim's [the protagonist's] actions, still others in argument, even in opposition. The deliberate fluctuations and "contradictions" are essential to the meaning of the book.

In writing *The Sexual Outlaw*, I attempted what I consider a new approach to the so-called non-fiction novel: I arranged random "real" experiences so that their structured sequence would stand for narrative development. Although there is a protagonist whom the book follows intimately, minute by recorded minute for a full weekend, there is no strict plot. Although there is a vast cast of characters, most are nameless and appear only briefly as their lives intersect with the short segment—virtually "pastless"—of Jim's life isolated for attention here. I wanted to create characters, including the protagonist, who might be defined "fully"—*by inference*—only through their sexual journeys.

This book was composed in two main parts: the "experiential" passages in which the protagonist, Jim, sexhunts throughout Los Angeles for three days and nights; and various "essay-style" sections. The "experiential" chapters were written first, straight through, with only noted designations of where a certain "essay" would be inserted later. Then I wrote the individual "essay" sections. (16–17)

The technique of concentrating action in a short but significant period of time, which slices through the lives of several "pastless" characters, is again used in Rechy's sixth novel, *Rushes*. The time is one long night at a "leather and Western bar" called Rushes, on a cruising strip along the decaying waterfront of an unnamed American city. Here, Rechy explores the varying sexual needs, habits, fears and concerns of his cast of characters, but is mainly interested in the exploration and evaluation of that aspect of the homosexual ethos that prizes macho types and attitudes above all. By internalizing society's predominant values, which prize masculinity and despise traits considered feminine in men, these homosexuals have moved to the opposite extreme from drag queens and their female costumes. All the uniforms of the most outstanding macho stereo-types are paraded in a sexual charade of dominance and submission: the cowboy, the lumberjack, the military hero, the motorcycle cop, the Nazi officer and that original uniform, which does not belong to any real-life character but is the composite and synthesis of machismo in clothes, the leatherman.

Ironically, the attitudes reflected in the uniforms reveal society's contempt for homosexuals stereotyped as sissies, but extending to the macho types as well. These attitudes are also shown in the sexual rites of dominance and submission, master and slave and sadomasochism, which assert the dominance of the macho man. Ironically, too, the book suggests, sexual freedom and gay liberation have led to the ghettoization of homosexuals, thus complying with society's repressive attitudes about them. They gather in the fringe of a society that rejects them, playing games that society imposes on them. Or perhaps not so happily, for the undercurrent of self-hatred that underlies these games overflows into contempt for all those who do not conform to an ideal of masculinity, beauty and youth—a contempt that nightly gnaws at the self-assurance of even the most macho but uncertain demigods. And yet, such a fringe world may seem a heavenly refuge, as a church would seem to the faithful: "No matter how cruel the Rushes may have been, it protected them from the vaster cruelty outside" (201).

On this level, the book can be read as the reenactment of a mystery play or sacramental rite. The book is divided in two parts, each introduced with a traditional blessing in Latin from the Catholic Mass. Each chapter also is introduced with an epigraph taken from the Mass, in praise of or expressing gratitude to the Lord. Fourteen chapters (the number of stations of the cross) begin with a recurrent sentence, "As often as he comes to the Rushes . . . " and a name introducing a character, thus underscoring the feeling of a recurrent ritual. Corresponding to the number of chapters, there is a recurrent reference to fourteen panels painted on the wall of the bar. These depict various scenes of a sexual nature with the theme of male dominance and submission. They, too, seem to have a religious connotation finally left unclear. There is an additional chapter, distinguished from the others in that it does not begin with the same sentence. In it, the tensions built up throughout the novel climax in a final scene of sadomasochism, violence and blood when some patrons of the bar are attacked by gay-bashing straights. This novel, written largely in dialogue form, has been turned into a play with the same title.

Rushes is Rechy's last novel dealing exclusively with a gay story. Subsequent works—*Bodies and Souls, Marilyn's Daughter* (1988), and *The Miraculous Day of Amalia Gómez* (1991)—present different aspects of life in Los Angeles, but all include gay and Chicano characters as part of the tapestry of life in "the city of lost angels" that has become a leitmotif in Rechy's work. The last two novels center on female protagonists and deal with what could be considered feminist themes. The last one is Rechy's first novel that deals mainly and explicitly with Chicano life.

Rechy has devoted most of his writings to the exploration and presentation of certain segments of marginalized, mainly homosexual, life in the United States. His approach to the subject has been explicit, anguished, sometimes sensationalist and quite intense. But some of his works have a documentary quality that moves critics to compare them to the social reform novel. Woven through them is the recurrent existential theme of the loss of salvation and the search for a substitute. Rechy's literature constitutes a gutsy report on the desperate agony of the social outcast in the midst of a repressive but lost society. Thus the plight of the outcast becomes, in a sense, a metaphor for the essentially lost nature of contemporary society and, in the final analysis, of the human condition and the individual's desperate and obsessive search for a substitute for salvation.

Rechy's seminal place in the development of gay literature is unquestionable. His first novel was ground-breaking. Successfully pulling together his sociological and literary interests, Rechy produced an extraordinary work that presented to the world in very explicit terms the heretofore hidden life of the gay culture. It was part of, and had an impact on, the development of the gay liberation movement of the 1960s and 1970s. Some of his works exposed the injustice of laws that condemned homosexual acts between consenting adults. Such laws were repealed in California in the 1970s by public referendum. The timeliness and quality of his writing have given Rechy the distinction of being one of the most successful and widely read gay writers. He has the same distinction, although not generally recognized, among Chicano writers.

WORKS

Bodies and Souls. New York: Carroll & Graf, 1983.
City of Night. New York: Grove Press, 1963.
"Conduct Unbecoming." *Nation* 202 (Feb. 21, 1966): 204–208.
"El Paso del Norte." *Evergreen Review* 2.6 (Autumn 1958): 127–140.
The Fourth Angel. New York: Viking, 1972.
"GIs for Peace." *Nation* 210 (Jan. 12, 1970): 8–12.
"I Was Always Mad at the World." *Nation* 200 (Mar. 8, 1965): 254–256.
"Jim Crow Wears a Sombrero." *Nation* 189 (Oct. 10, 1959): 210–213.
Marilyn's Daughter. New York: Carroll & Graf, 1988.
The Miraculous Day of Amalia Gómez. New York: Little, Brown, 1991.
Momma as She Became . . . But Not as She Was. One-act play. Produced New York, 1978.
"No Mañana for Today's Chicanos." *Saturday Review* 53.3 (Mar. 1970): 31–34.
Numbers. New York: Grove Press, 1967.
"Open Letter to Anita Bryant." *Human Behavior* 7 (July 1978): 11–12.
"Out of the Pages." *People*, May 22, 1978. pp. 61–62.
Rushes. New York: Grove Press, 1979. There is also an unpublished theatrical version.
The Sexual Outlaw: A Documentary. New York: Grove Press, 1977.
This Day's Death. New York: Grove Press, 1969.
Tigers Wild. Produced New York, 1986.
The Vampires. New York: Grove Press, 1971.

CRITICISM

Giles, James R., and Wanda Giles. "An Interview with John Rechy." *Chicago Review* 25 (Summer 1973): 19–31.
Lemon, Lee T. "You May Have Missed These." *Prairie Schooner* 45.3 (Fall 1971): 270–272.
Leyland, William. "John Rechy." In *Gay Sunshine Interviews*, 2.252–258. Ed. William Leyland. San Francisco: Gay Sunshine Press, 1978.

Nelson, E. S. "John Rechy, James Baldwin and the American Double Minority Litera-
    ture." *Journal of American Culture* 6 (Summer 1983): 70–74.
Satterfield, B. "John Rechy's Tormented World." *Southwest Review* 67 (Winter 1982):
    78–85.
Southern, Terry. "Rechy and Gover." In *Contemporary American Novelists*, 222–227.
    Ed. Harry T. Moore. Cabondale: Southern Illinois University Press, 1964.
"Special Section: A Focus on John Rechy." *Minority Voices* 3 (Fall 1979). Contains
    the following articles: Juan Bruce-Novoa, "In Search of the Honest Outlaw: John
    Rechy," 37–45; Charles M. Tatum, "The Sexual Underworld of John Rechy,"
    47–52; Carlos Zamora, "Odysseus in John Rechy's *City of Night*: The Episte-
    mological Journey," 53–62.
Steuervogel, T. "Contemporary Homosexual Fiction and the Gay Rights Movement."
    Journal of Popular Culture 20 (Winter 1986): 125–134.

Didier T. Jaén

REYNOSO, OSWALDO (Peru; 1932) ⎯⎯⎯⎯⎯

Reynoso was born in Arequipa, Peru. His only published volume of short stories
provides a portrait of the youth of Lima's lower classes, with an emphasis on
what middle-class values view as disordered passions spoken in a vulgar language. Rapid images and interior monologues serve as effective vehicles for a
narrative that is imbued with deep social pessimism. The adolescent bodies that
are the main characters of his narratives are shaped by abuse in a fierce apprenticeship of violence. "Cara de Angel" (Angel Face), from *Los inocentes*
(The Innocents; 1961), is the portrait of a beautiful adolescent who lives on the
line between gang delinquency and adult incomprehension. Although he refuses
to give his body to the rich old men who contemplate him lasciviously, his
sexuality is enmeshed in the structure of gang codes. Losers in games of chance
are obliged to masturbate in front of the others; there is no room here for
tenderness or friendship.

In his bitter novel *En octubre no hay milagros* (There Are No Miracles in
October; 1966) Reynoso attempts to demonstrate the inseparable connection
between sexual liberty and religious fervor in an ambitious social description of
both lower and upper social classes of Lima, embodied in two archetypal characters, one from each of two social poles: Miguel, a secondary school teacher
and Don Manuel, the head of a banking consortium, who is homosexual. They
both serve as signifiers of Peruvian bourgeois decadence. The sexuality of the
masses is signified by mass religious processions made up of an agglomeration
of bodies thrown together in unrestrained sexual contact. Other aspects of the
novel include violent sexual games in brothels and sexual commerce between
adolescents and adults. In both sexual worlds—that of the lower and that of the
upper social class—Reynoso details all possible forms of sexuality: voyeurism,
sadism, sodomy, masturbation and orgies. Within such a portrayal, woman is
described variously on the basis of two stereotypes: committed mother or pros-

titute. The use of sexuality for economic gain by Don Manuel is shown in its connection with religious beliefs that provide the moral basis for slavery and the promise to the slaves of a paradise in the next life. Peruvian society denies and represses desire in spite of the impulses that mark different social groups. There is no room, in Reynoso's often frustratingly clichéd and stereotyped view of sexual practices as deleterious social metonymy, for liberation within a social context that is displayed as racist, classist and spiritually alienated. In this sense, homosexuality is as pernicious as any other sexual practice of humiliation and exploitation; and Reynoso effectively, if overdramatically, plays on his reader's existing homophobic and antierotic prejudices.

In his most recent novel, *El escarabajo y el hombre* (The Beetle and the Man; 1970), Reynoso attempts to raise the consciousness of younger readers about freedom, politics and sexuality.

Following a long residence in China, Reynoso returned in the 1980s to Lima with a number of manuscripts he has yet to publish.

WORKS

El escarabajo y el hombre. Lima: Ediciones Universidad Nacional de Educación, 1970.
Los inocentes. 3rd ed. Lima: Narración, 1975. Orig. 1961. Also issued as *Lima en rock.* Lima: Populibros Peruanos, 1964.
En octubre no hay milagros. Lima: Wuaman Puma, 1966.

CRITICISM

Arguedas, José María. "Un narrador para un nuevo mundo." In Reynoso, *Los inocentes*, 9–12. 1975.
Villanueva-Collado, Alfredo. "Meta(homo)sexualidad e ideología en dos novelas anti-burguesas peruanas." *Confluencia* 7.2 (1992): 55–63.

Roberto J. Forns-Broggi

RIBEYRO, JULIO RAMÓN (Peru; 1929) _____

Ribeyro was born in Lima. From a very early age he has lived in Europe on various occasions, and in 1960 was appointed cultural attache in Paris. Despite his condition as an outsider, his narrative embraces the depth and extension of all of Peru's contemporary social diversity. It would not be inaccurate to state that Ribeyro is Peru's best short story writer, even though he is still unknown to a broad Latin American reading public. Some critics have cataloged him as an exponent of urban realism, but his stories reveal a great variety of social, imaginative, fantastic, satiric and even autobiographic themes. The unity of his narrative resides in his capacity to synthesize, his power of evocation and the handling of a technique that allows him effortlessly to achieve the desired effect.

The majority of Ribeyro's characters are marginal and forgotten individuals, condemned to exist without a voice. Ribeyro restores them to a lived space where they are able to express their eagerness, their desires and their rages. One of the aspects that characterizes this imagination is the complete absence of any ability to exercise sexual pleasure according to the dominant bourgeois molds of family and matrimony. Eroticism is always dealt with by Ribeyro with subtlety, indirectly through symbols and sexual references that are never explicit, that always border on the unconscious and the unknown. Even though brief passages in his novels have explicit pejorative references to homosexuality, Ribeyro's short stories are able to approach the subject with ambiguity and implication. Such is the case of extraordinary pieces like "Un domingo cualquiera" (Any Old Sunday) and "Terra incognita" from *La palabra del mudo* (The Mute's Word; 1973).

The first narrates a walk on the beach by two girls. Gabriella belongs to a well-to-do family, and Nelly comes from the lower social stratum. The situation presented is very suggestive; as they walk alone along the beach, Gabriella describes it as "the beach of delight," and she dives naked into the sea. Nelly watches her friend and also takes her clothes off; Gabriella talks about her experiences with past boyfriends, they touch, and compare their breasts. Nelly searches for seashells, Gabriella smokes, but nothing else happens. Social barriers and circumstances are stronger than Gabriella's erotic fever, and convert the ambiguous sensuality of the body language between the friendship and something unknown.

Ribeyro's second story is grounded in his recollection of a large black man from a low-class district in Lima who provided sexual favors to a rich bohemian gentleman from the capital's high society. Nevertheless, the story does not have any explicit sign of intercourse. Rather, it is centered on the ambiguity of a fictional character, Doctor Peñaflor (a name that combines *peña* [rock, a metaphor for male sexuality] and *flor* [flower, a metaphor for female sexuality]) who is at home reading Plato, alone and bored, while his family is traveling in Mexico and the United States. He decides to go out into the city, with which he is not very familiar. He has a few drinks, and his expectations toward the unknown grow. His attention is captured by three different persons: a lonely woman in a restaurant; a girl with very long hair who is wearing pants and sitting in the park, but who, upon closer examination, turns out to be a young man; and, sitting in a low-class bar, a large black man with whom he strikes up a conversation and whom he invites home to have a few more drinks. There the doctor insists on talking about Greek references that the black man does not understand. The stranger confesses that he is a religious man, but the body has its needs. Peñaflor shows him a nude image of Aristogiton, the Athenian tyrannicide who killed Pisistratus's son because he loved the same adolescent as Aristogiton. The black man falls asleep, and the doctor hesitates between putting him in the guest room and calling a taxi. Even though Peñaflor decides to do the latter and the black man, upon waking up, accepts the offer, the possibility of enjoying the black man's body still remains. Therefore, Peñaflor's inner being has been considerably changed by the end of the evening. Ribeyro, while he avoids explicit characterizations, nevertheless suggests the deepest desires and rages of his characters in order not to deny either their complexity or their sensuality.

WORKS

Atusparia. Lima: Rikchay, 1981.
Las botellas y los hombres. Lima: Populibros Peruanos, 1964.
Crónica de San Gabriel. Lima: Tawantinsuyu, 1960.
Dichos de Luder. Lima: Jaime Campodónico, 1989.
Los geniecillos dominicales. Lima: Populibros Peruanos, 1965. 2nd ed., Mexico City: Bogavante, 1969. 3rd ed., Lima: Milla Batres, 1973.
La juventud en la otra ribera. Lima: Mosca Azul, 1973.
La palabra del mudo. 4 vols. Lima: Milla Batres, 1973–1992. Selected English version as *Marginal voices.* Trans. Dianne Douglas. Austin: University of Texas Press, 1993.
Prosas apátridas. Barcelona: Tusquets/Cuadernos Marginales, 1975.
Prosas apátridas aumentadas. Lima: Milla Batres, 1978.
Sólo para fumadores. Lima: El Barranco, 1987.
La tentación del fracaso, I. Diario personal, 1950–1960. Lima: Jaime Campodónico Editor/COFIDE, 1992.
Tres historias sublevantes. Lima: Mejía Baca, 1964.

CRITICISM

Forgues, Roland. "La vida no es un hallazgo. Entrevista a Julio Ramón Ribeyro." In his *Palabra viva*, 1.107–126. Lima: Studium, 1988.
Higgins, James. *Cambio social y constantes humanas. La narrativa corta de Ribeyro.* Lima: Pontificia Universidad Católica, 1991.
Kristal, Efraín. "El narrador en la obra de Ribeyro." *Revista de crítica literaria latinoamericana* 20 (1984): 155–169.
Luchting, Wolfgang A. *Estudiando a Julio Ramón Ribeyro.* Frankfurt-am-Main: Vervuert, 1988.
———. *Julio Ramón Ribeyro y sus dobles.* Lima: Instituto Nacional de Cultura, 1971.
Ortega, Julio. "Los cuentos de Ribeyro." *Debate* 25 (1984): 56–58; 26 (1984): 52–59; 27 (1984): 70–72.

Roberto J. Forns-Broggi

RIO, JOÃO DO (Brazil; 1881–1921) ⸻⸻⸻⸻

Born Paulo Barreto in Rio de Janeiro, Rio was one of the most representative founding figures of Brazilian journalism. He introduced the interview, the personal chronicle with satirical dialogues and other modern forms into the daily press at the beginning of the century, publishing in a broad array of important papers. His highly ornamental style can be associated with what is generally called Art Nouveau and contains elements of what today would unquestionably be called camp. He translated Oscar Wilde's notorious play *Salomé* (1895) in 1905 and considered himself one of Wilde's first Brazilian followers. Rio also wrote dramas, short stories and two novels.

There is ample evidence of Rio's homosexuality, which was brutally satirized by his enemies, both by word of mouth and in the public press. He was called Madame Bicycle "because he always had someone on his back," and allegedly he was arrested one midnight for openly having sex with a black policeman in the street. He would dress all in white or all in green, in the fashion of Des Esseintes in Joris Karl Huysmann's *À rebours* (Adrift; 1884) or the title character in Jean Lorrain's *Monsieur de Phocas* (1901), an exquisite dandy in a Rio de Janeiro that was still basically provincial. Yet he did not openly flaunt his homosexuality, and he pursued a romantic liaison with a young Portuguese actress and even one with Isadora Duncan during her stay in Rio in 1916. According to legend, Duncan danced naked in the moonlight for him on a deserted Ipanema beach. In any event, they became close friends, and he is the only Brazilian she mentions in *My Life* (1928).

Rio rarely writes directly about homosexuality in his fiction, and his texts are more marked by a gay sensibility than by particular plot specifics: it is the narrator rather than the characters who bears a homosexual affiliation, as one finds in Wilde's writing or in the texts of Jean Lorrain, a forgotten French *maudit* who exercised a strong influence on Rio. His morbid view of life also links him to Octave Mirbeau, Pierre Loti, Edgar Allan Poe, Thomas de Quincey, Charles Baudelaire and Pierre Louys. Rio appears to be a unique case in Latin American literature: an individual who, despite his homosexuality, his condition as a mulatto and his political liberalism, achieved fame and fortune through his professional efforts and against great odds. He died of a heart attack at the age of thirty-nine. Although almost immediately forgotten, since 1980 there has been a project to rediscover and publish his voluminous work (over 2,500 press articles alone).

WORKS

Alma encantadora das ruas. Paris: Garnier, 1908. Also Rio de Janeiro: Secretaria Municipal de Cultura, 1988.

A bela Madame Vargas. Rio de Janeiro: Briguiet, 1912.

Cinematógrafo. Pôrto Alegre: Chardron, 1909.

A correspondência de uma estação de cura. Rio de Janeiro: Leite Ribeiro e Maurillo, 1918. Also Rio de Janeiro: Fundação Casa Rui Barbosa, 1992.

Dentro da noite. Paris: Garnier, 1910.

A mulher e os espelhos. Lisbon: Portugal/Brasil, 1919. Also Rio de Janeiro: Secretaria Municipal de Cultura, 1990.

Pall-Mall Rio de José Antonio José. Rio de Janeiro: Villas-Boas, 1917.

A profissão de Jacques Pedreira. Paris: Garnier, 1911. Also Rio de Janeiro: Fundação Casa Rui Barbosa, 1992.

Que pena ser só ladrão. Encontro. Um chá das cinco. Lisbon: Portugal/Brasil, n.d.

As religiões no Rio. Paris: Garnier, 1904.

O rosário da ilusão. Lisbon: Portugal/Brasil, 1921.

CRITICISM

Antelo, Raúl. *João do Rio: O dândi e a especulação*. Rio de Janeiro: Livrarias Taurus-Timbre Editores, 1989.

Broca, Brito. *A vida literária no Brasil, 1900*. 2nd ed., rev. and enl. Rio de Janeiro: Livraria José Olympio Editora, 1960.

Magalhães Júnior, Raimundo. *A vida vertiginosa de João do Rio*. Rio de Janeiro: Civilização Brasileira, 1978.

Paulo Barreto 1881–1921. Catálogo da exposição comemorativa do centenário de nascimento organizado pela seção de promoções culturais. Rio de Janeiro: Biblioteca Nacional, 1981.

Rodrigues, João Carlos. *Bibliografia completa de Paulo Barreto/João do Rio*. Rio de Janeiro: Secretaria Municipal de Cultura, 1993.

Secco, Carmen Lúcia Tindó. *Morte e prazer em João do Rio*. Rio de Janeiro: Livraria Francisco Alves Editora/SEEC, 1978.

João Carlos Rodrigues

RIOS, CASSANDRA (Brazil; date unknown)

Although Rios has written more than forty best-selling novels in Brazil, she is not well known outside of her native country, where she has been virtually ignored by academics due to the popular, sensationalist tone of her work. Rios's writing is produced at a fast pace for mass-market consumption. Her characters are hastily drawn, her plots tend to be contrived and untidy and her writing style, when she bogs down in philosophical conjectures and melodramatic exclamations about the nature of life and love, is far from polished. Nevertheless, Rios is unparalleled in her ability to capture the image of the sexually liberated life-style of Brazil's young urban set. Her books are primarily about sex, in all combinations and forms. From the most innocent to the most perverse, her characters cover the broad spectrum of sexual tastes and practices. Rios knows how to titillate her readers with detailed descriptions of erotic acts between all kinds of lovers.

It is not uncommon for sex scenes to go on for four or five pages, with enough adjectives and adverbs to make it very clear who is doing exactly what to whom. Dialogues about sex also are common. When her characters are not making love, they are talking about it. The use of popular slang, bits of songs, references to films and images borrowed from pop culture of the 1960s and 1970s creates the impression that Rios is telling it "like it is" when she talks about the sexual exploits of her characters. But whether her novels accurately reflect reality is open to debate. As David William Foster has observed, "Rios presents heroines who supplement the real urban situations of her readers by offering an image of personal sexual realization that, because it is the stuff of her novels, is not likely to be actual sociocultural fact" (120).

Foster's observation is especially astute in the way that it relates to Rios's portrayal of lesbian sex, for despite the abundance of lesbian lovers in her fiction, it is doubtful that Rios aims her work at a primarily lesbian audience. The positioning of the reader vis-à-vis the characters, as well as the treatment of homosexual desire in her novels, point toward traditional, heterosexual, male-biased viewing and reading habits. As Foster notes, it is clear that in her novels Rios "cannot decide whether female homosexuality is a good thing or not" (121). What is equally clear is that despite her stated intentions to show lesbianism as a natural practice, she cannot escape the cultural conditioning that brands it abnormal and deviant behavior.

In Rios's fiction, lesbians may enjoy good sex, but they seldom have good lives. She leaves no doubt that women who love women must pay a price for being different. They are alienated from their families, they live in fear of being exposed as lesbians, they have difficulty forming emotional bonds with others and they must deal with overt hostility from heterosexuals who despise them because of their sexual persuasion. Given the bleak picture Rios paints of lesbianism in Brazil, it is ironic that so many of her characters become lesbians. A look, a touch—and a formerly heterosexual woman falls into the arms of another woman. This recurrent pattern, rather than reflecting a widespread trend toward homosexuality in Brazil, more likely shows the relationship and interconnections between Rios's fiction and the conventions of male-oriented pornography.

One of the standard images of pornographic film and photography involves the girl-on-girl shot, the enactment of lesbian sex, but with the clear understanding that it is being carried out for the voyeuristic pleasure of the male viewer. It is a performance, a play conducted before an audience, in which the actors pretend they are oblivious to the spectators. Theoreticians of film have conjectured for some time that the image of the naked female body evokes the fear of castration in the male viewer, due to the female's lack of a male sex organ. In order to assuage the fear, the male has two options that often overlap and feed into one another: he can fetishize the female body, flattening the image into an icon that can be worshipped as something unreal in its perfection, and/or he can assume the position of voyeur, appropriating the phallic gaze and converting the female body into an object to be controlled by his decision to look/not look at any given part of it. In pornography, these two positions offer the male spectator a vehicle through which he can gratify his own desire. He can look at the body, fragment it through the close-up shot, dehumanize it by removing it from narrative content and assert his control over it by adopting the voyeur role. It exists to please him, rather than to please itself. Female sexuality is thus contained and defused, making it less dangerous and, at the same time, more thrilling to the male because his gaze has established him as master of the game. As Laura Mulvey has shown, the male-biased viewing position of most mainstream films leaves the female spectator in an awkward position. She must either learn to see like a male, or she is alienated from the process altogether.

Rios's fiction follows this pattern in many ways. In *Copacabana pôsto seis (a madrasta)* (Copacabana Beach, Station No. 6 [the Stepmother]; 1961), voyeurism is part of the novel. Simonni spies on her stepdaughter, Carla, as the girl engages in sex with a female friend. The servants spy on Simonni and Carla when they make love. And we, as readers, spy on them all as they go through these motions. Descriptions of Simonni's body are especially graphic. As the classic Hollywood femme fatale, every inch of her flesh is subjected to our gaze. We watch her fall under Carla's spell and engage in lesbian sex, but we also know that she is basically a heterosexual woman, because she says, "I always liked men, I could never accept this idea of . . . " (170). It is significant that she does not identify herself with the word *lesbian*. It is Carla, the androgynous but beautiful butch, who confesses, "I am a homosexual" at the end of the novel (210); the feminine Simonni "didn't say anything. She was afraid even to think" (211).

Voyeurism is also an explicit component of *Tessa, a gata* (Tessa, the Pussycat; 1968). Roberta's husband has supposedly corrupted her, forcing her to have sex with other people so that he can watch her. She has now become so used to providing a spectacle for others that she takes off her clothes and sprawls naked on the sofa in her husband's office, offering herself to Débora, a lesbian who works in the office as a secretary. Later, Roberta engages Débora in a sexual performance while her husband watches from the next room. Again, Roberta, the more feminine of the two, is the target of our gaze. We are offered detailed descriptions of her body and of the ways Débora uses it to satisfy her lust. But it is all carried out for the enjoyment of those who are watching/ reading, rather than for the benefit of those engaged in the act. The women show us what lesbians do in bed together; the descriptions of their movements, as well as the words they speak, set up a model so that we can know what lesbian love is like. What prevents this scene from becoming an authentic lesbian encounter is the fact that it is peripheral to what is supposedly the core of the narrative, Débora's search for love and understanding. It is a scene staged to excite the male viewer (and, by extension, those of us who look over his shoulder as he looks at them).

Once we return to the plot, the relationship between the two women quickly turns sour; Roberta murders her husband, and Débora blackmails her. The happy ending in which Débora is magically reunited with her first love, Tessa, is contrived and unconvincing. What will become of them is unclear. Débora dismisses their future by saying, "It was foolish to think. I would never reach any conclusion!'' (125). As was the case in *Copacabana pôsto seis*, the lesbian lovers of *Tessa, a gata* are silenced before they have come fully to terms with their sexual identity. They do not know what to say or what to think. Their number ends, the show is over, the lights are turned off on the metaphorical stage where they have been performing for our pleasure, the actors put on their clothes and they go home. There is little in the texts to indicate that they will end up in happy relationships, but they have not been constructed with enough conviction for us to care.

Mutreta (1972) uses lesbians in a similar way, as actors in a flimsy plot about contraband and murder, in which highly erotic sex scenes between women are inserted to provide narrative excitement. After engaging in numerous passionate but empty relationships, Amanda finds true love with Tarsa, but although a lesbian figures as the central character in the novel, it would be inaccurate to say that the book is really about lesbianism. The character of Amanda could easily be replaced by a heterosexual male, since her only function in the text is to act as a vehicle through which we have access to shots of beautiful women engaged in sexual activity. Voyeurism is also present in this work, both at the internal and at the external level. Amanda's lover, Lo, stands at the window and watches her make love to Ming Li in the garden. Ming Li knows that Lo is watching—she has arranged it so—and it is this knowledge that she is the spectacle to be looked at that excites her. The omniscient narrator also positions us, as readers, to see what Lo sees. In this and other scenes in the novel, we watch Amanda perform. It is through her eyes that the female body (of her lovers) is fetishized and turned into an object that can be offered to us for consumption.

It is important to note that in *Mutreta*, as well as in the novels just discussed, the narrative ends abruptly, just as the possibly permanent lesbian relationship seems about to begin. Rios offers no insight into what the daily life of these individuals might be like, what problems they face as a couple, what factors influence their decision to stay together or to part. The texts deal, for the most part, with the instability of past relationships, the inability of the characters to be monogamous, the lack of close ties between them and their previous lovers; instead, they focus on the way the characters are driven by passion to commit acts of folly. How they can be expected to settle down into meaningful relationships in light of their past history is never addressed. While popular novels in this vein seldom offer complex characterization or profound psychological insight into social relationships, it is clear that Rios is unable or unwilling to deal with lesbians as anything other than stereotypes or as fragmented body parts held up to the reader's gaze.

Tara (1970) proves the point quite well, for although it deals almost exclusively with the world of lesbians, it sheds little light on them as individuals, and does not move beyond the ''female attraction'' of their mating rituals. Tara's obsession with Alessandra and the difficulty of conquering her provides the main narrative thread of the novel. Tara is forced to behave seductively in one situation after another, to kiss and fondle and coax Alessandra into a physical relationship. The other women in the group all look on in silence as the drama unfolds between the two principal players. Once they form an alliance and "perform" for us in a variety of sexual acts, they are neatly eliminated from the plot by a jealous ex-lover who shoots them dead as they lie in each other's arms. Significantly, the novel ends with a voyeuristic scene that continues to frame the dead women as erotic objects: spectators look at the lovers, curled together in a tender embrace, and comment on how "incomprehensible" it is for women to love one another. The heterosexual relationship between two very minor characters in the book, Setubal and Luana, comes to the foreground, while the homosexual one is dismissed as "o fim das coisas impossíveis . . . sempre triste . . . sempre trágico" (214; the end of impossible things . . . always sad . . . always tragic).

The reluctance to speak the word *lesbian*, to identify oneself by that word, to embrace a lesbian life-style and to find positive value in it prevents Rios's characters from realizing their sexual identity as homosexual women. There is an abundance of supposedly bad girls in her books—prostitutes, murderers, blackmailers, sadomasochists, psychopaths—but there is not a single character who provides a truly admirable role model for real-life lesbians to follow. There is no one who shows the least interest in feminist concerns, in the role of women in society, or even in her own identity as a female. Female bonding rarely goes beyond the sexual. What appears on the surface to be a rejection of patriarchal order turns out to be a reconfirmation of it as lesbian lovers run off together, but take with them the formalized roles set up by mainstream heterosexual society. Despite her self-professed desire to explain homosexuality and make it comprehensible to her readers, Rios ultimately cannot resist the temptation to use her status as "the most banned author in Brazil" to become "the best-selling author in Brazil," reducing lesbianism to a commodity to be bought and sold in an economy dictated by masculine desire.

WORKS

Copacabana pôsto seis. Rio de Janeiro: Edições Spiker, 1961.
Marcellina. Rio de Janeiro: Distribuidora Record, 1980.
Mutreta. São Paulo: Editora Mundo Musical, 1972.
Tara. Rio de Janeiro: Distribuidora Record, 1970.
Tessa, a gata. São Paulo: Hemus, 1968.

CRITICISM

Foster, David William. *Gay and Lesbian Themes in Latin American Writing*, 120–124. Austin: University of Texas Press, 1991.
Mulvey, Laura. "Visual Pleasure and Narrative Cinema." *Screen* 18.3 (1975): 6–18.

Snitow, Ann, Christine Stansell and Sharon Thompson. *Powers of Desire: The Politics of Sexuality.* New York: Monthly Review Press, 1983.

Williams, Linda. *Hard Core: Power, Pleasure, and the "Frenzy of the Visible."* Berkeley: University of California Press, 1989.

Cynthia Duncan

ROBLES, MIREYA (Cuba; 1934) ————————————

Mireya Robles was born in Guantánamo. She studied civil and international law at the University of Havana before emigrating to the United States in 1957. She received her doctorate in Hispanic literature from the State University of New York and currently teaches Latin American literature at the University of Natal, Republic of South Africa. Robles has earned critical acclaim for two collections of poetry, *Tiempo artesano* (*Time, the Artisan*; 1973) and *En esta aurora* (In This Dawn; 1978), and a novel, *Hagiografía de Narcisa la bella* (Hagiography of Narcisa the Beautiful; 1985).

Robles's work contributes to a small but growing corpus of literature by Latin American women who deal with gender issues in spite of heterosexist societal pressure to suppress such topics. Her fiction in particular examines the influence of machista family structure on gender roles and sexual conduct of family members. Through satire that is at once imaginative and brutally honest, *Hagiografía de Narcisa la bella* reveals the internal oppression that such a family unit requires in order to exist. In Robles's poetry, on the other hand, the homosexual problematic is treated differently, in part because of the intensely subjective nature of the lyric voice. Her poems affirm the speaker's right to exist as a woman who loves another woman, in the very act of giving poetic expression to her love and desire.

As is frequently the case with poetry collections that employ a highly personal lyric voice, the twenty poems in *En esta aurora* reveal a questing process. The female speaker seeks to define herself and to affirm her existence through language and images, and the poems reflect her moments of pain and intense solitude. Many of the poems evoke the presence of a lover in order to achieve this affirmation, and in these love poems the obstacles to free expression of lesbian subjectivity become evident. Because the lover is also a woman, the love that is life-affirming to both women is unacceptable according to patriarchal societal norms. Yet the poems eloquently and defiantly construct this lesbian subjectivity through simultaneous processes of proclaiming desire for the absent lover and evoking her through language.

The first poem of the collection, "Cuando sólo se llenan las horas" (When All You Do Is Fill up the Hours), describes sensations of isolation, hunger and monotony—the spiritual emptiness that the speaker is struggling to replace with a sense of self. In the poems that follow, she begins, tentatively at first, to include the other in her poetic universe and to imagine the possibility of union with her: "el milagro desnudo de una palabra nuestra" (the naked miracle of a word of our own). Her lover is often associated with organic imagery ("jardines submarinos" [underwater gardens], "buganvilla silvestre" [wild bougainvillea], "las tempestades de los siglos" [the tempests of the centuries]), and love is portrayed as mystical, elusive ("tu sombra escapaba de mis manos" [your shadow escaped from my hands]), timeless ("Has llegado mañana y llegarás ayer" [You have arrived tomorrow and you will arrive yesterday]). In later poems, the speaker's love has intensified, as has her suffering when her lover is absent; the poems "Un momento" (One Moment), "Guardo de ti" (I Hold in You), "Escribo un verso" (I Write a Verse), "Si te fueras" (If You Were to Leave), and others reflect her deep sense of loss when separated from her beloved. She counters this absence by engaging her lover as interlocutor, re-creating her spirit and body in language.

The motif of absence plays a key role in the poems of *En esta aurora* because desire is experienced more powerfully in the absence of the lover. Even the poems that speak of fulfilled desire are permeated with a sadness born of longing for reunion, which serves to heighten the eroticism of the poems. In "Con los ojos perdidos" (With Lost Eyes), for example, she anticipates the dawn and her lover's farewell while reflecting on a just-ended erotic encounter. In the final poems of the collection, however, the bond between the two women seems to solidify, to become more tangible, as suggested by the proliferation of concrete images of daily life that contrast with the abstract nature imagery of earlier poems. The final poem, "Apuntes para una mañana" (Note for a Morning), expresses for the first time a sense of tranquillity, of hope, as the isolated I and you of previous poems have united to become we: "nos vimos crecer en la palabra" (we saw ourselves grow in the word). Although the speaker expresses solitude, unrequited desire and at times despair, she courageously proclaims her love—affirming her lesbian subjectivity—in defiance of societal taboos. As Eliana Rivero says in her introduction to *En esta aurora*, "The poetic texts take on depth through trying to name, through succeeding in naming, through joining two wills and two bodies by means of a language forged in artistic terrain claimed by no one" (6; my translation).

In contrast to the intimacy of Robles's poetry, biting satire at every level characterizes her novel *Hagiografía de Narcisa la bella*. As the title suggests, the text bears certain similarities to a traditional hagiography: the novel centers on the brief, tortured life of the misunderstood Narcisa, who is martyred by her own family at age fifteen. Like other saints, Narcisa possesses unusual powers, such as her ability to hear and comprehend her parents' conversation about her while she is still in the womb. Her father, Don Pascual, makes no secret of his adherence to the machista code that places supreme value on male offspring; before Narcisa's birth he is so vehement in his desire for a son that she arranges to be born wearing a diaper to cover her private parts. Narcisa is not a likely candidate for sainthood: the principal miracle that she performs is managing to survive in spite of her family's utter neglect and frequent abuse. Narcisa is an innocent victim, punished constantly for no apparent reason other than the fact that she was born female and homely. Her mother, Doña Flora, seems determined to test the limits of her daughter's tolerance for deprivation, ignoring her basic needs (food, hygiene, a place to sleep) and her emotional needs. When the family goes on an excursion to the beach, for example, Doña Flora and Don Pascual leave the infant Narcisa floating in the ocean for hours; when they finally retrieve her, their only response to the sodden child is to express annoyance when she soaks their clothes.

Robles's novel consists of a series of equally hyperbolic situations that deconstruct the bourgeois family unit and expose the repression generated within it. Narcisa's apparently average family consists of her mother, who is a fan of radio soap operas; her womanizing father; her sadistic older brother, Manengo; and her extremely status-conscious and demanding younger sister, Florita-ita. Although Florita-ita enthusiastically assumes an exaggerated feminine role, devoting her energies to maintaining her physical beauty, her siblings reject the traditional gender roles enacted by their primary male and female role models, Don Pascual and Doña Flora.

Manengo refuses to engage in the typical masculine activities that his father promotes, such as sports. When Don Pascual attempts to persuade his son to play baseball, "para ver si esto te enseña a ser un macho" (to see if this teaches you to be a macho; 57), Manengo infuriates him by putting on one of his mother's aprons and sticking his penis out through a hole in the cloth, shouting at his father, "Mira, viejo hipócrita, ¿así es cómo quieres que juegue a la pelota?" (Look, you old hypocrite, is this how you want me to play ball?; 58). Manengo further mocks his father's machista values through his sexual preference for boys. When he develops an obvious crush on a neighbor boy, Don Pascual calls him a *maricón* (faggot) and declares that his son needs straightening out. Manengo, on the other hand, appears unashamed of his desire, and during confession tells the priest that love between young men is beautiful. His father refuses to tolerate Manengo's homosexual activities, however. After receiving reports that his son has been seen having sex with other boys on a neighbor's patio, Don Pascual threatens to kill him, calling Manengo's behavior "la desgracia más grande, que no seas macho" (the worst disgrace, that you're not macho; 125). In spite of Don Pascual's disgust with and societal censure of Manengo's sexual orientation, he redeems himself by becoming a filmmaker, his studies financed by Narcisa's earnings as a bill collector.

Narcisa's own lesbian identity—evidence of her refusal to accept the stereotypical feminine role of passive sexual object for the dominant male—is developed more through her fantasies than through actual homoerotic encounters. As she becomes aware of her sexuality, Narcisa discovers that she agrees with her father that women are incredible (104) and imagines female romantic conquests. In fact, many of her fantasies involve emulation of Don Pascual; even as an infant she hopes one day to become the man of the house (26). She has an erotic dream about her friend Margarita after deciding that she should follow her father's model, taking women by surprise and seducing them, since according to Don Pascual, that is what they want. Later Narcisa speculates as to whether another friend, Glorita, likewise wants to be conquered; she masturbates while fantasizing about Glorita and about being with a woman in Manengo's favorite hideaway.

The lesbian problematic is explored in *Hagiografía de Narcisa la bella* at a symbolic level as well; Narcisa's name, for example, evokes the obvious connection with narcissism. In addition to the self-aggrandizement and egotism that characterize narcissism, its philosophical basis is the subject's infatuation with his/her own image, which can be interpreted as a form of homoerotic desire. Narcisa desires those in whom she sees herself reflected—other women—but she also develops an inflated sense of self-love in response to the absolute lack of love or compassion from other human beings. Intense solitude is the condition most familiar to Narcisa, as she is alienated from her family and unacknowledged by people on the outside. Her attempts to express herself through art are frustrated: when she laboriously composes a complex, unconventional essay on her family for a writing assignment, for example, her teacher gives her a low grade, declaring that the composition makes no sense.

The extreme degree to which Narcisa is silenced and rendered invisible is analogous to the treatment of lesbians within a heterosexist social order whose stability is threatened by their existence. Repeatedly throughout the novel, Narcisa encounters people who ignore her completely, and concludes that she must save herself from the solitude of abandonment. Yet her family and society are too powerful, and she cannot save herself; instead, Narcisa is silenced permanently, and Manengo's prophecy that her destiny is to forget her own name comes true within the novel. Ironically, however, each act of reading brings Narcisa back to life, allowing her to continue to speak. Thus the existence of the text assures her immortality, and her own prophecy is fulfilled: "Tal vez el eco de la voz hecha letra persista . . . y eso seré palabra que lleve a los demás a mundos desconocidos" (Perhaps the echo of the voice made into writing will persist . . . that's what I will be, I will be the word that takes others to unknown worlds; 104).

WORKS

En esta aurora. San Antonio, Tex.: M & A Editions, 1978.
Hagiografía de Narcisa la bella. Hanover, N.H.: Ediciones de Norte, 1985.
Tiempo artesano. Barcelona: Medinaceli, 1973. Trans. by Angela de Hoyos as *Time, the Artisan*. Austin, Tex.: Dissemination Center for Bilingual Bicultural Education, 1975.

CRITICISM

Collmann, Lilliam Oliva. "La estructura como acto subversivo: Un análisis de *Hagiografía de Narcisa la bella* de Mireya Robles." *Crítica hispánica* 9.1–2 (1987): 31–38.

Feal, Rosemary Geisdorfer. "Gender Identity and Feminine Creativity in *Hagiografía de Narcisa la bella* by Mireya Robles." *Literature and Psychology* 35.1–2 (1989): 1–18.

Rivero, Eliana S. Introduction. In Robles, *En esta aurora*, 5–7.

Sklodowska, Elzbieta. "El discurso de *Hagiografía de Narcisa la bella* de Mireya Robles en el contexto de la prosa femenina hispanoamericana." *Kwartalnik neofilologiczny* 33.4 (1986): 487–498.

Soto, Francisco. "Entrevista con Mireya Robles." *Mester* 20.2 (Fall 1991): 99–106.

———. "La representación del personaje femenino en *Hagiografía de Narcisa la bella* de Mireya Robles." *Mester* 20.2 (Fall 1991): 89–98.

Karen S. Christian

RODRIGUES, NELSON (Brazil; 1912–1980)

It is said that by the age of seven, the noted dramatist Nelson Rodrigues had already demonstrated signs of what would later become one of the dominant motifs of his writing. At that age he wrote his first story for a class project at the Prudente School in Tijuca. The story, later published in a two-volume collection of short stories titled *A vida como ela é* (Life as It Is; 1961), deals with a woman, in the mold of Emma Bovary, who is knifed to death by her husband. The response of his teacher can only be left to the imagination. Thus began the career of the man considered to be one of the most prominent Brazilian dramatists of the twentieth century. In addition to his sixteen plays, he wrote novels (many under the pseudonym Suzana Flag), short stories and newspaper pieces. His play *Vestido de noiva* (Wedding Gown; 1943) is considered one of the most significant works in the history of the Brazilian stage, as much for the direction of the play by Zbigniew Ziembinski—the Polish director regarded as the central force in bringing about a revolutionary transformation of Brazilian theater, principally through the use of expressionist techniques—as for its experimental content.

Rodrigues was born in Recife and early in life moved to Rio, where he later worked as a journalist. His theater and novels are heavily flavored with this journalistic formation. One of the recurring themes in both his plays and his novels is the danger of yellow journalism. His profession may also account for the sensationalist flavor in his writing. Criticism of Rodrigues's plays tends to center on questions of its connections to tragedy or innovative theatrical techniques. The theme that seems to crop up in virtually all of his work is the inability of the individual to mask the true nature of sexual inclinations due to the hegemonic social codes of patriarchy. These impulses somehow rise to the surface, unable to be confined within the parameters of supposedly proper behavior. The conflict between the social codes of morality and the putatively abnormal intimate impulses more often than not leads to an anguished death for Rodrigues's characters, either by their own hand or by someone else's.

Rodrigues's work may be read as a subversion of the patriarchal code of compulsory heterosexuality and the nuclear family. His plays, in spite of their tremendous success, were often banned for their perceived immorality during Brazil's military dictatorship (1965–1982). It is to be hoped that with the new focus on subaltern studies, a new interest will be kindled in the prevalence of allegedly sexually deviant characters in his plays. While homosexuality could be termed one of the dominant motifs in his writing, it remains virtually un-mentioned in the criticism.

Rodrigues wrote few novels. In the two-volume novel *Asfalto selvagem* (Savage Asphalt; 1960–1961), there is the ongoing obsession of Letícia with her husband's lover, Engraçadinha, protagonist of the novel. Their lesbian love relationship begins early in the first volume, subtitled *Engraçadinha dos 12 aos 18* (Engracadinha from 12 to 18) when the adolescents bathe together and Letícia becomes obsessed with Engraçadinha. The second volume, subtitled *Engraçadinha: Seus amores e seus pecados depois dos 30* (Engraçadinha: Her Loves and Sins After 30) ends with the suicide of Letícia, who leaves a note behind for Engraçadinha: "*Darling*: só te peço uma coisa: acredita no meu amor. E amor, e não tara. Na hora de morrer, eu não mentiria. E amor, *Darling*, só amor. Para sempre. Já morri e é amor. *I love you, I love you, I love you, Letícia*" (Italicized words in English in the original; Darling, I ask you only one thing: believe in my love. It is love, and not perversion. At the moment of my death, I would not lie. It is love, Darling, only love. Forever. I have already died and it is love.) There is an added twist to the narrative in that Letícia also has relations with Silene, Engraçadinha's daughter. Silene loses her virginity to Leleco, who kills Candelão when Candelão tries to use him as the passive partner in sex—to use him "as the woman." In *O casamento* (The Wedding; 1966), considered to be one of Rodrigues's better novels, there is yet another lesbian relationship, between Glorinha and María Inês.

Rodrigues's theater also has quite an array of homosexual figures, ranging from comical fags to the apparently heterosexual figures who reveal the alternative nature of their sexuality in often shocking and melodramatic ways. While these may be considered the more obvious examples of homosexual themes, Rodrigues also populates his plays with many characters who reflect a strong undercurrent of alternative sexuality (like the single aunts in *Toda nudez será castigada* (All Nudity Will be Punished; 1965) without its ever being made explicit textually.

One of the dramatist's first works, *Album de família* (Family Album; 1945) offers the adolescent lesbian relationship of Glória, fifteen years old, with Teresa, in the room that they share at a boarding school. When their relationship is discovered, they are expelled from the school and Glória returns home, triggering the events that compose the body of the play—most specifically, the subject of incest. The play was banned as immoral, and censorship was not lifted until 1965. In *Perdoa-me por me traíres* (Forgive Me for Your Cheating on Me; 1957), one of the minor characters is the gay black servant in a bordello with the ever-so-telling name Pola Negri (Black Pole). Glorinha and her friend

Nair go to the bordello to prostitute themselves. Nair becomes pregnant as a result of the experience, and when she goes to have an abortion, there is an echo of what would later be the central theme in *Beijo no asfalto* (A Kiss on the Pavement; 1960)—the illicit kiss: "E se eu morrer, quero que tu me beijes, apenas isso: quero ser beijada, um beijo sem maldade, mas que seja um beijo!" (And if I die, I want you to kiss me, just that: I want to be kissed, an innocent kiss, but nonetheless a kiss!) (141). It is insinuated in the text that the homosexuality of Nair is the result of having experienced the masculine brutality of the bordello.

In *Os sete gatinhos* (The Seven Cats; 1958), Rodrigues's Rio tragedy, a lower-middle-class family headed by the patriarch Noronha is composed of sisters who are prostitutes, except the youngest, Silene. When Silene becomes pregnant, the family seeks revenge upon the one who stained the only point of honor the family had, Silene's purity. Arlete is Silene's lesbian sister, who, much like Nair, it is insinuated, turns to lesbianism to avoid the brutalities of men and to distance herself from her prostitution. In the sensationalist ending, the sisters find out that the man who impregnated Silene was none other than their father, Noronha, the one who most fervently had demonstrated his desire for revenge.

Toda nudez será castigada calls into question the spectator's ability to discern the sexual identity of the characters. The play revolves around Herculano, the patriarch, living with his three old maid aunts and his devious brother, and mourning the loss of his wife to breast cancer. Patrício sets a trap for Herculano, getting him involved with a prostitute, Geni, with whom he later falls in love and marries. Herculano's son, Serginho, meanwhile, sees the two making love in the garden and goes out drinking; he ends up in jail, where he is raped by a Bolivian thief. To avenge what he sees as his father's lack of respect for the memory of his dead mother, Serginho decides that he will agree to the marriage of his father to Geni, then get revenge by taking her as his lover. In a typical Rodrigues ending, Serginho decides to abandon Geni and leave the country with the Bolivian thief, triggering her suicide. The play begins and ends with Herculano listening to a tape Geni had made for him before her death, explaining everything, while the play is seen as a flashback.

The play text has clues planted throughout, pointing to the cracks in the patriarchal mask that lead to the ending. Moreover, the text seems to indicate homosexuality in both Serginho and Herculano. It is interesting to note that in Arnaldo Jabor's enormously successful screen adaptation of the play (1973), the allusions have all but vanished. *Beijo no asfalto* remains probably the foremost work in Rodrigues's theater in terms of its treatment of homosexual themes. The text offers a Kafkaesque view of a respectable bourgeois man's progressive descent into hell as a result of having kissed a dying man on the street. The moment is caught by the yellow-press journalists, who write about it under the inflammatory title "Beijo no asfalto." The journalists, seeking to satisfy the voyeuristic urges of the community, invent a story of the long and torrid love affair between Arandir and the dead man. The result is a seething wave of homophobia that engulfs the protagonist. He loses his job, and his wife is tortured in an interrogation about his manliness. Soon she also is engulfed in doubt as to the nature of the kiss, and her husband is forced to go into hiding to avoid persecution. In the final explosive scene, his sister-in-law comes to the hotel where he is staying to voice her love for him. His father-in-law enters, orders his daughter to leave, and kills Arandir, but not before confessing his own secret love for him.

Rodrigues paints a fascinating picture of homophobia and its ability to dehumanize the other. He also seems to be making yet another scathing commentary on the nature of patriarchal masks. Aprígio, Arandir's father-in-law, weaves his masculine identity so tightly that only in rereading the play text does the reader perceive the clues distributed throughout to indicate the nature of his feelings. Only then do the elements of homosexual panic become obvious, like his insistent curiosity about the sex life of his daughter, his jealousy at the thought of Arandir with another man and his rather hypersensitive justification of his actions and feelings under the guise of ''The Father.''

One of the most ingenius aspects of the play is that everything takes place *after* the kiss. The omission of the determining event around which all of the play revolves cleverly forces spectators to call into question their own judgment based on the evaluation of the event by the other characters. The error, as seen in 1993, is that the injustice of the persecution of what many critics have called Rodrigues's first truly sympathetic character is tied to his perceived heterosexuality. Given the sociohistoric framing of the play, the sympathetic treatment of homosexuality is to be commended. Yet it falls short of being truly revolutionary because of the implied connection between the claimed purity of the kiss and the inhumanity of Arandir's treatment by others in relation to his heterosexual identity. A truly remarkable play would have allowed for the possibility that purity and homosexuality are not at odds.

What is most consistently repeated by critics with regard to the explosive nature of the themes and characters in Rodrigues's plays and novels is that the author has an overwhelming desire to unmask the defects of the hegemonic social code of behavior. For this reason, possibly, his theater has been termed disagreeable. While his characters today may be seen as rather superficially conceived, lacking profound psychological delineation, when we take into account the sociohistorical context of his writing, Rodrigues's work stands as a monument to gay literary/theatrical tradition in Brazil.

WORKS

Album de família. In *Teatro completo*. Vol. 2: *Peças míticas*, 51–120. Ed. Sábato Magaldi. Rio de Janeiro: Nova Fronteria, 1981.

Asfalto selvagem I. Engraçadinha dos 12 aos 18. Rio de Janeiro: Nova Fronteria, 1980.

Asfalto selvagem II. Engraçadinha: Seus amores e seus pecados depois dos 30. Rio de Janeiro: Nova Fronteira, 1980.

Beijo no asfalto. In *Teatro completo.* Vol. 4: *Tragedias cariocas II*, 87–153. Ed. Sábato
   Magaldi. Rio de Janeiro: Nova Fronteira, 1981.
O casamento. Rio de Janeiro: Eldorado, 1966.
100 contos escolhidos: A vida como ele é. Rio de Janeiro: J. Ozon, 1961.
Os sete gatinhos. In *Teatro completo.* Vol. 3: *Tragedias cariocas*, 181–254. Ed. Sábato
   Magaldi. Rio de Janeiro: Nova Fronteira, 1981.
Perdoa-me por me traíres. In *Teatro completo.* Vol. 3: *Tragedias cariocas*, 122–179.
   Ed. Sábato Magaldi. Rio de Janeiro: Nova Fronteira, 1981.
Toda nudez será castigada. In *Teatro completo.* Vol. 4: *Tragedias cariocas II*, 155–242.
   Ed. Sábato Magaldi. Rio de Janeiro: Nova Fronteira, 1981.
Vestido de noiva. In *Teatro completo.* Vol. 1: *Peças psicológicas*, 11–124. Ed. Sábato
   Magaldi. Rio de Janeiro: Nova Fronteira, 1981.

CRITICISM

Canales, Luis. "O homossexualismo como tema no moderno teatro brasileiro." *Luso-
   Brazilian Review* 18.1 (1981): 173–180.
Carneiro, María José. "A desagradável família de Nelson Rodrigues." In *Uma nova
   família?*, 69–82. Ed. Sévulo A. Figueira. Rio de Janeiro: Jorge Zahar, 1987.
George, Nelson. Os comediantes and *Bridal Gown.*" *Latin American Theatre Review*
   21.1 (1987): 29–41.
———. "Nelson 2 Rodrigues." *Latin American Theatre Review* 21.2 (1988): 79–83.
Johnson, Randal. "Nelson Rodrigues as Filmed by Arnaldo Jabor." *Latin American
   Theatre Review* 16.1 (1982): 15–28.
Lins, Ronaldo Lima. *O teatro de Nelson Rodrigues: Uma realidade em agonia.* Rio de
   Janeiro: Livraria Francisco Alves Editora; Brasília: Instituto Nacional do Livro,
   1979.
Magaldi, Sábato. *Nelson Rodrigues: Dramatúrgia e encenações.* São Paulo: Perspectiva
   Universidade de São Paulo, 1987.
Mileto, Thales de. "Nelson Rodrigues." *Revista de teatro* 460 (1988): 24–25.
Süssekind, Flora. "Nelson Rodrigues e o fundo falso." In *I Concurso nacional de mon-
   ografias—1976*, 5–42. Brasília, Ministério da Educação e Cultura, Fundação Na-
   cional de Arte, Serviço Nacional de Teatro, 1977.
Vogt, Carlson, and Berta Waldman. *Nelson Rodrigues.* São Paulo: Brasiliense, 1985.
Waldman, Berta. "A cena e o cio nacional (uma leitura dos romances folhetins de Nelson
   Rodrigues)." In *Toward Socio-Criticism: Luso-Brazilian Literatures*, 76–85. Ed.
   Roberto Reis. Tempe: Center for Latin American Studies, Arizona State Univer-
   sity, 1991.
Waldman, Berta, Jorge Aguade and Carlson Vogt. "Nelson Rodrigues en escena." *Es-
   critura* 14.28 (1989): 477–489.

                                                            Melissa A. Lockhart

RODRÍGUEZ-MATOS, CARLOS A.
(Puerto Rico; 1949) _____

Rodríguez-Matos, who lives in New York, has published two collections of
poetry, *Matacán* (1982) and *Llama de amor vivita: Jarchas* (Flame of Living

Love, Jarchya; 1988), as well as poems in anthologies. In addition, he is the author of *El narrador pícaro: Guzmán de Alfarache* (The Picaresque Narrator: Guzmán de Alfarache; 1985) and the editor of *Simposio: Clemente Soto Vélez* (Symposium on Clemente Soto Vélez; 1990). He also has published articles of literary criticism. Since 1979 he has been a professor of Spanish and Spanish literature at Seton Hall University.

Through his poetic work as well as in his literary criticism, Rodríguez-Matos has focused his effort on an understanding of the specificity of homoerotic discourse. He has pointed to the impact of societal repression on homosexuals and the inevitable guilt that is manifested in their writing. With his characteristic humor, Rodríguez-Matos ("Encuentro," 1988) affirms that "Upon writing an openly gay or lesbian poem one still experiences the feelings of stirring up mischief, if not of committing a crime."

This idea is thematically presented in his poetry through the creation of an Arcadian ideal that permits the free expression of same-sex love. The Arcadian ideal has been valued by the homosexual imagination from Virgil's *Second Eclogue* to contemporary poetry, for it provides a space within which homosexuality is not viewed as censurable and homoeroticism is freely expressed. Those who seek an Arcadian ideal long for a secret paradise isolated from the world that will liberate them from society-reflected guilt (Fone).

A metaphoric space emerges within various poems in *Matacán* and *Llama de amor vivita* in which homoeroticism is constructed as a nonmarginal discourse. From this space the prejudices of a homophobic society are challenged and subverted. This poetry's great singularity lies in the utilization of the idyllic space in order to create a dual code: on the surface, the verses do not appear to confront the established order; the poetic subject is seldom identified as masculine, and when it is, the gender of the beloved remains unstated. Nevertheless, the homoerotic relationship is revealed beneath the surface in all its intensity, thus achieving the transgression. For example, "Ritos" (Rites), in *Matacán*, appears at first glance to be a poem about the arrival of spring. However, a more careful reading reveals a sexual encounter in the lines that describe the poet–subject's metamorphosis into a tree: "my lover's hand/a well aimed magic/awakened the buds/the trunk/a spark for my log/a provocation to life/a mouth dampened my roots/root against root intertwined/the savia responded with fire."

The metaphoric space evokes the Puerto Rican landscape. For example, in "Para llegarte" (To Meet You), in the section of the same title in *Matacán*, the poetic subject affirms: "and, if I were a carpenter of words/I would build an immense, gigantic verse to reach you/with jasmine and dew/bird's songs, fairies, wands/fragments of rainbows, bushes and mountains/foam from the ocean and seaweed/the coquí's song, coffee incenses . . . " (13). This Puerto Rican landscape is part of an offering of gifts that, according to Byrne Fone, is included in the symbolic rituals for the Arcadian who seeks to overcome obstacles in order to liberate the beloved. The longed-for freedom is noted in the last verse as the poetic voice affirms: "and I, reclaimed, beside your hand" (13).

It is not possible to love outside the idyllic space because society's circumstances conspire to separate the lovers. Significantly, the first two poems of the "Para llegarte" section are both titled "Distancias" (Distances). The first expresses the origin of the obstacles that must be overcome in order to reach the beloved. "Only you and I/in between, a serpent of waves" (11). The serpent, associated in Judeo-Christian tradition with transgression, alludes to the condemnation imposed by this tradition on homoerotic relationships. As Julia Kristeva has stated, "Judaism prescribed heterosexual love, basing its ethic on the family, on reproduction, and the chosen number of those who understand word of the Father" (1987, 60).

If the creation of an Arcadian space in Rodríguez-Matos's poetry is a response to the censorship to which homoeroticism is subjected, the tone of the poems seeks to combat this very censorship. The use of a ludic and humoristic tone challenges the conventions of traditional poetry by depriving it of its solemnity. This suggests an aggressive thematic stance that attempts to confront a society that marginalizes its members through prejudice. The very title *Matacán* provides the initial coordinates of meaning. *Matacán* means, among other things, "a poisonous compound that kills dogs; a stone to be lifted and thrown by the hand"; there is also a definition of the sense in which the Arabic term *jarcha* is used: "the jarchya has to have a few lines delivered by someone else besides the poet; better that it be a small dove or something else—like a woman, for example. And if that weren't enough, the jarchya should move like a streetwalker, coarsely and recklessly, like baby talk, or like a drunk or a Puerto Rican talking" (51). Rodríguez-Matos constructs poems distinguished by their humor, thus placing his poetry within that current of Puerto Rican literature that uses laughter as a tool for undermining and subverting.

Matacán's third part, "Llama de amor vivita. Jarchas" was expanded into Rodríguez-Matos's second collection, of the same title. Here, the poetic space is created through the image of a house that gives form to the intimate values of an interior space. These poems thus express a more transcendental preoccupation: the impossibility of a life that permits the expression of love and the development of creativity, particularly of writing. To welcome the beloved, the house must be stripped of a technology that has dehumanized it and that is symbolic of a consumer society. The house has ceased to symbolize the internal space because it impedes creativity. It becomes necessary to destroy it. It is possible that the house is reminiscent of the paternal home and thus is associated with death. Within that familiar realm the first repression appears: "Ríos" (Rivers) of *Matacán* evokes the mother's room, described as a cemetery where the poetic subject has been buried, its true identity lost to the falsehood of the portraits she keeps. The eradication of a false life in which society reduces homosexuals to a marginal existence, and its replacement by one in which the erotic will be experienced as a transforming desire that leads to freedom, constitutes the objective of Rodríguez-Matos's work.

WORKS

El narrador pícaro: Guzmán de Alfarache. Madison, Wis.: Hispanic Seminary of Medieval Studies, 1985.

"Encuentro de dos mundos: Puerto Rican Writing in Puerto Rico and New York." City College of New York, Nov. 18–19, 1988.

Llama de amor vivita. Jarchas. South Orange, N.J.: Ediciones Ichali, 1988.

Matacán. Madrid: Playor, 1982.

Simposio: Clemente Soto Vélez. San Juan, P.R.: Instituto de Cultura Puertorriqueña, 1990.

CRITICISM

Fone, Byrne R. S. "This Other Eden: Arcadia and the Homosexual Imagination." In *Essays on Gay Literature*, 13–34. Ed. Stuart Kellogg. New York: Harrington Park Press, 1983.

Kristeva, Julia. *Tales of Love*. Trans. Leon S. Roudiez. New York: Columbia University Press, 1987.

Ana Sierra

RODRÍGUEZ-MATOS, RAFAEL (Puerto Rico; 1951)

Rafael Rodríguez-Matos was born in Naranjito. He holds a B.A. from Interamerican University and is enrolled in the graduate program of Hispanic studies at the University of Puerto Rico–Río Piedras. He teaches in the public school system in Río Piedras. Rodríguez-Matos wrote the third book of poems with an explicit homosexual speaking subject in the history of Puerto Rican literature, *Anhelo de infinitos* (Desire for Infinite Limits; 1976), in the same year as Víctor Fragoso's *Ser islas* (Being Islands). The speaker in *Anhelo* is not gay in the sociohistorical sense of Fragoso's subject in *El reino de la espiga* (The Realm of the Ear of Grain; 1973), which marks the constitution of a gay speaking subject in Puerto Rican poetry. In contrast to Fragoso, who lived in New York City before, during and after the Stonewall riots that began the gay liberation movement in the United States, Rodríguez-Matos has always lived in Puerto Rico, and until recently, in the mountains of Naranjito, away from cosmopolitan San Juan and its gay subculture. In most of the poems of *Anhelo*, the lyric speaker is the neuter I addressing a neuter you so common in poetry and popular songs, pronouns with whom either males or females can identify. There is only one untitled poem that has an explicitly male you.

This homosexual I (and here one is assuming that the I who speaks in the poems and the poet who writes them are one and the same) represents in the other poems the love that did not dare speak its name, the lover who had to be neutered or lower his revealing voice. The ambiguity of the neutral I–you is one of many strategic devices of communication/expression employed by the oppressed to represent their situation. Many of Rodríguez-Matos's poems have the existential anguish experienced by so many homosexuals who felt condemned to a well of loneliness in this world, reduced to mere living dead, lonesome, afraid but not defeated. And if humans become evil, nature and poetry will provide salvation.

WORKS

Anhelo de infinitos (antología). Santo Domingo: Polly, 1976.
"Diario." 1975. Unpublished MS.
"Endechas o una canción triste y lamentable." 1974. Unpublished MS.
"Flor de mi pelvis." 1981. Unpublished MS.
"Lo que sobró del vaso." 1974. Unpublished MS.
"Raíz oscura." 1985. Unpublished MS.
"Voces silvestres." 1975. Unpublished MS.
Various poems. In *Poesía universitaria 1982–1983*, 40–41. Ed. Marcos Reyes Dávila and Manuel de la Puebla. Río Piedras, P.R.: Mairena, 1983.

CRITICISM

Rodríguez-Matos, Carlos A. "Apuntes para un acercamiento a la poesía puertorriqueña contemporánea: 1962–1986." *Revista del Instituto de cultura puertorriqueña* 94 (Oct.–Dec. 1986): 45–55.

Carlos A. Rodríguez-Matos

ROFFÉ, REINA (Argentina; 1951) ⸻⸻⸻⸻⸻

Reina Roffé was born in Buenos Aires; she currently resides in Madrid. She belongs to the generation of writers who came of age during one of the darkest periods of Argentine history, the Process of National Reorganization (1976–1983), led by a neofascist military government.

In 1969, at the age of seventeen, Roffé wrote her first novel, *Llamado al puf* (Call[ed] to the Ottoman), which met with immediate critical acclaim and won the Pondal Ríos Prize in Buenos Aires in 1975 for the best novel by a young writer. *Llamado al puf* chronicles many of the events in the author's life. She has termed it an "análisis casero de mi infancia" (a homegrown analysis of my infancy). In it Roffé exposes the bourgeois Buenos Aires family, in all of its misery and ridiculous hopes, all of its pain and failures. The family is seen as an example of a world in decay. After the success of *Llamado al puf*, literary circles in Buenos Aires anxiously awaited Roffé's next novel, which came in 1976.

Monte de Venus (Mons of Venus) was published at the inception of the new military government in 1976 and was immediately banned. The experience was devastating for Roffé. She wrote little in the way of fiction in the years that followed, conserving her attachment to the literary field by working as a journalist, editor and book reviewer for such newspapers as *Clarín* (Clarion), *Convicción* (Conviction), and *La Opinión* (Opinion). In 1979 Roffé won the Borges Prize of the Givre Foundation in Buenos Aires for her short story "Profanación" (Profanation), which uncovers the profound parallel isolation and silence of two apparently dissimilar Buenos Aires women. In 1981 she was granted a Fulbright Scholarship to study in the United States at the University of Iowa as part of its International Writing Program. In 1987, eleven years after her last novel was published, *La rompiente* (The Breaking Surf) appeared.

The theme of homosexuality emerges in Roffé's second novel, *Monte de Venus*, which may have accounted in part for its banning by the censors. The novel is about a group of women who decide to return and finish high school, each attempting to better her life through the system. There are two stories that emerge. The first, narrated in the third person, is that of Barú, one of the returning students, who finds her voice through politicization; the second, that of Julia Grande, concerns a lesbian who finds her voice through recounting her life story into a tape recorder for Victoria Sáenz Ballesteros, one of the instructors, who takes a personal interest in Julia's life as the possible subject of a novel.

All of these characters in one way or another are subalterns in a world that does not recognize that they have a voice or control over their destinies. All of them attempt to assume some form of self-empowerment but are greeted with failure and humiliation, presenting a pathetic if not grotesque image to the reader. For example, when the women decide to return to school, they are placed in a classroom with infantile decor and miniature furniture, which only serves to heighten their sense of shame. When, in the microcosm of Argentina that the school represents, Barú opts for politicization, it is for the right to wear pants. This privilege is granted through the benevolence of the oppressors—the school administrators—who later capriciously decide to take it away. Thus, the message is that any power the subaltern may believe s/he has to change the system is an illusion. The hegemonic cultural prohibitions deny the women any opportunity to define an identity that does not fall within prescribed parameters. Roffé presents the reader with an inflammatory text, feminist and radical because it signals that change within the system is impossible.

Julia Grande is probably the most tragic figure in Roffé's novel. She is the "love-'em-and-leave-'em" cliché of masculinity. Julia is stuck in the binary paradigm that dictates that the only way to exist is to play the "feminine" or the "masculine" role. In order to survive economically, Julia becomes a prostitute after being raped by a man she had thought was her friend. The experience brings her to the point of suicide; the supreme degradation of being nothing more than an *agujerito* (little hole), to use the word of her rapist, causes her to rethink her life and attempt to better herself and her prospects for the future by receiving an education. Julia soon falls in love with her teacher, Victoria Sáenz

Ballesteros. When the latter approaches Julia about recording the events of her life as the possible subject of a novel, Julia feels valued for the first time. However, in the course of telling her story, Julia admits that she killed a man by accident. Ballesteros blackmails her with the information in order to take away Julia's child.

Roffé's treatment of lesbian sexuality is explicit. Julia is in many ways a parody of a man, representing the worst that masculinist ideology has to offer. Each lover is another notch on her belt. Adopting a masculine stance is an attempt to enter the realm of phallocentric power. This transvestism is a critique of binary fissure, calling attention to its own constructed nature. Julia breaks with the erotic and social role assigned to her, proving in the process that the model is flawed, incapable of fixing any identity, be it heterosexual or homosexual.

In *Monte de Venus*, Roffé speaks openly about the sexual and political frustrations of women in a society that exploits and oppresses them. With her writing, like Barú with her politics and Julia Grande with her sexuality, Roffé dares to enter into the masculine sphere of power, and fails. She deconstructs the mechanisms and myths of patriarchy that serve to subject the individual to phallocentric tyranny and exposes the few options that exist for self-fulfillment within this system. The novel ends, however, on what may be considered a positive note: with anger—anger at having been deceived; Julia's anger at her situation, her misery, her poverty. And anger may be seen as a positive step toward social change.

One of the most interesting elements in *Monte de Venus* is the description of Julia's engagement to her lover, Paola. The subject of gay marriages following the lines of heterosexual marriages remains a heated debate within the gay and lesbian community. Julia's engagement party is a replication of heterosexual constructs within nonheterosexual frames. This calls attention to the utterly constructed status of the sociocultural heterosexual original. The transvestism is a critique of binary sex and gender distinctions as it seeks to stabilize and defamiliarize them. This in turn sets up what will become the dominant structure of Roffé's third novel, *La rompiente*.

While *La rompiente* does not deal with homosexuality per se, we still may see it as a logical extension of *Monte de Venus*, for if the characters in *Monte de Venus* are circumscribed by the binary structure of patriarchy, in *La rompiente* Roffé blurs the binarisms. The text, in and of itself, deals with the plurality of identity, the plurality that is a process. In *La rompiente*, the composition of self and of text is like the fragments of a broken mirror. There is a rewriting of the narrative as dialogue. In this sense the text is truly postmodern, placing itself in opposition to the master narrative, the story, by allowing for a multiplicity of stories, some inconsequential, to be a part of the schema. Thus *La rompiente* places itself in opposition to the unified, androcentric model of literary production that insists upon lineal progression and fixed interpretation. The novelty of *La rompiente* is that it converts the reader into the protagonist. The story

of the protagonist is dictated *to* her. When she is allowed to speak, the interlocutor interrupts, criticizing the novel as it is being told to her. The effect is
disconcerting, yet authentic. *La rompiente* received immediate critical acclaim,
winning the International Prize for Short Novel in 1986.

La rompiente, a multiplicity of texts in the most postmodern of senses, is
resistant to one interpretation. It is divided into three parts. First, there is the
story of a trip. The last part revolves around the time of silence and isolation
following the trip, crossed with assorted memories. The second part, titled "The
Novel," also carries many separate stories—some read, some spoken, interrupted and commented upon—revolving around a literary group of friends who
gather to play cards, and the persecution and disappearance of one. If *Monte de
Venus* issued a scathing condemnation of the binary social structure, then *La
rompiente* takes the revolutionary step of blurring the structure, showing how
identity is no longer thinkable in the rather simplistic terms of the male/female,
hetero/homo dialectic. Finding a voice, the dominant motif in the writing of
Roffé, entails finding one's voices. For this reason, *La rompiente* is relevant to
the discussion of lesbian and gay theories by exposing the fragmented nature of
the hegemonic binary structure. It calls attention to the artificiality of the structure that does not allow for the continuum of sexualities—bisexuality, transvestism, transsexualism, polysexualism—to be brought into the realm of the visible.
La rompiente erodes the polarizing fragmentation hetero/homo to acknowledge
that identity is process, resistant to any definitive narrativization. The text may
be seen as showing the progression of identity, not always lineal, subject to
challenge and revision, resistant to being controlled. In this way it refuses entry
into oppressive identity categories. Following the contemporary shift of homosexual theoretical studies, *La rompiente* consciously refuses to be regulated,
constrained and controlled by the reader/critic. The homosexual subject, like the
text, is a discursive product, the result of a multiplicity of discourses, less a
matter of discovery than of continual reinvention and performance.

WORKS

Llamado al puf. Buenos Aires: Pleamar, 1972.
Monte de Venus. Buenos Aires: Corregidor, 1976.
"Omnipresencia de la censura en la escritura argentina" *Revista iberoamericana* 51,
      131–133 (1985): 909–920.
La rompiente. Buenos Aires: Puntosur, 1987.

CRITICISM

Foster, David William. *Alternative Voices in the Contemporary Latin American Narra-
      tive*, 76–81. Columbia: University of Missouri Press, 1985.
———. "The Demythification of Buenos Aires in Selected Argentine Novels of the
      Seventies." *Chasqui* 10.1 (1980): 3–25.

González, Ester Gimbernat. "*La rompiente* o la integración de la escritura." In her *Aventuras del desacuerdo: Novelistas argentinas de los '80*, 186–190. Buenos Aires: Danilo Albero Vergara, 1992.

Gramuglio, María Teresa. Aproximaciones a *La rompiente*." In Roffé, *La rompiente*, 127–135.

Masiello, Francine. "Contemporary Argentine Fiction: Liberal (Pre-)texts in the Reign of Terror." *Latin American Research Review* 16.2 (1981): 218–224.

Szurmuk, Mónica. "La textualización de la represión en *La rompiente* de Reina Roffé." *Nuevo texto crítico* 3.5 (1990): 123–129.

Melissa A. Lockhart

ROFFIEL, ROSAMARÍA (Mexico; 1945) ⸻

Born in the port city of Veracruz, Roffiel has worked primarily as a journalist for the newspaper *Excélsior* and as a regular contributor to the journals *Proceso* (Process) and *fem*. In addition, she has edited women's writing published by small presses. As an outgrowth of her newspaper reportage, she is coauthor of a book on the role of religion in Iran's fundamentalist revolution and author of an eyewitness testimonial account of Nicaragua under the Sandinistas. Roffiel has two volumes of poetry to her credit as well.

Her first novel, *Amora*, has been identified as "the first lesbian novel published in Mexico" (Foster, 115), a status conferring particular importance on this text. Provocatively mixing autobiographical anecdotes, references to the organization of a rape crisis center (GRAPAV) and pamphlets in defense of women's rights, an essay on menopause written at the request of a representative of *fem*'s cooperative, dialogues among women of different origins and backgrounds and the story of a developing attraction between two women, Roffiel has created a hybrid narrative that begins as one-sided, unrequited anguish and ends in triumphant consummation, based on the central issue of lesbian identity politics. The tale of Guadalupe/Amora and Claudia is set in contemporary Mexico City, an urban environment characterized by critical issues like domestic violence, the difficulty of finding suitable and affordable housing, daily rape statistics and a frightening scarcity of employment, all of which lead to women forming alliances and support networks. So it is that the "discovery" of feminism and her entry in 1979 into the Movimiento de la Liberación de la Mujer (Woman's Liberation Movement), along with her daring to leave home and move out on her own, begin Guadalupe's experiences with sexual politics and lead her to form a new kind of "family" with two other women.

Amora insists on collectivity: there are women in pairs, groups, organizations, neighborhoods and communities; there is an omnipresent use as well of *nosotras* (we women), especially by Guadalupe, who counts herself among the pioneers of Mexican feminism. In each of these venues, women discuss their relationships with (and without) men, macho visions of the world, society's identification of feminists with lesbians, the spoiled life of wealthy women who exploit other women to do their domestic work, the nearly impossible task of reconciling feminist theory and practice, women as victims of the male-dominated judicial system, whether to reject men altogether, as potential rapists, or consider some of them possible allies and the constant need to invent their own identities as lesbians in a culture that still denies equal rights to many of its members. Moreover, the stereotyping of lesbian sexuality as just a copycat version of cinematic macho conduct, and the medical community's consideration of homosexuality as a "chemical imbalance" or sickness, come under scrutiny in collective readings of the contents of the morning newspaper as points of departure for the day. In a broad sense, *Amora* is a vindication of the rights and practices of lesbians and a challenge to this community to forge ahead with its resistance to everyday harassments and violence perpetrated by a "democratic" society.

With its glossary of colloquial terminology scattered throughout, *Amora* functions as an excellent linguistic primer for the uninitiated reader as well as a public affirmation of collective identity and presence through shared language. Naming specific practices and preferences excised from "proper" speech (and literature) except as vulgar jokes or insults, *Amora* confers a radical presence on the various experiences of gay women in Mexico. Turning traditional heterosexual perspective on its head, Guadalupe speaks of "others" who may attempt to naturalize and normalize gender identity across the board, but who do not and cannot represent the desires or feelings of all women. Specifically, *bugas* (straights)—women who, at least on the surface, proclaim their interest in sexual relations with men only—are displaced from the center to be relativized in the context of *closeteras* (closet homosexuals), *bicicletas* (bisexuals), *masocas* (masochists) and other participants in a true atmosphere of sexual democracy.

Claudia, the U.S.-educated daughter of a petit bourgeois Mexican family, embodies the crisis of self-denial in the subject who lives a schizophrenic life, masquerading as a loyal wife and mother and as a committed feminist who desires, but at the same time fears, sexual relations with Guadalupe. The narrator coaxes, then challenges, her to embrace the risk of complete commitment to her true feelings, not a half-lived existence on two margins, and she recognizes the crucial need to forge a language capable of representing this relationship. For example, the word *amora* is coined, a feminine form of the masculine term of endearment, *amor*, which becomes a foreign, or at least peripheral, referent in this context. The search for self-expression parallels the process of constructing the text out of hybrid elements: fiction and essay, high and low culture, monologic and dialogic narration. In other words, sexual politics (identity politics) and textual politics (experimentation with genres and other conventions) are interwoven issues leading to the reconsideration of cultural survivals (codes, norms, conduct, customs, tradition) and the potential for alternative discourses on both fronts, the individual and the collective.

Although scant in quantity, critical response to Roffiel's novel has focused primarily on the texture of the narrative, in particular the juxtaposition of a plurality of feminist discourses, and on its ground-breaking treatment of lesbians' lives. Foster refers to *Amora* as a "testimonial of voices" (117) that speak to and about the daily lives of women who generally have been heard from rarely, if at all, throughout either history or literary history; Elena Martínez applauds the open-ended structure of the text (it ends with a question) as one of its strongest contributions to the depriveleging of one discourse on sexuality over another. By avoiding the pitfalls of heterosexual erotic literature—with scene after scene of formulaic and repetitive sexual encounters—*Amora* refuses to prescribe patterns of conduct and instead offers options. It does not lack eroticism, but accommodates it within a multiplicity of discourses that appeal to reason as well as to affect.

Two other Mexican reviewers, Pablo Salvador Martínez and Luis Rojas Cárdenas, judge Roffiel's first attempt at a novel a failure, owing to her taking too many "liberties" (Martínez, 13) with structure and style while hinting that they find much of the content unacceptable. Martínez singles out the long monologues and autobiographical references by the author as inappropriately overbearing for the realistic re-creation of these prohibited themes, whose exposition, in his opinion, can be justified only if presented in a more orthodox and objective form. Yet he paradoxically begins the review by stating the need to separate this negative criticism from his admitted enjoyment of the book—perhaps an overt case of attraction/repulsion toward the themes presented in the novel. Or perhaps the double-edged commentary reveals an ideological difference, since the politics of identity and the more traditional politics of the Left (espoused in *La jornada semanal*, where the review appears) frequently do not find a common ground on which to work for change. Rojas Cárdenas, on the other hand, expresses his disappointment over the novel's conventionality, its portrayal of passive women like Lupe who wait for their object of desire to come running into their open arms at the (happy) end of the love story, the fragmented tales used as fillers for the main event, and what he calls a tendency to categorize things as black or white (relationships with men/relationships with women). This judgment seems to overlook Guadalupe/Amora as the bridge between such polarities.

Either way, Roffiel's debut as a novelist promises to fuel additional debate over the form and content of her writings; they merit much more detailed analysis in light of what may (or may not) follow with regard to the representation of gay women in Latin America.

WORKS

Amora. Mexico City: Editorial Planeta Mexicana, 1989.

CRITICISM

Foster, David William. *Gay and Lesbian Themes in Latin American Writing.* Austin: University of Texas Press, 1991: 114–118.

Martínez, Elena. Review of *Dos mujeres* (Sara Levi Calderón) and *Amora* (Rosamaría Roffiel). *Letras femeninas* 18.1–2 (Spring–Autumn 1992): 175–179.

Martínez, Pablo Salvador. "Atracción fatal." *La jornada semanal* 19 (Oct. 1989): 13.

Rojas Cárdenas, Luis. "Militancia feminista." *Sábado*, supp. to *Unomásuno*, Oct. 28, 1989, p. 13.

                                                    Claudia Schaefer-Rodríguez

ROSA, JOÃO GUIMARÃES (Brazil; 1908–1967)

The work of Rosa (usually identified as Guimarães Rosa) has a place in this volume for two main reasons. First, we may consider his writing as going against the mainstream of patriarchal writing, in the sense that it decenters and problematizes meaning. To allude to the title of a famous Rosa story, all of his rivers have "three banks." By exploring the potentialities of the linguistic system, by incorporating words from other languages into Portuguese, by revitalizing terms and expressions that have fallen into disuse, by using the language of the backlands of his native state of Minas Gerais, by creating neologisms, forging syntax and experimenting with new resonances of alliteration, Rosa elaborates his own unmistakable diction. He turns Portuguese inside out, confers on it a new expressive stature, and liberates language, in his own words, "from the mountains of ashes under which it lies."

But the care taken with language reaches beyond the aesthetic and the ludic in that, for Rosa, language possesses a metaphysical dimension. Words have their own "third bank." Rosa sees language as a weapon in the defense of human dignity. By renovating language, the world is renovated. The sense of life may be recovered via a reconstruction of language whereby the latter has restored to it its naming and creative power, the original act of poiesis by which being is founded through the word. Concomitantly, Rosa rejects Cartesian rationality in favor of a greater role for intuition, revelation, inspiration, enchantment and magic. As a consequence, there is a rejection of certain weaknesses of Western thought and its reliance on binary oppositions like reason vs. emotion, good vs. evil and so on. Rosa shows how "everything is and nothing is," how each thing carries within it its own contrary and how the "third bank" may be seen as a privileged space, a utopian territory in which contradictions are abolished. Neither this bank nor that bank and both at the same time, the "third bank" is the place where the subject wanders, where he explores the different–same waters of the river of life, free from the confines of temporality.

Nevertheless, one might say, following Consuelo Albergaria's suggestion (although she does not explore her findings in this direction), that in Rosa's fiction the fictional author is in control of the meanings that circulate therein. Rosa disguises himself in his characters and is always "present" in what he writes. By the same token, we cannot deny that his fiction still belongs to a patriarchal tradition very much rooted in Brazilian society. For instance, in *Grande sertão Veredas* (*The Devil to Pay in the Backlands*; 1956) women are always at home, waiting for the *jagunços* (bandits from the backlands), knights whose place is on horseback or in the backlands, fighting. Robert Krueger reveals some of the sociological aspects implied in Rosa's works, and refers to a correspondence between Rosa and a friend that introduces us to a less-known aspect of his personality, that of the capitalist entrepreneur.

In *Grande sertão* there is a homosexual attraction between Riobaldo and Diadorim throughout the novel. It is easy to imagine the transgressive quality of such love, since we are among *jagunços*, for whom heterosexual manhood is an unquestionable matter of honor. But, in the end, Diadorim, murdered in a duel, reveals his true female identity. As happens in another novel, Lúcio Cardoso's *Crônica da casa assassinada* (Chronicle of the Murdered House; 1959)—and in a different way in other literatures (one thinks here of Jean Genet)—*Grande sertão* steps back from the issue of homosexual attraction, paying tribute to the conservative nature of Brazilian society. We are left with an ambiguity that has not yet been resolved by the critics, despite the enormous number of pages written on Rosa: Is his work a tributary of the mainstream of Brazilian literary tradition, the swan song of traditional Brazil retold in a poetic saga? Or is his literature a unique example that breaks down a conservative pattern in Brazilian literature, standing as a masterpiece of the twentieth century? Since we do not have many sociological inquiries about his work, the question regarding whether Rosa represents a true rupture remains unsolved.

WORKS

Grande sertão: Veredas. Rio de Janeiro: José Olympio, 1956. English version as *The Devil to Pay in the Backlands*. Trans. James L. Taylor and Harriet de Onís. New York: Knopf, 1963.

Primeiras estórias. Rio de Janeiro: Livraria José Olympio, 1962. English version as *The Third Bank of the River, and Other Stories*. Trans. Barbara Shelby. New York: Knopf, 1968.

Sagarana. Rio de Janeiro: Editora Universal, 1946. English version as *Sagarana*. Trans. Harriet de Onís. New York: Knopf, 1966.

CRITICISM

Albergaria, Conseulo. "O autor como instância de poder." In *Toward Socio-Criticism: Luso-Brazilian Literature*. Roberto Reis, ed. Tempe: Center for Latin American Studies, Arizona State University, 1991, pp. 175–182.

Candido, Antonio. "Jagunços mineiros de Cláudio a Guimarães Rosa." In his *Vários escritos*, 133–160. São Paulo: Duas Cidades, 1970.

Galvão, Walnice Nogueira. *As formas do falso: um estudo sobre a ambigüidade no Grande sertão: Veredas*. São Paulo: Perspectiva, 1972.

Garbuglio, José Carlos. *O mundo movente de Guimarães Rosa*. São Paulo: Atica, 1972.

Also as *El mundo mágico de Guimarães Rosa.* Buenos Aires: García Cambeiro, 1973.

Krueger, Robert. "Ideology and Esthetics in *Grande sertão, veredads*, by João Guimarães Rosa." Ph.D. dissertation, University of Minnesota, 1978.

Nunes, Benedito. "O amor na obra de Guimarães Rosa." In his *O dorso do tigre*, 143–170. São Paulo: Perspectiva, 1969.

Roberto Reis

ROSERO DIAGO, EVELIO (Colombia; 1958)

Evelio Rosero Diago, born in Bogotá and now living in Barcelona, has worked as a journalist and has received several literary prizes. Although all of his narratives contain sexual overtones and childlike narrators, none does so in such an explicit way as *Juliana los mira* (Juliana Watches Them; 1987). The narrator is a nine-year-old girl from an upper-middle-class Bogotá family, her father is a member of the president's cabinet, and her mother is a bored and alcoholic society matron. Juliana has a fascination for her friend Camila. Camila constantly attempts to undress Juliana, hold her close, and initiate her into the joys of sexual activities; Juliana is more than willing to participate in Camila's games.

The title of the novel comes from Juliana's main activity throughout the novel; she watches. She observes everything that the adults do. She studies everything that Camila tells her, and all of these activities are relayed to the reader through her nine-year-old eyes and language structure. Juliana sees her mother and the chauffeur having sex each afternoon, and she sees Camila's mother gamble her possessions in endless card games. She also sees the president of the country snort cocaine and lust after her, Camila and the girls' mothers. She sees two female performers from a children's television show kiss each other lasciviously during a cocaine and marijuana high while at a party in her house. Because she relays to the reader all that she sees and feels, she is initially a passive player in the sexual activities with Camila. The games that the two girls play imitate the adult world and highlight its depravity. Juliana allows Camila to touch her and arouse her without fully understanding the repercussions of the activities. Once Camila penetrates Juliana with a doll and causes her to bleed, Juliana takes control of Camila and all the adults around her. She even goes so far as to try to replace her mother as the object of her father's physical affection.

The lesbian relationship that Rosero Diago sets up between the two girls in this novel is used only to highlight a totally depraved society. The girls imitate society, but they do so in Camila's locked room, thereby indicating that the games that they act out are representative of the side of society that must not be seen. Although Juliana seems to feel affection toward Camila initially, that affection is lost when it is seemingly not reciprocated by Camila and after Juliana is raped with the doll. Juliana then tries to dominate Camila, her father and all who surround her, and she appears to seek only physical pleasure from everyone and everything around her. Once again she apparently imitates the adults that she observes. The lesbian relationship is thus used as a vehicle to clarify the author's disgust toward the events in the country. Juliana's transformation from innocent to seductress, from passive player to active one, is seen as exemplifying the degradation and corruption inherent at all levels of Colombian society.

WORKS

Juliana los mira. Barcelona: Editorial Anagrama, 1987.

Steven M. DuPouy

S

SAENZ, JAIME (Bolivia; 1921–1986)

Saenz, one of the most important Bolivian writers, was born, lived, and died in La Paz, a city that became his vital space and the most permanent background of his work. His life and his literary work provided Bolivian culture with a distinctive pattern during the second part of the century, projecting a powerful image of himself as an enfant terrible. For many years, and before writing his major works, Saenz lived as an alcoholic, wandering the marginal zones of La Paz in the company of Indians, beggars, sorcerers and other characters excluded from La Paz society in the 1950s. These experiences are at the heart of his writing. However, Saenz went beyond biographical data to create a universe of his own that is unique in Bolivian and Latin American literature.

Saenz's works can be seen as the attempt to construct a totality, something he called *la obra* (the work), both in the sense of a mystic and esoteric work and in the sense of a lasting and self-sufficient aesthetic object. Thus, his writings can be seen in terms of a unity in which recurrent subjects like death, alcohol, writing, music and the search for transcendence cannot be separated. One implies the others, and many times they all become one in the representation of a poetic subjectivity. To these subjects, emphasized by critics and commentators of his work, we now can add that of a gay sensibility and/or identity after the posthumous publication of his last novel, *Los papeles de Narciso Lima Achá* (Narciso Lima Achá's Papers; 1991). This last characteristic is not, however, just one further aspect of his work; it is the centerpiece and the clarifying element of his poetic world.

Saenz started his career by writing poetry. From his early book *El escalpelo* (The Scalpel; 1955) to such later books as *Las tinieblas* (The Darkness; 1978) and *La noche* (The Night; 1984), his poetry is mainly the exploration of death

(Mitre) by means of a permanent dialogue with an undefined you. Interpretations of this other have ranged from metaphysical explanation to linguistic analysis. However, all critics seem to agree that many times this other is a double of the poetic I (Antezana; Wiethüchter; Mitre). The relationship with a double acquires a more defined representation in Saenz's novel *Felipe Delgado* (1979). The eponymic protagonist, an alcoholic in search of his identity and the meaning of life and death, is recurrently assaulted by the presence of a diabolic being. This double many times acquires the appearance of the protagonist himself in different stages of his life (a younger or an older Felipe). The climax of these appearances occurs during a night of drunkenness and hallucinations. Felipe confuses his female lover (Ramona) with a male lover of the same name (Ramón) who, in the end, reveals himself to be another representation of his disturbing double.

The first sign of a conflictive definition of gender roles and sexual identity in Saenz's writings points toward how homosexuality will be defined in his last novel. However, it is still difficult to see in Felipe Delgado how important homosexuality is in understanding Saenz's poetics. Similarly, in all his other books there are few or no references to homosexuality. There is, however, an interesting passage in *La piedra imán* (The Magnet; 1989), to some extent an autobiographical narration, in which Saenz tells of an experiment with a servant. At an early age Saenz tried to inflate her through her anus, creating a lot of pain for the unfortunate Indian and producing no significant result to satisfy his own curiosity. This incident of his life is fictionalized in *Los papeles de Narciso Lima Achá* with himself as the one who is inflated, indicating some kind of anal fixation that later was an important component in his representation of male homosexuality.

Homosexuality is a major topic only in Saenz's last novel, *Los papeles de Narciso Lima Achá*. The book is divided in two parts with a different narrator/author for each part, following the "found manuscript" technique. The first part consists of the writings of Carlos María Canseco, a friend of Narciso Lima Achá; the latter is the author of the second part. Carlos María tells the story of Lima Achá from the moment he meets him until his death. Some time after Narciso's death, Carlos María receives his manuscript, which is an autobiography. The heart of Narciso's manuscript is the narration of his love and sexual life as a young man. The narrative, constructed in the tradition of the bildungsroman, is a voyage of learning and of passage to adulthood. It starts as a trip from La Paz to Germany, first by train and then by boat, in 1933, at the time of the rise of Nazism. On board ship Narciso meets and falls in love with a German, Elbruz Ulme. They have similar characteristics: they are young (less than twenty years old), intelligent, from similar social backgrounds (the bourgeoisie) and concerned with the same kind of search, the defining of an identity. From this moment until the day of his return from Germany to Bolivia, Narciso tries to understand love, life, death and himself. The events that follow during his travels through Germany, the other male and one female lover, will be part of this search.

Saenz traveled to Germany during the Hitler regime, full of admiration for some aspects of Nazism, mainly its antirationalism. Probably this trip provided him with the episode that is fictionalized in the novel. It is unknown if he ever had a gay affair on this trip or at any other time in his life. What is known is that Saenz married a German woman who had a daughter by him. So German culture, including its dark side (Nazism), had a strong attraction for Saenz, a good reason to use that country as the stage for his intimate book. An origin for this attraction can be seen in his appreciation of German culture, which has been integrated in his works, as the title of one of his poetry books makes explicit: *Bruckner* (1978) is a portrait of the German composer as the paradigm of the true artist. In this aspect Saenz reflects an ideology popular among the Bolivian ruling class: its admiration of German civilization. From the many possible examples that could be used, we need only mention the many times that the Bolivian army has relied on German instructors and officials, as was the case in the Chaco War with Paraguay (1932–1935).

Los papeles de Narciso Lima Achá is a very complex book, not only because Saenz's poetics obscure and sometimes esoteric, but also because it brings together disturbing themes like homosexuality and Nazism while trying to maintain an objective distance from such matters, which clearly are taboo in Bolivia. The need to avoid any implication of homosexuality in the real Saenz forces the author to place himself as a character in the novel, assuring the reader that Saenz is not Narciso Lima Achá and is not gay like his character. Still, this does not erase the impression that this text has a strong dose of personal experience and/or knowledge of male homosexuality. It is clearly difficult for a writer in Bolivia to voice his own sexuality (especially if it is not the prescribed heterosexual behavior). From this perspective Saenz's novel, by bringing these topics to light, is a trailblazing text.

Male homosexuality is the dominant subject in the second part of *Los papeles de Narciso Lima Achá*. Besides the main story of the young Narciso and his first male love, Elbruz Ulme, he has affairs with other young men in Germany. Even his uncle, a traditional patriarchal figure, with whom he is traveling, shows a clear sexual attraction toward young men. Furthermore, for Narciso himself homosexuality is not a circumstantial experience, but something inherent in his personality. He recalls one of his first sexual experiences in his childhood: a male friend offered to be his girlfriend, and they had a mutual masturbation encounter. But the importance of homosexuality for Narciso's life transcends the biographical and points toward an ontological view of the universe. Narciso lives his sexual orientation as a path to knowledge and metaphysical transcendence. Saenz introduces a serious exchange of ideas and feelings between Narciso, Elbruz and other characters in order to understand the (transcendental, universal) meaning of male homosexuality. Here is where Saenz's gay sensibility can be linked to his writing. Both his sexuality and his aesthetic experiences seem to carry him through the same kinds of topics: darkness, death, platonic love and alcohol. In the novel, as in many other works by Saenz, characters drink alcohol all the time.

This can best be exemplified by the most important love story in the novel, the one between Narciso and Elbruz. From the moment they meet, there is a strong mutual attraction, and at the same time a need for confrontation and differentiation. A gypsy who reads their hands says, "They are brothers who are not brothers" (324). Narciso seems to be more in the position of the learner, while Elbruz appears to possess well-structured thoughts about his life; he is the voice of the master. Narciso, on the other hand, will have a dominant sexual role; he is the active male partner in all his relationships. Saenz appears to want to compensate with the power of the sexual role for the power of Elbruz's knowledge. However, they accept from the beginning that both are one in two persons, a certainty that will nourish their relationship. This feeling of unity will motivate a continuous discussion about the meaning of male love, life and knowledge. A certitude grows out of this discussion that male love leads to the devil's path, the path of darkness, but also to the path of knowledge. It is important to emphasize that for Saenz, *tinieblas* has a very positive meaning: it is the realm of knowledge, art and reality, where the final understanding of life can be acquired. For Elbruz and Narciso, homosexuality and metaphysics are united, and one leads to the other.

It is important to remember that homosexuality is always defined as universal love, true love, beyond gender and, many times, beyond flesh, space and time. Following this argument, Narciso realizes that in universal love, women can also be loved and desired. At one point he finds that in the image of Elbruz he also sees a woman, and his desire for the woman in his friend becomes almost unbearable. Later in the novel Narciso falls in love with a woman, Mariana Wolf. This love gives him a time of peace and reconciliation with his life, which has lost meaning after Elbruz's suicide. Mariana is his final love in Germany before he returns to Bolivia. Narciso learns during this time to admire Hitler's project, because he discovers another bedeviled person in the figure of the Führer. For Narciso, Hitler represents absolute solitude, both a bad joke and a superior destiny for humanity, a destiny related to universal laws and goals. However, Saenz makes clear that Narciso's admiration of Hitler is based on emotional grounds and that he does not share the political doctrines of National Socialism (again seeking a self-protective distance from a taboo subject in Bolivia).

The trip to and the stay in Germany are the center of the story narrated by Narciso in his papers. The story is an exploration of love from a Platonic point of view. Love is universal and therefore transcends genders. However, in opposition to an orthodox Platonism, true love is not an idea but an experience. For Saenz, life and love are experiences from which he will disclose the real meaning of his being in this world. Homosexuality is privileged as the first real experience, the one that opens a new way of understanding reality. Narciso's life will always be marked by this experience, and his sensibility is of this kind. Consequently, Saenz puts male homosexual love as the first experience of knowledge, a foundation for the development of subsequent poetic subjects.

This is true of most of the works by Saenz. All the complexity and richness of his novels and poems seem to share this sensibility: homosexual love. From this perspective, *Los papeles de Narciso Lima Achá* is one of the most illuminating texts of his poetics and perhaps the key to understanding his universe.

WORKS

Al pasar un cometa. Poemas (1970–72). La Paz: Ediciones Altiplano, 1982.
Aniversario de una visión. La Paz: n.p., 1960.
"El aparapita de La Paz." *Mundo nuevo* 26–27 (1968): 4–8.
Bruckner. Las tinieblas. La Paz: Editorial Difusión, 1978.
Los cuartos. La Paz: Ediciones Altiplano, 1985.
El escalpelo. La Paz: El Progreso, 1955.
Felipe Delgado. La Paz: Editorial Difusión, 1979.
El frío. Muerte por el tacto. Aniversario de una visión. La Paz: Imprenta Burillo, 1967.
Imágenes paceñas. Lugares y personas de la ciudad. La Paz: Editorial Difusión, 1979.
La noche. La Paz: Talleres de Don Bosco, 1984.
Obra poética. La Paz: Biblioteca del Sesquicentenario, 1975.
Los papeles de Narciso Lima Achá. La Paz: Instituto Boliviano de Cultura, 1991.
La piedra imán. La Paz: Editorial Huayna Potosí, 1989.
Recorrer esta distancia. La Paz: Imprenta Burillo, 1973.
Vidas y muertas. La Paz: Editorial Huayna Potosí, 1986.
Visitante profundo. La Paz: Imprenta Burillo, 1964.

CRITICISM

Antezana, J., Luis H. "*Felipe Delgado* de Jaime Saenz." In his *Ensayos y lecturas*, 333–354. La Paz: Ediciones Altiplano, 1986.
————. "Hacer y. cuidar." In *El paseo de los sentidos. Estudios de literatura boliviana contemporánea*, 107–128. Ed. Leonardo García Pabón and Wilma Torrico. La Paz: Instituto Boliviano de Cultura, 1983.
García Pabón, Leonardo. "Las memorias y el lenguaje de *Felipe Delgado*." In *El paseo de los sentidos*, 259–267.
Mitre, Eduardo. *El árbol y la piedra. Poetas contemporáneos de Bolivia*, 34–43. Caracas: Monte Avila, 1986.
Ortega, José. "Fantasmagoría boliviana: *Felipe Delgado* de Jaime Saenz." In *El paseo de los sentidos*, 269–276.
Rivera Rodas, Oscar. "La poesía de Jaime Saenz." *Inti* 18–19 (1983–1984): 59–82.
Taller Hipótesis. "Dos novelistas contemporáneos: Jesús Urzagasti y Jaime Saenz." *Revista iberoamericana* 134 (1986): 279–284.
————. "Escribir antes y después de la muerte (sobre la obra poética de Jaime Saenz)." *Revista iberoamericana* 134 (1986): 285–289.

Wiethüchter, Blanca. "Las estructuras de lo imaginario en la obra poética de Jaime
    Saenz." In *Obra poética*, 267–425.
————. *Memoria solicitada*. La Paz: Ediciones Altiplano, 1989.
————. "Poesía boliviana contemporánea: Oscar Cerruto, Jaime Saenz, Pedro Shimose,
    Jesús Urzagasti." In *Tendencias actuales de la literatura boliviana*, 75–114. Ed.
    Javier Sanjinés. Minneapolis: Institute for the Study of Ideologies and Literature,
    1985.

                                                                    Leonardo García-Pabón

SALAS, FLOYD (United States; 1931) ————————

The son of Edward Salas and Anita Sánchez, born in Walsenburg, Colorado,
Salas attended California College of Arts and Crafts, Oakland Junior College,
the University of California at Berkeley, and San Francisco State University.
He has been a lecturer at San Francisco State University and an instructor in
creative writing at the University of California, Berkeley, where he has also
been an assistant boxing coach. His literary work has brought him several grants
and honors: a 1958 Rockefeller Foundation scholarship to the Centro Mexicano
de Escritores (Mexican Writers' Center) and fellowships from the National Endowment for the Arts in 1978 and the Bay Writing Project in 1984 (Ryan).

If, as suggested by literary critics, formal Chicano literature took shape no
earlier than 1966 (Cuéllar), then Salas's novel *Tattoo the Wicked Cross* (1967)
stands as precursor of this movement. In fact, Juan Bruce-Novoa considers this
work third in chronological importance in the development of Chicanismo—a
Chicano cultural identity (*Chicano Authors*, 4). Still, Salas's literary production
has failed to attract major analysis, although he has received overwhelmingly
positive press reviews of his novels. Bruce-Novoa has questioned Salas's absence from a canonical list of Chicano writers, pointing to the possibility that
the early Chicano movement's insistence on issues exclusive to ethnic identity
might have predisposed contemporary Chicano criticism to ignore the significance of Salas's writing (1990, 133).

Indeed, Salas's works are not particularly oriented to the traditional Latino
motifs (e.g., the Catholic-oriented values of the traditional Hispanic family) or
to the political struggle for the civil rights of the economically strained Chicano
population. Salas's novels develop multiple male characters, many of them Chicanos, whose major existential confrontation is not their ethnic marginality but
their struggle for sexual individuation. This is the case in *Tattoo the Wicked
Cross*, which re-creates a documented case of homosexual rape of an adolescent
in a reform school. As he explained to this critic, Salas based the story on
incidents personally witnessed while he was in juvenile halls and jails, a total
of nine months, when he was "threatened by homosexuals and had to beat them
up to make them leave me alone" (all quotations are from a written questionnaire answered by Salas in November 1992). Although he insists that his literary

treatment of homosexuality is not consciously that of a Latino writer and, therefore, that this issue is not part of a political or sexual agenda, "it does, upon
reflection, reflect Latino values of fear and dislike of homosexuality."

As he points out, Salas's homosexual characters "are part of the world I write
about"—a juvenile penal institution (*Tattoo the Wicked Cross*), the arena of
amateur boxing (*Lay My Body on the Line*; 1978), and his own family background in an extensive autobiographical memoir (*Buffalo Nickel*; 1992). In the
best tradition of the bildungsroman, *Tattoo the Wicked Cross*'s protagonist, fif-
teen-year-old Aaron D'Aragon, faces the brutal atmosphere of the Golden Institute of Industry and Reform, where he is an inmate because of his involvement
with violent street gangs. In spite of his efforts to resist sexual advances, eventually he is violently gang-raped. His revenge comes unnoticed to his attackers,
as he poisons all of the perpetrators with rat poison, an incident that leads to
one death. The restrictive space of penal institutions, like society at large, contributes to the development of a violent homosexual culture, which runs parallel
to the construction of another marginalized group—the Chicano underground
group of the Pachucos.

Violence and death stand as clear leitmotifs in Salas's work. His straight
young protagonists (e.g., Roger in *Lay My Body on the Line* and the self-
portrayed Floyd in *Buffalo Nickel*) suffer similar paramount experiences: the
death of the mother at an early age and the suicide of a fatherlike figure, the
older brother. Salas's own confrontation with his older brother's suicide at age
thirty on account of his bisexuality has determined, in large part, his literary
handling of homosexuality: "So my interest lies not in being Latino but in being
a normal male who has suffered the death of a brother and seeks to understand
it in order to live with the sadness of the death."

These two novels present the bildungsroman's view of a male protagonist
who encounters the destructive societal behavioral codes toward homosexuality
in a concrete space: his own home. Although a character of minor importance
in the plot development, Eddy in *Lay My Body* discloses his bisexuality to his
younger brother in an explanation of the aloofness and coldness in his relationship with his father. In fact, Eddy's sexual orientation is equated with a tragic
flaw, for which he is punished in spite of his success as a business entrepreneur
and political activist: "But you see, men will feel your manliness and they'll
give you more respect, they'll open a bigger world for you" (15). Subsequently,
Eddy commits suicide, a decision that his brother, an emerging young artist,
recognizes as climactic in the fixation of his own self.

Salas's interest in developing strong-willed male characters (not necessarily
homosexuals) is evident in his projected book on an ex-con rapist, with references to sporadic homosexual experiences in prison. Although not a homosexual, the protagonist "commits homosexual acts in prison and beats the
homosexual up in fear and hatred of him." In an interesting turn of events, "he
doesn't hurt the women he rapes, though he does force them to submit and
makes them fear for their lives." Salas's male characters (Latinos or not) show

distinctive patterns of marginality (sexual or ethnic), and their individual confrontation with their community leads to a deconstruction of societal sexual values.

WORKS

Bronka Stooler Boo Boo Boo. Ed. Floyd Salas. Berkeley, Calif.: Mother's Hen, 1986.

Buffalo Nickel. A Memoir. Houston: Arte Público Press, 1992.

Lay My Body on the Line. Berkeley, Calif.: Y'Bird, 1978.

Tattoo the Wicked Cross. New York: Grove Press, 1967. An excerpt appeared as "Dead Time." In *Chicano Voices*, 126–132. Ed. Carlota Cárdenas de Dwyer. Boston: Houghton Mifflin, 1975.

To Build a Fire: A Commemorative Anthology of 77 Writers in, from & About a Geographical Place Known as Oakland, California. Ed. Floyd Salas. Oakland: M. Ross, 1976.

What Now My Love. New York: Grove Press, 1969. Reprinted: Houston: Arte Público Press, 1994.

"The Politics of Poetry" (poem; 117–120), "Dead Lion or Live Dog. The Artist in American Society. Some Reflections on the Suicide of Richard Brautigan" (essay; 225–235), "Steve Nash Homosexual Transient Executed San Quentin Gas Chamber August 21st 1959 for Killing Eleven Men and a Little Boy" (poem; 297–302), "Kid Victory" (short story; 491–509). In *Stories and Poems from Close to Home.* Ed. Floyd Salas. Berkeley: Calif.: Ortalda & Associates, 1986.

CRITICISM

Bruce-Novoa, Juan. *Chicano Authors: Inquiry by Interview.* Austin: University of Texas Press, 1980.

———. *RetroSpace: Collected Essays on Chicano Literature Theory and History.* Houston: Arte Público Press, 1990.

Cuéllar, Alfredo. "The Chicano Movement." In *From the Barrio: a Chicano Anthology*, 3–10. Ed. Luis Omar Salinas and Lillian Faderman. San Francisco: Canfield, 1973.

Ryan, Bryan, ed. "Salas, Floyd (Francis)." In *Hispanic Writers: A Selection of Sketches from Contemporary Authors*, 422–423. Detroit: Gale Research, 1991.

Rafael Ocasio

SANABRIA SANTALIZ, EDGARDO
(Puerto Rico, 1951) _____

Edgardo Sanabria Santaliz was born in San Germán, Puerto Rico. Shortly after his birth, his family moved to metropolitan San Juan and later to the suburbs, a decision that deeply shaped Sanabria's literature. In 1978 he published a story in an anthology produced by the writer Emilio Díaz Valcárcel's workshop, *17 de taller* (17 from a Workshop), and his first book of short stories, *Delfia cada tarde* (Delfia Every Afternoon), appeared. Sanabria is one of the least studied prose writers of his literary generation (sometimes called Generation of '70 or Generation of '75), although he has published three volumes of stories and several essays in important collections like *El tramo ancla* (Anchor Drag; 1989), edited by Ana Lydia Vega, and *Imágenes e identidades* (Images and Identities; 1985), edited by Asela Rodríguez de Laguna.

Sanabria's writing often consists of long and baroque sentences, cinematic cuts and ellipses, an uncanny poetic quality, and a set of recurrent themes and structures pointing to contradictory desires framed by a Catholic ideological matrix. Although his discourse on the purpose of literature in his essay "Sangre y palabras" (Blood and Words; 1989) points to rigid moral dichotomies in which the writer has the obligation to edify readers by showing them a mirror of human perversity, ambiguity often complicates the goal of edification and instead produces a tense weaving of contradictory desires. Thus, while the language of gay desire is often sensual and arousing, same-sex pleasure is consistently represented as perverse, unconsented and forced. In addition, while most of Sanabria's texts tend to be incantations mourning the loss of community and the family, the idealized construction of the people also serves as a resistance to the fear of uncharted territory, including gay male desire and death present in stories of male–male relationships.

There are several texts in which gay desire or mediation produces illness, instability and/or death. These include the title story, "Delfia cada tarde," in which a gay man symbolizes the deadly absence of normalized heterosexuality; "1898" (1984), a story of a young man who seeks to remove a tattoo that was forced upon him by his mother's boyfriend, symbolically linking male-to-male eroticism to child rape; and "Borinquen Restaurant" (1988), one of the few stories in contemporary Puerto Rican literature where a butch woman (potentially a lesbian) is represented in ambiguous terms associated with both justice and death. In the following pages, I will concentrate on two stories, "Antes del último día" (Before the Last Day; 1978) and "La tercera noche" (The Third Night; 1984), since they point to the central modes of representation of male homosexual desires in Sanabria's work to date.

In "Antes del último día," an unnamed high-school-age male character who volunteers time to an institution for the elderly is forced to confront the lust of an older man, the priest Castillo. Superficially, this story has been read as the tale of a perverted priest who preys on young and innocent men. However, the language of the text suggests a richness of associations, ambiguities and sexual slippages that map the subtleties of power and desire in homosexual encounters as contradictory pleasurable experiences for young male protagonists still struggling with strong oedipal family context (in the most traditional and psychoanalytical sense).

Once the young man enters the institution, he is met by Sor Prudencia (Prudence), who seems to him to be "two different people" because there is a white part and a black part to her nun's habit. This metaphor is a productive one for this story, since the narrator's account of his experience textualizes contradictory desires. After he has shaved four old men, Sor Prudencia calls the young man and leads him to see Father Castillo. This summoning legitimizes the character's intense sensation of having been watched by someone while he shaved the old men. At the same time, the feeling of being the object of Castillo's gaze produces a certain satisfaction in the telling of the experience of being watched. Thus, for example, the narrator sees the priest reflected in the soapy water as he walks away after listening to huffing and puffing sounds, a metaphoric allusion to masturbation and ejaculation. In describing the feeling of the priest's gaze, he alludes to the gaze "as a hoarse bird freed from his cage," a description that could represent both men's sexual tension.

Going up the stairs, a classic symbol for sexual intercourse in Freudian terms, the young man holds on to Sor Prudencia's hanging crucifix to continue on the "right path." The meaning of the pendant is ambiguous, since it can simultaneously be read as a need for protection and a guidance from darkness, and the caressing of the penis. The religious symbolic ambiguity of this passage is also present in the fact that both characters are going up (closer to God), but when the priest opens the door, he blocks the light. The narrator is terrified by the man's face and feels Castillo's gaze "piercing" his face. Despite the initial repulsion due to the priest's physical appearance (he is asthmatic, smalls bad, and his hands stink of cigars), he admits to being seduced by the authority of the priest, whom he allows to take his hands (as he has taken cigars before, another phallic symbol). His fear of being taken and possibly violated increases when he seeks Sor Prudencia's support in fleeing the priest and finds instead a toothless mouth receding to close the door behind her and scaring the seagulls outside. The toothless mouth suggests both castration anxiety and the impotence of the nun to stop Castillo's desires, which scare the seagulls (social taboos) outside of the room. The woman's retreat also points to a potential complicity between nun and priest that underlines the critique of religious authority as corrupt and hypocritical.

The priest, fearful of his own desire, decides to read for an hour before speaking to the young man again. When he addresses the young man, the latter feels persecuted because the priest is attempting to obtain information about himself and his family. As in other stories where gay male desire is represented, the priest and the narrator are reproducing the confessional experience, something that simultaneously shames and seduces the young man. The questioning tongue and the gaze of the priest, which have transformed water into sperm in the young man's imagination, now produce palpitations that "struggle to deform my body." Sweat "licks" his hands, toes "play" with the leather of his shoes and "displace himself within." The knowledge of his arousal makes the narrator want to avoid the seductive "sweet and authoritarian" gaze that is making him blush. Ultimately, it is the knowledge/power of the priest that arouses the man and makes him identify with priests as a potential escape from the gaze of the mother. Despite the rejection of the mother, the priest ultimately is simultaneously female and male, suggesting the difficulties of fleeing certain desiring structures produced within nuclear middle-class heterosexual families in Sanabria's texts.

In this passage, the tensions between a woman's socially castrating gaze (the mother) and a man's penetrating gaze are symbolically released when the priest asks the man to shave him, a task that, after some hesitation, he accepts. However, as he notes the priest's habit as a "giant black flower" and sees a "hand looking like a pistil" come out from under the priest's garments and grab his own, he cuts the priest's face. The description of the priest's habit and the hand emerging from under his clothing suggests an erection, while the cutting off is more complex. While castration may be the simplest way of reading this, there is a contradiction in that the hand (penis) looks like a pistil, which is the *female* organ of plants, and therefore (in traditional psychoanalytic discourse) is already castrated. Another reading may suggest that the cutting alludes simultaneously to the penetration of the flesh (where the priest is feminized) and a fear of being feminized by allowing gay desire to be acted upon. The young man's response to the contradictory feelings the encounter has produced in him is to flee the scene (the scene of a crime in the most literal sense) and run home, another recurrent symbolic solution to the possible explosion of gay male desire in Sanabria's texts.

"La tercera noche" is the only story by Sanabria to date in which desire is represented in explicit sexual terms, although it is also rejected as a possible source of pleasure. The narrator (Aureo) is a middle-class young man who decides to leave home because of an abusive father. On the third day he goes into a piano bar, where a southern American woman, Sara Lee, is playing the piano. The language of this passage is rich with sexual imagery and suggests a disposition of the narrator to the sexually suggestive.

As in "Antes del último día," the homosexual seduction begins through confession. Sara Lee's assistant, René, a submissive younger man, goes over to Aureo and begins to talk to him and buy him liquor. With some hesitation, Aureo tells René his story and circumstances, feeling both guilt and relief. After René manages to get Aureo drunk, the latter beings to lose his sense of reality and allows René to lead him to Sara Lee's room. In a more radical sense than in "Antes del último día," the only context for gay desire is coercion or loss of consciousness by young men who are led on and seduced by authority or confusion.

Aureo's narration of René's leading him to the room does not suggest that René has in any way sexually seduced or touched Aureo (at the bar or in the room). However, during his recollection of what occurred the night before, Aureo rewrites the story as a dual seduction by René and Sara Lee. The contrast between versions suggests various reading possibilities, reflecting the deep ambiguities Aureo experiences over what occurred. The straightforward version suggests that Aureo could have had sex with both, but was too drunk to know it, and it is only after finding himself in the room with two naked bodies that he realizes what happened. This reading is justified by the allusion to an allegedly unfamiliar pleasure during the narration of the sexual experience without identifying it in any detail. A second reading is that Aureo had sex only with Sara Lee and/or only with René, and imagined either/both experiences in order to match his own desire. If it was only with Sara Lee, this may explain the concrete allusions to her body. In all versions, however, the representation of sexual experience with the woman is distinctly unpleasant, and her body is mostly described with unappealing metaphors; René's body (specifically his penis), however, is represented in arousing terms as a "humid, hot and ascending animal," even the next day when the pleasure of his looks causes strong stomach pains for Aureo.

Thus, once Aureo wakes up and presents the narrative of homosexual desire to himself, the narrator flees the scene (as in "Antes del último día"), as if he had committed a crime. He runs from the room and down the stairs, feeling shame not only at what he supposedly did, but also at the possibility that people will immediately know that he enjoyed having sex with a man. This knowledge, pleasure among men and the fear of pleasure, makes Aureo pick up the phone to call home, where his platonic oedipal sexuality will keep him from engaging in sin. Consistent with other representations in Sanabria's work, homosexual desire is represented as traumatic to the lives of young men (particularly of the middle class), deadly if it intervenes in the lives of heterosexuals and socially dangerous as a source of sexual pleasure.

WORKS

Cierta inevitable muerte. Buenos Aires: Ediciones de la Flor, 1988.
"Con los pies en la tierra." In *El tramo ancla: Ensayos puertorriqueños de hoy*, 211–215. Ed. Ana Lydia Vega. Río Piedras: Universidad de Puerto Rico, 1989.
Delfia cada tarde. San Juan, P.R.: Huracán, 1978.
El día que el hombre pisó la luna. San Juan. P.R.: Editorial Antillana, 1984.
"Las dos casas habitadas." In *Imágenes e identidades: El puertorriqueño en la literatura*, 141–146. Ed. Asela Rodríguez de Laguna. San Juan, P.R.: Huracán, 1985.

CRITICISM

"Cierta inevitable muerte." *El Mundo* (San Juan, P.R.), Jan. 15, 1988, p. 9.
Ríos Avila, Rubén. "Puertorriqueños: Álbum de la sagrada familia literaria." *El Mundo* (San Juan, P.R.), spec. supp., Jan. 14, 1990, pp. 34–36.
Vega, José Luis. "Reseña: Edgardo Sanabria Santaliz." *Revista de estudios hispánicos* 5 (1978): 293–295.
———. *Reunión de espejos*. San Juan: Editorial Cultural, 1983, 27–28, 185–186.

Frances Negrón-Muntaner

SÁNCHEZ, LUIS RAFAEL (Puerto Rico; 1936)

Trained in theater arts at the University of Puerto Rico, Sánchez is considered Puerto Rico's most distinguished dramatist and fiction writer. He holds a master's degree in Spanish literature from New York University and a doctorate from the University of Madrid, and he has held distinguished university appointments in the United States. One of the few Puerto Rican writers to have attained an international readership (his books have been published in the United States, Cuba, Mexico, Argentina and Spain, in part the consequence of self-censorship practiced by writers and publishers in Puerto Rico, a society of generally conservative views), and several of his works have been translated into English.

Sánchez's works have not as a rule dealt with traditionally defined homosexual topics, although one significant exception is a story in *En cuerpo de camisa* (Body Show; 1966). "¡Jum!" is a brief text, essentially a litany of voices connected by transitions provided by the narrator, that describes a boy's suicide because of the accusations against him of effeminacy and sexual deviance. The litany consists of reiterated accusations, based typically on Puerto Rican sexual slang, and the narrator's transitions record Jum's reactions to those accusations, culminating in his suicide by drowning. It is irrelevant to the text whether Jum is in fact gay, since the point of the story is the psychological consequences of a language of attribution: Jum is accused of being gay, and in a sense he accepts this attribution by responding with the act demanded of a seriously flawed— suicide, which is necessitated by a secondary acceptance of the attribution of direness to homosexuality demanded by the society in which Jum exists. The story neither discusses a sexual identity for Jum in counterpoint to societal accusations nor details what it is about Jum that leads to the deafening crescendo of hounding accusations, although given conventional identifications of homosexuality on the basis of metonymic physical features and/or corporal bearing, it is not difficult to speculate on what the correlation might be between the commonplace accusations and Jum's social performance, conscious or not, spontaneous or studied.

Where Sánchez's writing is of particular relevance for queer theory beyond congealed images, identities and plot schemata is in the area of the display of sexual turbulence, shifting sexual models and an eroticism that is transgressive in the ways it transcends and overcomes the attempts to contain it in a conservative, repressive society and in the ways it is fundamentally at odds with circumscribed sexual identities and behaviors. For example, Sánchez's most famous novel, *La guaracha del Macho Camacho* (*Macho Camacho's Beat*; 1976), a best-seller in its original Argentine edition and now carried by a Spanish publisher, is still considered, almost thirty years after it was written, a scandal in Puerto Rico, although it is probably the most read work of contemporary Puerto Rican literature. Built around a *guaracha*, a popular song characterized by a heavy musical beat and by lyrics consisting of repeated phrases that border on the meaningless, Sánchez's novel is a mosaic of the protean flux of contemporary urban life in San Juan. Moving back and forth, in the typical modernist fashion of the Latin American new novel, between various individuals and their social and physical settings, the highly stylized narration juxtaposes the trivialness of the *guaracha*'s lyrics to its isn't-life-great-in-the-sexy-sunwashed-tropics message, with a probing amplification of the premises of the lyrics that deconstructs their silly perspective on island life to reveal the social and cultural conflicts that contradict them and that they, in the nature of much of commercial culture, seek to gloss over and to conceal.

The representation of the breakdown of social hierarchies, which may continue to exercise their oppressive control but no longer have any ideological pertinence; the disordered nature of private and public lives that defies the strict moral code to which a conservative, Catholic Puerto Rican petite bourgeoisie adheres in its attempts to project an image of decency; and the chaotic plasma of an inner realm of sexual desire that, while it may not be specifically homoerotic, escapes the boundaries of the facile heterosexism of the guaracha are all dimensions of *La guaracha del Macho Camacho* that constitute openings toward the broad agenda of queer theory.

In an essay Sánchez published in 1981, "Apuntación mínima de lo soez" (Minimal Notes on the Dirty), he defends a revindication of what Puerto Rican society considers dirty as a form of what today would be called cultural resistance: words, expressions, social styles, themes and beliefs that become repressed in favor of a norm of decency, which mostly means adherence to a U.S.-based, white, middle-class value system in which whatever is historically and typically Puerto Rican is, with an optic of social, linguistic and racial discrimination, considered inferior, if not dirty.

For Sánchez, the process of whitening decency normalizes Puerto Rican society in such a way that true human experience is lost, with the result by implication being the confused personal and social identities portrayed in *La guaracha del Macho Camacho*, where the superficiality of the *guaracha* may be false, but the chaos of so-called real life, despite its undeniably vital undercurrents, is the consequence of the violent conflict resulting from Puerto Rico's precarious existence between Hispanic and Anglo cultures, a circumstance only exacerbated by its geographic position as an island on the fringe of the Caribbean.

The play *Quíntuples* (Quintuplets; 1985) is the counterimage of patriarchal regulation. Consisting of monologues (at the very least, a mark of breakdown of interpersonal dialogue) by the five children of the actor the Great Mandrake, *Quíntuples* is characterized over and over again by signs of erotic and sexual identity that are excesses of heterosexist normalcy, culminating in the frankly homophobic image of Baby, Mandrake's effeminate son, who seems to signal the refusal to reproduce his father's authoritarian masculinity.

Sánchez's most interesting text is his last novel, *La importancia de llamarse Daniel Santos* (The Importance of Being Named Daniel Santos; 1988), which is drenched in homoeroticism. Significantly, like *Quíntuples*, its first Spanish-language edition was in the United States, although it was subsequently published in 1989 by Editorial Diana, one of a few major companies in Mexico willing to publish explicitly erotic writing. Based on the life of the Puerto Rican bolero singer of the 1940s and 1950s whose talent brought him fame throughout Mexico, Central America, the Caribbean and the United States, the text is typical of a form of contemporary hybrid writing in which documentary material is intercalated with fictional extrapolations that allow for a field of biographical and cultural interpretation that is not legitimated by the historical record: the novel is significantly subtitled *fabulación* (fabulation). This allows Sánchez to develop a narrative for Santos that focuses on the impact on others of his charismatic nature, the multiple meanings represented by his macho aura and complicated relations with real and imagined sexuality and, most particularly, Santos and his music as a form of display of sexuality, of performative erotics, that triggers multiple sexual reactions in his audiences, male and female.

While an interpretation confirmed by conventional sexual roles would emphasize Santos's appeal to women as an alluring potential sex partner and to men as a powerful role model of masculine affirmation, the complexities of the eroticism his persona unleashes cannot be so neatly defined nor so easily contained. The key here is the nature of the bolero. In contrast to the Argentine tango and the Mexican *canción ranchera* (ranch song, the equivalent of a country/western song), the two other most famous forms of Latin American music, the bolero's lush sensuality and dreamy sentimentality render the lines of sexual identity and erotic reaction more problematical. The tango is essentially a song and dance of rough sex. It may involve a male lament of abandonment, but there is no mistaking the putatively exciting violence of macho control that lies so close to the surface in its stark, jarring rhythms and its often brutal lyrics, both in their semantics and in their customary mode of articulation. The Mexican *canción ranchera* may be more harmonious, more lyrical in a traditional sense of the love song, but it typically speaks of clearly defined heterosexual roles and plot relations (although a male singer like Juan Gabriel and a female singer like Chavela Vargas have brought both implicit and explicit homoeroticism to this most popular of Mexican song forms).

By contrast, the bolero involves a singing narrative voice that is frequently interchangeable with regard to masculine/feminine behavioral markers, in an underdifferentiated romanticism or sentimentality that transcends harsh daily realities: a masculinist world is alleviated by a feminizing song in which feelings are possible, in which men may cry in emotional pain (as opposed to the male rage of the tango and, to a certain extent, of the *canción ranchera*), and in which the public display of eroticism by the man in ways other than command and control is as desirable as it is feasible. Again, all of this may not be homoerotic, but the sexual charge stimulated by the intense emotionalism of the bolero generates a cultural space in which the stark sexual differentiation of masculine imposition and feminine acquiescence, of what is customarily called the active and the passive, begins to blur under the sway, to cite a commonplace of another Caribbean bolero king, of "cherry pink and apple-blossom white."

WORKS

"Apuntación mínima de lo soez." In *Literature and Popular Culture in the Hispanic World: A Symposium*, 9–14. Ed. Rose S. Minc. Gaithersburg, Md.: Hispamérica; Upper Montclair, N.J.: Montclair State College, 1981.

En cuerpo de camisa. San Juan: Lugar, 1966.

La guaracha del Macho Camacho. Buenos Aires: Ediciones de la Flor, 1976. English version as *Macho Camacho's Beat*. Trans. Gregory Rabassa. New York: Pantheon, 1988.

La importancia de llamarse Daniel Santos. Hanover, N.H.: Ediciones del Norte, 1988.

Quíntuples. Hanover, N.H.: Ediciones del Norte, 1985.

CRITICISM

Alonso, Carlos J. "*La guaracha del Macho Camacho*: The Novel as Dirge." *Modern Language Notes* 100.2 (1985): 348–360.

Aparicio, Frances. "Entre la guaracha y el bolero: Un ciclo de intertextos en la nueva narrativa puertorriqueña." *Revista iberoamericana* 162–163 (1993): 73–89.

Arrigoitia, Luis de. "Una novela escrita en puertorriqueño." *Revista de estudios hispánicos* (Río Piedras) 5 (1978): 71–89.

Arrilaga, María. "Enajenación social y lingüística en *La guaracha del Macho Camacho*." *Hispamérica* 34–35 (1983): 155–164.

Beauchamp, José Juan. "*La guaracha del Macho Camacho*: Lectura política y visión del mundo." *Revista de estudios hispánicos* (Río Piedras) 5 (1978): 91–128.

Cachán, Manuel. "*En cuerpo de camisa* de Luis Rafael Sánchez: La antiliteratura alegórica del otro puertorriqueño." *Revista iberoamericana* 162–163 (1993): 177–186.

Cruz, Arnaldo. "Repetition and the Language of the Mass Media in Luis Rafael Sánchez's *La guaracha del Macho Camacho*." *Latin American Literary Review* 26 (1985): 35–48.

Gelpí, Juan. "La cuentística antipatriarcal de Luis Rafael Sánchez." *Hispamérica* 43 (1986): 113–120.

González, Aníbal. "Luis Rafael Sánchez." In *Spanish American Authors: The Twentieth Century*, 795–798. Ed. Angel Flores. New York: H. W. Wilson, 1992.

López-Baralt, Luce. "*La guaracha del Macho Camacho*: Saga nacional de la 'guarachita' puertorriqueña." *Revista iberoamericana* 130–131 (1985): 103–123.

Roffé, Reina. "Luis Rafael Sánchez." In *Espejo de escritores*, 175–194. Hanover, N.H.: Ediciones del Norte, 1985.

Vázquez Arce, Carmen. "Sexo y mulatería: Dos sones de una misma guaracha." *Sin nombre* 12.4 (1982): 51–63.

Waldman, Gloria F. *Luis Rafael Sánchez: Pasión teatral*. San Juan: Instituto de Cultura Puertorriqueña, 1988.

David William Foster

SANDOVAL-SÁNCHEZ, ALBERTO
(Puerto Rico; 1954) _____

Poet, essayist, literary critic and professor, Sandoval-Sánchez was born in San-turce. After two years at the University of Puerto Rico, he moved in 1973 to Wisconsin, where he completed a B.A. at Carroll College in 1975 and an M.A. at the University of Wisconsin–Madison in 1976. He holds a Ph.D. in Golden Age theater (with a dissertation on Pedro Antonio de Alarcón) from the University of Minnesota (1983). He has been teaching at Mount Holyoke College since 1983.

The poetry of Sandoval-Sánchez is theatrical in the sense that it stages a sort of spectacle that can by lyrical, dramatic, comical, melodramatic, farcical and even tragic. The city of New York (which, more than a place, is a state of mind) is the unifying element in *Nueva York tras bastidores/New York Backstage*, written between 1983 and 1986. It is the stage for characters and scenes represented behind the stage: we are not on Broadway anymore. Rather, the whole city (the world) is a Broadway theater (a stage). New York, and the mockingly ironic voice that makes fun of it, are the stage, the actor and the action; like the eyes that never dare to make direct contact with other eyes in the subway ("Eighth Avenue," "The New York Look") but look every other way, revealingly/distortingly/deconstructively. A list of characters: "a desperate graffiti," "a victim of rape," "She," "a subway rider," "bar patron," "eyes," "father and son," "the poet," "legs/hands/eyes," "aspiring actors," "The Statue of Liberty," "a peep-show dancer," "un-identified voices," "a baglady," "umbrellas," "The old-maid of Manhattan," "the rush-hour," "5 PM," "The Brooklyn Bridge," "Poetry in New York," "a traffic light," "A Chorus of Whores," "the Front Page of the *New York Times*." Everything and everyone auditions for the chorus line of the desperate musical of insomniacs that is life in the City That Never Sleeps; but everything and everyone are the reflection of the seeing/speaking subject (and vice versa).

The mirror reappears in "Tantrum de la muerte" (Death Tantrum; from the book in progress, "Side Effects"). This time the stage, the action and the number of characters are reduced. "Tantrum" seems like a dramatic monologue in which one actor represents several characters who are really one and the same: in this case "he," "I," "you" and Death—different roles/reflections of the speaking subject; a person with AIDS. If living in the city of *New York Backstage* is a constant, dehumanizing performance, a sort of burlesque, living with AIDS/dying of AIDS is also a performance, not exempt from elements of the burlesque. The refraction of voices/speaking subjects/objects/images that composes/decomposes, veils/reveals (the fragments of) The City now propitiates a postmodern version of the "Dance of Death" ("Danza de la muerte") closely related to the plagues that decimated Europe's population during the late Middle

Ages and early Renaissance. To the Hispanic poetic tradition of the subject of death, from the fifteenth-century Jorge Manrique to the late romantic Gustavo Adolfo Bécquer and others, Sandoval-Sánchez adds elements from contemporary (American) culture: the disco of the late 1970s, Hollywood, Washington, the "peep shows," Broadway and AIDS. The result is a carnivalization of death, which becomes a protean entity, a kind of transvestite siren ("sirena travestí") who will play disco diva Donna Summer singing "I Love to Love You, Baby," as well as George Bush playing Uncle Sam seducing young men with "Read my lips: I want you!" But at the center of the stage is the tragic confrontation between the protagonist and Death, with the realization that the "he" looking at his own image in the mirror and the speaking subject "I" are one (and one is the other, and the other is all); and that what the "he" is looking at in the mirror is (his own) Death, which is looking at "he" from inside the mirror with desire. So, instead of remaining a passive object of desire, a victim, "he" becomes the writing subject of his own death, embroidering his shroud with the ink of his blood: the poem that would tattoo Death with the initials "A.I.D.S."

WORKS

Nueva York tras bastidores/New York Backstage. Santiago, Chile: Cuarto Propio, 1993.
"Side Effects." Unpublished ms.
"Tantrum de la muerte." In Carlos A. Rodríguez-Matos. "Retazos: Poesía del sida en lengua hispana." *Sidahora* 13 (Winter 1992): 21–27, 55.

CRITICISM

Ortega, Eliana. "Otro poeto en Nueva York." In Sandoval-Sánchez, *Nueva York tras bastidores*, 9–11.

                                                          Carlos A. Rodríguez-Matos

SANT'ANNA, VERA DE (Brazil; 1929) ⎯⎯⎯⎯⎯

Painter, actress, political activist and autobiographer, Vera de Sant'Anna is best known for her participation in avant-garde movements and liberation fronts of the 1960s and 1970s in Brazil. She has developed both scholarly and popular careers. As an ambitious, innovative painter, she contributed to official mainstream exhibitions in Rio de Janeiro and Salvador between 1949 and 1959. As a pioneer artist, she brought her works to the squares and parks for display and sale. Coordinating bureaucratic efforts for others to be able to do the same, she sought to narrow the distance between the artists and the public, and to make virtually all forms of art available to the masses. Band performances, circus acts, regional dances, puppet shows and theater (which often mocked the military dictatorship) came to be presented free in the open air, an initiative unmatched in other parts of the country until the early 1970s.

One of Sant'Anna's most notorious techniques as a painter resembles that of Flemish watercolor, which she and her partner Cláudio Bataglia studied under Pumm Devez in the Netherlands in 1973. The procedure consists of overlaying several coats of transparent ink on canvas. Using the name of Sant'Clau, which combines their names, the two Brazilians produced what critic Míriam Alencar has called "fantastic painting, without the oneiric quality that characterizes surrealism."

In tune with the Dada Manifesto (1918), Oswald de Andrade's Cannibalist Manifesto (1928), and Gilberto Gil and Caetano Veloso's *Tropicalismo* of the late 1960s, Sant'Anna's creative process aims at art from a unique standpoint. It commands a complex, distorting and iconoclastic understanding of the world, which, in turn, ends up destroying its own power to judge, exclude and categorize. In certain pieces, "deviations" like dadaism seem to be overwhelming— for instance, a Madonna wearing a beard, with Baby Jesus looking underneath her skirt. He wants to know what is inside, whether that person is male or female; breasts and facial hair together, of course, can be misleading (*Quase baixo*, 214).

Like her plastic art, humor and iconoclasm comprise the backbone in *Quase baixo* (Nearly Low), Sant'Anna's 1983 autobiography. Among a variety of institutions and values attacked by her sharp and irreverent prose are the Catholic dogmas and sacraments and, in particular, the notions of "proper" sexuality. Complying with the author–narrator–protagonist direct line of referentiality (though often twisted by carnivalization), this uncanny text unveils an epigraph that sums up the main theme of the piece: "This book is a Declaration of Lust. I confess that since the age of seven all I can think of is sex" (7). The epigraph alludes to the painting on the cover. *L'Âge d'or* (1973) mischievously portrays a naked, brown-skinned, gray-haired woman with her right hand on her genitalia. The epigraph clarifies that the canvas represents the moment when Sant'Anna's body reached its peak sexual dexterity. As she entered The *Age of Gold* (English title of the painting), continues the opening voice, her hair turned silver. One is tempted to relate this portrait to a later passage in *Quase baixo*. At the age of fifty, the narrator exclaims, "[I have] nothing against dyeing," when she comes across a first, frustrating gray pubic hair. She pulls it out, then puts her glasses on—only to realize there are many others. She finally says, "Was it about time for me to ask my partner in bed for a dimming light? How distressing!" (194).

The onset of the narrative also cements the colloquial, carnivalized tone prevailing in the piece: "On a certain 20th of April I knocked on the door of my mother's womb. I was already fed up with so much darkness, placenta, fat, etc. and so on" (11). Moving mockingly between serious and comic discourse, Sant'Anna uses a metaphor of *carnaval* to describe her birth. The German midwife "*foi logo abrindo alas pra eu passar* [was quick in spreading the wings for me to pass through] from bad to worse" (11). Sant'Anna was an unusually opinionated child. She was expelled from a Catholic boarding school at the age of nine. Among other "sins," she dared to question the mother superior as to why the French nuns mistreated the orphan children working in the school. The last straw that caused her to break with Roman Catholicism came when, at fourteen, she confessed to a priest that she had been masturbating for many years. She learned from him, for the first time, not only that people of the same sex could play with their bodies together, but also that it was all right. She also became extremely angry when he gave her heavy penance for doing it with a boy instead of a girl. "The world cannot go on like this, my darling, with so many unmarried mothers," the priest informed her (19).

Sex, which had been such a powerful impulse for her, now turned out to be a mysterious matter, a source of awe enhanced by her boyfriend's comments on what the priest had said. "Huh . . . it makes sense when Dad says every priest is a fag." She tried to avoid the topic, but he continued: "Girl, the gay fever is out there, fancy-free. But we men are safe. We sometimes mess around with one of those queers, here and there, but we are always on top, you know. But on the bottom? . . . no way! There is always a faggot around for that" (17).

The intricacies of male homosexuality seem to have played an enormous role in Sant'Anna's quest for understanding sex. She has often asked straight men whether they have been penetrated; the initial answer is inevitably "Never." After a few drinks, the majority of them, she says, reconfirm they have never been "bottoms," then confess they have been "tops" when they were children. She also mentions, with some irony, that she has yet to come across that type of young man who fulfills the widespread lust supposedly found in religious boarding schools and seminaries: "the little fag, who escapes guilt by cultivating a macho image" (49).

Sant'Anna's bewilderment at human sexuality remained strong well into her late thirties, when she opted for a drastic experience. In 1969, while earning a steady living as a stenographer for the State House of Representatives, she established an unusual learning center. She called it the Laboratory for Sexual Research. The series of experiments she conducted was not an orgy or bacchanal, as the mainstream press had reported, and she explains why. The project was launched by four women and a man. All naked in the bathroom of her apartment, they ranged on the social scale from filmmaker to model to prostitute. Before they had sex, they smoked marijuana. Their conversations were plain and unpretentious, and she realized that "One who's nude doesn't talk hermeneutics or cybernetics; it's embarrassing to show erudition when the person is bare-assed" (52).

For Sant'Anna, at least, their sexual deeds were scientific. Whether such performances were enjoyed or not, they were always followed by a high-level debate on learnings and sensations. One of her realizations was that to be "able to choose what one wishes to do with his or her body is the minimum right any human being deserves" (53). She herself came to grips with her "real preference—proven by action—in the complicated field of sexuality" (52). After savoring the big breasts of a shy woman in the group, while being penetrated by another with a rubber penis, the sexologist felt she needed the only man present in the scene to achieve a "sobbing orgasm." But that was not all. She learned that "erogenous zones are not gender-bound" and that she has a craving for breasts. "I started to think that if men had full breasts, they'd be nature's perfection" (54).

The laboratory experiences taught Sant'Anna mostly about issues of heterogeneity and disguise in the so-called homosexual and heterosexual behaviors. She charges, for instance, that "Every fanatic heterosexual is either a closeted fag or a closeted dyke." On the other hand, "The moderate heterosexual, who gets by all right with pederasts and lesbians of all sorts and has nothing against them (but just doesn't like the same things), may be a bisexual." This bisexual, however, "may like the opposite sex so much that he or she won't even try new stuff," especially if the bisexual "is more than satisfied (with what he or she knows) and is free (from prejudice)" (53). Sant'Anna's education in terms of sex and gender also took place outside Brazil, when she traveled extensively through the Middle East, Latin America, Europe and Africa. Some of her most shocking discernments came in Arab countries, where homosexuality and machismo coexisted in the oppression of women. Syrian women, for instance, seemed to implore Sant'Anna for help by suggesting that "Men of this country have habits which benefit them alone; they treat us like animals that neither sit at the table to eat nor enter a mosque to pray" (135). In various Arab countries, adds Sant'Anna, boys do painful exercises in order to ready themselves for anal sex; they mean to broaden the opening of their sphincters and better manage their expansion and contraction abilities. In the meantime, not only is sex with women pursued for procreation only, but young girls also have their clitorises cut off, "so that women's pleasure is restricted to the womb-house, where maternal pleasure resides" (135).

Much to the reader's astonishment, Sant'Anna, single and childless, feels acquiescent, surprisingly close to death upon closing her autobiography. In 1980, at the age of fifty-one, she reveals her dissatisfaction with her book. It remains exquisitely powerful, nevertheless. One can plausibly argue that the voice in charge now is another dadaistic persona. A small dose of carnivalization is interspersed with bittersweet sentimentality and self-pity. Humor and heat are dim, and attempts at enhancing them betray the persona's mood, fearful and sad. "I wish this will and testament to be hot in all senses," the voice declares in regard to the last segment of the text, titled "Will." Yet following this rerun of sexual allusions (an echo of the epigraph), Sant'Anna, the persona, turns defensive and urges the reader to respect the "cheerful style" and "sort of alternative content" of her writing, for that is the way her life had been (197).

In reality, the penchant for multiple sex, scientific or not, is replaced by an appeal to the grotesque. Sant'Anna apologizes to worms and cockroaches for bequeathing her properties to her living parents; she also draws images of people buried alive, feeding on their own flesh. In the meantime, a weird faith trivial metaphysics is her walking stick: "I've got a replica of the Cheops Pyramid on my bedside table, in order to unclog my brain and light up my dreams" (198). She explains, "Thanatos finally decided to sneak into every little corner of my apartment in search of Eros (198)."

WORKS

Quase baixo. Rio de Janeiro: Codecri, 1983.

CRITICISM

Alencar, Míriam. "As praças aos artistas." *Jornal do Brasil*, sec. B, July 9, 1975, n.p. Cited in Sant'Anna 160–161.
Dicionário brasileiro de artistas plásticos, 4.160. Ed. Walmir Ayala. Brasília: Instituto Nacional do Livro, 1980.

Dário Borim, Jr.

SANTIAGO, SILVIANO (Brazil; 1936) _____

The emergence of the journal *Tendência* (Tendency; 1957) in Belo Horizonte brought many artists together, among them Silviano Santiago, born in Formiga, Minas Gerais. In the early 1960s *Tendência* engaged in a polemic with some of the more institutionalized sectors of Brazilian culture. These included the concrete as well as neoconcrete poets and other writers who stood apart from any particular literary or poetic style. The poetic predecessors of Santiago's writing date from this period, and their production continues to remain strong even today.

In 1960, Santiago and three other young poets, Affonso Romano de Sant' Anna, Terezinha Alves Pereira, and Domingos Muchon, published their first volume of poetry, *4 poetas* (4 Poets). Their artistic production demonstrated a strong formal preoccupation, and introduced in embryonic form what would later become the "deemotionalization" of poetry. These poems, written between 1955 and 1959, manifest signs of what would later become the tense and dramatic dialectic between story and history, a relation that would become radicalized in later texts.

Duas faces (Two Faces; 1961), Santiago's second book, was a joint publication with Ivan Ângelo, one of the principal representatives of Brazilian prose in the 1970s. This volume contains two stories told in the first person, "Pai e filho" (Father and Son) and "Olivia." The first is the story of the antagonism between two generations, and the second concerns a romance between adolescents. The texts attest to Santiago's growing preoccupation with the relationship between the individual and the social, showing how the two can no longer be separated in identity. The stories also mark the beginning of what would become his concentration on the double articulation between the individual's story and history.

After spending time outside Brazil as a professor of French, Portuguese and Brazilian literature in France, Canada and the United States, Santiago returned to Brazil in the early 1970s and published two new books, *Salto* (Jump; 1970), a collection of poetry, and *O banquete* (The Banquet; 1970), a collection of short stories. The first was a concrete experience in which a harsh criticism of the establishment's poetic language is rendered. Santiago's criticism was of an emphasis on the signifier as a result of specific historical contingencies. In writing these experimental poems, Santiago combined various elements in the search for a distinct expression: deautomatized, deconstructive and derealized. Geometric language, which was first introduced in *4 poetas*, is accentuated in these poems and used as a vehicle for a criticism of language through the use of language. *Crescendo durante a guerra numa província ultramarina* (Growing up During the War in an Overseas Province; 1978) is anticipated by *4 poetas*. *Crescendo* attempts to reveal how language functions in terms of the antiquated mental structures of society.

O banquete, Santiago's second book, is a collection of twelve stories. In its second edition (1977), the text provoked considerable critical interest. If in 1970, due to the political situation of the country, the book had not received much in the way of formal criticism, the response to its second edition was overwhelming. Many critics were quick to find in this banquet an anthropophagic interpretation of neodependent culture. The title immediately establishes the intense dialogue between two of the principal lines of thought in Brazilian modernism, represented, respectively, by Oswald de Andrade (*antropofagia*, cannibalism) and Mário de Andrade (*poesia universal experimental*, experimental universalist poetry).

O olhar (The Gaze; 1974) reflected the *nouveau roman* style that Santiago used in exploring yet another genre: the novel with a strong experimental character. If in poetry he had already demonstrated an interest in a well-elaborated formal character, this work may be considered a radicalization of this practice in prose. Beginning with a banal triangle—mother, father, son—and the rewriting of many oedipal myths drawn from Minas Gerais, Santiago's text concerns the repressed eroticism that violently invades the organization of the family. At this point his examination of the subject as an erotic entity may be considered to emerge in this text.

During the period in which there was talk of the dictatorship loosening its grip, *Crescendo durante a guerra numa província ultramarina* provided the reader with the opportunity to reflect upon memory, exile and personal and social experience. The text showed how they are all bound up together with Brazilian neodependence that emerged during the postwar period. The question of repressed sexuality is evident in some of the poems, in the form of castration, diseased sex and other putatively perverse modalities of Minas Gerais society.

Em liberdade (In Freedom; 1981) is the fictional story or the historical fiction of two days of freedom in 1937 of the writer Graciliano Ramos in Rio de Janeiro, after he had been in prison for nine months. The novel may be considered a continuation of an interpretive–memorialist project on Brazil, utilizing in this specific case the cultural term coined by the writer Antônio Cândido, the *corrida de revezamento* (relay race). In 1946 Ramos wrote *Memória do cárcere* (Memory of Prison; 1953), which was not published until after his death. Silviano continued the story with *Em liberdade*, and what—or rather, who—is born, as Nélson Motta astutely observes, is Ramos. Any relation between Silviano's text and the writing of James Joyce, V. I. Lenin, and Tristan Tzara is no mere coincidence. The presence of the body as it is connected to the positive image of the happy Baby Jesus, and not to the pathetic or tragic suffering of Christ crucified, becomes apparent in this novel, and is developed as one of the dominant motifs in Silviano's writing.

Stella Manhattan (1985) is Silviano's first novel with an explicit homosexual theme. Here the connection between story and history is exceptionally clear. Eduardo da Costa e Silva is a middle-class Brazilian from a traditional family in Minas Gerais. When the family discovers that he is homosexual, they arrange for him to obtain a position as a clerk in the Brazilian consulate in New York. He becomes involved with the consulate's military attaché, who has a penchant for sadomasochism. The entire spectrum of New York's underground subculture is examined in a penetrating and thorough manner, in an attempt to probe the specificity of this sexual option. *Stella Manhattan* explores how the bonds between sexuality, history and literary representation are established. Inexplicably, Eduardo suddenly disappears from the novel, and the narrator offers the reader a series of discursive possibilities with respect to his disappearance. Everything (running the gamut from story to history) becomes discourse, seen as a monster that contaminates daily reality.

In the context of the lack of a particularly strong tradition of homosexual literature (possibly due to the repressive nature of Brazilian society), *Stella Manhattan* represents the first Brazilian novel that attempts a lucid comprehension of how to establish the dialectic bonds between history and sexuality. Via a postmodern optic, the author attempts to present the reader with a simple picture (and yet at the same time a very complex one) of the two discursive elements of sexuality and history. The categories of race, gender, class and sexual options appear intimately connected, as if to demonstrate for the reader the enormous webs that entangle the individual in this post-everything world. *Stella Manhattan* represents the radicalization of the process of writing that utilizes allegedly aberrant sexuality as its basic metaphor (using Freudian theory with care). Beyond this, peripheral spaces (in this case, Brazil), are seen through the eyes of others, who, in a radical or different manner, reinterpret the diverse discourses produced in the metropolis and exported acritically to the periphery. Eduardo da Costa e Silva, or Stella Manhattan, dramatizes through his own body the many contradictions of a writing that, produced on the fringes of the Western world, anthropophagically swallows its enemies.

Uma história de família (A Family History; 1992) is the account of an extremely ill man attempting to carry on a lucid conversation with his deranged uncle. The framework of the novel enables it to be understood that he is dying of AIDS. Once again, the questions of story and history inhabit this short novel, in which a superhuman effort is made to understand their multiple and irreconcilable differences.

It may be said that the focus of Santiago's works falls primarily on the relationship between history and sexuality. His body of work on the whole is a meditation on the many labels that are imposed, sometimes freely, sometimes not, by incessant discursive constructions.

WORKS

O banquete. 2nd ed. São Paulo: Atica, 1977.

Carlos Drummond de Andrade. Rio de Janeiro: Vozes, 1976.

Crescendo durante a guerra numa província ultramarina. Rio de Janeiro: Francisco Alves, 1978.

4 poetas. Silviano Santiago, Affonso Romano de Sant'Anna, Terezinha Alves Pereira, Domingo Muchon. Belo Horizonte: Gráfica da Universidade de Minas Gerais, 1960.

Duas faces. Written with Ivan Ângelo. Belo Horizonte: Itatiaia, 1961.

Em liberdade. Rio de Janeiro: Paz e Terra, 1981. 3rd ed., 1985.

Uma história da família. Rio de Janeiro: Rocco, 1992.

Uma literatura nos trópicos. São Paulo: Perspectiva, 1978.

Nas malhas da letra. São Paulo: Companhia das Letras, 1989.

O olhar. Belo Horizonte: Edições Tendências, 1974. 2nd ed. São Paulo: Global, 1983.

Salto. Belo Horizonte: Imprensa Oficial, 1970.

Stella Manhattan. Rio de Janeiro: Nova Fronteira, 1985.

Vale quanto pesa. Rio de Janeiro: Paz e Terra, 1982.

CRITICISM

Lopes, Francisco Caetano, Jr. "A obra de Silviano Santiago: A possibilidade do corpo." *Paunch* 65–66 (1991): 189–200.

———. "*Stella Manhattan*: Uma subjetividade outra." *Brasil/Brazil* 5.4 (1991): 54–78.

———. "Uma subjetividade outra." In *Towards Sociocriticism: Luso-Brazilian Literatures, a Socio-critical Approach*, 67–74. Ed. Roberto Reis. Tempe: Center for Latin American Studies, Arizona State University, 1991.

Miranda, Wander de Melo. *Corpos escritos*. São Paulo: Editora da Universidade de São Paulo, 1992.

Süssekind, Flora. "Ficção 80: Dobradiças e vitrines." *Revista do Brasil* 5 (1986): 82–89.

Villaça, Nízia. "Feminino/masculino." *Revista do Brasil* 5 (1986): 122–124.

Francisco Caetano Lopes, Jr.

SARDUY, SEVERO (Cuba; 1937–France 1993) _____

In an interview in *Quimera* in 1991, Mihály Dés asked Sarduy about homosexuality. Sarduy responded that he considered it strictly a matter of personal taste, something like being a diabetic or a stamp collector, not worthy of even mentioning. One may feel that he is nonchalantly brushing aside the issue. His readers should overcome the temptation to interpret his work from a strictly autobiographical perspective. What should be relevant is that Sarduy invites the reader to search and discover how he, an author, chooses to address and treat homosexual issues.

Sarduy often develops such questions through the use of sardonic humor and/or the art of simulation, simulating the seriousness with which he considers the literary presentation of nontraditional Latin American issues like racial and sexual discrimination, the contributions of African and Chinese elements to Cuban culture and the fear of AIDS. Why he opts for the mask of humor is for his readers to debate but not to judge. He denounces problems as he sees fit, artistically, but he is neither a preacher nor a moralizer.

Sarduy was born in Camagüey and died in Paris, a French citizen. He was not only one of Latin America's leading writers but also a critic, a translator, a painter, a reader for Paris publishing houses and the host of a Radio France International program. The reflection of this chameleonic existence can be found in Sarduy's texts, in which, to the dismay of many readers, allusions to Cuban food, music or the Chinese lottery appear next to mentions of European, Latin American or Oriental art, Buddhism, literary references, scientific data or Derrida's deconstruction, to mention just a few. Sarduy began his public writing career with the publication of a poem in 1953. In 1956 his family moved to Havana, where Sarduy studied medicine. There, he quickly became active in the literary movement around the review *Ciclón* (Cyclone; 1955–1957; 1959). He wrote articles mostly on painting. Fidel Castro and the Cuban Revolution affected not only the island's history but Sarduy's life as well. Because of his commitment, his literary and artistic endeavors increased, and he directed a page in the newspaper *Lunes de revolución* (Revolutionary Monday). In 1962 the Cuban government awarded him a scholarship to study art history and criticism in Europe. While in Rome, he met the French philosopher François Wahl. In Paris, Wahl introduced Sarduy to Roland Barthes. This opened the doors to other significant meetings, mostly with members of Philippe Sollers's Tel Quel (Just That Way; 1960–1982) group.

Of his published works, the novel *Gestos* (Gestures; 1963) is unique in that it follows the prescriptions of the so-called French new novel and attempts to apply the principles of action painting in writing. The action is set in prerevolutionary Cuba, and the narrative focus is on the protagonist, a black woman singer and launderess who is placing bombs in Havana. Although the text emphasizes her actions, and at first glance the novel may not seem pertinent to this discussion, one can find recurring leitmotifs that are part and parcel of Sarduy's presentation of homosexual concerns. There is, for example, mention of a Japanese transvestite artist, Musmut. In that short passage there is a roster of Sarduyan preoccupations, and the staccato rhythm and the elliptic terms are significant components of the style and lexicon Sarduy utilizes to present a being hiding behind many masks. By using such techniques, Sarduy insists on diminishing the importance of knowing what the gender, and by extension, what the sexual inclination, of a character may be. Bodies, and not only those of transvestites, often appear lavishly decorated, inscribed or tattooed, amid the accumulation of trite details of the neobaroque—in other words, simulated.

Subsequent characters, like Cobra, who starts as a transvestite unhappy with her/his feet, undergoes castration and resurfaces as the leader of a motorcycle gang; Cadillac, another transvestite transformed as Dr. Ktazob, responsible for Cobra's castration (both in *Cobra* [1972]); and Colibrí, the beautiful young man who one day appears in a bar, sumo wrestles a big Japanese, escapes to the jungle, becomes a painter of fleas in the city and returns to the bar (in *Colibrí* [Hummingbird; 1984]) represent not only the changing nature of writing but also the existence of figures for androgynous and homosexual beings who undertake a search for a body better suited or transformed to accommodate their sexual likings or needs. The goal is to establish or explain their origin per se, as well as the direction of the literary search for such a body, as parodic, tortuous or uncertain as it may seem to some readers. The artifice of Musmut's synthesis of the male and female personae is limited to that brief staged illusion of the transvestite. Yet in a way, Musmut is quite literally the opening act of the next stagings of simulations, or rather the search for appropriate setting(s) for Sarduy's ever-changing sexually complex characters.

Perhaps the periplus undertaken by the majority of the characters in *De donde son los cantantes* (*From Cuba with a Song*; 1967), *Cobra*, *Maitreya* (1978) and *Colibrí* reflect the literary meanderings Sarduy requires to present issues related to homosexuality. These novels seem to perpetuate the roundabout Latin American way of addressing homosexual topics. A close reading of a crucial passage of *De donde son los cantantes* may dispel this perception and serve as a potential model for reading applicable to the rest of Sarduy's literary corpus. Sarduy sets the reader to try to use known guideposts (like *santería* [witchcraft] beliefs, Cuban slang, popular culture or even linear plots) in order to find the way out of the maze of his writings.

Most critics establish that the intention of *De donde son los cantantes* is to parody Cuban writers who have tried to define, with strict paradigms, what it means to be Cuban. In Sarduy's novel the traditional, typical Cuban is represented (as heterosexual literature tends to do) by a righteous white Spaniard, a macho man chasing what he thinks is an Oriental, thus exotic, woman through Havana's nightclubs. In a passage at the close of the "Curriculum cubense," the first section of the novel, Sarduy sets out to undo the commonplace mentality of a dominant race (and gender). The putting together of four disparate characters occurs underneath an imaginary mirror that the reader is called to place above the head of the checkout clerk, and off which one is supposed to see the collision of the characters. Other than the three races, the Yoruban symbols and the allusion to Heidegger, the text, thanks to the mirror of the imagination, suggests to the reader the possibility of seeing past the binary male/female union, since the genders of some of the characters are not specified or are purposely presented in both masculine and feminine terms. The genders of Auxilio, the representative of Death, and Socorro, Auxilio's constant companion, are elusive (both names mean aid/help/mercy). In much the same way, Flor de Loto Junto al Río de Cenizas de Rosa (Lotus Flower Next to the River of Rose Ashes) is described to the macho general by Auxilio and Socorro as "a mirage, a flower in vitro . . . a pure absence, she is what she is not; she is not the answer" (38).

In this novel, as well as in *Cobra* and *Maitreya*, Sarduy describes or places the homosexual being within Oriental or pseudo-Oriental settings, as if asking the reader to consider that a foreign or exotic being (a Latin American homosexual) is one of the many components of society, whether it is out in the open or not. The allusions to castrations, sadomasochistic rituals and transformations are always present. The Orient and tantric rituals, in particular, serve as a foil to the presentation of homosexuality in the West. Through the presentation of the Chinese transvestite character chased by the libidinous general, Sarduy may be suggesting that if she is not what she seems to be (a female prey for the general), then perhaps she is the contrary; and the general, blinded and bound by his heterosexual tradition, refuses to see in his imaginary mirror that he is experiencing homoerotic impulses. His desire to see Flor de Loto dead, once she eludes him, could be the reflection of his unfulfilled erotic impulses. He does not succeed in achieving any of his expected masculine goals. He neither gets her nor kills her. Contrary to his set role as a male, he wants to cry, only to be criticized by the ever-present Auxilio and Socorro, who remind him of his dilemma: if he were a man, he would not cry. In the passage from "Curriculum," Sarduy points to an array of sexual inclinations and combinations, including the possibility of homosexual desire in all.

Cocuyo (1990) completes the cycle of Sarduy's novels to date, and its central transgression is that of a child who tries to kill his family with rat poison, falls in love with beautiful Ada and ends up seeing her as one of the women in a bordello where men come as voyeurs in order to masturbate. The women are to be seen, not touched. As one of the characters explains, it is an ocular pleasure. And although *El Cristo de la rue Jacob* (The Christ of Jacob Street; 1987), a collection of *epifanías* (epiphanies) and commentaries, does not quite fit the category of fiction, these short narratives deal with some of the serious aspects of today's homosexuality: the fear of contracting AIDS, the loss of friends and artists to the disease and the seeming ineffectiveness of a writer to contribute a solution. Sarduy removes the mask of humor and concentrates on the suffering, the emptiness and the devastation that surround him. Several passages illustrate the melancholy tone of the writer, in this most personal test. The lightheartedness of the sexual encounters in the novels is absent. Fear seems to permeate the relationships in these narratives. The first-person narrator of "Una limpieza" (A Cleansing) goes to a forest, where he meets a trucker. Contrary to the playful accumulations of Sarduy's neobaroque novels, the descriptions are direct and to the point. The sense of helplessness is repeated in another context, where Sarduy describes a girl, trapped in lava, whose image is beamed to television viewers around the globe. They watch, in dismay, the unsuccessful efforts of the rescuers. The girl dies buried in lava. But Sarduy could very well be alluding to the uselessness of writing, which cannot immediately save those with AIDS.

Sarduy's writing, like his characters, changes from one sentence to the next, and it challenges assumptions about sexuality, even if this is not immediately evident. He stated that writing is useless, yet kept writing, and his words disseminated his insistence on the presentation and acceptance of sexual differences. In light of this, one can understand his commentary on homosexuality: it is but one of many sexual possibilities, so he feels no need to single it out.

WORKS

Barroco. Buenos Aires: Sudamericana, 1974.
Cobra. Buenos Aires: Sudamericana, 1972. English version as *Cobra.* Trans. Suzanne Jill Levine. New York: Dutton, 1975.
Cocuyo. Barcelona: Tusquets Editores, 1990.
Colibrí. Barcelona: Argos Vergara, 1984.
El Cristo de la rue Jacob. Barcelona: Edicions del Mall, 1987.
De donde son los cantantes. Mexico City: Joaquín Mortiz, 1967. English version as "From Cuba with a Song." Trans. Suzanne Jill Levine. In *Triple Cross*, 231–329. New York: Dutton, 1972.
Escrito sobre un cuerpo: Ensayos de crítica. Buenos Aires: Sudamericana, 1969.
Gestos. Barcelona: Seix Barral, 1963.
Maitreya. Barcelona: Seix Barral, 1978.
La simulación. Caracas: Monte Avila, 1982.

CRITICISM

Costa, Horacio. "Sarduy: La escritura como *épure.*" *Revista iberoamericana* 154 (1991): 275–300.
Dés, Mihály. "Una autobiografía pulverizada entrevista." *Quimera* 102 (1991): 32–38.
González Echevarría, Roberto. "Interview/Severo Sarduy." *Diacritics* 2.2 (1972): 41–45.
———. *La ruta de Severo Sarduy.* Hanover, N.H.: Ediciones del Norte, 1987.
Kushigian, Julia A. *Orientalism in the Hispanic Literary Production. Dialogue with Borges, Paz, and Sarduy.* Albuquerque: University of New Mexico Press, 1991.

Levine, Suzanne Jill. "Escritura, traducción, desplazamiento: (Un acercamiento a *Maitreya*)." *Revista iberoamericana* 154 (1991): 309–315.

Márquez, Enrique. "*Cobra*: De aquel oscuro objeto del deseo." *Revista iberoamericana* 154 (1991): 301–307.

Méndez-Rodenas, Adriana. *Severo Sarduy: El neobarroco de la transgresión*. Mexico City: Universidad Nacional Autónoma de México, 1983.

Prieto, René. "The Ambiviolent Fiction of Severo Sarduy." *Symposium* 32.1 (1985): 49–60.

Ríos, Julián, ed. *Severo Sarduy*. Madrid: Editorial Fundamentos, 1976.

Rivero Potter, Alicia. "Algunas metáforas somáticas—erótico-escripturales—en *De donde son los cantantes* y *Cobra*." *Revista iberoamericana* 123–124 (1983): 497–508.

Santí, Enrico Mario. "Textual Politics: Severo Sarduy." *Latin American Literary Review* 16 (1980): 152–160.

Seager, Denis. "Conversation with Severo Sarduy: A Dialogue." *Dispositio* 15–16 (1980–1981): 129–142.

Ulloa, Justo C., and Leonor A. de Ulloa. "Proyecciones y ramificaciones del deseo en 'Junto al río cenizas de rosa.'" *Revista iberoamericana* 92–93 (1975): 569–578.

Mary Ann Gosser-Esquilín

SCHÓÓ, ERNESTO (Argentina; 1925) ──────

Schóó was born into one of Argentina's oldest families. He describes his early years and his cultural formation in the following fashion: "I had a comfortable and happy childhood. I learned to read when I was three years old, making out the letters in a book my father would read to me at night, [the Nicaraguan] Rubén Darío's *Odas profanas* [*Profane Odes*; 1917]. I studied law and philosophy, but I never finished either degree. I speak English, French, and Italian, and I consider myself self-taught."

Schóó began a lifelong career in journalism at the age of eighteen. His first publication, in the literary supplement of *La gaceta de Tucumán* (Tucumán Gazette, was a review of Jorge Luis Borges's translation of Walt Whitman's *Leaves of Grass*. In the 1960s he was one of the most important members of the DiTella Group, a private institute of intellectuals and creative minds based in Buenos Aires. At the same time he was writing songs that were popularized by the divas of the DiTella vanguard, Marikena Monti and Nacha Guevara.

In 1956 Schóó's short story "La isla" (The Island) won first place in a contest sponsored by the Sociedad Argentina de Escritores (Argentine Society of Writers) and the Esso Oil Company. At the time it was the highest award in the genre given in Argentina. The jury was composed of Borges, Manuel Mujica Lainez, and Juan Manuel Villarreal. "Despite having won this award, my timidity and my constant self-criticism held me back as a writer. I was never satisfied with what I wrote, and everything ended up stored away in desk drawers."

In 1976 Schóó finally decided to publish his first novel, which had been written between 1973 and 1975. *Función de gala* (Gala Event) is a fragmentary work constructed on the basis of a family history that the author had heard told in hushed voices during his childhood. The plot is episodic, with images presented in rapid succession that detail the way in which the characters intensely live the emptiness of their world and the commanding need to appear to be someone else. Their lives are so fictive that they become confused as to their identity and in the end have no idea who they are.

Función narrates three stories tied together by Pupé, a woman from the most decadent sphere of Buenos Aires high society. Pupé travels through Europe with her homosexual companion, Tony. Each has an affair with the outrageous Ludwig II. Also told is the story of Juan, the son of the cook in the Sánchez Olaguer household, where he is raised as one of their children. Beginning in childhood, Juan maintains sexual relations with Francisco, the oldest son of Doña Josefina, the lady of the house. After the cook's death, the lovers are discovered, and the family decides to evict Juan from the mansion in order to avoid a scandal. Juan moves into a tenement in the Boca district of Buenos Aires, where he meets Antonio, a handsome greengrocer who takes Juan in until the latter grows tired of Antonio's jealousy and his greed. Juan lands a good job, steals Antonio's savings, and abandons him.

Schóó also introduces us to Lolo Irazábal and his friend Maneco, two upper-class homosexuals who function as the sarcastic commentators on the events surrounding Pupé and Tony, the Sánchez Olaguers, and Juan. The author refrains from making direct criticisms, since they are eloquently made in an implicit fashion. The story in its totality provides a satiric vision of Buenos Aires during the 1930s and, as Schóó says, it does so "with much personal delirium." The year 1976 was not the most propitious time to publish this sort of novel. As a consequence of the military coup in March of that year, the press in certain cases preferred to refrain from publishing a review, or would publish "damning reviews that would be signed, which is rather an unusual practice."

Between 1975 and 1978, Schóó devoted himself to writing his second novel, *El baile de los guerreros* (The Dance of the Warriors; 1979), a historical fantasy based on real events. It is a tragicomic view of Argentine history spanning a century. Its characters enact situations in which they move between terror and the ridiculous. Since the novel did not deal with individuals or scenes that posed a threat to "morality in those times," it enjoyed a good critical reception. According to Schóó, "This novel was an homage to my Argentine literary mentors: [Domingo Faustino] Sarmiento, [Arturo] Cancela, and [Manuel] Mujica Lainez"; the novel is dedicated to Mujica Lainez.

Schóó's third novel, *El placer desbocado* (Runaway Pleasure; 1988) tells the story of Marcelo Cabrera, an Argentine diplomat who, in order to advance personally and professionally, drops his father's surname in favor of his mother's, which is more distinguished. Marcelo is a repressed homosexual who lives the isolation of his consular post in the Aeolian (Lipari) Islands in the Mediterranean. His actions and his thoughts are based exclusively on appearances, discretion, lies and simulacra. He attempts to lead a double life by clinging to the social principles that have been inculcated in him since infancy, and these prejudices force him to see his homosexuality as monstrous. His sole sexual activity consists of looking at naked Italian youths photographed at the beginning of the century by Baron Gloeden in his villa on Capri. Also, in order to keep up appearances, every Thursday he pays a visit to Rosalía, the local prostitute, who recommends he take Chinito, an Oriental homosexual known as the Sidewalk Queen, into his service. Chinito and Rosalía attempt to convince Marcelo to give free rein to his repressed sexuality but never achieve satisfactory results.

The young diplomat lives tied to memories of his country, his childhood and his family life. Although he is literally lost in the "other place" he always wants to inhabit, he is incapable of being himself. But then a figure totally the opposite of Marcelo visits the island. Dino Bernini, a friend from Argentina, is a homosexual painter who lives his condition openly and unproblematically. Dino, who is free of social ties, defines homosexuality in the following terms: "A man can make love with another man and still continue to be a man. There are no faggots, only human beings" (105).

Although Marcelo at first deplores Dino's intrusion into his life, his friend finally enables the diplomat to see the reality of his life. Marcelo decides to liberate himself before it is too late, and he begins to be more understanding toward Dino. The last chapter of the novel leaves open the possibility that Marcelo attains his liberation. He exchanges his maternal surname for the paternal one he had kept hidden, and he ends up recognizing that his is the story of "a poor man who knows what he doesn't want to be and is still ignorant of what he will be" (216). *El placer desbocado* was well received by the critics and enjoyed considerable popular readership.

Ciudad sin noche (City Without Night; 1990) is a satiric and erotic novel that deals with the amorous misfortunes of two samurais. It received honorable mention in Editorial Tusquets's erotic series, Sonrisa Vertical (Vertical Smile).

WORKS

El baile de los guerreros. Buenos Aires: Ediciones Corregidor, 1979.
Ciudad sin noche. Buenos Aires: Editorial Planeta, 1991.
Coche negro, caballos blancos. Buenos Aires: Ediciones de la Flor, 1989.
Función de gala. Buenos Aires: Editorial Sudamericana, 1976.
El placer desbocado. Buenos Aires: Emecé, 1988.
Quotes from Ernesto Schóó are taken from my personal interview with him in Buenos Aires, August 20, 1989.

Osvaldo R. Sabino

SILÉN, IVÁN (Puerto Rico; 1944) ⎯⎯⎯⎯⎯⎯

There is one phrase that could very well describe Iván Silén's writings: irreverence to the utmost degree. Regardless of the genre, Silén writes to upset and to shock. However, as he says in his "Poética" (Poetics), irreverence is only an aspect of his work, perhaps the first step into something else. He calls himself a "pariahnic" poet: a literary outcast with political and poetical dimensions. Writing from this distanced perspective—a conscious position of exile—Silén resists the preestablished linguistic system in order to explore and perhaps discover a new, asystematic linguistics.

Silén was born in Santurce, and he has lived both in San Juan and in New York, where, as a result of his contact with the Nuyorican poets, he edited an anthology of their poems, *Los paraguas amarillos* (Yellow Umbrellas; 1984). He also edited, during his stay in New York, the journals *Lugar sin límite* (Unbounded Place) and *Caronte* (Charon). He has written several collections of poetry, the genre that has attracted most of the few critics who have written about him: *Después del suicidio* (After Suicide; 1970), *El pájaro loco* (The Crazy Bird; 1971), *Los poemas de Filí-Melé* (Filí-Melé's Poems; 1976), *El miedo del pantócrata* (Fear of the Pantocrat; 1980), *Las mariposas de alambre* (Wire Butterflies; 1992), *El último círculo* (The Last Circle; 1992) and *El libro de los místicos* (The Book of Mysteries; 1992).

Death and poetry seem to be the overriding obsessions of Silén in these works, along with the political implications of sex and the body. These themes persist in his other works, especially in his essays *El llanto de las ninfómanas/The Wail of the Nymphomaniacs* (1981) and *Nietzsche o la dama de las ratas* (Nietzsche or the Rat Lady; 1986), a series of philosophical, psychoanalytical and poststructuralist writings. Silén has also written three novels in the mode of what he calls *realismo esquizo* (schizo realism), a disjunctive narration loaded with hallucinations and mythological intrusions, in which the characters (if that is what they are) are merely the fractured remains of a subject. *La biografía* (The Biography) was published in 1986. *La casa de Ulimar* (Ulimar's House; 1987), an essayistic novel full of conversations about art and writing, deals with a Puerto Rican nationalist revolution and a series of political murder attempts, with the narrative based on the life of Christ. *Las muñecas de la calle del Cristo* (The Christ Street Dolls; 1989) is in a way a rewriting of *La casa de Ulimar*, although here the revolution becomes the background, and the central figure is an unemployed musician who seduces both the Puerto Rican first lady and the hermaphrodite daughter of a senator.

Throughout Silén's writings, sexuality always serves as a rebellious factor. The Christ figure in *La casa de Ulimar* is corporal and intensely involved in sexual practices. The hermaphrodite is also a favorite subject, especially in his novels. What is curious about Silén's novels is that the homosexual as rebel or social violator is absent, except in insignificant moments (there are some fleeting gay demonstrations in *La casa de Ulimar* and *Las muñecas*). The homosexual is, instead, a social outrage and an embarrassment, a symbol of decadent and apocalyptic times. Is Silén, then, writing within a homophobic discourse? Absolutely not. He places his narrative perspective on the side of the scandalized, of the repressed subject that is terrorized by the homosexual, and of the homosexual who considers himself a social outrage. Silén's writing generates the exhibition of hysteria toward the homosexual within an apocalyptic world— without, however, any interest in systematically dismantling the homophobic mind's mechanisms. Silén is never systematic; he is *esquizo*.

This take on homosexuality is clear in *Las muñecas de la calle del Cristo*, in which the president of the United States and the governor of Puerto Rico are gay lovers. Their relationship is one of master and slave, Governor Tavárez being the colonial inferior to Ricky, the president: "This is the truth," declares the governor, "what I am for you is what Puerto Rico is for the United States" (192). Silén compares the colonial status of the island to a type of sodomy in which there is a giver and a taker and no possibility for change. But even though Tavárez seems desperately in love with his bugger, he refuses to admit that he is gay. His wife at one point asks him, "Why don't you accept the fact that you are homosexual?" He replies, "You know that that is impossible. You know I'm the Governor" (12–13). To what does that impossibility refer? The fact that he is gay, or the fact that he should accept his homosexuality? In either case, the governor denies homosexuality as a social possibility. At the end of the novel, the governor and the president are kidnapped and killed; later, a love letter written by the governor is published in the newspapers. What infuriates people is not the fact that the governor was gay, but that his orientation was made public, that the scandal was revealed. Homosexuality, in the decaying society of *Las muñecas de la calle del Cristo*, cannot be made known, since as a perversion, it must remain in the closet.

WORKS

La biografía. Mexico City: Villicaña, 1986.
Después del suicidio. San Juan, P.R.: n.p., 1970.
La casa de Ulimar. Mexico City: Villicaña, 1988.
El llanto de las ninfómanas/The Wail of the Nymphomaniacs. Editorial El Libro Viage, 1981.
El miedo del Pantócrata. Santo Domingo: Luna Cabeza Caliente, 1980.
Las muñecas de la calle del Cristo. Buenos Aires: Ediciones de la Flor, 1989.
Nietzsche o la dama de las ratas. Mexico City: Villicaña, 1986.
El pájaro loco. Río Piedras, P.R.: Ediciones Librería Internacional, 1971.
La poesía como libertá. San Juan: Instituto de Cultura Puertorriqueña, 1992. (Contains *El libro de los místicos, Las mariposas de alambre, El miedo del pantócrata, Los poemas de Filí-Melé,* and *El último círculo*.)

"Poética." In *Papiros de Babel: Antología de la poesía puertorriqueña en Nueva York*, 256–258. Ed. Pedro López Adorno. Río Piedras: Editorial de la Universidad de Puerto Rico, 1991.

Carmelo Esterrich

T

TELLES, LYGIA FAGUNDES (Brazil; 1923)

Telles's fiction concerns moments of crisis. While death may be considered to be one of the dominant motifs in her writing, it is presented not only as the end of physical life but also as a site for the playing out of internal contradictions and pulsions in the characters' lives. Even though matters related to choice in sexual orientation are not prominent in Telles's fiction, one of the most frequent characteristics of her work is that women are always talking, figuring things out together, fighting against an unknown—death or a hostile society—that, if not faced and defeated, will destroy them. Sometimes death is a symbolic presence, as in "As formigas" (The Ants), in which two cousins find strength in each other to flee the apartment where a male skeleton is slowly being put together by ants. Other times, death is very real, as in "Antes do baile verde" (Before the Green Dance, in a collection of the same name; 1970), when employer and maid sew a costume for a carnival dance while they are both painfully aware of the impending death of the employer's father in the other room. In these stories, even though there is no lesbian relationship as such, there are hints of a lesbian continuum, of a nonsexual female bonding that is extremely important for the characters: women join forces and find consolation and help in one another. In another work, *As meninas* (*The Girl in the Photograph*; 1973), one of the main characters, Lia, has been initiated into a sexual life by another woman; later in the same work, she is shown as the most generous and most powerful of the group of three women.

In "Tigrela" (Tigress), a short story first included in *Seminário dos ratos* (Rat Seminar; 1977) and incorporated in *Tigrela and Other Stories* (1986), Telles discusses a lesbian relationship. In the story, Romana, a woman who has been married five times, talks to a former high school friend in a bar. Her subject is not her marriages, but a tigress she says she has raised in her apartment. This animal is "just a little bigger than a cat, the kind with tawny fur and toast-colored stripes, golden eyes" (131), and has developed such a close relationship with Romana that she is jealous of Aninha, the maid. She has only lately accepted Aninha because, unlike the other, younger maid, Aninha is old and ugly.

As in other stories, in "Tigrela" there is also the presentation of a fantastic atmosphere in a way that makes it seem natural. In this atmosphere, Telles can discuss love, hatred, life and death. For instance, when Romana tells her friend that Tigrela "adores velvet" (133), is calmed by the perfume of incense, likes Bach (especially the *Passion According to St. Matthew*), prefers classic clothes and even helps Romana choose her attire for parties, these things become acceptable within the general framework of the narrative. We are even told that now the tigress walks around the apartment wearing one of Romana's amber necklaces.

Romana is restless during this conversation with the unnamed female friend. She drinks whiskey and every now and then asks the waiter the time. When Romana loosens the knot in her scarf, her friend sees a purple bruise on her neck. The scarf is quickly tied again, and Romana comments that Tigrela doesn't like cheap whiskey and once broke a bottle that contained a brand that gives Romana hallucinations. The friend, who instills a note of common sense in the story and asks the questions that make Romana's story more out of the ordinary, says that it would be more humane to send Tigrela to a zoo. She insists that Romana has enslaved the tigress, and herself in the process. Romana replies that freedom is comfort and that Tigrela is aware of this. Suddenly, Romana starts talking quickly, and the friend has to ask her to slow down. Then Romana tells her that lately Tigrela has been consumed by jealousy. Yasbeck, a former lover, has reappeared in Romana's life, and Tigrela knows it. She lies awake waiting for Romana, sniffs her body, finds the man's smell and goes wild.

By this point of the narrative, it is clear that Romana is not talking about an animal but about a human being who speaks to her, watches her, reads her thoughts, someone "full of fervor" (137). Today Tigrela had chewed the phone cord to prevent Yasbeck from calling, and she things that at this moment Romana is with Yasbeck. "She's so unpredictable," Romana says. She adds that she will go back to the apartment trembling, because she never knows whether or not "the porter's coming to tell me that a young lady has thrown herself off one of the terraces, naked except for an amber necklace" (137).

In this seven-page short story, Telles provides the reader with a dense psychological drama impregnated with mystery and a touch of magic. It is as if, to relate a story of a lesbian relationship, Romana has to metamorphose the lover into a ferocious animal. In this process, however, Telles calls our attention to the paradoxes that constitute this love: on the one hand, there is no room for Romana and Tigrela in exterior society—their life is completely played out in Romana's apartment. On the other hand, however, the exterior society makes itself present in Romana's apartment through the presence of the maid (necessarily another woman) and, especially, through Tigrela's reproduction of Romana's heterosexual relationship in their homosexual relationship. Tigrela appropriates the "authority" commonly understood to be the prerogative of the male: she is jealous, possessive, violent.

However, Telles calls our attention also to the fact that the story is being narrated by Romana. Tigrela's testimony is never heard; therefore there is a sense in which it is Romana who is jealous, possessive and violent against Tigrela. After all, Romana—and it is not idle to observe the appropriateness of the name: Roman, imperial, domineering—keeps her lover in the apartment, provokes her jealousy and finally locks her up at a moment when Tigrela can kill herself out of desperation. At the end of the story, there is the sensation that a final resolution will not be presented in the text. The reader does not know whether Tigrela—beast or woman—has played the final lines of her love for Romana, or whether Romana will finally accept the humanity of her love for another woman.

WORKS

Antes do baile verde. Rio de Janeiro: Nova Fronteira, 1970.

O cacto vermelho. Rio de Janeiro: Mérito, 1949.

Ciranda de pedra. Rio de Janeiro: Nova Fronteira, 1954. English version as *The Marble Dance*. Trans. Margaret A. Neves. New York: Avon Books, 1986.

A disciplina do amor. Rio de Janeiro: Nova Fronteira, 1978.

Filhos pródigos. Rio de Janeiro: Nova Fronteira, 1978.

"Gaby." In *Os sete pecados capitais: Novelas*. Rio de Janeiro: Editora Civilização Brasileira, 1954.

Histórias do desencontro. Rio de Janeiro: José Olympio, 1958.

Histórias escolhidas. São Paulo: Boa Leitura Editora, 1961.

As horas nuas. Rio de Janeiro: Nova Fronteira, 1989.

O jardim selvagem. São Paulo: Martins, 1965.

Os melhores contos de Lygia Fagundes Telles. São Paulo: Global Editora, 1984.

As meninas. Rio de Janeiro: Nova Fronteira, 1973. English version as *The Girl in the Photograph*. Trans. Margaret A. Neves. New York: Avon Books, 1982.

Mistérios. Rio de Janeiro: Nova Fronteira, 1981.

Praia viva. São Paulo: Livraria Martins, 1944.

Seleta. Ed. Nelly Novaes Coelho. Rio de Janeiro: José Olympio, 1971.

Seminário dos ratos. Rio de Janeiro: Nova Fronteira, 1977. English version as *Tigrela and Other Stories*. Trans. Margaret A. Neves. New York: Avon Books, 1977.

Trilogia da confissão. Rio de Janeiro: Nova Fronteira, 1968.

Verão no aquário. São Paulo: Martins, 1963.

CRITICISM

Aguiar, Adonias (Adonias Filho, pseud.). *Modernos ficcionistas brasileiros*, 161–168. Rio de Janeiro: O Cruzeiro, 1958.

Ataíde, Vicente de Paula. *A narrativa de ficção*, 91–111. 2nd ed., rev. São Paulo: Mc-Graw-Hill do Brasil, 1973.

Brown, Richard L. "Lygia Fagundes Telles: Equalizer of the Sexes." *Romance Notes* 32.2 (Winter 1991): 157–161.

Carvalho, Alfredo Leme Coelho de. "A densidade simbólica e sugestiva em dois contos de Lygia Fagundes Telles." *Mimesis* 3 (1977): 81–88.

"Entrevista a Lygia Fagundes Telles." *Plaza* 13 (1987): 1–11.

Josef, Bella. "El arte de Lygia Fagundes Telles." *Nueva narrativa hispanoamericana* 5.1–2 (1975): 185–188.

Medina, Cremilda de Araújo. *A posse da terra: Escritor brasileiro hoje*, 59–67. São Paulo: Secretaria da Cultura do Estado de São Paulo, 1985.

Oliveira, Kátia. *A técnica narrativa em Lygia Fagundes Telles*. Pôrto Alegre: Universidade do Rio Grande do Sul, 1972.

Perez, Renard. *Escritores brasileiros contemporâneos. 2a. série*, 211–217. 2nd ed., rev. Rio de Janeiro: Civilização Brasileira, 1971.

Silva, Antonio Manoel dos Santos. "Existência e coisificação nos contos de Lygia Fagundes Telles." *Revista de letras* 26–27 (1986–1987): 1–16.

Tolman, Jon M. "Lygia Fagundes Telles." *Review* 30 (1981): 65–66.

Van Steen, Edla. "The Baroness of Tatuí." *Review* 36 (1986): 30–33.

Eva Paulino Bueno

THOMAS, PIRI (pseud. of John Peter Thomas; United States; 1928) _____

Painter, filmmaker, social activist, poet, playwright, short-story writer and autobiographer born in New York City, Piri Thomas stands out as the Puerto Rican author best known to English-speaking readers. *Down These Mean Streets*, his 1967 autobiography with millions of copies in print, is considered by many critics to be a masterpiece. It offers a personal view of the depression of the 1930s, when young Thomas experienced first hand discrimination and a disturbing sense of racial and ethnic displacement.

An African–Puerto Rican born and raised in the United States, Thomas learned to survive in the violent Spanish Harlem streets of New York City as a gang member and a drug dealer; in 1950 he was jailed for armed robbery and attempted murder. He served seven years in New York state penitentiaries, where he began his rehabilitation as a religious advocate, painter and author. While on parole at the age of twenty-eight, Thomas became a youth counselor. He worked with Spanish Harlem street thugs and addicts. Later, he began lecturing at universities throughout the country. Apart from its remarkable reception by the general public, *Mean Streets* has been widely praised by the critics. The work, however, is a classic case of extraordinary craft that has been extensively reviewed and commented upon, yet lacks in-depth, comprehensive analyses. In this regard, Yanis Gordils argues that "Thomas is not exempt from the established categorization of literature by minority authors as works of greater sociological than literary interest'' (317). Thomas's skills as a writer are likewise overshadowed by those who interpret his work within ''preconceptions and stereotypes established by Anglo portrayals of Puerto Rican communities . . . the so-called culture of poverty of the unemployed, welfare-dependent, drug- and crime-ridden Hispanic'' (318–319).

According to a large number of critics, however, Thomas's interest in sharing a ''truthful'' account of his painfully adventurous life, from street fights to spiritual salvation in jail, does not obliterate his creativity. There seems to be an even balance in his narrative, inasmuch as his literary options make the text both stylish and convincingly informative. Thomas manages to get the reader into the heart and mind of a younger persona. The effects of poetry and action, proximity and empathy turn his debut work into a rare example of highly creative yet realist autobiography. Some of *Mean Streets*'s most fascinating aspects involve the usage of metaphorical imagery and poignant language, features that render the narrator/protagonist's self both a multifaceted artistic construct and a down-to-earth portrait of a noncelebrity individual. For Thomas, writing *Mean Streets* for five years, there appears to be no need to forge an image of redemption and to erase what has been ugly about his former frame of mind. He narrates alluring searches for a place to belong, among which stands a mighty appeal to ''maleness.'' The part of the narrator's personality that has to do with understanding sex seems to escape very seldom, if at all, from male chauvinism. He displays blatant hypocrisy in his jealousy toward Trina, for example, while making out with another girl at the same party. Furthermore, while expecting the love of his life to remain a virgin until they marry (a notion he cherishes until late in the book), he has impregnated a stranger. Most significantly, young Thomas rejects the son born of that encounter.

Thomas eventually overcomes some of his machismo, which is pervasive in *Mean Streets* in the recurrent bashing of male homosexuals. It would be a mistake, however, to relate the narrator's jeers to the author's personal attitude toward gays. Written under the idea of producing sequels, *Mean Streets* does not account for Thomas's subsequently changed views. During an interview in 1980 he declared that, in prison, inmates ''knock you down or they hold you and then they rape you. . . . [I]t's all right if I want to give it away, but to be taken is a terrible thing.'' Thomas then suggests further detachment from homophobia: ''I knew once you got into homosexuality you get to like it. I didn't want to be torn and my machismo was still very, very strong in me, even though I was gentle'' (Binder, 69).

The third of Thomas's three overlapping autobiographical narratives, *Seven Long Times* (1974), insinuates that his attitude toward gays started to shift while he was serving time. *Seven* articulates a personal, profound investigation into the dehumanizing effects of repressed sexuality during an experience from which, as he puts it, most people ''come out with a doctorate in crime, hardened by an overdose of brutality, twisted by racism, or physically and emotionally scarred by forced homosexuality'' (224). Thomas appears to understand the dynamics of coerced seduction and rape, survival and sexual fulfillment in the so-called rehabilitation centers. If he demonstrates respect for the homosexuals who come into prison as proud gays, his sympathy for the indignities and debasement suffered by ''joy-boys'' is unequivocal. Having the highest rate of suicide and mental illness among all convicts, these young individuals ''accepted another inmate's help of fist power against his enemies only to find he eventually had to fight off his erstwhile benefactor because the payment demanded for the assistance was sexual'' (140). Joy-boys were also victims of the pimplike ''gorillas,'' who, ''by right of might, threats, or treats, would commit sodomy with their victims'' as well as put them out to ''hustle their favors on other inmates in exchange for jailhouse goodies'' (137). According to Thomas, anyone could be led into a role as joy-boy. He managed to avoid that by imposing a gender-stereotypical cliché on his bullies. To a man in the shower who harassed him, and subsequently to many others, he replied, ''I'm a man, diggit. I came in here my father's son and I'll be damned if I go out my mother's daughter'' (66).

Even though Thomas refrains from passing moral judgment against his attackers, the brutal experience of rape was routinely present in his life, as he listened to and agonized over youngsters' screams and shame somewhere down the hall. ''Cupping my hands to my mouth and doing my best to disguise my voice, I yelled across the echoing cellblock, 'man in trouble on the flats.' '' Another voice coerced Thomas into keeping quiet. As nothing happened to save the victim, Thomas realized nobody, from the warden down, cared, ''as long as it's just cons eating up cons'' (75).

''Love is where you find it, but in prison, most times, it's in your head and hand,'' writes Thomas. As this implies, masturbation is the greatest outlet for the frustration caused by sexual abstinence and, through the years, ''becomes the greatest sense of lonely pain next to the agonized yearning for freedom'' (136). Since sex normally becomes an all-out obsession, many substitutes apply. Apart from fantasizing romance and heterosexual action, Thomas took to the widespread yet clandestine habit of channeling such imagination into art. Artists ran the risk of severe punishment for altering women's portraits in magazine photographs. They would bleach out the parts of the body that were clothed. ''Eventually, after some important touchups here and there with colored pencils, a most saleable pinup was created'' (138). Gays were doing the same with pictures of men. Thomas humorously writes that some of them got so carried away with the touchup jobs ''that even King Kong would have been envious at the size of the added manhood in the photographs'' (139).

Despite his reluctance to engage in homosexual acts, Thomas acknowledges his yearning for gays. To him, it was ''*mucho* hard after being locked up for a long time not to start looking at them [gay men] with almost the same kind of feelings that a man would put out toward a woman'' (146). Indeed, one of the most compelling scenes in *Seven* closes a chapter entitled ''Nothing like the Real Thing,'' a direct allusion to women and sexual substitutes. In that emotionally charged sequence, the narrator feels ''the most fantastic urge'' to hold

Alec in his arms. He "was like a woman, his mannerisms and the softness of voice, and his build was slender" (148). Thomas's hands reached out to caress Alec's face, hair. "I began to feel my nostrils dilating . . . my breath was starting to come out in short heavy gasps" (148–149). When Alec's lips started to purse and a kiss was imminent, Thomas sprang back as if he had "touched a red-hot oven." To Alec's question of what was the matter, Thomas explained, "It's not you. It's me. I can't cut this. Sorry, Alec." The narrator adds, "I hadn't been putting Alec down for his way of living but I couldn't put down my way of living either" (149).

All in all, *Seven* may be construed as a plea for the humanization of penitentiaries; restoring a sense of identity through sex and love is one of Thomas's requests. If society will not allow conjugal visits or weekend passes home, "then it should at least make men's and women's prisons co-ed. . . . It would ease the pain of loneliness and fulfil the human right to feel love and express emotions" (140). For Thomas, substitutes for heterosexual relationships in prison "do not make the inmates perverted. It is society that is perverted by perpetuating this negation of normal expression of love" (141).

WORKS

Down These Mean Streets. New York: Vintage Books, 1991.
"A Neorican in Puerto Rico: Or Coming Home." In *Images and Identities: The Puerto Rican in Two World Contexts*, 153–156. Ed. Asela Rodríguez de Laguna. New Brunswick, N.J.: Transaction, 1987.
"A Nightmare Night in 'Mi Barrio.' " *New York Times Magazine*, Aug. 13, 1967, pp. 16ff.
Savior, Savior Hold My Hand. Garden City, N.Y.: Doubleday, 1972.
Seven Long Times. New York: Praeger, 1974.
Stories from El Barrio. New York: Knopf, 1978.

CRITICISM

Binder, Wolfgang. "An Interview with Piri Thomas." *Minority Voices*. 4.1 (1980): 63–78.
Gordils, Yanis. "Thomas, Piri." In *Biographical Dictionary of Hispanic Literature in the United States*, 311–312. Ed. Nicolás Kanellos. Westport, Conn.: Greenwood Press, 1989.
Gunton, S., ed. *Contemporary Literary Criticism*, 17.497–502. Detroit: Gale Research, 1981.
Gussow, Mel. "Theater: A New Play by Piri Thomas [review of *The Golden Streets*]. *New York Times*, Aug. 14, 1970, p. 21.
Holte, James Craig. "Piri Thomas: *Down These Mean Streets*." In *The Ethnic I*, 167–171. Westport, Conn.: Greenwood Press, 1988.
Mohr, Eugene V. "Lives from El Barrio." *Revista Chicano-Riqueña* 8.4 (1980): 60–79.

Rodriguez, Joe E. "The Sense of Mestizaje in Two Latino Novels." *Revista chicano-requeña* 12.1 (1984): 57–63.

Dário Borim, Jr.

TRABA, MARTA (Argentina; 1930–1983) _____

Traba lived in Argentina, Bolivia, Colombia, France, Italy, Puerto Rico, Spain, the United States, Uruguay and Venezuela. More an art critic than a writer of fiction, she was nevertheless able to interrelate the two disciplines. According to Damián Bayón, as a critic she was a judge, a militant and a theorist. In spite of her many biases, she was always open to discussion, ready to change her position and challenge her audience. Her most obvious defect was a tendency to avail herself of the lapidary sentences that foreshortened the thrust of her analysis. In one interview she said, "America is a continent of apologetics . . . there is almost a painful need for criticism. I believe that the root of our evils is the lack of critical spirit" (*Marta Traba*, 340). This proposition runs through her literature. According to Elena Poniatowska, "She is a cultural agitator at a time when culture is a closed circle. It is not just that she champions an unknown topic in Latin America, modern art, but that she promotes it and even praises those who are labeled as madmen. She belongs to the avant-garde: she is a revolutionary" (9). For instance, Traba was one of the first Latin American intellectuals to use television to promote culture and to create new institutions like Colombia's Museum of Modern Art. She said, "I believe in feminine literature, in a tender regard for detail that is not perceived by men. . . . I believe that women perceive reality more keenly than men; they grasp what lies in between the cracks. Man encompasses more and possesses a well-ordered, organized intellect. But women behold what is interstitial; it is a very specific, tender, feminine view, and one that I share" (Garfield, 126).

Debra Castillo has systematized Traba's thought about feminine literature according to her "Hipótesis sobre una escritura diferente" (Hypothesis About a Different Writing):

[Traba] suggests that women's writing attends to a second, equally profound and valuable set of criteria. First, women's literature can serve a mediating function: "If the feminine text has been situated in proximity to . . . the culturally marginalized . . . it can, like all countercultures, mediate perfectly between the solitary producer and the untrusting receiver. . . ." Second, says Traba, following upon the recognition of the woman writer's role as a representative of the margin and an intermediary with the center, the woman writer can learn to speak for herself. . . . Women reading/women writing provide, then, a viable, profound, and morally defensible alternative to the dominant cultural mode. (50)

Las ceremonias del verano (Summer Rites; 1966) received the Cuban Casa de las Américas Award. The first part, "Il trovatore" (The Troubador), is an autobiographical account of the early adolescence of a fourteen-year-old girl in a Buenos Aires neighborhood and her love of literature. *Los laberintos insolados* (Sunstroke Labyrinths; 1967) is an uninteresting Proustian novel. *Homérica latina* (Latin Homerics; 1979) is an attempt to grasp the totality of the Latin American reality that fails to respect the limit memory imposes upon the novel. *Conversación al sur* (*Mothers and Shadows*; 1981), Traba's masterpiece, is a novel of repression and torture. It relates the conversation between two women: Dolores, a defeated young woman who has lost her husband and has miscarried as the result of having been tortured; and Irene, the seductress, an actress of forty who discovers through her family and friends the real meaning of the military's so-called dirty war against subversion, and whose son seems to be among the "disappeared" in Chile. According to Elia Kantaris, "The conversation reaches out towards a deeper, unmediated communication: the trusting, loving relationship which the two women build. This is reflected in the past by Dolores' love for Victoria, the leader of the resistance in Buenos Aires. On this level, language and desire (love) both partake of the vital urge to reclaim the plurality of whole areas of existence (including the possibility of lesbian love) negated by the possessive logic of the phallus" (258). *Conversación* is a novel of words, the first words after mute repression, a basic conversation to remind the protagonists and readers that there is still life. The protagonists are "disappeared" by the end of the novel, so that the reader has to keep the conversation open in order not to lose the right to words.

En cualquier lugar (Anyplace; 1984) is a novel of exile that is interesting because it is an open attack on the Left and its dogmatisms. Traba distinguishes between a canonical masculine literature and a marginal feminine one. She writes both in her collections of short stories *Pasó así* (It Happened like That; 1968) and *De la mañana a la noche (cuentos norteamericanos)* (From Morning to Night: North American Short Stories; 1986).

Despite the opinionated nature of Traba's writings, it is difficult to classify them. Although she sought a feminine mode of writing, she refused to label herself as a feminist, perhaps to avoid the common Latin American tendency of equating lesbianism and feminism. Traba is a writer conscious of differences between male and female points of view. When she writes using the point of view of a man, she is more successful in the short stories of *De la mañana a la noche*—teenage literature of manners in the present-day United States—than in *Homérica latina*, her unsuccessful attempt to write a total novel like Julio Cortázar's *Rayuela* (*Hopscotch*; 1963). Traba said that *Homérica latina* "is a desperate and poetic global attempt to relate, like a chronicle, man's [sic] terrible relationships to power" (Garfield, 140). She uses "detail" in *De la mañana a la noche* because "although I am no feminist, I believe in feminine literature, in a tender regard for *detail* that is not perceived by man" (Garfield, 128), while in *Homérica latina* she uses the fragment in the fashion of Cortázar—the fragment as a Latin American phenomenon. She claims that "the irrationality of myths may be depicted by fragmentation" (Garfield, 132).

In *Conversación al sur*, lesbianism is a delayed and denied presence, and its denial suspends the romantic happy ending of an erotic affair between Dolores and Irene. The bursting of the policemen into the house where the two women meet and the disappearance of both of them destroys this possibility. Thus, lesbianism becomes an open sign, a utopian alternative to the dirty war being conducted by the military. This ending can be compared to that of *Las púberes canéforas* (The Pubescent Maidens; 1983) by José Joaquín Blanco, in which La Gorda is "disappeared" by Mexico City police after an erotic encounter: Blanco attempts to equate gay and police repression.

WORKS

Las ceremonias del verano. Havana: Casa de las Américas, 1966.
Conversación al sur. Mexico City: Siglo XXI, 1981. English version as *Mothers and Shadows*. Trans. Jo Labanyi. London: Readers International, 1986.
De la mañana a la noche (cuentos norteamericanos). Montevideo: Monte Sexto, 1986.
En cualquier lugar. Bogotá: Siglo XXI, 1984.
"Hipótesis sobre una escritura diferente." In *La sartén por el mango*, 21–26. Ed. Patricia Elena González and Eliana Ortega. Río Piedras, P.R.: Huracán, 1984.
Homérica latina. Bogotá: Carlos Valencia, 1979.
Los laberintos insolados. Barcelona: Seix Barral, 1967.
Marta Traba. Bogotá: Planeta Colombiana, 1984.
Pasó así. Montevideo; Arca, 1968.

CRITICISM

Bayón, Damián. "El espléndido no conformismo de Marta Traba." *Sin nombre* 14.3 (1984): 92–96.
Castillo, Debra. *Talking Back: Toward a Latin American Feminist Literary Criticism*, 49–50, 57–58. Ithaca, N.Y.: Cornell University Press, 1992.
Garfield, Evelyn Picon. "Marta Traba." In her *Women's Voices from Latin America*, 115–140. Detroit: Wayne State University Press, 1985.
Kantaris, Elia. "The Politics of Desire: Alienation and Identity in the Work of Marta Traba and Cristina Peri Rossi." *Forum for Modern Language Studies* 25.3 (1989): 248–264.
Poniatowska, Elena. "Marta Traba o el salto al vacío." In Traba, *En cualquier lugar*, 7–28.

Salvador A. Oropesa

U

UMPIERRE-HERRERA, LUZ MARÍA
(Puerto Rico; 1947)

Born in 1947 in Santurce, Umpierre grew up in a household that included two aunts, an uncle, a grandmother and eight cousins. After attending a private high school, she enrolled in the University of the Sacred Heart with several scholarships. Majoring in Spanish, she graduated cum laude in 1970 and went on to study law at the Catholic University of Ponce and then at the law school in Río Piedras. In 1974, one semester short of her law degree, Umpierre left Puerto Rico to study Latin American literature at Bryn Mawr, where she wrote that university's first dissertation on Puerto Rican literature. She published her first book of poetry during this time. After a year of teaching at Immaculata College in Pennsylvania, Umpierre was given a tenure-track position at Rutgers University. In 1984 the Rutgers administration forced the Spanish department to award her tenure, but in 1988 the university attempted to rescind her tenure because of her refusal to undergo psychiatric evaluation. Allowed back into the Spanish department, she was nevertheless denied office space. In 1989 Umpierre accepted the chair of modern languages and intercultural studies at Western Kentucky University, but she left in 1991 for the State University of New York at Brockport, where she chairs the Spanish department and holds the rank of full professor.

Umpierre's first volume of poetry, *Una puertorriqueña en Penna* (A Puerto Rican in Penna [Penna = Pennsylvania; Penna also = pena = pain]; 1979), was incorporated almost entirely into her second volume, *En el país de las maravillas* (In the Country of Marvels; 1982), a volume divided into three parts: "Exodo (una puertorriqueña en Penna)" (Exodus [A Puerto Rican in Penna]), "Jueces" (Judges) and "Lamentaciones de Luz María" (Luz María's Lamentations). Some of the pieces are written in Spanglish, a technique that brings to the lines a satiric humor special to Umpierre, particularly in poems like "Rubbish" and "Oración ante una imagen derrumbada" (Prayer Before a Fallen Image). Three poems are arranged on the page as pictures: "Título sobreentendido" (Understood Title; spelling the English word "ghetto"), "Writer's Block" (using Spanish text) and "Sol bricua" (Puerto Rican Sun; using musical solfeggio). The combination of wit and righteous anger has become a trademark of Umpierre's life and poetry. Her third collection, . . . *Y otras desgracias/And Other Misfortunes*, appeared in 1985 and contains almost no Spanish. "Mishaps," the first part of the volume, contains twenty-nine pages of poems written in English. The remainder of the sixty-seven-page book contains poems in Spanish. Umpierre's fourth collection, *The Margarita Poems* (1987), contains only nine poems, the last and longest, titled "The Mar/Garita Poem," covers seven pages. In a preface Umpierre defends the shortness of the volume and attacks those who "question the volume of this collection instead of what it represents for Puerto Rican literature, its importance, the pain that brought it together, the thought that went into it."

Umpierre has been lauded by critics perceptive enough to appreciate the brutal power of her special craft. Nancy Mandlove has commented on the "double-bladed axe that both destroys and creates . . . the labrys that cuts through centuries of patriarchal oppression to create a path for new ways of being" (ix). There is in the poet an ongoing battle against authority, and Mandlove sees in Umpierre some of the frozen candor of Stéphane Mallarmé struggling against the absurd challenge of "living and creating on the edge of nothing." Eliana Rivero has noted Umpierre's puns aimed against Bryn Mawr and Pennsylvania, her wordplay, her use of Spanglish, and her onomatopoeic sound effects. Julia Alvarez reads Umpierre's *Margarita Poems* as an invitation to poets lost on a quest or stuck in ivory towers. The poems are an invitation to find one's personal voice. Roger Platizky finds in this same collection the trademarks of Umpierre's special style to be "bristling frankness and lyrical angst, dystonic imagery of pleasures and pain, Amazonic voices of assertion and fetal whispers of longing, semiotic incantations and cosmic humor, the themes of societal oppression and the need to combat it at all costs, even at the cost of losing one's mind" (12). He explicates the two female voices, Julia and Margarita, and sees in the collection a movement toward ultimate reconciliation of the disparate voices when light ("Luz") fuses with the sea ("Mar").

Umpierre's lesbian voice does not really surface until *The Margarita Poems*. In this collection, with antipatriarchal invective from earlier poems as background, she finally brings the reader to understand her sexual preference: "What I needed to verbalize is the fact that I am, among many other things, a Lesbian. Second, I wanted to communicate in some viable form with some One who came to represent all women to me" (1). Her most obviously lesbian poem is "Immanence," in which she searches for Julia, her alter ego. She is frantic for Julia to lose herself in her sexuality and to surface as herself, as a lesbian woman. With the poem's finale, Umpierre finds herself able to love herself, the first step toward healing. It is not until the last poems in the collection, however, that Umpierre finds herself really free when she discovers "LUZ Y MAR, sin olas" (LIGHT AND SEA, without waves). Then she can finally pinpoint her day of liberation as December 10, 1985. The necessity of finding and going public with her lesbian voice in poetry thus gives significance to the entire Umpierre corpus.

WORKS

En el país de las maravillas. Bloomington, Ind.: Third Woman Press, 1982.
The Margarita Poems. Bloomington, Ind.: Third Woman Press, 1987.
Una puertorriqueña en Penna. San Juan: Masters, 1979.
. . . *Y otras desgracias/And Other Misfortunes.* Bloomington, Ind.: Third Woman Press, 1985.

CRITICISM

Alvarez, Julia. "Freeing La Musa: Luzma Umpierre's *The Margarita Poems.*" In Umpierre, *The Margarita Poems*, 4–7.
Mandlove, Nancy. "In Response." In Umpierre, . . . *Y otras desgracias/And Other Misfortunes*, ix–xiii.
Platizky, Roger. "From Dialectic to Deliverance: *The Margarita Poems.*" In Umpierre, *The Margarita Poems*, 12–15.
Rivero, Eliana. "De maravillas, oraciones y sofritos: La poeta cautiva." In Umpierre, *En el país de las maravillas*, i–iv.
Rodríguez, Carlos. "Por el río a la mar, todo por Margarita." In Umpierre, *The Margarita Poems*, 8–11.

George Klawitter

V

VALERO, ROBERTO (Cuba; 1955) _____

Valero was among the 10,800 Cubans who entered the Peruvian embassy in Havana in 1980 and shortly thereafter left the island through the Mariel boat exodus. Since his arrival in the United States, he has published five books of poetry: *Desde un oscuro ángulo* (From an Obscure Corner; 1982), *En fin, la noche* (At Long Last, the Night; 1984), *Dharma* (1985), *Venías* (You Were Coming; 1990) and *No estaré en tu camino* (I Will Not Be on Your Road; 1991). The latter was a finalist for Spain's Adonais Award. In 1989 Valero won the Letras de Oro (Golden Letters) Literary Prize for his critical study *El desamparado humor de Reinaldo Arenas* (The Forlorn Humor of Reinaldo Arenas; 1991). At present Valero has two unpublished manuscripts: "... pero nadie sabe su nombre" (... But Nobody Knows His Name), a lengthy mythological poem that articulates fundamental ideas concerning God, love (both sacred and secular) and creation by utilizing different world mythologies as a poetic framework, and "Este viento de cuaresma" (This Wind of Lent; finalist for Spain's 1989 Nadal Prize), a novelistic account of the Cuban Revolution as seen through the eyes of a young man who has never experienced any other political system.

In 1985 Valero published "Había una vez" (Once Upon a Time), a short story in which male homosexuality is utilized for a specific literary end. The story's title functions ironically, as the reader soon discovers that this story is not a fairy tale but a sadistic portrayal of repressed homosexual desire. The story is told through the voice of an omniscient narrator who describes how one day "el glorioso Comandante" (the Glorious Commander), a military symbol of ethical (heterosexual) incorruptibility, arrives at the torture cell to interrogate a political prisoner accused of being an enemy of the state. The prisoner is described as being handsome, tall, virile and dressed only in his underwear, having refused to put on the uniform of the common prisoners. Upon seeing the prisoner, the commander asks the soldiers to tie him to the bed and to leave them alone, after which he proceeds to fondle and kiss the prisoner's muscular body and then to masturbate the man. After the prisoner has ejaculated, the commander composes himself, beats the man violently, and finally puts a bullet through his mouth. This short narrative piece exposes the brutality of a dominant military heterosexual discourse that sanctions violence in order to repress all expressions of homosexual desire.

Valero's poetry revolves around several themes: nostalgia for a lost childhood, love/death, traveling as a physical and emotional movement away from memories and man's inner struggle between good and bad. In the prologue to the poet's first collection, *Desde un oscuro ángulo*, Reinaldo Arenas wrote that Valero's poetry could be defined by one mysterious word: beauty, a beauty that challenges and strengthens the reader. Many of the poet's most beautiful poems are sensual/erotic/love poems in which the poetic voice addresses itself to both men and women. This bisexual sensibility can be seen, for example, throughout *No estaré en tu camino*: "Tú, María Eugenia, Ileana, Eduardo, Erik, María Elena . . . /mientras te adornas con las plumas más exóticas" (17; You, María Eugenia, Ileana, Eduardo, Erik, María Elena . . . /while you adorn yourself with the most exotic feathers). The motif of bisexual love is presented by the alternation of male and female names that are evoked for more than a page. Later we read: "También tú eres cruz,/serpiente suave,/cueva y racimos de uvas,/y los sexos no estaban definidos,/sólo el amor nadaba entre las algas,/entre las olas sin color" (27; You are also a cross, a soft serpent,/a cave and a cluster of grapes,/and the sexes were not defined,/only love swam among the algae,/among the colorless waves). Both the serpent and the cave (obvious symbols of male and femal sexual organs) are unconstrained by traditional gender roles and are allowed to "swim freely" in the ocean waters; water is yet another sexual symbol.

In Valero's most recent collection, *Venías*, we again see an example of ambiguity in regard to sexual preference. This time, however, in the poem "Venías por la noche con tus rostras," it is not the poetic voice that is ambiguous in its desire but the object of desire itself, a woman so alluring that she is pursued by both sexes: "Venías bordeada de lanzas suaves y profundas,/deseada por los teenagers,/los biólogos, los deportistas, [. . .] los hombres todos/y todas las mujeres" (flanked by soft and deep spears you came,/desired by teenagers,/biologists, athletes, [. . .] every man/and every woman) (16). The sexual ambivalence of these verses is further underscored by attributing what have been traditionally feminine characteristics (soft and deep) to a phallic symbol (spears).

"Este viento de cuaresma" is a stirring narrative that is highly evocative and poetic. It is the story of Jaime Valdés, a young man growing up in revolutionary Cuba who not only must face the perplexing questions of young adulthood, but must do so within a system that carefully monitors appropriate revolutionary behavior. Jaime is presented in the novel as bisexual, engaging in sexual acts and fantasies with both sexes. Scenes of male same-sex relations are explicitly present throughout the novel—for instance, in the chapter entitled "Noviembre 13 de 1968," the date when Jaime first masturbates. In a society that is hostile to any form of unorthodox behavior, homosexual desire must be sublimated. Around him Jaime Valdés sees that individuals unsympathetic to the Revolution are accused of being *maricones* (queers); also, at one point in the novel, the secret police threaten Jaime and hold over his head his questionable friendship with "that tall blond boy from Las Villas." At other moments in the text the repressive forces of the rural population conceal homosexual desire, as is the case when Jaime's aunt tells him that his father was caught with a friend "doing you know what."

In both his poetry and his novel Valero is purposefully ambiguous in regard to sexual orientation, thus challenging and resisting traditional Cuban society, which has sought to exclude all forms of sexual orientation that is not heterosexual.

WORKS

El desamparado humor de Reinaldo Arenas. North Miami: University of Miami, Hallmark Press, 1991.
Desde un oscuro ángulo. Madrid: Editorial Playor, 1982.
Dharma. Miami: Editorial Universal, 1985.
En fin, la noche. Miami: Editorial Solar, 1984.
"Este viento de cuaresma." Unpublished novel.
No estaré en tu camino. Madrid: Ediciones Rialp, 1991.
"Había una vez." *Mariel,* Winter 1985, p. 33.
" . . . pero nadie sabe su nombre." Unpublished poem.
Venías. Madrid: Editorial Betania, 1990.

CRITICISM

Arenas, Reinaldo, "El ángulo se ilumina." In Valero, *Desde un oscuro ángulo,* 7–9.
Florit, Eugenio. "Cinco notas en busca de un prólogo." *Mariel,* Fall 1984, p. 10.
Maratos, Daniel C. *Cuban Exile Writers: A Biobibliographic Handbook,* xi, xvi, 7, 283, 345. London: Scarecrow Press, 1986.
Soto, Francisco, "*Venías.*" *Linden Lane Magazine* 10.3 (1991): 26–27.

Francisco Soto

VALLEJO, FERNANDO (Colombia; 1942)

Vallejo, born in Medellín, lives and works in Mexico. Besides writing novels, he has studied and written on poetry and grammar. In Mexico he has worked in the film industry, directing and writing scripts for films dealing with the recurrent violence in Colombia.

Vallejo's four narratives to date fall under the encompassing title *El río del tiempo* (The River of Time). They mark specific time frames in this river and in the narrator's development. The narrator, the recurring episodes and place-names give unity to the four novels, which also maintain thematic unity. They serve as an analysis of Colombia's political and social structure and at the same time point out the ongoing struggle of the main character/narrator, Fernando, to live in a society that condemns his sexual orientation but accepts constant violence and death as the norm. The narrator in all four novels addresses the reader or someone referred to as Doctor, "you" or Bruja, his dog. This directed monologue or confession serves to break down the distance between reader and text, and allows the reader to follow the narrator in his evocation of past events.

The first novel, *Los días azules* (Clear Days; 1987), introduces the reader to Fernando's family and deals mostly with his early childhood. Essentially it serves to present characters and places and to establish the family relationships that are referred to in the later novels. There is no mention of any type of homosexual relationship; the novel dwells instead on the childhood innocence of the narrator and his loving relationship with his family, especially his grandparents.

Second in the series is *El fuego secreto* (The Secret Fire; 1987). This novel highlights Fernando's late adolescent years and takes place almost entirely in the hidden gay world of Medellín and in Bogotá. Fernando takes the reader on a tour of bars and cruising areas. At the same time he tears apart the false morality that he sees evident at all levels of Colombian society. In this way a division is established between two layers of Colombian society. On the one hand, there is the apparent Colombia that is pious, respects family and is outwardly critical of any deviation from the established values. On the other hand, there is a Colombia that must be hidden, that must create its own space and must function in small, darkened bars in order to exist. Both levels of this Colombia constantly interact, and the socially accepted one is characterized as false because it criticizes and ostracizes the gay reality while actively participating in it. No level of Colombian society is left untouched, from the highest political officials to the church, the armed forces and the literati. Fernando is critical of each facet of official Colombian life because it forces a false morality or vision on the populace while actively engaging in the very act it condemns.

Although on one level the novel attacks Colombian society, on another it tells Fernando's story of his search for a romantic involvement or a true love, not just sexual encounters. This search focuses on young men from fifteen to nineteen years old. Fernando is especially fascinated with watching Junín Street in Medellín and observing the flow of people in it after the various high schools have let out. He compares the street to a river that, with its ebb and flow, can produce objects of beauty. Fernando's search for love eventually forces him into direct confrontation with his family, and he is placed in a mental institution to undergo psychiatric evaluation and therapy. He escapes, and returns to his search for a romantic involvement. The search eventually leads him back to one of his favorite bars, El Miami, where he meets the love of his life, Jesús Lopera. This meeting ends his search, and the bar, the entire Junín neighborhood, and finally the statue of Simón Bolívar, symbol of the oppressive patriarchal society, are consumed in a cleansing fire that signals Fernando's release from his past. The fire allows him to break all ties and feel totally liberated.

The sequence of novels continues with *Los caminos a Roma* (All Roads Lead to Rome; 1988). Fernando wins a scholarship to study film in Rome. While there, he matures and at the same time acts on his desires toward young men. He travels throughout Europe and manages to have a sexual encounter in every major city, but finds that without romance the encounter leaves him feeling empty. When he finally is accepted in Cinecittà, the Italian film school, he throws himself into his studies. At the same time, he fantasizes about an Italian boy he met on a train in northern Spain. Before he leaves Italy, he visits him. This visit, at first the romance that Fernando had been waiting for, turns into a complete failure, and he returns to Colombia disillusioned. As the novel ends, he tells his grandmother that he is happiest when he is with her and hopes to never leave the family again.

The final novel, *Años de indulgencia* (Years of Indulgence; 1989), takes place in New York City. The narrative style and the narrator are the same as in the previous novels, but the tone of the novel is much darker. Fernando curses everything: the United States, New York City, Colombia, the film industry. All serve as topics for him to vent his rage. In New York he lives in an apartment building that he helps his brother manage while they teach African Americans skills that will help them enter the work force. Fernando's brother, also gay, is in charge of the program. Fernando ridicules the program and despises the participants. He covers the gay cruising scenes of New York, taking the reader to the docks, Central Park, the Continental Baths, and several discos in Greenwich Village. Although a brief mention is made of the disease that would appear within a few years, the action takes place before the onset of AIDS.

Fernando is unhappy with everything, and his rage is aimed at all levels of Colombian and North American society. The focus does not have to do with his position as a gay male within society, but with his loss of youth and of family. He seemingly longs for the security that he felt growing up and is unsure of his role in life. In the end, to wipe away all vestiges of a life he dislikes, he sets fire to the building where he lives. This episode, unlike the one in *El fuego secreto,* is more an act of sheer anger or lunacy than of rebellion against the patriarchal society. Fernando seems to want to destroy everything because he has lost his focus in life.

All four of Vallejo's novels are very explicit. The narrator never seems ashamed of his sexual orientation, but instead seems comfortable with the outsider position it affords him. Also, he is comfortable with the rebellious character he assumes because of his orientation. The narratives are challenging for the reader. There is a general lack of chronological ordering, and many episodes are repeated. The directed monologue forces the reader to select information in order to establish validity and a narrative thread. Vallejo's texts effectively point out the repression that a highly organized patriarchal society imposes on those who do not conform. At the same time, by subverting the narrative structure and not conforming to traditional narrative modes, the narrator or authorial force appears to use the text as another arm in his intent to disrupt or destroy the societal norm. The text then serves Vallejo as an additional way to subvert and break the patriarchal society. All four novels clearly point to this intent on the part of the author.

WORKS

Años de indulgencia. Bogotá: Planeta Colombiana, 1989.
Los caminos a Roma. Bogotá: Planeta Colombiana, 1988.
Los días azules. Bogotá: Planeta Colombiana, 1987.
El fuego secreto. Bogotá: Planeta Colombiana, 1987.

CRITICISM

Foster, David William, *Gay and Lesbian Themes in Latin American Writing,* 124–128. Austin: University of Texas Press, 1991.
———. Review of *Los caminos a Roma. Revista de estudios colombianos* 7 (1989): 63–64.
Pineda-Botero, Alvaro. *Del mito a la postmodernidad: La novela colombiana del siglo XX,* 114–117. Bogotá: Tercer Mundo Editores, 1990.

Steven M. DuPouy

VARGAS VICUÑA, ELEODORO (Peru; 1924) _____

Vargas Vicuña, born in Acombamba de Tarma, a small town in the Peruvian highlands of the province of Arequipa, is a representative of Lima's marginal gay bohemia. Like the Mexican novelist Juan Rulfo (1918–1986), he wrote a brief work designed to promote an understanding of the deep reality of the human being; he has not published anything since then. Vargas Vicuña writes in order to come to terms with a body from which he seems about to separate. He is an immigrant from the highlands who lives in Lima and writes about the people he knows, their origins, and their forms of existence.

Vargas Vicuña considers that the fullness of existence is poetry, which explains why his short stories and poems have a subdued poetic atmosphere in which each animal, plant, hill, person and spirit takes on a meaning charged with earthy vitality. His writings represent a subtle work with language in which the syntax is underlain by Quechua. Yet unlike the writings of fellow Peruvian

José María Arguedas (1911–1969), Vargas Vicuña's Spanish is polished and concentrated. He recovers the sententious speech of the peasant and elaborates a magic, mythical map of the agrarian world. The sensations come from a harmonious agony stemming from the cycles of animal and vegetable life. Sexuality is understood as a mysterious energy that travels throughout all of life's elements proper to the world of the highland inhabitant.

In "Un grano de sal" (A Grain of Salt), from the series "El cristal con que se mira" (The Crystal in Which You Can See Yourself; in *Ñahuin*), a disembodied gaze is cast over the dead, and specifically over the city of Lima as the place where Peruvians from all over the country migrate to die. Here Vargas Vicuña examines the multiplicity of sex, the energy that surges through diverse matter, the copulation of the animals that carry on the ritual of life and death. The sense of all his narrative is summarized in one Quechuan word, *ñahuin* (her/his eyes), a transformation of the word *ñawi* (first leaves, the beginning of the creative order). The anxious eyes that order the narrative are similar to characters in other short stories: they want to know their reality, their identity. This permanent search answers to a cosmic sense of creation that it is very important to safeguard today. Against the threats of the technological world destroying nature, the wise and loving words of Vargas Vicuña's people are heard. They are corporeal words of creation that deserve to be heard for their clear tenderness.

WORKS

Ñahuin. Narraciones ordinarias (del amor, la pasión, el agua, la tierra, el árbol, el viento, el toro y el hombre) 1950/1975. 2nd ed. Lima: Milla Batres, 1978. Orig. 1975.
Taita Cristo. Lima: Populibros Peruanos, 1963.
Zora, imagen de poesía. Cajamarca, Peru: Departamento de Publicaciones de UNTC, 1971.

CRITICISM

Delgado, Washington. "La subyugante intensidad poética de Vargas Vicuña. Prólogo." In Vargas Vicuña, *Ñahuin*, 17–21.
Forgues, Roland. "El sentido adánico de la creación. Entrevista a Eleodoro Vargas Vicuña." In his *Palabra viva*, 1.51–63. Lima: Studium, 1988.

Roberto J. Forns-Broggi

VARO, CARLOS (Spain–Puerto Rico; 1936) _____

Carlos Varo was born in Ría de Arosa, a small fishing town in the Spanish province of Pontevedra in Galicia. Educated primarily in Jesuit schools, after his graduation from high school, he enrolled in a Jesuit novitiate in Veruela, in the northern region of Aragon. That experience, "spiritually and aesthetically sublime," took place in the same monastery where the Spanish Romantic poet, Gustavo Adolfo Bécquer, wrote his *Cartas desde mi celda* (Letters from My Cell; 1864) during his recuperation from tuberculosis. A year later, Varo was sent to Cochabamba, Bolivia, where he studied Quechua and the humanities. Two years later he was transferred to the Instituto Superior de Humanidades Clásicas, where in 1959 he obtained a doctoral degree. In 1961 he left the Society of Jesus, a traumatic decision; "my heart still bleeds," he has said.

In 1966 Varo accepted an invitation to teach literature at the University of Puerto Rico. His published doctoral dissertation, *Génesis y evolución del Quijote* (Genesis and Evolution of *Don Quixote*), in 1967 received the Isidoro Bonsoms Prize from the Diputación de Barcelona (Barcelona City Council). In 1970 he became a visiting professor at the City University of New York and Barnard College. Since 1977 he has been in Puerto Rico, teaching the humanities and comparative literature at the Colegio Universitario Tecnológico de Bayamón. Varo is also the founder and director of *Plural,* a multidisciplinary journal for the University of Puerto Rico's college system.

Varo has stressed that his Jesuit education, with its emphasis on spirituality and the humanities, is evident in *Rosa mystica* (Mystical Rose; 1987), his first novel. An observer of human behavior, he says that the work came into existence by "accident." Varo had heard about a beautiful woman (in reality a transsexual) who had captivated Tangier's society. In response to that story Varo remarked that transsexuals traditionally have chosen between opposite pathlike life-styles: either that of a devoted and faithful wife or that of a prostitute. He added that sex-altering operations will be believable only when a "queer, after a sex-change becomes a nun with perpetual chastity vows."

In this spiritually and socially subversive text Varo's initial purpose was to create a short story in the tradition of François Rabelais, Voltaire, or Denis Diderot's *La religieuse* (The Nun; 1760); but he soon realized that his "festive and irreverent" story required the broader dimension of a novel for its confrontation of "the sacred and the profane, the divine and the human in a religious crisis where my own faith had to be rethought." *Rosa mystica* may be viewed as a traditional "thesis novel," with numerous texts drawn from Western and Eastern philosophical and literary sources that give weight to the arguments analyzed. The novel also openly deconstructs human sexuality—specifically, the object of homosexual desire—in a burlesque game of gender voices (biased and unbiased) and presents a reinterpretation of the body politic.

Unorthodox male characters (women have no important roles in the plot) portray various degrees of abusive conditions that lead to gender-role plays. This is the case of the two protagonists, Rosa Mystica and Divina. The first, formerly Antoñito, is a turn-of-the-century Spanish orphan in a shelter run by nuns who initiate him into the pleasures of religious cross-dressing as he delightedly plays angels of dubious gender and impersonates novice nuns; later he is raped by an uncle who has adopted him. As if following a call, at age twenty-five he abandons the family fortune, self-induces a mental sex change and lives as a self-created nun. Rosa Mystica undergoes a series of exorcisms, receives training in spiritual exercises, builds a shelter for abused women and experiences a mystic death, including the ultimate mystical kiss.

Rosa Mystica's counterpart, Divina, a Puerto Rican drag queen, presents the theme of the delicate boundaries of gender identity and sexual pleasure. Perhaps the most tragic and most crudely presented story (with clear echoes of contemporary Puerto Rican neorealism) is that of a lower-class macho peasant who becomes involved in drug trafficking, is arrested, is forced to become a ''woman'' in jail, and, subsequently, becomes a world-famous transvestite. In a literary game of supposed identities, the burlesque elements in *Rosa mystica* come alive through the cross-dressing of male and female voices. There are two unusual plot lines: Puerto Rican sexual codes, physically exhibited by a transvestite; and the body/temple dichotomy of the religious experience, sustained by a transsexual mystic. These build a semiotic text in which the discursive power of traditional sexual signs is interpreted, allowing the existence of a homoerotic discourse in these two opposed environments. Unconventional as it may seem, real cross-gender texts are present—for example, those of John of the Cross, the homoerotic mystic poet ironically described by Teresa de Jesús as *medio fraile* (half a friar). As for Divina, a self-created and self-taught cabaret singer and dancer, her cross-dressing instructs her in her role as a woman, experimenting with sources of sexual pleasure unknown, or at least unexplored, by traditional women.

Clearly, *Rosa mystica*, in Michel Foucault's terms, leads to the ''transformation of sex into discourse.'' Varo has proposed to become a storyteller like those in the Djemaa el-Fna, a plaza in Marrakesh, a raconteur or ''herald of a gospel, of good tidings.'' Toward that goal, his ongoing project is a novel titled ''En soledad, de amor herido'' (In Solitude, Wounded by Love), inspired by a poem by John of the Cross. It narrates the secret homosexual biography of Juba II, the Roman-raised king of Mauritania Tingitana (Tangier). In Varo's own words, this project proposes to ''elevate the theme of homosexuality, both in aesthetics, in literature, and in dignity and respect,'' since Juba II was well-known and respected, and the author of numerous learned books in Greek. Varo's novel, researched and developed for an expected period of six to eight years, will go against the social stereotypes, presenting ''a furious and crazy faggot, a mischievous queer, a suicidal gay, mentally ill people whose genitals are gleaned by the neurotic pimp.''

WORKS

Génesis y evolución del Quijote. Madrid: Alcalá, 1968.
Rosa mystica. Barcelona: Seix Barral, 1987.
  All quotations are from a questionnaire answered by Varo in December 1992.

Rafael Ocasio

VEGA, ANA LYDIA (Puerto Rico; 1946) ———————

Vega is an essayist, short story writer, coauthor of a movie script and professor who was born in Santurce. She has won several literary prizes, including Cuba's Casa de las Américas (House of the Americas) and Mexico's Juan Rulfo Internacional. Her narrative style is marked by the humorous incorporation of Puerto Rican slang, elements of contemporary popular Puerto Rican culture, the use of Spanglish and elevated prose. Her intentions are not merely ludicrous, and she is aware of the responsibility she has as a woman writer of a colonized island.

Vega focuses on the candid presentation of women's issues. Cellulitis, varicose veins and housecleaning are important components of a woman's life, just like feminism, equal rights, sexual liberation and a straightforward view of the macho man. She also deals with the problems of migration to the mainland, exile, uprooted families, racism and misunderstanding among the islanders of the Caribbean. Her writings reveal a profound respect for the rights and liberties of all human beings. Some passages demonstrate her sensibility to the harassment faced by lesbians. Others suggest that perhaps heterosexual relationships are not for everybody. The protagonist of "Puerto Príncipe abajo" (Going Down Port-au-Prince) in *Vírgenes y mártires* (Virgins and Martyrs; 1981), is a black Puerto Rican teacher with nationalist inclinations who wins a trip to Haiti. Her fellow travelers are "matronas urbanizadas . . . con los maridos a cuesta" (92; urban matrons with their husbands on their backs). Because she is alone, she immediately becomes the focus of interest, gossip and speculation, and the narrative implies that a stereotypical heterosexual middle-class person quickly assigns labels, with no regard for the feelings of the nonconventional other. In this passage Vega demonstrates that sexual misconceptions are just as crippling as political or racial persecutions.

In the story "Tres aeróbicos para el amor" (Three Love Aerobics) in *Pasión de historia y otras historias de pasión* (Passion for History and Other Stories of Passion; 1987), the text goes further in suggesting sexual possibilities other than those offered by heterosexual relationships, which are not always satisfactory. The story is divided into three parts. Una, the protagonist of the first section, is a divorced, middle-aged woman who needs the male's gaze to feel like a woman. The second section has El and Ella (He and She) as protagonists. These two seem to be lovers and become sexually excited by telling each other of their sexual exploits, which include porno movies, orgies, voyeuristic experiences, anal penetration, lesbian experimentation and intercourse with fruits and animals.

The third section is the most interesting. A first-person-plural voice tells the story, and the reader is led to assume that a very satisfied couple narrates how they have been together for ten years, whereas the rest of the world is divorced or in the process of getting a divorce. Their friends are very annoyed because they cannot unveil the secret of the success of this marriage. The narrative voice is made up of three people. Here the author suggests the possibility of a variety of sexual and social arrangements, not just those dictated by a limiting tradition.

To date the explicit presentation of lesbian or heterosexual issues is not the central concern of Vega's writing, yet there is profound respect and acceptance whenever they are addressed. Tolerance of sexual differences is part of Vega's philosophy of writing and choice of topics.

WORKS

Encancaranublado y otros cuentos de naufragio. 3rd ed. Río Piedras, P.R.: Editorial Antillana, 1983.
Falsas crónicas del sur. Río Piedras: Editorial de la Universidad de Puerto Rico, 1991.
Pasión de historia y otras historias de pasión. Buenos Aires: Ediciones de la Flor, 1987.
El tramo ancla: Ensayos puertorriqueños de hoy. Ed. Ana Lydia Vega. Río Piedras: Editorial de la Universidad de Puerto Rico, 1988.
Vírgenes y mártires. Río Piedras, P.R.: Editorial Antillana, 1981.

CRITICISM

Barradas, Efraín. "La necesaria innovación de Ana Lydia Vega: Preámbulo para lectores vírgenes." *Revista iberoamericana* 51.132–133 (1985): 547–556.
Handelsman, Michael H. "Desnudando al macho: Un análisis de 'Letra para salsa y tres sonetos por encargo.' " *Revista/Review interamericana* 12.4 (1982–1983): 559–564.
Panico, Marie J. "Dos escritoras puertorriqueños: Entrevistas a Ana Lydia Vega y Myrna Casas." *Revista del Instituto de cultura puertorriqueña* 97 (1987): 43–46.
Romero, Ivette. "The Voice Recaptured: Fiction by Dany Bebel-Gisler and Ana Lydia Vega." *Journal of Caribbean Studies* 8.3 (1992): 159–165.
Santos Silva, Loreina. " 'Cuatro selecciones por una peseta': Patrones de sexismo machista." *Revista/Review interamericana* 12.4 (1982–1983): 515–520.
Vélez, Diana L. " 'Pollito Chicken': Split Subjectivity, National Identity and the Articulation of Female Sexuality in a Narrative by Ana Lydia Vega." *The Americas Review* 14.2 (1986): 68–76.

Mary Ann Gosser-Esquilín

VILLANUEVA, ALFREDO (Puerto Rico; 1944)

Alfredo Villanueva was born in Puerto Rico but moved at an early age to Caracas, Venezuela. He has lived in New York City since the early 1970s, and is a professor of English at Hostos Community College in the South Bronx.

Villanueva has written short stories, literary criticism and poetry in Spanish and English. As a literary critic, he has published extensively on the relationship between sexuality and power in the Latin American novel. His short stories deal with (homo)sexual experience(s), as well as the Puerto Rican experience in Puerto Rico and the United States. These thematic interests are at the core of his seven books of poetry: *Las transformaciones del vidrio* (The Transformations of Glass; 1984), *Grimorio* (Book of Spells; 1988), *En el imperio de la papa frita* (The Potato Chip Empire; 1987), *La guerrilla fantasma* (The Ghost Guerilla; 1989), *La voz de la mujer que llevo dentro* (The Voice of the Woman Inside Me; 1990), *Pato Salvaje* (Wild Duck; 1991) and "Angel en el circo" (Angel in the Circus; 1986).

The theme of homosexual love appears impressionistically throughout *Las transformaciones del vidrio*. At the center of this first book is the concept of transformation, essential to the poetics of Villanueva. Here, the lyric subject contemplates different objects, particularly iridescent vases but also a man sleeping next to the speaker. It is nighttime, and the interplay of light and darkness erases borderlines and definitions. Everything is movement and becoming. A glass—and a poem—is a fragment of movement.

The idea of transformation is implicit in the title of the second book, *Grimorio*—the alchemist's book of magic with instructions for transmuting base metals into gold. In this book of poems, the lyric voice is not the passive observer (or at times the observed one) of *Las transformaciones*. It now assumes an active (and at times aggressive) role of an alchemist/magician seeking to transmute his experience of (homosexual) love into poetry.

Grimorio is a book of love poetry. But since it exposes the artificial borders between the realm of the personal and the realm of the political, it is also a book about sexual politics. (The author confesses his admiration for French feminism in the prologue, which he calls "a guerrilla text.") The gold of love, sex and poetry is covered with the excrement of politics/power. The poet/alchemist must unveil and extract it. Poetry (as well as lovemaking and growing up) is purification: not the end result, but the continuous process of becoming, of which a sexual encounter, an act of love or a poem is a fragment.

From *Grimorio* on, Villanueva's poetry embraces the search, the way, with its anguish, excrement and joy. By accepting the risks of aesthetic impurities and rejecting the pure metaphor as the ultimate aim of poetry, his poetic language is galvanized with the urgency of a mocking prophet, part Diogenes, part Jeremiah. The eye/I that in *Las transformaciones* observes/is observed at night in a room full of all sorts of glass objects becomes in *Grimorio* the eye/I of the magician capable of separating the macho from the man, of restoring the pleasure to the text/body. It becomes in *El imperio de la papa frita* the cynical lantern of a displaced Diogenes, revealing the spectacle of Puerto Rico according to the myths and realities of the colony. In *La guerrilla fantasma* it is the terrifying notes of a requiem for the "vast cemetary that is America," a countersong to

Neruda's *Canto general* (General Song; 1950), composed/decomposed by a Jeremiah–Verdi while it emerges as a hermaphrodite in *La voz de la mujer que llevo dentro*, looking through the eye/I of its multiple sexuality at the politics of gender, including the politics of feminism. Even in books like *El imperio* and *La guerrilla*, in which the theme of (homo)sexuality is not at the center of the text, sexual politics is the generating discourse. Imperialism, war, assassination, sexism—all are manifestations of the patriarchal order.

Villanueva's most recent book, *Pato salvaje*, is a tribute to his lover of seventeen years who died in 1988, and a diary of the AIDS plague. Like *Grimorio*, it is a book of love poetry (for Víctor Amador) and a book of political/social poetry for the homosexuals dying of/living with AIDS. If *Grimorio* begins by separating the object of the poems from the rejected possibilities, *Pato salvaje* begins by defining the lyric subject: a scared, mature man in front of the mirror, weaving a shroud with words for his own body/corpse and for the others. The text continues by separating the poet it takes to write the poems that follow from the coward–poets. If *Grimorio* is a book of homosexual love as well as the diary of a homosexual person/poet, *Pato salvaje* is, like *La guerrilla*, a book of death, the death of loved ones and the death of the poet. Like *Grimorio*, *Pato salvaje* is a book of transformations, a book of magic. At the end, the man in the mirror, the poet/fly who sings/sees the dead everywhere, will join the flock of wild ducks guided by his lover, after singing his own death in a duo with Puerto Rican poet Julia de Burgos, after prophesying with Jeremiah the holocaust of the tribe, after officiating a mass for the dead, after experiencing the mystical processes of the alchemy of nature and after conducting his dead like a modern day Hermes. If *Grimorio* provides instructions on how to live and love as a homosexual, *Pato salvaje* instructs on how to live, love and die proudly, liberated. The fly trapped in the greased paper of the mirror (your death, my death, your death), is transmuted by the poet/alchemist into a wild duck flying free in the last page of his book, conducting an ever-increasing flock for the V of Víctor Amador, the "Vicky Lover" of *La voz de la mujer que llevo dentro*. In the process the *pato* (literally, duck, but in Puerto Rico, faggot) is transformed from the passive, victimized domestic animal that eats scum and is slaughtered and stewed, into a free, wild being.

WORKS

"Angel en el circo." 1986. Unpublished ms.
En el imperio de la papa frita. Santo Domingo: Colmena, 1989.
Grimorio. Barcelona: Murmurios, 1988.
La guerrilla fantasma. New York: Moria, 1989.
"Machismo vs Gayness: Latin American Fiction." *Gay Sunshine* 29–30 (1976): 22.
Pato salvaje. New York: Arcas, 1991.
Las transformaciones del vidrio. Mexico City: Oasis, 1985.
La voz la mujer que llevo dentro. New York: Arcas, 1990.

CRITICISM

Cancel, Mario R. "Para una poética del exilio: La poesía de Alfredo Villanueva." *Claridad (en rojo)*, April 14–20, 1989, p. 24.

Justicia, Teresa. "Exile as 'Permanent Pain': Alfredo Villanueva's *El imperio de la papa frita.*" In *Paradise Lost or Regained: The Literature of Hispanic Exile*, 183–191. Ed. Fernando Alegría and Jorge Rufinelli. Houston: Arte Público, 1991.

Rodríguez-Matos, Carlos A. "Apuntes para un acercamiento a la poesía puertorriqueña contemporánea, 1962–1986." *Revista del Instituto de cultura puertorriqueña* 94 (1986): 45–55.

Torres-Saillant, Silvio. "Overview of Three Immigrant Writers." *Punto 7 Review* 2 (1989): 147–152.

Trempe, Lady Rojas. "*La guerrilla fantasma.*" *Explicación de textos literarios* 19.2 (1990–1991): 93–95.

Carlos A. Rodríguez-Matos

VILLAURRUTIA, XAVIER (Mexico; 1903–1950)

Villaurrutia, who was born in Mexico City, belongs to the avant-garde poetry group called Los Contemporáneos (The Contemporaries). As a founder of the Ulises (Ulysses) theater organization (1928), he attempted to renew the Mexican stage by writing modern plays, training actors who were able to perform non-melodramatic and slapstick plays and teaching a new generation of theatergoers to understand the artistic forms of modernity. He also founded Grupo de Orientación (Orientation Group) in 1932 and other small theater groups in the 1930s and 1940s, in an attempt to create a valid, authentic and modernist Mexican theatrical tradition. In his private papers Villaurrutia wrote:

Anyone who pauses to consider how poor life is will be deeply hurt. And, if the anxiety of his soul does not make him follow the blind path of everyday ugliness, deafening him to the horrible noises of present-day mechanical existence, he will find it necessary to convey that hurt in Art. He will find a way to forget, and even though it is fleeting, it will be more desirable than reality. Reality makes existence an unbearable spectacle, a play for people with no more sense than their own common sense. (*Obras*, 601)

Nostalgia de la muerte (Nostalgia for Death; 1938) is Villaurrutia's most famous collection of poems. "Nocturno amor" (Love Nocturne) is an outstanding poem formed by new images in Spanish (the armpit, ear and artery as synecdoches of the body and the mouth as a metonymy of sex) to tell a story of the passion and conflict between lovers. "Nocturno de los ángeles" (Nocturne of the Angels) is a poem about the gay world of sailors in Los Angeles. Other important poems in this regard are "Nocturno mar" (Sea Nocturne) and "Nocturno de la alcoba" (Nocturne of the Bedroom).

In prose Villaurrutia wrote *Dama de corazones* (Queen of Hearts; 1928), a Proustian exercise. *El amor es así* (Love Is Like That; ca. 1930) is a melodrama about the life of working-class immigrants in Mexico City. *Variedad* (Variety; ca. 1930) is a key text for understanding the influence of André Gide on the Contemporáneos group, for it was through Gide's example that these poets gave artistic and literary expression to their homosexuality. *Cartas de Villaurrutia a Novo* (Letters from Villaurrutia to Novo; 1966) is a collection of letters important for their literary qualities that Villaurrutia sent to Salvador Novo while Villaurrutia was studying theater at Yale University in the mid-1930s.

Autos profanos (Profane Acts; 1943) is a collection of one-act plays. *¿En qué piensas?* (What Are You Thinking?; 1938) is interesting because critics, following what the male characters in the play say, consider it to be a study about the ideal woman, whose main characteristic is that she is unable to think. But the plot reveals the opposite; María Luisa is in control, and she is in charge of deconstructing the notion of romantic love. *Sea usted breve* (Be Brief; 1938) uses absurd elements to denounce an attempt by authorities to promote birth control without taking into account the opinion of women. The play works with the official construction of feminine gender, and criticizes the public concealment of the prostitute (herself a product of machismo) and the compulsoriness of marriage for women. *El ausente* (The Absent Man; 1943) criticizes machismo among the working class and advocates the right of women to live by themselves.

La mulata de Córdoba (The Mulatto Woman from Córdoba; 1939) is a melodrama by Villaurrutia and his male companion, the painter Agustín Lazo. Written in the style of the Mexican movie scripts of the 1930s, it uses melodrama in the attempt to resolve the social conflicts of the period. This technique enables the authors to write about issues, like gender, that had been neglected by the novel focusing on the Revolution of 1910. The opera version of this play elevates the popular culture of the golden age of Mexican cinema to the rank of high culture. *La hiedra* (Ivy; 1941) is a Victorian drama whose main purpose is to Mexicanize bourgeois European high culture. *La mujer legítima* (The Legitimate Wife; 1942), *Invitación a la muerte* (Invitation to Death; 1943) and *El yerro candente* (The Burning Error; 1944) are bourgeois dramas based on Greek myths with powerful heroines, an effective strategy for depicting dysfunctional families; at the same time they present the family as the site where conflicts must be solved. *El pobre Barba Azul* (Poor Blue Beard; 1946) and *Juego peligroso* (Dangerous Game; 1949) are comedies that present the problems of family and gender construction, although in a comic way. Villaurrutia wrote more than five hundred movie reviews and examples of the *género chico* (little genre; a hybrid genre similar to the cabaret sketch). He was also a literary and art critic. He and the other members of the Contemporáneos opened Mexican literature to the most important tendencies of the twentieth century.

As a gay writer, Villaurrutia challenged the definition of gender given by the Mexican Revolution: the combination of indigenous and Hispanic machismo, along with the virility of the Soviet Revolution, ended up in the petit bourgeois conservatism of Manuel Ávila Camacho's presidency (1940–1946). In order to mount his challenge, Villaurrutia introduced into Mexico a European modernity with the feminine/homoerotic prose of Marcel Proust and André Gide, with its sensitive male characters and modern women. In theater he postulated a markedly sophisticated upper-class melodrama with similarly marked characters that stood in opposition to the traditional drama of honor, with its rigidly defined male and female roles. Villaurrutia's melodramas blur such roles, for example, in the use of wit and the image of active women.

But while in many cases Villaurrutia's prose and theater are intellectual exercises, in his poetry he sets aside any stance of distance in order to focus on a personalized or autobiographical subjectivity in an urban and urbane context. In this context his use of humor and popular culture finds its justification: these are realms not dominated by the emergent conservative middle class, but spaces with greater freedom in gender and class issues. Because of the nature of power relations in Mexico City, based on an opposition between oppressor and oppressed, the possibility of a gay writer making use of public spaces, such as the theater or newspapers, and solidifying his status as a professional writer becomes essential to his survival and the recognition of his writing.

WORKS

Cartas de Villaurrutia a Novo. Mexico City: Instituto Nacional de Bellas Artes, 1966.
Obras. 2nd ed. Ed. Miguel Capistrán, Alí Chumacero and Luis Mario Schneider. Mexico City: Fondo de Cultura Económica, 1966.

CRITICISM

Blanco, José Joaquín. "La crítica de Villaurrutia." In his *La paja en el ojo ajeno: Ensayos de crítica*, 81–92. Puebla, Mexico: Universidad Autónoma de Puebla, 1980.
Dauster, Frank. *Xavier Villaurrutia*. New York: Twayne, 1971.
Paz, Octavio. "Xavier se escribe con equis." In Xavier Villaurrutia, *Antología*, 91–61. Ed. Octavio Paz. Mexico City: Fondo de Cultura Económica, 1991.

Salvador A. Oropesa

VIÑAS, DAVID (Argentina; 1929) ⸻⸻⸻

Viñas has dealt with the problems of homoerotic and homosocial relationships since his first novel, *Los años despiadados* (The Merciless Years; 1956). He is one of the few Latin American writers to explore the relationship of males to themselves in terms of a feminine/masculine topography of their bodies; to create a homosexual bildungsroman, fearlessly examining the relationship between male sexuality and military institutions; and to study the social role of homosexuals in Argentinean society and culture.

Los años despiadados, one of the best descriptions of homosexual awakening, tells the story of Rubén, a twelve-year-old who is gang-raped by a band of street urchins. His father, an invalid for many years, dies, and Rubén is left with his mother and sister. After the father's funeral, the man with whom Rubén rides to the cemetery tries to fondle him. Rubén wants to be hard like his friend Mario, the janitor's son, who becomes his male role model and teaches him about masturbation. Mario assumes the dominant role in their relationship by the time-honored macho method of beating Rubén up. Rubén, however, is powerful through the use of the imaginative faculty, and he lures Mario by allowing him to explore the countless trunks filled with objects from his family's past.

Mario dresses up in petticoats and thus gives Rubén a measure of masculinity by becoming a girl in his eyes. Afterward, Mario exposes himself to Rubén. The gang rape occurs when Rubén leaves home, searching for Mario, and finds him with his friends, who tease them about their relationship. Among machos in groups, females are objects to be shared; Mario cannot and does not rebel against the code. The boys beat Rubén up because he is blond, white and weak. Rubén's father and a neighbor girl already had questioned his maleness. Rubén is not safe from women either; coming home after the rape, bruised and bleeding, he is stopped by a woman who performs fellatio on him. The novel ends with Rubén's discovery of his body as an object of desire and power, and with Mario's tormented surrender to Rubén's will.

Dar la cara (Show Your Face; 1962) begins with a homosexual rape among army recruits the night before they are released from duty. The victim is singled out because of his whiteness and softness. Later on, some intellectuals discuss homosexuality; one of them attacks queers: they are loud, promiscuous and overprotective of each other. Another defends them, pointing out that they have the courage to show they do not believe in dominant discourse. A third, De Vito, himself a homosexual, states that all sexuality is a private affair and that no one has a right to discuss it.

De Vito is a loner, but he is also a survivor. He cruises the streets looking for a sex partner, either a James Dean or a Marlon Brando. Boy prostitutes make fun of him as he goes by: male whores must humiliate their clients. Gloeber, a friend, reports that he has been picked up by the police, but refuses to be humbled. Gloeber blames homosexuals for corruption in government, but he is last seen allowing De Vito to kiss him in public. Pelusa, an actress, serves as Viñas's mouthpiece by stating that homosexuals are no worse off than blacks or Jews.

In *Jauría* (Pack of Dogs; 1974), Viñas explores the pathology of the macho. Simón, the protagonist, equates weapons with the phallus. He forces a soldier to suck the barrel of his gun and remarks that killing a man is like fucking a woman. He rapes a young boy before killing him. Conversely, for the macho to be wounded or killed means becoming like a woman. Any subordinate position affects the macho's sexual identity. Arminia, Simón's prostitute girlfriend, summarizes Simón's submissive sexual relationship to the General, whom he later kills. The relationship between softness, youth and effeminacy had already been explored by Viñas in *Los dueños de la tierra* (The Owners of the Land; 1958), in which a young criminal develops an attachment to an older man, a labor organizer. Their relationship is carefully underplayed, with no hints of physical intimacy. The younger man shows his feelings for the older man by dying in his place, which effectively ends and immortalizes the relationship.

In *Los hombres de a caballo* (Men on Horseback; 1968) Viñas explores the homoerotic drives of the military in a manner reminiscent of Mario Vargas Llosa. These professional soldiers are obsessed with the size and shape of the phallus, which they view as the objective correlative of the virtues associated with their way of life. They dream of having penises as long as their rifles. At the same time, they are obsessed with fear of queers, who must be beaten up and raped at every possible opportunity. When the protagonist, Emilio, is making love to his girlfriend, she threatens to turn him into a queer by assuming an active role (possibly by fellatio). Emilio, on the other hand, shows an unconscious capacity for responding erotically to men, as he does when given a body rub by a masseur. Sex between men happens only when one male wants totally to humiliate another; however, Viñas makes it clear that both parties enjoy the game. Cadets learn to dance with one another, underlining the sexual ambiguity and paradoxical nature of male desire in Viñas's novels: only through violence are males able to express homoerotic desires and act upon them.

WORKS

Los años despiadados. Buenos Aires: Letras Universitarias, 1956.
Cosas concretas. Buenos Aires: Editorial Tiempo Contemporáneo, 1969.
Dar la cara. Buenos Aires: Editorial Jamcana, 1962.
Los dueños de la tierra. Buenos Aires: Editorial Schapire, 1967.
Los hombres de a caballo. Mexico City: Siglo XXI, 1968.
Jauría. Buenos Aires: Granica Editor, 1974.
La semana trágica. Buenos Aires: Ediciones Siglo XX, 1975.

CRITICISM

Rosa, Nicolás. "Sexo y novela: David Viñas." In his *Crítica y significación*, 7–99. Buenos Aires: Editorial Galerna, 1970.

Alfredo Villanueva

W

WACQUEZ, MAURICIO (Chile; 1939) _____

Wacquez has explored gay themes in all of his fiction, although the fiction written in Barcelona in the years since the Chilean coup is more gay-affirmative than his earlier Chilean writings. David William Foster has considered *Toda la luz del mediodía* (All the Light of Midday; 1964), a novel about a ménage à trois, in *Gay and Lesbian Themes in Latin American Writing*. *Paréntesis* (Parenthesis; 1975) concerns two straight couples and their explorations of perversity. *Ella o el sueño de nadie* (She, or the Dream of No One; 1983) is again concerned with a ménage à trois, this one composed of three circus performers, Reina, Marcio and Julián. I will focus here on what I consider Wacquez's most audacious novel, *Frente a un hombre armado (Cacerías de 1848)* (Facing an Armed Man [1848 Hunts]; 1981).

Frente a un hombre armado is a sort of gay male *Orlando*, a historical novel that sweeps from 1848 through World War II to Mexico and Algeria. Narrated by a French aristocrat, Juan de Warni, it revolves around the central images of hunting and being hunted, considered as sexual possession and class exploitation. The interest of the novel resides in the way the historical reflection on class struggle, violence and treachery is linked with a more intimate reflection on seduction and sexual possession. Wacquez relates the revolutions of 1848 to the French Revolution of 1789, though he presents the events of 1848 as a pretext for revenge by the aristocrats. The narrator and the mysterious Prince under whom he serves in the latter half of the book are sodomites and aesthetes whose tastes run to the lower classes. The central romance in the novel (as in D. H. Lawrence's *Lady Chatterley's Lover* and E. M. Forster's *Maurice*) is between social unequals: Juan de Warni becomes involved with Alexandre, a young peasant who is one of his attendants on his hunting parties.

The link between desire and death (so eloquently explored by Georges Bataille) is further developed in the text in an explanation provided by an unidentified (and not wholly convincing) second narrator, who informs the reader that the greater part of the novel occurs in Juan de Warni's mind in the instant after he has been shot by Alexandre. If this assertion is true, Juan dies at the moment he first feels transfixed by desire, and the rest of the action is a utopian or dystopian projection into the near and more distant future, a future in which that desire is realized repeatedly, with all the permutations and combinations permitted in erotic literature. If the second narrator's assertion is false, it is a castrating gesture by a puritanical censor who arrives too late to thwart the reader's pleasure, although the interruption may provoke reflection and guilt. In any case, what is interesting about the constellation provided in the novelistic situation—desire/sexual violence/death—is the eroticization of death and the linking of violence and desire. The hunting metaphor that runs throughout the novel (even the later sequences when the old aristocratic order has finally crumbled and Juan de Warni has become a fierce and willing mercenary) offers a vision of homosexual desire that is inextricably linked to exploitation and death. As such, it can hardly be offered as the most liberated example of gay fiction. Yet precisely the upsetting or unsettling aspects of the book are the ones that demand discussion.

At one point Warni describes an encounter with a soldier with whom "se deja sodomizar como una imagen santa" (he lets himself be sodomized as if he were a holy image), a phrase in which the lack of a precise equivalence—due to the fact that marble or wooden images of saints are not frequently penetrated—again evokes a symbolic equivalence between mystical rapture and anal penetration. As in much erotic literature, the preliminaries to sexual intercourse are more satisfying than possession. Since possession is linked in the novel to subjugation, desire exists as such only until it is interrupted by physical contact. The verb used to describe Juan de Warni's looking at Alexandre—*contemplar* (contemplate)—opposes contemplation to action, glance to touch, much as the religious imagery already examined links sex with mystical rapture.

Perhaps the most disturbing of the erotic scenes in the book involves Juan de Warni, his mother and his patron, the Prince. The scene begins with the Prince making love to Juan's mother, who is holding her young son. Then the Prince forces the child to perform oral sex. The Prince penetrates the boy, who in turn penetrates his mother; the mother is so excited by this development that the previous stages of the sexual encounter seem to her no more than grotesque parodies of pleasure. That the scene is ultimately attributed by Warni to a nightmare suffered by his mother only displaces the erotic jolt, leaving unresolved the manner in which Warni came to know—or invent—his mother's dreams.

Since the sexual encounters are presented from Juan de Warni's point of view and are expressions of his obsession with power, the only alternative really offered to that other, to Alexandre, is murdering his master. What is troubling about the end of the novel is that it suggests that this murder also is a fantasy controlled by Juan, yet another means for maintaining his dominant position. In the last of the many versions offered of the death scene, after Juan has been shot by Alexandre, he manages to inflict a mortal wound on his servant, and as they bleed to death together, Juan reflects "that force is only force, that, outside of imagination and dreaming, it cannot be thought as a complement or ornament to pleasure, that ultimately force does not arise except as an absolute, inevitable evil, to flee from which he had to weave together a future in which all the dangers would be exorcised at the very moment they threatened him" (250). This conclusion is another utopian projection into the future, but one in which the bourgeois subject is still very much in control.

WORKS

Cinco y una ficciones. Santiago, Chile: Aranciba Hermanos, 1963.
Ella o el sueño de nadie. Barcelona: Tusquets, 1983.
Excesos. Santiago, Chile: Editorial Universitaria, 1971.
Frente a un hombre armado (cacerías de 1848). Barcelona: Bruguera, 1981.
Paréntesis. Barcelona: Barral, 1975.
Toda la luz del mediodía. Santiago, Chile: Zig-Zag, 1964.

CRITICISM

Donoso, José. "Prólogo." In Wacquez, *Paréntesis,* 9–14.
Foster, David William. *Gay and Lesbian Themes in Latin American Writing,* 58–61. Austin: University of Texas Press, 1991.
Marco, Joaquín. "Mauricio Wacquez, *Frente a un hombre armado* (1981)." In his *Literatura hispanoamercana: Del modernismo a nuestros días,* 469–473. Madrid: Espasa-Calpe, 1987.
Santos, Danilo. "Aproximación a una novela de Mauricio Wacquez, *Frente a un hombre armado*: Indagación del lenguaje en torno a la muerte y el erotismo." *Revista chilena de literatura* 41 (1993): 119–122.

Daniel Balderston

WILCOCK, JUAN RODOLFO
(Argentina; 1919–1978) ──────────────

Wilcock was a highly esteemed young writer, particularly known as a poet, when he went into exile, first in England, then in Italy, in 1953 (he died in Lubriano). His homosexuality had as much to do with his decision to go into exile as his opposition to Juan Perón's government. During his two decades in Italy, Wilcock became an Italian writer of considerable importance, a friend of Alberto Moravia and Pier Paolo Pasolini; he published a dozen books in Italian. He also appeared in Pasolini's *Gospel* in the role of the head rabbi. Some of

Wilcock's Italian poems have appeared in anthologies of gay Italian poetry, and his short stories and novels in that language often explore perversity, sexual or otherwise. This article focuses on Wilcock's production in Spanish, most of which is prior to his Italian work.

Wilcock's initial reputation rested on a series of books of elegant neoromantic poems, many of them love poems. One of the young poet's principal themes is the need to hide his love from the eyes of all but the beloved. The early poems are sometimes addressed to women—"princess," he writes once—but are increasingly gender neutral in their address. *Paseo sentimental* (Sentimental Stroll; 1946) begins with an epigraph from Tennyson's "In Memoriam," a poem famous in part for its guarded expression of homosexual love; the whole of this book avoids identifying the gender of the beloved, a game that, because it is so difficult to sustain in Spanish, is tantamount to an admission that the beloved is male. *Sexto* (Sixth; 1953), the last of Wilcock's books of poems published in Argentina, is again a series of love poems whose homoerotic nature is betrayed only by an occasional reference to Antinoüs or Endymion; it culminates in an epithalamium that imagines the public union of poet and beloved sanctified by Saturnal rites, though the real ending of that story was a suicide and an exile.

In the 1950s Wilcock began to write stories; his Spanish stories were eventually published as *El caos* (Chaos; 1974) and in Italian translation in the same year as *Parsifal*. Of interest here are three stories: "El caos," "La fiesta de los enanos" (The Dwarves' Party) and "La engañosa" (The Deceitful Woman). Their dates are uncertain, but the coded references in some of them to Peronism and existentialism suggest that they were composed in the 1950s. "El caos" is the story of an existentialist philosopher–prince who seeks a hidden order in the universe, only to discover, in a series of ever more absurd and fanciful misadventures, that the only order is chaos. He then gleefully turns his realm into a kingdom of surprises, centered on orgiastic parties at which every religious and sexual preference is equally indulged, people switch professions on whim and the one who enjoys himself the most is the prince, now turned from philosopher to voyeur. "La fiesta de los enanos" tells of the rupture of the idyllic life enjoyed by a wealthy Buenos Aires woman and her two dwarves when the woman's young nephew comes to visit. The dwarves are shocked when the relation between aunt and nephew becomes carnal, and plot revenge for the exclusion they have suffered. The plot goes awry, and the dwarves eventually torture the boy to death. Their orgy of eating, drinking and torturing is narrated with wicked glee, and the effect of Grand Guignol is perhaps unsurpassed in modern Spanish-American literature. "La engañosa" is the misogynistic counterpoint to the story of the dwarves, a tale of misbegotten love between a randy male agricultural worker and a Spanish woman who turns out to have a quite liberal *vulva dentata* and many other unpleasant parts besides. Taken together, the stories of *El caos* reveal Wilcock as a master of a variety of queer discourses, from camp to sadism.

One of Wilcock's Italian works deserves mention here because it is set in

Argentina and rewrites a national myth as polymorphous perversity: *L'ingegnere* (The Engineer; 1975). The narrator of this epistolary novel is a young Buenos Aires engineer who is working in a remote Andean town on the reconstruction of the trans-Andean railroad. In letters to his beloved grandmother, he tells of the events of his daily life, and of the splendid solitary feasts he prepares for himself on holidays like Christmas and Easter. Since nothing is available in the remote location but mutton, he prepares his feasts (but does not tell his grandmother this directly) from the tender flesh of the male children of the railroad workers. The novel plays with echoes of the nineteenth-century nation-building texts about "civilization and savagery," particularly Domingo Sarmiento's *Facundo* (1845) and José Hernández's "Camino trasandino" (The Trans-Andean Railroad; 1872), suggesting that in Argentina, civilization consists of a delicate mixture of cannibalism and pederasty. As Wilcock's farewell to Argentine literature, the novel is an ironic masterpiece.

WORKS

El caos. Buenos Aires: Editorial Sudamericana, 1974.
Ensayos de poesía lírica. Buenos Aires: n.p., 1945.
Los hermosos días. Buenos Aires: Emecé, 1946.
L'ingegnere. Milan: Rizzoli, 1975.
"Introducción." In Ruggero Guarini, *Parodia*, 9–12. Barcelona: Editorial Anagrama, 1981. Essay on pornography.
Libro de poemas y canciones. Buenos Aires: Editorial Sudamericana, 1940.
Il libro dei mostri. Milan: Adelphi Edizioni, 1978.
Paseo sentimental. Buenos Aires: Editorial Sudamericana, 1946.
Persecución de las musas menores. Buenos Aires: n.p., 1945.
Poesie. Milan: Adelphi Edizioni, 1980.
Sexto. Buenos Aires: Emecé, 1953.
La sinagoga degli iconoclasti. Milan: Adelphi Edizioni, 1972.
Lo stereoscopio dei solitari. Milan: Adelphi Edizioni, 1972.

CRITICISM

Balderston, Daniel. "Civilización y barbarie: Un topos reelaborado por J. R. Wilcock." *Discurso literario* 4.1 (1986): 57–61.
———. "Los cuentos crueles de Silvina Ocampo y Juan Rodolfo Wilcock." *Revista iberoamericana* 125 (1983): 743–752.
———. "La literatura antiperonista de J. R. Wilcock." *Revista iberoamericana* 135–136 (1986): 573–581.
———. "Wilcock, el museo de los recuerdos." *Hispamérica* 44 (1986): 55–57.

Daniel Balderston

Z

ZAPATA, LUIS (Mexico; 1951) ⸺⸺⸺⸺⸺⸺⸺⸺

Born in Chilpancingo, Guerrero, Zapata studied at the Universidad Nacional Autónoma de México, where he specialized in medieval French literature. Since the 1970s he has published several collections of short stories, seven novels, a number of works for the theater, and a translation into Spanish of the first gay novel in Latin America, Brazilian Adolfo Caminha's *Bom-Crioulo* (1895). He has been a frequent contributor to several Mexican newspapers and journals, including *Punto de partida* (Point of Departure) and *Alianza francesa* (French Alliance). Zapata, currently living in Cuernavaca, concedes that over the years the greatest influences on his writing have been films.

From his earliest writings through his most recent novel, Zapata's texts raise crucial questions regarding the facile stereotyping of sexual identity by bringing the social margins into the cultural center. In placing what have traditionally been condemned as indecent or obscene human desires at the core of these narratives (Blanco, "Zapata"), Zapata relativizes such polarized categories as his characters examine their feelings and passions in counterpoint to the forces of bourgeois morality that are the source of such negative judgments. Through a consistent emphasis on the dignity and respectability—which also indicate a literary "worthiness"—of the erotic, the sensual and the sexual, his works must be viewed as liberating influences on the taboos of Mexican culture that have censored positive portraits of gay life out of so-called serious literature by relegating such topics to the realm of tabloid sensationalism, cantina stories, graffiti and caricature.

This is not to say that Zapata promotes a division between elite and popular notions of culture; on the contrary, as he strives to incorporate discourses on sexuality into different genres, he does so by using lively dialogue, colloquial expressions, biting humor and the wordplay so frequently found in spoken language. But instead of descending into ridicule or insult, Zapata's language and style elevate and humanize his characters so that they become a natural part of the multitudes that compose the metropolis of Mexico City in the late twentieth century. Indeed, José Joaquín Blanco concludes that this attitude of professionalism that proposes the exercise of equal rights to literary discourse for homosexual as well as heterosexual narrators is one of the factors triggering the reaction of moral outrage and economic boycott in the face of the publication of *Las aventuras, desaventuras y sueños de Adonis García, el vampiro de la colonia Roma (Adonis García: A Picaresque Novel)* in 1979 (Blanco, ''Zapata''). But although this novel is a watershed in the representation of the repressed and the oppressed of Mexican society, it neither appears out of the blue nor sets up an inviolable aesthetic for all future texts. In fact, one of the virtues of Zapata's writings is their experimentation.

His first novel, *Hasta en las mejores familias* (Even in the Best of Families; 1975), has been characterized by some as of little consequence (Brushwood) for its reduction of the narrative sequences to episodic and undeveloped fragments and to the personalized realm of the family. Influenced by the stream-of-consciousness writers of La Onda (literally, The Wave—the avant-garde of the 1960s and 1970s), this is a pun-filled, sarcastic, first-person narrative quest to discover (uncover) the mechanisms functioning in the middle-class Mexican family in order to seek a liberation from them. (The stories contained in *Ese amor que hasta ayer nos quemaba* [That Love That Even Yesterday Burned Us; 1989] are less jocose, more morbidly serious, versions of the same type of situations.)

From the child's frozen photograph on the first page to the discovery of his father's homosexuality, the narrator, Octavio Rivera, moves like a sleepwalker through his daily routines, finding no personal satisfaction in any of them: he sleeps with his lover, Leni, expresses anguish and frustration over a comfortable but meaningless life, organizes a cinema club, visits his heavily made-up mother and listens to family stories about his father's exemplary life in the Colegio Militar (Military Academy). Between his parents' projections as role models for their son and his visions of everyday events through the filter of screen images from Pier Paolo Pasolini, Federico Fellini and the like, identity is constantly revealed to Octavio as appearance, masquerade, pretense and surface; it is something akin to the extravagant clothing worn by invited guests at a family wedding. This feeling is compounded when Octavio inadvertently intercepts a telephone call meant for his father and discovers the hidden life he has led as a member of the Caballeros Rectos (Straight Gentlemen), a secret fraternity of gay men and transvestites. When they finally confront each other, Octavio confesses that he resents the mask of authority and perfection his father has always forced his son to conform to, not the fact that he is gay. It is the father's lack of affection and understanding toward Octavio, while he prefers to spend his time with other young men, that the son rejects by leaving home and family.

Rather than a disconnected narrative, this novel of a character's coming out of middle-class sexual repression and the mundane psychodramas of daily life plants the seeds for *Las aventuras, desventuras y sueños de Adonis García, el vampiro de la colonia Roma* (the full title of *Vampiro*), Zapata's revolutionary novel that exploded on the literary scene in 1979. Having set up homosexuality in *Hasta en las mejores familias* as something "no tan mala como tú piensas" (not as bad as you think it is; 186), as Javier tells Octavio (who, ironically, doesn't think of it in those terms at all)—unless, of course, one succumbs to the societal pressures to hide one's outlaw sexuality—Zapata moves on to explore the life of a gay male prostitute in Mexico City. At the same time he searches for a narrative form appropriate and adequate to tell this story without regressing into the closet (literally, a patio) of Octavio's father, who could never seem to find the language to share his real desires with his son.

Adonis García, the protagonist of *Vampiro*, lives for the enjoyment of the pleasures his body can offer and receive. Fleeing the stultifying atmosphere of the provinces, he looks for the brightest lights of paradise and finds life on the streets of Mexico City a banquet of adventures and passions from which he eagerly samples at will. In the promising glow of each streetlight, Adonis seeks encounters with the men who savor the hours of darkness to fulfill the sexual fantasies repressed or disguised (in more acceptable forms) during the day. The central districts of this urban capital become a carnival of carnal delights for him, with no need for apologies or justifications ever entering the narrative picture. Adonis García, a living ode to the beauty of the human body and all of its surfaces, radiates youth, energy and exuberance; even when he becomes the victim of economic exploitation (orgies of wealth and luxury vie with the pleasures of the flesh on these pages), he looks with optimism toward the next experience and admonishes those who would wallow in self-pity.

Far from the apologetic tone of Octavio's father's confession of his secret in *Hasta en las mejores familias*, Adonis's guileless honesty in telling his stories fills the pages of this novel—as it does the streets of the colonia Roma—with a gay sexuality that is neither eccentric (as were the descriptions of the Caballeros Rectos in the first novel) nor morbidly clinical in its details, but totally natural for the narrating voice, just as it is a moral part of the human landscape of this city. In juxtaposing the two novels, the reader could find more tragedy in Javier's duplicitous life than in Adonis's daily immersion in a social world filled with individuals pursuing their dreams.

Based on six hours of taped interviews and conversations with a young street hustler that Zapata then edited and reworked, *Vampiro* is a first-person narrative whose elements have reminded some critics of a twentieth-century version of the picaresque genre (see, for example, Blanco, 1981; Jaén). The episodes are organized around the outlaw character who lost his family while still relatively young and has had to confront life using all his survival skills—thus his turn to prostitution—ever since, even if in this case his economic background is more bourgeois than disadvantaged and he seems to enjoy hustling rather than finding it a degrading chore. Each of the sections or tapes is framed by an epigraph from classic texts of the tradition of the free-spirited *pícaro*, all of which point to the attractions inherent in this life for those who wish to participate in "adventures, misadventures, and [the pursuit of] dreams," and not merely contemplate the vital experiences of others secondhand. Thus Adonis freely chooses what we might call the subculture of the streets.

While appealing to the reader on one level as an unrehearsed and undisciplined free-associating series of tales in the most direct, popular 1970s Mexican slang, the spontaneity of Adonis's monologue is carefully structured to reproduce the sound—a spoken, not written version—of immediate and unmediated experience, with all of the grammatical liberties, sarcasm, hesitations and repetitions this might imply. By these means, Zapata liberates the gay experience from the domain of back rooms, demeaning jokes, vicious rumors and accusations and tragic or sentimentalized endings. There is no doubt from the very beginning: Adonis is gay, and that is that. Zapata simultaneously opens up the novel to alternative forms of storytelling to represent alternative sectors of society. It is, at least in part, the narrative respectability (Blanco, 1990) accorded homosexuality and eroticism in this novel that so disturbed critics and public alike in 1979; their reaction may also have had something to do with Adonis's will to survive against all odds and even dare to fantasize about the future. Interestingly, the English translation, *Adonis García*, was confiscated by the authorities in London as recently as 1986 for being "indecent, pornographic, and obscene" while more supposedly tasteful versions of homosexuality were not censored.

Following the scandalous reception created by *Vampiro*, particularly its being awarded the Grijalbo Literary Prize and the money that came with it, Zapata published two shorter novels. The first, *De pétalos perennes* (Perennial Petals; 1981), is based on dialogues between a woman and her servant, Tacha. Through their own words we witness struggles for power, each in her own realm of possibilities: the wealthy bourgeois employer who dictates the lives of those around her, and the prettier, more desirable maid who has the power of youth on her side. Each searches for affection and physical gratification by placing personal classified advertisements in the newspaper—that is, they translate their desires and fantasies into literature of a sort—and each ends up having sexual relations with Jaime, a young man from the provinces whom they both see as the answer to their frustrations and loneliness. The characters and their competition for the same object of desire are reminiscent of popular television soap operas (*telenovelas*) in which women of the upper and lower classes of society are frequently pitted against each other. In the end, no matter what experiences or sentiments they might share, the hierarchy is reestablished and class wins out over beauty since, as Señora Adela reminds Tacha, "no soy tu igual" (I am not your equal; 195).

As the flip side to this story of two women, *Melodrama* (1983) is a sentimental novel (*novela rosa*) or, more accurately, a parody of the genre, based on the passionate attraction between two men, one of whom is a private detective hired to investigate and correct the conduct of the other. When a mother overhears her son speaking on the telephone, using adjectives with feminine endings when referring to himself, she immediately jumps to the conclusion (a logical one, in her own mind) that he is selling drugs undercover, thereby explaining both the need to use code names and the change in behavior she has noticed in him. The narrative sequence of clichés progresses, with the physically and emotionally frustrated detective, Axel Romero, falling in love with the *hijo de familia* (mama's boy) Alex Rocha. Just as in film melodramas, this forbidden relationship unleashes the opposition of both families—Alex's mother and Axel's wife (who uses the situation to try to extort money from the overprotective parent). The abundance of details, such as the decor of the family home (with an omnipresence of alabaster, marble vestibules, endless curtains and pastel tones), and the self-consciously studied poses of Alex's mother, down to the delicately orchestrated position of her hands as she sleeps, are combined with dialogues modeled on the scripts of popular Mexican films, in which exaggerated emotion is an expected convention, to playfully demythicize the sentimental genre as nothing more than stylized and commercialized postures as far from a realistic representation of characters and situations as can be imagined.

On entering this fictional universe, the reader encounters the language of the silver screen: from the first paragraph of stage directions, to the fade-ins and fade-outs throughout the episodes in the text, to the word FIN (The End) on the last page. Recriminations of a tormented mother who blames her son and his so-called aberrations for causing her suffering alternate with confrontations between the two male lovers—Axel and Alex—whose tone of expression never descends from the exaggerated heights of exclamation points, question marks, elliptical accusations, slashes, hyphens and other insinuations of constant anguish or distress in their relationship. There remains no doubt at any time about the artificiality and theatricality of this textual world that is constructed on a parody of stereotyped excess. Therefore, any attempt to equate the *novela rosa* with some kind of natural discourse for homosexuality is disarmed and dismissed by Zapata's insistence on an irreverent vision of this aesthetic world.

After his overt questioning of literary representations of sexual fantasy, it seems only logical that Zapata's next novel would combine the search for erotic expression with the quest for form once again. He does just that in *En jirones* (In Tatters; 1985), in what has been described as a "double helix" (Foster, 1991) whose strands constantly intersect and then pull apart to form a text filled with couplings and uncouplings, in terms of both physical relationships and stylistic conventions. If his first novel is composed of an extended interior monologue, *Vampiro* is an attempt to transcribe the lapses and revelations of spoken language onto the written page (just as the body of the text stands for the actions of a sexual body), and *Melodrama* takes on the exaggerated caricatures of popular culture, then *En jirones* embodies exactly what the title implies—fragments of passion presented in the impassioned narrative fragments.

First in his private diary, then as an individual "en jirones," as the second part is titled (to be understood as broken up, emotionally distraught, radically fragmented as a subject or self), the narrator, Sebastián, confesses the heights and depths of his feelings toward the object of his desire, identified only as A, with one eye on his own countenance reflected in the mirror and one eye on A himself. The concept of rupture orders this narrative. Rather than being left with a sense of completion or wholeness or the definitive reassembly of the psychological and narrative fragments, we find a vortex of movement, of endless process, throughout Sebastián's story, ending with the obsessive repetition of their frenzied sexual encounters "hasta el fin del siglo de los siglos de los siglos por los siglos de los siglos" (until the end of all time, for ever and ever and ever and ever; 274), leaving no insinuation of possible resolution.

Judged as "by far the most sexually explicit gay novel published so far in Mexico" (Foster, 1991), *En jirones* revolves more around the characters' psychological responses to their physical confrontations than around the axis of a traditional plot structure. Stating that he fervently wishes to leave some kind of material trace, some visible proof, of what he is living and feeling, Sebastián struggles with language to represent what he ultimately terms the victimization, the possession, the enslavement, the sacrifice, the compulsion and the fascination that come together in passions such as he experiences with A. Verging on a psychological disruption that could be associated with traumatic mental illness (a *locura de amor* [love madness] perhaps), Sebastián is barely able to function in his everyday surroundings—work, parties, art theaters and cafés. He can do so only through their association with his lover, an individual so at war with himself over the sexual arousal provoked in him by another man that he lives in violent denial to the point of physically abusing Sebastián (for being a constant reminder of these feelings) and entering into a marriage of convenience with a woman of some social reputation. So complete is his focus on the corporal desire for A that Sebastián describes their first sexual encounter—a utopian moment frustratingly postponed time after time—as his proof of the existence of God. Physical ecstasy and an almost mystical rapture are personified in the meeting of their flesh, leaving a permanent (psychological) mark on the narrator that he represents in terms of human skin burned by the kiss of the devil, the fallen angel of temptation.

Writing and sex are the acts through which Sebastián feels alive, and he describes each in vivid detail to form a "novela intimista" (intimate novel; Teichmann) focused on the pleasure and pain derived by the subject from these relationships of power and possession (over one's own body, over the body of another, over the words and images taking the place of acts). The crisis of representation comes under scrutiny, therefore, in terms of his desire for A as well, since the latter refuses any identification with homosexuality; rather than categorizing or classifying what he feels under some corresponding (if inadequate) set of words, A isolates his acts from one another in a perfect embodiment of "the sex which dare not speak its name." Content with calling Sebastián a "friend," A is threatened by any suggestion that their relationship is more, a situation accepted by his sometimes excruciatingly passive lover, who seems willing to submit to much (or all) of the humiliation inflicted by A as long as he continues to be the object of the other's obsessive love. Sebastián seeks but finds no substitute for A, after recognizing his own submission as more painful than pleasurable. Cruising bars and night spots, fantasizing that each disembodied organ really belongs to the absent A, the narrator decides to dedicate these intimate confessions to that very absence who cannot overcome his fears of self-identity and social identification, and who is convinced he will outgrow this adolescent phase of same-sex attraction.

In response, the second part of *En jirones* is a narrative conjured up to combat the anxiety produced by the ruptures of the first part. Here, Sebastián finds in the lyrics of popular songs by the Mexican singer Juan Gabriel (who is openly gay) one way to express the overwhelming loss he feels. By having him do so, Zapata also parodies the false identification of the masses with such commercialized sentiment. Abandoned by the city that once seduced him, Sebastián finds his world reduced to the individual components and biological functions of his own body that he tries to organize into a coherent whole, but that seem only to operate at different and competing rhythms, never in harmony. In this way, they form a metaphorical version of the narrative fragments in constant contention (though not in total futility, given the concrete existence of this text).

The bridge between all of Zapata's previous novels and *La hermana secreta de Angélica María* (Angélica María's Secret Sister; 1989) is film and the power of popular cinema to promote and sustain stereotyped images of gender and sexuality in the social body. In an overwhelmingly parodic narrative laced with heavy doses of recycled versions of the 1960s teen movie heroine Angélica María ("la novia de toda América Latina" [the sweetheart of all Latin America]), the three episodes of this novel trace the life of aspiring singer and actress Alba María/small town movie addict and androgynous figure Alvaro/nightclub performer Alexina ("la sensualidad encarnada, la exuberancia hecha mujer" [sensuality incarnate, exuberance become woman; 29]), three facets of one and the same protagonist. Mythicizing her physical attributes as the incarnation of feminine perfection, Alvaro/Alba/Alexina attempts to live in an everyday reality, far removed from the utopia of the motion picture screen, in the guise of an Angélica María wanna-be. The result is a series of tragicomic encounters between the commercial media's fantasy world of pleasure and fulfillment and a society based on relationships of exploitation, violence, domination and macho brutality. When Alba María and Alvaro are both almost raped, one by a boyhood friend and the other by a tabloid reporter, they respond by killing their aggressors. No sexual act is attempted or consummated in the text without incurring similarly disastrous consequences. The only real locus of pleasure or desire is the cinema, where no such threat of violation is ever suggested and where all passion is portrayed as decent, to adopt Alba María's favorite expression. But film is, after all, only representation; desire is therefore always deferred and postponed, never present but always future.

Through the use of camp exaggeration, the cultivated bad taste of stereotyped conventions of gender identity, Zapata destroys any possible notion that these qualities are inherent in any human being. Instead, he offers the reader a look at the consequences of taking the culture industry's images as literal truths and trying to apply them to real life. When Alba María reaches the conclusion that the only valid—or harmonious—reality exists on celluloid, this cannot lead to anything but a discourse of kitsch in which the artifacts of feminine beauty can be endlessly and banally mass-produced, creating the illusion that anyone and everyone can live the life of Angélica María by buying (and buying into) certain goods and ideas: makeups, lingerie, perfumes, cosmetic surgery, the youth cult and ultimately sex-reassignment surgery to become what the narrator calls the new Eve. The doctor promises Alvaro/Alba that the result will be the physical re-creation of a double of movie star idol Angélica María, "la mujer de tus sueños" (the woman of your dreams; 121).

As neither androgynous child nor transvestite adult nor postoperative hyper-feminine object of desire Alexina does this character find happiness in his/her own body, since it is always the source of pain, contradiction, secrecy and discontent, and the reminder of the desire to be what one is not. *La hermana secreta* leaves us on the doorstep of the postmodern, then, with its appropriation of the radically fragmented or disintegrated subject; the narrative ends with transsexual Alexina in a mental hospital, believing that she is really acting in a film by a famous director, while her doctor plays along with her delusions. Disillusioned by the world, she finds herself repeating the same monologues and scenes to the other inhabitants of the ward while taking refuge in the solace of sleep (dreams). The reader is left questioning whether there is any space for the erotic in the realm of the everyday or only in the idealized vision of film, and whether any attempt at integrating mind and body is doomed to failure, violence or the asylum.

Zapata's latest novel, *¿Por qué mejor no nos vamos?* (Why Don't We Just Leave?; 1992), consists of a running dialogue between a narrative voice assigned feminine adjectives and one belonging to a gay man. In a barrage of colloquial language, each line containing numerous examples of puns and double meanings, we are told of a seemingly infinite variety of sexual experiences between men in the aging hotels, cafés, bars and movie theaters of the port city of Veracruz. The voices belong to two longtime acquaintances who have just turned 40 and whose look back at the 1960s relentlessly parodies the cultural assumptions and clichés of their generation. They have made a pact to recount (or invent?) their sexual adventures in order to counteract nights of insomnia.

In a lengthy series of detailed episodes, the homosexual narrator repeats his encounters with other men from all walks of life (although he seems to obsess on *indios* [Indians] and men of the lower classes) until they become rituals whose language, actions and descriptions vary little if at all from scene to scene. But instead of the adolescent narrators of *Vampiro* or *Melodrama* or *En jirones*, who are in the process of acting on their desires, this character already has a history full of concrete experiences that here are reduced to an almost predictable pattern: surreptitious meeting, sexual intercourse, heart-to-heart conversation. While some critics have regarded the novel as "un monumento al lugar común de la pornografía homosexual" (a monument to the commonplaces of homosexual pornography; Trejo Fuentes, 10), the very appearance of these "commonplaces" might be considered in another light—as a portrait of narrative maturity in their ironic demythicization of the past hopes and fears of a generation whose sexual practices and identities were in desperate search of modes of self-expression while believing in the freedom available to all in the 1960s. From the vantage point of middle age, the years of sexual experimentation and excess run together and lose their distinguishing characteristics or individual identities; they become instead a recognizable, comfortable and nostalgically exaggerated litany to lull the listener to sleep (in place of the habitual dose of Valium): "No puedo dormir. Cuéntame algo" (I can't sleep. Tell me a story; 81), the narrator is told throughout the text. He obliges, returning time and again to rituals of sexual pleasure at all hours of the day or night, and conquests of willing bodies in all imaginable public places.

The play between past and present, between youthful utopian visions and the vicissitudes of actual life (like aging and emotional disillusionment), between a continual state of adolescent excitation and more mature ideas of pleasure, is reflected constantly in their conversations and in confessions regarding situations that, by inference, no longer hold true or were true only in appearance to begin with. And the changes in personal behavior and social tolerance are reflected in linguistic terms as well, in particular the references to sexual preference and orientation, which before were unspeakable and now proliferate at all levels of culture. The obvious question remains, however, as to whether linguistic liberties of the social body mirror real liberation of the physical bodies of which it is composed.

The state of constant motion reflected in the title of his latest novel in a sense summarizes all of Zapata's writings, since they confront norms, stereotypes and traditional models of behavior in order to move beyond, even if the direction of that movement is not always clear from the outset: away from bourgeois family values, from censorship of the body and its desires, from overly melodramatic representations of sexual identity as literal portraits, from publicly sanctioned images of allegedly proper conduct and ultimately from the rarefied sanctity of the literary work as incompatible with the obviously parodied sexual excesses of what some have classified as pornography.

Each step in this "destape" (uncovering: Trejo Fuentes) or liberating project has contributed to the diversity of speaking subjects represented in Zapata's texts, some overtly professing a gay identity and others more subtly exploring (and exploding) issues of sexuality in more general terms. The quantity of criticism addressing these texts lags far behind the amount of primary material, and it tends to be polarized into camps either for or against the inclusion of such allegedly marginal themes in works of literature, or debates over the amount of delicacy with which sexuality and homoeroticism should be handled. Others have examined Zapata's novels in terms of their appropriation of specific literary genres for their passionate explorations of life (Jaén), the parallels between the search for avenues of expression in the terrains of the erotic and the aesthetic (Foster, 1991), the possibilities of imagining (and representing) an alternative future space for the socially marginalized and ways to survive in the meantime (Schaefer-Rodríguez) and the reconsideration of the vampire figure of the colonia Roma in the shadow of the specter of AIDS (Blanco, 1990).

WORKS

Las aventuras, desventuras y sueños de Adonis García, el vampiro de la colonia Roma. Mexico City: Editorial Grijalbo, 1979. English version as *Adonis García: A Picaresque Novel.* Trans. E. A. Lucey. San Francisco: Gay Sunshine Press, 1981.

De amor es mi negra pena. Mexico City: Panfleto y Pantomima, 1983.

De pétalos perennes/Melodrama. Mexico City: Editorial Posada, 1987. First editions 1981/1983.

En jirones. Mexico City: Editorial Posada, 1985.

Ese amor que hasta ayer nos quemaba. Mexico City: Editorial Posada, 1989.

Hasta en las mejores familias. Mexico City: Organización Editorial Novaro, 1975.

La hermana secreta de Angélica María. Mexico City: Cal y Arena, 1989.

¿Por qué mejor no nos vamos? Mexico City: Cal y Arena, 1992.

"Prólogo." In Adolfo Caminha, *Bom-Crioulo*, 9–22. Mexico City: Editorial Posada, 1987.

CRITICISM

Blanco, José Joaquín. "La carne se destruye en el desamor (*En jirones*)." *La jornada* Nov. 9, 1984, p. 20.

———. Introduction. In Luis Zapata, *Adonis García*, 5–8.

———. Review of *El vampiro de la colonia Roma. Unomásuno*, Mar. 15, 1979, p. 6.

———. "Zapata: El vampiro en los años del SIDA." In his *Las intensidades corrosivas*, 187–193. Villahermosa, Mexico: Gobierno del Estado de Tabasco, 1990.

Brushwood, John S. *La novela mexicana (1967–1982).* Mexico City: Grijalbo, 1984.

Foster, David William. *Gay and Lesbian Themes in Latin American Writing*, 37–42. Austin: University of Texas Press, 1991.

———. Review of H. Ernest Lewald, ed. and trans., *The Web: Short Stories by Argentine Women*; Winston Leyland, ed., *My Deep Dark Pain Is Love: A Collection of Latin American Gay Fiction*; Review of Luis Zapata, *Adonis García: A Picaresque Novel* [E. A. Lacy, trans.]. *Chasqui* 13.1 (Nov. 1983): 90–92.

Jaén, Didier T. "La neo-picaresca en México: Elena Poniatowska y Luis Zapata." *Tinta* 1.5 (1987): 23–29.

Reyes, Juan José. "Luis Zapata, duelos de ingenio." *El semanario cultural de novedades*, 544 (Sept. 20, 1992): 6.

Schaefer-Rodríguez, Claudio. "The Power of Subversive Imagination: Homosexual Utopian Discourse in Contemporary Mexico." *Latin American Literary Review* 33 (1989): 29–41.

Schneider, Luis Mario. "El tema homosexual en la nueva narrativa mexicana." *Casa del tiempo* 5.49/50 (Feb.–Mar. 1985): 82–86.

Sefchovich, Sara. *México: País de ideas, país de novelas. Una sociología de la literatura mexicana.* Mexico City: Grijalbo, 1987.

Teichmann, Reinhard. Interview with Luis Zapata. In his *De La Onda en adelante: Conversaciones con 21 novelistas mexicanos*, 355–374. Mexico City: Editorial Posada, 1987.

Trejo Fuentes, Ignacio. "Las joterías de Luis." *Sábado*, supp. to *Unomásuno* 793 (Dec. 12, 1992): 10.

Claudia Schaefer-Rodríguez

Selected Bibliography

Acevedo, Zelmar. *Homosexualidad: Hacia la destrucción de los mitos*. Buenos Aires: Ediciones del Ser, 1985.

Almaguer, Tomás. "Chicano Men: A Cartography of Homosexual Identity and Behavior." *Différences* 3.2 (Summer 1991): 75–100.

Argüelles, Lourdes, and B. Ruby Rich. "Homosexuality, Homophobia, and Revolution: Notes Toward an Understanding of the Cuban Lesbian and Gay Male Experience." *Signs* 9.4 (1984): 683–699; 11.1 (1985): 120–136.

Bautista, Juan Carlos. "La sonrisa de Sor Juana." *Fem* 14.95 (1990): 13–16.

Bellini, Ligia. *Mulher, sodomia e inquisição no Brasil colonial*. São Paulo: Editora Brasiliense, 1989.

Blanco, José Joaquín. *La paja en el ojo: Ensayos de crítica*. Puebla, Mexico: ICUAP, Centro de Estudios Contemporáneos, Editorial Universidad Autónoma de Puebla, 1980.

Bruce-Novoa, Juan. "Homosexuality and the Chicano Novel." *Confluencia: Revista hispánica de cultura y literatura* 2.1 (1986): 69–77. Also in *European Perspectives on Hispanic Literature of the United States*, 98–106. Ed. Genvieve Fabre. Houston: Arte Público Press, 1988.

Chicana Lesbians: The Girls Our Mothers Warned Us About. Ed. Carla Trujillo. San Francisco: Aunt Lute Books, 1991.

Compañeras: Latina Lesbians (an Anthology). Comp. and ed. Juanita Ramos. New York: Latina Lesbian History Project, 1987.

Foster, David William. *Contemporary Argentine Cinema*. Columbia: University of Missouri Press, 1992.

————. *Gay and Lesbian Themes in Latin American Literature*. Austin: University of Texas Press, 1991.

————. "El lesbianismo multidimensional: Conflicto lingüistico, conflicto cultural y conflicto sexual en *Giving up the Ghost: Teatro in Two Acts* de Cherríe Moraga." Forthcoming.

————. Review of Luis Zapata, *Adonis García: A Picaresque Novel* [E. A. Lacey, trans.]; and Winston Leyland, ed., *My Deep Dark Pain Is Love: A Collection of Latin American Gay Fiction*. *Chasqui* 13.1 (Nov. 1983): 90–92.

————. "Social Pact and Lesbian Writing in Mexico." In *Literatura mexicana/Mexican*

Literature. José Miguel Oviedo, ed. Philadelphia: The University of Pennsylvania, 1993, pp. 92–103.

———. "Some Proposals for the Study of Gay Culture in Latin America." Chapter 2 of his *Essays in Latin American Cultural Diversity*. Albuquerque: University of New Mexico Press, 1994.

Foster, Stephen Wayne. "Latin American Studies." *Cabirion and Gay Books Bulletin* 11 (1984): 2–7, 29.

Fry, Peter. "Da hierarquia à igualdade: A construção histórica da homossexualidade." In his *Para inglês ver: Identidade e política na cultura brasileira*, 87–115. Rio de Janeiro: Zahar, 1982.

———. "Léonie, Pompinha, Amaro e Aleixo, prostituição, homossexualidade e raça em dois romances naturalistas." In his *Caminhos cruzados: Linguagem, antropologia, ciências naturais*, 33–51. São Paulo: Editora Brasiliense, 1982.

Gregorich, Luis. *Literatura y homosexualidad y otros ensayos*. Buenos Aires: Editorial Legasa, 1985.

Howes, Robert. "The Literature of Outsiders: The Literature of the Gay Community in Latin America." In *Latin American Masses and Minorities: Their Images and Realities*, 1.288–304; 580–591. Ed. Dan C. Hazen. SALALM no. 30. Madison: SALALM Secretariat, Memorial Library, University of Wisconsin, 1985.

Jáuregui, Carlos Luis. *La homosexualidad en la Argentina*. Buenos Aires: Ediciones Tarso, 1978.

Jockl, Alejandro. *Ahora, los gay*. Buenos Aires: Ediciones de la Pluma, 1984.

Leyland, Winston, ed. *My Deep Dark Pain Is Love: A Collection of Latin American Gay Fiction*. San Francisco: Gay Sunshine Press, 1983.

———. *Now the Volcano: An Anthology of Latin American Gay Literature*. Translated Erskine Lane, Franklin D. Blanton and Simon Karlinsky. San Francisco: Gay Sunshine Press, 1979.

Lima, Délcio Monteiro de. *Os homoeróticos*. Rio de Janeiro: Francisco Alves, 1983.

Lumsden, Ian. *Homosexualidad: Sociedad y estado en México*. Mexico City: Solediciones; Toronto: Canadian Gay Archives, 1991.

Machado, Luiz Carlos. *Descansa en paz, Oscar Wilde*. Rio de Janeiro: Editora Codecri, 1982.

Míccolis, Leila, and Herbert Daniel. *Jacarés e lobisomens: Dois ensaios sobre a homossexualidade*. Rio de Janeiro: Achiamé, 1983.

Monsiváis, Carlos. *Amor perdido*. Mexico City: Era, 1977.

———. *Días de guardar*. 4th ed. Mexico City: Era, 1971.

———. *Escenas de pudor y liviandad*. 9th ed. Mexico City: Grijalbo, 1988.

Moraga, Cherríe. *Loving in the War Years: Lo que nunca pasó por sus labios*. Boston: South End, 1983.

Mott, Luiz. *Escravidão, homossexualidade e demonologia*. São Paulo: Icone, 1988.

Murray, Stephen O., ed. *Male Homosexuality in Central and South America*. San Francisco: Instituto Obregón; New York: GAU-NY, 1987.

Parker, Richard G. *Bodies, Pleasures, and Passions: Sexual Culture in Contemporary Brazil*. Boston: Beacon Press, 1990.

Paz, Octavio. *Sor Juana Inés de la Cruz o las trampas de la fe*. Mexico City: Fondo de Cultura Económica, 1982.

Pérez, Emma. "Sexuality and Discourse: Notas from a Chicana Survivor." In *Chicana Lesbians: The Girls Our Mothers Warned Us About*, 159–184.

Perlongher, Néstor Osvaldo. *O negócio do michê: Prostituição viril em São Paulo*. São Paulo: Editora Brasiliense, 1987.

Puig, Manuel. "El error gay." *El porteño* (Sept. 1990): 32–33.

Reinhardt, Karl J. "The Image of Gays in Chicano Prose Fiction." *Explorations in Ethnic Studies* 4.2 (1981): 41–55.

Rodríguez, Jesusa. "La gira mamal de Coatlicue." *Debate feminista* 1 (Sept. 1990): 400–403.

Ruiz Esparza, Jorge. "Homotextualidad: La diferencia y la escritura." In *Coloquio internacional: Escritura y sexualidad en la literatura hispanoamericana*, 233–252. Poitiers: Université de Poitiers, Centre de Recherches Latino-Américaines, 1990.

Schaefer-Rodríguez, Claudia. "The Power of Subversive Imagination: Homosexual Utopian Discourse in Contemporary Mexican Literature." *Latin American Literary Review* 33 (1989): 29–41.

Schneider, Luis Mario. "El tema homosexual en la nueva narrativa mexicana." *Casa del tiempo* (Mexico City) 49–50 (1985): 82–86.

Schwartz, Kessel. "Homosexuality as a Theme in Representative Contemporary Spanish American Novels." *Kentucky Romance Quarterly* 22 (1975): 247–257.

Shaw, Donald A. "Notes on the Presentation of Sexuality in the Modern Spanish-American Novel." *Bulletin of Hispanic Studies* 59 (1982): 275–282.

Smith, Paul Julian. *Laws of Desire: Questions of Homosexuality in Spanish Writing and Film 1960–1990*. Oxford: Clarendon Press, 1992.

Soto, Francisco. "Reinaldo Arena's Literary Legacy." *Christopher Street* 156 (1991): 12–16.

This Bridge Called My Back: Writings by Radical Women of Color. Ed. by Cherríe Moraga and Gloria Anzaldúa. New York: Kitchen Table/Women of Color Press, 1981.

Trevisan, João S. *Perverts in Paradise*. Trans. Martin Foreman. London: GMP Publications, 1986. Originally published as *Devassos no paraíso* (1986).

Villanueva, Alfredo. "Machismo vs. Gayness: Latin American Fiction." *Gay Sunshine* 29–30 (1976): 22.

Williams, Walter L. "The Abominable Sin: The Spanish Campaign Against 'Sodomy,' and Its Results in Modern Latin America." In his *The Spirit and the Flesh: Sexual Diversity in American Indian Culture*, 131–151. Boston: Beacon Press, 1986.

Yarbro-Bejarano, Yvonne. "Reclaiming the Lesbian Body: Cherríe Moraga's *Loving in the War Years*." *Out/Look* 12 (1991): 74–79.

Young, Allen. *Gays Under the Cuban Revolution*. San Francisco: Grey Fox Press, 1981.

Index

Bold indicates the page numbers for the entry on the author.

About the Editor and Contributors

DAVID WILLIAM FOSTER is Regents' Professor of Spanish at Arizona State University, where he is Director of Spanish graduate studies. He has published extensively on Hispanic literature, with an emphasis on narrative and theater in Argentina and popular culture in Latin America in general. His research interests also include Jewish culture and queer theory in Latin America. His book, *Gay and Lesbian Themes in Latin American Writing*, was published in 1991.

DANIEL ALTAMIRANDA is Assistant Professor at the University of Buenos Aires and Professor of modern literature at the Instituto Nacional de Enseñanza Superior No. 1, where he directs the graduate program in literature. He has published on literary theory, contemporary Latin American writing and Golden Age drama.

DANIEL BALDERSTON is Professor and Chair of Spanish and Portuguese at Tulane University. His most recent books are *The Latin American Short Story: An Annotated Guide* (Greenwood, 1992) and *Out of Context: Historical Reference and the Representation of Reality in Borges* (1993). He has translated books of fiction by José Bianco, Silvina Ocampo, Sylvia Molloy, Juan Carlos Onetti and Ricardo Piglia, and is the author of numerous articles.

A. ALEJANDRO BERNAL teaches Latin American literature in the Department of Spanish, Italian and Portuguese and the Latin American studies program at the University of South Carolina. He has published articles on Latin American authors and currently is working on a book on José Donoso.

DÁRIO BORIM, JR. has taught language and literature at the University of Minnesota since 1988, and is presently completing his Ph.D. there. He has contributed to international journals, such as *Chasqui*, *Quadrant*, and *Brasil/Brazil*. His research focuses on contemporary autobiographies and the conflict of individual versus community.

EVA PAULINO BUENO was born in Brazil. She teaches Spanish at Pennsylvania State University–DuBois. Her research interests are Latin American women writers of the twentieth century and Brazilian literature of the nineteenth century.

ANA GARCÍA CHICHESTER teaches in the Department of Modern Foreign Languages at Mary Washington College.

KAREN S. CHRISTIAN is a doctoral candidate in Spanish at the University of California–Irvine and was a 1993 fellow with the University of California Humanities Research Institute Minority Discourse Initiative. She has published articles on Chicano and Cuban-American literature, and edited the 1991 *Irvine Chicano Literary Prize* anthology.

ROLANDO COSTA PICAZO is Professor of literature at the University of Buenos Aires. A professional translator, he has rendered over fifty books from English into Spanish, among them fiction by William Faulkner, Ernest Hemingway, Truman Capote, Norman Mailer, and Jean Rhys, as well as poems by W. H. Auden, Frank O'Hara, Joseph Brodsky and William Carlos Williams. He has published a book on the poetry of Auden and numerous articles on literature and culture.

ROSELYN COSTANTINO is Assistant Professor of Spanish at Pennsylvania State University–Altoona. She has published on Argentine film and on women and women writers in Mexican society, with a focus on the playwright, poet and novelist Sabina Berman and the poet, novelist and playwright Carmen Boullosa. She is working on a manuscript on new trends in the Mexican theater.

ANDRÉ COYNÉ is Honorary Professor at the University of Lima. He taught at various universities between 1949 and 1985, including Universidades Clásicas de Buenos Aires, Madrid, Lisbon, Ecole Normale Supérieure in Abidjan, Ivory Coast and Costa de Marfil.

CARMEN DOMÍNGUEZ was born in Spain. She currently lectures in Spanish at the University of Paisley, Scotland.

CYNTHIA DUNCAN teaches in the Department of Foreign Languages at the University of Tennessee.

STEVEN M. DUPOUY is Assistant Professor of Latin American literature and Spanish at Georgia State University, where he is the director of the translation and interpretation programs. His research interests center on contemporary Latin American literature, and he has published articles on Manuel Puig and Lourdes Sifontes.

BRADLEY EPPS is currently Assistant Professor of Romance languages at Harvard University. He has published a number of articles on contemporary Spanish narrative and film, and his book, *Significant Violence: Oppression and Resistance in Juan Goytisolo's Recent Fiction*, is forthcoming.

CARMELO ESTERRICH is an Assistant Professor of Spanish and Portuguese at Denison University. He is currently writing on the rhetoric of exile and home in the novels of Reinaldo Arenas.

ROBERTO J. FORNS-BROGGI was born in Lima. He has taught literature in Peruvian high schools and universities, and has published a book and articles about reading and creative writing. He has studied at Arizona State University since 1991, where he is working on a dissertation on Roberto Juarroz's poetry.

DARÍO GALAVIZ QUEZADA (1951–1993) was born in Guaymas, Mexico. Coauthor of *Protagonistas y coprotagonistas de la literatura sonorense*, he was active in the promotion of literature and in the academic criticism of regional cultural production.

LEONARDO GARCÍA-PABÓN is an Assistant Professor at the University of Oregon. His research focuses on Bolivian literature and the colonial period in Latin America. He has served as editor of *Ideologies and Literature* (1987) and *Hipótesis. Revista boliviana de literatura* (1981–1988).

GUSTAVO GEIROLA was Professor at the University of Salta, the University of Tucumán, and the Catholic University of America. At present he is completing his dissertation at Arizona State University. He has published in international journals and *La Gaceta* of Tucumán, and is the author of *El tatuaje invisible: Ensayos sobre la escritura del horror en Hispanoamérica* (1994).

KAREN S. GOLDMAN teaches Spanish and Latin American literature at Pitzer College in Claremont, California. She has written and lectured about contemporary Latin American women writers, Latin American and Spanish cinema, and popular culture in Latin America. She is currently working on a manuscript about the Spanish filmmaker Luis Buñuel.

GILBERTO GÓMEZ OCAMPO teaches at Wabash College.

MARY ANN GOSSER-ESQUILÍN teaches in the Department of Foreign Languages and Linguistics at Florida Atlantic University.

LIBRADA HERNÁNDEZ is Associate Professor of Spanish at Furman University, Greenville, South Carolina. She specializes in nineteenth-century Spanish literature and has written on Cuban women poets living in the United States. At present, she is doing research on feminism in Hispanic letters and is studying the works of Gertrudis Gómez de Avellaneda.

MANUEL DE JESÚS HERNÁNDEZ-GUTIÉRREZ is an Assistant Professor of foreign languages and a Research Faculty member of the Hispanic Research Center at Arizona State University, he has contributed articles to various journals and books, including *The Bilingual Review*, *Culturas hispanas de los Estados Unidos* (1990), and *Chicano Discourse* (1992). His latest book, *El colonalismo interno en la narrativa chicana* (1994), offers a provocative theory on the Chicano novel.

ELIZABETH ROSA HORAN directs the program in comparative literature at Arizona State University. She has published monographs on Gabriela Mistral forthcoming from the University of Texas Press and the Biblioteca Latino Americana Series published by the Organization of American States.

ROBERT HOWES was born in Bristol, England. He studied at the Universities of Cambridge, British Columbia and Sheffield. He has been a librarian in the British Library and Cambridge University Library, and currently is at the University of Sussex Library. He works as a volunteer in the London Friend lesbian and gay counseling organization.

DIDIER T. JAÉN is a Professor of Spanish at the University of California–Davis.

ANNLOUISE KEATING teaches multiethnic U.S. literature, women's studies and critical theory at Eastern New Mexico University. She has published on black feminist theory, Paula Gunn Allen, Gloria Anzaldúa, Audre Lorde, contemporary Chicana writers, Ralph Waldo Emerson and Herman Melville. She is completing a book-length study of Allen, Anzaldúa and Lorde.

GEORGE KLAWITTER is Associate Professor in the English Department of Viterbo College. He has edited a volume of the poetry of Richard Barnfield (1990) and has published *Adapted to the Lake: Letters by the Brother Founders of Notre Dame, 1841–1849* (1993).

CHRISTOPHER TOWNE LELAND is Professor of English at Wayne State University. He is the author of four novels, the most recent being *The Professor of Aesthetics* (forthcoming), as well as the critical study *The Last Happy Men: The Generation of 1922, Fiction, and the Argentine Reality* (1986).

MELISSA A. LOCKHART was raised in San Francisco in the brief but pivotal period following the assassination of Councilman Harvey Milk and prior to the onset of AIDS. She has conducted research on homosexual themes in the theater of Nelson Rodrigues and is working on her doctoral dissertation at Arizona State University.

FRANCISCO CAETANO LOPES, JR. Until he died of AIDS in March 1994, Lopes was Assistant Professor of Luso-Brazilian literature at Stanford University.

DOMINIQUE M. LOUISOR-WHITE, born in France, has been Assistant Professor of Spanish at California State University–San Bernardino since 1993.

LILLIAN MANZOR-COATS is an Assistant Professor in the programs of comparative literature and women's studies at the University of California–Irvine. She is a Latin American cultural critic specializing in interdisciplinary studies and feminist theory. She has published in *World Literature Today*, *Gestos* and

Latin American Literary Review. She is completing a book manuscript on U.S. Cuban theater, *Marginality Beyond Return.*

ELENA M. MARTÍNEZ is Assistant Professor at Baruch College (CUNY). She has published *El discurso dialógico en* La era imaginaria *de René Vásquez Díaz* (1991) and *Onetti: Estrategias textuales y operaciones del lector* (1992). She is currently working on a book called *Lesbian Voices from Latin America.*

JOHN C. MILLER, Professor of Spanish and Chair of the Languages and Cultures Department at the University of Colorado–Colorado Springs, is a specialist in Hispanic literature of the United States. Having worked in Hispanic theater in New York, he is currently dedicating his research to gay and lesbian U.S. Hispanic writers, U.S. Cuban writing and a popular press "gay fathers" manuscript.

MARTHA ELENA MUNGUÍA ZATARAIN teaches literature at the University of Sonora.

ELÍAS MIGUEL MUÑOZ is a widely published prose writer and poet. His published works include two books of literary criticism, the highly regarded novels *Crazy Love* and *The Greatest Performance* and two poetry collections. Muñoz has contributed to several anthologies of U.S. Latino literature, including the critically acclaimed *Iguana Dreams.*

MANUEL MURRIETA SALDÍVAR is from Hermosillo, Mexico. Journalist and writer, he is currently working on a Ph.D. at Arizona State University. He has written newspaper works about northwest Mexico and the United States. His essay *Mi letra no es en inglés* and his chronicles *De viaje en Mex-América* won first prize in the Sonora Book Award (1990 and 1991).

FRANCISCO NÁJERA is an independent scholar who has published articles on Latin American literature. His book-length study of Rafael Arévalo Martínez's work was published in 1993 in Guatemala. He also has written several books of poetry and short stories.

FRANCES NEGRÓN-MUNTANER is a Philadelphia-based Puerto Rican writer and filmmaker. She is currently a Ph.D. candidate in comparative literature at Rutgers University, and finishing a one-hour film on Puerto Rican identities, *Brincando el charco*, and has completed editing an anthology of Latino poets in Philadelphia, *Shouting in a Whisper.*

GUILLERMO NÚÑEZ NORIEGA was born in Sonora, Mexico. He completed studies in sociology at the University of Sonora and, is currently completing an M.A. in humanities at Arizona State University. He has published research on ethnography about sexual culture in Mexico. His book *Sexo entre varones. Poder y resistencia en el campo sexual* was published in April 1994.

RAFAEL OCASIO is Assistant Professor of Spanish and adviser of the Latin

American Studies Program at Agnes Scott College. His research includes Afro-Cuban literatures, *santería*, and revolutionary children's literature. He is at work on a critical monograph on Reinaldo Arenas and on a course on gay and lesbian Latino and Latin American literatures.

SALVADOR A. OROPESA, born in Málaga, Spain, teaches Peninsular literature and Latin American culture at Kansas State University. He is the author of a book on the Chilean writer Ariel Dorfman and has published articles on women writers like Rosa Montero, Laura Esquivel and Angeles Mastretta.

MARINA PÉREZ DE MENDIOLA is Assistant Professor of Latin American literature and culture at the University of Wisconsin–Milwaukee. She is the author of several articles on contemporary Mexican literature. She is currently completing a book-length manuscript on the evolution of different discourses on sexuality and sexual identities in contemporary Mexican literature.

ÁNGEL PUENTE GUERRA has published in *La Nación, Sur, Cuadernos hispanoamericanos,* and *Hispamérica.*

ROBERTO REIS, born in Rio de Janeiro, is Professor of Brazilian studies at the University of Minnesota. He has published fiction and literary criticism both in Brazil and abroad. Among his recent publications are *Toward Sociocriticism* (1991), of which he was editor, and *The Pearl Necklace* (1992).

JOÃO CARLOS RODRIGUES was born in Rio de Janeiro. A journalist and film critic who has published many articles in the Brazilian press, his published works include *O negro brasilerio e o cinema* (1988), *Pequena história da Africa negra* (1991), and *João do Rio e la Belle-Époque no Rio* (1994).

CARLOS A. RODRÍGUEZ-MATOS was born in Naranjito, Puerto Rico. He teaches Spanish language and literature at Seton Hall University. He has published two books of poetry: *Matacán* (1982) and *Llama de amor vivita: Jarchas* (1988), and his books on criticism include *El narrador pícaro: Guzmán de Alfarache* (1985) and, as editor, *Simposio: Clemente Soto Vélez* (1990).

OSVALDO R. SABINO is Assistant Professor of Spanish at Marygrove College in Detroit. In addition to numerous short stories and scholarly articles in a variety of journals, he is the author of two collections of poetry and the study *Borges: Una imagen del amor y de la muerte.*

CLAUDIA SCHAEFER-RODRÍGUEZ teaches Hispanic literature and culture at the University of Rochester. Her publications include *Textured Lives: Women, Art, and Representation in Modern Mexico* (1992) and numerous studies on twentieth-century Spain and Latin America. She is currently finishing a book about gay and lesbian writers in contemporary Mexico.

JUAN ANTONIO SERNA is working on a doctoral dissertation concerning adolescent language use in the contemporary Mexican novel at Arizona State University.

GLENN SHELDON is Publications Director of the Latin American Studies Association at the University of Pittsburgh. His poetry has appeared in numerous literary journals, including *Evergreen Chronicles* and *James White Review*.

ANA SIERRA teaches in the Department of Modern Languages at Seton Hall University.

FRANCISCO SOTO is Assistant Professor of Spanish at the College of Staten Island (CUNY) and the author of *Conversación con Reinaldo Arenas* (1990) and the forthcoming *Reinaldo Arenas: The Pentagonía*.

DANIEL TORRES teaches Spanish at Ohio University. His areas of research include baroque and contemporary Latin American poetry. His gay novel *Morirás si da una primavera* (1993) won the Letras de Oro award (1991–1992).

VÍCTOR F. TORRES is head librarian of the Caribbean and Latin American Studies Library of the University of Puerto Rico–Río Piedras. He has contributed articles to *Mester* and the *Inter-American Review of Bibliography*, and is writing a doctoral dissertation on Luis Zapata.

MARY JANE TREACY is Professor of Spanish and women's studies at Simmons College. She specializes in Latin American women's literature and looks primarily at the place of women within the state and state violence against women. She is working on biographies and narratives by women political prisoners and guerrilla fighters.

ALEJANDRO VARDERI teaches Spanish language, literature and film at New York University. His books of criticism include *Estado e industia editorial*, *Anotaciones sobre el amor y el deseo*, and *Anatomía de una seducción: Reescrituras de lo femenino*. His novels include *Para repetir una mujer* and *Amantes y reverentes*. He is currently working on a book on excess in Severo Sarduy's writing and Pedro Almodóvar's films.

ALFREDO VILLANUEVA is a poet and teaches comparative literature at Hostos Community College, CUNY, where he is Chair of English. He is the author of *Pato salvaje* and *La voz de la mujer que llevo dentro*, among others, and the winner of the 1993 NEMLA/Peter Lang Award for "Discurso hermético y modernismo hispanoamericano: *De sobremesa*, de José Asunción Silva."

DAVID WETSEL is Associate Professor of French at Arizona State University. His publications include *L'Ecriture et le reste . . .* (1981), *Pascal and Disbelief* (1994) and the chapter on France in Emmanuel Nelson, ed., *AIDS: The Literary Response* (1992).

ISBN 0-313-28479-2

90000>

EAN

9 780313 284793

HARDCOVER BAR CODE